GROSS!

rick kirkman
jerry scott

Scrapbook

NO. 33

Andrews McMeel
Publishing®

a division of Andrews McMeel Universal

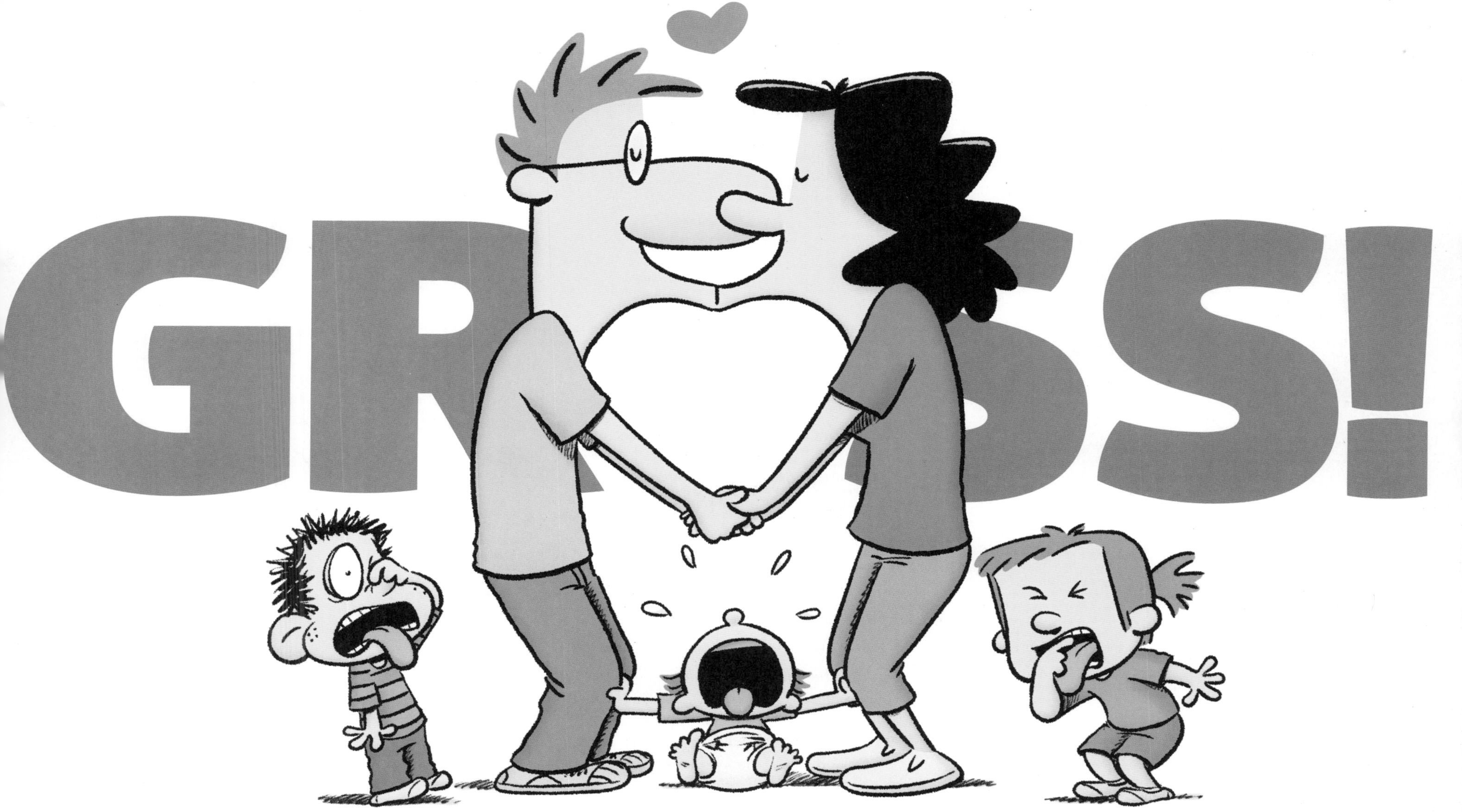
GR
SS!

Other Baby Blues® Books from Andrews McMeel Publishing

Guess Who Didn't Take a Nap?
I Thought Labor Ended When the Baby Was Born
We Are Experiencing Parental Difficulties . . . Please Stand By
Night of the Living Dad
I Saw Elvis in My Ultrasound
One More and We're Outnumbered!
Check, Please . . .
threats, bribes & videotape
If I'm a Stay-at-Home Mom, Why Am I Always in the Car?
Lift and Separate
I Shouldn't Have to Scream More Than Once!
Motherhood Is Not for Wimps
Baby Blues®: Unplugged
Dad to the Bone
Never a Dry Moment
Two Plus One Is Enough
Playdate: Category 5
Our Server Is Down
Something Chocolate This Way Comes
Briefcase Full of Baby Blues®
Night Shift
The Day Phonics Kicked In
My Space
The Natural Disorder of Things
We Were Here First
Ambushed! In the Family Room
Cut!
Eat, Cry, Poop
Scribbles at an Exhibition
Bedlam
Wetter, Louder, Stickier
No Yelling!

Treasuries

The Super-Absorbent Biodegradable Family-Size Baby Blues®
Baby Blues®: Ten Years and Still in Diapers
Butt-Naked Baby Blues®
Wall-to-Wall Baby Blues®
Driving Under the Influence of Children
Framed!
X-Treme Parenting
BBXX: Baby Blues: Decades 1 and 2

Gift Book

It's a Boy
It's a Girl

To Mell

—R.K. & J.S.

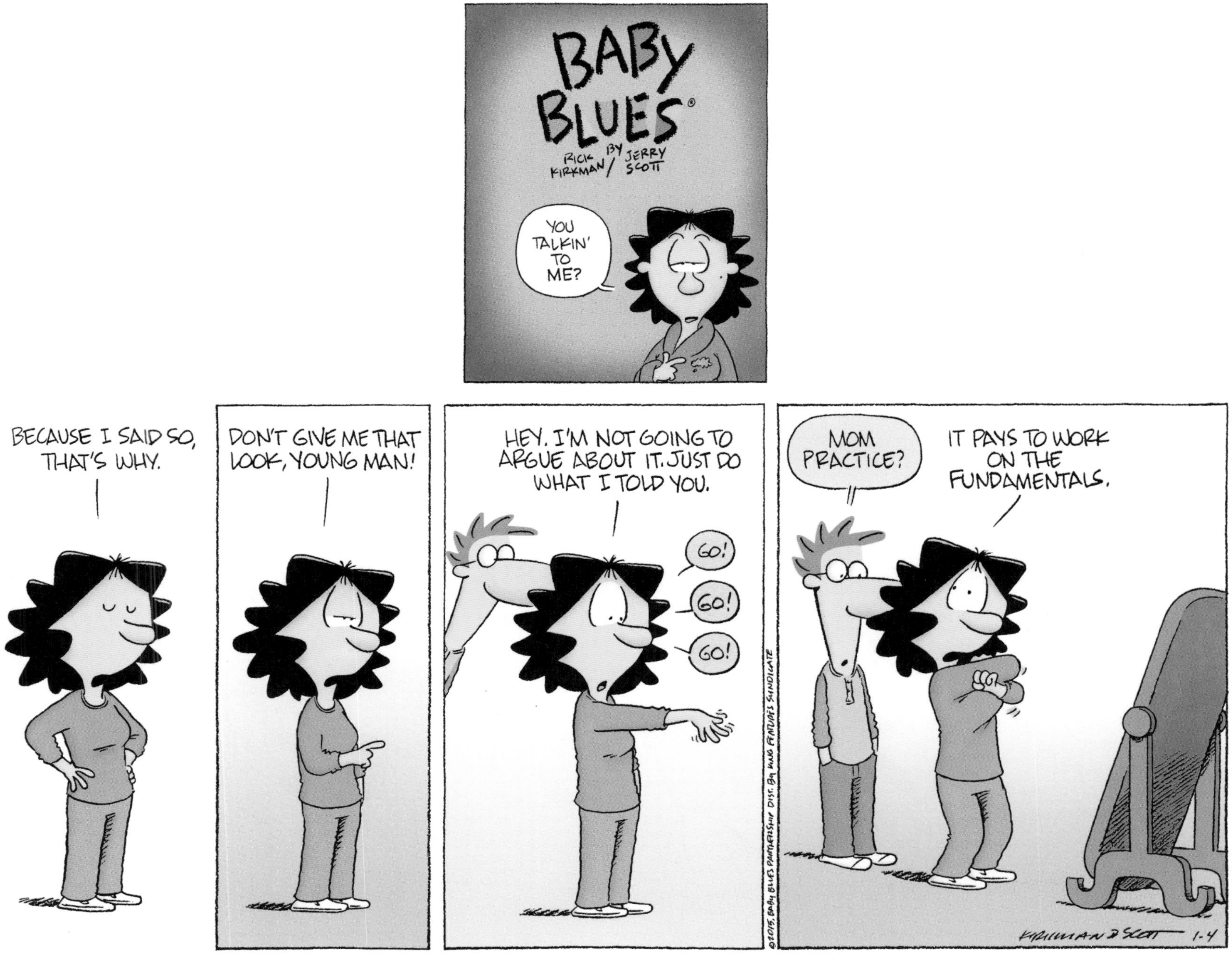
BABY BLUES®
BY RICK KIRKMAN / JERRY SCOTT
YOU TALKIN' TO ME?
BECAUSE I SAID SO, THAT'S WHY.
DON'T GIVE ME THAT LOOK, YOUNG MAN!
HEY. I'M NOT GOING TO ARGUE ABOUT IT. JUST DO WHAT I TOLD YOU.
GO!
GO!
GO!
MOM PRACTICE?
IT PAYS TO WORK ON THE FUNDAMENTALS.
KIRKMAN & SCOTT 1-4

Rick: Title panel: Wanda doing *Taxi Driver*, with Robert De Niro's mole.

Jerry: It wouldn't be right if I said that this idea came from years of watching my wife rehearsing kid lectures under her breath. Nope, it wouldn't be right at all.

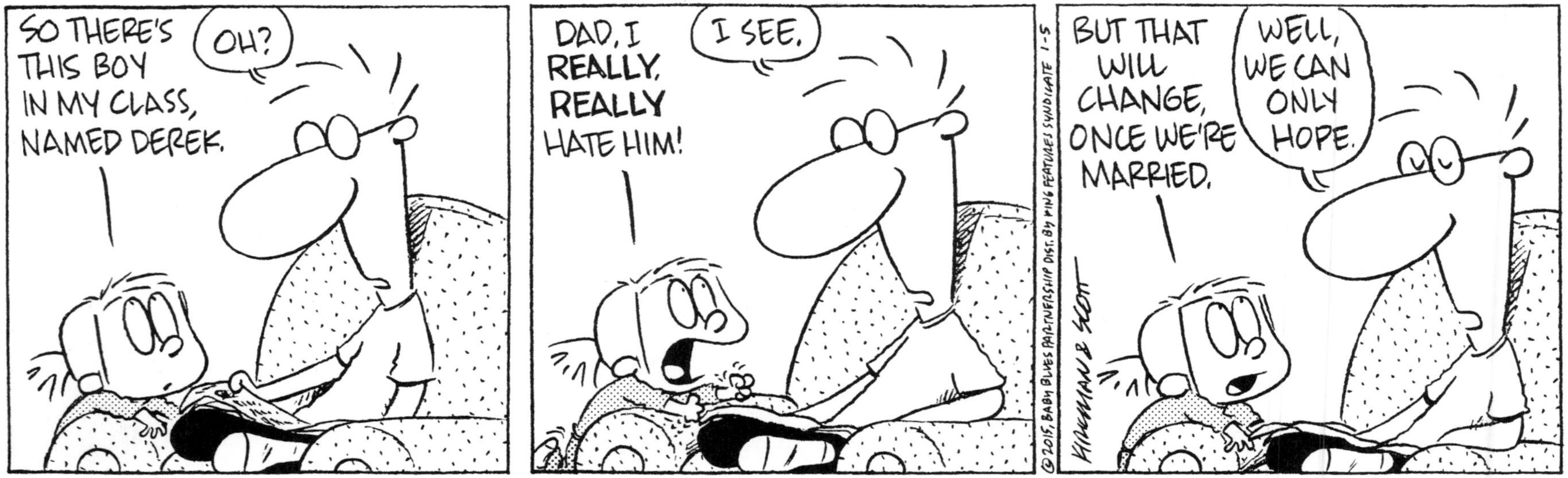
SO THERE'S THIS BOY IN MY CLASS, NAMED DEREK.
OH?
DAD, I **REALLY**, **REALLY** HATE HIM!
I SEE.
BUT THAT WILL CHANGE, ONCE WE'RE MARRIED.
WELL, WE CAN ONLY HOPE.
© 2015, BABY BLUES PARTNERSHIP DIST. BY KING FEATURES SYNDICATE 1-5
KIRKMAN & SCOTT

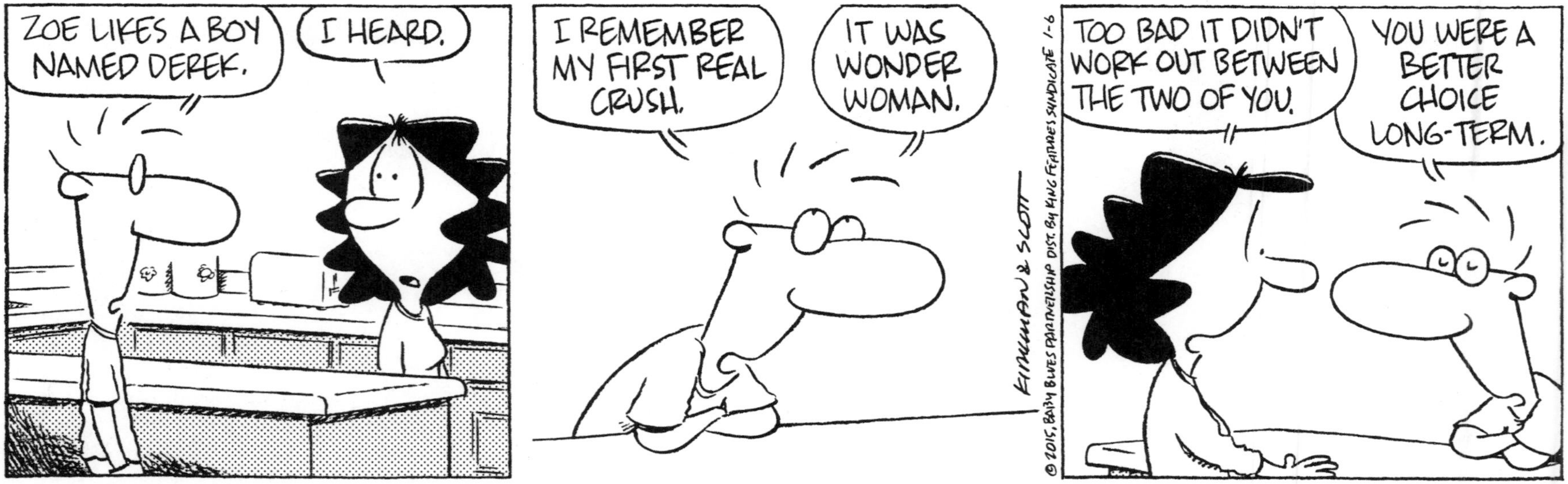
ZOE LIKES A BOY NAMED DEREK.
I HEARD.
I REMEMBER MY FIRST REAL CRUSH.
IT WAS WONDER WOMAN.
TOO BAD IT DIDN'T WORK OUT BETWEEN THE TWO OF YOU.
YOU WERE A BETTER CHOICE LONG-TERM.
KIRKMAN & SCOTT
© 2015, BABY BLUES PARTNERSHIP DIST. BY KING FEATURES SYNDICATE 1-6

Rick: Wonder Woman could be difficult to be married to, with that whole Lasso of Truth thing.

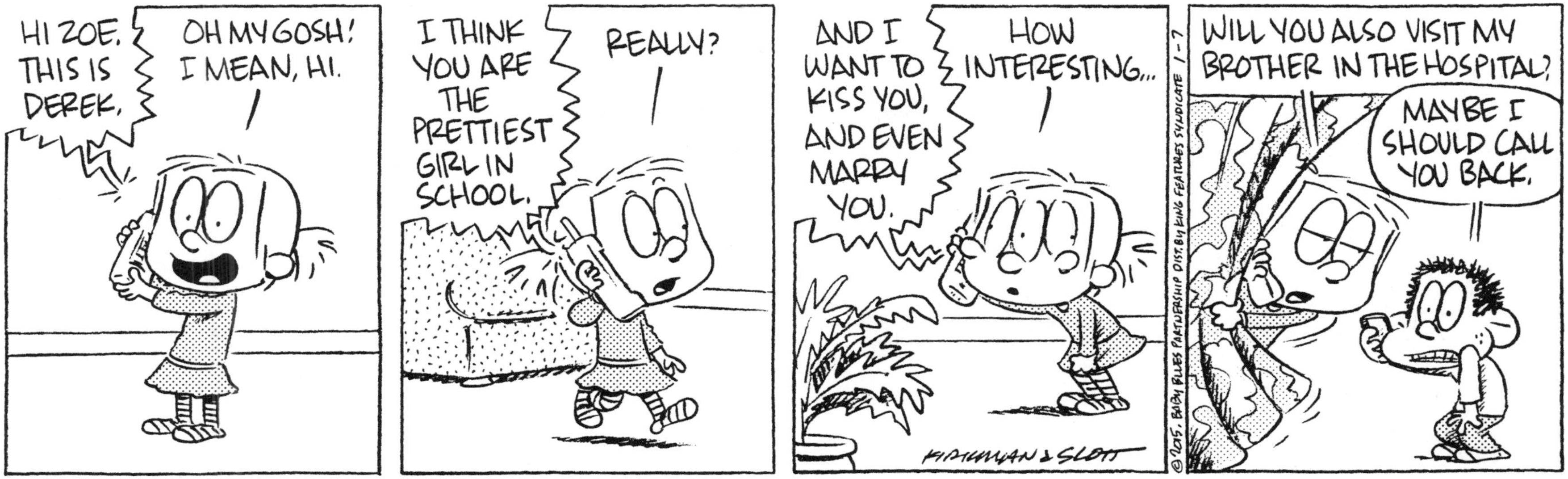
HI ZOE. THIS IS DEREK.
OH MY GOSH! I MEAN, HI.
I THINK YOU ARE THE PRETTIEST GIRL IN SCHOOL.
REALLY?
AND I WANT TO KISS YOU, AND EVEN MARRY YOU.
HOW INTERESTING...
KIRKMAN & SCOTT
©2015, BABY BLUES PARTNERSHIP DIST. BY KING FEATURES SYNDICATE 1-7
WILL YOU ALSO VISIT MY BROTHER IN THE HOSPITAL?
MAYBE I SHOULD CALL YOU BACK.

Rick: And a morning DJ is born.

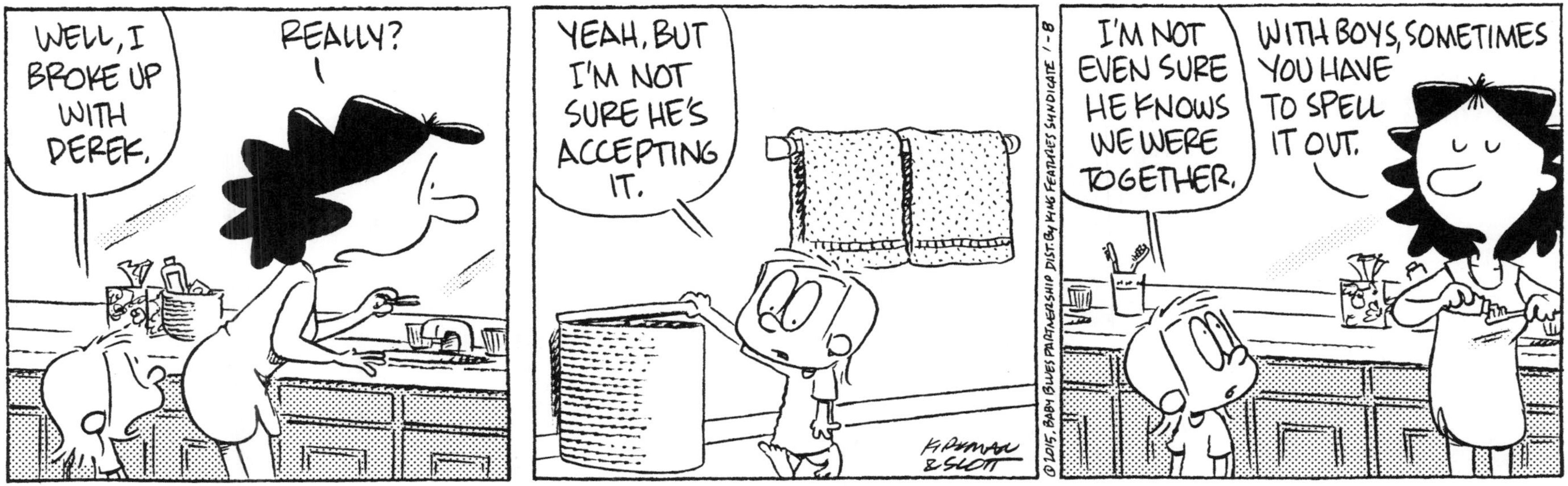
WELL, I BROKE UP WITH DEREK.
REALLY?
YEAH, BUT I'M NOT SURE HE'S ACCEPTING IT.
KIRKMAN & SCOTT
©2015, BABY BLUES PARTNERSHIP DIST. BY KING FEATURES SYNDICATE 1-8
I'M NOT EVEN SURE HE KNOWS WE WERE TOGETHER.
WITH BOYS, SOMETIMES YOU HAVE TO SPELL IT OUT.

Jerry: Nothing personal, you Dereks of the world. I just like the way the name looks in print. Oh, and watch out for Zoes.

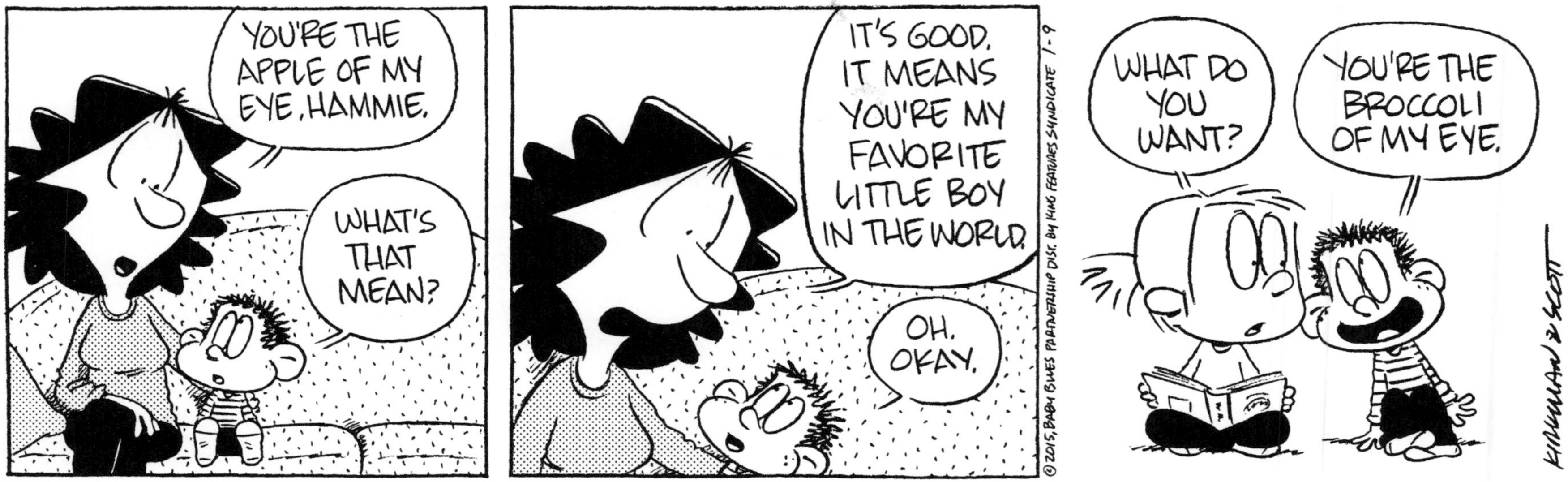
YOU'RE THE APPLE OF MY EYE, HAMMIE.
WHAT'S THAT MEAN?
IT'S GOOD. IT MEANS YOU'RE MY FAVORITE LITTLE BOY IN THE WORLD.
OH. OKAY.
©2015, BABY BLUES PARTNERSHIP DIST. BY KING FEATURES SYNDICATE 1-9
WHAT DO YOU WANT?
YOU'RE THE BROCCOLI OF MY EYE.
KIRKMAN & SCOTT

Rick: I don't get it . . . I love broccoli.

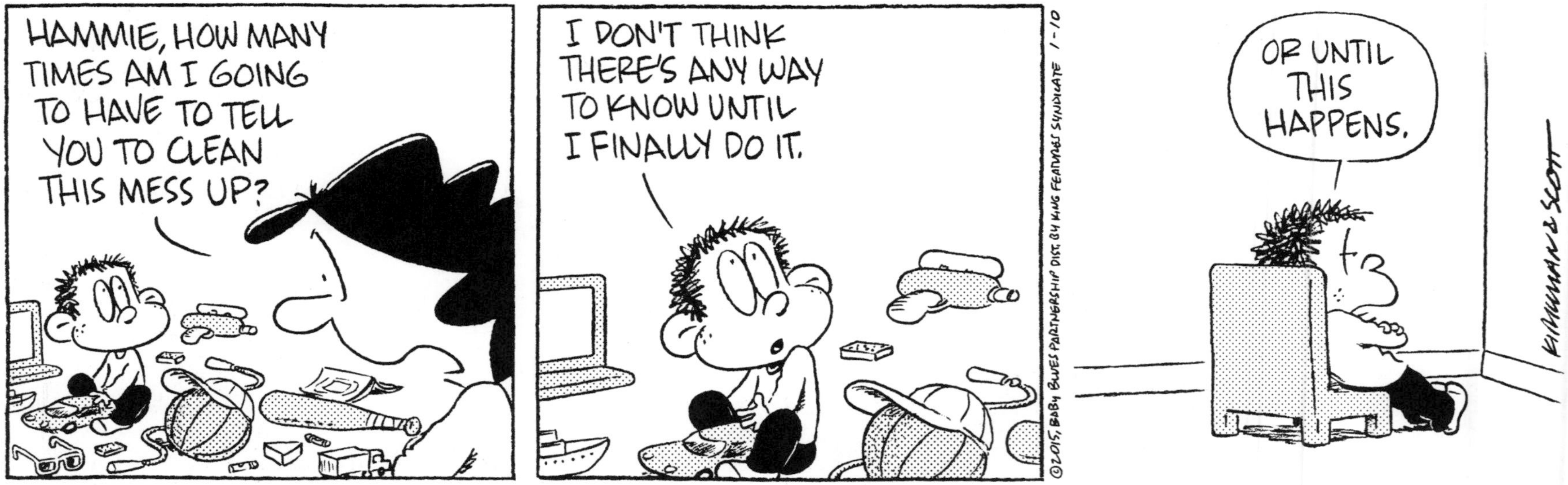
HAMMIE, HOW MANY TIMES AM I GOING TO HAVE TO TELL YOU TO CLEAN THIS MESS UP?
I DON'T THINK THERE'S ANY WAY TO KNOW UNTIL I FINALLY DO IT.
©2015, BABY BLUES PARTNERSHIP DIST. BY KING FEATURES SYNDICATE 1-10
OR UNTIL THIS HAPPENS.
KIRKMAN & SCOTT

Rick: The burden of having a literal mind . . .

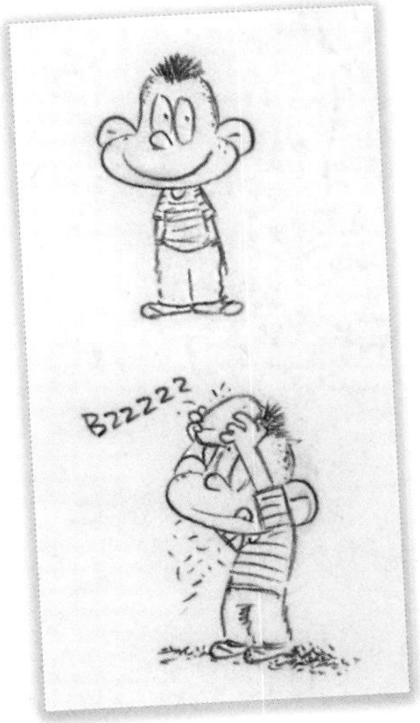
BZZZZZ

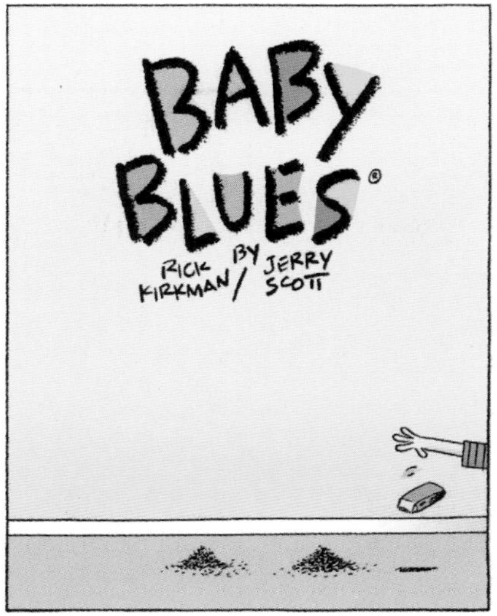
BABY BLUES®
BY RICK KIRKMAN / JERRY SCOTT

Rick: This strip stemmed from a sketch I made that I thought was funny, of Hammie shaving his head. I'd seen a kid in a waiting room with that haircut, and it got me thinking how it happened.

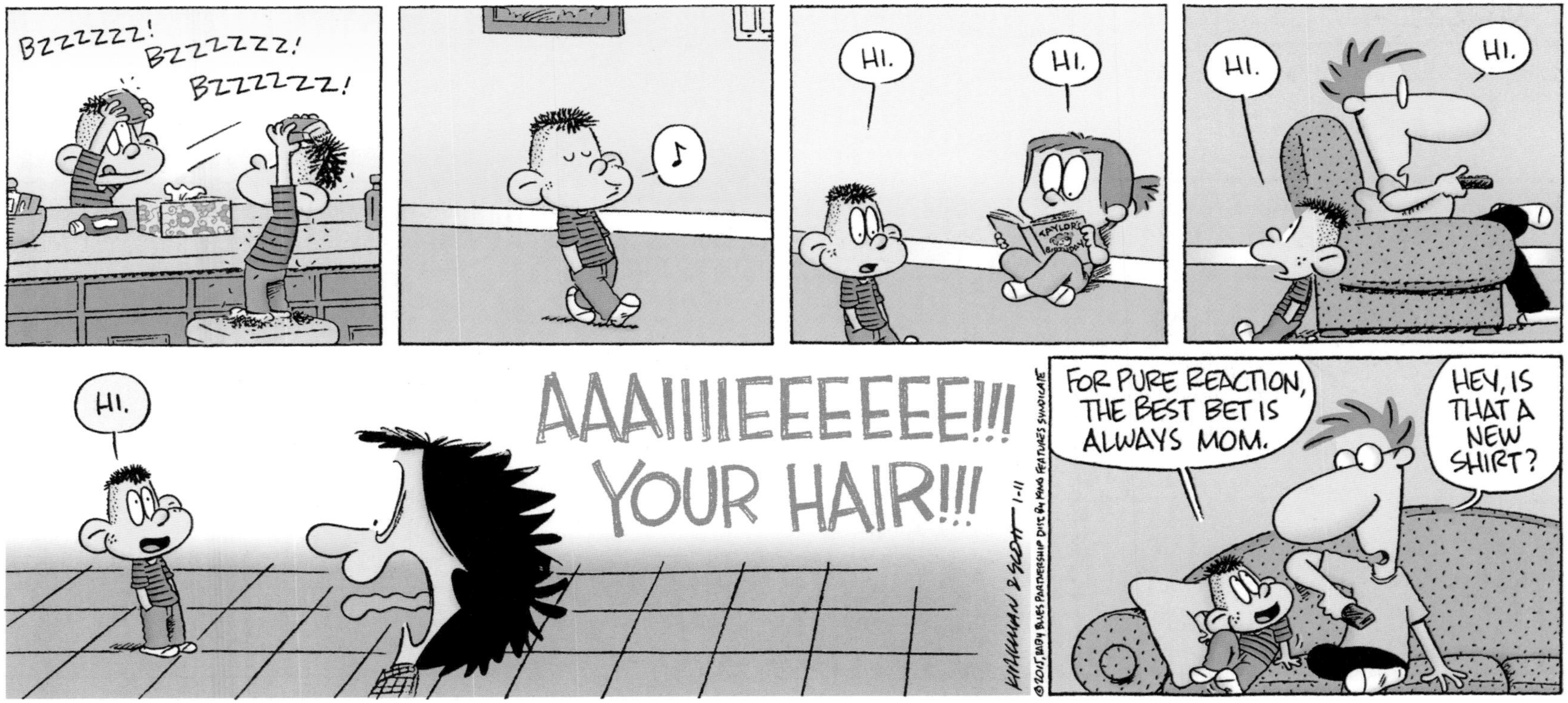
BZZZZZZ!
BZZZZZZ!
BZZZZZZ!
♪
HI.
HI.
HI.
HI.
HI.
AAAIIIIIEEEEEE!!! YOUR HAIR!!!
KIRKMAN & SCOTT 1-11
©2015, BABY BLUES PARTNERSHIP DIST. BY KING FEATURES SYNDICATE
FOR PURE REACTION, THE BEST BET IS ALWAYS MOM.
HEY, IS THAT A NEW SHIRT?

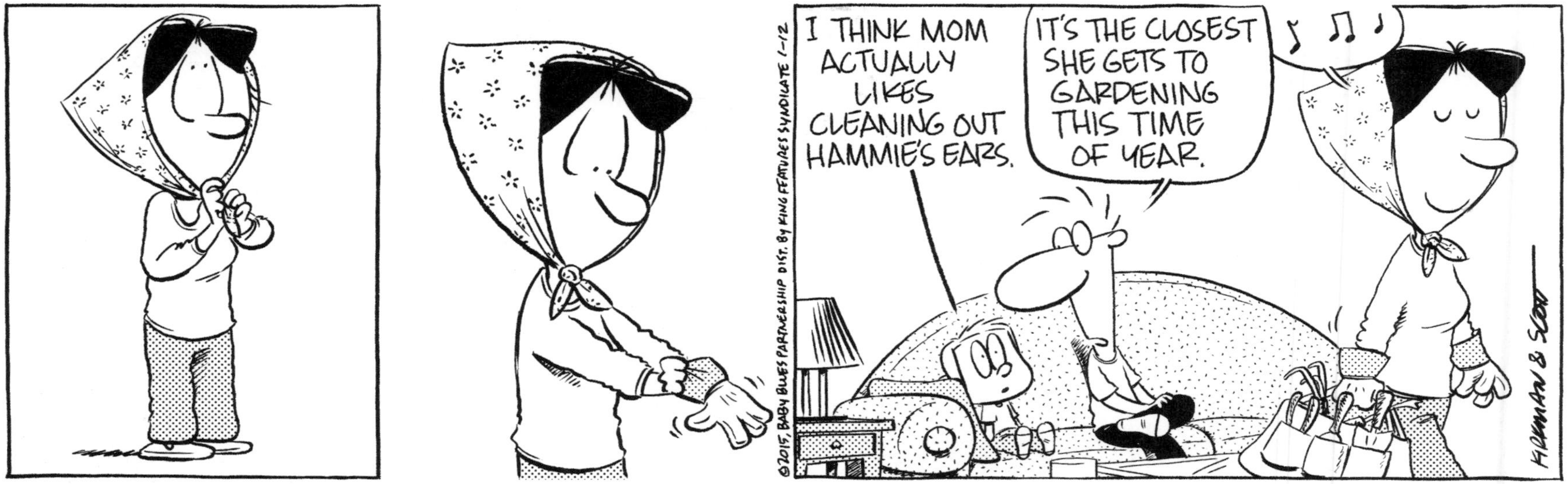
I THINK MOM ACTUALLY LIKES CLEANING OUT HAMMIE'S EARS.
IT'S THE CLOSEST SHE GETS TO GARDENING THIS TIME OF YEAR.
©2015, BABY BLUES PARTNERSHIP DIST. BY KING FEATURES SYNDICATE 1-12
KIRKMAN & SCOTT

Jerry: My mom used to say I had enough dirt in my ears that she could grow potatoes in them. Ridiculous. It was wheat.

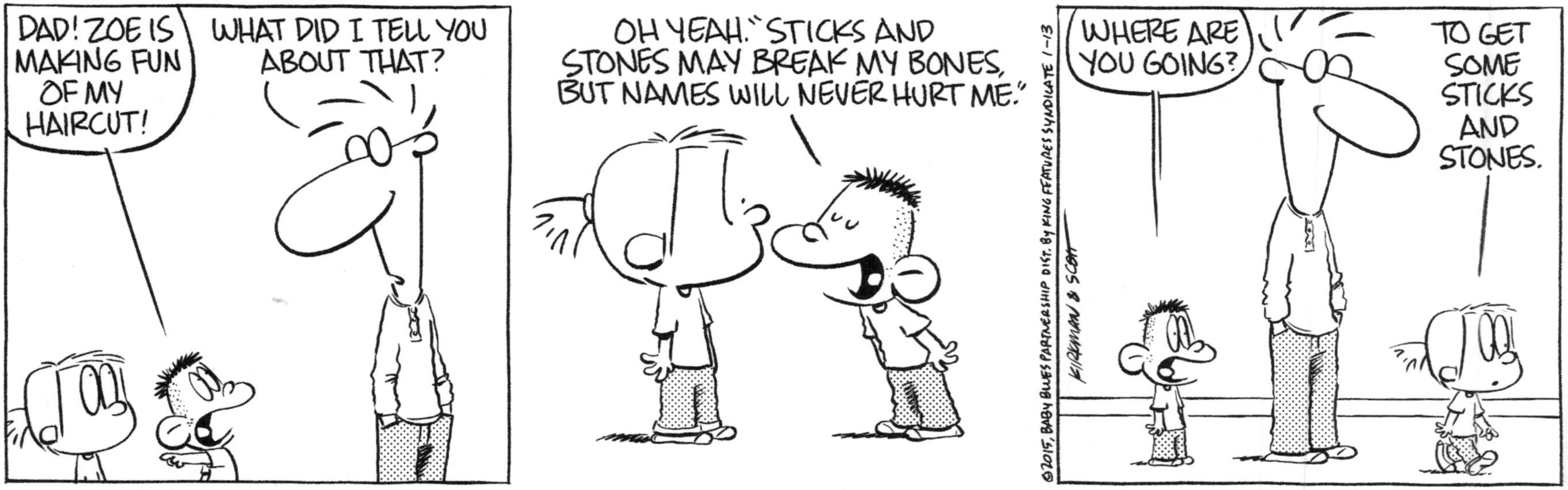
DAD! ZOE IS MAKING FUN OF MY HAIRCUT!
WHAT DID I TELL YOU ABOUT THAT?
OH YEAH. "STICKS AND STONES MAY BREAK MY BONES, BUT NAMES WILL NEVER HURT ME."
WHERE ARE YOU GOING?
TO GET SOME STICKS AND STONES.
©2015, BABY BLUES PARTNERSHIP DIST. BY KING FEATURES SYNDICATE 1-13
KIRKMAN & SCOTT

Rick: This began several weeks of me worrying about forgetting about Hammie's haircut, and absentmindedly drawing all his hair in. I forgot, though, that we had scheduled vacation strips in the midst of this series. So Hammie's hair came back briefly, despite my worry.

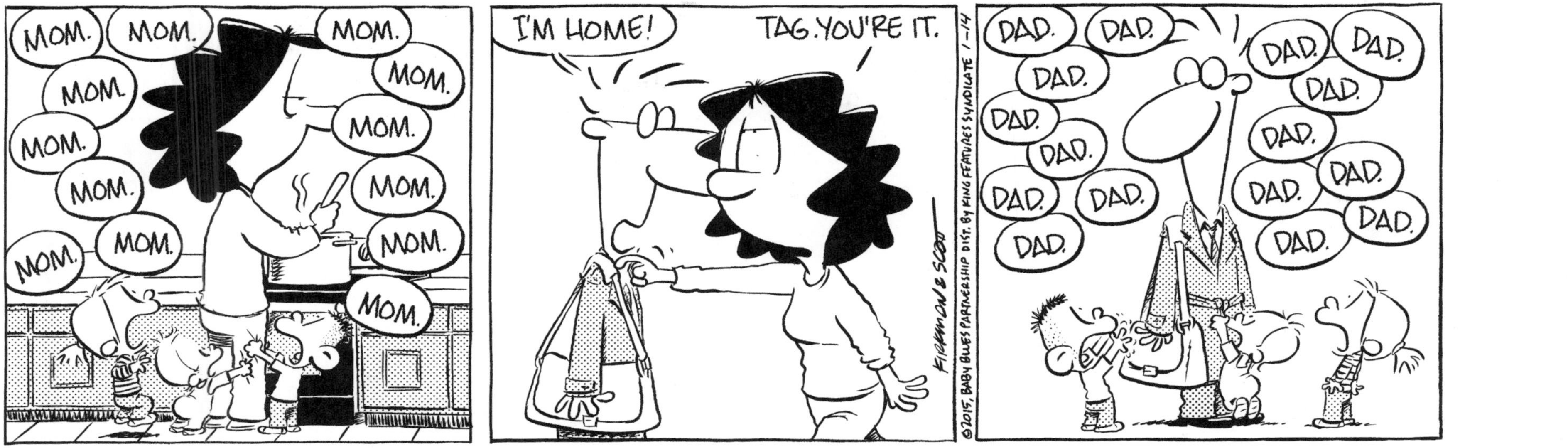
MOM.
MOM.
MOM.
MOM.
MOM.
MOM.
MOM.
MOM.
MOM.
MOM.
MOM.
MOM.
MOM.
MOM.
I'M HOME!
TAG. YOU'RE IT.
KIRKMAN & SCOTT
©2015, BABY BLUES PARTNERSHIP DIST. BY KING FEATURES SYNDICATE 1-14
DAD.
DAD.
DAD.
DAD.
DAD.
DAD.
DAD.
DAD.
DAD.
DAD.
DAD.
DAD.
DAD.
DAD.
DAD.

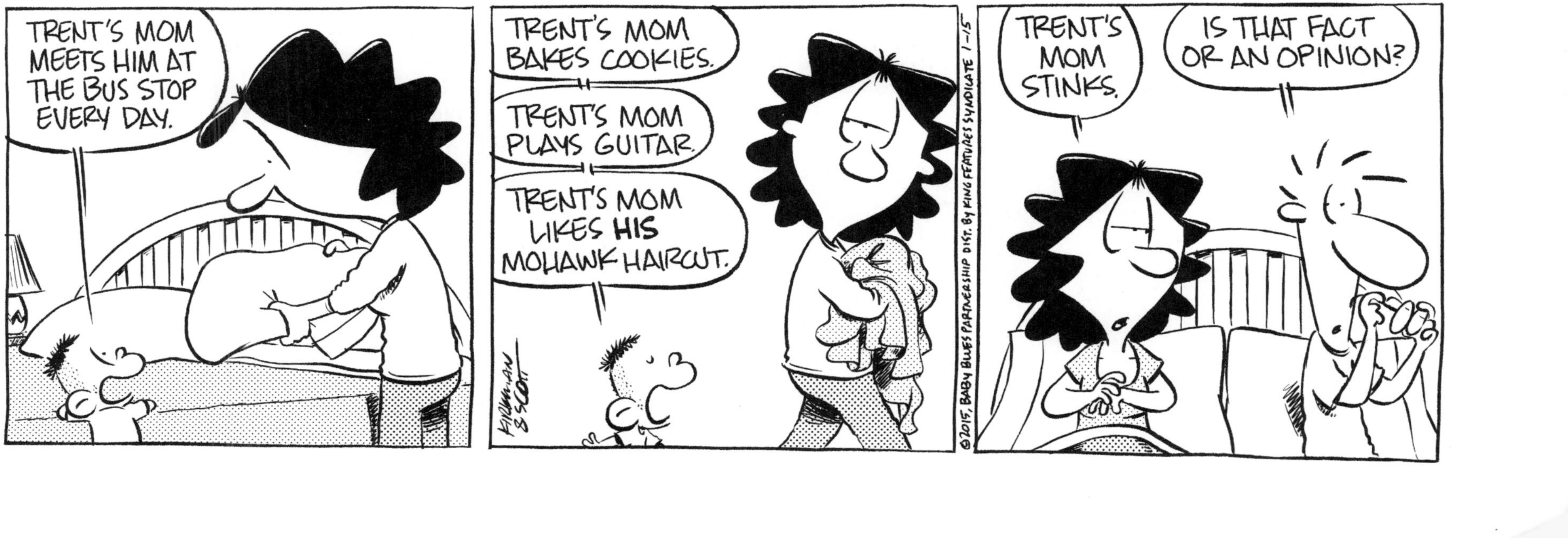
TRENT'S MOM MEETS HIM AT THE BUS STOP EVERY DAY.
TRENT'S MOM BAKES COOKIES.
TRENT'S MOM PLAYS GUITAR.
TRENT'S MOM LIKES **HIS** MOHAWK HAIRCUT.
KIRKMAN & SCOTT
©2015, BABY BLUES PARTNERSHIP DIST. BY KING FEATURES SYNDICATE 1-15
TRENT'S MOM STINKS.
IS THAT FACT OR AN OPINION?

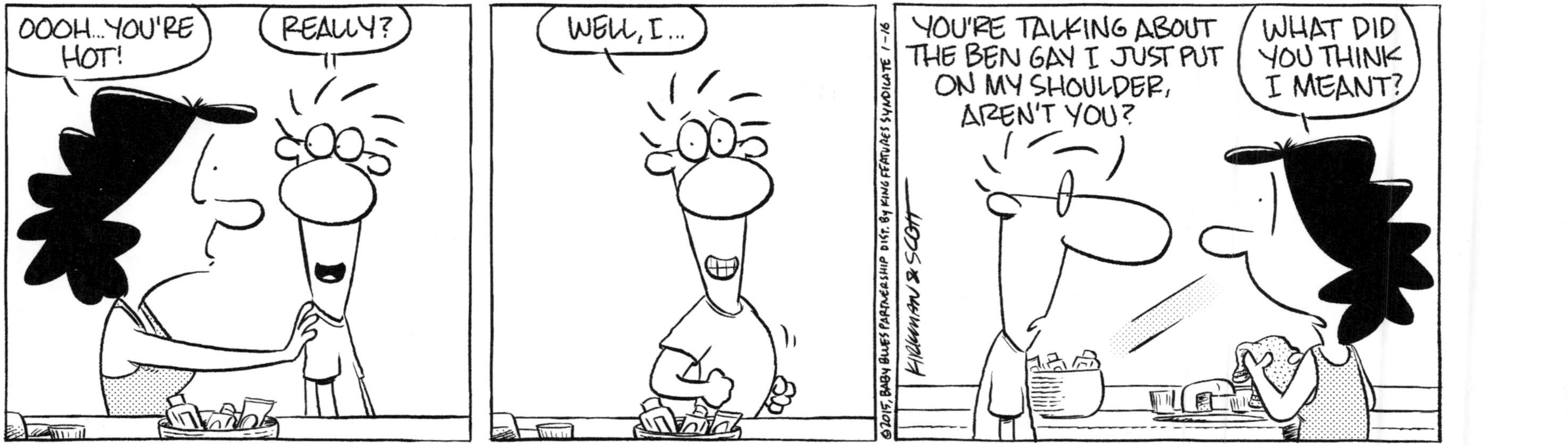
OOOH...YOU'RE HOT!
REALLY?
WELL, I...
YOU'RE TALKING ABOUT THE BEN GAY I JUST PUT ON MY SHOULDER, AREN'T YOU?
WHAT DID YOU THINK I MEANT?
©2015, BABY BLUES PARTNERSHIP DIST. BY KING FEATURES SYNDICATE 1-16
KIRKMAN & SCOTT

Jerry: Ripped from the pages of my life.

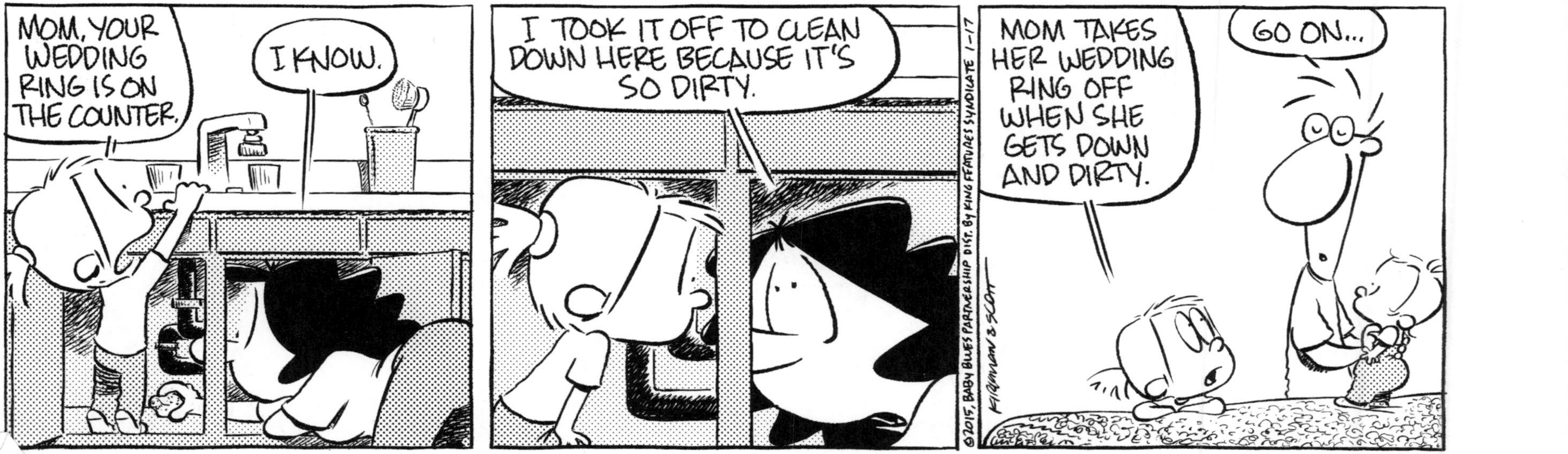
MOM, YOUR WEDDING RING IS ON THE COUNTER.
I KNOW.
I TOOK IT OFF TO CLEAN DOWN HERE BECAUSE IT'S SO DIRTY.
MOM TAKES HER WEDDING RING OFF WHEN SHE GETS DOWN AND DIRTY.
GO ON...
©2015, BABY BLUES PARTNERSHIP DIST. BY KING FEATURES SYNDICATE 1-17
KIRKMAN & SCOTT

Baby Blues®

by Rick Kirkman and Jerry Scott

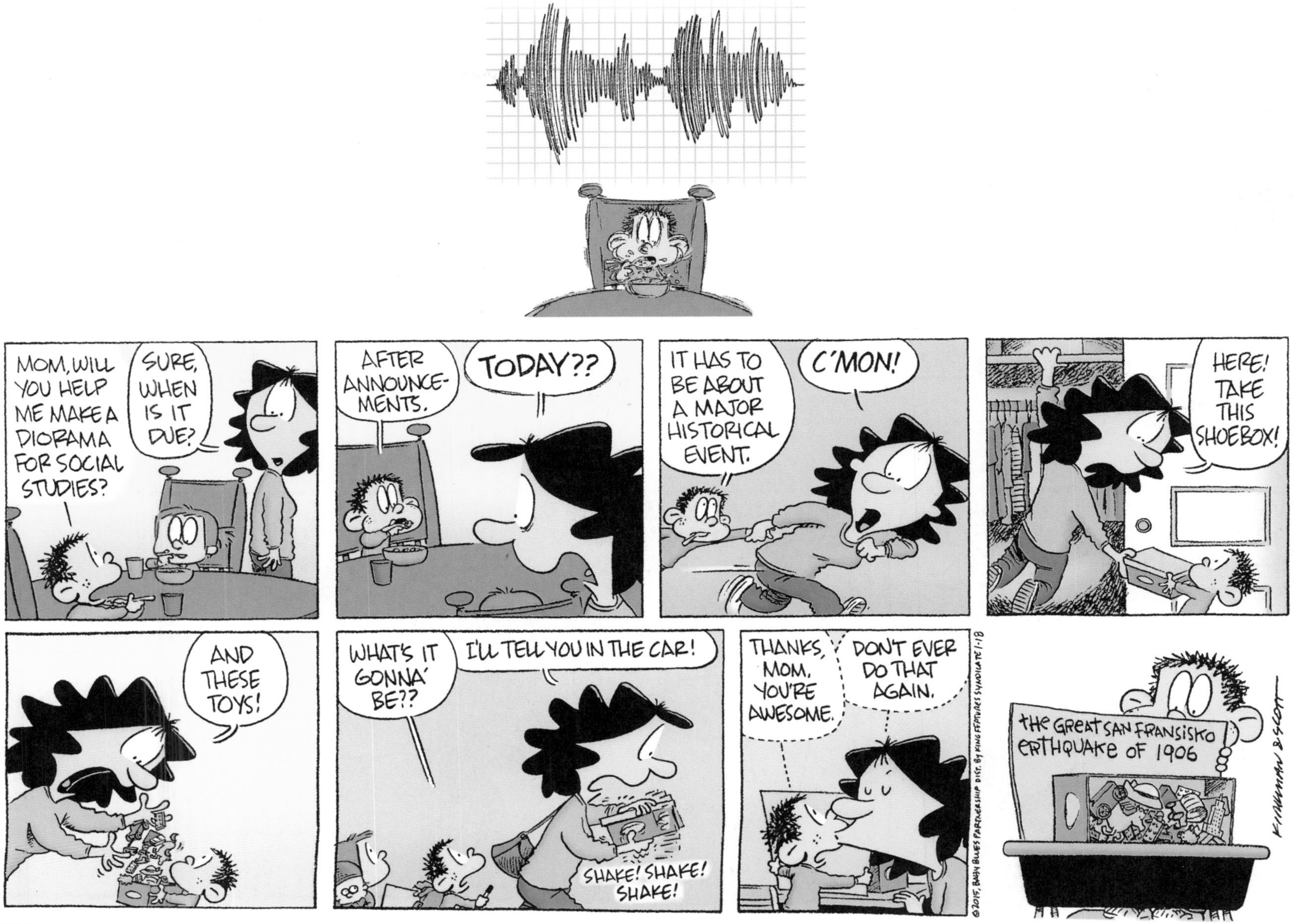
MOM, WILL YOU HELP ME MAKE A DIORAMA FOR SOCIAL STUDIES?
SURE, WHEN IS IT DUE?
AFTER ANNOUNCEMENTS.
TODAY??
IT HAS TO BE ABOUT A MAJOR HISTORICAL EVENT.
C'MON!
HERE! TAKE THIS SHOEBOX!
AND THESE TOYS!
WHAT'S IT GONNA' BE??
I'LL TELL YOU IN THE CAR!
SHAKE! SHAKE! SHAKE!
THANKS, MOM. YOU'RE AWESOME.
DON'T EVER DO THAT AGAIN.
THE GREAT SAN FRANSISKO ERTHQUAKE OF 1906
KIRKMAN & SCOTT

Rick: It's harder to draw a seismograph recording than you would think.

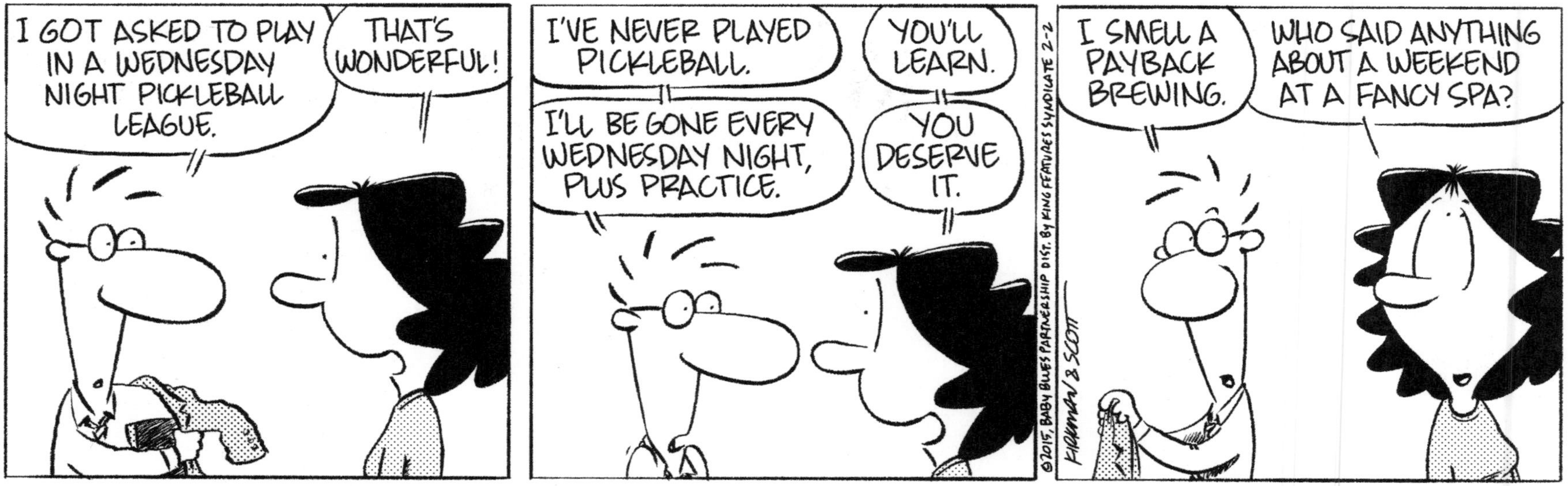
I GOT ASKED TO PLAY IN A WEDNESDAY NIGHT PICKLEBALL LEAGUE.
THAT'S WONDERFUL!
I'VE NEVER PLAYED PICKLEBALL.
YOU'LL LEARN.
I'LL BE GONE EVERY WEDNESDAY NIGHT, PLUS PRACTICE.
YOU DESERVE IT.
© 2015, BABY BLUES PARTNERSHIP DIST. BY KING FEATURES SYNDICATE 2-2
KIRKMAN & SCOTT
I SMELL A PAYBACK BREWING.
WHO SAID ANYTHING ABOUT A WEEKEND AT A FANCY SPA?

Rick: I was unfamiliar with Pickleball when I got this gag from Jerry. At first, I thought he made it up. Off to the Internet for research . . .

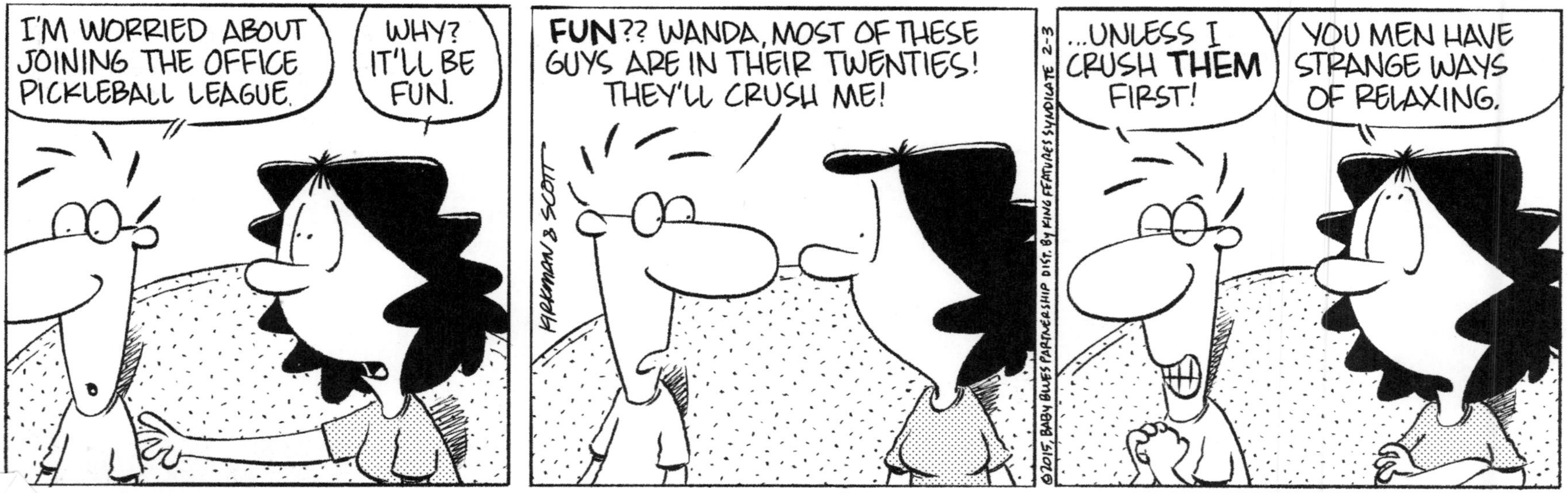
I'M WORRIED ABOUT JOINING THE OFFICE PICKLEBALL LEAGUE.
WHY? IT'LL BE FUN.
FUN?? WANDA, MOST OF THESE GUYS ARE IN THEIR TWENTIES! THEY'LL CRUSH ME!
KIRKMAN & SCOTT
© 2015, BABY BLUES PARTNERSHIP DIST. BY KING FEATURES SYNDICATE 2-3
...UNLESS I CRUSH **THEM** FIRST!
YOU MEN HAVE STRANGE WAYS OF RELAXING.

Since then, I've watched some Pickleball players in person. was definitely in trouble.

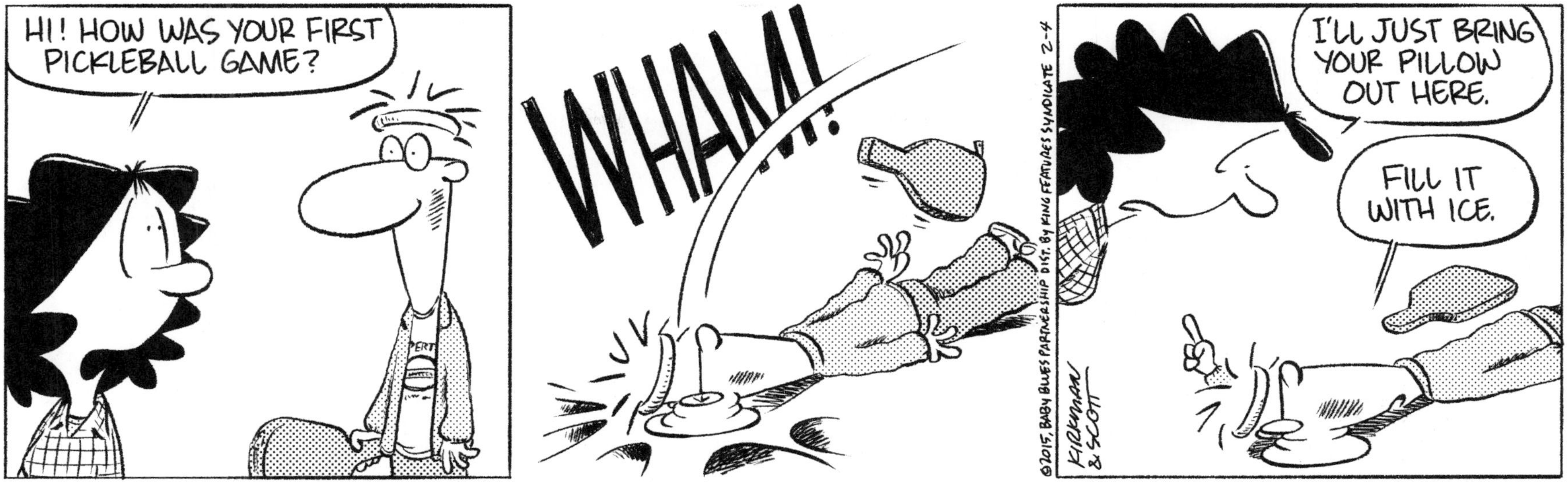
HI! HOW WAS YOUR FIRST PICKLEBALL GAME?
WHAM!
©2015, BABY BLUES PARTNERSHIP DIST. BY KING FEATURES SYNDICATE 2-4
KIRKMAN & SCOTT
I'LL JUST BRING YOUR PILLOW OUT HERE.
FILL IT WITH ICE.

Rick: Typical response to new sports in middle age—at least for me.

Jerry: This is how I used to feel when Rick and I played racquetball back in the day.

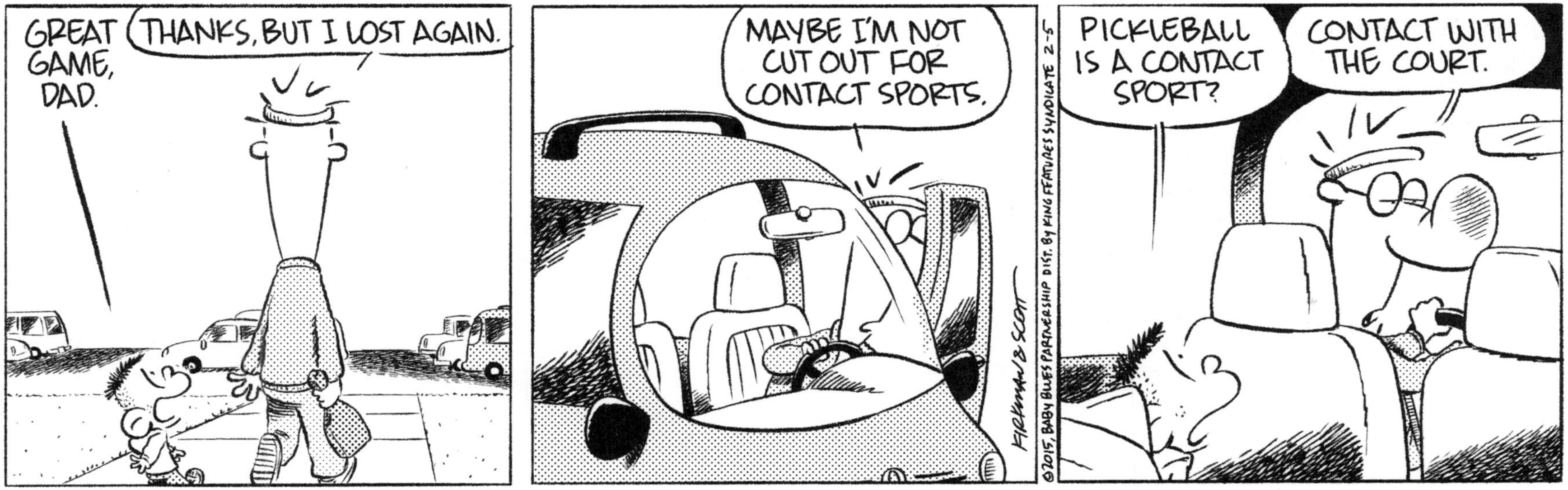
GREAT GAME, DAD.
THANKS, BUT I LOST AGAIN.
MAYBE I'M NOT CUT OUT FOR CONTACT SPORTS.
KIRKMAN & SCOTT
©2015, BABY BLUES PARTNERSHIP DIST. BY KING FEATURES SYNDICATE 2-5
PICKLEBALL IS A CONTACT SPORT?
CONTACT WITH THE COURT.

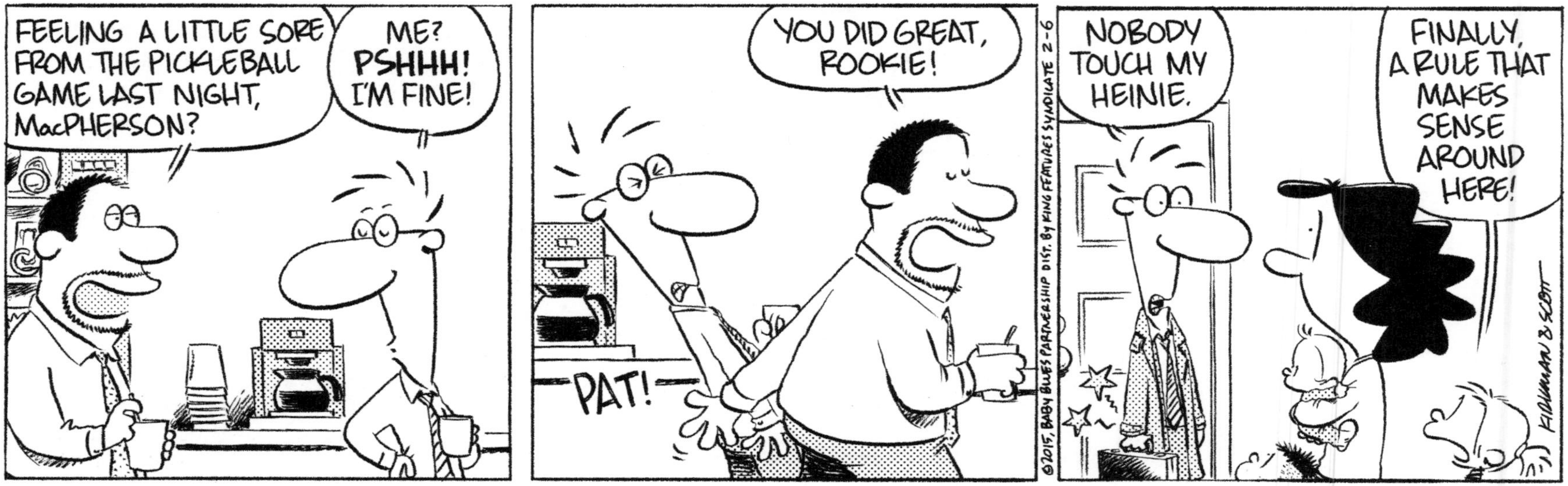
FEELING A LITTLE SORE FROM THE PICKLEBALL GAME LAST NIGHT, MacPHERSON?
ME? PSHHH! I'M FINE!
PAT!
YOU DID GREAT, ROOKIE!
©2015, BABY BLUES PARTNERSHIP DIST. BY KING FEATURES SYNDICATE 2-6
NOBODY TOUCH MY HEINIE.
FINALLY, A RULE THAT MAKES SENSE AROUND HERE!
KIRKMAN & SCOTT

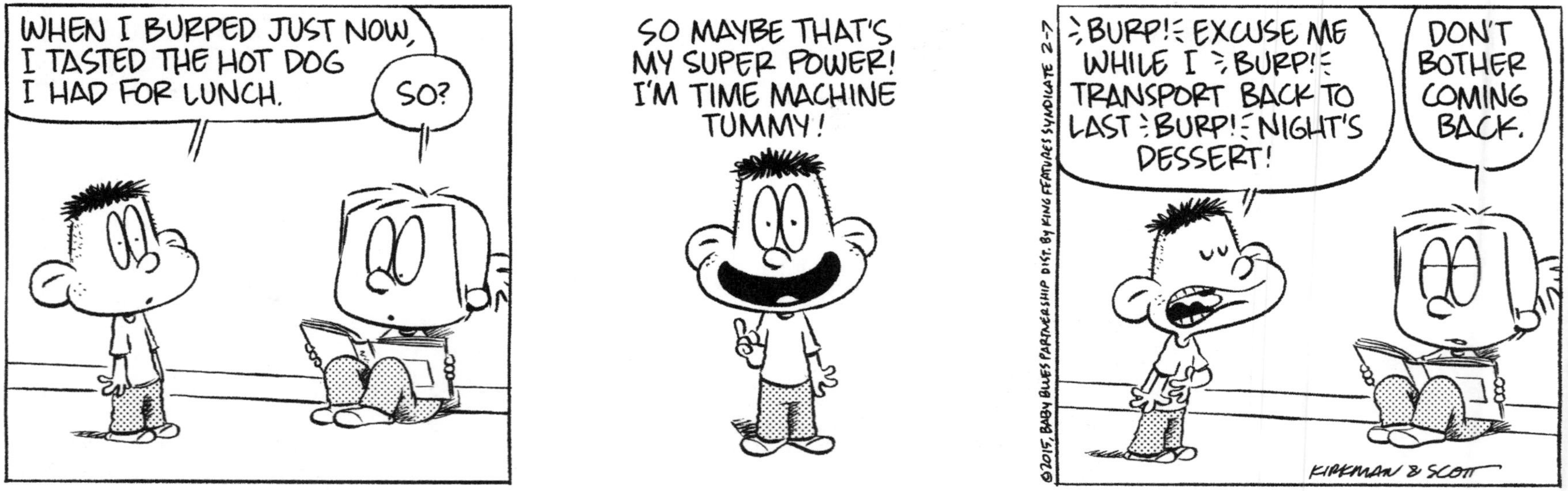
WHEN I BURPED JUST NOW, I TASTED THE HOT DOG I HAD FOR LUNCH.
SO?
SO MAYBE THAT'S MY SUPER POWER! I'M TIME MACHINE TUMMY!
©2015, BABY BLUES PARTNERSHIP DIST. BY KING FEATURES SYNDICATE 2-7
BURP! EXCUSE ME WHILE I BURP! TRANSPORT BACK TO LAST BURP! NIGHT'S DESSERT!
DON'T BOTHER COMING BACK.
KIRKMAN & SCOTT

Rick: Mmmm. Time-traveling gut. How appetizing.

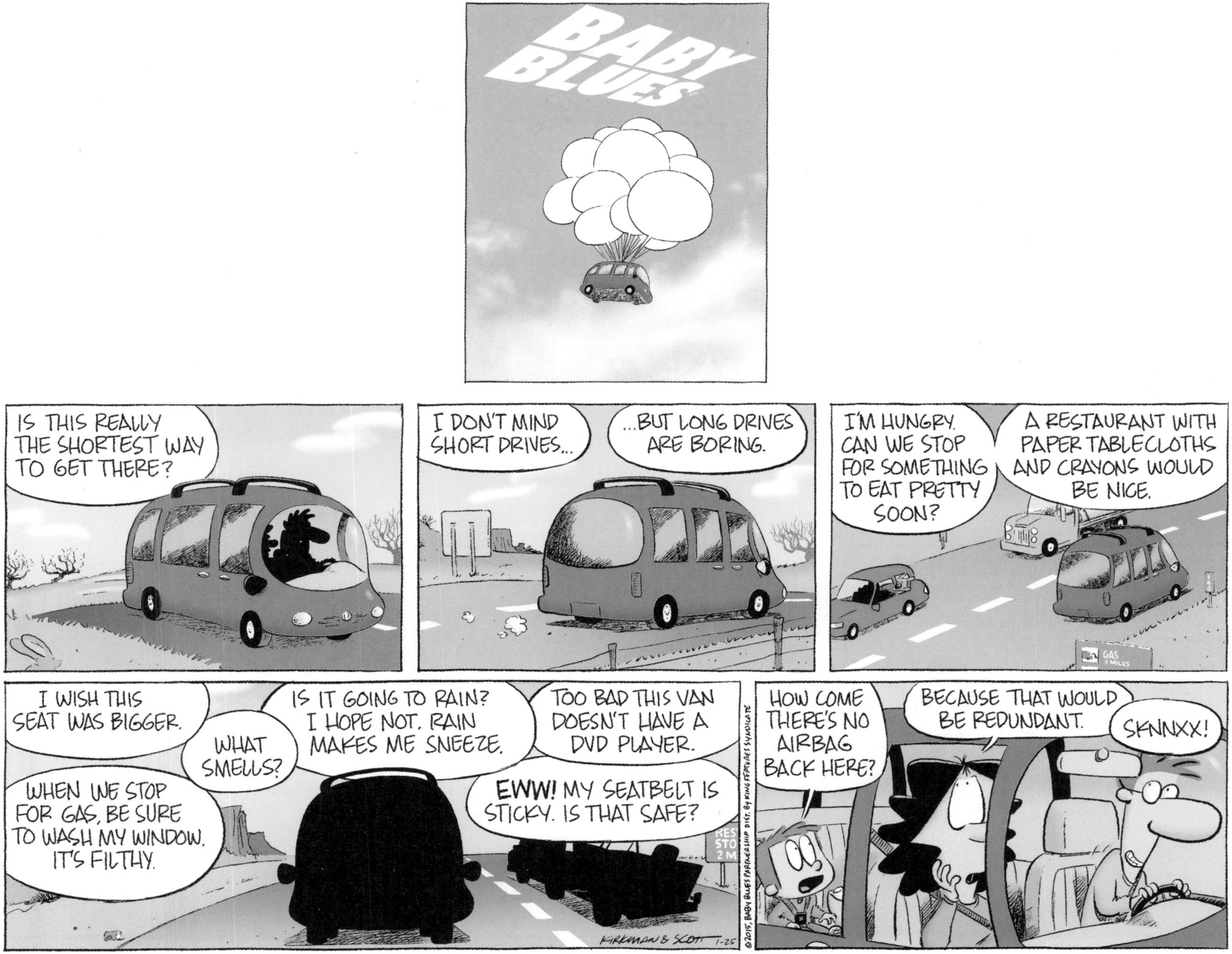
BABY BLUES
IS THIS REALLY THE SHORTEST WAY TO GET THERE?
I DON'T MIND SHORT DRIVES...
...BUT LONG DRIVES ARE BORING.
I'M HUNGRY. CAN WE STOP FOR SOMETHING TO EAT PRETTY SOON?
A RESTAURANT WITH PAPER TABLECLOTHS AND CRAYONS WOULD BE NICE.
GAS
I WISH THIS SEAT WAS BIGGER.
WHAT SMELLS?
IS IT GOING TO RAIN? I HOPE NOT. RAIN MAKES ME SNEEZE.
TOO BAD THIS VAN DOESN'T HAVE A DVD PLAYER.
WHEN WE STOP FOR GAS, BE SURE TO WASH MY WINDOW. IT'S FILTHY.
EWW! MY SEATBELT IS STICKY. IS THAT SAFE?
KIRKMAN & SCOTT 1-25
©2015, BABY BLUES PARTNERSHIP DIST. BY KING FEATURES SYNDICATE
HOW COME THERE'S NO AIRBAG BACK HERE?
BECAUSE THAT WOULD BE REDUNDANT.
SKNNXX!

Rick: A little nod to the Pixar movie *Up* in the title panel.

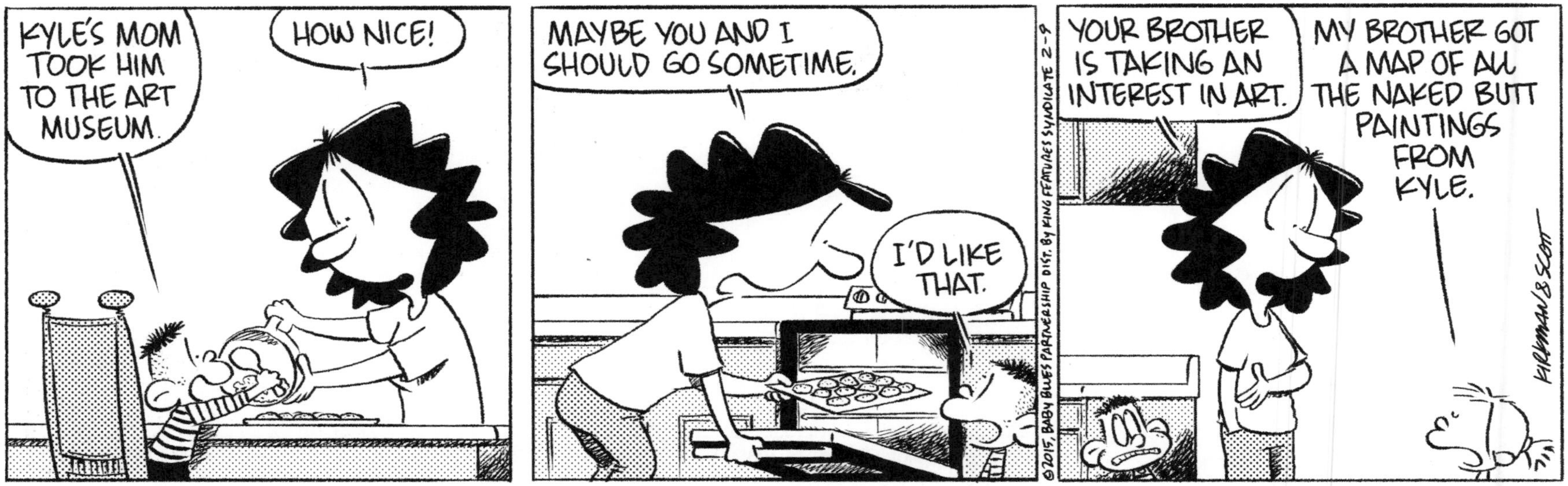
KYLE'S MOM TOOK HIM TO THE ART MUSEUM.
HOW NICE!
MAYBE YOU AND I SHOULD GO SOMETIME.
I'D LIKE THAT.
©2015, BABY BLUES PARTNERSHIP DIST. BY KING FEATURES SYNDICATE 2-9
YOUR BROTHER IS TAKING AN INTEREST IN ART.
MY BROTHER GOT A MAP OF ALL THE NAKED BUTT PAINTINGS FROM KYLE.
KIRKMAN & SCOTT

Rick: Older than the paintings: The tradition of sisters ratting on brothers.

Jerry: Guys like Kyle provide a valuable and time-saving service. I wouldn't mind having one of those maps.

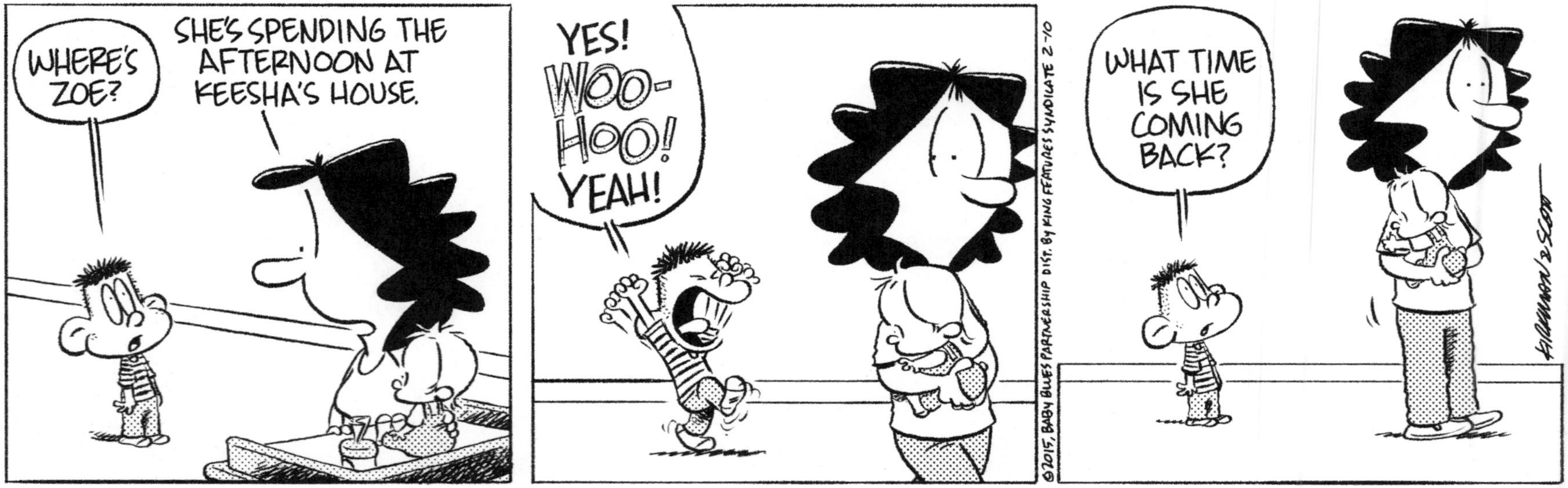
WHERE'S ZOE?
SHE'S SPENDING THE AFTERNOON AT KEESHA'S HOUSE.
YES! WOO-HOO! YEAH!
©2015, BABY BLUES PARTNERSHIP DIST. BY KING FEATURES SYNDICATE 2-10
WHAT TIME IS SHE COMING BACK?
KIRKMAN & SCOTT

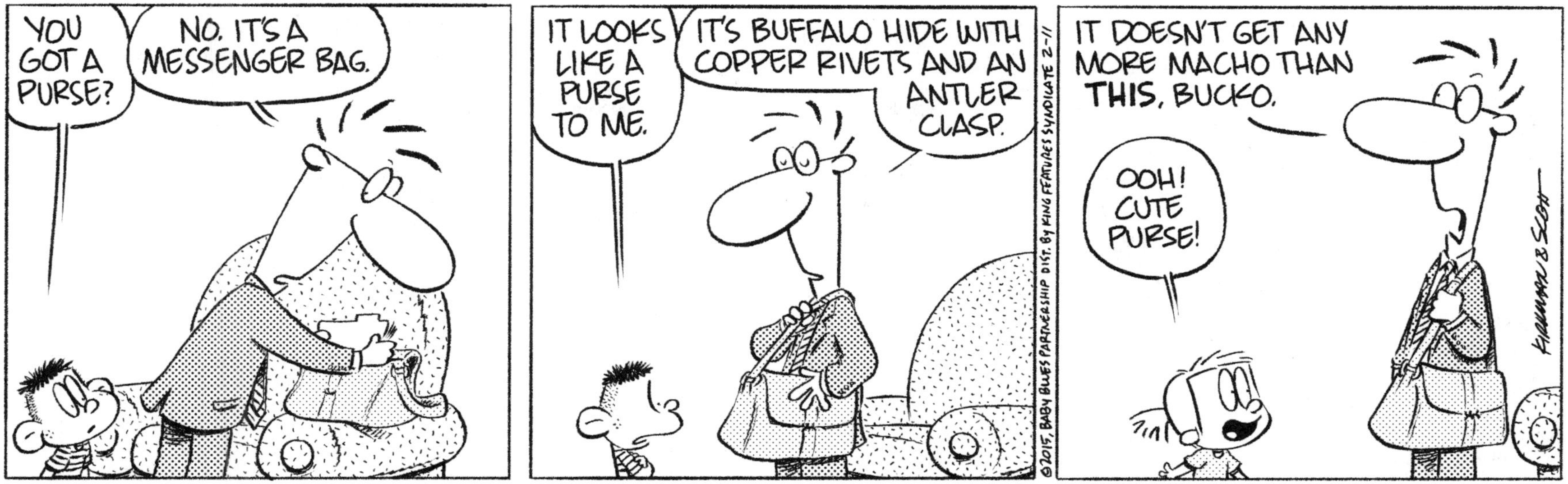
YOU GOT A PURSE?
NO. IT'S A MESSENGER BAG.
IT LOOKS LIKE A PURSE TO ME.
IT'S BUFFALO HIDE WITH COPPER RIVETS AND AN ANTLER CLASP.
IT DOESN'T GET ANY MORE MACHO THAN **THIS**, BUCKO.
OOH! CUTE PURSE!
©2015, BABY BLUES PARTNERSHIP DIST. BY KING FEATURES SYNDICATE 2-11
KIRKMAN & SCOTT

Jerry: I got a leather shoulder bag for Christmas. Buffalo leather, copper rivets, testosterone buckles . . . and I still kinda feel like I'm carrying a purse.

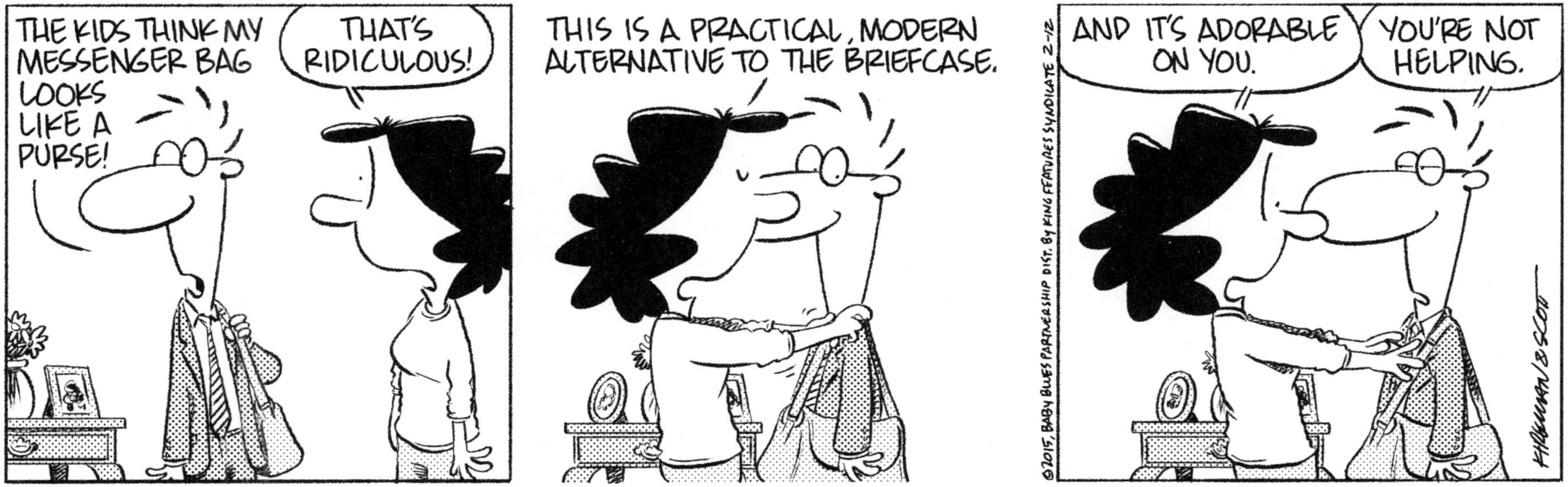
THE KIDS THINK MY MESSENGER BAG LOOKS LIKE A PURSE!
THAT'S RIDICULOUS!
THIS IS A PRACTICAL, MODERN ALTERNATIVE TO THE BRIEFCASE.
AND IT'S ADORABLE ON YOU.
YOU'RE NOT HELPING.
©2015, BABY BLUES PARTNERSHIP DIST. BY KING FEATURES SYNDICATE 2-12
KIRKMAN & SCOTT

Rick: Darryl, I think that's called a consensus.

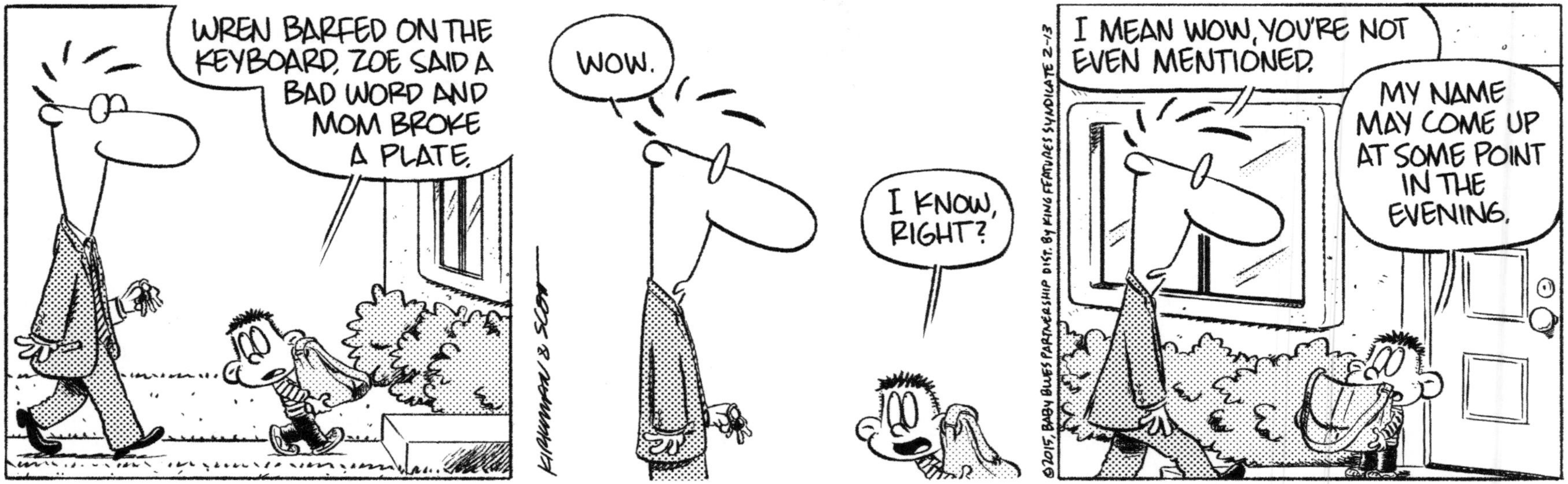
WREN BARFED ON THE KEYBOARD, ZOE SAID A BAD WORD AND MOM BROKE A PLATE.
KIRKMAN & SCOTT
WOW.
I KNOW, RIGHT?
©2015, BABY BLUES PARTNERSHIP DIST. BY KING FEATURES SYNDICATE 2-13
I MEAN WOW, YOU'RE NOT EVEN MENTIONED.
MY NAME MAY COME UP AT SOME POINT IN THE EVENING.

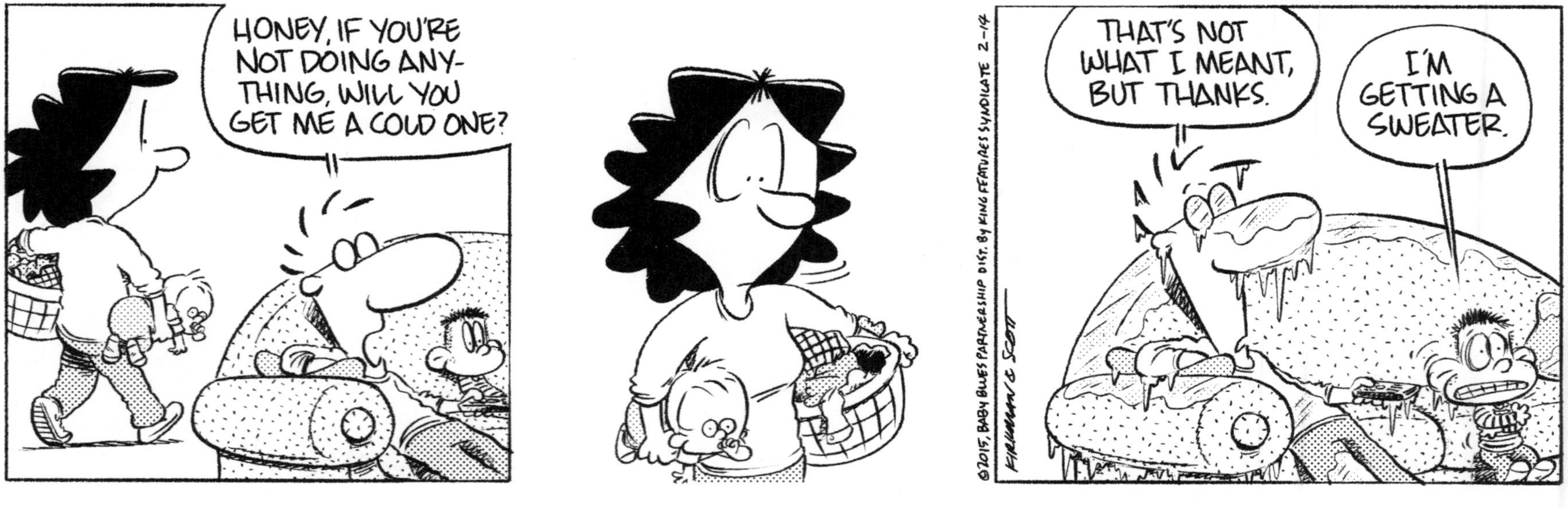
HONEY, IF YOU'RE NOT DOING ANY-THING, WILL YOU GET ME A COLD ONE?
©2015, BABY BLUES PARTNERSHIP DIST. BY KING FEATURES SYNDICATE 2-14
KIRKMAN & SCOTT
THAT'S NOT WHAT I MEANT, BUT THANKS.
I'M GETTING A SWEATER.

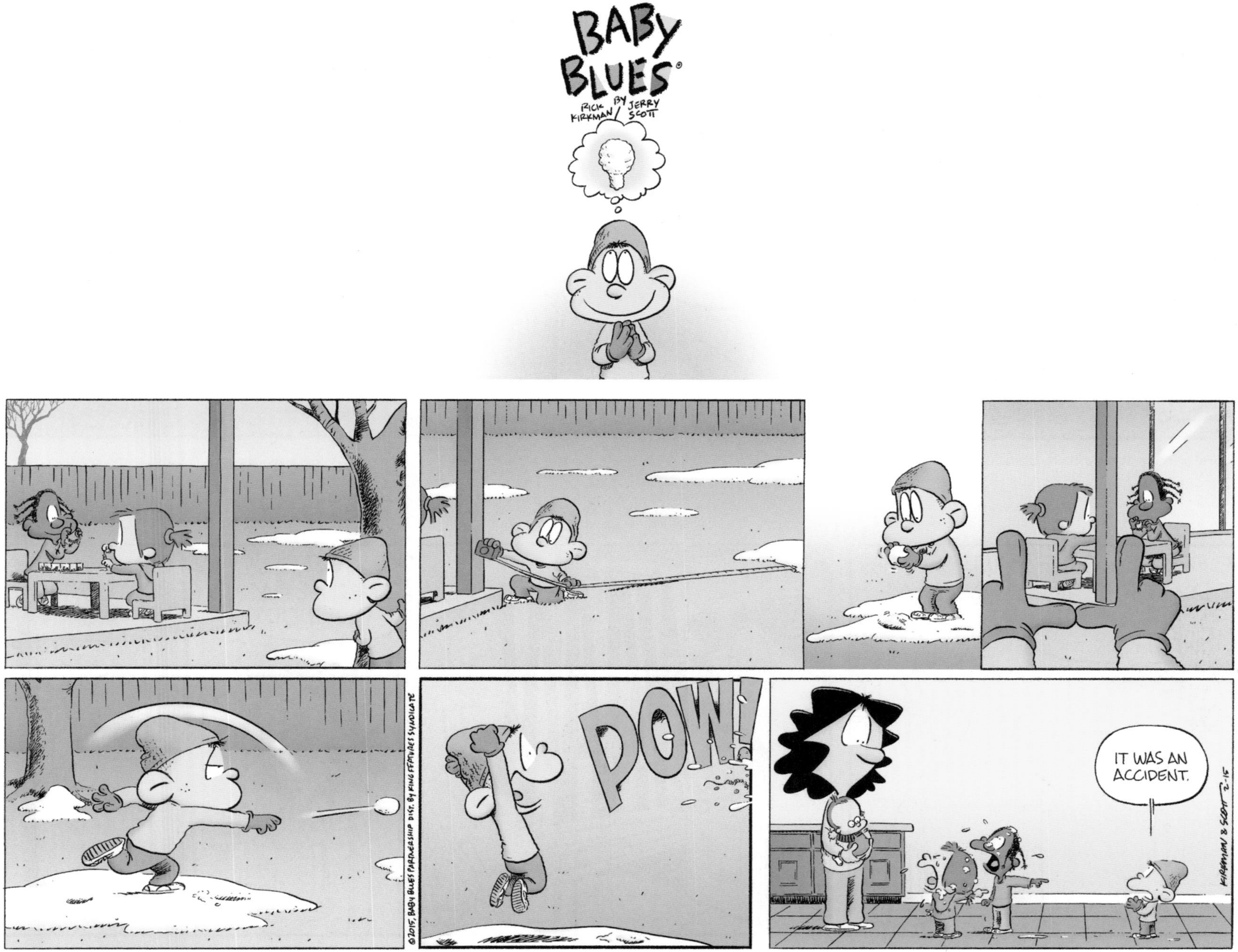
BABY BLUES®
RICK KIRKMAN / BY JERRY SCOTT
©2015, BABY BLUES PARTNERSHIP DIST. BY KING FEATURES SYNDICATE
POW!
IT WAS AN ACCIDENT.
KIRKMAN & SCOTT 2-15

Rick: The MacPhersons live in that magical land where last Sunday they were in the desert, and this Sunday, there's a little snow on the ground.

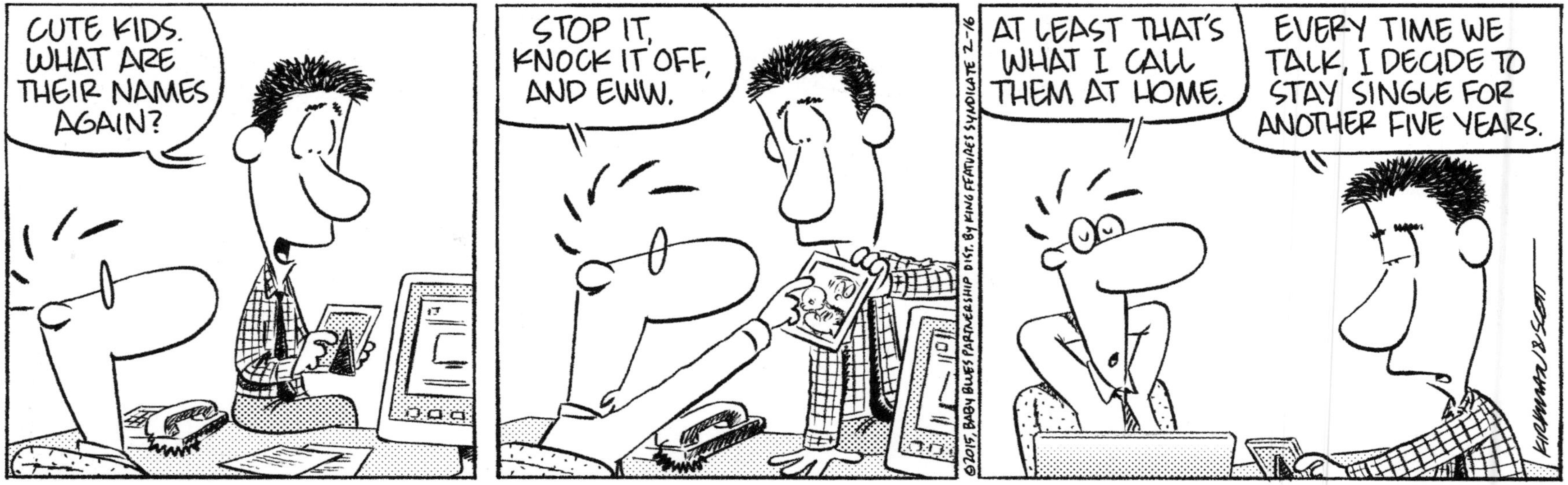
CUTE KIDS. WHAT ARE THEIR NAMES AGAIN?
STOP IT, KNOCK IT OFF, AND EWW.
AT LEAST THAT'S WHAT I CALL THEM AT HOME.
EVERY TIME WE TALK, I DECIDE TO STAY SINGLE FOR ANOTHER FIVE YEARS.
©2015, BABY BLUES PARTNERSHIP DIST. BY KING FEATURES SYNDICATE 2-16
KIRKMAN & SCOTT

Rick: We'll leave it to you to decide which one is which.

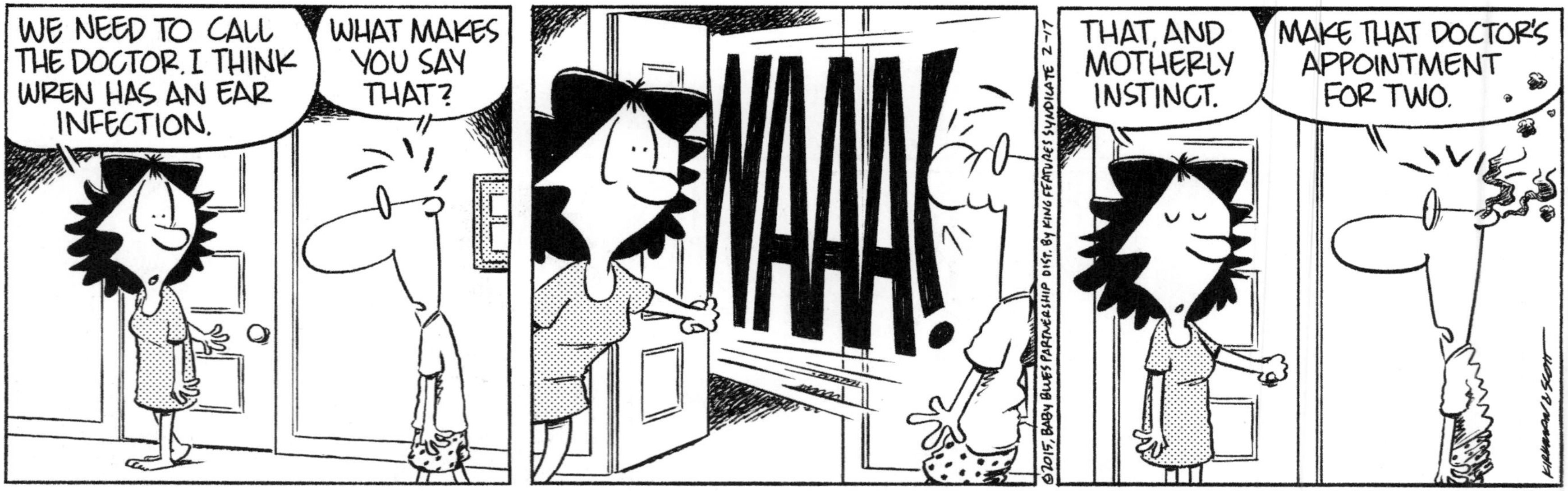
WE NEED TO CALL THE DOCTOR. I THINK WREN HAS AN EAR INFECTION.
WHAT MAKES YOU SAY THAT?
WAAA!
THAT, AND MOTHERLY INSTINCT.
MAKE THAT DOCTOR'S APPOINTMENT FOR TWO.
©2015, BABY BLUES PARTNERSHIP DIST. BY KING FEATURES SYNDICATE 2-17
KIRKMAN & SCOTT

Rick: Jerry's gag read, "A wall of sound hits Darryl in the face." I took that literally.

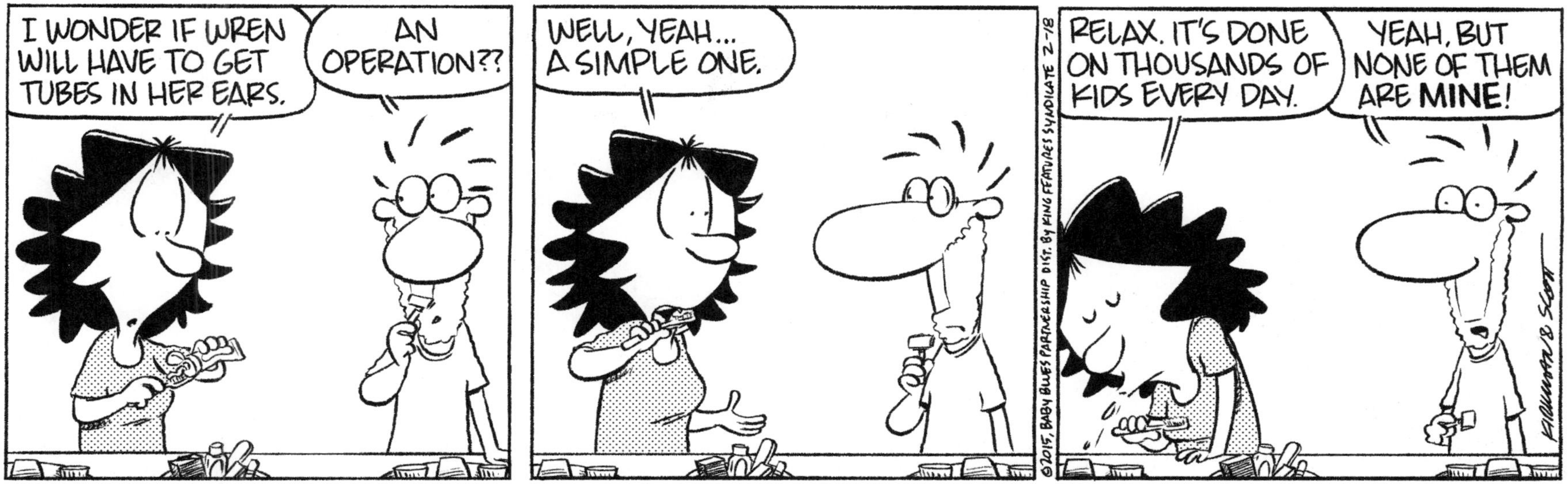
I WONDER IF WREN WILL HAVE TO GET TUBES IN HER EARS.
AN OPERATION??
WELL, YEAH... A SIMPLE ONE.
RELAX. IT'S DONE ON THOUSANDS OF KIDS EVERY DAY.
YEAH, BUT NONE OF THEM ARE **MINE**!
©2015, BABY BLUES PARTNERSHIP DIST. BY KING FEATURES SYNDICATE 2-18
KIRKMAN & SCOTT

Rick: Seemed like half the kids had tubes in their ears when our kids were that age.

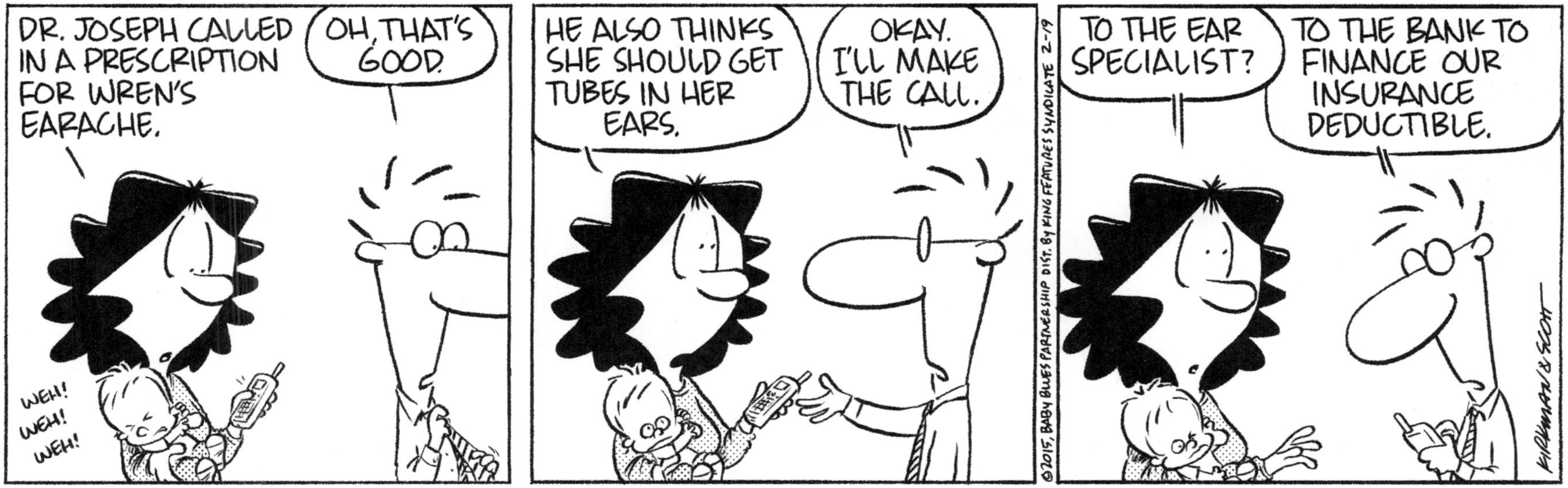
DR. JOSEPH CALLED IN A PRESCRIPTION FOR WREN'S EARACHE.
OH, THAT'S GOOD.
WEH! WEH! WEH!
HE ALSO THINKS SHE SHOULD GET TUBES IN HER EARS.
OKAY. I'LL MAKE THE CALL.
TO THE EAR SPECIALIST?
TO THE BANK TO FINANCE OUR INSURANCE DEDUCTIBLE.
©2015, BABY BLUES PARTNERSHIP DIST. BY KING FEATURES SYNDICATE 2-19
KIRKMAN & SCOTT

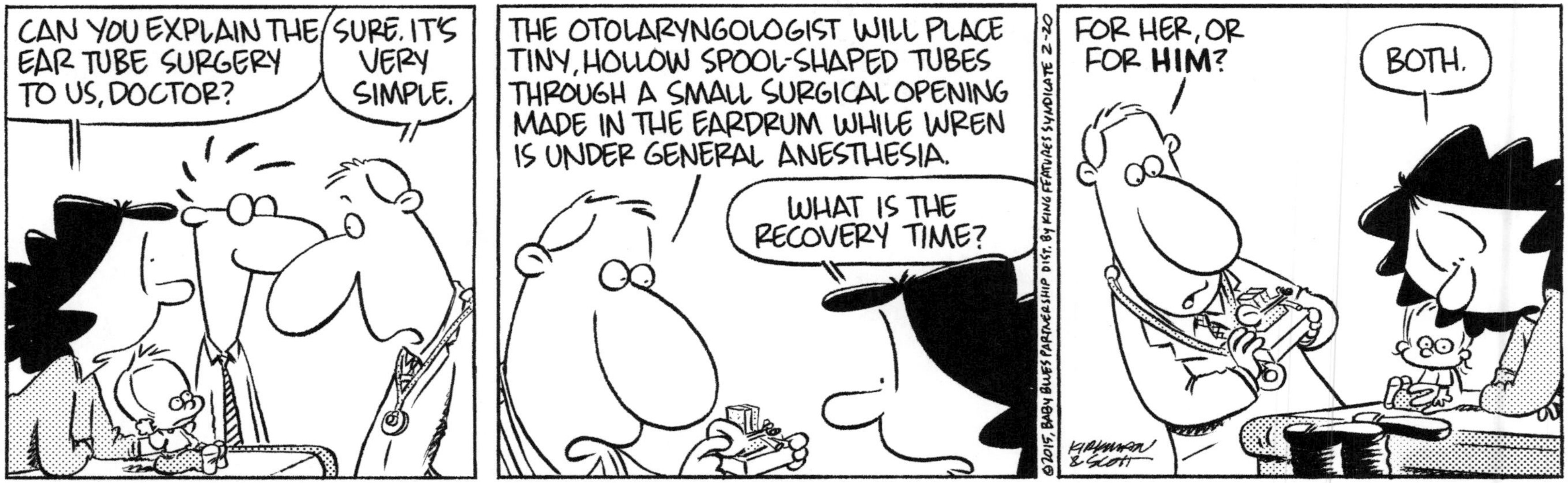
CAN YOU EXPLAIN THE EAR TUBE SURGERY TO US, DOCTOR?
SURE. IT'S VERY SIMPLE.
THE OTOLARYNGOLOGIST WILL PLACE TINY, HOLLOW SPOOL-SHAPED TUBES THROUGH A SMALL SURGICAL OPENING MADE IN THE EARDRUM WHILE WREN IS UNDER GENERAL ANESTHESIA.
WHAT IS THE RECOVERY TIME?
FOR HER, OR FOR **HIM**?
BOTH.
©2015, BABY BLUES PARTNERSHIP DIST. BY KING FEATURES SYNDICATE 2-20
KIRKMAN & SCOTT

Rick: I only passed out when I got a cost estimate from a doctor's office.

Jerry: I have such a weak stomach when it comes to any medical thing. I once passed out talking to a doctor about somebody else's X-ray.

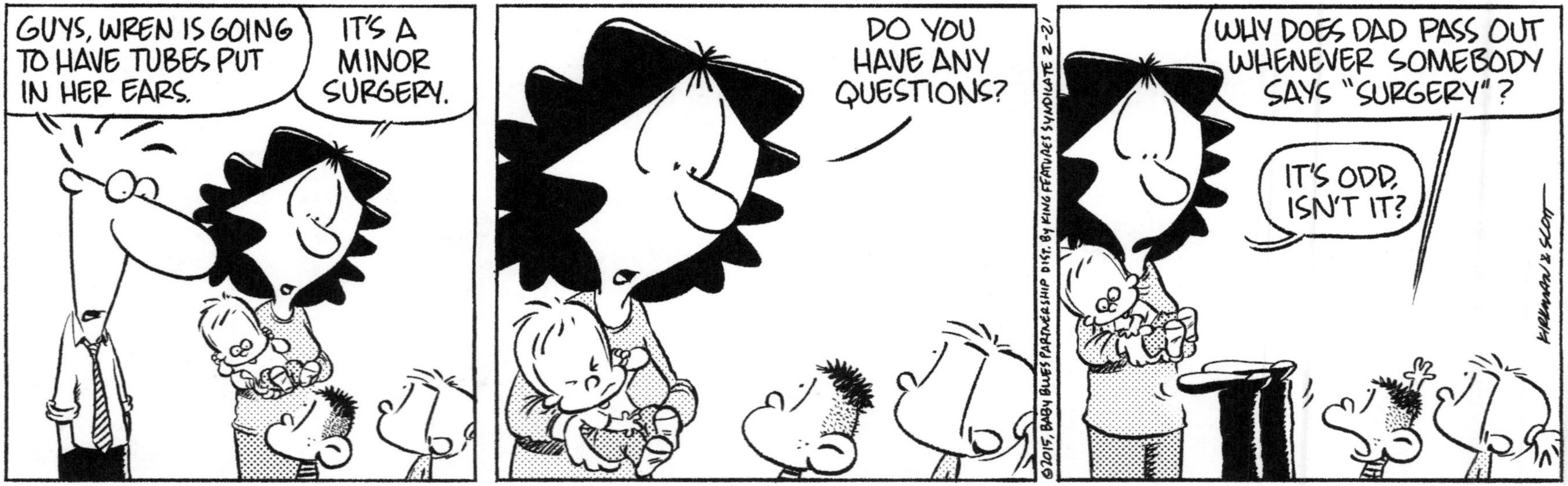
GUYS, WREN IS GOING TO HAVE TUBES PUT IN HER EARS.
IT'S A MINOR SURGERY.
DO YOU HAVE ANY QUESTIONS?
WHY DOES DAD PASS OUT WHENEVER SOMEBODY SAYS "SURGERY"?
IT'S ODD, ISN'T IT?
©2015, BABY BLUES PARTNERSHIP DIST. BY KING FEATURES SYNDICATE 2-21
KIRKMAN & SCOTT

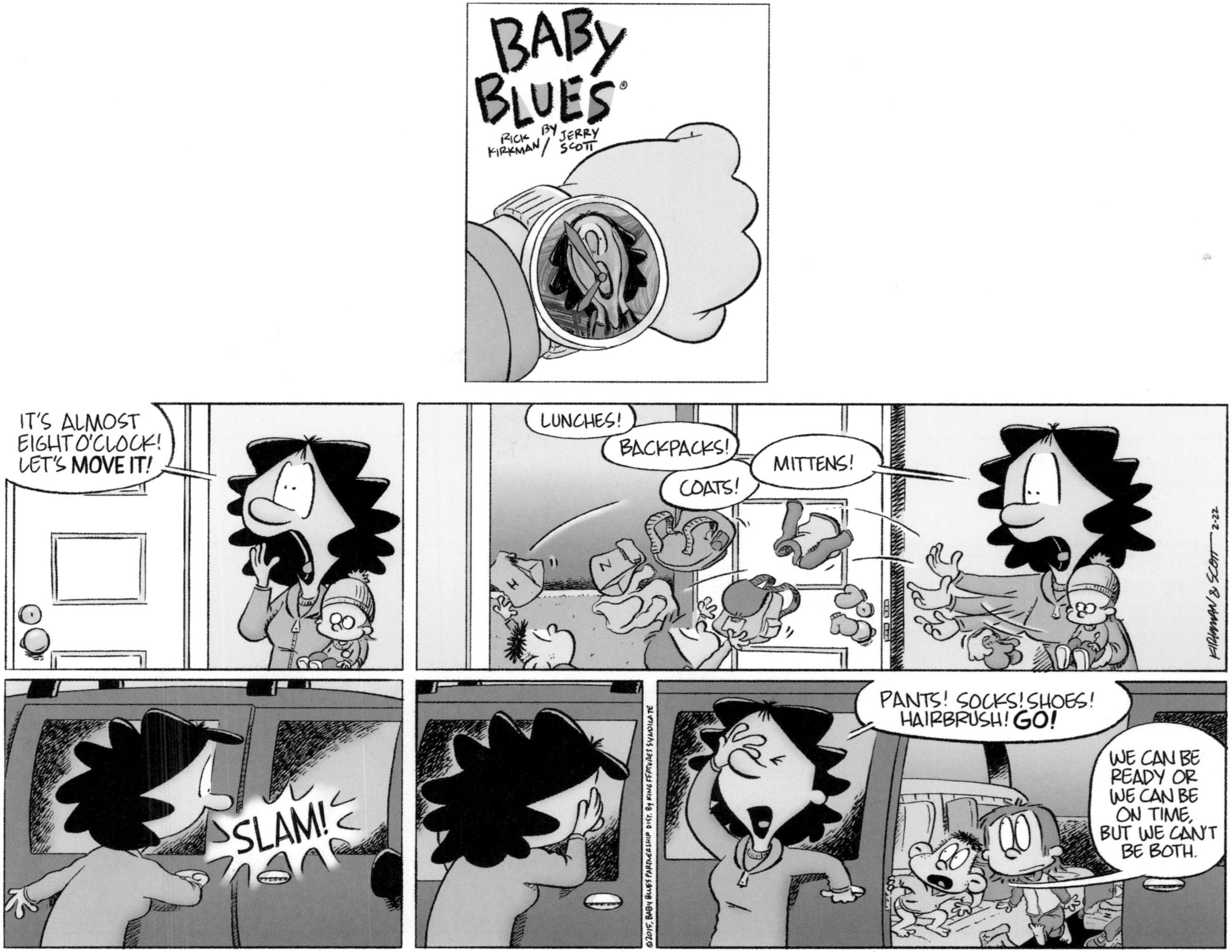
BABY BLUES®
BY RICK KIRKMAN / JERRY SCOTT
IT'S ALMOST EIGHT O'CLOCK! LET'S MOVE IT!
LUNCHES!
BACKPACKS!
COATS!
MITTENS!
SLAM!
PANTS! SOCKS! SHOES! HAIRBRUSH! GO!
WE CAN BE READY OR WE CAN BE ON TIME, BUT WE CAN'T BE BOTH.

Rick: Wanda starring in Edvard Munch's *The Scream* on a watch face in the title panel.

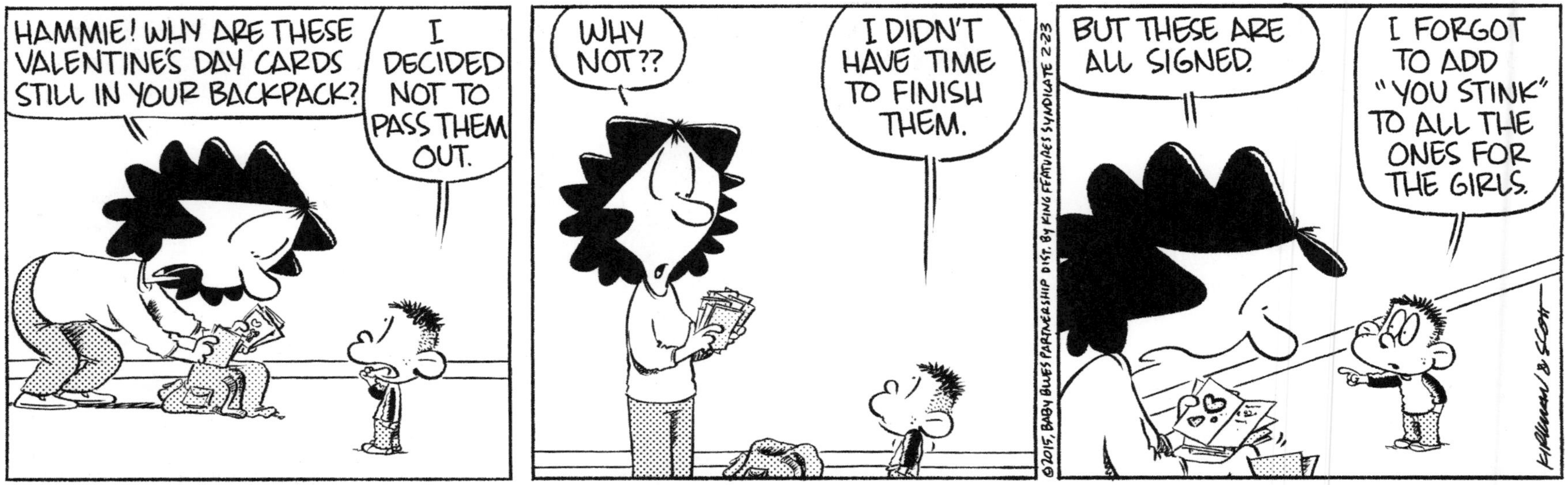
HAMMIE! WHY ARE THESE VALENTINE'S DAY CARDS STILL IN YOUR BACKPACK?
I DECIDED NOT TO PASS THEM OUT.
WHY NOT??
I DIDN'T HAVE TIME TO FINISH THEM.
©2015, BABY BLUES PARTNERSHIP DIST. BY KING FEATURES SYNDICATE 2-23
BUT THESE ARE ALL SIGNED.
I FORGOT TO ADD "YOU STINK" TO ALL THE ONES FOR THE GIRLS.
KIRKMAN & SCOTT

Rick: Well, you wouldn't want one to get the inscription and leave out the rest. Hammie has such a sense of fairness.

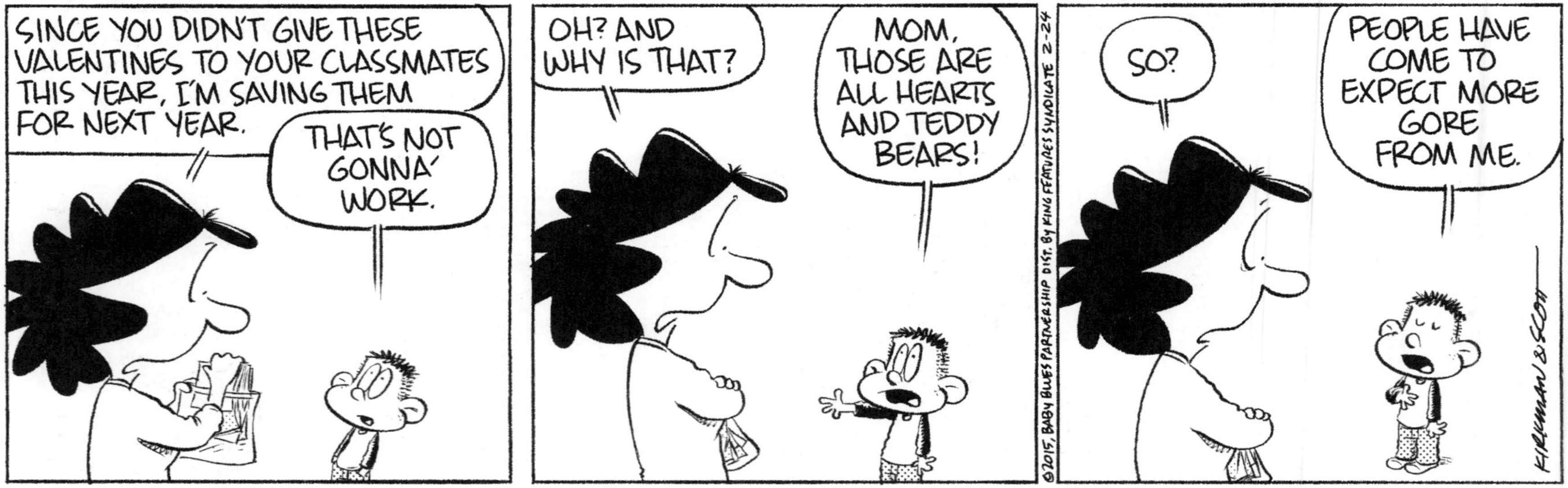
SINCE YOU DIDN'T GIVE THESE VALENTINES TO YOUR CLASSMATES THIS YEAR, I'M SAVING THEM FOR NEXT YEAR.
THAT'S NOT GONNA' WORK.
OH? AND WHY IS THAT?
MOM, THOSE ARE ALL HEARTS AND TEDDY BEARS!
©2015, BABY BLUES PARTNERSHIP DIST. BY KING FEATURES SYNDICATE 2-24
SO?
PEOPLE HAVE COME TO EXPECT MORE GORE FROM ME.
KIRKMAN & SCOTT

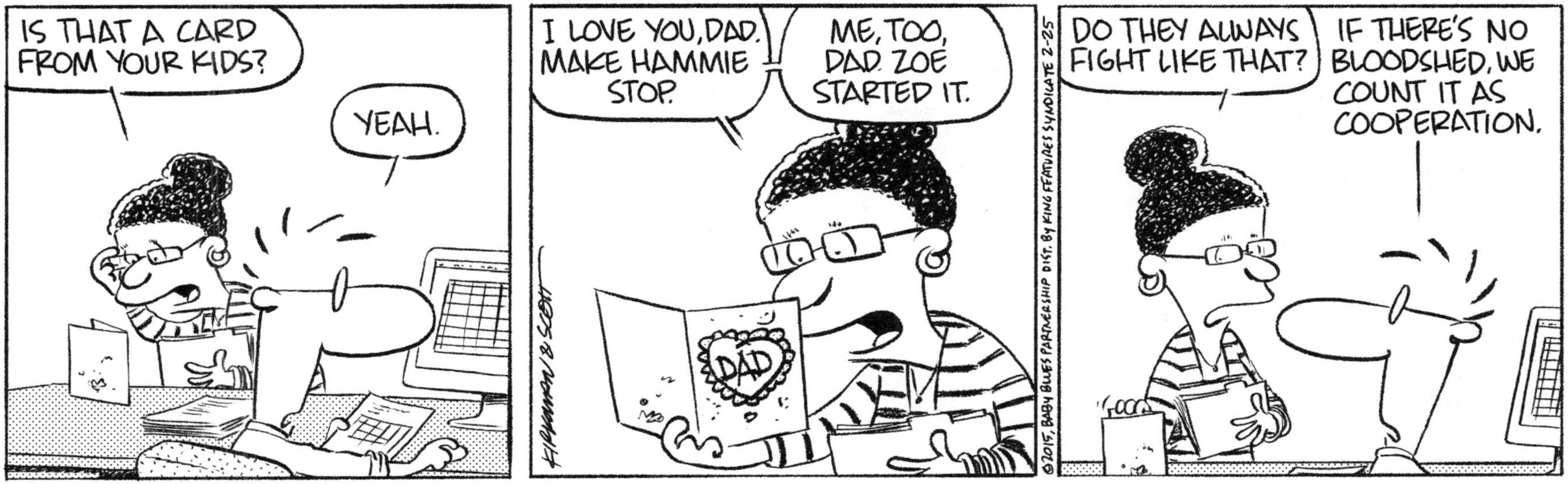
IS THAT A CARD FROM YOUR KIDS?
YEAH.
I LOVE YOU, DAD. MAKE HAMMIE STOP.
ME, TOO, DAD. ZOE STARTED IT.
DAD
DO THEY ALWAYS FIGHT LIKE THAT?
IF THERE'S NO BLOODSHED, WE COUNT IT AS COOPERATION.
KIRKMAN & SCOTT
©2015, BABY BLUES PARTNERSHIP DIST. BY KING FEATURES SYNDICATE 2-25

Jerry: I love that Zoe and Hammie are fighting in a greeting card here. So silly, but kinda believable.

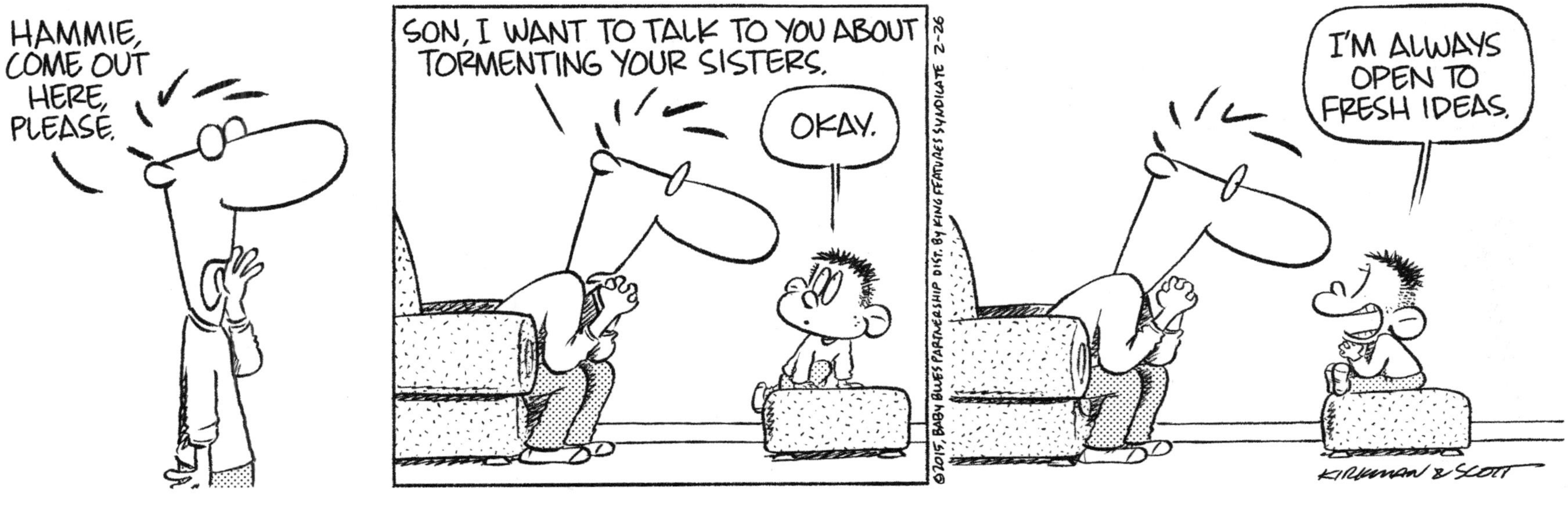
HAMMIE, COME OUT HERE, PLEASE.
SON, I WANT TO TALK TO YOU ABOUT TORMENTING YOUR SISTERS.
OKAY.
I'M ALWAYS OPEN TO FRESH IDEAS.
©2015, BABY BLUES PARTNERSHIP DIST. BY KING FEATURES SYNDICATE 2-26
KIRKMAN & SCOTT

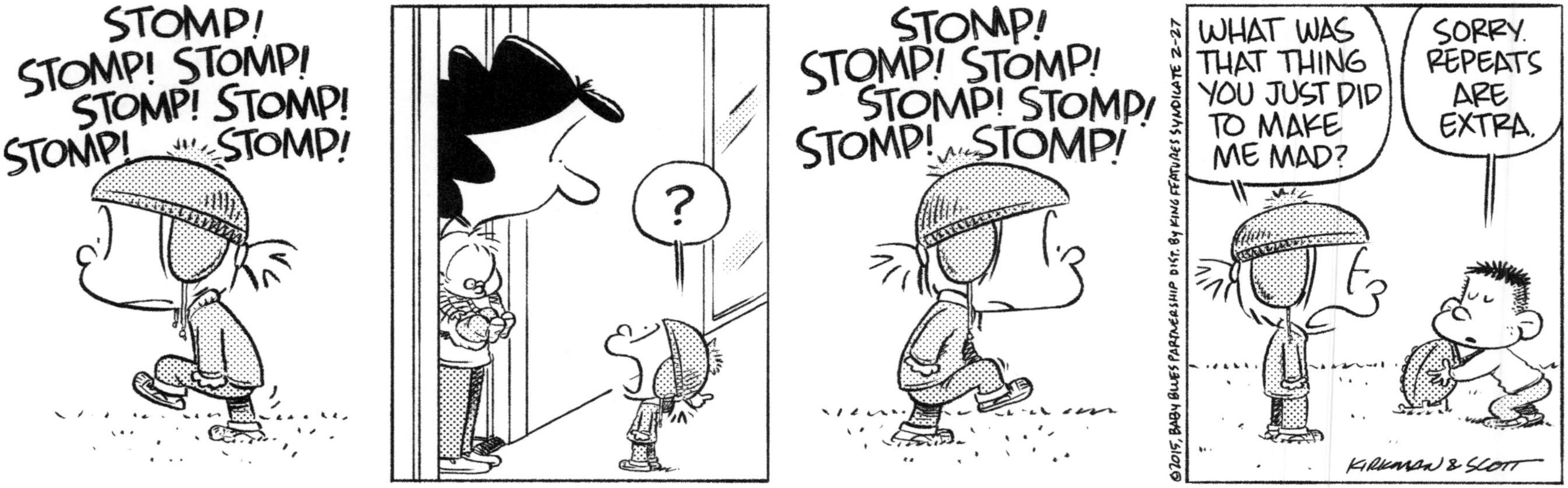
STOMP! STOMP! STOMP! STOMP! STOMP! STOMP! STOMP!
?
STOMP! STOMP! STOMP! STOMP! STOMP! STOMP! STOMP!
©2015, BABY BLUES PARTNERSHIP DIST. BY KING FEATURES SYNDICATE 2-27
WHAT WAS THAT THING YOU JUST DID TO MAKE ME MAD?
SORRY. REPEATS ARE EXTRA.
KIRKMAN & SCOTT

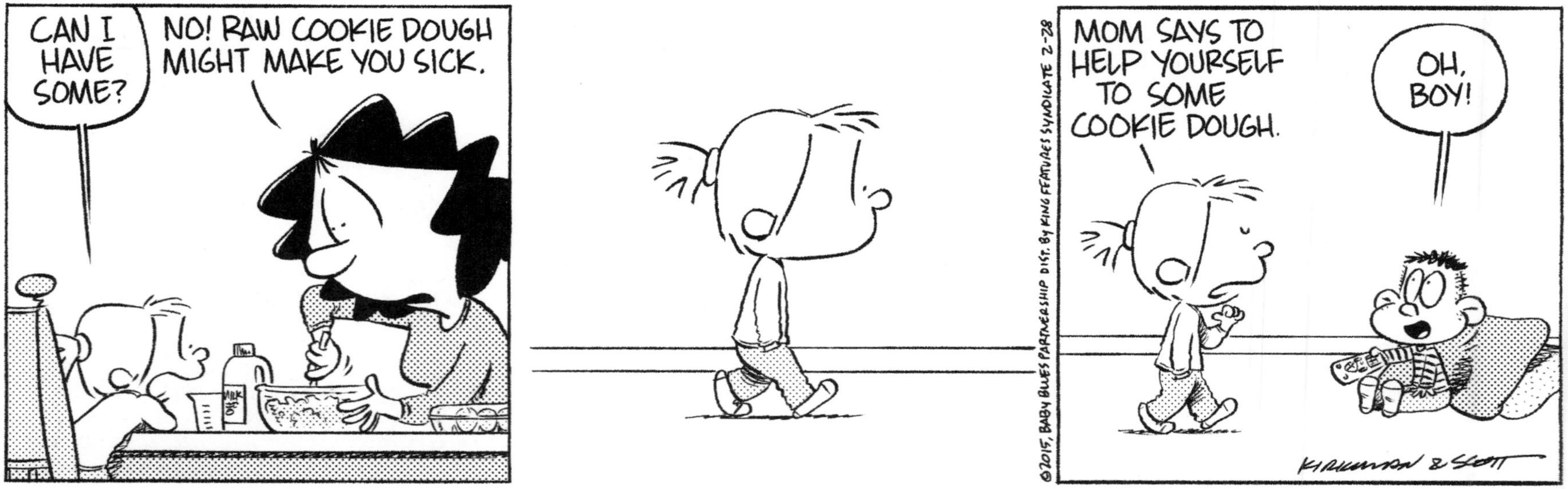
CAN I HAVE SOME?
NO! RAW COOKIE DOUGH MIGHT MAKE YOU SICK.
©2015, BABY BLUES PARTNERSHIP DIST. BY KING FEATURES SYNDICATE 2-28
MOM SAYS TO HELP YOURSELF TO SOME COOKIE DOUGH.
OH, BOY!
KIRKMAN & SCOTT

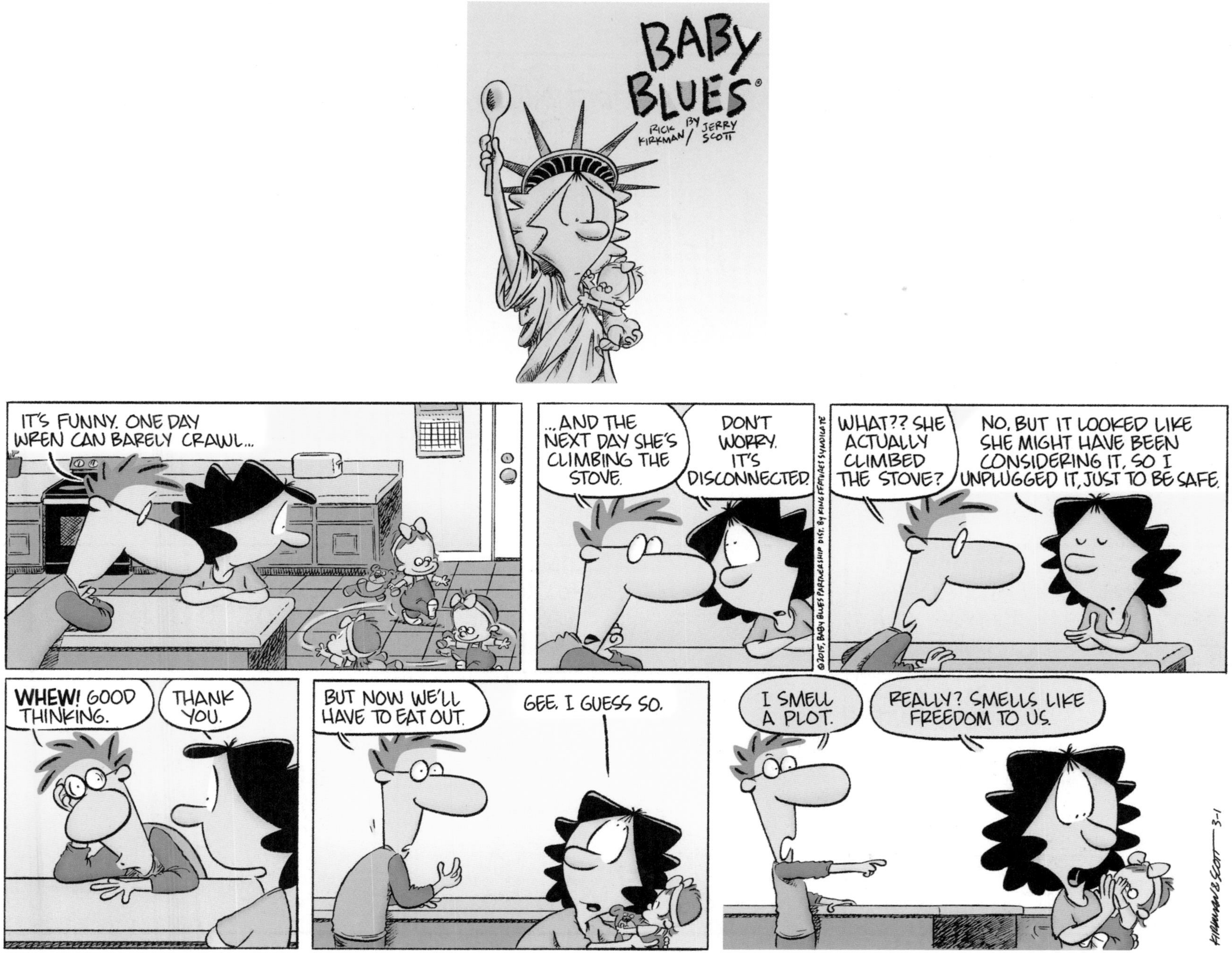
BABY BLUES®
BY RICK KIRKMAN / JERRY SCOTT
IT'S FUNNY. ONE DAY WREN CAN BARELY CRAWL...
...AND THE NEXT DAY SHE'S CLIMBING THE STOVE.
DON'T WORRY. IT'S DISCONNECTED.
©2015, BABY BLUES PARTNERSHIP DIST. BY KING FEATURES SYNDICATE
WHAT?? SHE ACTUALLY CLIMBED THE STOVE?
NO, BUT IT LOOKED LIKE SHE MIGHT HAVE BEEN CONSIDERING IT, SO I UNPLUGGED IT, JUST TO BE SAFE.
WHEW! GOOD THINKING.
THANK YOU.
BUT NOW WE'LL HAVE TO EAT OUT.
GEE. I GUESS SO.
I SMELL A PLOT.
REALLY? SMELLS LIKE FREEDOM TO US.
KIRKMAN & SCOTT 3-1

Rick: Give me your tired, your sore, your huddled mommies yearning to go out to eat . . .

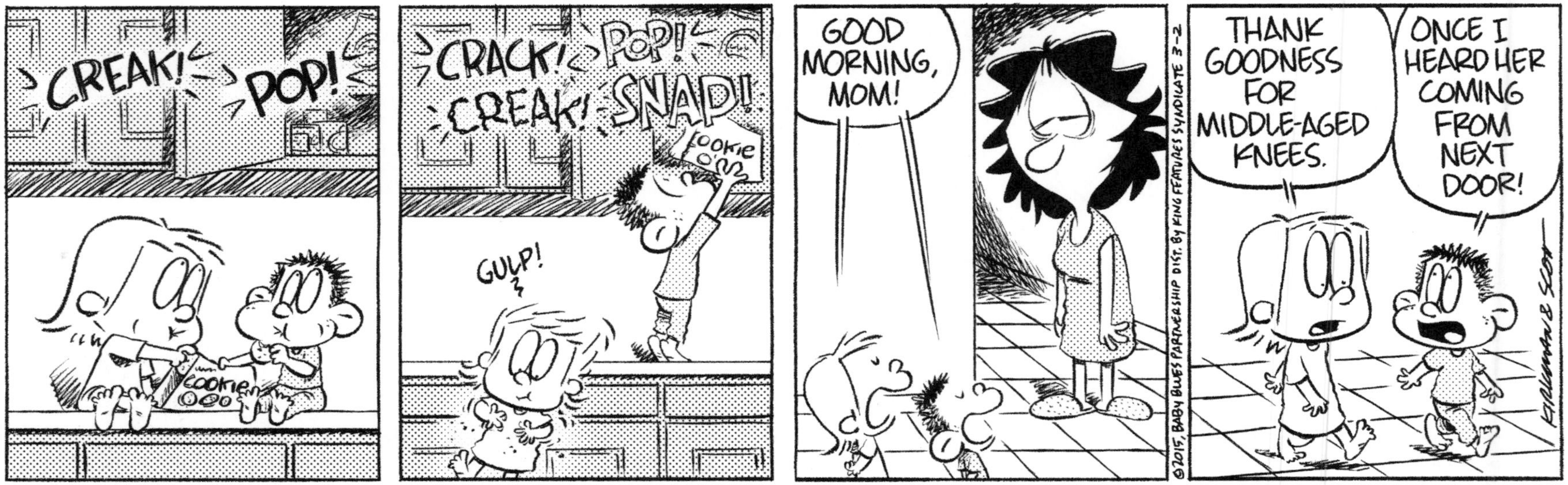
CREAK!
POP!
CRACK!
POP!
CREAK!
SNAP!
COOKIE
GULP!
GOOD MORNING, MOM!
THANK GOODNESS FOR MIDDLE-AGED KNEES.
ONCE I HEARD HER COMING FROM NEXT DOOR!
©2015, BABY BLUES PARTNERSHIP DIST. BY KING FEATURES SYNDICATE 3-2
KIRKMAN & SCOTT

Rick: The truth in that is almost as painful as my knees.

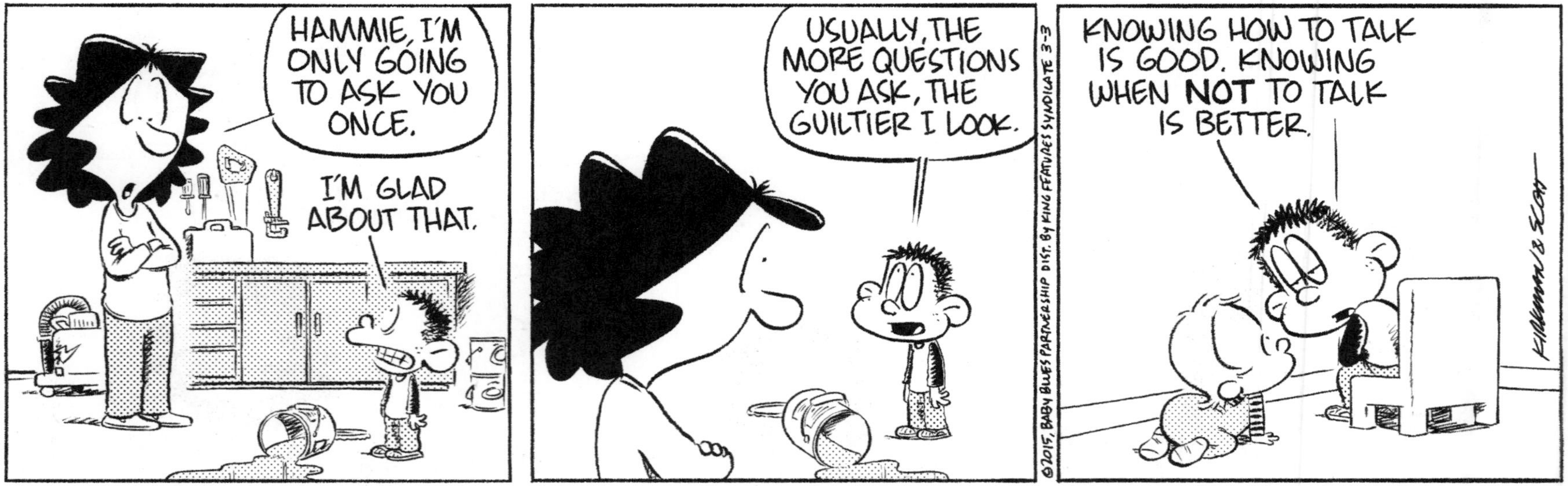
HAMMIE, I'M ONLY GOING TO ASK YOU ONCE.
I'M GLAD ABOUT THAT.
USUALLY, THE MORE QUESTIONS YOU ASK, THE GUILTIER I LOOK.
©2015, BABY BLUES PARTNERSHIP DIST. BY KING FEATURES SYNDICATE 3-3
KNOWING HOW TO TALK IS GOOD. KNOWING WHEN **NOT** TO TALK IS BETTER.
KIRKMAN & SCOTT

Rick: A valuable lesson to learn early.

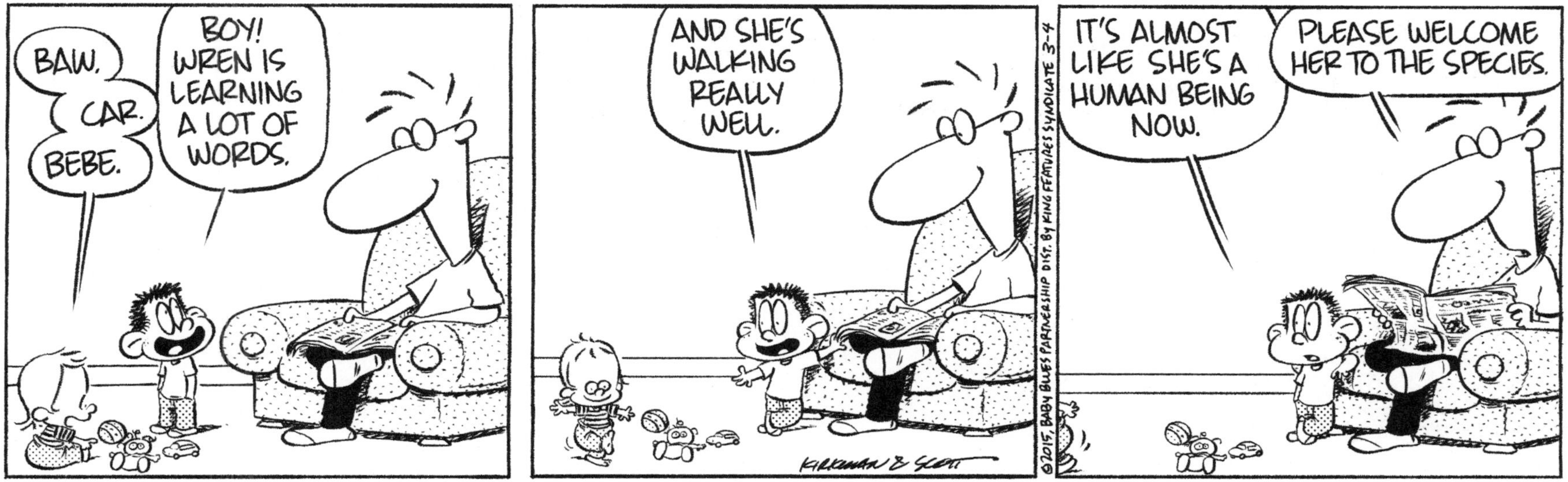
BAW.
CAR.
BEBE.
BOY! WREN IS LEARNING A LOT OF WORDS.
AND SHE'S WALKING REALLY WELL.
KIRKMAN & SCOTT
©2015, BABY BLUES PARTNERSHIP DIST. BY KING FEATURES SYNDICATE 3-4
IT'S ALMOST LIKE SHE'S A HUMAN BEING NOW.
PLEASE WELCOME HER TO THE SPECIES.

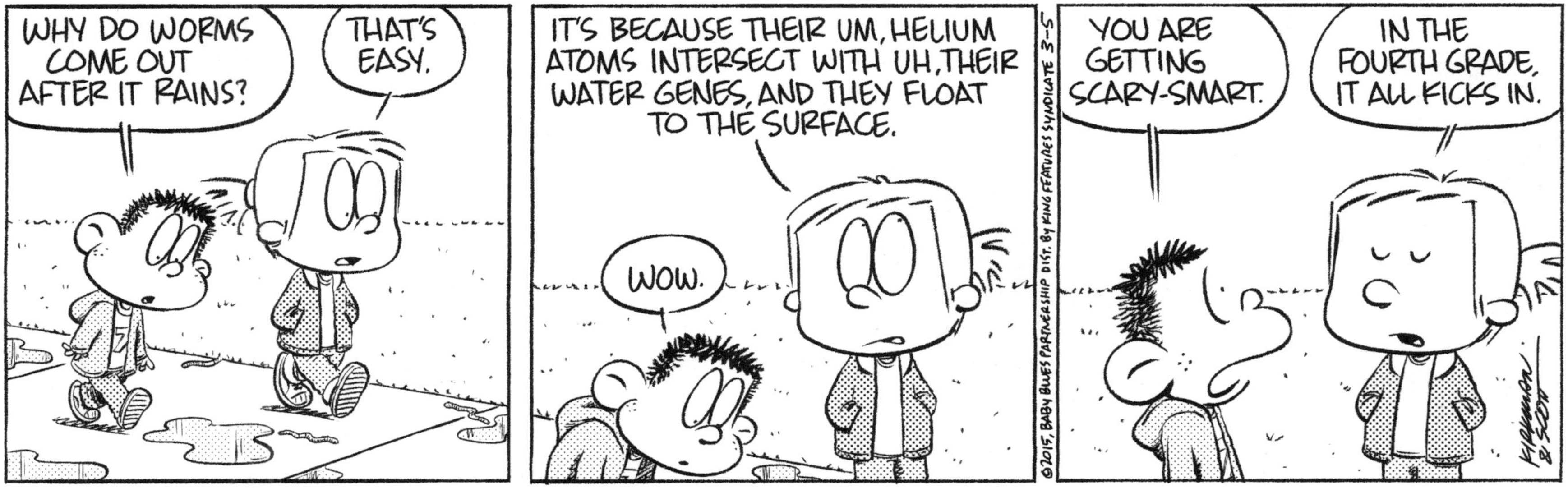
WHY DO WORMS COME OUT AFTER IT RAINS?
THAT'S EASY.
IT'S BECAUSE THEIR UM, HELIUM ATOMS INTERSECT WITH UH, THEIR WATER GENES, AND THEY FLOAT TO THE SURFACE.
WOW.
©2015, BABY BLUES PARTNERSHIP DIST. BY KING FEATURES SYNDICATE 3-5
YOU ARE GETTING SCARY-SMART.
IN THE FOURTH GRADE, IT ALL KICKS IN.
KIRKMAN & SCOTT

Rick: With the emphasis on "scary."

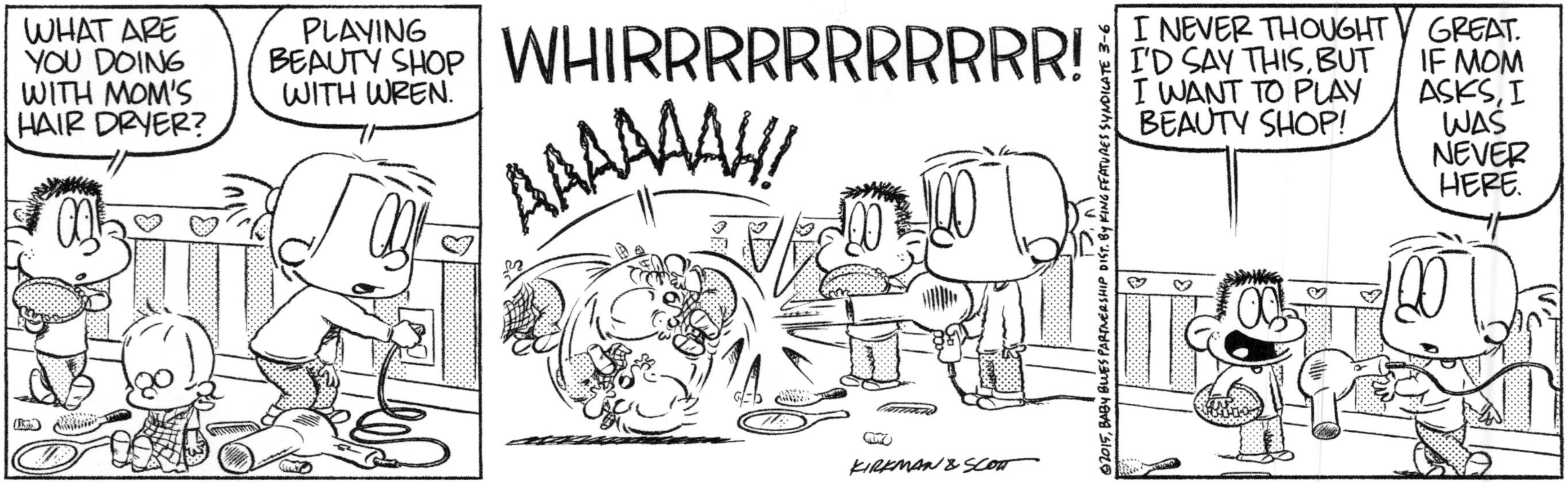
WHAT ARE YOU DOING WITH MOM'S HAIR DRYER?
PLAYING BEAUTY SHOP WITH WREN.
WHIRRRRRRRRRRRR!
AAAAAAH!
KIRKMAN & SCOTT
©2015, BABY BLUES PARTNERSHIP DIST. BY KING FEATURES SYNDICATE 3-6
I NEVER THOUGHT I'D SAY THIS, BUT I WANT TO PLAY BEAUTY SHOP!
GREAT. IF MOM ASKS, I WAS NEVER HERE.

Rick: In case you hadn't noticed, Hammie's hair is back this week.

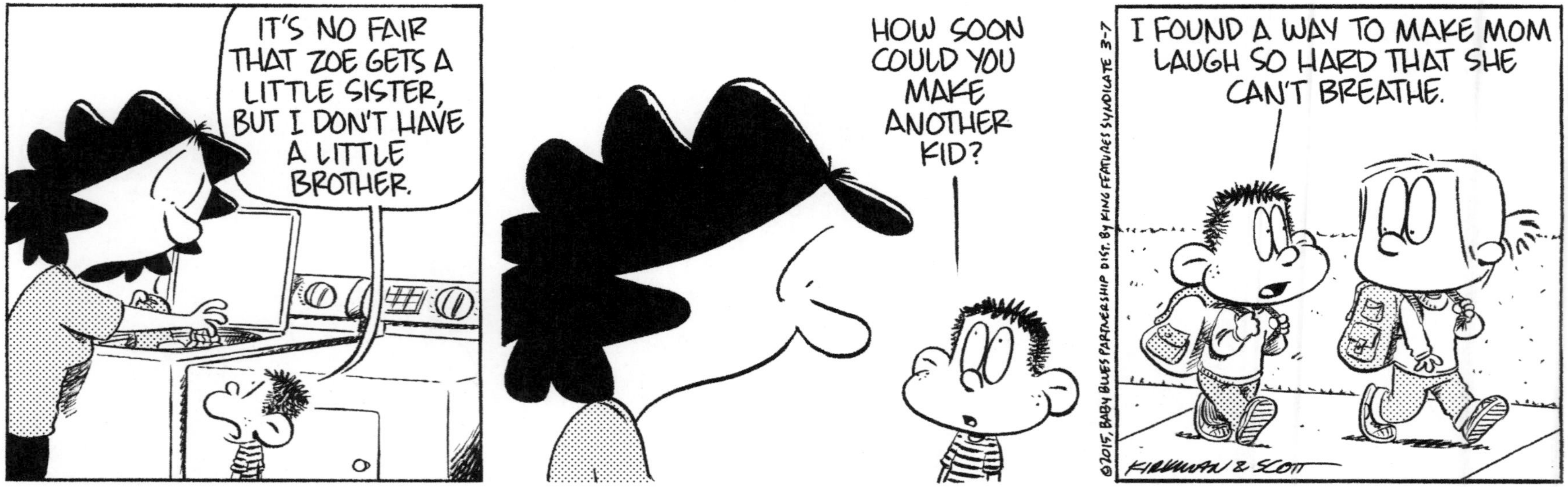
IT'S NO FAIR THAT ZOE GETS A LITTLE SISTER, BUT I DON'T HAVE A LITTLE BROTHER.
HOW SOON COULD YOU MAKE ANOTHER KID?
©2015, BABY BLUES PARTNERSHIP DIST. BY KING FEATURES SYNDICATE 3-7
I FOUND A WAY TO MAKE MOM LAUGH SO HARD THAT SHE CAN'T BREATHE.
KIRKMAN & SCOTT

Rick: That has to be one of my favorite questions from the kids.

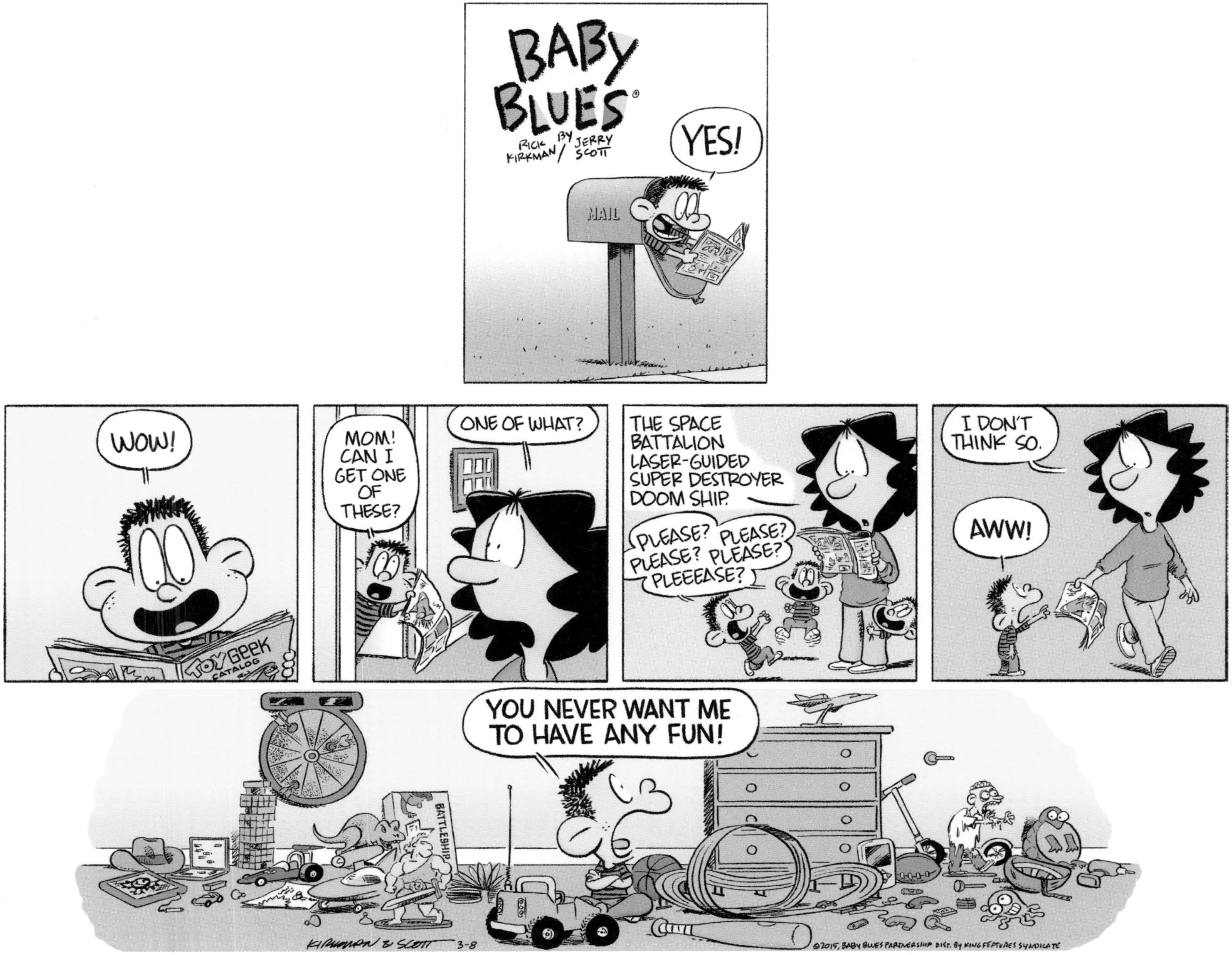
BABY BLUES®
RICK KIRKMAN / BY JERRY SCOTT
YES!
MAIL
WOW!
TOY GEEK CATALOG
MOM! CAN I GET ONE OF THESE?
ONE OF WHAT?
THE SPACE BATTALION LASER-GUIDED SUPER DESTROYER DOOM SHIP.
PLEASE? PLEASE? PLEASE? PLEASE? PLEEEASE?
I DON'T THINK SO.
AWW!
YOU NEVER WANT ME TO HAVE ANY FUN!
BATTLESHIP
KIRKMAN & SCOTT 3-8
©2015, BABY BLUES PARTNERSHIP DIST. BY KING FEATURES SYNDICATE

Jerry: Rick hates it when I write gags that involve words like "a roomful of toys." It's partly his fault because he's so good at drawing stuff like that.

Rick: Thanks a lot, Jerry. Although I do like how the zombie and the turtle came out. I think you owe me a Space Battalion Laser-Guided Super Destroyer Doom Ship.

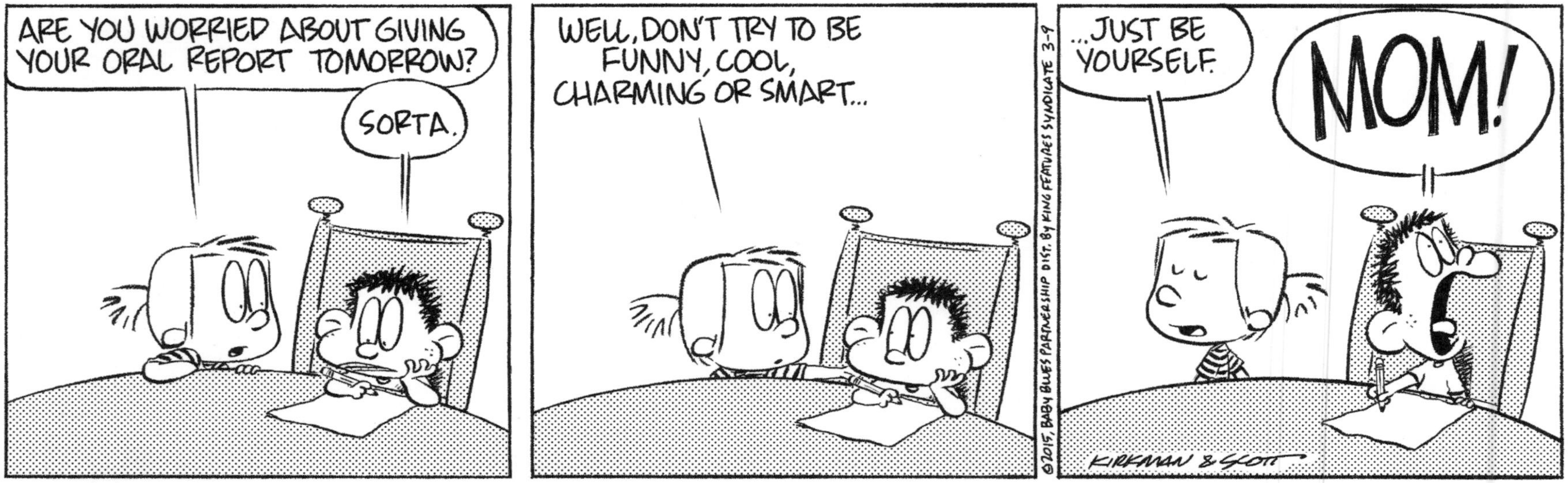
ARE YOU WORRIED ABOUT GIVING YOUR ORAL REPORT TOMORROW?
SORTA.
WELL, DON'T TRY TO BE FUNNY, COOL, CHARMING OR SMART...
©2015, BABY BLUES PARTNERSHIP DIST. BY KING FEATURES SYNDICATE 3-9
...JUST BE YOURSELF.
MOM!
KIRKMAN & SCOTT

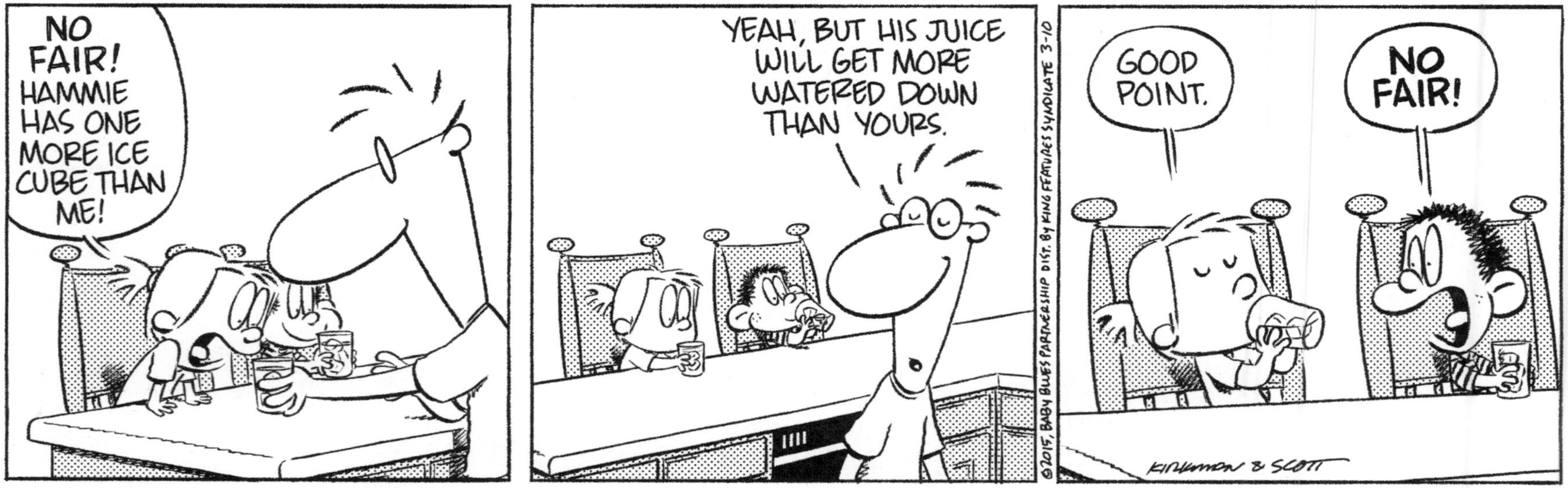
NO FAIR! HAMMIE HAS ONE MORE ICE CUBE THAN ME!
YEAH, BUT HIS JUICE WILL GET MORE WATERED DOWN THAN YOURS.
©2015, BABY BLUES PARTNERSHIP DIST. BY KING FEATURES SYNDICATE 3-10
GOOD POINT.
NO FAIR!
KIRKMAN & SCOTT

Rick: Knowing the upside of everything is key to dealing with siblings.

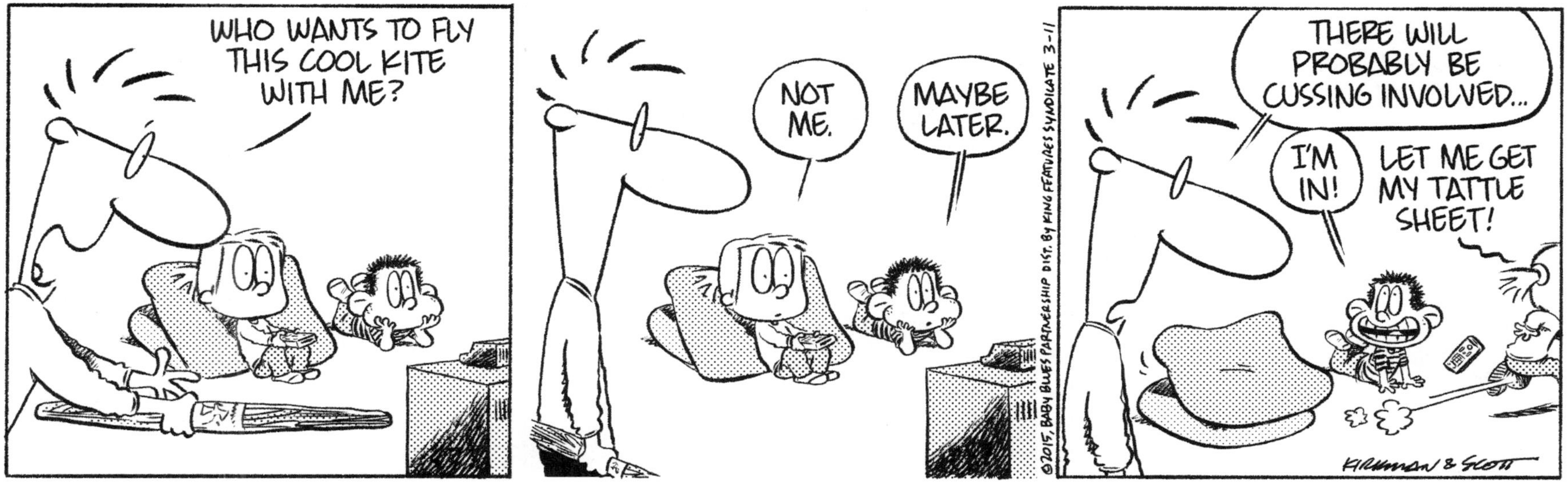
WHO WANTS TO FLY THIS COOL KITE WITH ME?
NOT ME.
MAYBE LATER.
THERE WILL PROBABLY BE CUSSING INVOLVED...
I'M IN!
LET ME GET MY TATTLE SHEET!
©2015, BABY BLUES PARTNERSHIP DIST. BY KING FEATURES SYNDICATE 3-11
KIRKMAN & SCOTT

Jerry: Is it even possible to fly a kite without at least a little cussing? Maybe . . . but I've never seen it happen.

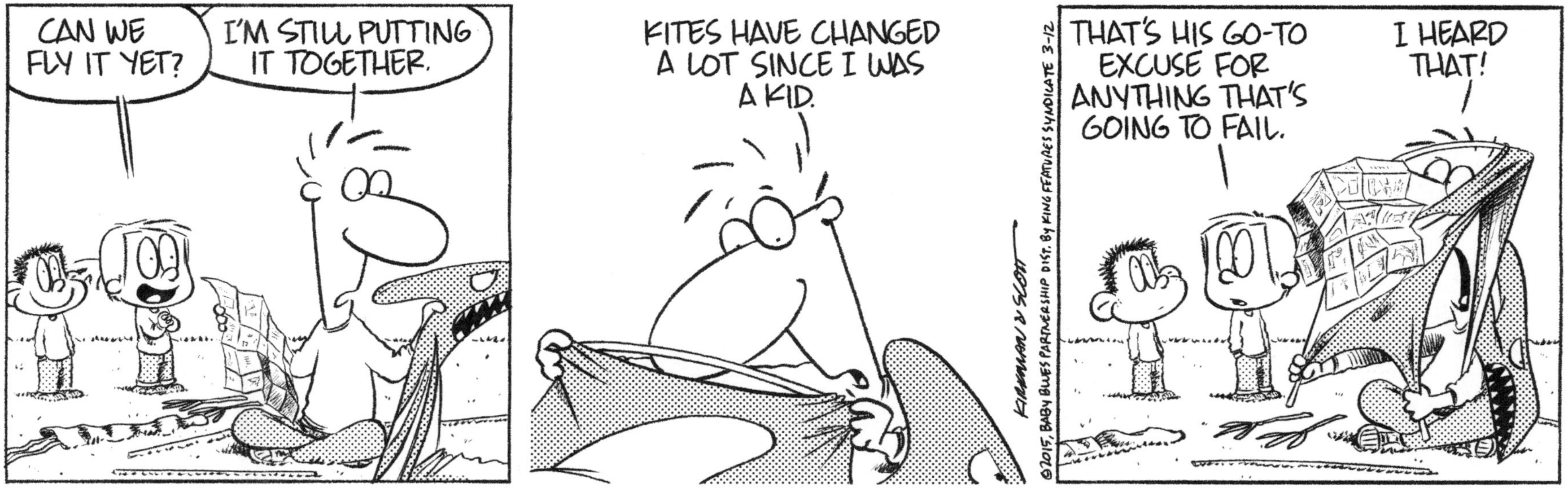
CAN WE FLY IT YET?
I'M STILL PUTTING IT TOGETHER.
KITES HAVE CHANGED A LOT SINCE I WAS A KID.
THAT'S HIS GO-TO EXCUSE FOR ANYTHING THAT'S GOING TO FAIL.
I HEARD THAT!
©2015, BABY BLUES PARTNERSHIP DIST. BY KING FEATURES SYNDICATE 3-12
KIRKMAN & SCOTT

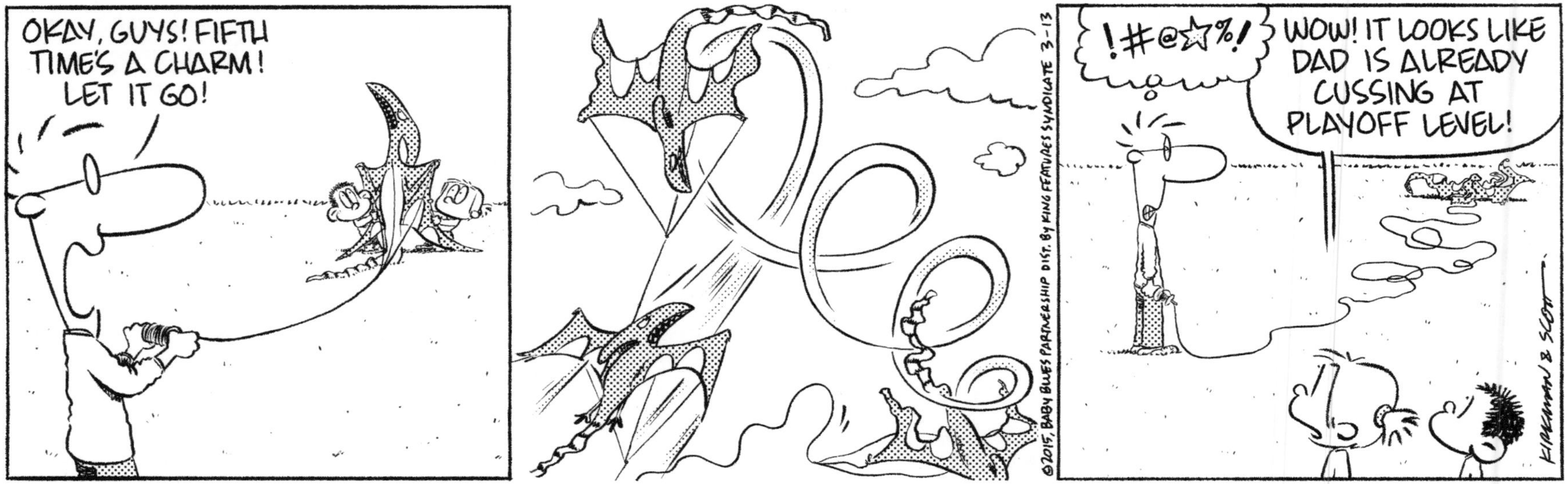
OKAY, GUYS! FIFTH TIME'S A CHARM! LET IT GO!
©2015, BABY BLUES PARTNERSHIP DIST. BY KING FEATURES SYNDICATE 3-13
!#@☆%!
WOW! IT LOOKS LIKE DAD IS ALREADY CUSSING AT PLAYOFF LEVEL!
KIRKMAN & SCOTT

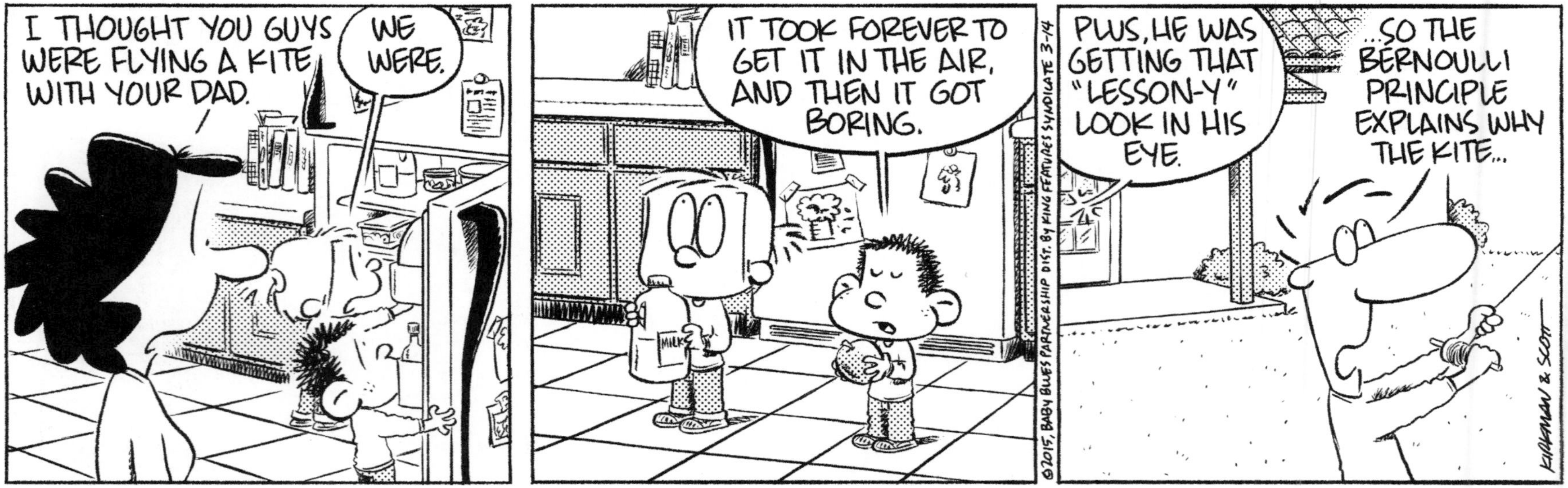
I THOUGHT YOU GUYS WERE FLYING A KITE WITH YOUR DAD.
WE WERE.
IT TOOK FOREVER TO GET IT IN THE AIR, AND THEN IT GOT BORING.
©2015, BABY BLUES PARTNERSHIP DIST. BY KING FEATURES SYNDICATE 3-14
PLUS, HE WAS GETTING THAT "LESSON-Y" LOOK IN HIS EYE.
...SO THE BERNOULLI PRINCIPLE EXPLAINS WHY THE KITE...
MILK
KIRKMAN & SCOTT

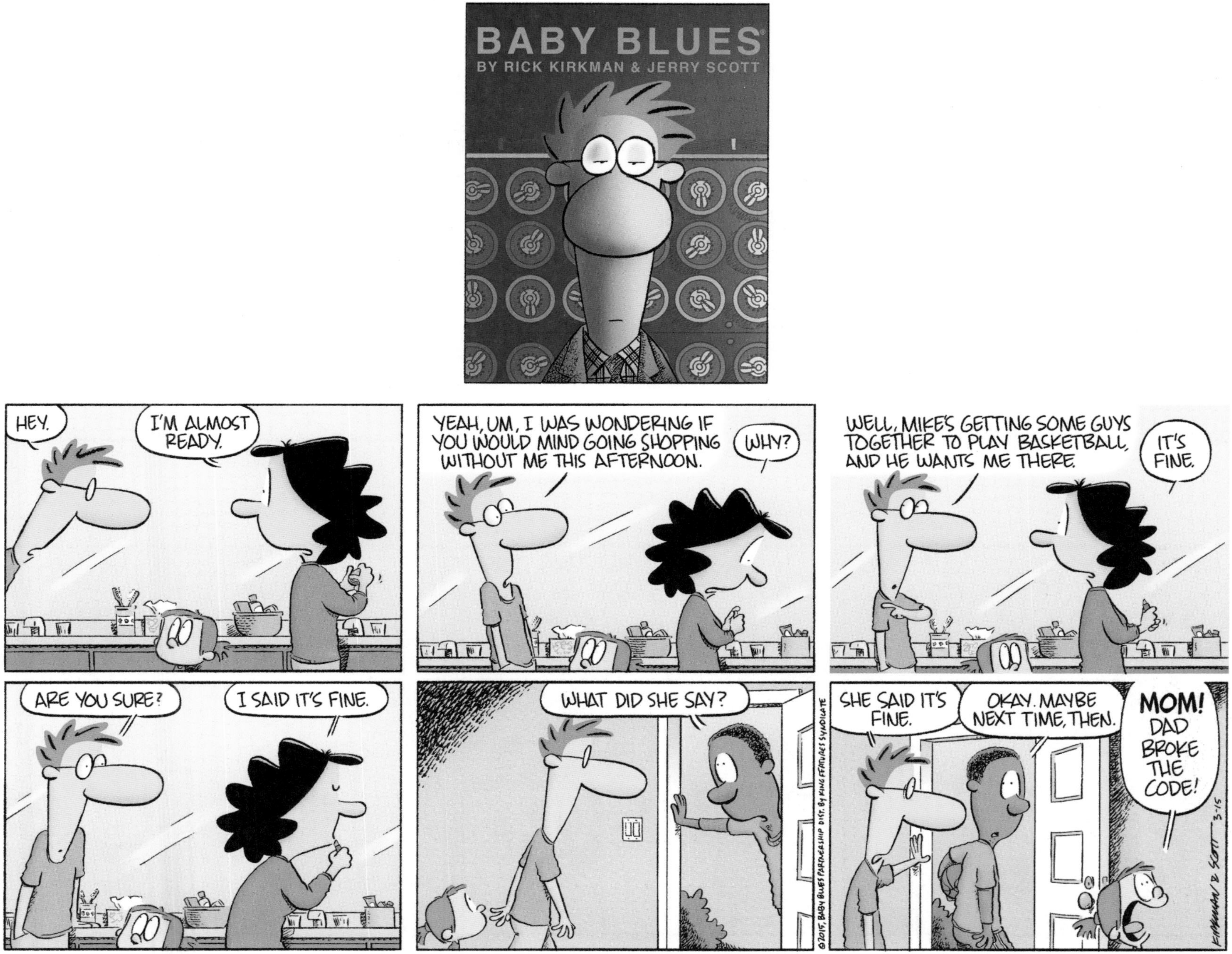
BABY BLUES®
BY RICK KIRKMAN & JERRY SCOTT
HEY.
I'M ALMOST READY.
YEAH, UM, I WAS WONDERING IF YOU WOULD MIND GOING SHOPPING WITHOUT ME THIS AFTERNOON.
WHY?
WELL, MIKE'S GETTING SOME GUYS TOGETHER TO PLAY BASKETBALL, AND HE WANTS ME THERE.
IT'S FINE.
ARE YOU SURE?
I SAID IT'S FINE.
WHAT DID SHE SAY?
©2015, BABY BLUES PARTNERSHIP DIST. BY KING FEATURES SYNDICATE
SHE SAID IT'S FINE.
OKAY. MAYBE NEXT TIME, THEN.
MOM! DAD BROKE THE CODE!
KIRKMAN & SCOTT 3-15

Rick: After I started that idea for the title panel being taken from the movie poster for *The Imitation Game*, I realized it was more work than I had bargained for. By that time, it was too late—I had to finish it, probably taking as long as the rest of the strip. Later, I found a much simpler poster for the movie. Sigh.

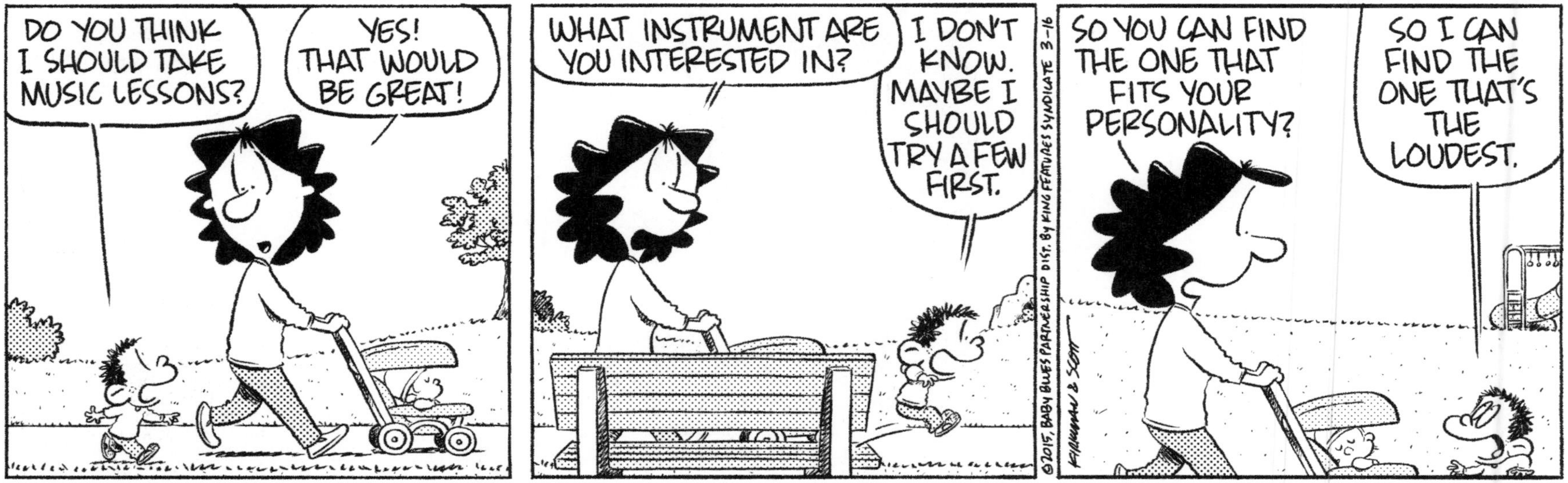
DO YOU THINK I SHOULD TAKE MUSIC LESSONS?
YES! THAT WOULD BE GREAT!
WHAT INSTRUMENT ARE YOU INTERESTED IN?
I DON'T KNOW. MAYBE I SHOULD TRY A FEW FIRST.
©2015, BABY BLUES PARTNERSHIP DIST. BY KING FEATURES SYNDICATE 3-16
KIRKMAN & SCOTT
SO YOU CAN FIND THE ONE THAT FITS YOUR PERSONALITY?
SO I CAN FIND THE ONE THAT'S THE LOUDEST.

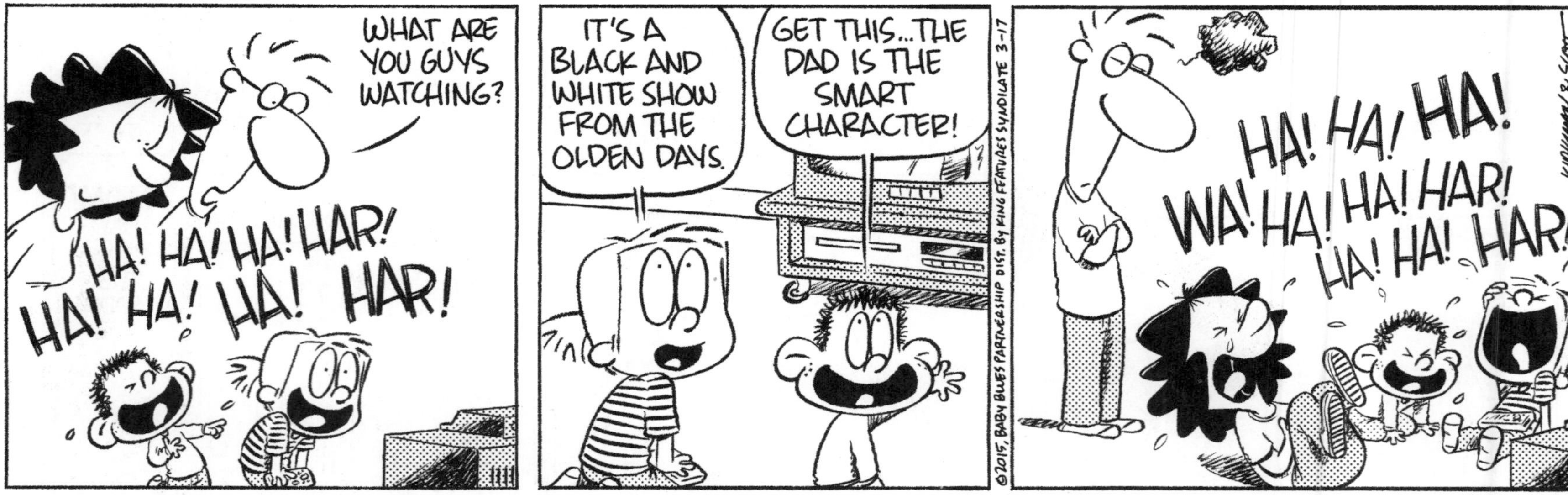
WHAT ARE YOU GUYS WATCHING?
HA! HA! HA! HAR!
HA! HA! HA! HAR!
IT'S A BLACK AND WHITE SHOW FROM THE OLDEN DAYS.
GET THIS...THE DAD IS THE SMART CHARACTER!
©2015, BABY BLUES PARTNERSHIP DIST. BY KING FEATURES SYNDICATE 3-17
KIRKMAN & SCOTT
HA! HA! HA!
WA! HA! HA! HAR!
HA! HA! HAR!

Rick: Considering the amount of media time given to the wise-father character in the "olden days," I suppose it's only fair.

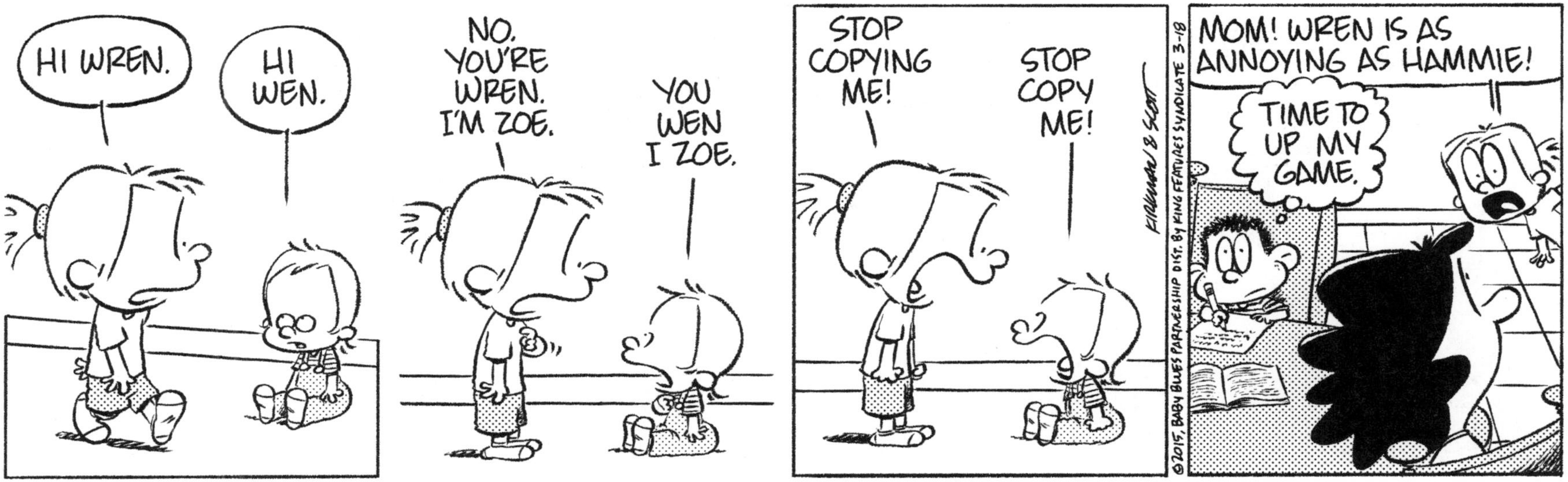
HI WREN.
HI WEN.
NO. YOU'RE WREN. I'M ZOE.
YOU WEN I ZOE.
STOP COPYING ME!
STOP COPY ME!
KIRKMAN & SCOTT
©2015, BABY BLUES PARTNERSHIP DIST. BY KING FEATURES SYNDICATE 3-18
MOM! WREN IS AS ANNOYING AS HAMMIE!
TIME TO UP MY GAME.

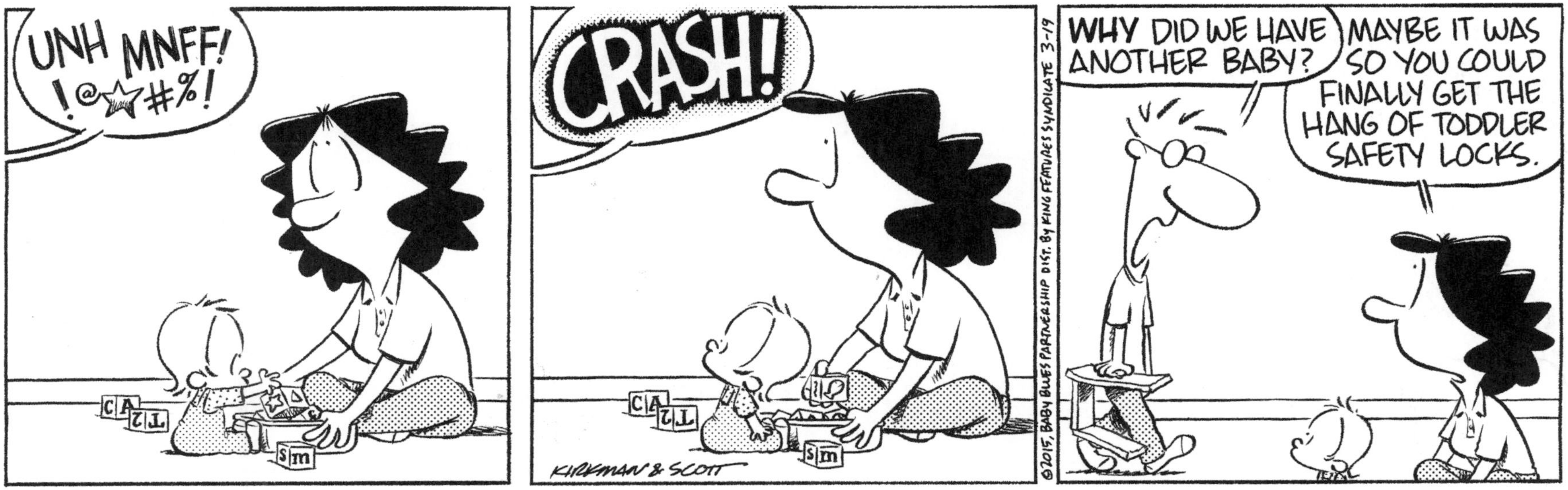
UNH MNFF! !@☆#%!
CRASH!
KIRKMAN & SCOTT
©2015, BABY BLUES PARTNERSHIP DIST. BY KING FEATURES SYNDICATE 3-19
WHY DID WE HAVE ANOTHER BABY?
MAYBE IT WAS SO YOU COULD FINALLY GET THE HANG OF TODDLER SAFETY LOCKS.

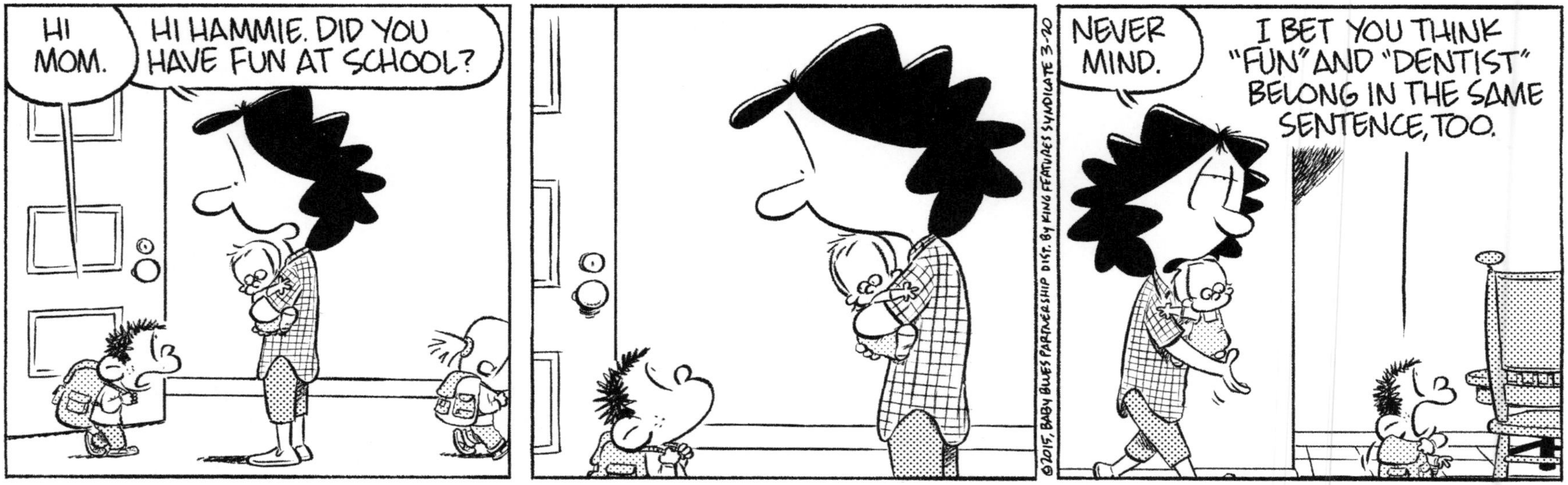
HI MOM.
HI HAMMIE. DID YOU HAVE FUN AT SCHOOL?
©2015, BABY BLUES PARTNERSHIP DIST. BY KING FEATURES SYNDICATE 3-20
NEVER MIND.
I BET YOU THINK "FUN" AND "DENTIST" BELONG IN THE SAME SENTENCE, TOO.

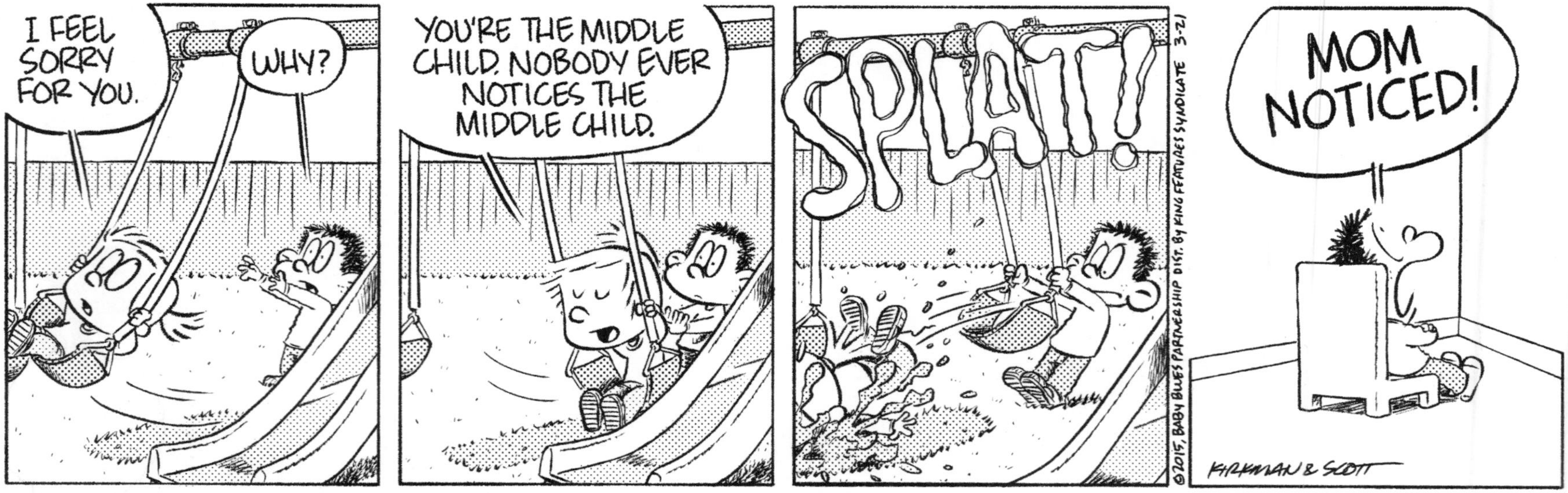
I FEEL SORRY FOR YOU.
WHY?
YOU'RE THE MIDDLE CHILD. NOBODY EVER NOTICES THE MIDDLE CHILD.
SPLAT!
©2015, BABY BLUES PARTNERSHIP DIST. BY KING FEATURES SYNDICATE 3-21
MOM NOTICED!
KIRKMAN & SCOTT

Rick: Zoe learns not to be so careless as to impart dangerous knowledge.

Jerry: As a middle child, I feel it's my duty to strike a blow for my kind once in a while.

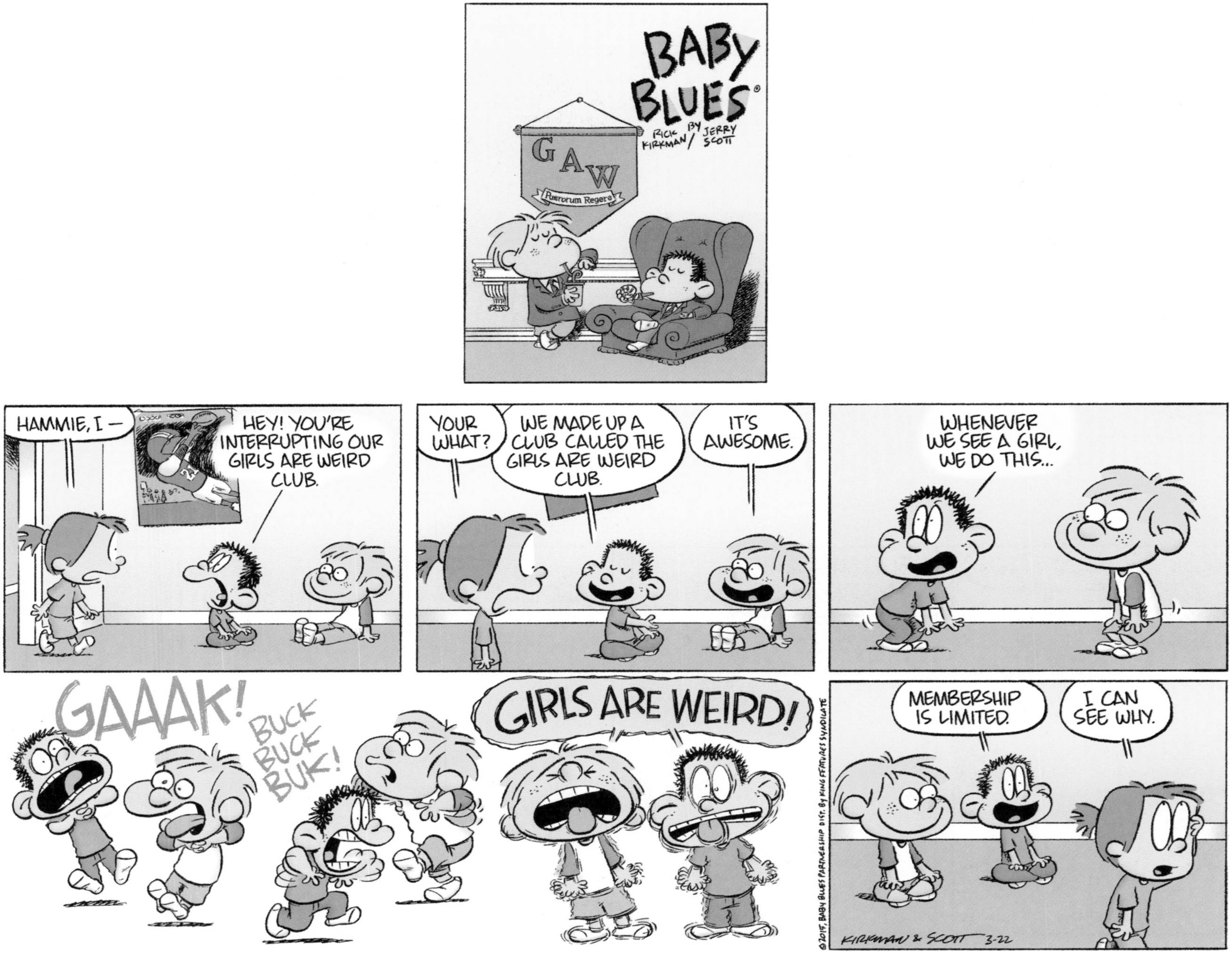
BABY BLUES®
RICK KIRKMAN / BY JERRY SCOTT
G A W
Puerorum Regere
HAMMIE, I —
HEY! YOU'RE INTERRUPTING OUR GIRLS ARE WEIRD CLUB.
YOUR WHAT?
WE MADE UP A CLUB CALLED THE GIRLS ARE WEIRD CLUB.
IT'S AWESOME.
WHENEVER WE SEE A GIRL, WE DO THIS...
GAAAK!
BUCK BUCK BUK!
GIRLS ARE WEIRD!
©2015, BABY BLUES PARTNERSHIP DIST. BY KING FEATURES SYNDICATE
MEMBERSHIP IS LIMITED.
I CAN SEE WHY.
KIRKMAN & SCOTT 3-22

Rick: I love drawing action vignettes with crazy faces. All you Latin geeks, have fun with the coat of arms. If it's wrong, I blame Google.

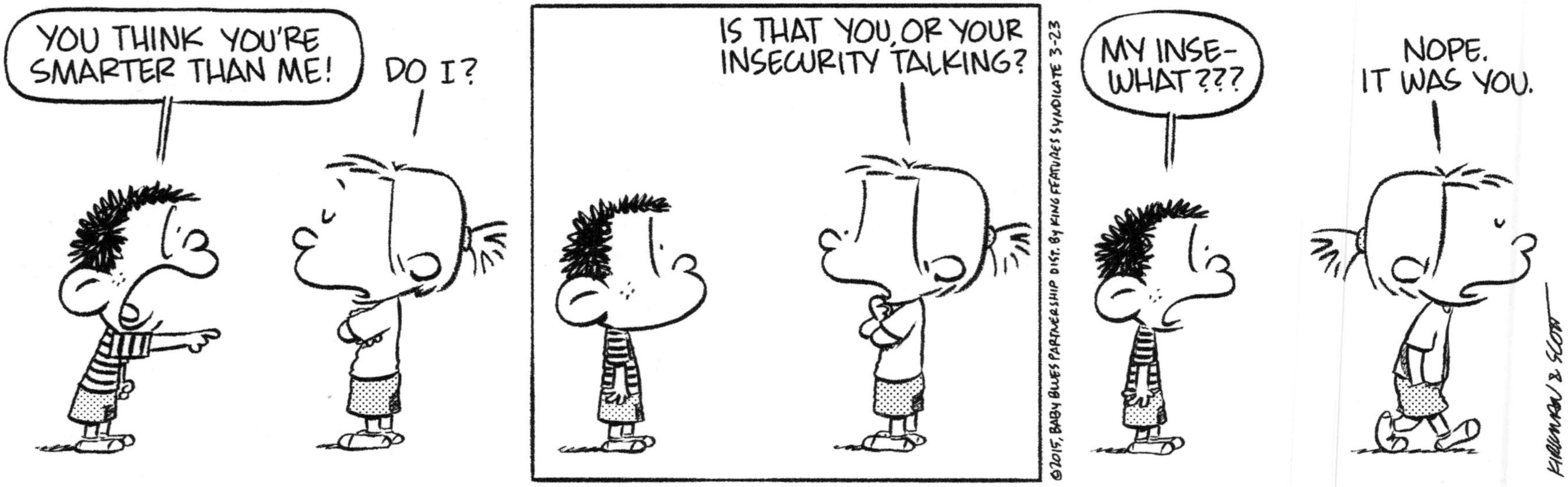
YOU THINK YOU'RE SMARTER THAN ME!
DO I?
IS THAT YOU, OR YOUR INSECURITY TALKING?
MY INSE-WHAT???
NOPE. IT WAS YOU.
©2015, BABY BLUES PARTNERSHIP DIST. BY KING FEATURES SYNDICATE 3-23
KIRKMAN & SCOTT

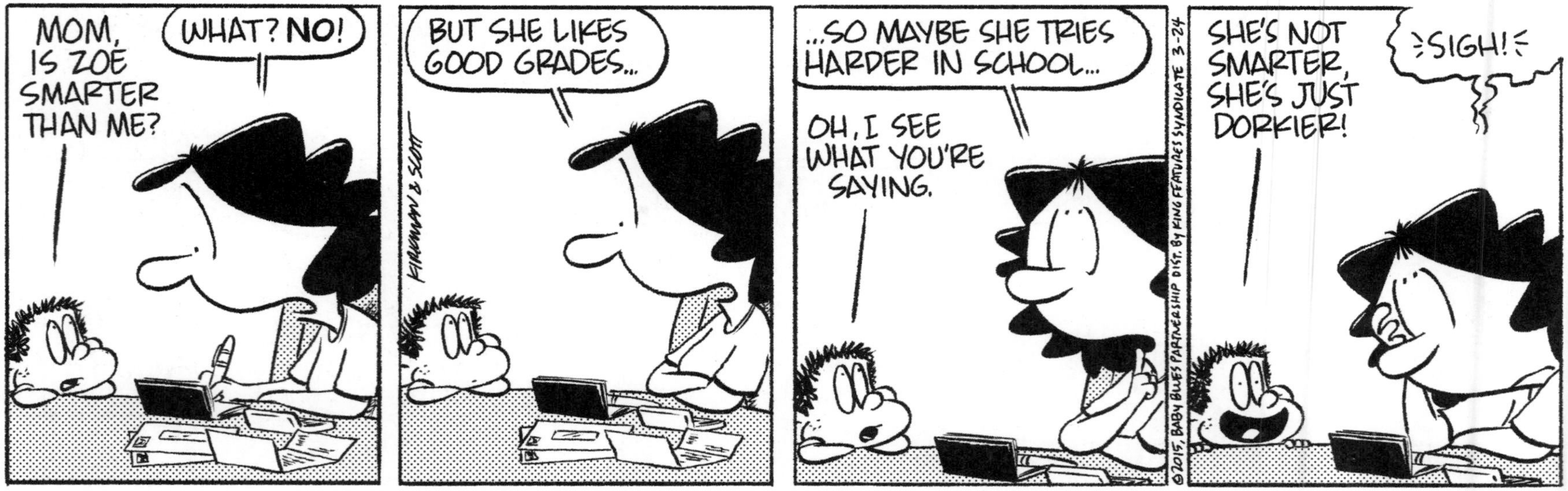
MOM, IS ZOE SMARTER THAN ME?
WHAT? **NO**!
BUT SHE LIKES GOOD GRADES...
KIRKMAN & SCOTT
...SO MAYBE SHE TRIES HARDER IN SCHOOL...
OH, I SEE WHAT YOU'RE SAYING.
©2015, BABY BLUES PARTNERSHIP DIST. BY KING FEATURES SYNDICATE 3-24
SHE'S NOT SMARTER, SHE'S JUST DORKIER!
SIGH!

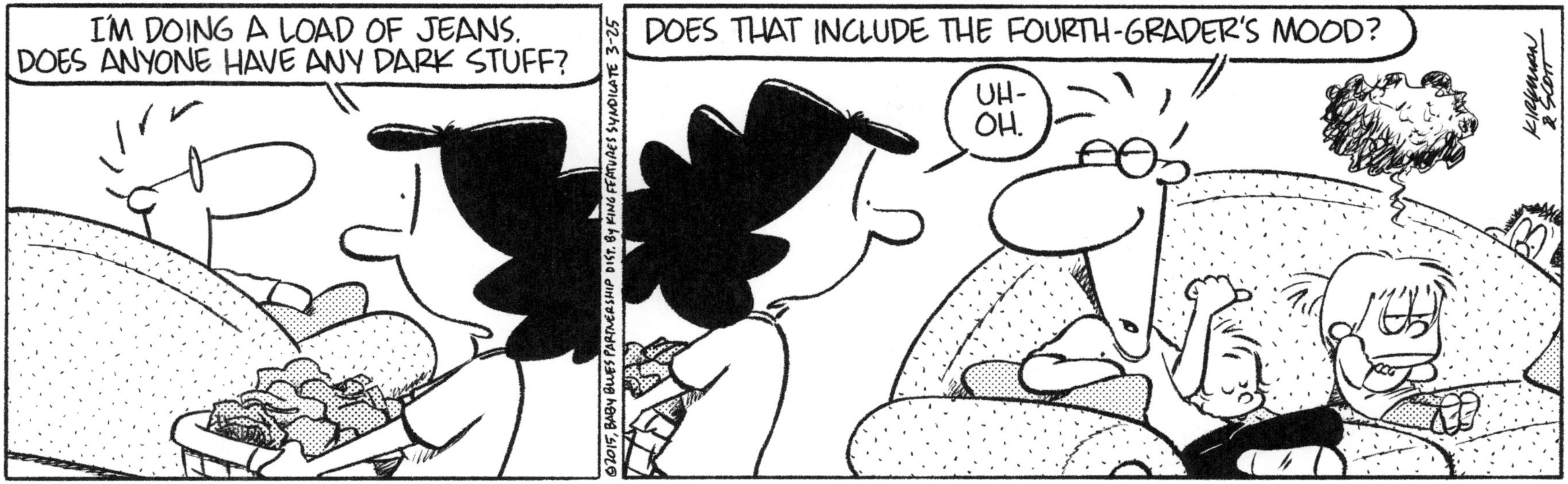
I'M DOING A LOAD OF JEANS. DOES ANYONE HAVE ANY DARK STUFF?
©2015, BABY BLUES PARTNERSHIP DIST. BY KING FEATURES SYNDICATE 3-25
DOES THAT INCLUDE THE FOURTH-GRADER'S MOOD?
UH-OH.
KIRKMAN & SCOTT

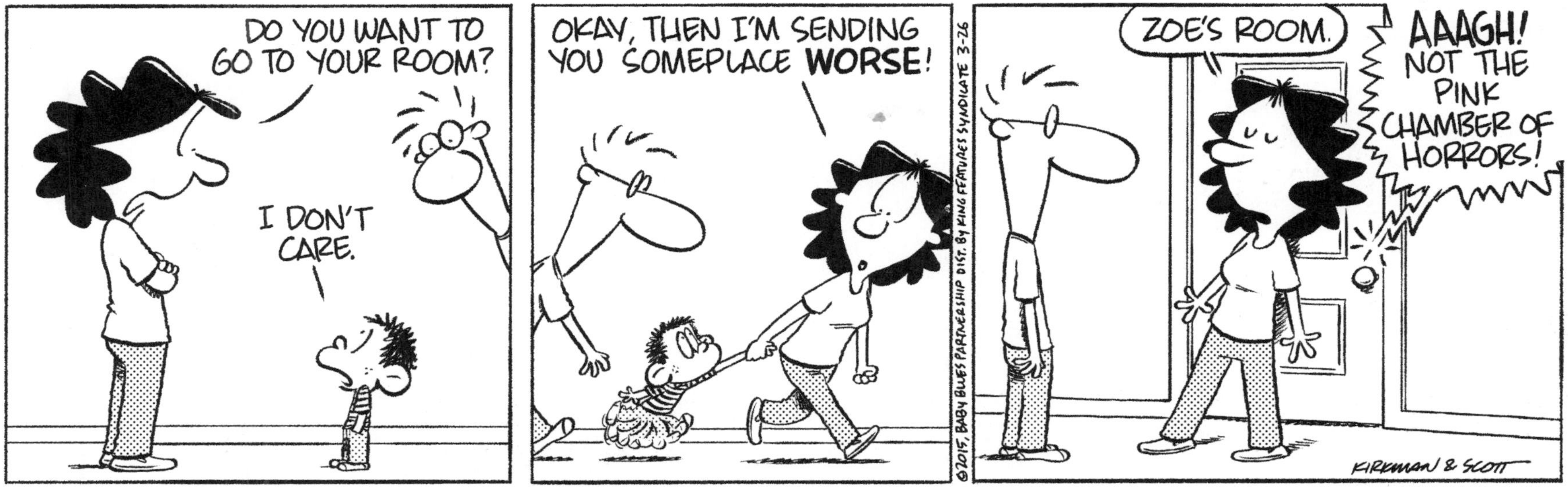
DO YOU WANT TO GO TO YOUR ROOM?
I DON'T CARE.
OKAY, THEN I'M SENDING YOU SOMEPLACE **WORSE**!
©2015, BABY BLUES PARTNERSHIP DIST. BY KING FEATURES SYNDICATE 3-26
ZOE'S ROOM.
AAAGH! NOT THE PINK CHAMBER OF HORRORS!
KIRKMAN & SCOTT

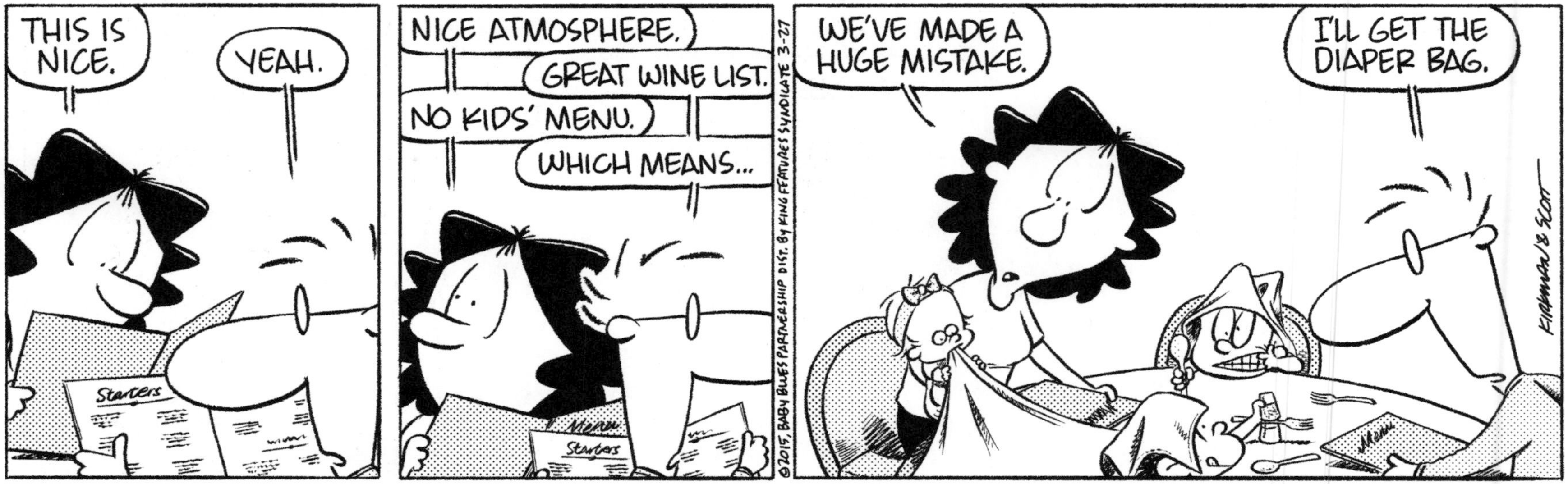
THIS IS NICE.
YEAH.
NICE ATMOSPHERE.
GREAT WINE LIST.
NO KIDS' MENU.
WHICH MEANS...
©2015, BABY BLUES PARTNERSHIP DIST. BY KING FEATURES SYNDICATE 3-27
WE'VE MADE A HUGE MISTAKE.
I'LL GET THE DIAPER BAG.
KIRKMAN & SCOTT

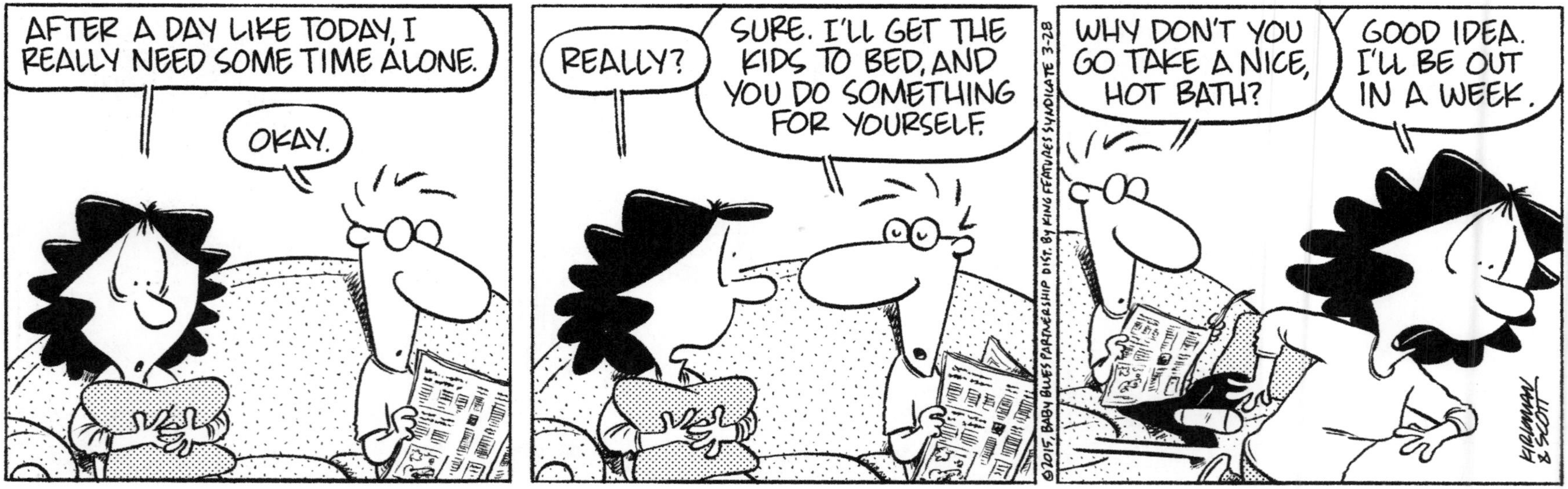
AFTER A DAY LIKE TODAY, I REALLY NEED SOME TIME ALONE.
OKAY.
REALLY?
SURE. I'LL GET THE KIDS TO BED, AND YOU DO SOMETHING FOR YOURSELF.
©2015, BABY BLUES PARTNERSHIP DIST. BY KING FEATURES SYNDICATE 3-28
WHY DON'T YOU GO TAKE A NICE, HOT BATH?
GOOD IDEA. I'LL BE OUT IN A WEEK.
KIRKMAN & SCOTT

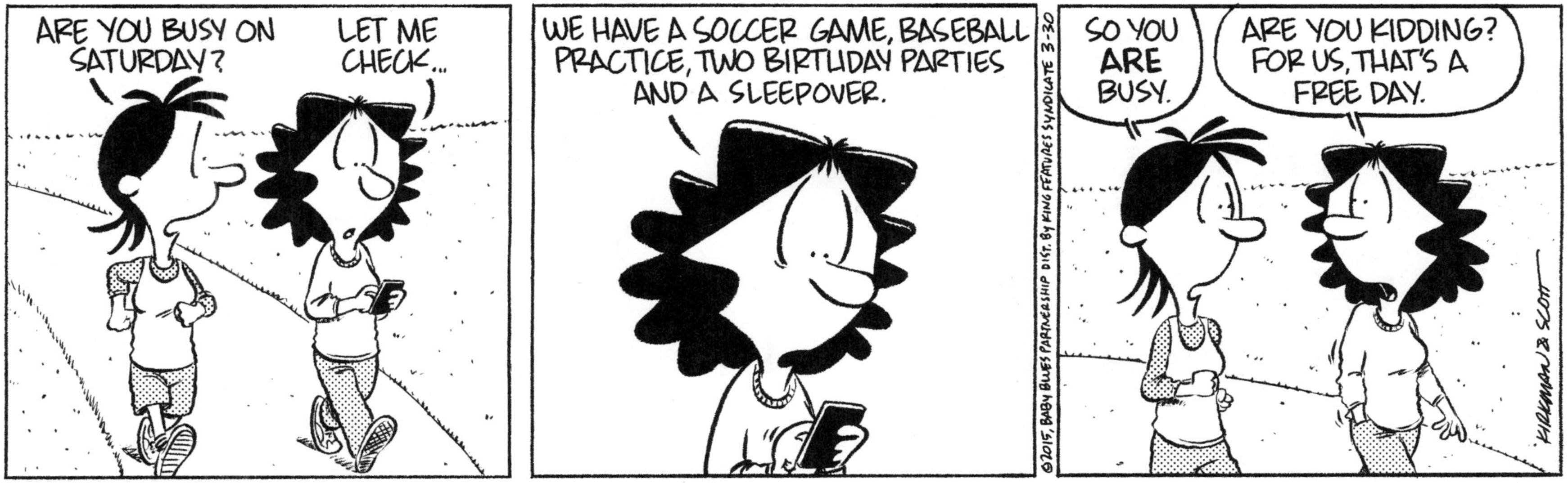
ARE YOU BUSY ON SATURDAY?
LET ME CHECK...
WE HAVE A SOCCER GAME, BASEBALL PRACTICE, TWO BIRTHDAY PARTIES AND A SLEEPOVER.
SO YOU **ARE** BUSY.
ARE YOU KIDDING? FOR US, THAT'S A FREE DAY.
©2015, BABY BLUES PARTNERSHIP DIST. BY KING FEATURES SYNDICATE 3-30
KIRKMAN & SCOTT

Rick: The threshold of "busy" is directly proportional to the number of kids.

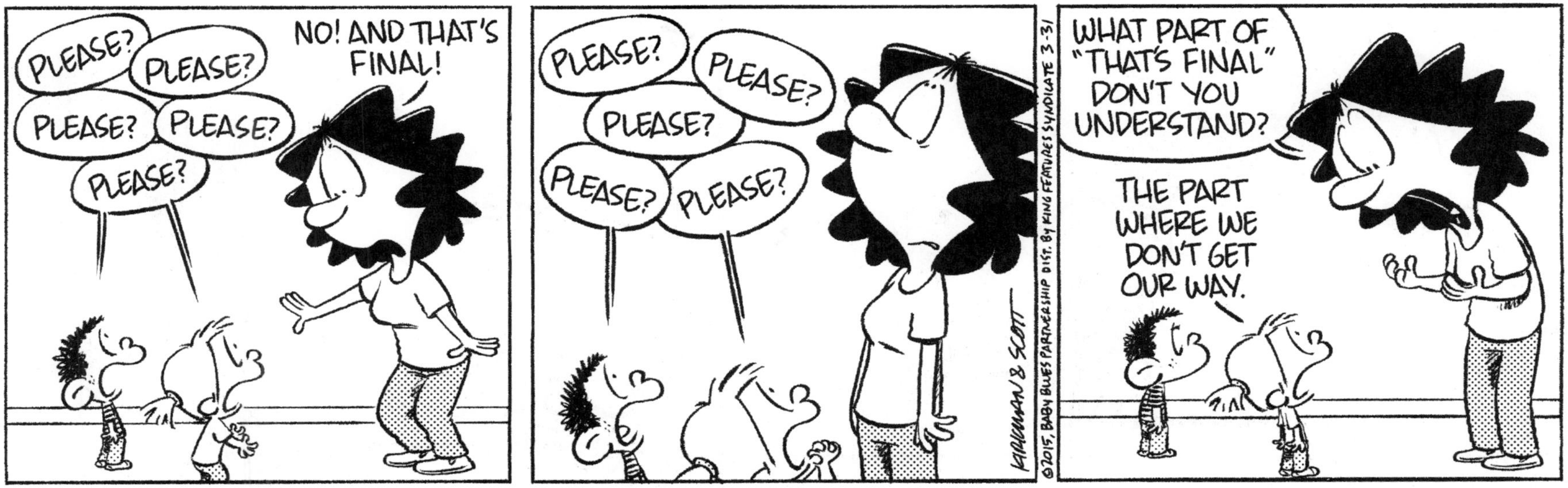
PLEASE?
PLEASE?
PLEASE?
PLEASE?
PLEASE?
NO! AND THAT'S FINAL!
PLEASE?
PLEASE?
PLEASE?
PLEASE?
PLEASE?
KIRKMAN & SCOTT
©2015, BABY BLUES PARTNERSHIP DIST. BY KING FEATURES SYNDICATE 3-31
WHAT PART OF "THAT'S FINAL" DON'T YOU UNDERSTAND?
THE PART WHERE WE DON'T GET OUR WAY.

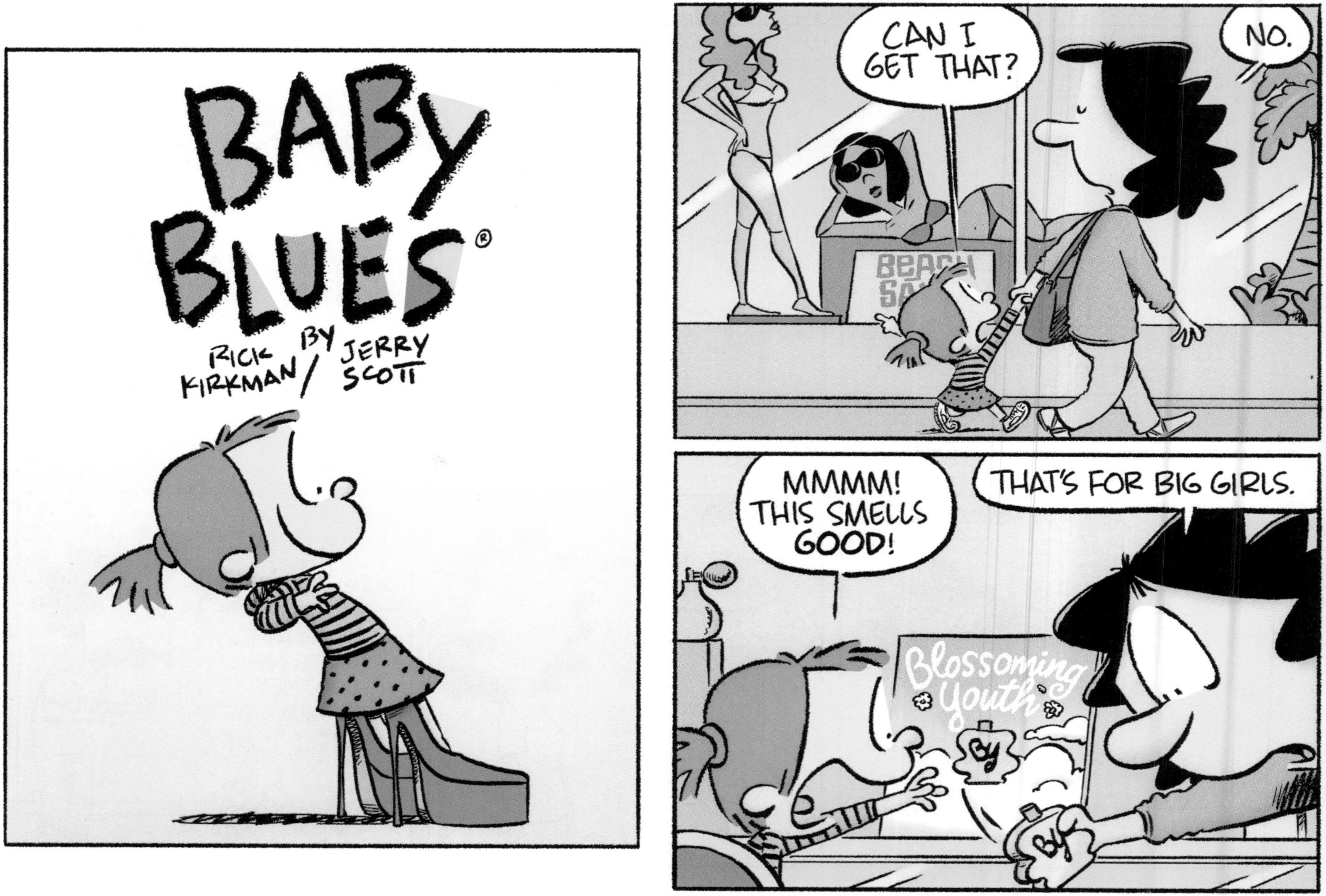
BABY BLUES®
BY RICK KIRKMAN / JERRY SCOTT
CAN I GET THAT?
NO.
MMMM! THIS SMELLS GOOD!
THAT'S FOR BIG GIRLS.
Blossoming Youth

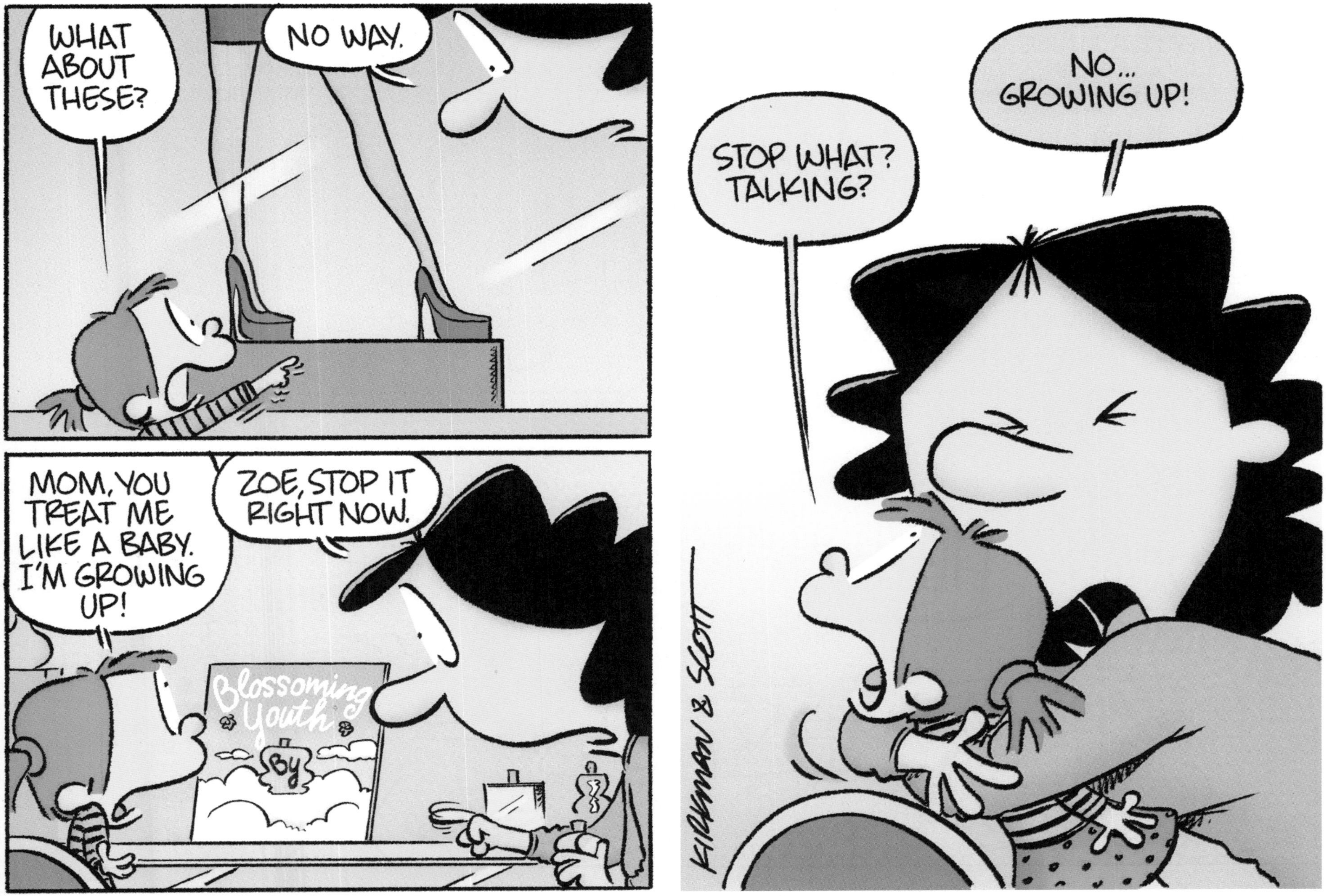
WHAT ABOUT THESE?
NO WAY.
MOM, YOU TREAT ME LIKE A BABY. I'M GROWING UP!
ZOE, STOP IT RIGHT NOW.
Blossoming Youth
By
STOP WHAT? TALKING?
NO... GROWING UP!
KIRKMAN & SCOTT

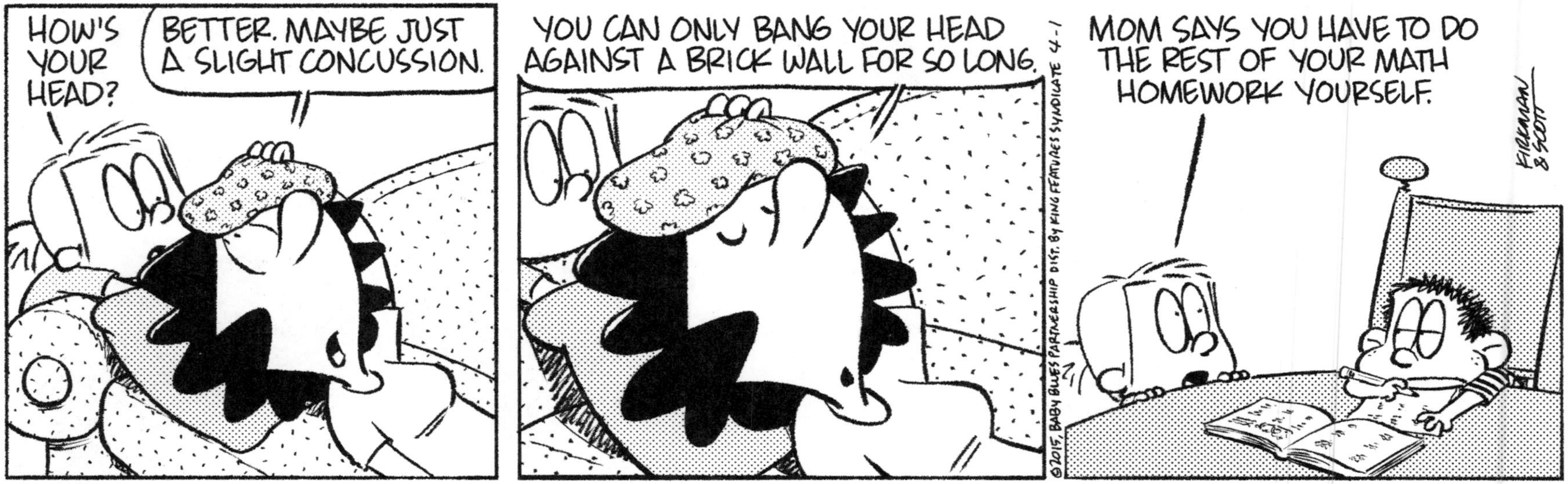
HOW'S YOUR HEAD?
BETTER. MAYBE JUST A SLIGHT CONCUSSION.
YOU CAN ONLY BANG YOUR HEAD AGAINST A BRICK WALL FOR SO LONG.
©2015, BABY BLUES PARTNERSHIP DIST. BY KING FEATURES SYNDICATE 4-1
MOM SAYS YOU HAVE TO DO THE REST OF YOUR MATH HOMEWORK YOURSELF.
KIRKMAN & SCOTT

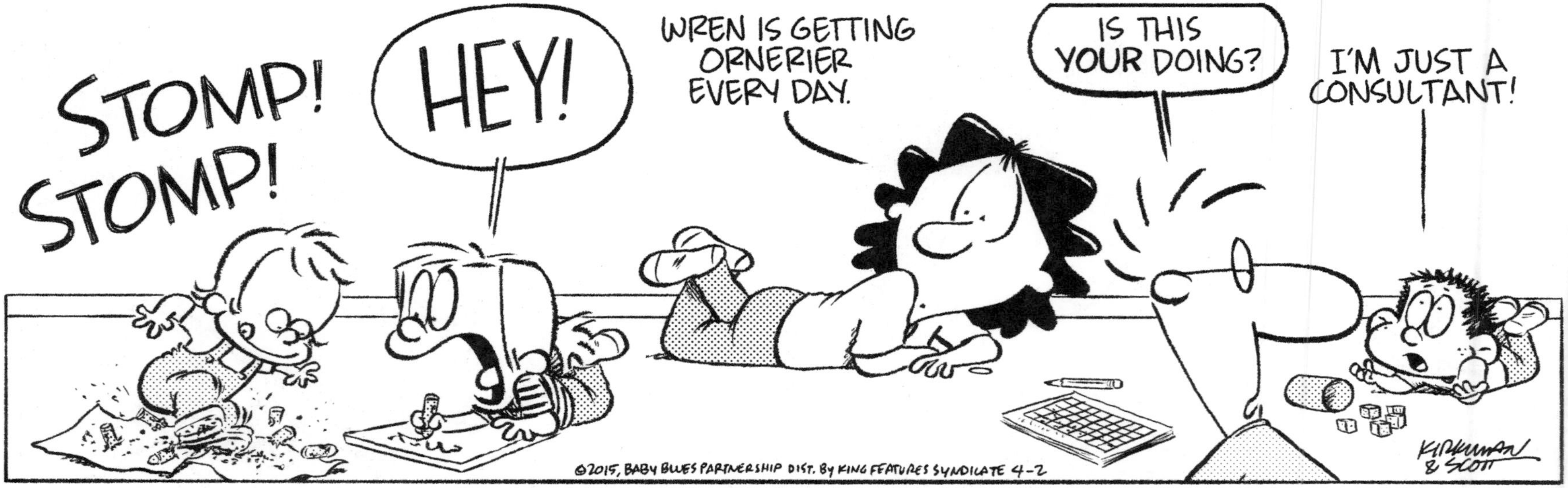
STOMP! STOMP!
HEY!
WREN IS GETTING ORNERIER EVERY DAY.
IS THIS YOUR DOING?
I'M JUST A CONSULTANT!
©2015, BABY BLUES PARTNERSHIP DIST. BY KING FEATURES SYNDICATE 4-2
KIRKMAN & SCOTT

Rick: Consultants: All of the influence, and none of the blame.

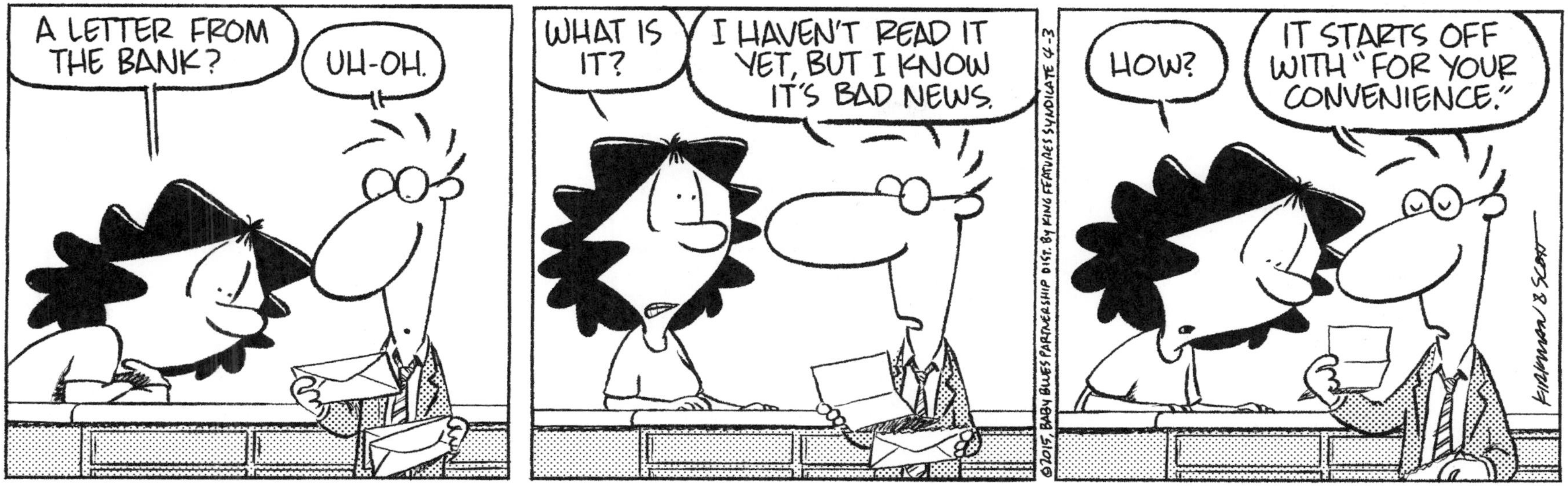
A LETTER FROM THE BANK?
UH-OH.
WHAT IS IT?
I HAVEN'T READ IT YET, BUT I KNOW IT'S BAD NEWS.
HOW?
IT STARTS OFF WITH "FOR YOUR CONVENIENCE."
©2015, BABY BLUES PARTNERSHIP DIST. BY KING FEATURES SYNDICATE 4-3
KIRKMAN & SCOTT

Jerry: Ranks right up there with "Your call is important to us . . ."

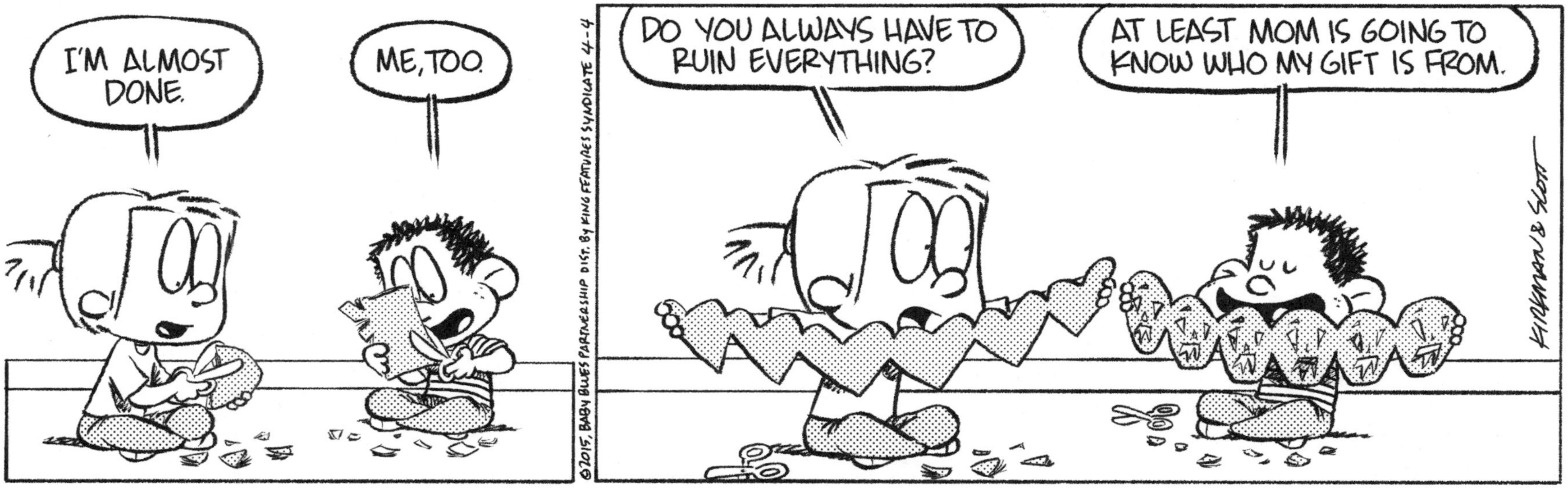
I'M ALMOST DONE.
ME, TOO.
DO YOU ALWAYS HAVE TO RUIN EVERYTHING?
AT LEAST MOM IS GOING TO KNOW WHO MY GIFT IS FROM.
©2015, BABY BLUES PARTNERSHIP DIST. BY KING FEATURES SYNDICATE 4-4
KIRKMAN & SCOTT

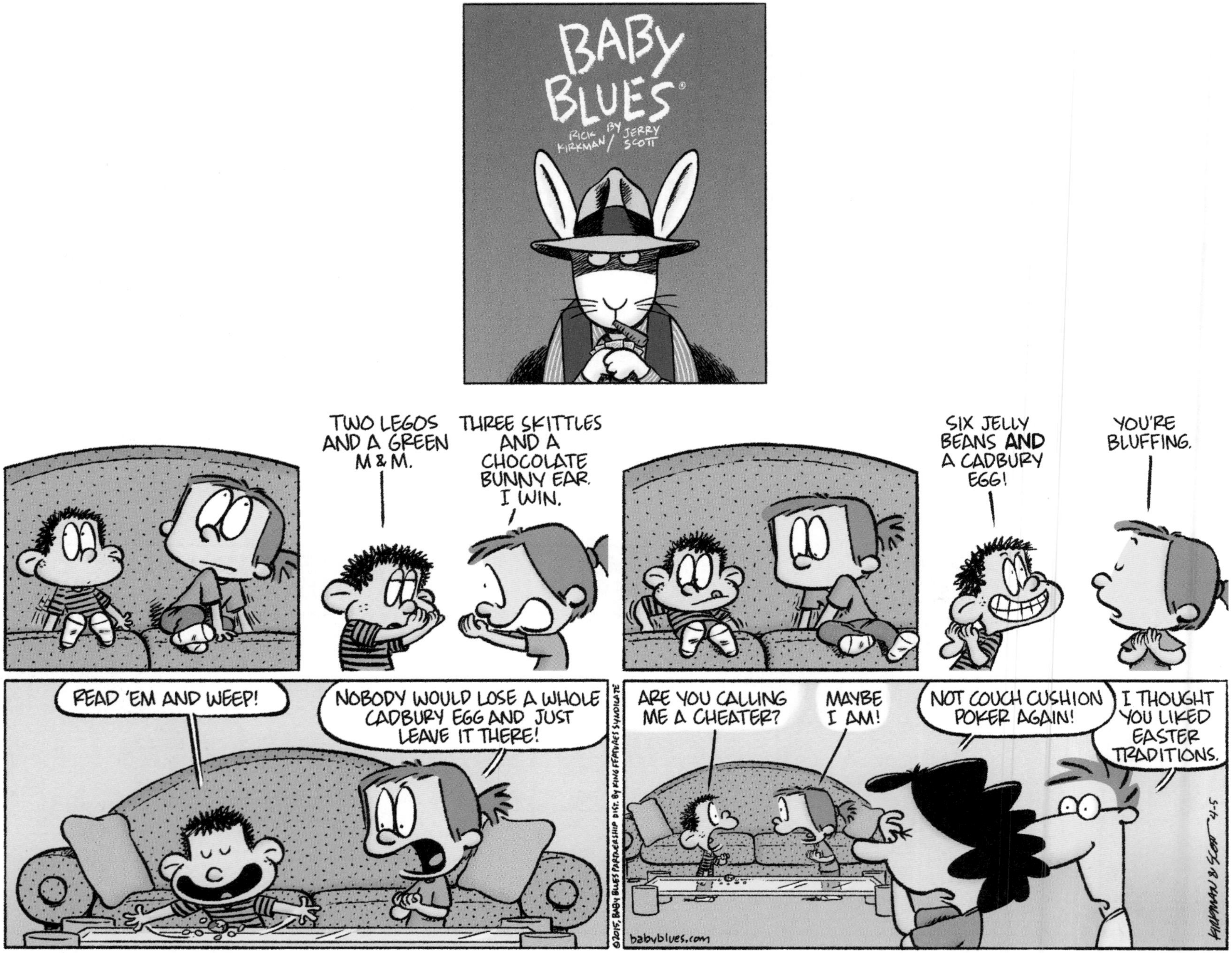
BABY BLUES®
BY RICK KIRKMAN / JERRY SCOTT
TWO LEGOS AND A GREEN M & M.
THREE SKITTLES AND A CHOCOLATE BUNNY EAR. I WIN.
SIX JELLY BEANS AND A CADBURY EGG!
YOU'RE BLUFFING.
READ 'EM AND WEEP!
NOBODY WOULD LOSE A WHOLE CADBURY EGG AND JUST LEAVE IT THERE!
©2015, BABY BLUES PARTNERSHIP DIST. BY KING FEATURES SYNDICATE
ARE YOU CALLING ME A CHEATER?
MAYBE I AM!
NOT COUCH CUSHION POKER AGAIN!
I THOUGHT YOU LIKED EASTER TRADITIONS.
babyblues.com
KIRKMAN & SCOTT
5-4

Rick: Poker + Easter = The Easter Bunny filtered through Paul Newman from *The Sting* for the title panel.

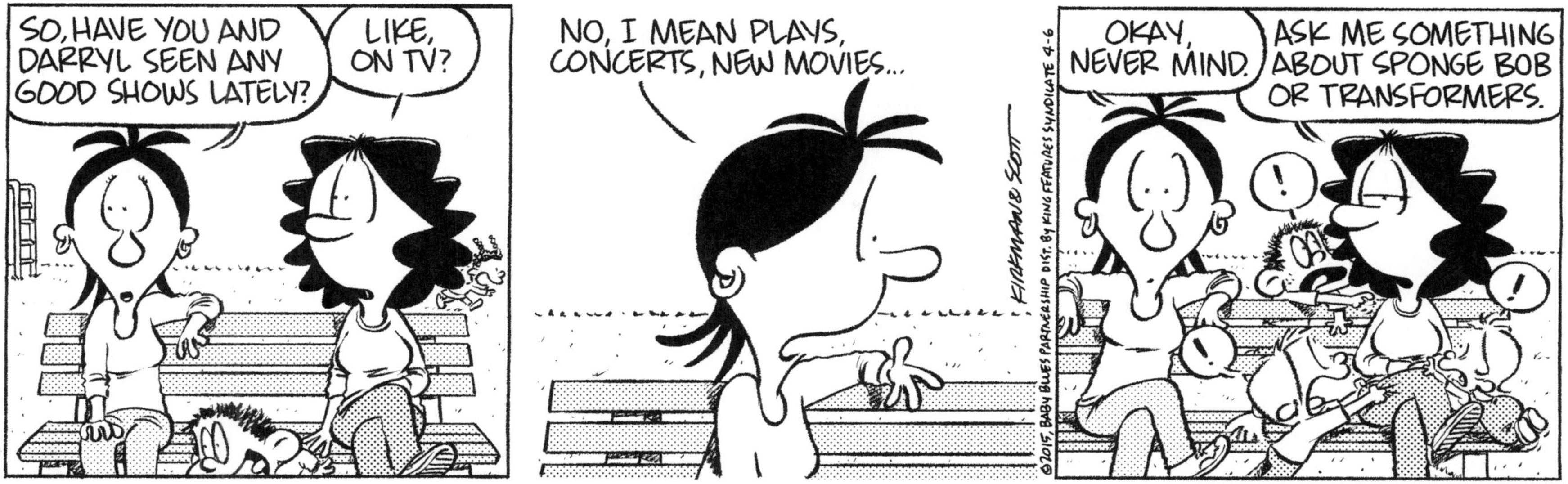
SO, HAVE YOU AND DARRYL SEEN ANY GOOD SHOWS LATELY?
LIKE, ON TV?
NO, I MEAN PLAYS, CONCERTS, NEW MOVIES...
OKAY, NEVER MIND.
ASK ME SOMETHING ABOUT SPONGE BOB OR TRANSFORMERS.
KIRKMAN & SCOTT
©2015, BABY BLUES PARTNERSHIP DIST. BY KING FEATURES SYNDICATE 4-6

Rick: The cultural Lost Years of Parenthood.

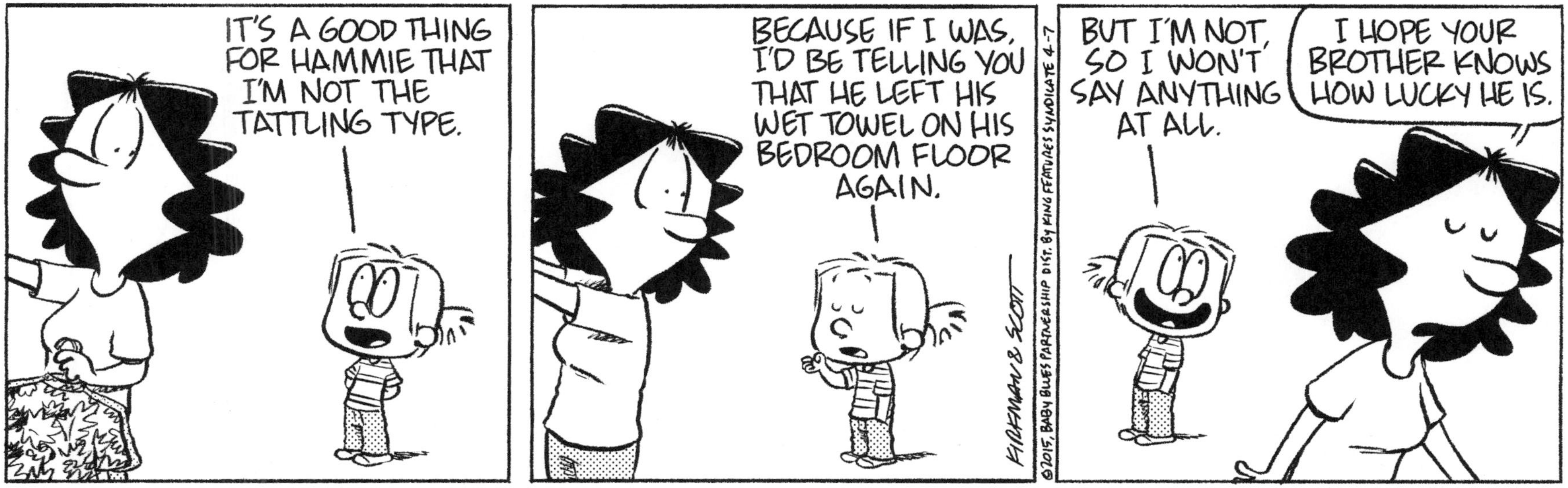
IT'S A GOOD THING FOR HAMMIE THAT I'M NOT THE TATTLING TYPE.
BECAUSE IF I WAS, I'D BE TELLING YOU THAT HE LEFT HIS WET TOWEL ON HIS BEDROOM FLOOR AGAIN.
BUT I'M NOT, SO I WON'T SAY ANYTHING AT ALL.
I HOPE YOUR BROTHER KNOWS HOW LUCKY HE IS.
KIRKMAN & SCOTT
©2015, BABY BLUES PARTNERSHIP DIST. BY KING FEATURES SYNDICATE 4-7

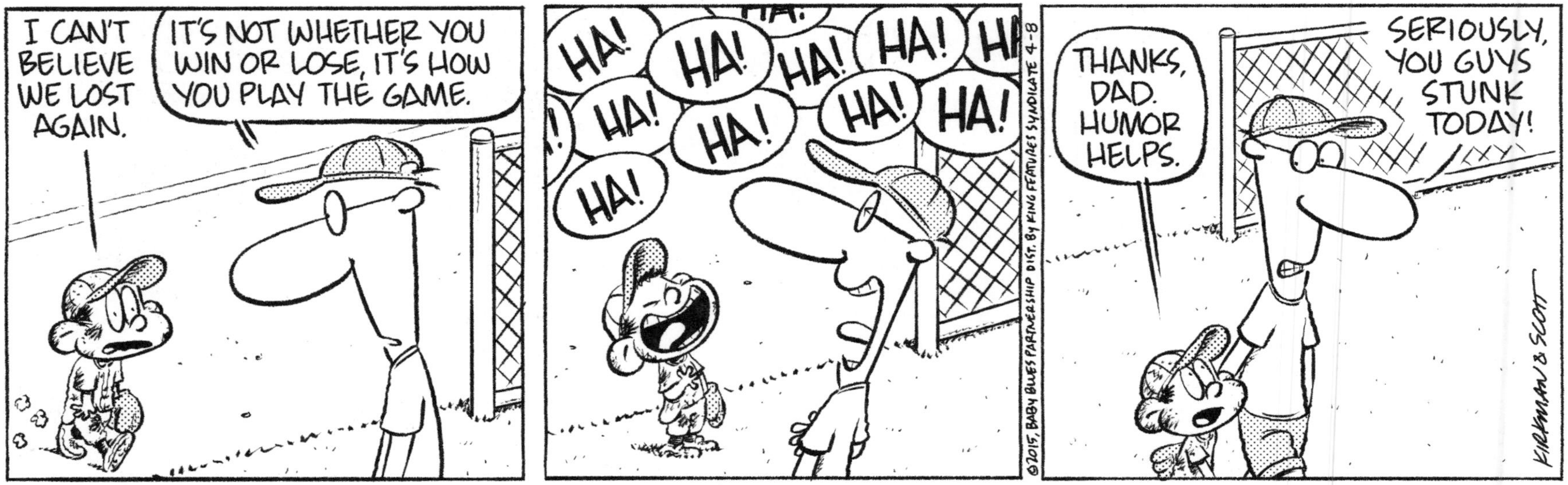

I CAN'T BELIEVE WE LOST AGAIN.
IT'S NOT WHETHER YOU WIN OR LOSE, IT'S HOW YOU PLAY THE GAME.
HA!
HA!
HA!
HA!
HA!
HA!
HA!
HA!
HA!
©2015, BABY BLUES PARTNERSHIP DIST. BY KING FEATURES SYNDICATE 4-8
THANKS, DAD. HUMOR HELPS.
SERIOUSLY, YOU GUYS STUNK TODAY!
KIRKMAN & SCOTT

Rick: There is something to knowing where you stand.

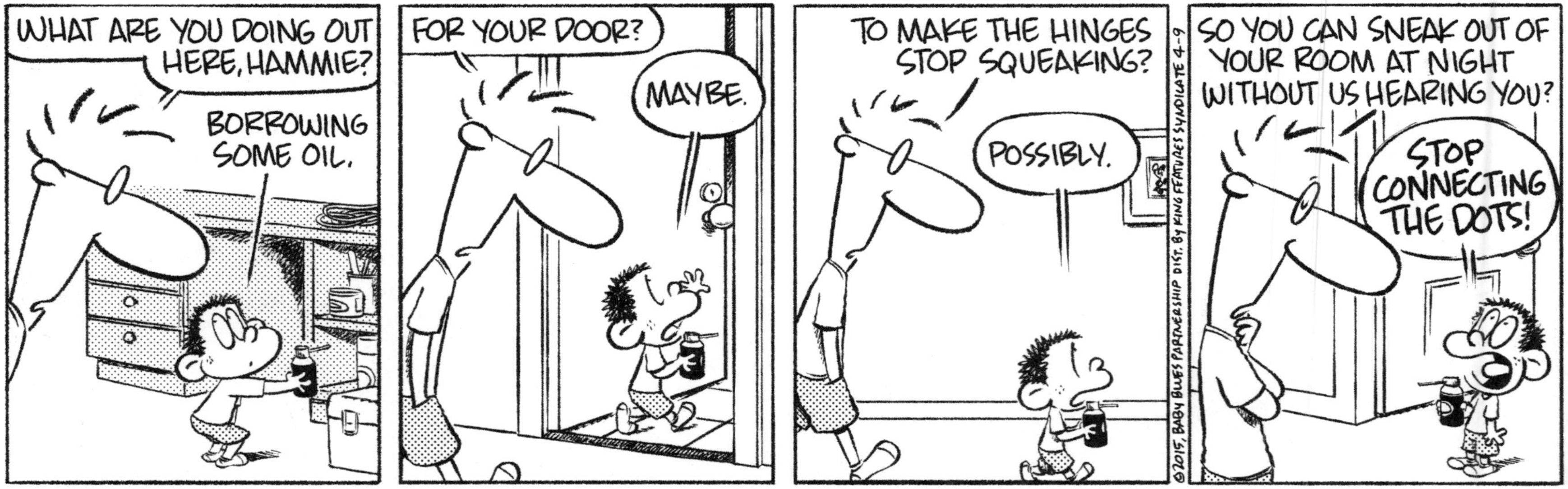

WHAT ARE YOU DOING OUT HERE, HAMMIE?
BORROWING SOME OIL.
FOR YOUR DOOR?
MAYBE.
TO MAKE THE HINGES STOP SQUEAKING?
POSSIBLY.
©2015, BABY BLUES PARTNERSHIP DIST. BY KING FEATURES SYNDICATE 4-9
SO YOU CAN SNEAK OUT OF YOUR ROOM AT NIGHT WITHOUT US HEARING YOU?
STOP CONNECTING THE DOTS!

Rick: Parents have to be part-detective . . .

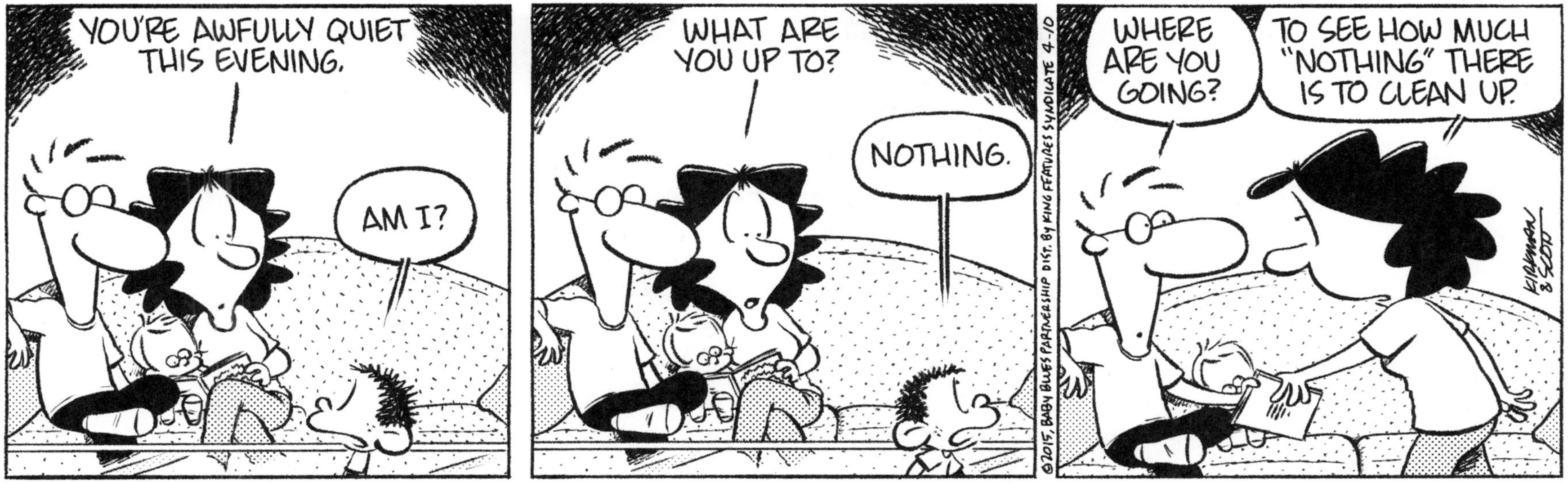
YOU'RE AWFULLY QUIET THIS EVENING.
AM I?
WHAT ARE YOU UP TO?
NOTHING.
©2015, BABY BLUES PARTNERSHIP DIST. BY KING FEATURES SYNDICATE 4-10
WHERE ARE YOU GOING?
TO SEE HOW MUCH "NOTHING" THERE IS TO CLEAN UP.
KIRKMAN & SCOTT

Rick: . . . and learn to read between the lines.

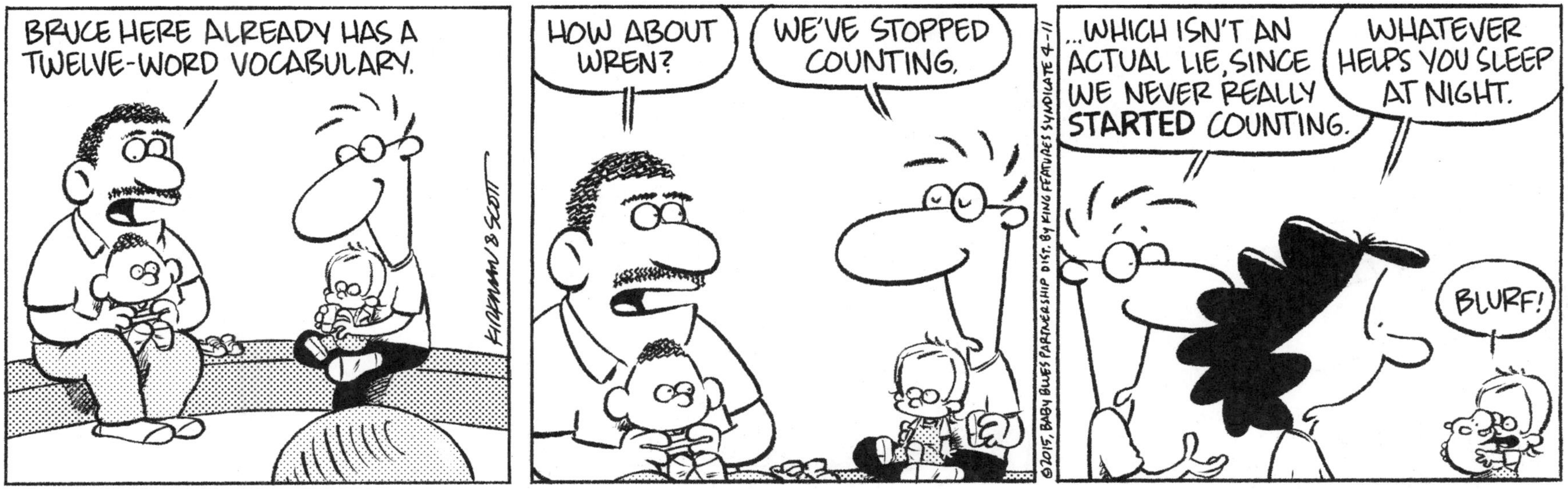
BRUCE HERE ALREADY HAS A TWELVE-WORD VOCABULARY.
KIRKMAN & SCOTT
HOW ABOUT WREN?
WE'VE STOPPED COUNTING.
©2015, BABY BLUES PARTNERSHIP DIST. BY KING FEATURES SYNDICATE 4-11
...WHICH ISN'T AN ACTUAL LIE, SINCE WE NEVER REALLY STARTED COUNTING.
WHATEVER HELPS YOU SLEEP AT NIGHT.
BLURF!

Rick: I like that other kid's look. I may have to bring him back again.

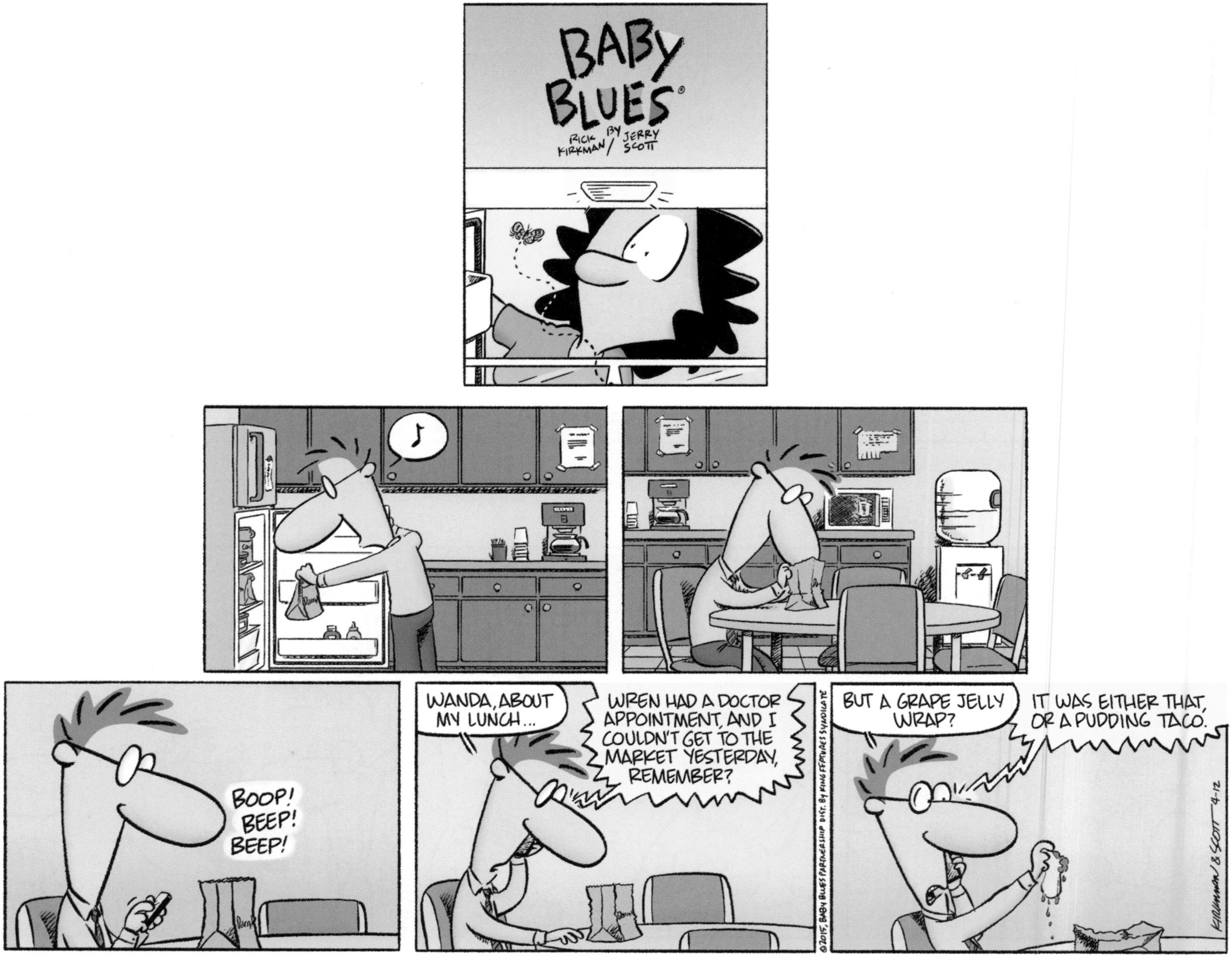
BABY BLUES®
RICK KIRKMAN / BY JERRY SCOTT
BOOP! BEEP! BEEP!
WANDA, ABOUT MY LUNCH...
WREN HAD A DOCTOR APPOINTMENT, AND I COULDN'T GET TO THE MARKET YESTERDAY, REMEMBER?
BUT A GRAPE JELLY WRAP?
IT WAS EITHER THAT, OR A PUDDING TACO.
©2015, BABY BLUES PARTNERSHIP DIST. BY KING FEATURES SYNDICATE
KIRKMAN & SCOTT 4-12

Jerry: Hey! Those are my recipes!

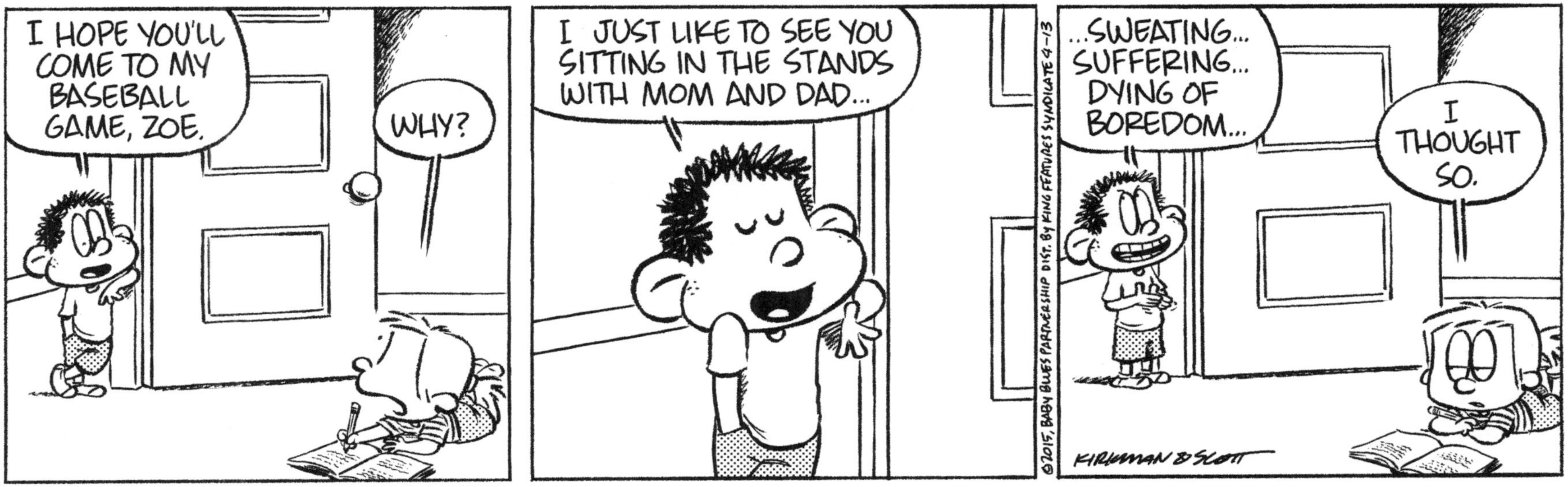
I HOPE YOU'LL COME TO MY BASEBALL GAME, ZOE.
WHY?
I JUST LIKE TO SEE YOU SITTING IN THE STANDS WITH MOM AND DAD...
©2015, BABY BLUES PARTNERSHIP DIST. BY KING FEATURES SYNDICATE 4-13
...SWEATING... SUFFERING... DYING OF BOREDOM...
I THOUGHT SO.
KIRKMAN & SCOTT

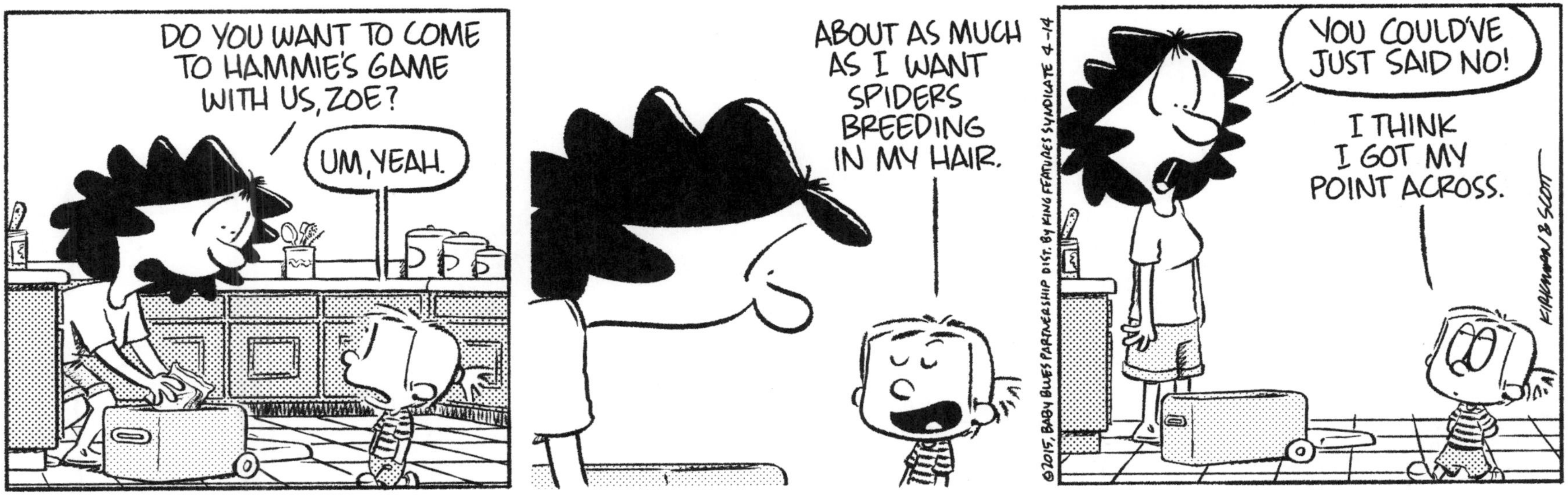
DO YOU WANT TO COME TO HAMMIE'S GAME WITH US, ZOE?
UM, YEAH.
ABOUT AS MUCH AS I WANT SPIDERS BREEDING IN MY HAIR.
©2015, BABY BLUES PARTNERSHIP DIST. BY KING FEATURES SYNDICATE 4-14
YOU COULD'VE JUST SAID NO!
I THINK I GOT MY POINT ACROSS.
KIRKMAN & SCOTT

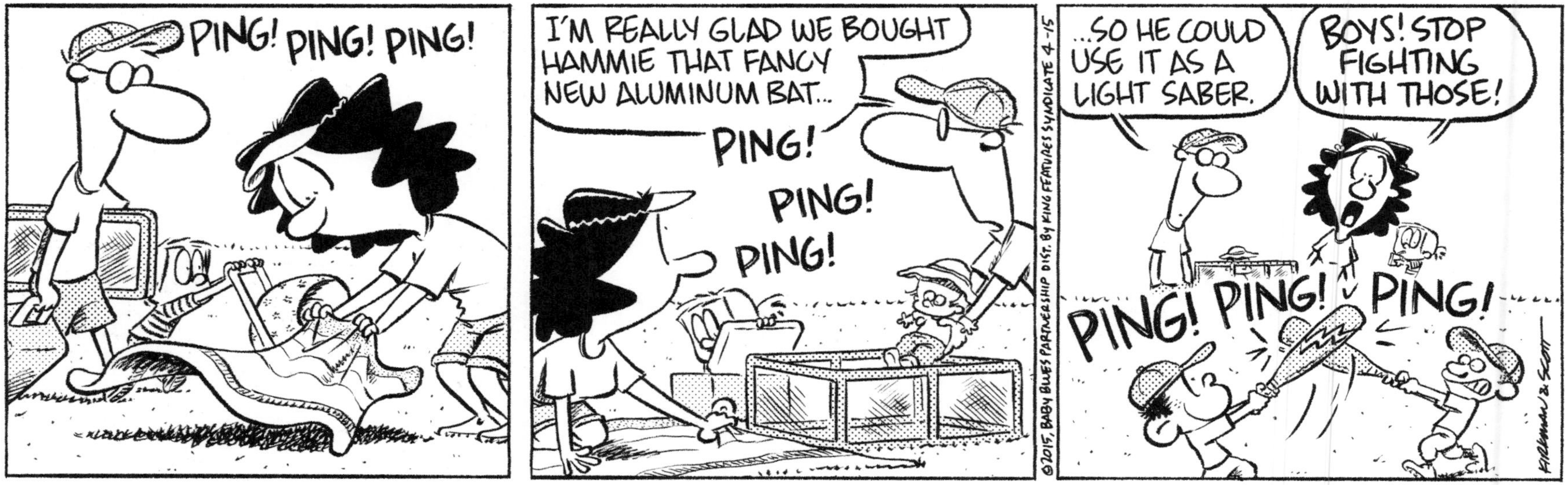
PING! PING! PING!
I'M REALLY GLAD WE BOUGHT HAMMIE THAT FANCY NEW ALUMINUM BAT...
PING!
PING!
PING!
...SO HE COULD USE IT AS A LIGHT SABER.
BOYS! STOP FIGHTING WITH THOSE!
PING! PING! PING!
©2015, BABY BLUES PARTNERSHIP DIST. BY KING FEATURES SYNDICATE 4-15
KIRKMAN & SCOTT

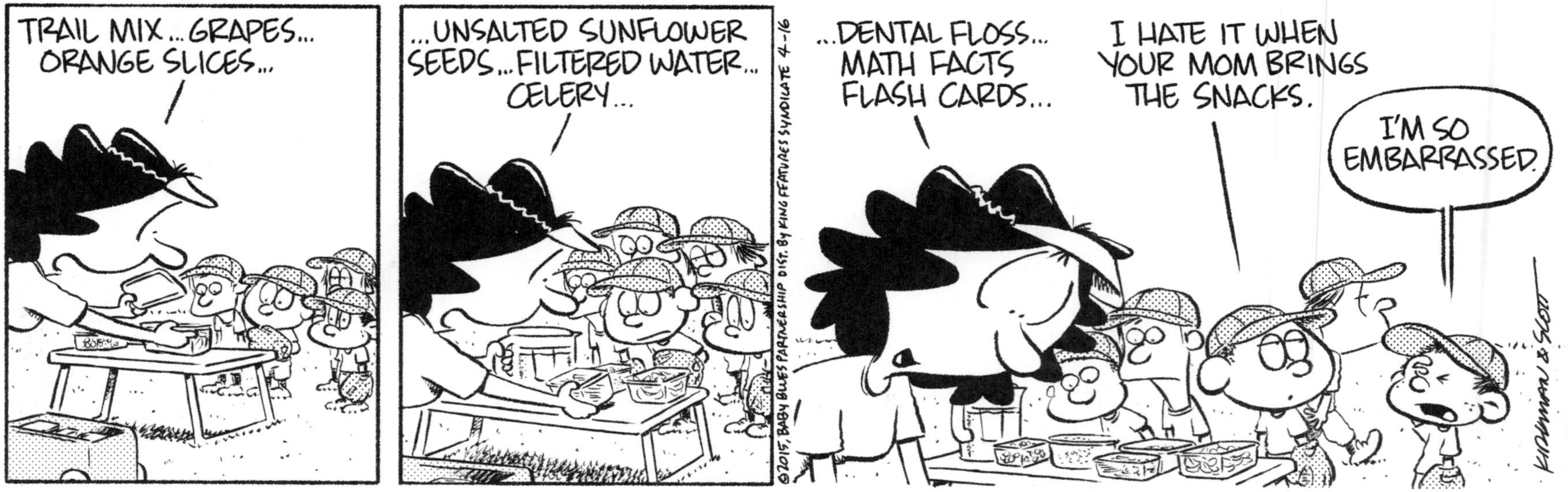
TRAIL MIX... GRAPES... ORANGE SLICES...
...UNSALTED SUNFLOWER SEEDS... FILTERED WATER... CELERY...
...DENTAL FLOSS... MATH FACTS FLASH CARDS...
I HATE IT WHEN YOUR MOM BRINGS THE SNACKS.
I'M SO EMBARRASSED.
©2015, BABY BLUES PARTNERSHIP DIST. BY KING FEATURES SYNDICATE 4-16
KIRKMAN & SCOTT

Rick: The curse of the Too-Conscientious Mom.

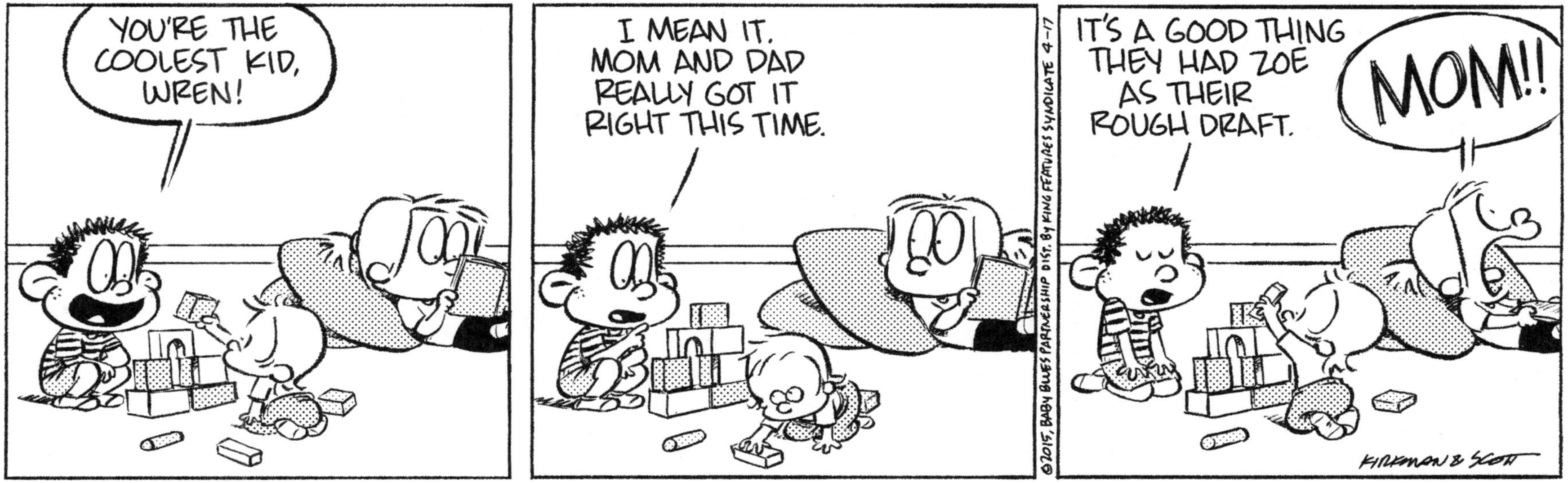
YOU'RE THE COOLEST KID, WREN!
I MEAN IT. MOM AND DAD REALLY GOT IT RIGHT THIS TIME.
©2015, BABY BLUES PARTNERSHIP DIST. BY KING FEATURES SYNDICATE 4-17
IT'S A GOOD THING THEY HAD ZOE AS THEIR ROUGH DRAFT.
MOM!!
KIRKMAN & SCOTT

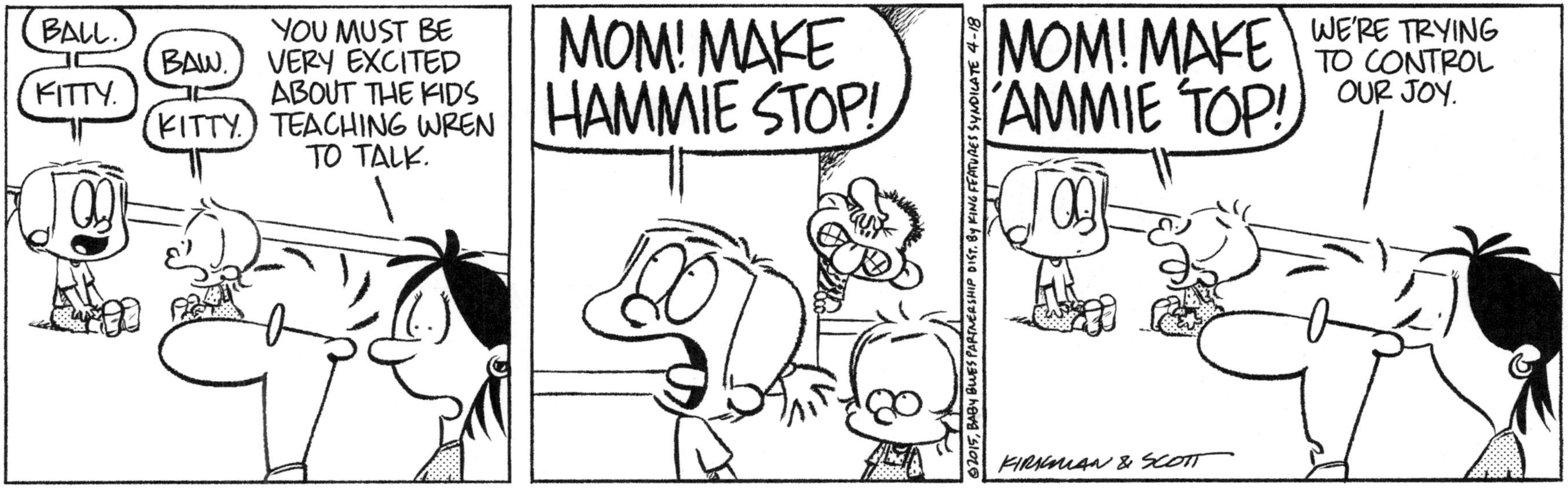
BALL.
KITTY.
BAW.
KITTY.
YOU MUST BE VERY EXCITED ABOUT THE KIDS TEACHING WREN TO TALK.
MOM! MAKE HAMMIE STOP!
©2015, BABY BLUES PARTNERSHIP DIST. BY KING FEATURES SYNDICATE 4-18
MOM! MAKE 'AMMIE 'TOP!
WE'RE TRYING TO CONTROL OUR JOY.
KIRKMAN & SCOTT

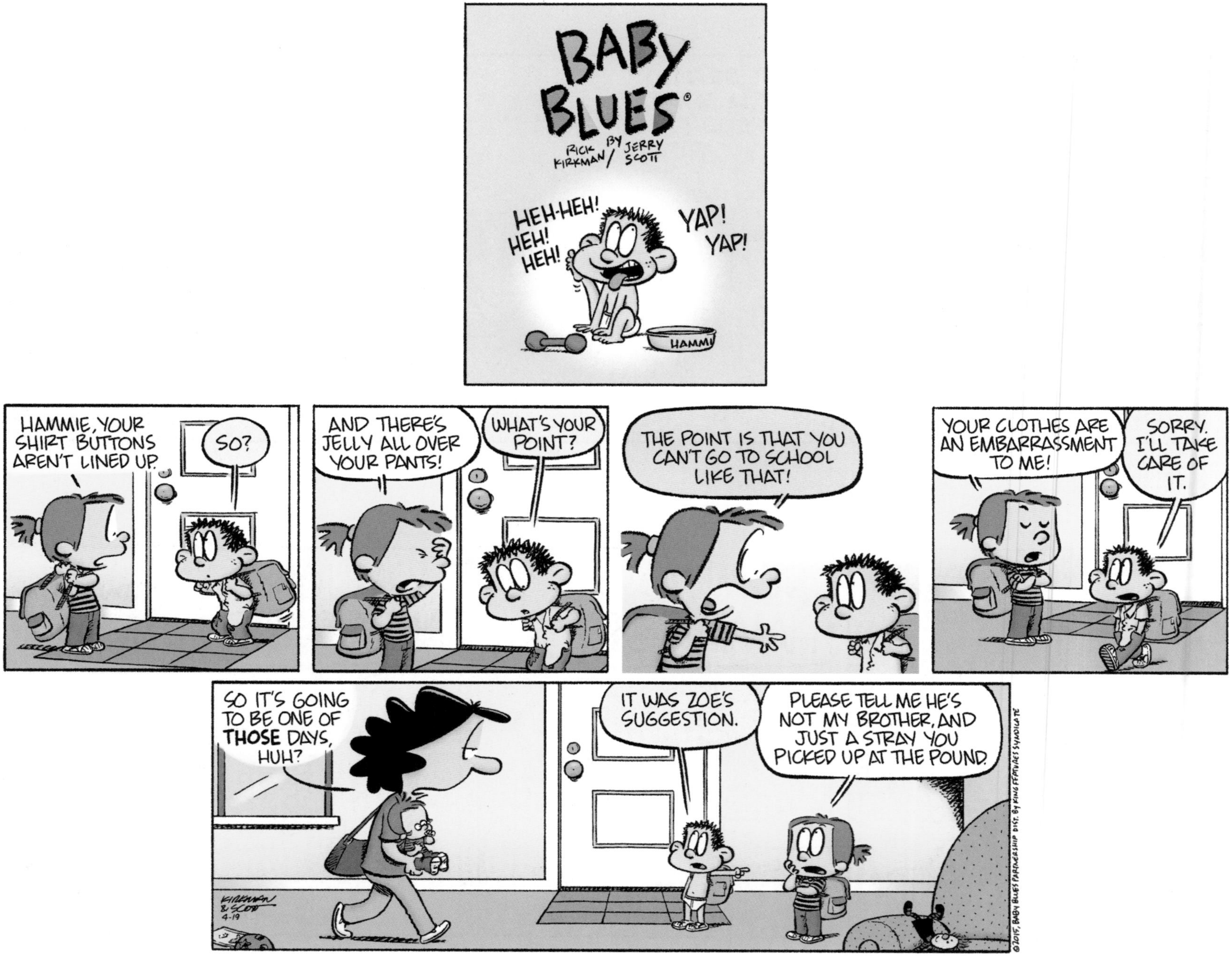
BABY BLUES®
RICK KIRKMAN / BY JERRY SCOTT
HEH-HEH! HEH! HEH!
YAP! YAP!
HAMMIE
HAMMIE, YOUR SHIRT BUTTONS AREN'T LINED UP.
SO?
AND THERE'S JELLY ALL OVER YOUR PANTS!
WHAT'S YOUR POINT?
THE POINT IS THAT YOU CAN'T GO TO SCHOOL LIKE THAT!
YOUR CLOTHES ARE AN EMBARRASSMENT TO ME!
SORRY. I'LL TAKE CARE OF IT.
SO IT'S GOING TO BE ONE OF **THOSE** DAYS, HUH?
IT WAS ZOE'S SUGGESTION.
PLEASE TELL ME HE'S NOT MY BROTHER, AND JUST A STRAY YOU PICKED UP AT THE POUND.
KIRKMAN & SCOTT 4-19
©2015, BABY BLUES PARTNERSHIP DIST. BY KING FEATURES SYNDICATE

Rick: Hey, they always wanted a dog.

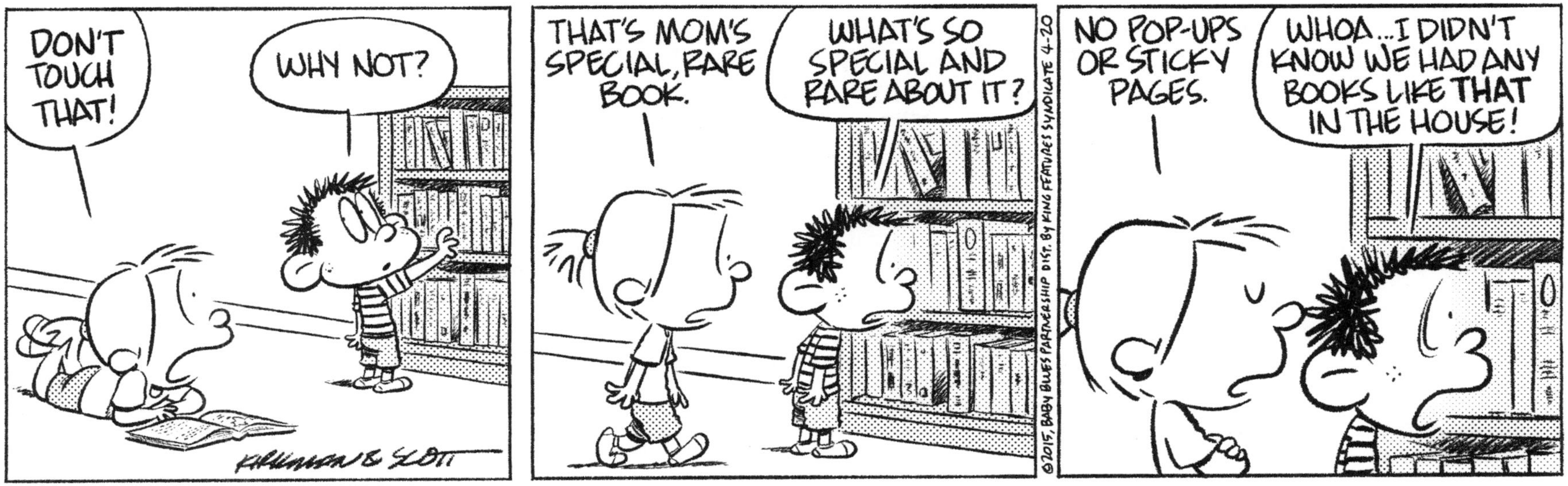
DON'T TOUCH THAT!
WHY NOT?
KIRKMAN & SCOTT
THAT'S MOM'S SPECIAL, RARE BOOK.
WHAT'S SO SPECIAL AND RARE ABOUT IT?
©2015, BABY BLUES PARTNERSHIP DIST. BY KING FEATURES SYNDICATE 4-20
NO POP-UPS OR STICKY PAGES.
WHOA...I DIDN'T KNOW WE HAD ANY BOOKS LIKE THAT IN THE HOUSE!

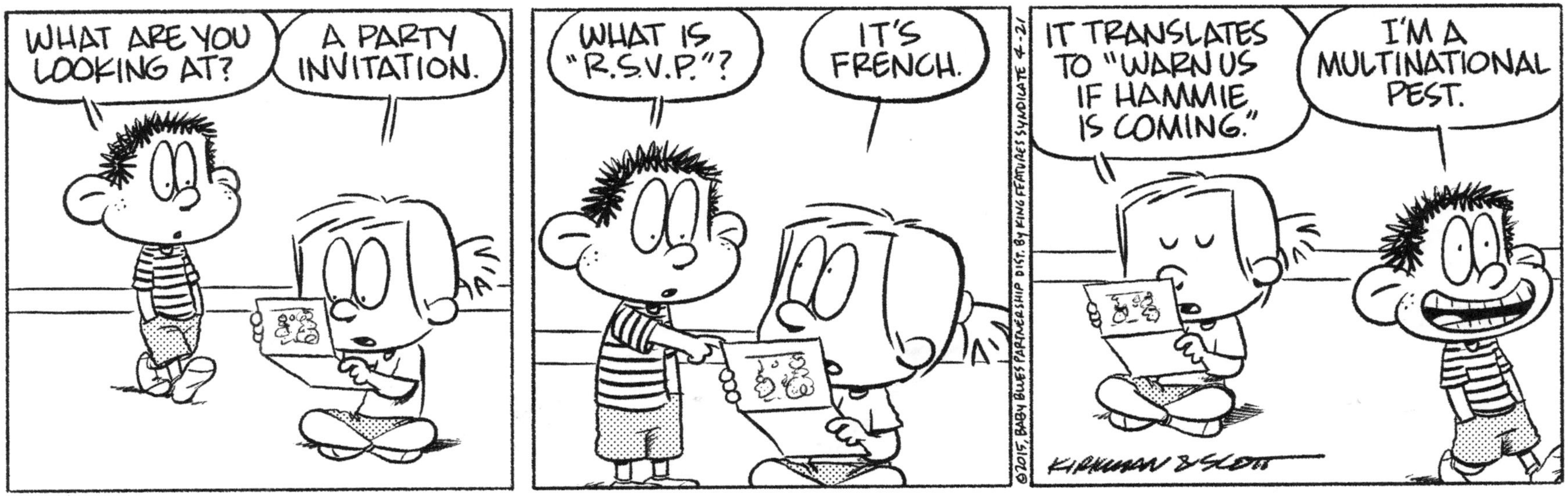
WHAT ARE YOU LOOKING AT?
A PARTY INVITATION.
WHAT IS "R.S.V.P."?
IT'S FRENCH.
©2015, BABY BLUES PARTNERSHIP DIST. BY KING FEATURES SYNDICATE 4-21
IT TRANSLATES TO "WARN US IF HAMMIE IS COMING."
I'M A MULTINATIONAL PEST.
KIRKMAN & SCOTT

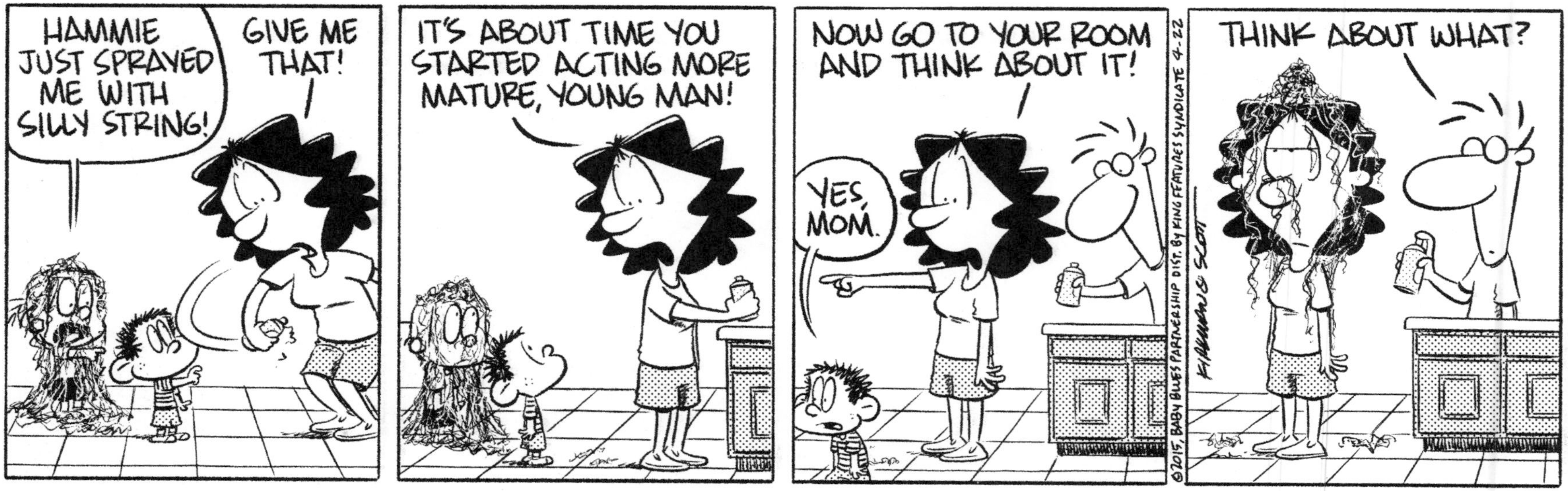
HAMMIE JUST SPRAYED ME WITH SILLY STRING!
GIVE ME THAT!
IT'S ABOUT TIME YOU STARTED ACTING MORE MATURE, YOUNG MAN!
NOW GO TO YOUR ROOM AND THINK ABOUT IT!
YES, MOM.
THINK ABOUT WHAT?

Rick: That was a first—I'd never drawn Silly String before.

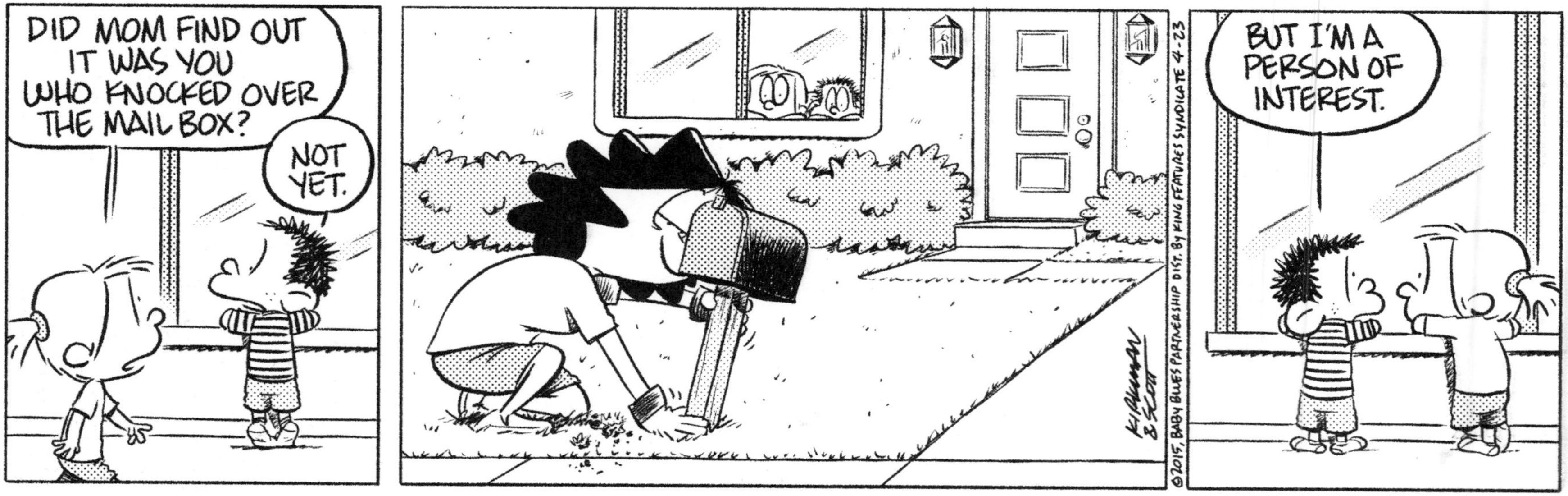
DID MOM FIND OUT IT WAS YOU WHO KNOCKED OVER THE MAIL BOX?
NOT YET.
BUT I'M A PERSON OF INTEREST.

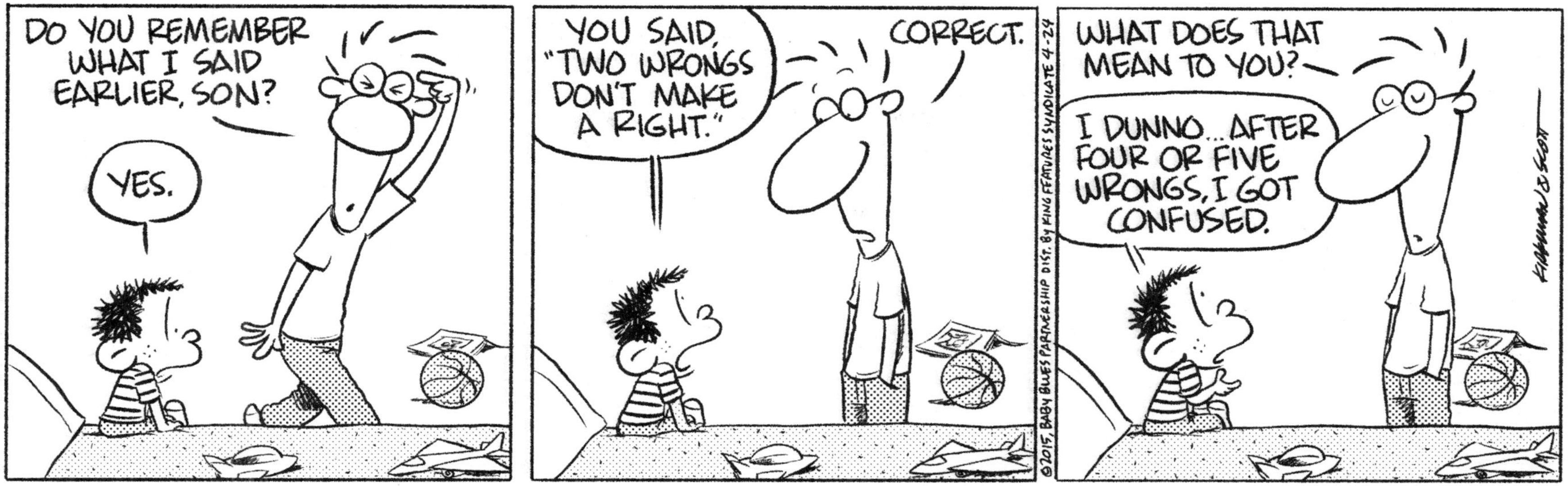
DO YOU REMEMBER WHAT I SAID EARLIER, SON?
YES.
YOU SAID, "TWO WRONGS DON'T MAKE A RIGHT."
CORRECT.
WHAT DOES THAT MEAN TO YOU?
I DUNNO... AFTER FOUR OR FIVE WRONGS, I GOT CONFUSED.
©2015, BABY BLUES PARTNERSHIP DIST. BY KING FEATURES SYNDICATE 4-24
KIRKMAN & SCOTT

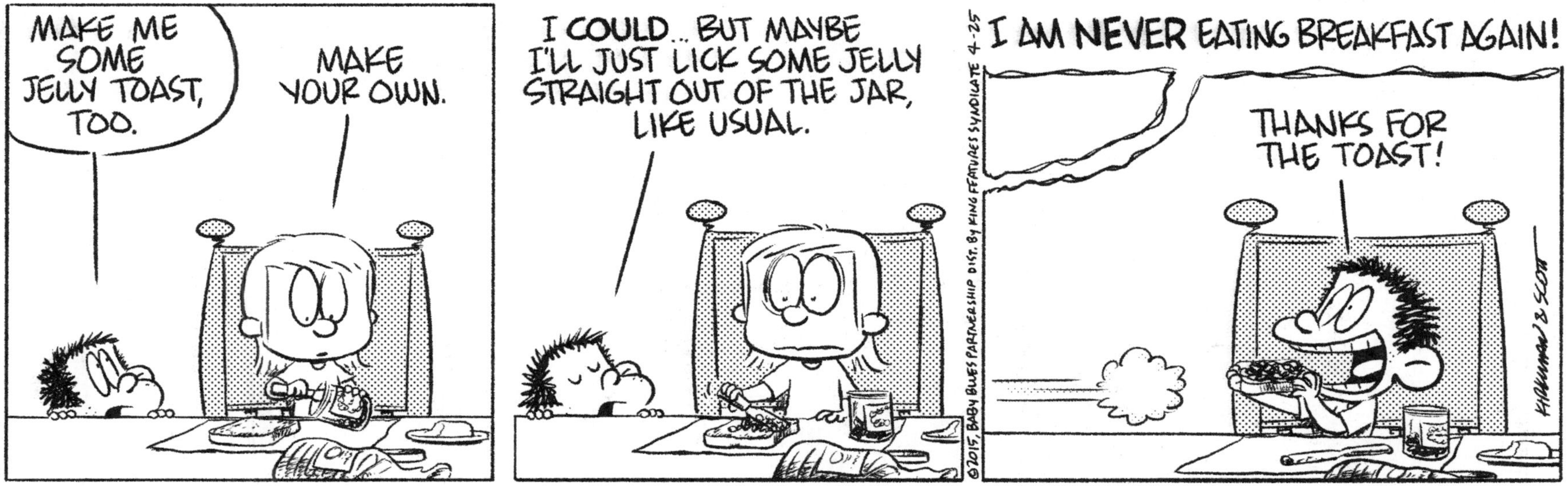
MAKE ME SOME JELLY TOAST, TOO.
MAKE YOUR OWN.
I **COULD**... BUT MAYBE I'LL JUST LICK SOME JELLY STRAIGHT OUT OF THE JAR, LIKE USUAL.
I AM **NEVER** EATING BREAKFAST AGAIN!
THANKS FOR THE TOAST!
©2015, BABY BLUES PARTNERSHIP DIST. BY KING FEATURES SYNDICATE 4-25
KIRKMAN & SCOTT

Rick: Saliva—a brother's (or sister's) secret weapon.

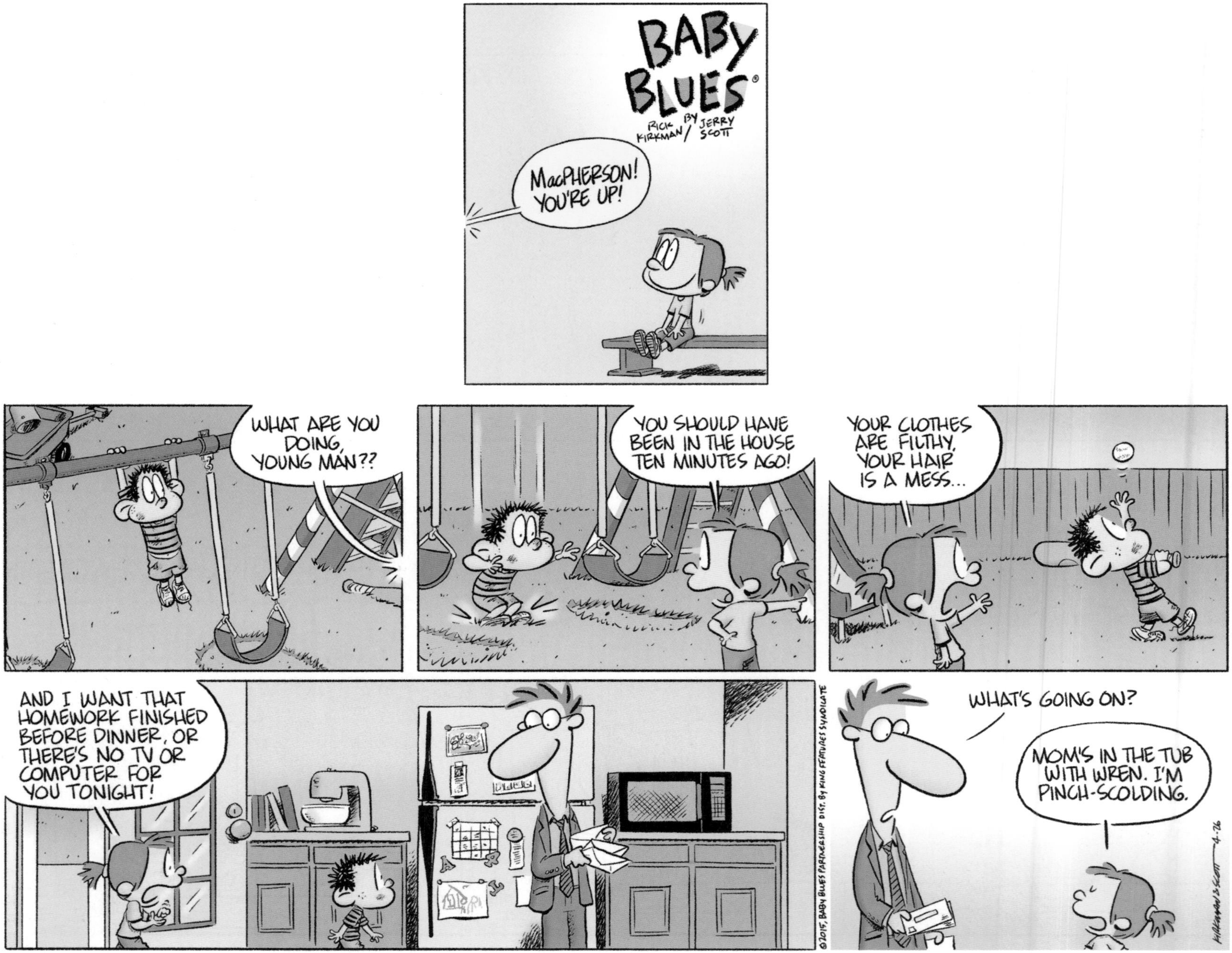
BABY BLUES®
BY RICK KIRKMAN / JERRY SCOTT
MacPHERSON! YOU'RE UP!
WHAT ARE YOU DOING, YOUNG MAN??
YOU SHOULD HAVE BEEN IN THE HOUSE TEN MINUTES AGO!
YOUR CLOTHES ARE FILTHY, YOUR HAIR IS A MESS...
AND I WANT THAT HOMEWORK FINISHED BEFORE DINNER, OR THERE'S NO TV OR COMPUTER FOR YOU TONIGHT!
©2015, BABY BLUES PARTNERSHIP DIST. BY KING FEATURES SYNDICATE
WHAT'S GOING ON?
MOM'S IN THE TUB WITH WREN. I'M PINCH-SCOLDING.
4-26
KIRKMAN & SCOTT

Rick: The MacPhersons' house and yard is based on the one our kids grew up in. Sometimes it's such a déjà vu experience seeing it in a cartoon.

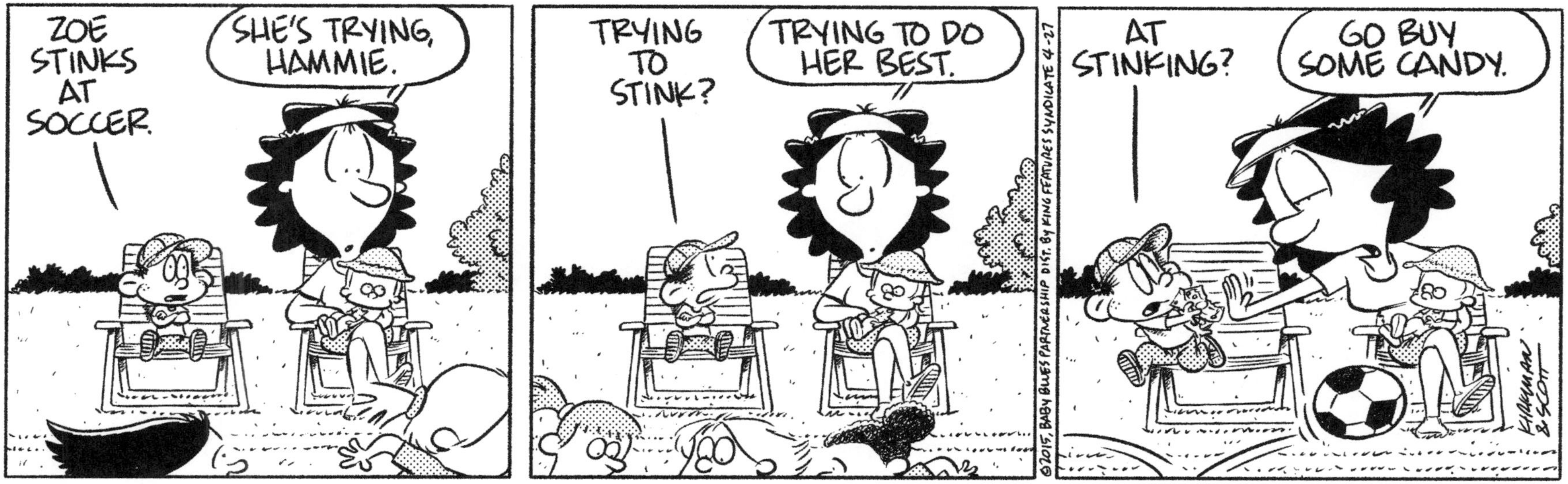
ZOE STINKS AT SOCCER.
SHE'S TRYING, HAMMIE.
TRYING TO STINK?
TRYING TO DO HER BEST.
AT STINKING?
GO BUY SOME CANDY.
©2015, BABY BLUES PARTNERSHIP DIST. BY KING FEATURES SYNDICATE 4-27
KIRKMAN & SCOTT

Jerry: This should land Hammie in the Annoying Little Brother Hall of Fame.

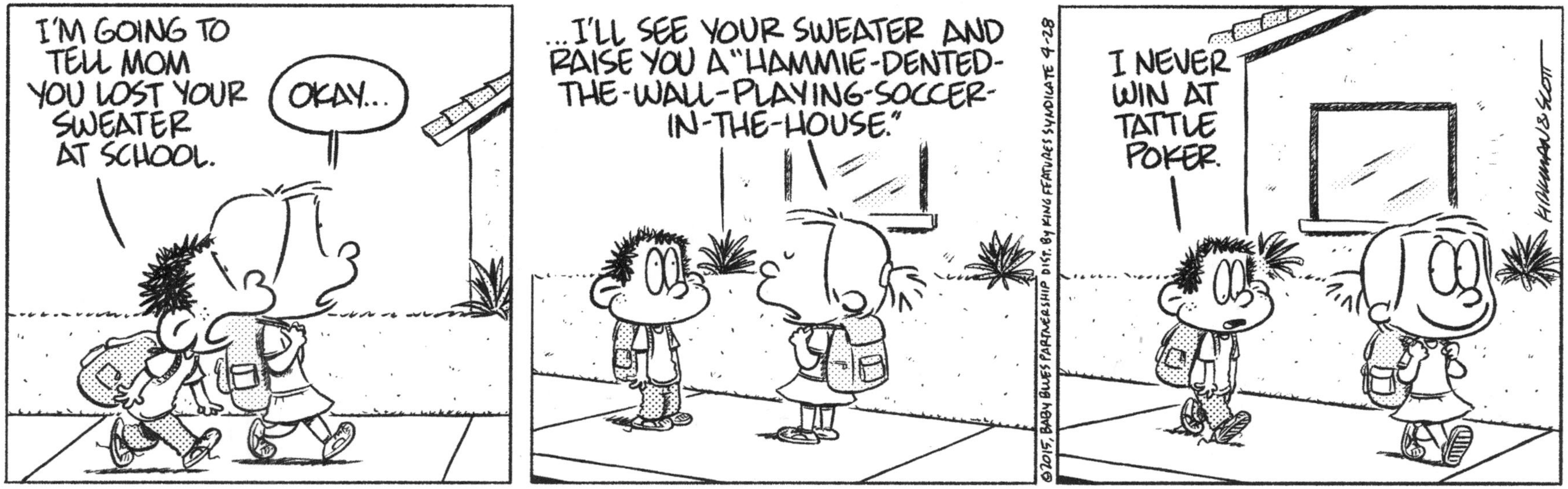
I'M GOING TO TELL MOM YOU LOST YOUR SWEATER AT SCHOOL.
OKAY...
...I'LL SEE YOUR SWEATER AND RAISE YOU A "HAMMIE-DENTED-THE-WALL-PLAYING-SOCCER-IN-THE-HOUSE."
I NEVER WIN AT TATTLE POKER.
©2015, BABY BLUES PARTNERSHIP DIST. BY KING FEATURES SYNDICATE 4-28
KIRKMAN & SCOTT

Rick: I wanna see that on TV—The World Series of Tattle Poker.

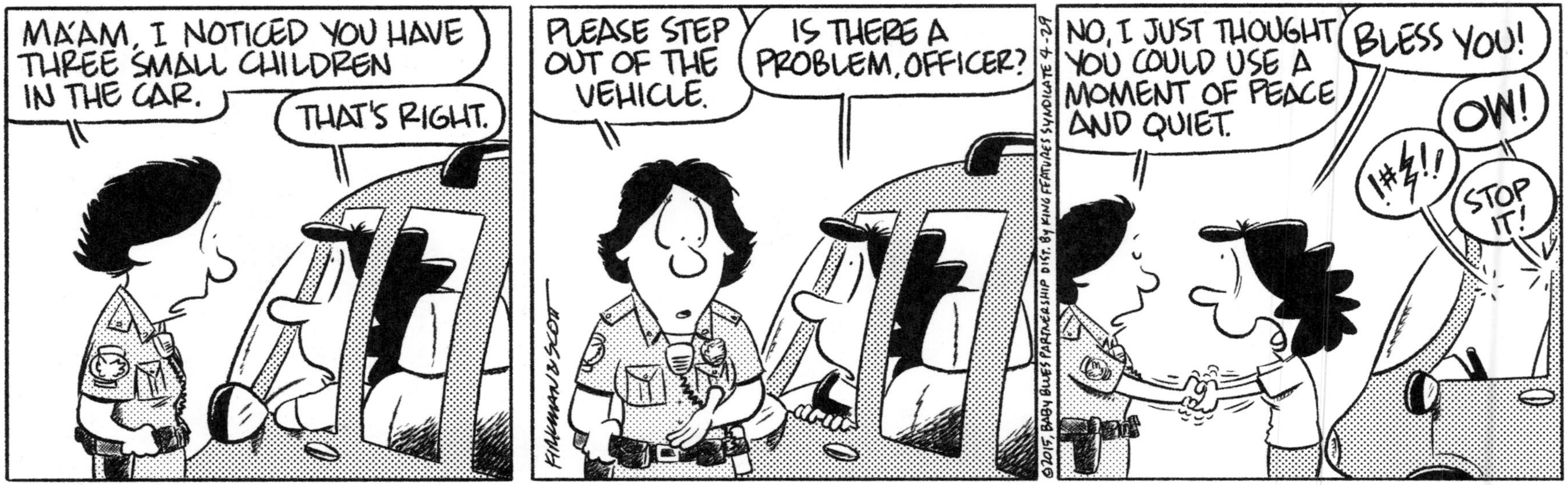
MA'AM, I NOTICED YOU HAVE THREE SMALL CHILDREN IN THE CAR.
THAT'S RIGHT.
PLEASE STEP OUT OF THE VEHICLE.
IS THERE A PROBLEM, OFFICER?
KIRKMAN & SCOTT
©2015, BABY BLUES PARTNERSHIP DIST. BY KING FEATURES SYNDICATE 4-29
NO, I JUST THOUGHT YOU COULD USE A MOMENT OF PEACE AND QUIET.
BLESS YOU!
OW!
!#$!!
STOP IT!

Rick: Now that's a hero.

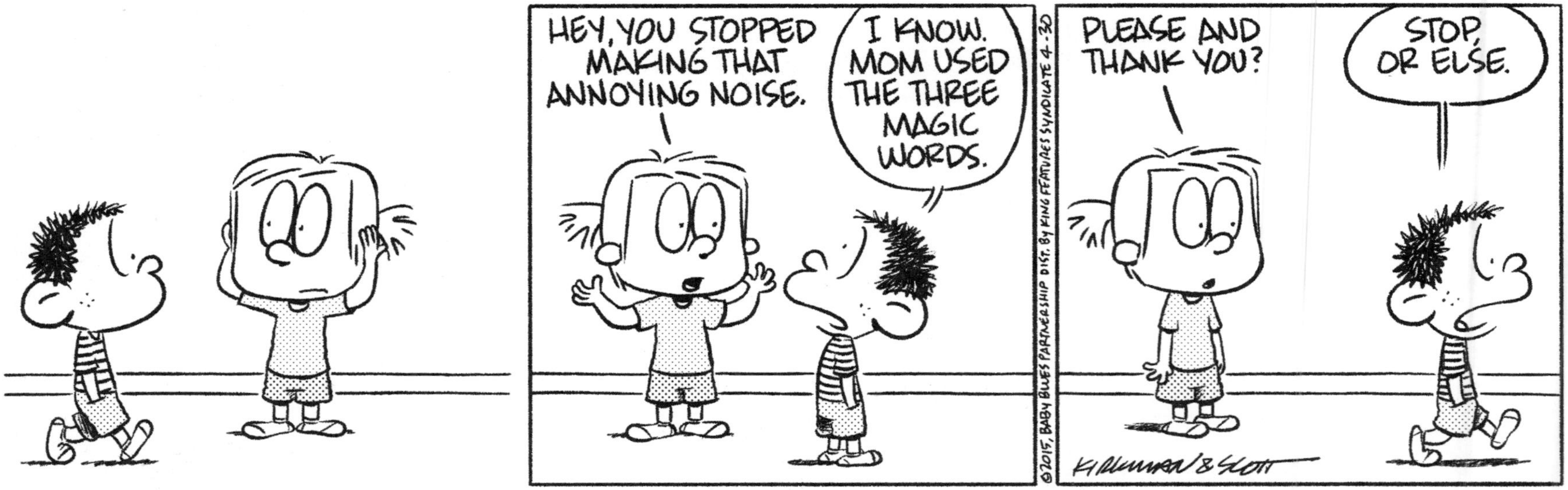
HEY, YOU STOPPED MAKING THAT ANNOYING NOISE.
I KNOW. MOM USED THE THREE MAGIC WORDS.
©2015, BABY BLUES PARTNERSHIP DIST. BY KING FEATURES SYNDICATE 4-30
PLEASE AND THANK YOU?
STOP, OR ELSE.
KIRKMAN & SCOTT

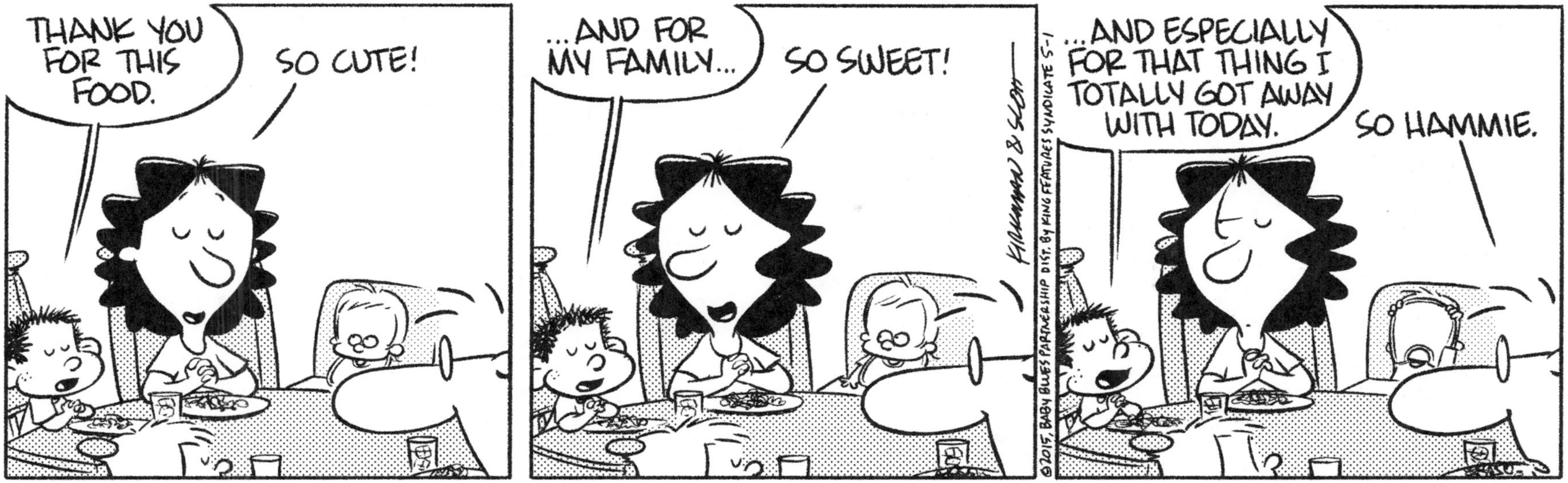
THANK YOU FOR THIS FOOD.
SO CUTE!
...AND FOR MY FAMILY...
SO SWEET!
KIRKMAN & SCOTT
©2015, BABY BLUES PARTNERSHIP DIST. BY KING FEATURES SYNDICATE 5-1
...AND ESPECIALLY FOR THAT THING I TOTALLY GOT AWAY WITH TODAY.
SO HAMMIE.

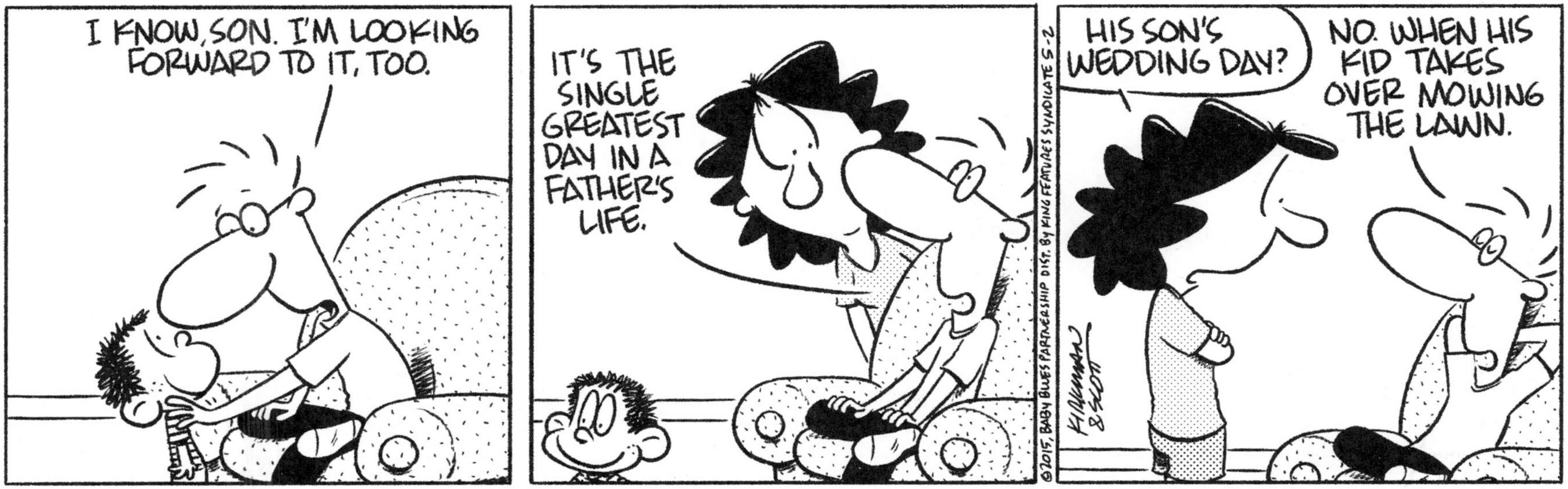
I KNOW, SON. I'M LOOKING FORWARD TO IT, TOO.
IT'S THE SINGLE GREATEST DAY IN A FATHER'S LIFE.
©2015, BABY BLUES PARTNERSHIP DIST. BY KING FEATURES SYNDICATE 5-2
KIRKMAN & SCOTT
HIS SON'S WEDDING DAY?
NO. WHEN HIS KID TAKES OVER MOWING THE LAWN.

Rick: Didn't work for me and my dad. I ended up being allergic to grass.

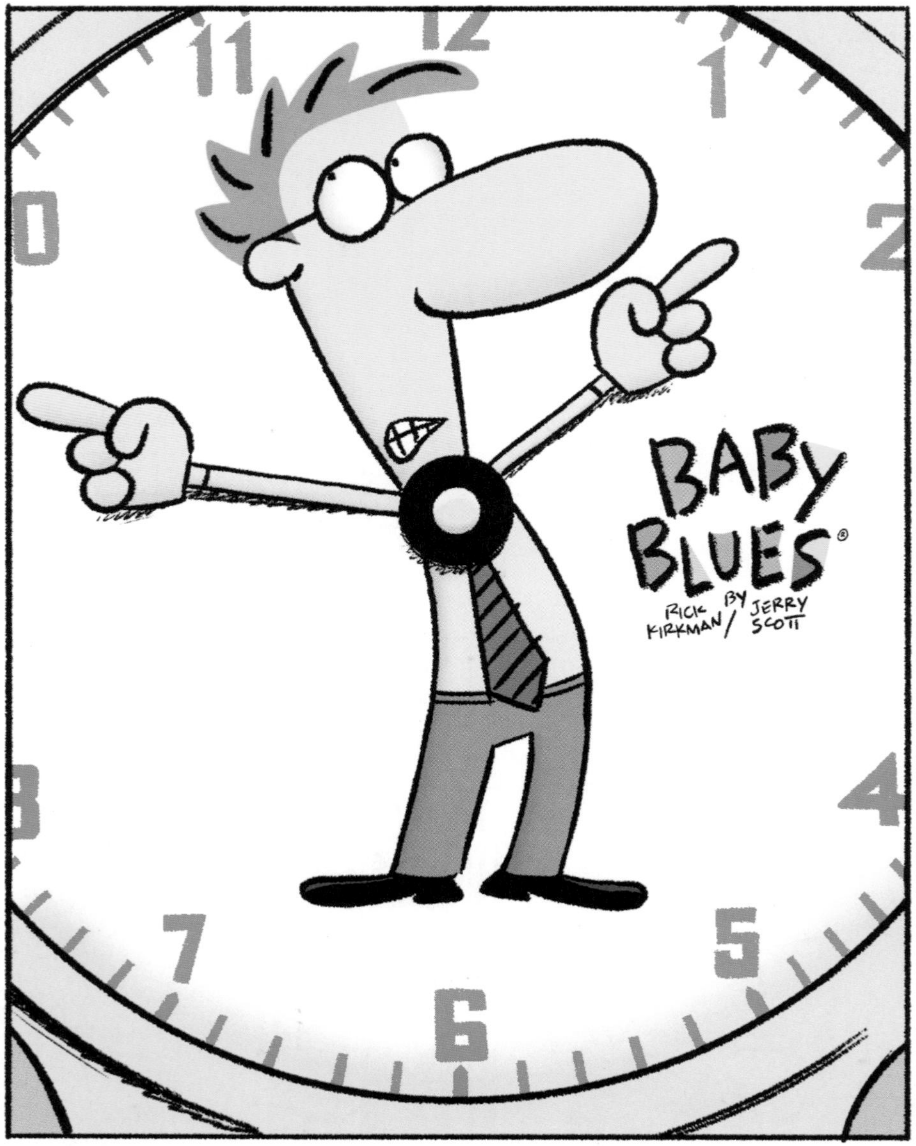
BABY BLUES®
RICK KIRKMAN / BY JERRY SCOTT

Jerry: Moment captured. Nice job, Rick!

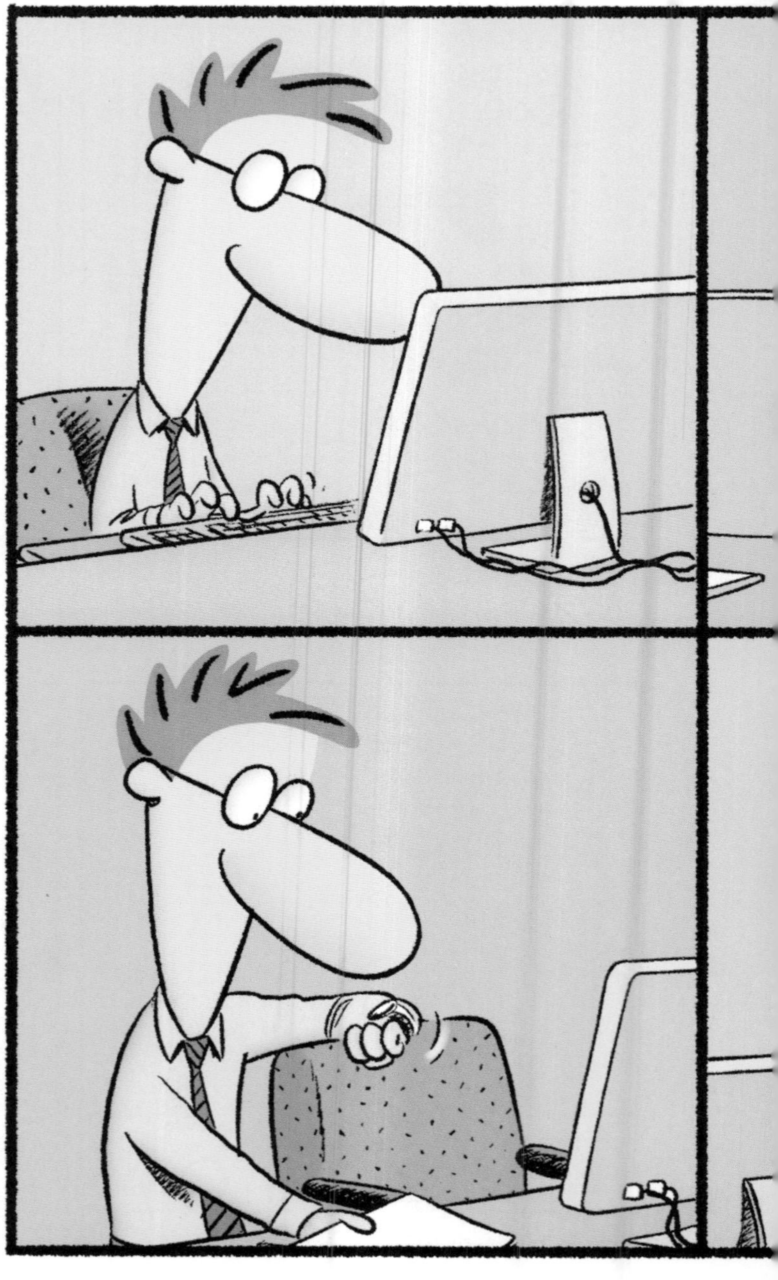

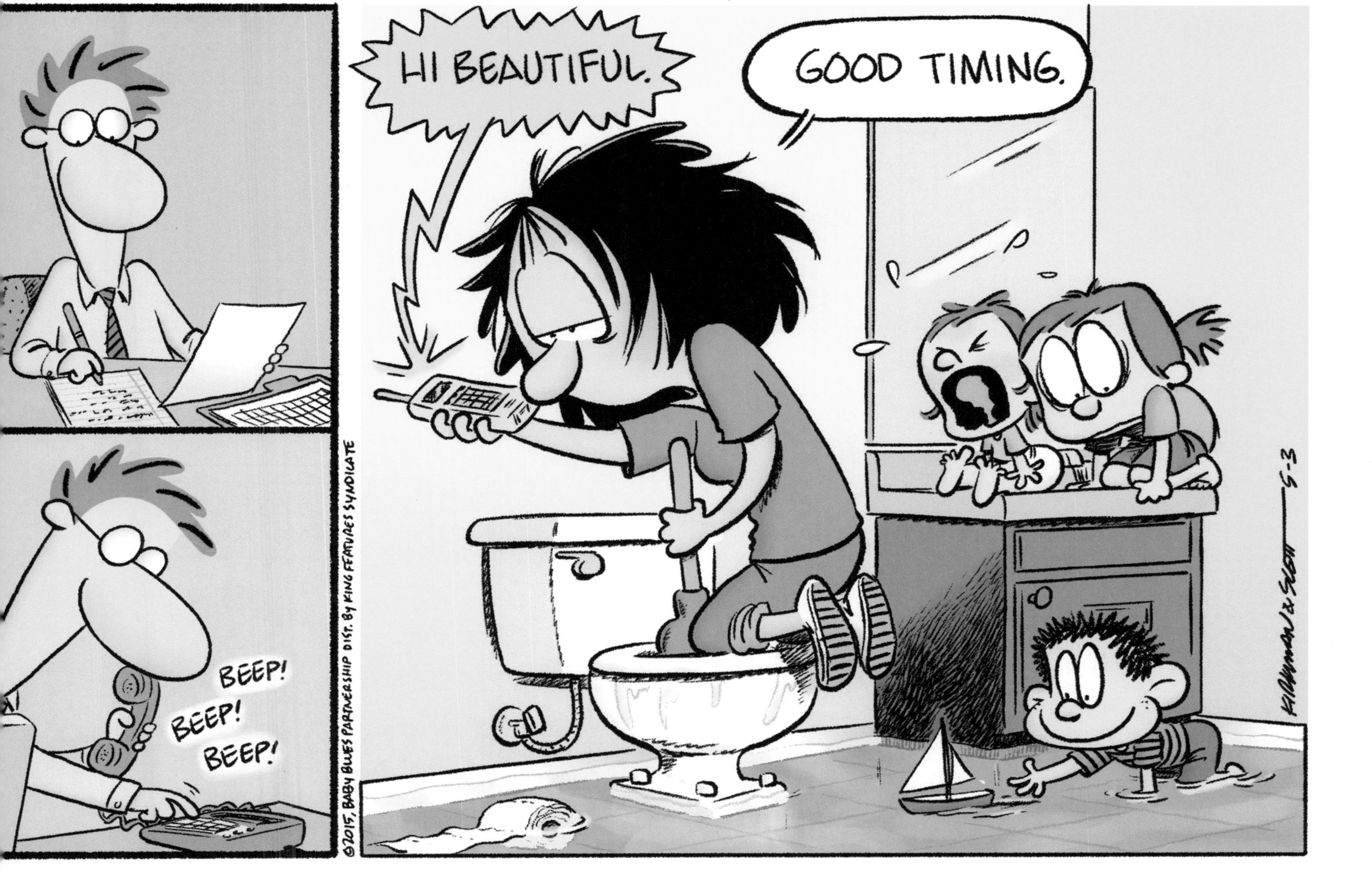
BEEP!
BEEP!
BEEP!
HI BEAUTIFUL.
GOOD TIMING.
KIRKMAN & SCOTT
5-3

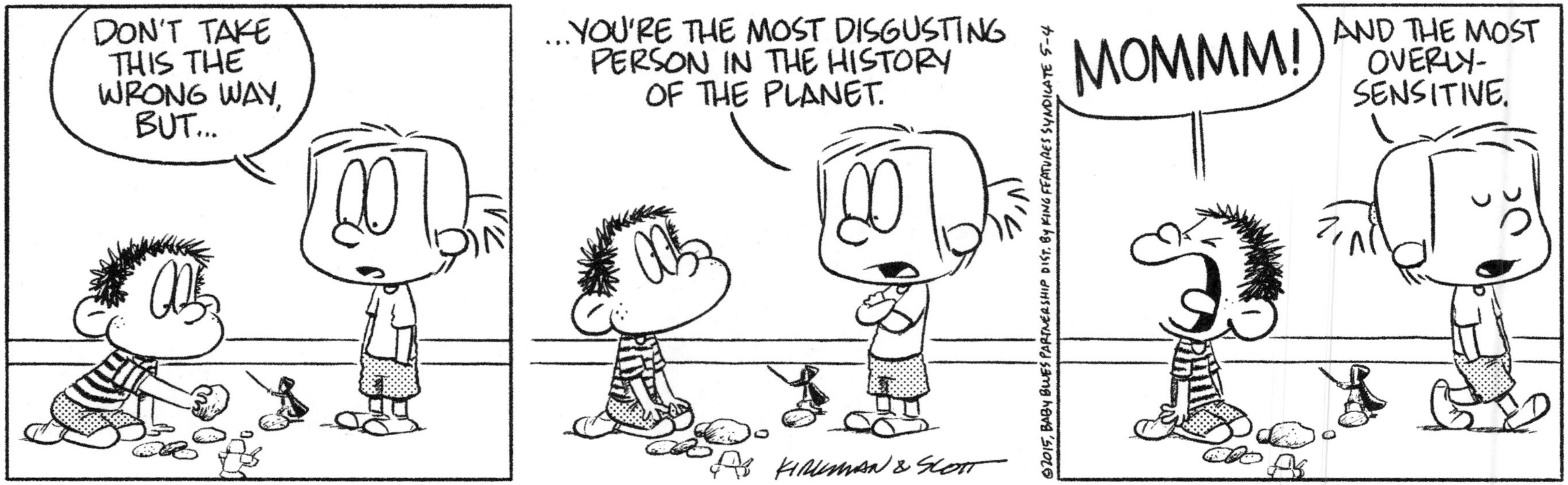
DON'T TAKE THIS THE WRONG WAY, BUT...
...YOU'RE THE MOST DISGUSTING PERSON IN THE HISTORY OF THE PLANET.
KIRKMAN & SCOTT
©2015, BABY BLUES PARTNERSHIP DIST. BY KING FEATURES SYNDICATE 5-4
MOMMM!
AND THE MOST OVERLY-SENSITIVE.

Jerry: Sisters can be so diplomatic.

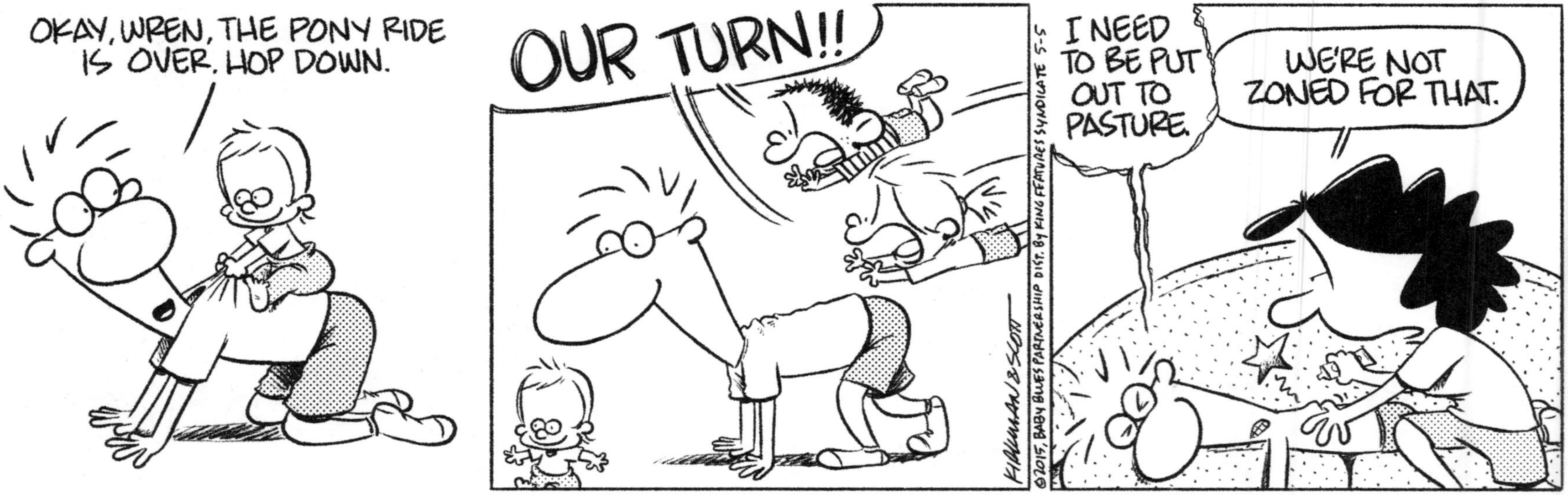
OKAY, WREN, THE PONY RIDE IS OVER. HOP DOWN.
OUR TURN!!
KIRKMAN & SCOTT
©2015, BABY BLUES PARTNERSHIP DIST. BY KING FEATURES SYNDICATE 5-5
I NEED TO BE PUT OUT TO PASTURE.
WE'RE NOT ZONED FOR THAT.

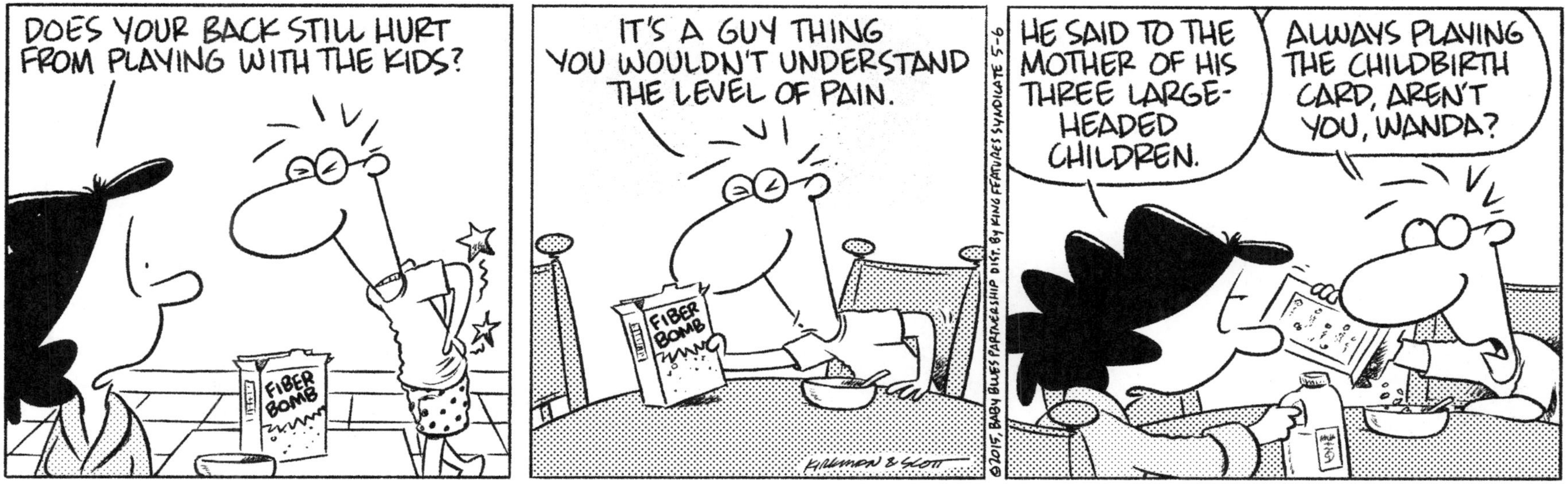
DOES YOUR BACK STILL HURT FROM PLAYING WITH THE KIDS?
FIBER BOMB
IT'S A GUY THING YOU WOULDN'T UNDERSTAND THE LEVEL OF PAIN.
FIBER BOMB
KIRKMAN & SCOTT
©2015, BABY BLUES PARTNERSHIP DIST. BY KING FEATURES SYNDICATE 5-6
HE SAID TO THE MOTHER OF HIS THREE LARGE-HEADED CHILDREN.
ALWAYS PLAYING THE CHILDBIRTH CARD, AREN'T YOU, WANDA?

Rick: Love that last line. Of Wanda's! Of Wanda's!

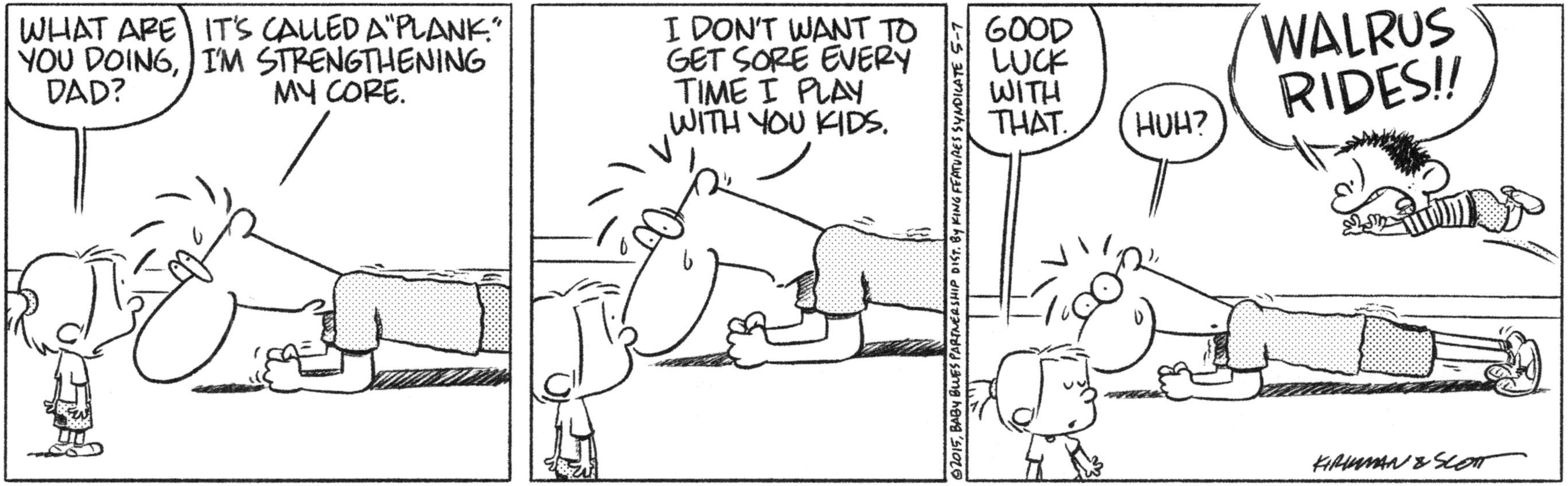
WHAT ARE YOU DOING, DAD?
IT'S CALLED A "PLANK." I'M STRENGTHENING MY CORE.
I DON'T WANT TO GET SORE EVERY TIME I PLAY WITH YOU KIDS.
©2015, BABY BLUES PARTNERSHIP DIST. BY KING FEATURES SYNDICATE 5-7
GOOD LUCK WITH THAT.
HUH?
WALRUS RIDES!!
KIRKMAN & SCOTT

Rick: There goes that perfect form.

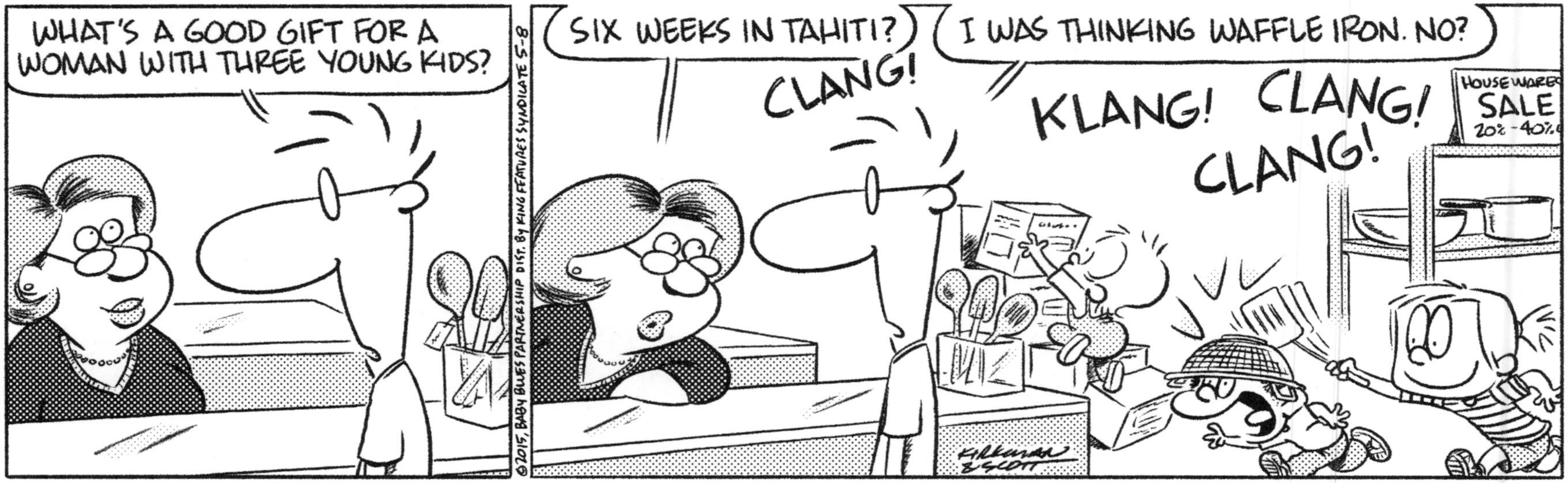
WHAT'S A GOOD GIFT FOR A WOMAN WITH THREE YOUNG KIDS?
SIX WEEKS IN TAHITI?
I WAS THINKING WAFFLE IRON. NO?
CLANG!
KLANG! CLANG!
CLANG!
SALE
©2015, BABY BLUES PARTNERSHIP DIST. BY KING FEATURES SYNDICATE 5-8
KIRKMAN & SCOTT

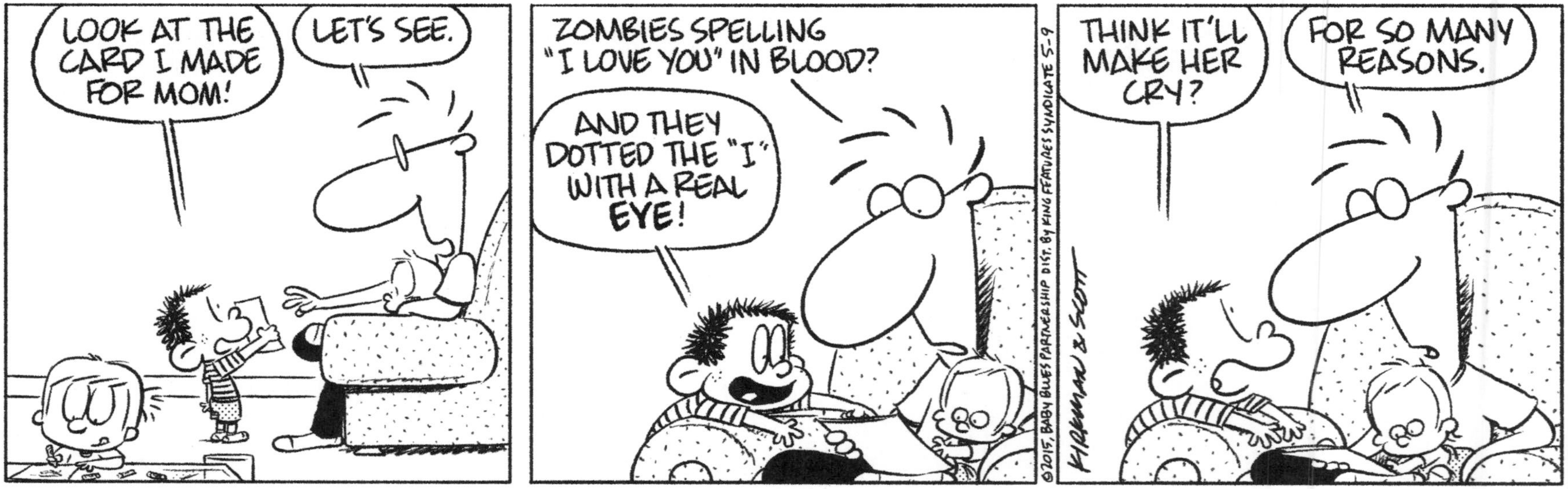
LOOK AT THE CARD I MADE FOR MOM!
LET'S SEE.
ZOMBIES SPELLING "I LOVE YOU" IN BLOOD?
AND THEY DOTTED THE "I" WITH A REAL EYE!
THINK IT'LL MAKE HER CRY?
FOR SO MANY REASONS.
©2015, BABY BLUES PARTNERSHIP DIST. BY KING FEATURES SYNDICATE 5-9
KIRKMAN & SCOTT

Rick: Now there's a missed opportunity—*Walking Dead* Mother's Day cards.

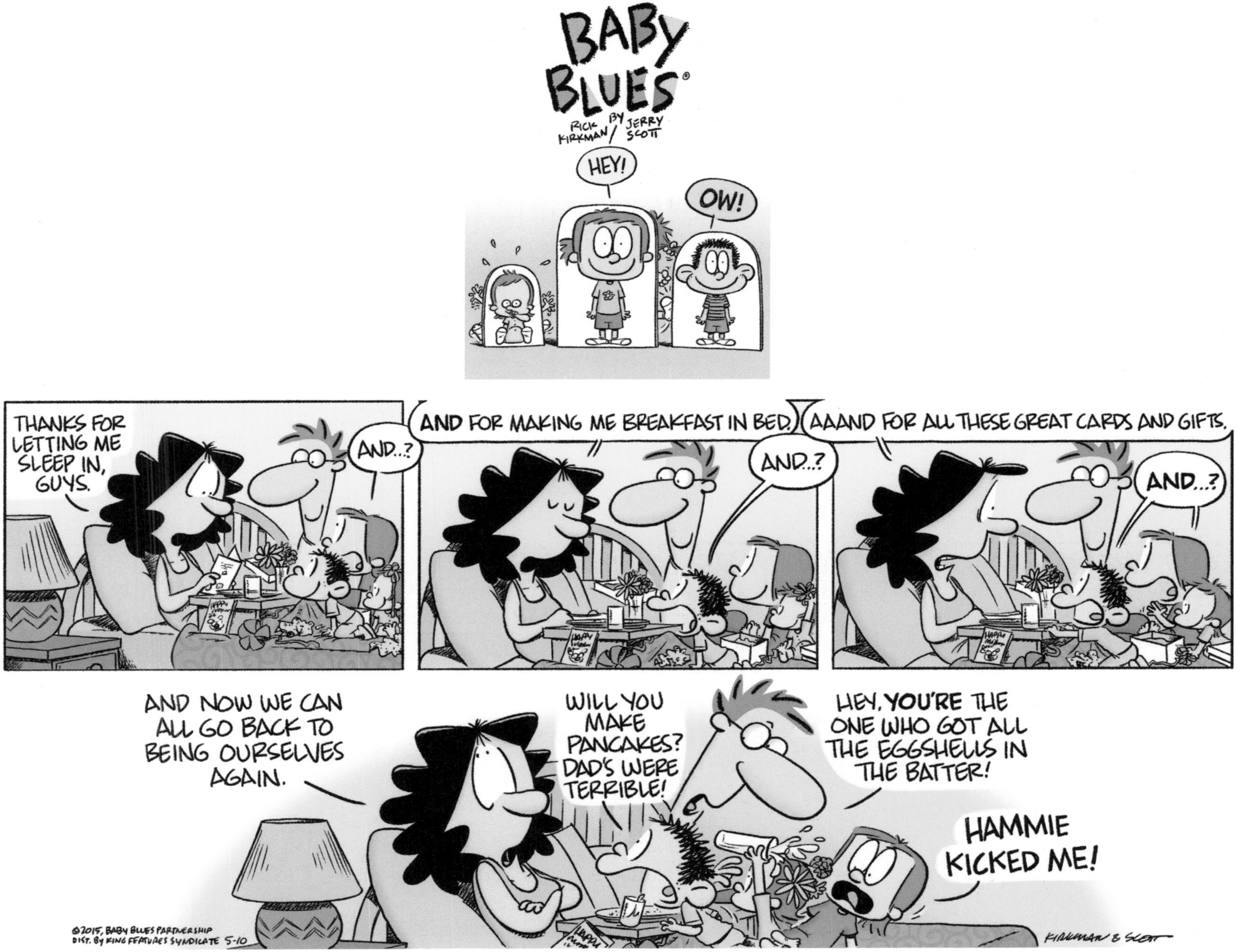
BABY BLUES®
RICK KIRKMAN / BY JERRY SCOTT
HEY!
OW!
THANKS FOR LETTING ME SLEEP IN, GUYS.
AND...?
AND FOR MAKING ME BREAKFAST IN BED.
AND...?
AAAND FOR ALL THESE GREAT CARDS AND GIFTS.
AND...?
AND NOW WE CAN ALL GO BACK TO BEING OURSELVES AGAIN.
WILL YOU MAKE PANCAKES? DAD'S WERE TERRIBLE!
HEY, YOU'RE THE ONE WHO GOT ALL THE EGGSHELLS IN THE BATTER!
HAMMIE KICKED ME!
©2015, BABY BLUES PARTNERSHIP DIST. BY KING FEATURES SYNDICATE 5-10
KIRKMAN & SCOTT

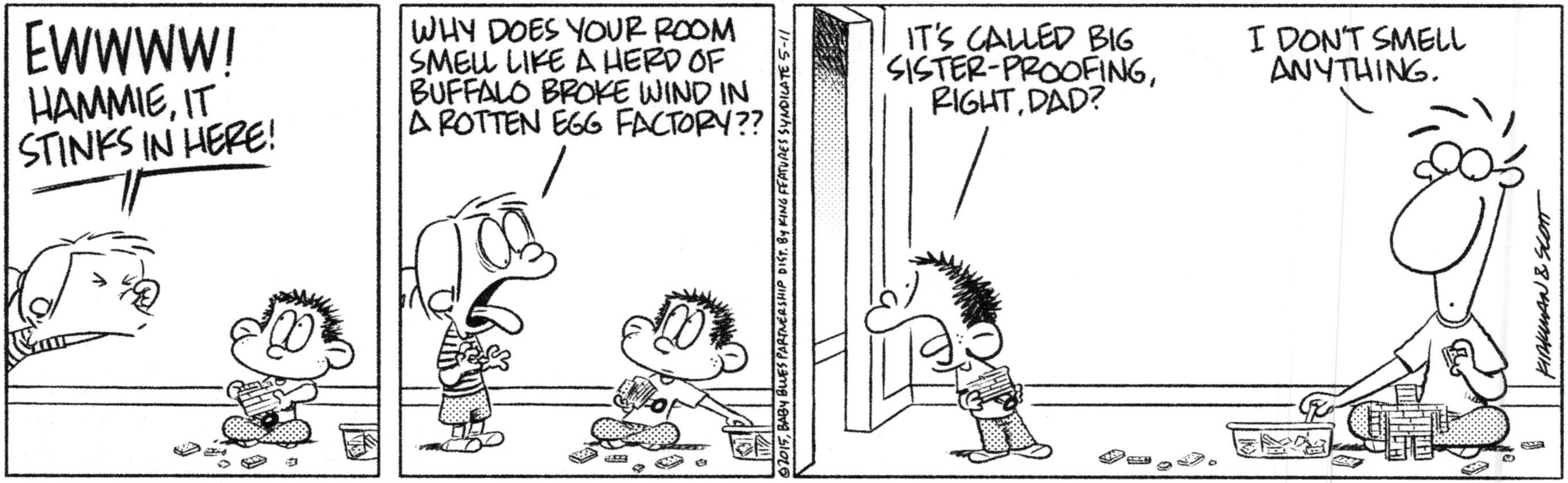
EWWWW! HAMMIE, IT STINKS IN HERE!
WHY DOES YOUR ROOM SMELL LIKE A HERD OF BUFFALO BROKE WIND IN A ROTTEN EGG FACTORY??
©2015, BABY BLUES PARTNERSHIP DIST. BY KING FEATURES SYNDICATE 5-11
IT'S CALLED BIG SISTER-PROOFING, RIGHT, DAD?
I DON'T SMELL ANYTHING.
KIRKMAN & SCOTT

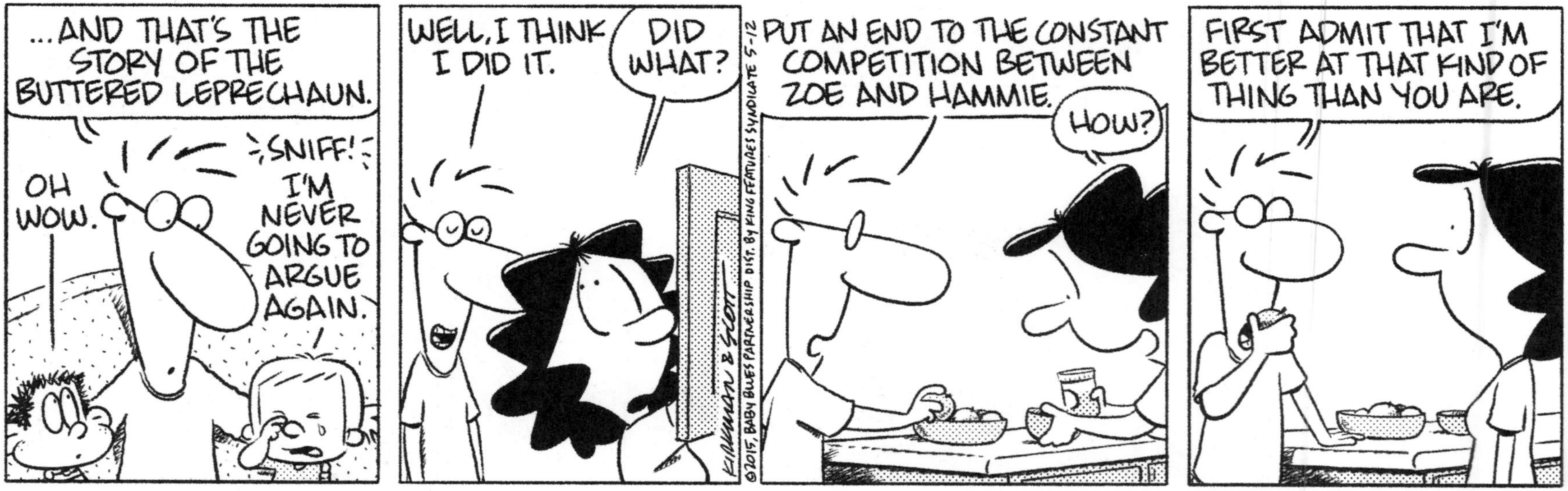
...AND THAT'S THE STORY OF THE BUTTERED LEPRECHAUN.
OH WOW.
SNIFF! I'M NEVER GOING TO ARGUE AGAIN.
WELL, I THINK I DID IT.
DID WHAT?
KIRKMAN & SCOTT
©2015, BABY BLUES PARTNERSHIP DIST. BY KING FEATURES SYNDICATE 5-12
PUT AN END TO THE CONSTANT COMPETITION BETWEEN ZOE AND HAMMIE.
HOW?
FIRST ADMIT THAT I'M BETTER AT THAT KIND OF THING THAN YOU ARE.

Rick: I really want to know the story of The Buttered Leprechaun.

Jerry: I thought of the title. Somebody else has to write the story.

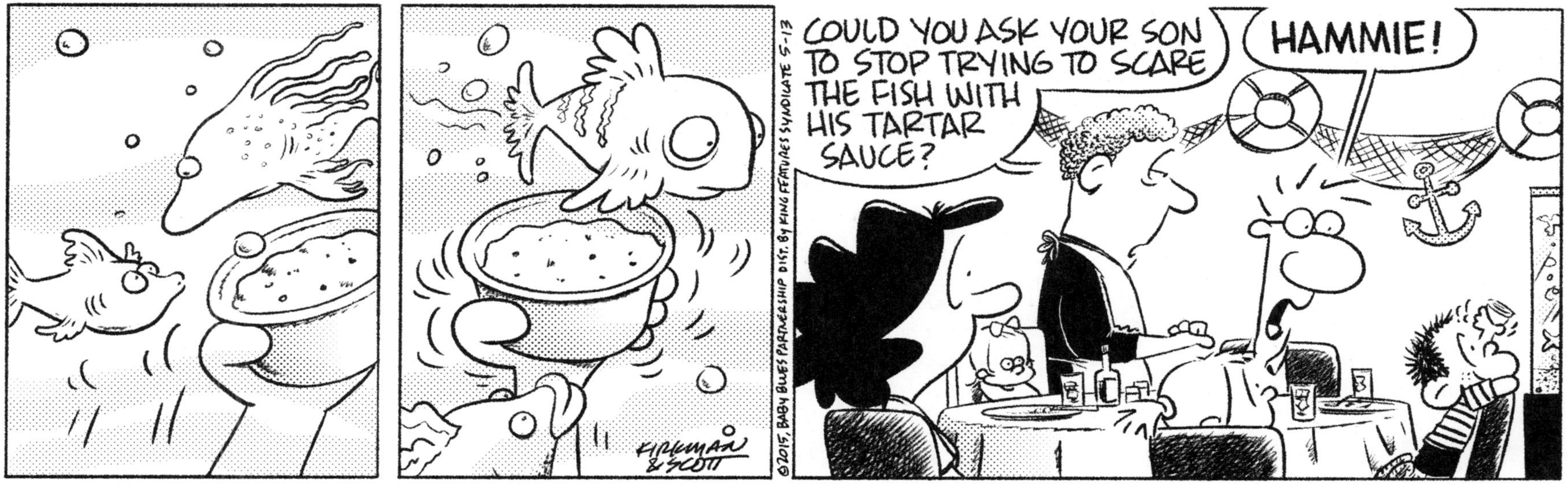
©2015, BABY BLUES PARTNERSHIP DIST. BY KING FEATURES SYNDICATE 5-13
KIRKMAN & SCOTT
COULD YOU ASK YOUR SON TO STOP TRYING TO SCARE THE FISH WITH HIS TARTAR SAUCE?
HAMMIE!

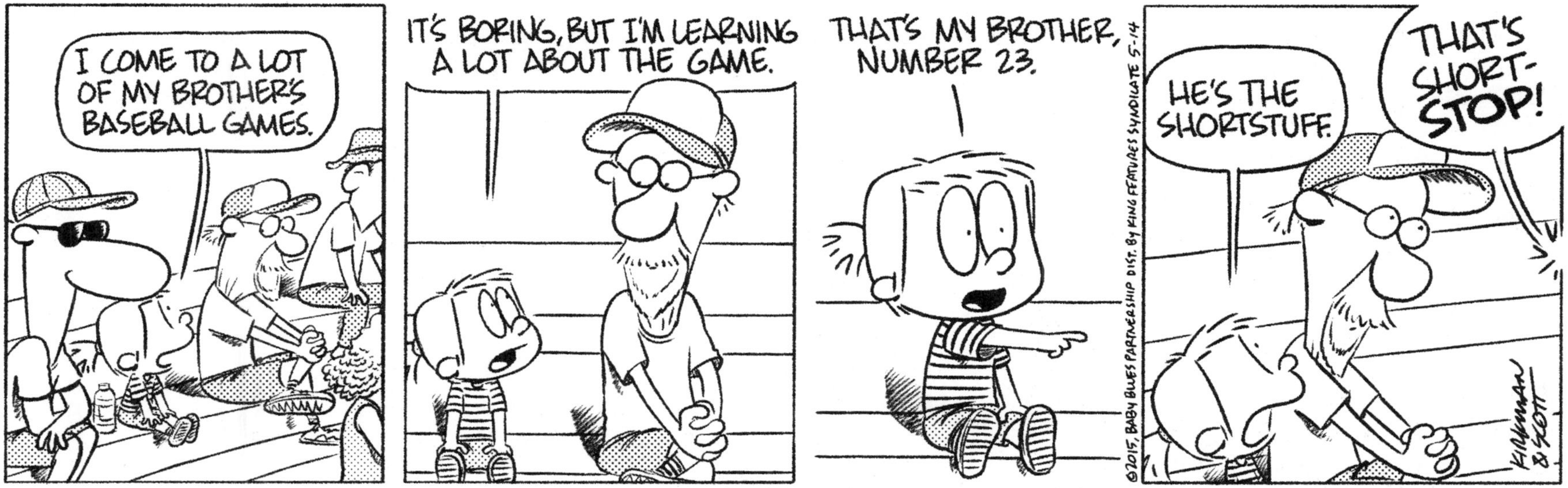
I COME TO A LOT OF MY BROTHER'S BASEBALL GAMES.
IT'S BORING, BUT I'M LEARNING A LOT ABOUT THE GAME.
THAT'S MY BROTHER, NUMBER 23.
©2015, BABY BLUES PARTNERSHIP DIST. BY KING FEATURES SYNDICATE 5-14
HE'S THE SHORTSTUFF.
THAT'S SHORT-STOP!
KIRKMAN & SCOTT

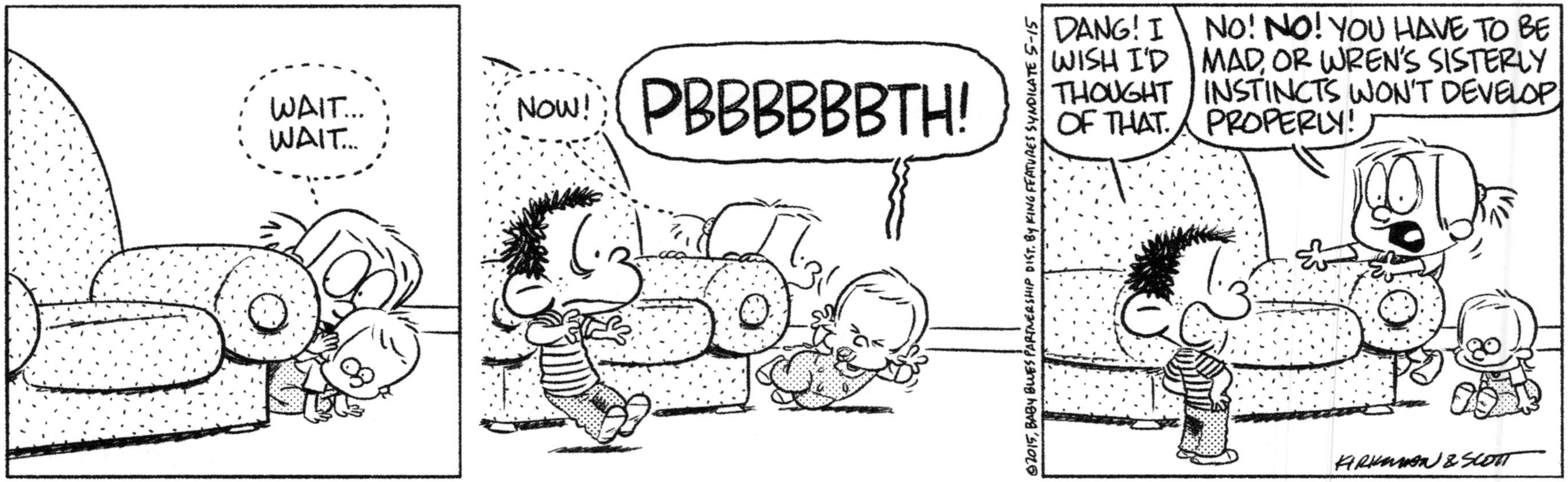
WAIT... WAIT...
NOW!
PBBBBBBTH!
DANG! I WISH I'D THOUGHT OF THAT.
NO! **NO**! YOU HAVE TO BE MAD, OR WREN'S SISTERLY INSTINCTS WON'T DEVELOP PROPERLY!
©2015, BABY BLUES PARTNERSHIP DIST. BY KING FEATURES SYNDICATE 5-15
KIRKMAN & SCOTT

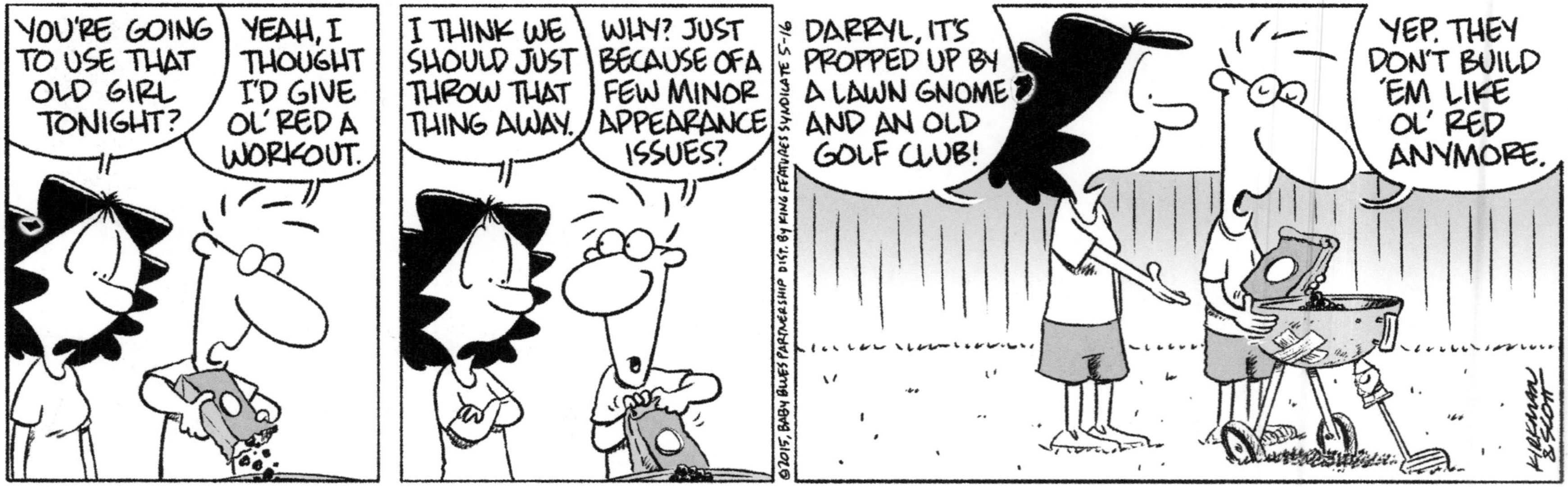
YOU'RE GOING TO USE THAT OLD GIRL TONIGHT?
YEAH, I THOUGHT I'D GIVE OL' RED A WORKOUT.
I THINK WE SHOULD JUST THROW THAT THING AWAY.
WHY? JUST BECAUSE OF A FEW MINOR APPEARANCE ISSUES?
©2015, BABY BLUES PARTNERSHIP DIST. BY KING FEATURES SYNDICATE 5-16
DARRYL, IT'S PROPPED UP BY A LAWN GNOME AND AN OLD GOLF CLUB!
YEP. THEY DON'T BUILD 'EM LIKE OL' RED ANYMORE.
KIRKMAN & SCOTT

Rick: It's just getting broken in!

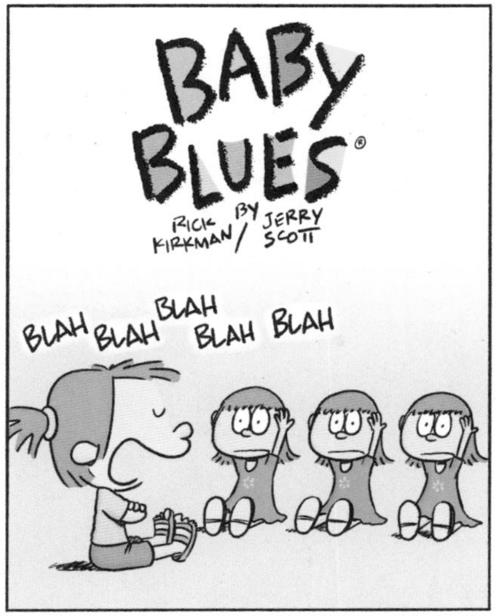
BABY BLUES®
RICK KIRKMAN / BY JERRY SCOTT
BLAH BLAH BLAH BLAH BLAH

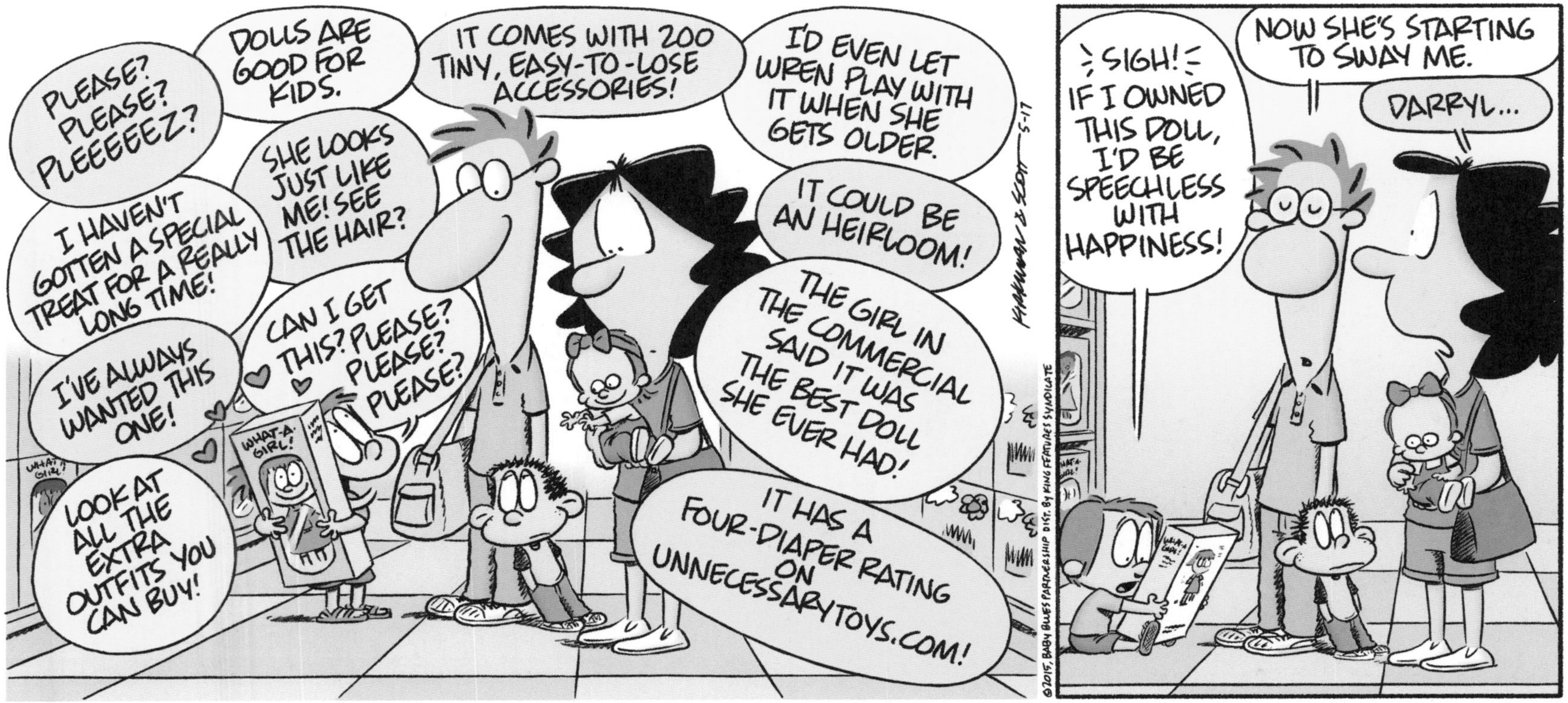
PLEASE? PLEASE? PLEEEEEZ?
DOLLS ARE GOOD FOR KIDS.
IT COMES WITH 200 TINY, EASY-TO-LOSE ACCESSORIES!
I'D EVEN LET WREN PLAY WITH IT WHEN SHE GETS OLDER.
I HAVEN'T GOTTEN A SPECIAL TREAT FOR A REALLY LONG TIME!
SHE LOOKS JUST LIKE ME! SEE THE HAIR?
IT COULD BE AN HEIRLOOM!
I'VE ALWAYS WANTED THIS ONE!
CAN I GET THIS? PLEASE? PLEASE? PLEASE?
THE GIRL IN THE COMMERCIAL SAID IT WAS THE BEST DOLL SHE EVER HAD!
LOOK AT ALL THE EXTRA OUTFITS YOU CAN BUY!
IT HAS A FOUR-DIAPER RATING ON UNNECESSARYTOYS.COM!
WHAT-A-GIRL!
KIRKMAN & SCOTT 5-17
©2015, BABY BLUES PARTNERSHIP DIST. BY KING FEATURES SYNDICATE
SIGH! IF I OWNED THIS DOLL, I'D BE SPEECHLESS WITH HAPPINESS!
NOW SHE'S STARTING TO SWAY ME.
DARRYL...

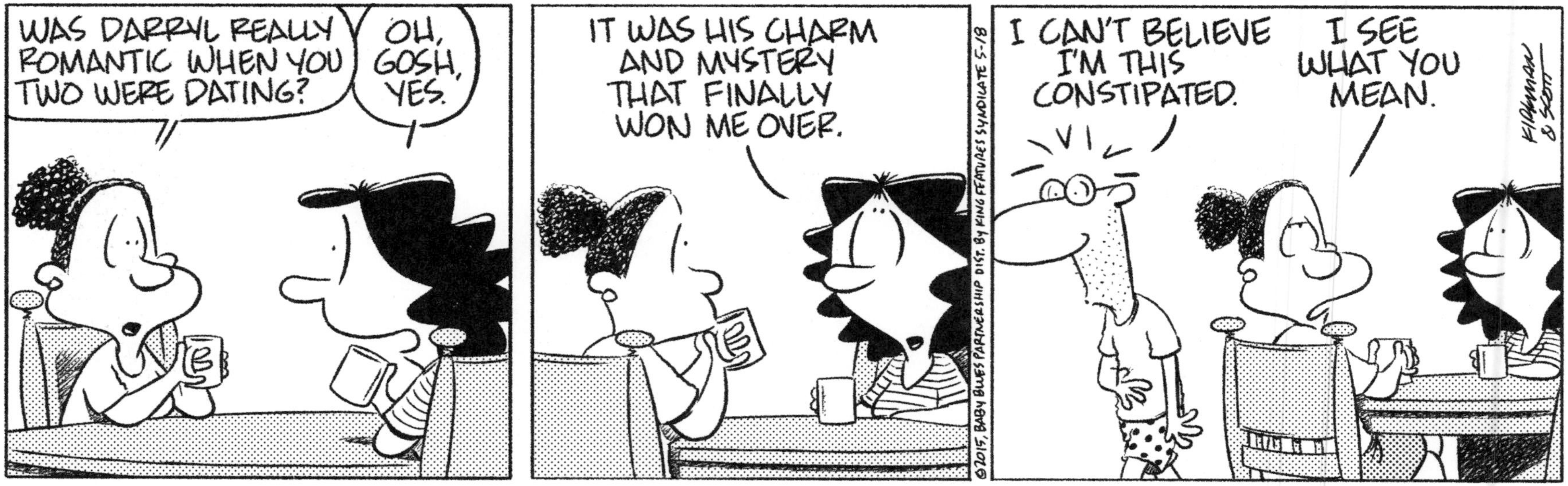
WAS DARRYL REALLY ROMANTIC WHEN YOU TWO WERE DATING?
OH, GOSH, YES.
IT WAS HIS CHARM AND MYSTERY THAT FINALLY WON ME OVER.
I CAN'T BELIEVE I'M THIS CONSTIPATED.
I SEE WHAT YOU MEAN.
KIRKMAN & SCOTT
©2015, BABY BLUES PARTNERSHIP DIST. BY KING FEATURES SYNDICATE 5-18

Rick: I think this was the first strip with a new hairstyle for Yolanda.

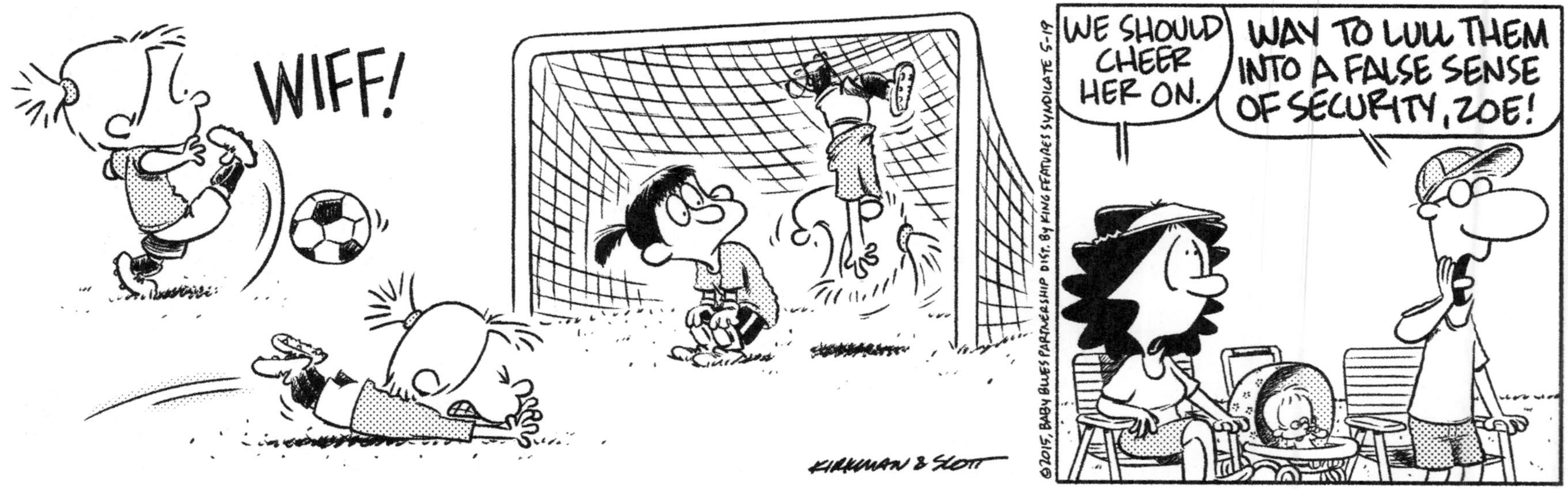
WIFF!
KIRKMAN & SCOTT
©2015, BABY BLUES PARTNERSHIP DIST. BY KING FEATURES SYNDICATE 5-19
WE SHOULD CHEER HER ON.
WAY TO LULL THEM INTO A FALSE SENSE OF SECURITY, ZOE!

Jerry: Well, maybe not a FALSE sense of security . . .

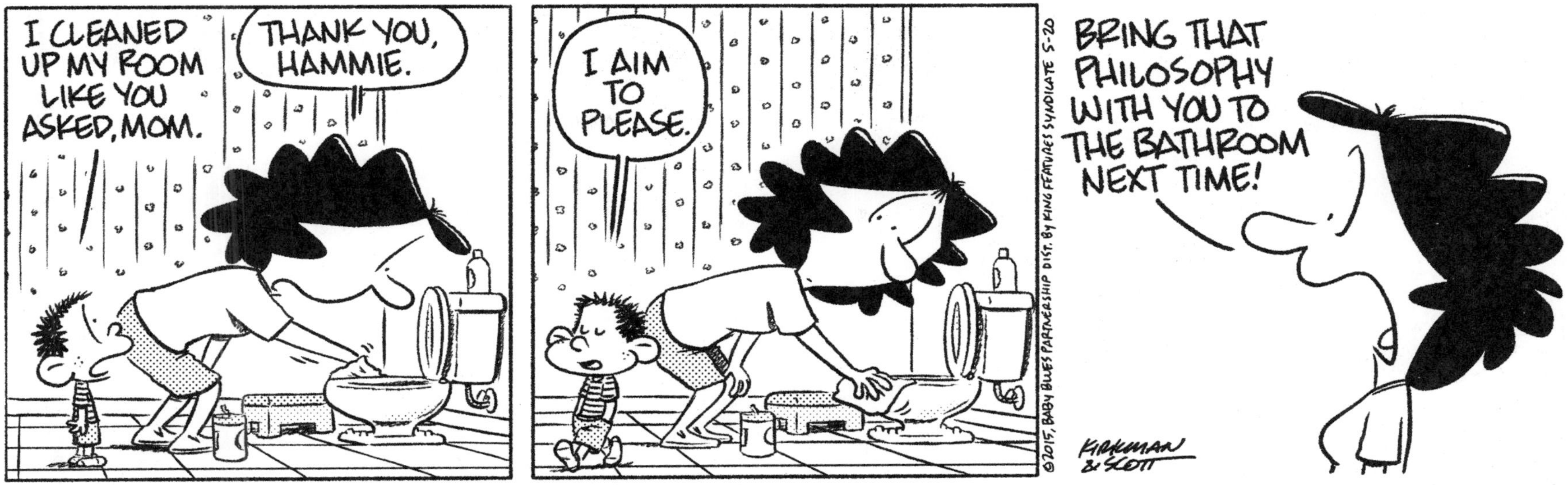
I CLEANED UP MY ROOM LIKE YOU ASKED, MOM.
THANK YOU, HAMMIE.
I AIM TO PLEASE.
BRING THAT PHILOSOPHY WITH YOU TO THE BATHROOM NEXT TIME!
KIRKMAN & SCOTT
©2015, BABY BLUES PARTNERSHIP DIST. BY KING FEATURES SYNDICATE 5-20

Jerry: Bathroom humor has no place in newspaper comic strips, except this one.

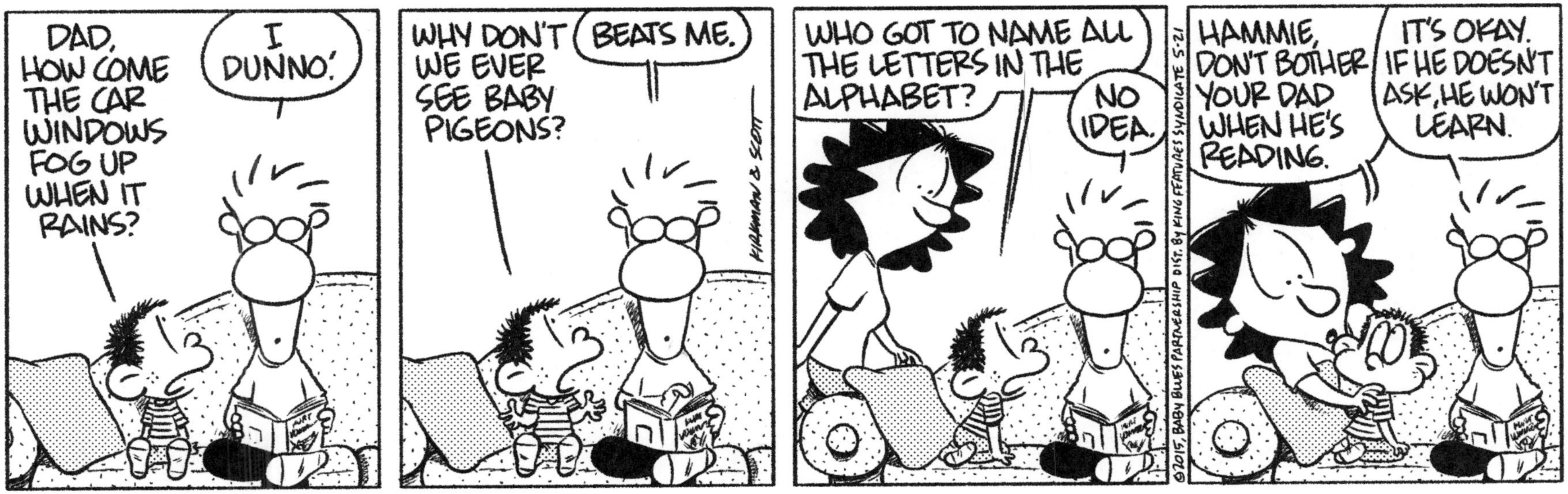
DAD, HOW COME THE CAR WINDOWS FOG UP WHEN IT RAINS?
I DUNNO.
WHY DON'T WE EVER SEE BABY PIGEONS?
BEATS ME.
KIRKMAN & SCOTT
WHO GOT TO NAME ALL THE LETTERS IN THE ALPHABET?
NO IDEA.
©2015, BABY BLUES PARTNERSHIP DIST. BY KING FEATURES SYNDICATE 5-21
HAMMIE, DON'T BOTHER YOUR DAD WHEN HE'S READING.
IT'S OKAY. IF HE DOESN'T ASK, HE WON'T LEARN.

Rick: Why is Darryl reading Kurt Vonnegut? Probably because I was at the time—*Cat's Cradle*, I think.

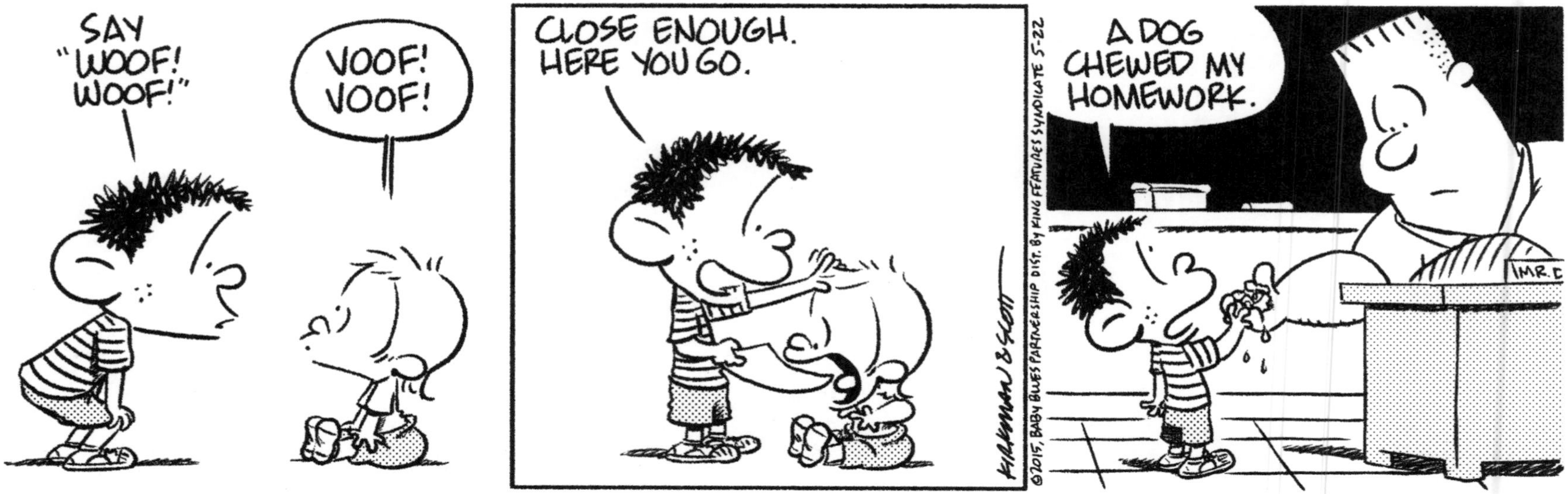
SAY "WOOF! WOOF!"
VOOF! VOOF!
CLOSE ENOUGH. HERE YOU GO.
KIRKMAN & SCOTT
©2015, BABY BLUES PARTNERSHIP DIST. BY KING FEATURES SYNDICATE 5-22
A DOG CHEWED MY HOMEWORK.

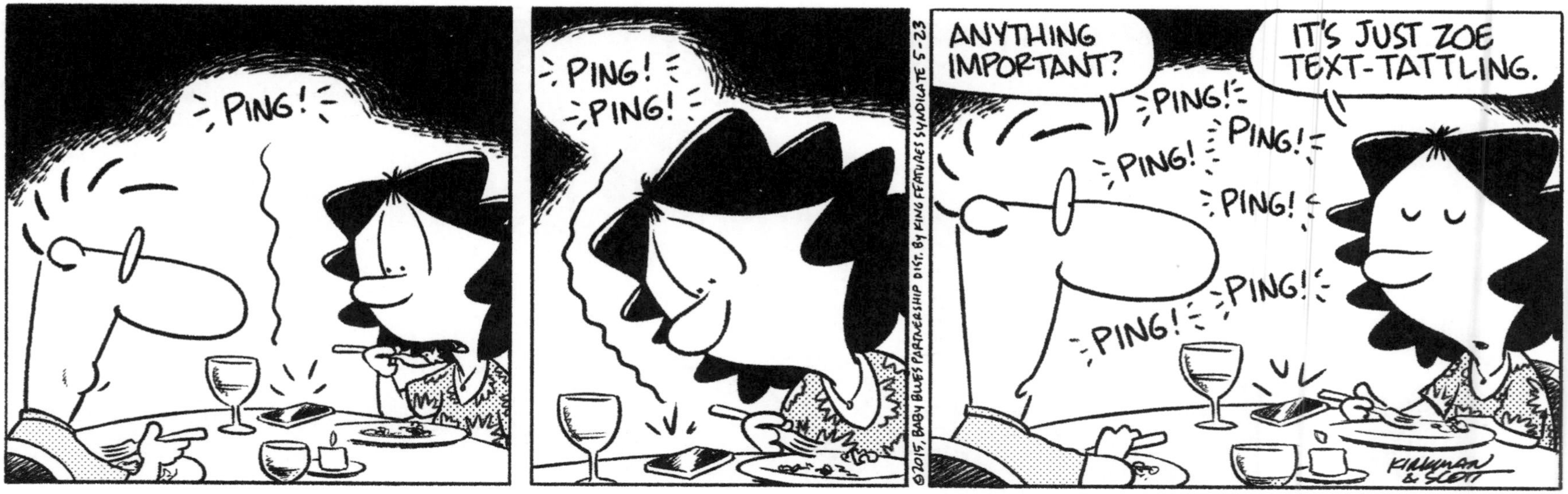
PING!
PING!
PING!
©2015, BABY BLUES PARTNERSHIP DIST. BY KING FEATURES SYNDICATE 5-23
ANYTHING IMPORTANT?
PING!
PING!
PING!
PING!
PING!
PING!
IT'S JUST ZOE TEXT-TATTLING.
KIRKMAN & SCOTT

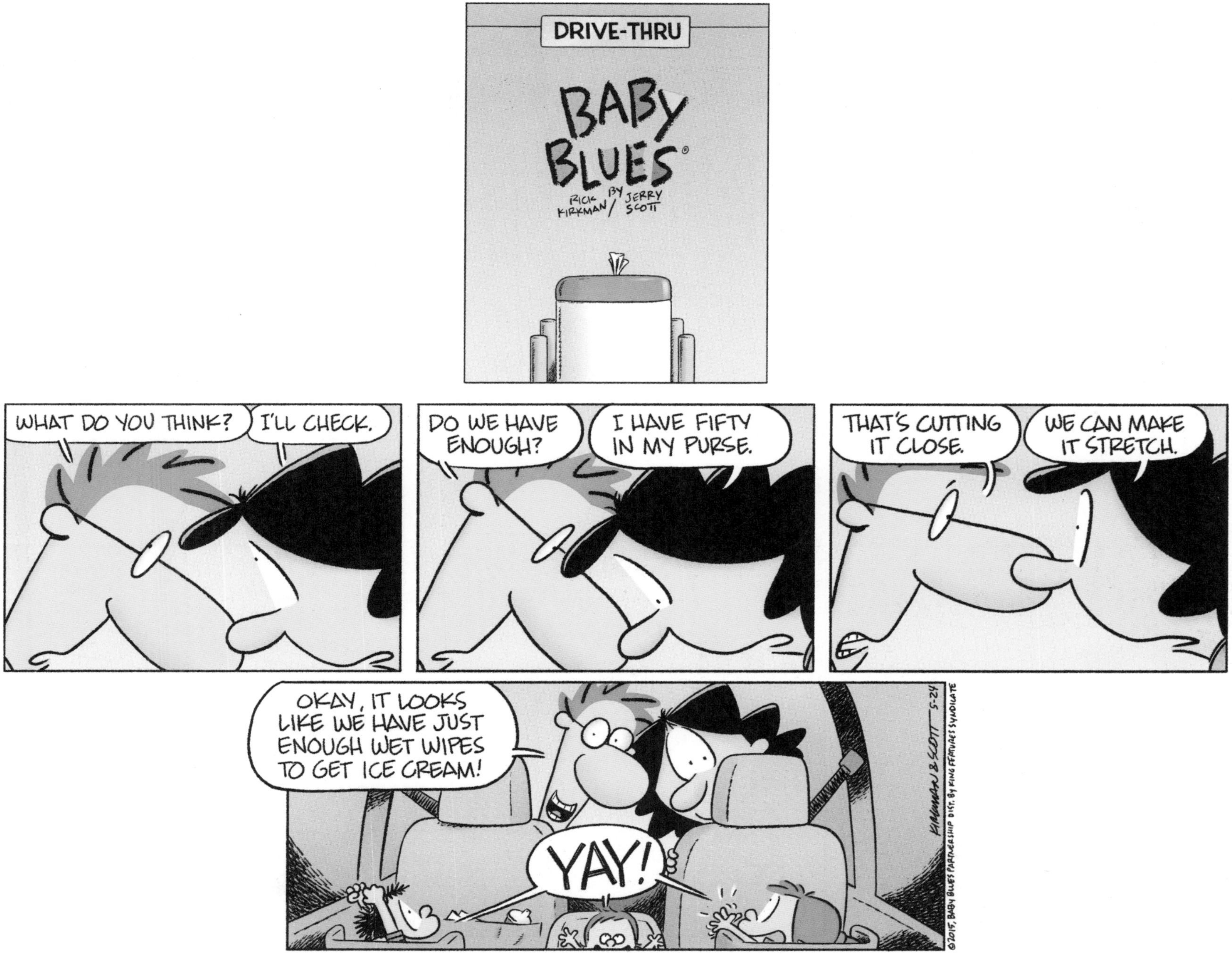
DRIVE-THRU
BABY BLUES®
BY RICK KIRKMAN / JERRY SCOTT
WHAT DO YOU THINK?
I'LL CHECK.
DO WE HAVE ENOUGH?
I HAVE FIFTY IN MY PURSE.
THAT'S CUTTING IT CLOSE.
WE CAN MAKE IT STRETCH.
OKAY, IT LOOKS LIKE WE HAVE JUST ENOUGH WET WIPES TO GET ICE CREAM!
YAY!
KIRKMAN & SCOTT 5-24
©2015, BABY BLUES PARTNERSHIP DIST. BY KING FEATURES SYNDICATE

Rick: Parental currency based on the Wet-Wipe Standard. I love it.

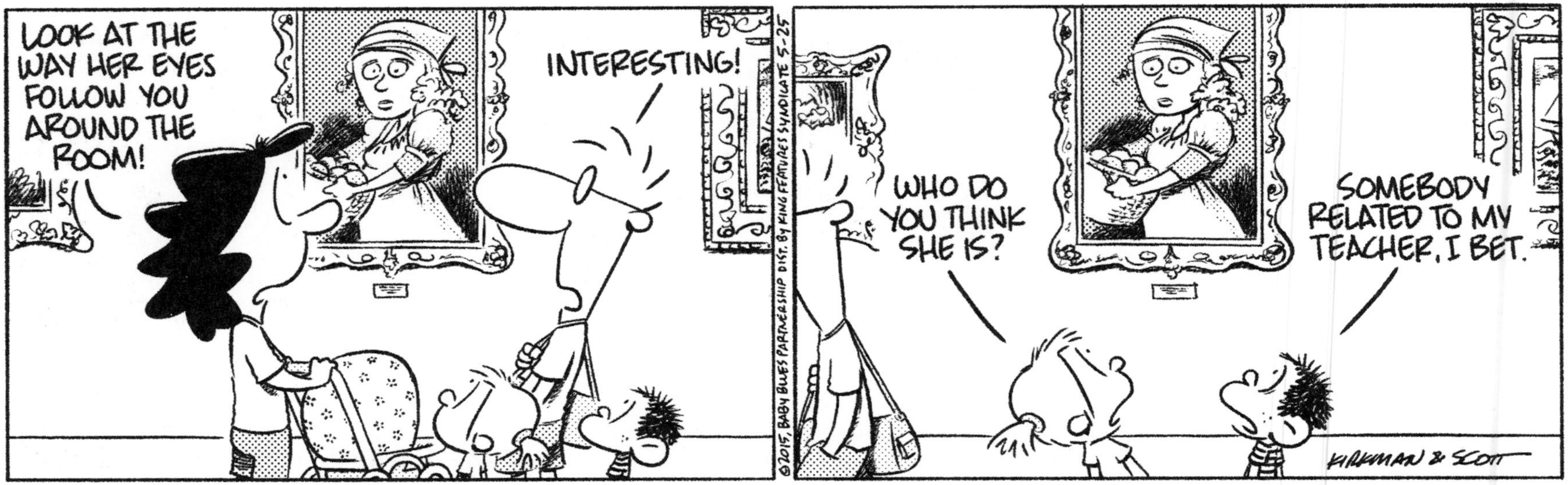
LOOK AT THE WAY HER EYES FOLLOW YOU AROUND THE ROOM!
INTERESTING!
©2015, BABY BLUES PARTNERSHIP DIST. BY KING FEATURES SYNDICATE 5-25
WHO DO YOU THINK SHE IS?
SOMEBODY RELATED TO MY TEACHER, I BET.
KIRKMAN & SCOTT

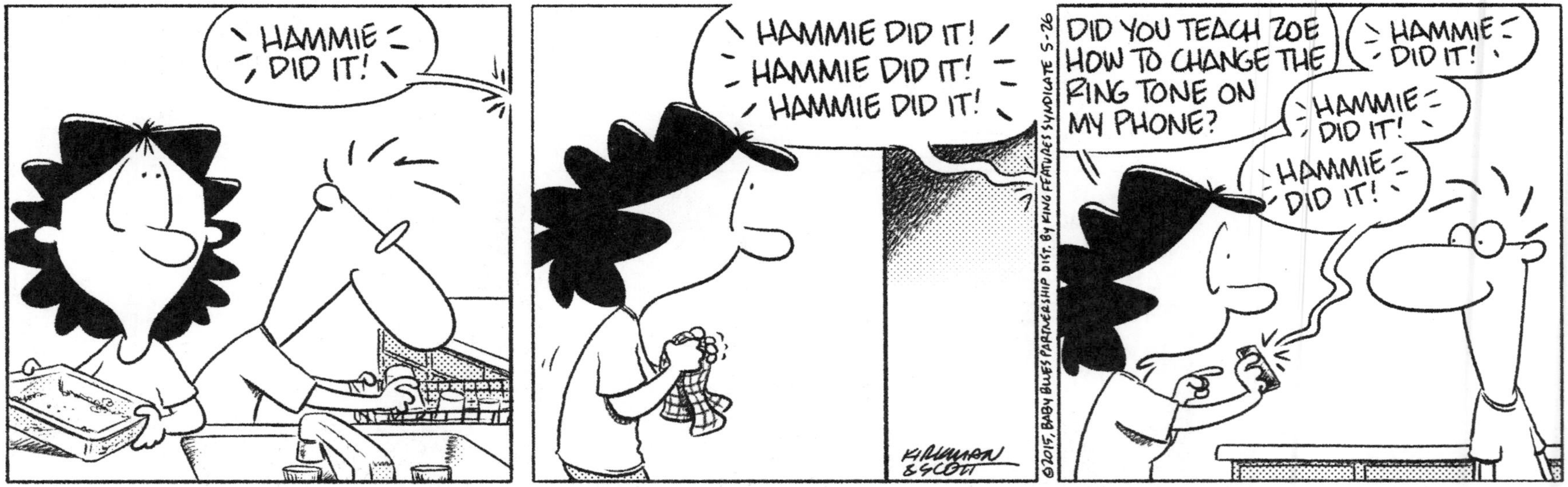
HAMMIE DID IT!
HAMMIE DID IT! HAMMIE DID IT! HAMMIE DID IT!
KIRKMAN & SCOTT
©2015, BABY BLUES PARTNERSHIP DIST. BY KING FEATURES SYNDICATE 5-26
DID YOU TEACH ZOE HOW TO CHANGE THE RING TONE ON MY PHONE?
HAMMIE DID IT!
HAMMIE DID IT!
HAMMIE DID IT!

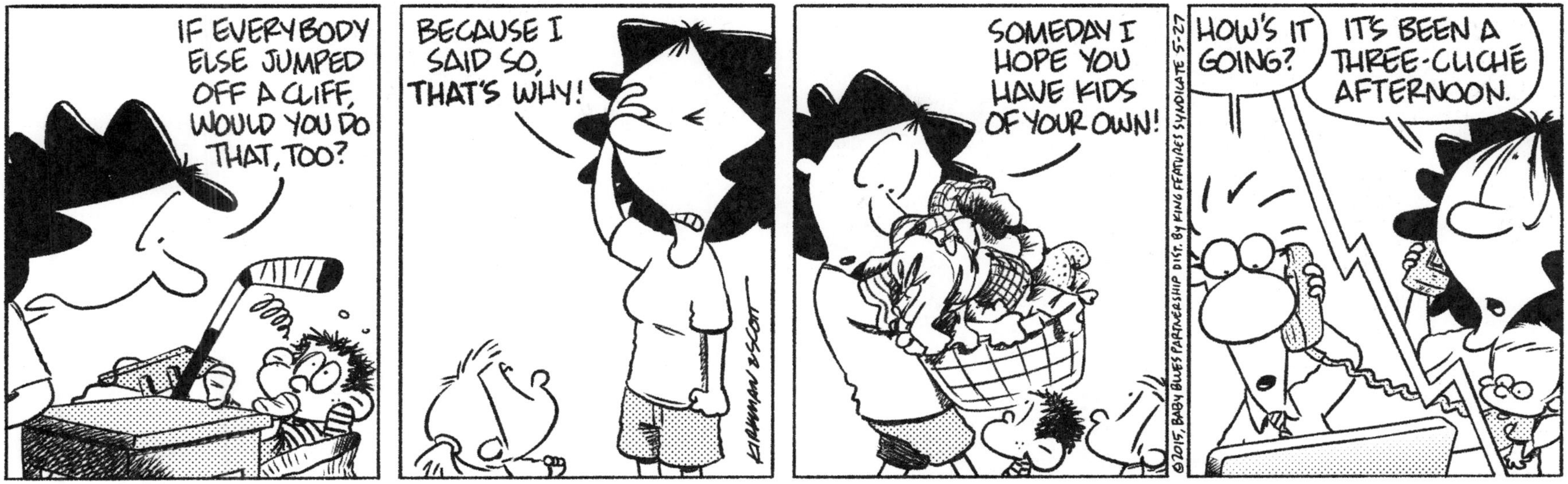
IF EVERYBODY ELSE JUMPED OFF A CLIFF, WOULD YOU DO THAT, TOO?
BECAUSE I SAID SO, THAT'S WHY!
KIRKMAN & SCOTT
SOMEDAY I HOPE YOU HAVE KIDS OF YOUR OWN!
©2015, BABY BLUES PARTNERSHIP DIST. BY KING FEATURES SYNDICATE 5-27
HOW'S IT GOING?
IT'S BEEN A THREE-CLICHE AFTERNOON.

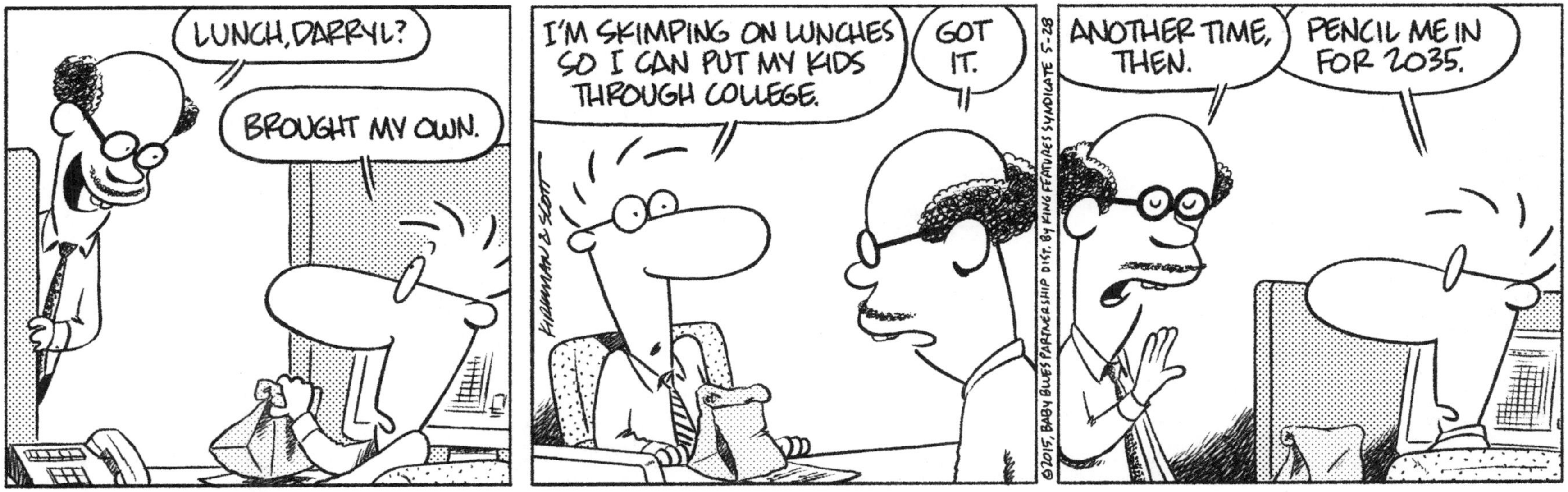
LUNCH, DARRYL?
BROUGHT MY OWN.
I'M SKIMPING ON LUNCHES SO I CAN PUT MY KIDS THROUGH COLLEGE.
KIRKMAN & SCOTT
GOT IT.
©2015, BABY BLUES PARTNERSHIP DIST. BY KING FEATURES SYNDICATE 5-28
ANOTHER TIME, THEN.
PENCIL ME IN FOR 2035.

Rick: Sometimes I look at a drawing I did a while back and think, "I have no idea where that came from." That's what I think about Darryl's coworker.

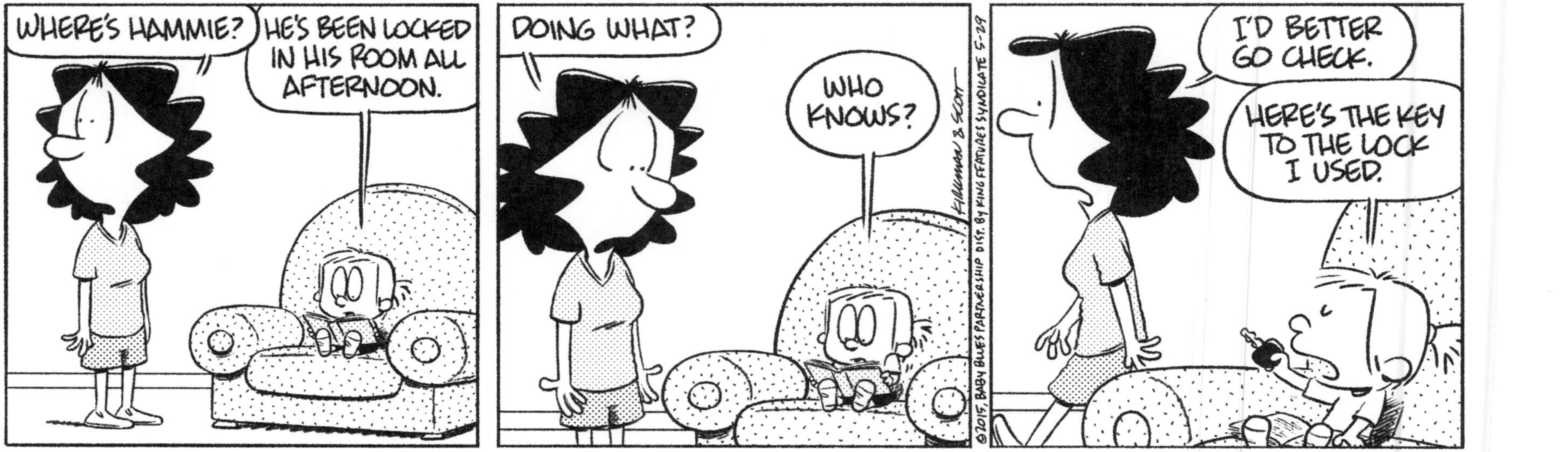
WHERE'S HAMMIE?
HE'S BEEN LOCKED IN HIS ROOM ALL AFTERNOON.
DOING WHAT?
WHO KNOWS?
KIRKMAN & SCOTT
©2015, BABY BLUES PARTNERSHIP DIST. BY KING FEATURES SYNDICATE 5-29
I'D BETTER GO CHECK.
HERE'S THE KEY TO THE LOCK I USED.

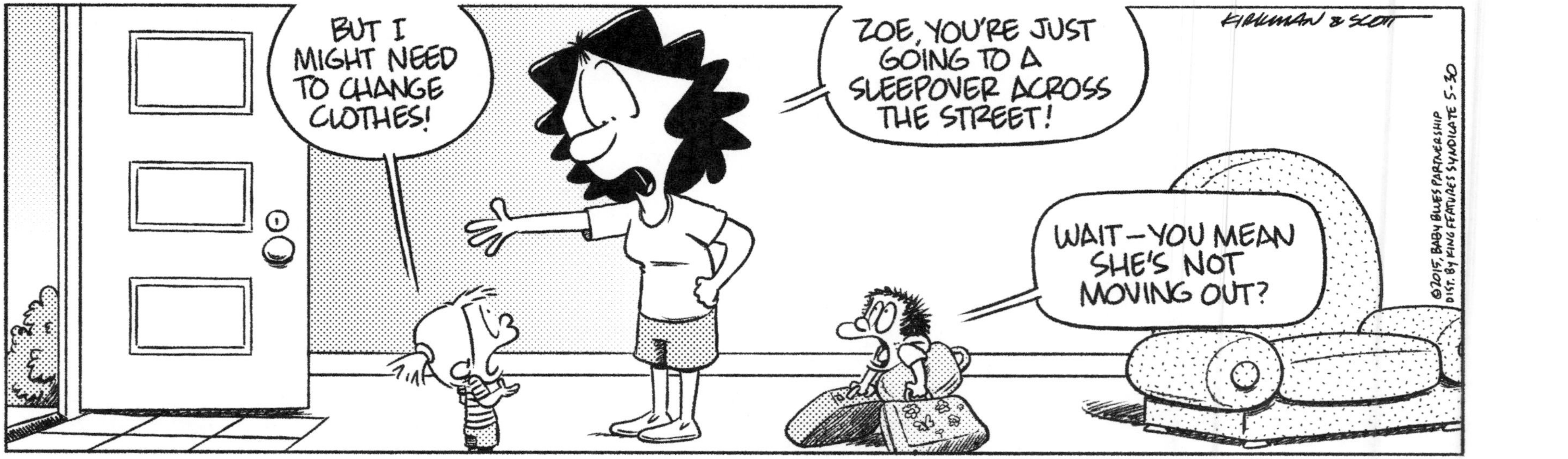
BUT I MIGHT NEED TO CHANGE CLOTHES!
ZOE, YOU'RE JUST GOING TO A SLEEPOVER ACROSS THE STREET!
KIRKMAN & SCOTT
©2015, BABY BLUES PARTNERSHIP DIST. BY KING FEATURES SYNDICATE 5-30
WAIT—YOU MEAN SHE'S NOT MOVING OUT?

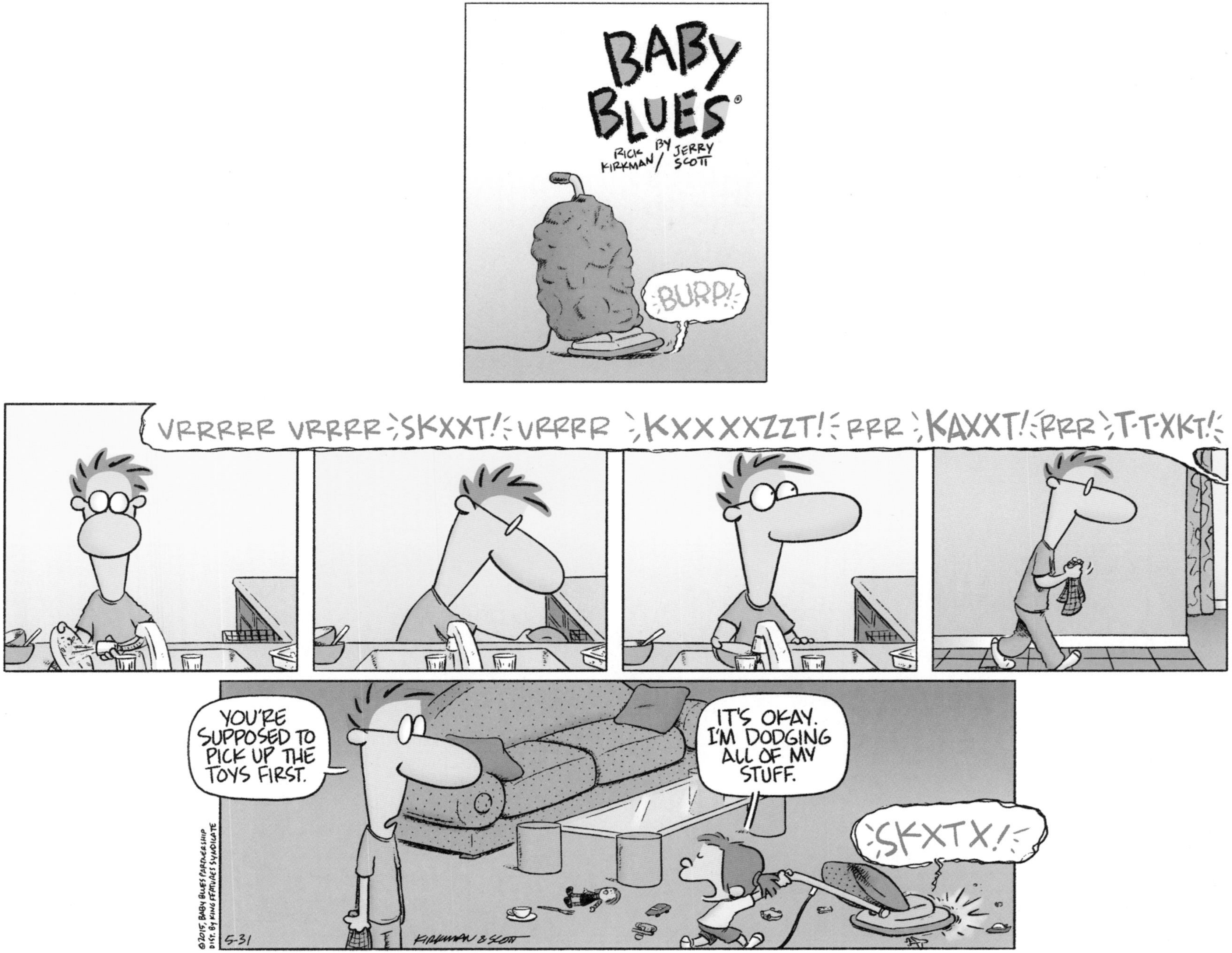

BABY BLUES®
BY RICK KIRKMAN / JERRY SCOTT
BURP!
VRRRRR VRRRR SKXXT! VRRRR KXXXXZZT! RRR KAXXT! RRR T-T-XKT!
YOU'RE SUPPOSED TO PICK UP THE TOYS FIRST.
IT'S OKAY. I'M DODGING ALL OF MY STUFF.
SKXTX!
©2015, BABY BLUES PARTNERSHIP
DIST. BY KING FEATURES SYNDICATE
5-31
KIRKMAN & SCOTT

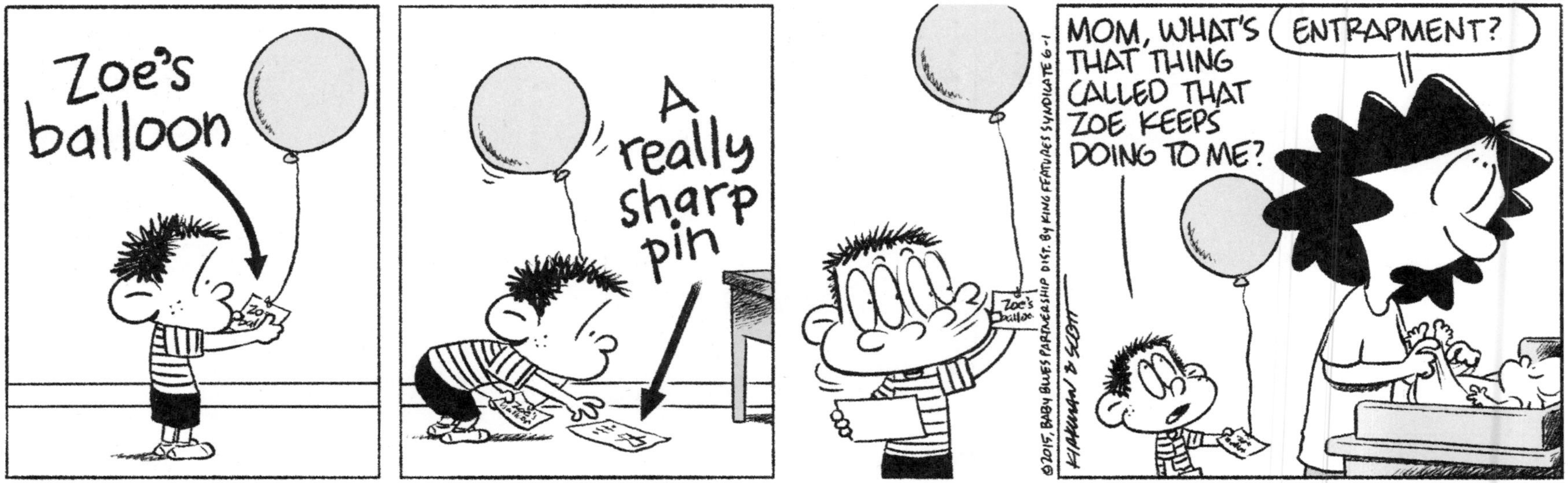
Zoe's balloon
A really sharp pin
©2015, BABY BLUES PARTNERSHIP DIST. BY KING FEATURES SYNDICATE 6-1
KIRKMAN & SCOTT
MOM, WHAT'S THAT THING CALLED THAT ZOE KEEPS DOING TO ME?
ENTRAPMENT?

Rick: Walk. Away. Hammie.

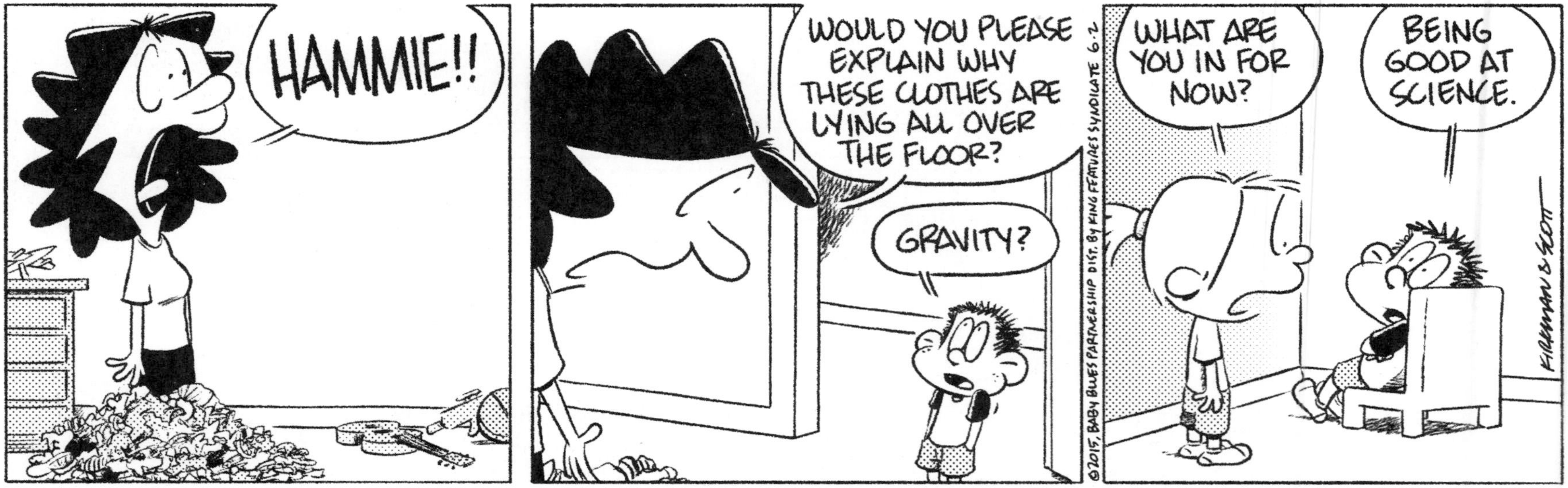
HAMMIE!!
WOULD YOU PLEASE EXPLAIN WHY THESE CLOTHES ARE LYING ALL OVER THE FLOOR?
GRAVITY?
©2015, BABY BLUES PARTNERSHIP DIST. BY KING FEATURES SYNDICATE 6-2
WHAT ARE YOU IN FOR NOW?
BEING GOOD AT SCIENCE.
KIRKMAN & SCOTT

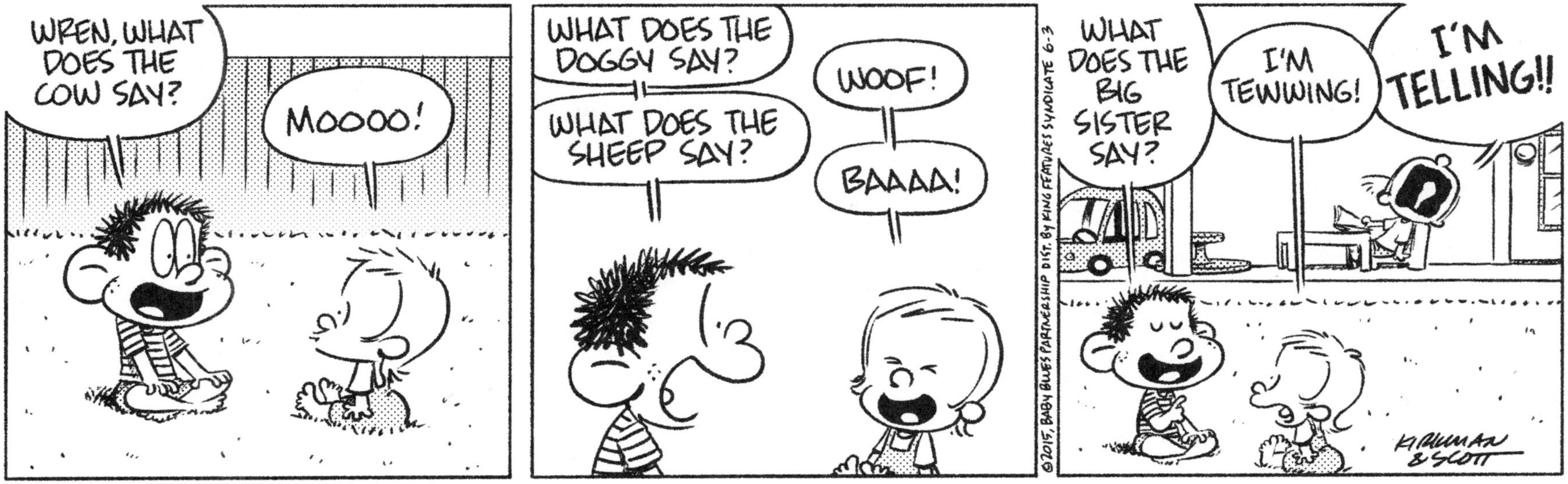
WREN, WHAT DOES THE COW SAY?
MOOOO!
WHAT DOES THE DOGGY SAY?
WOOF!
WHAT DOES THE SHEEP SAY?
BAAAA!
WHAT DOES THE BIG SISTER SAY?
I'M TEWWING!
I'M TELLING!!
©2015, BABY BLUES PARTNERSHIP DIST. BY KING FEATURES SYNDICATE 6-3
KIRKMAN & SCOTT

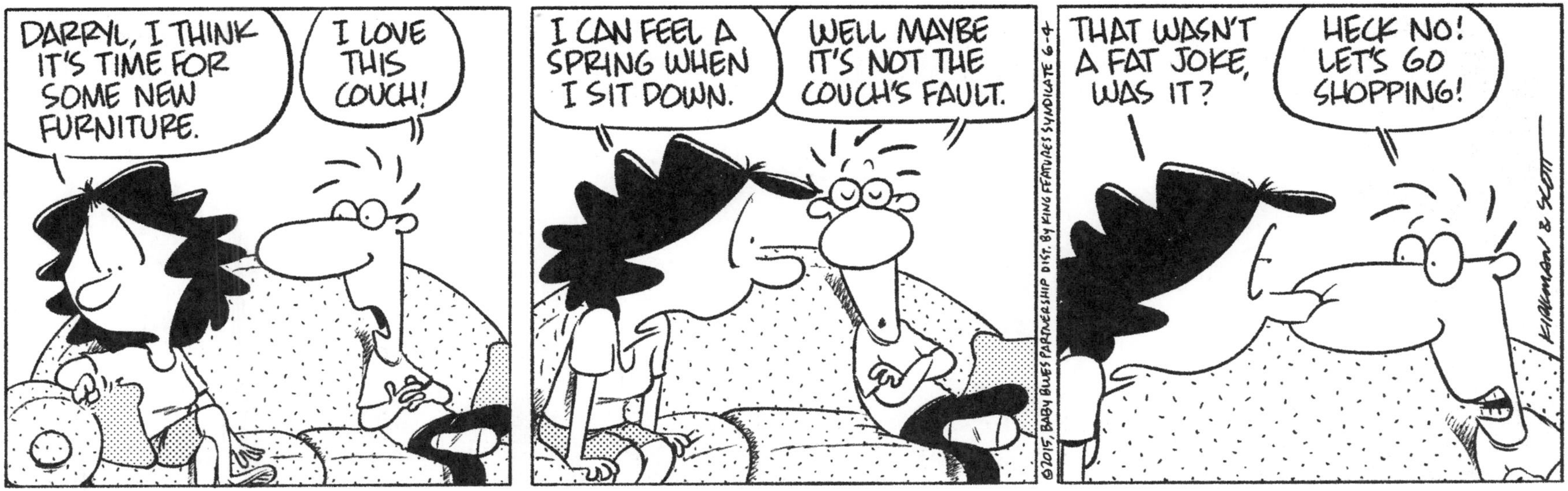
DARRYL, I THINK IT'S TIME FOR SOME NEW FURNITURE.
I LOVE THIS COUCH!
I CAN FEEL A SPRING WHEN I SIT DOWN.
WELL MAYBE IT'S NOT THE COUCH'S FAULT.
THAT WASN'T A FAT JOKE, WAS IT?
HECK NO! LET'S GO SHOPPING!
©2015, BABY BLUES PARTNERSHIP DIST. BY KING FEATURES SYNDICATE 6-4
KIRKMAN & SCOTT

Rick: Uh-oh. Without warning, I have to come up with some new furniture.

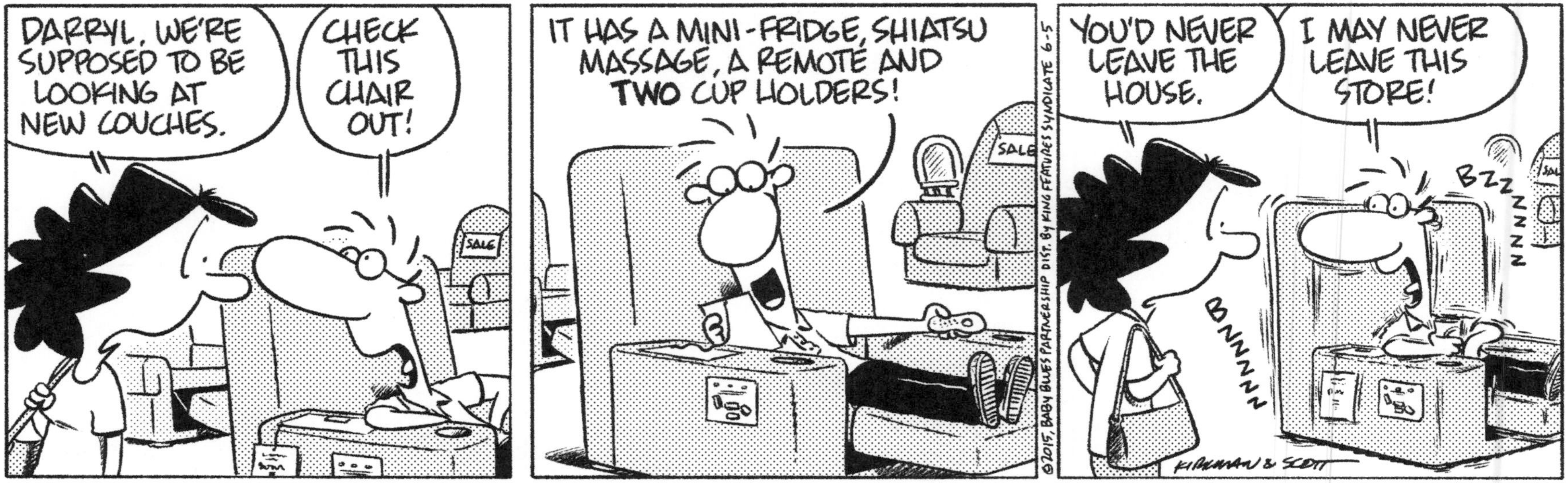
DARRYL, WE'RE SUPPOSED TO BE LOOKING AT NEW COUCHES.
CHECK THIS CHAIR OUT!
SALE
IT HAS A MINI-FRIDGE, SHIATSU MASSAGE, A REMOTE AND **TWO** CUP HOLDERS!
SALE
©2015, BABY BLUES PARTNERSHIP DIST. BY KING FEATURES SYNDICATE 6-5
YOU'D NEVER LEAVE THE HOUSE.
I MAY NEVER LEAVE THIS STORE!
BNNNNN
BZZZZZ
KIRKMAN & SCOTT

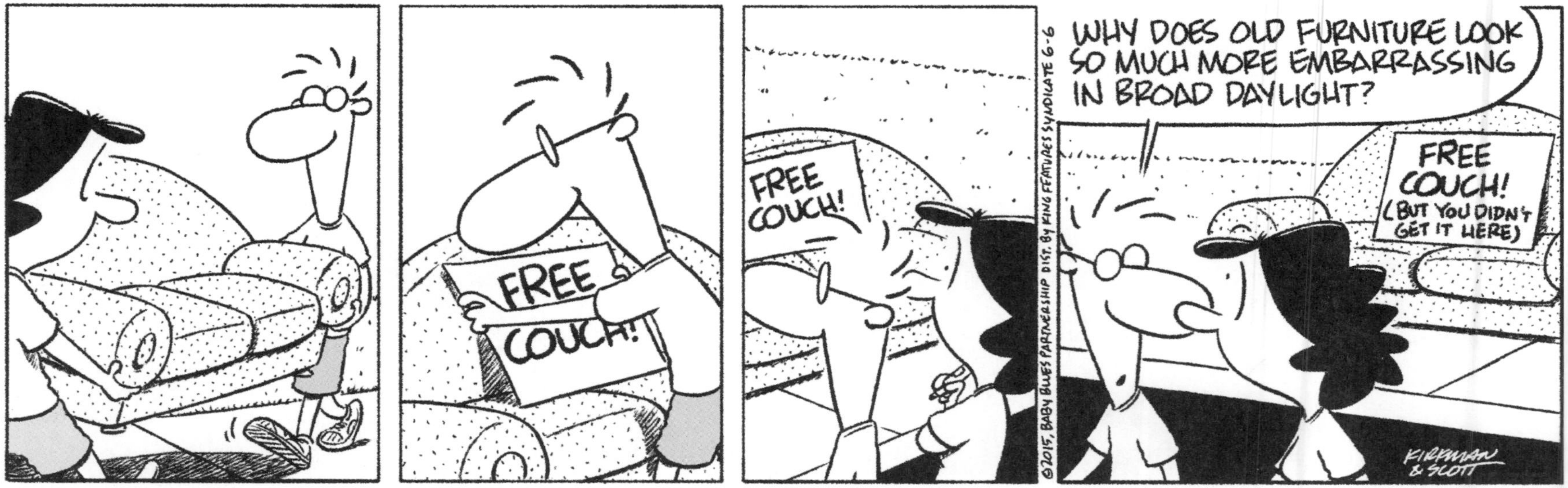
FREE COUCH!
FREE COUCH!
©2015, BABY BLUES PARTNERSHIP DIST. BY KING FEATURES SYNDICATE 6-6
WHY DOES OLD FURNITURE LOOK SO MUCH MORE EMBARRASSING IN BROAD DAYLIGHT?
FREE COUCH! (BUT YOU DIDN'T GET IT HERE)
KIRKMAN & SCOTT

Rick: *Sniff!* Goodbye, old couch.

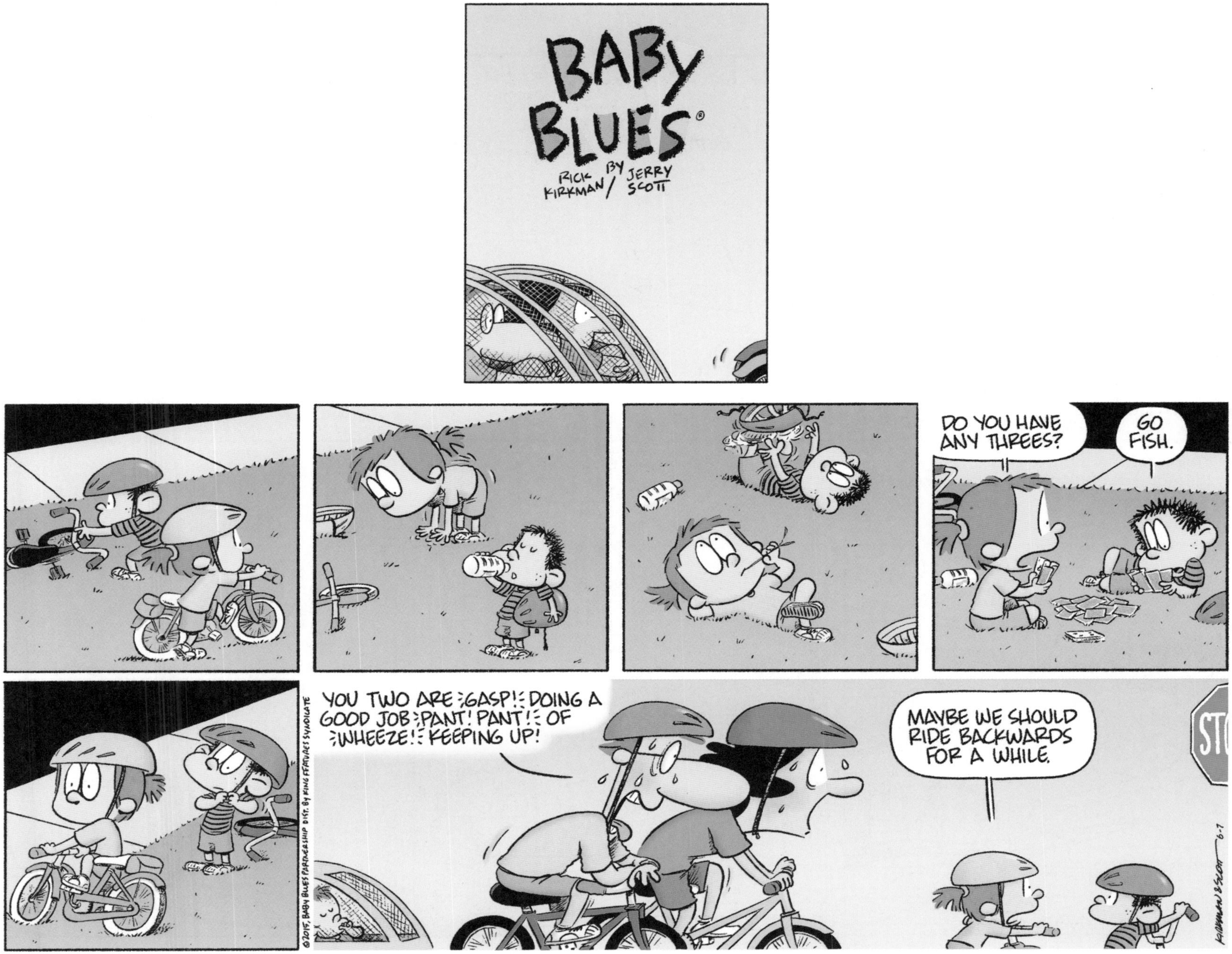
BABY BLUES®
BY RICK KIRKMAN / JERRY SCOTT
DO YOU HAVE ANY THREES?
GO FISH.
©2015, BABY BLUES PARTNERSHIP DIST. BY KING FEATURES SYNDICATE
YOU TWO ARE GASP! DOING A GOOD JOB PANT! PANT! OF WHEEZE! KEEPING UP!
MAYBE WE SHOULD RIDE BACKWARDS FOR A WHILE.
STO
KIRKMAN & SCOTT
6-7

Rick: Despite my intense dislike of drawing bicycles, I was really happy with this strip . . . mainly because Jerry wrote such a good gag. Nice timing and understatement.

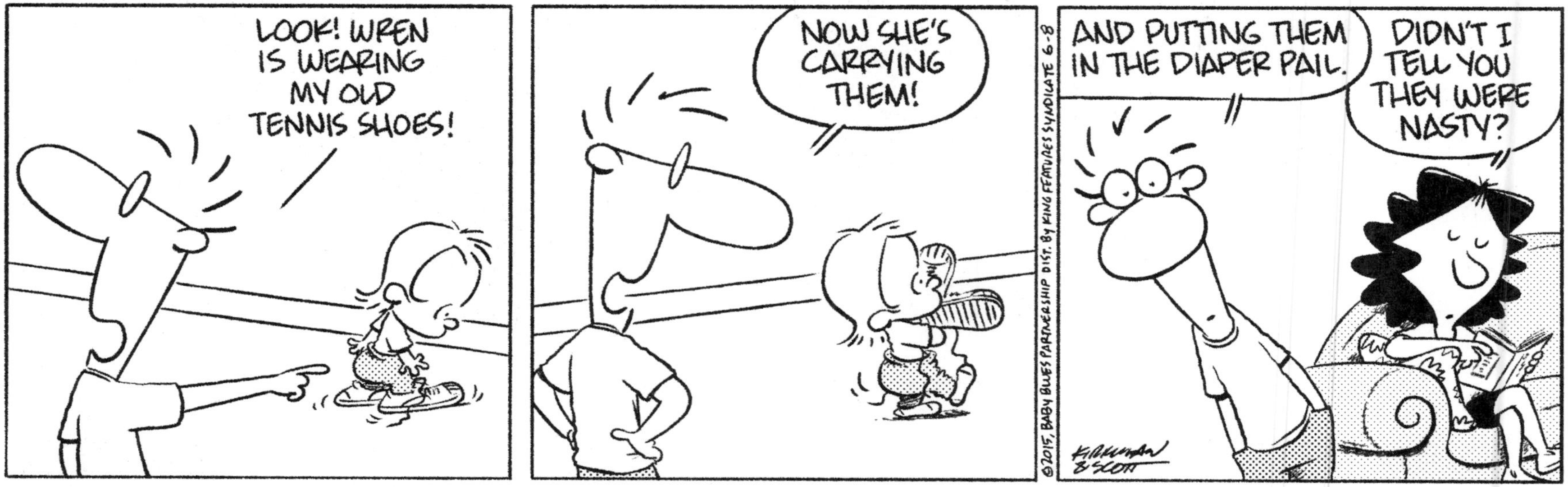
LOOK! WREN IS WEARING MY OLD TENNIS SHOES!
NOW SHE'S CARRYING THEM!
AND PUTTING THEM IN THE DIAPER PAIL.
DIDN'T I TELL YOU THEY WERE NASTY?
©2015, BABY BLUES PARTNERSHIP DIST. BY KING FEATURES SYNDICATE 6-8
KIRKMAN & SCOTT

Rick: Bingo! New furniture. This time I was smart and didn't make furniture that required making hundreds of little tick marks inside each time I drew it.

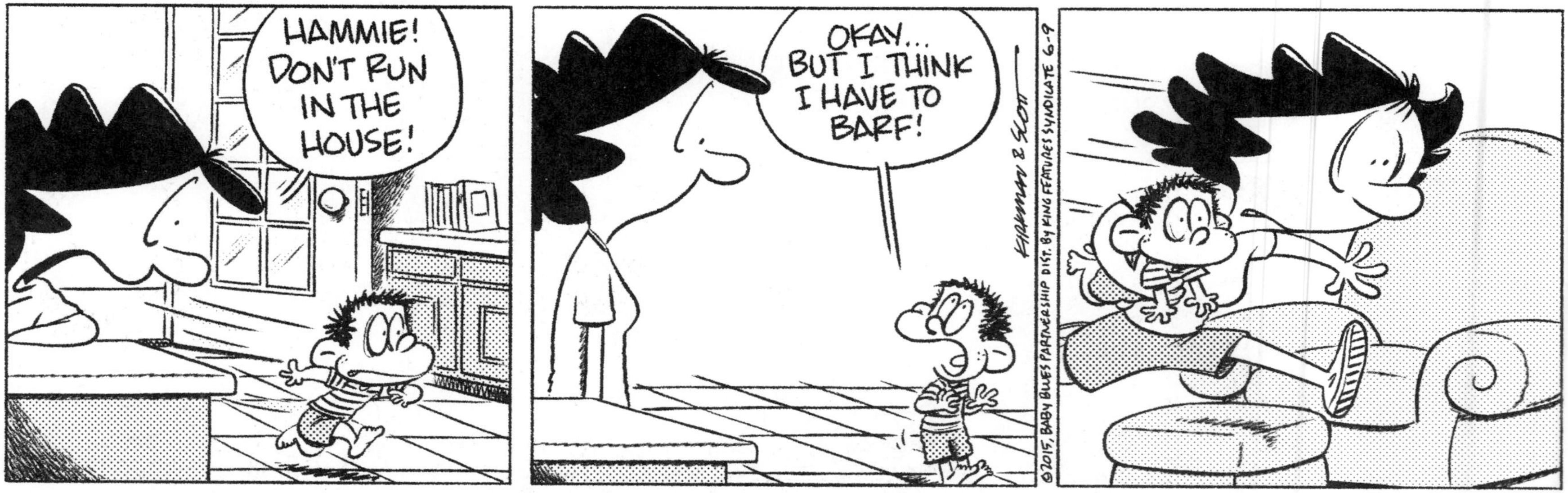
HAMMIE! DON'T RUN IN THE HOUSE!
OKAY... BUT I THINK I HAVE TO BARF!
©2015, BABY BLUES PARTNERSHIP DIST. BY KING FEATURES SYNDICATE 6-9
KIRKMAN & SCOTT

Rick: Oh, yeah . . . we parents all know that look of panic in the last panel.

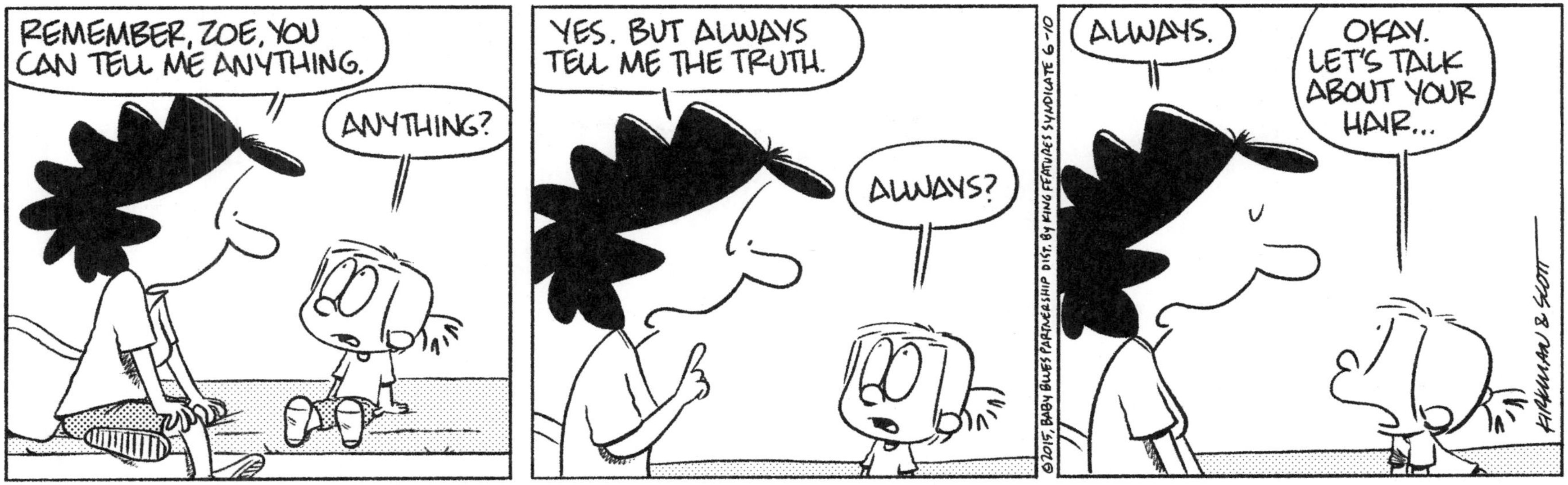
REMEMBER, ZOE, YOU CAN TELL ME ANYTHING.
ANYTHING?
YES. BUT ALWAYS TELL ME THE TRUTH.
ALWAYS?
©2015, BABY BLUES PARTNERSHIP DIST. BY KING FEATURES SYNDICATE 6-10
ALWAYS.
OKAY. LET'S TALK ABOUT YOUR HAIR...
KIRKMAN & SCOTT

Jerry: Okay, not always.

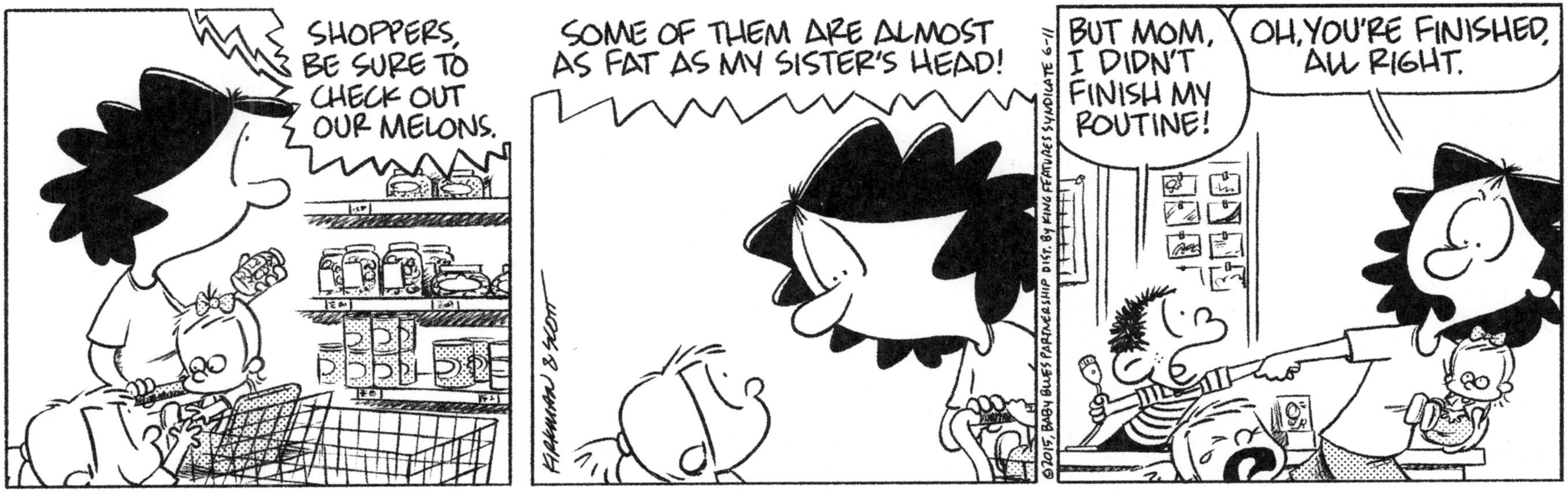
SHOPPERS, BE SURE TO CHECK OUT OUR MELONS.
KIRKMAN & SCOTT
SOME OF THEM ARE ALMOST AS FAT AS MY SISTER'S HEAD!
©2015, BABY BLUES PARTNERSHIP DIST. BY KING FEATURES SYNDICATE 6-11
BUT MOM, I DIDN'T FINISH MY ROUTINE!
OH, YOU'RE FINISHED, ALL RIGHT.

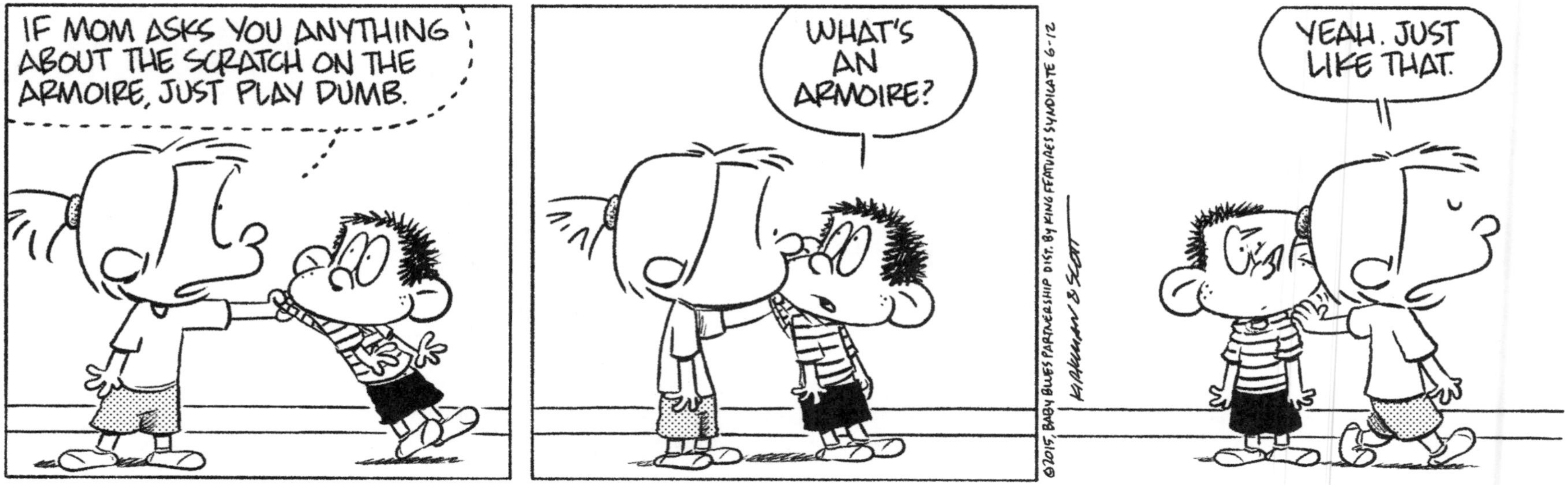
IF MOM ASKS YOU ANYTHING ABOUT THE SCRATCH ON THE ARMOIRE, JUST PLAY DUMB.
WHAT'S AN ARMOIRE?
©2015, BABY BLUES PARTNERSHIP DIST. BY KING FEATURES SYNDICATE 6-12
KIRKMAN & SCOTT
YEAH. JUST LIKE THAT.

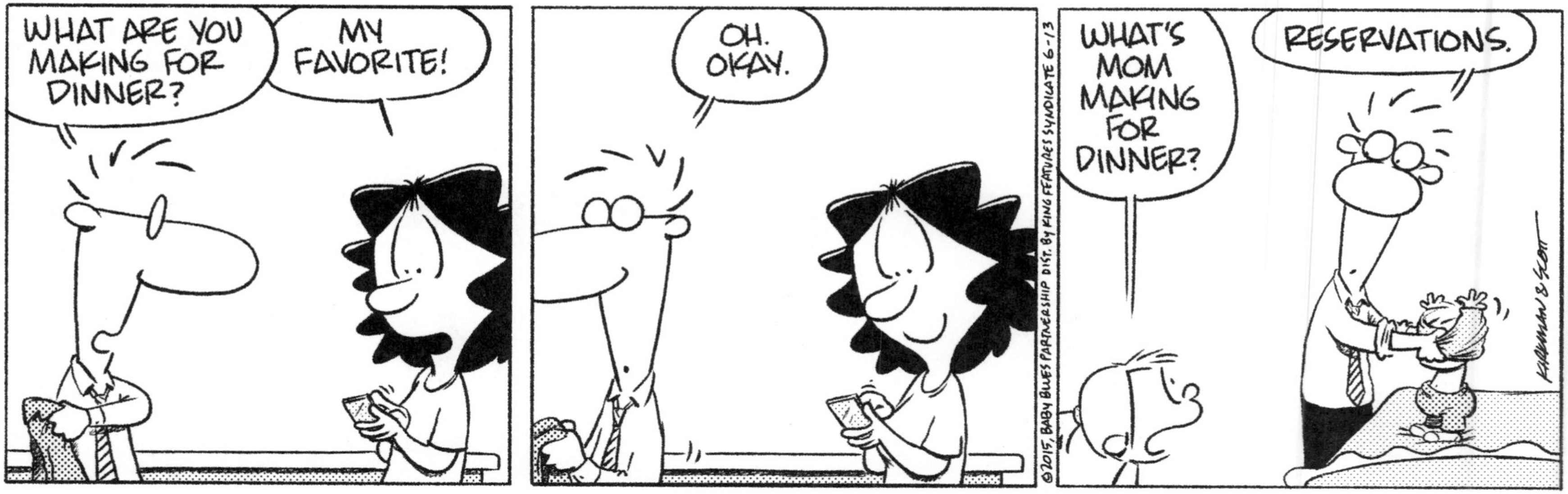
WHAT ARE YOU MAKING FOR DINNER?
MY FAVORITE!
OH. OKAY.
©2015, BABY BLUES PARTNERSHIP DIST. BY KING FEATURES SYNDICATE 6-13
WHAT'S MOM MAKING FOR DINNER?
RESERVATIONS.
KIRKMAN & SCOTT

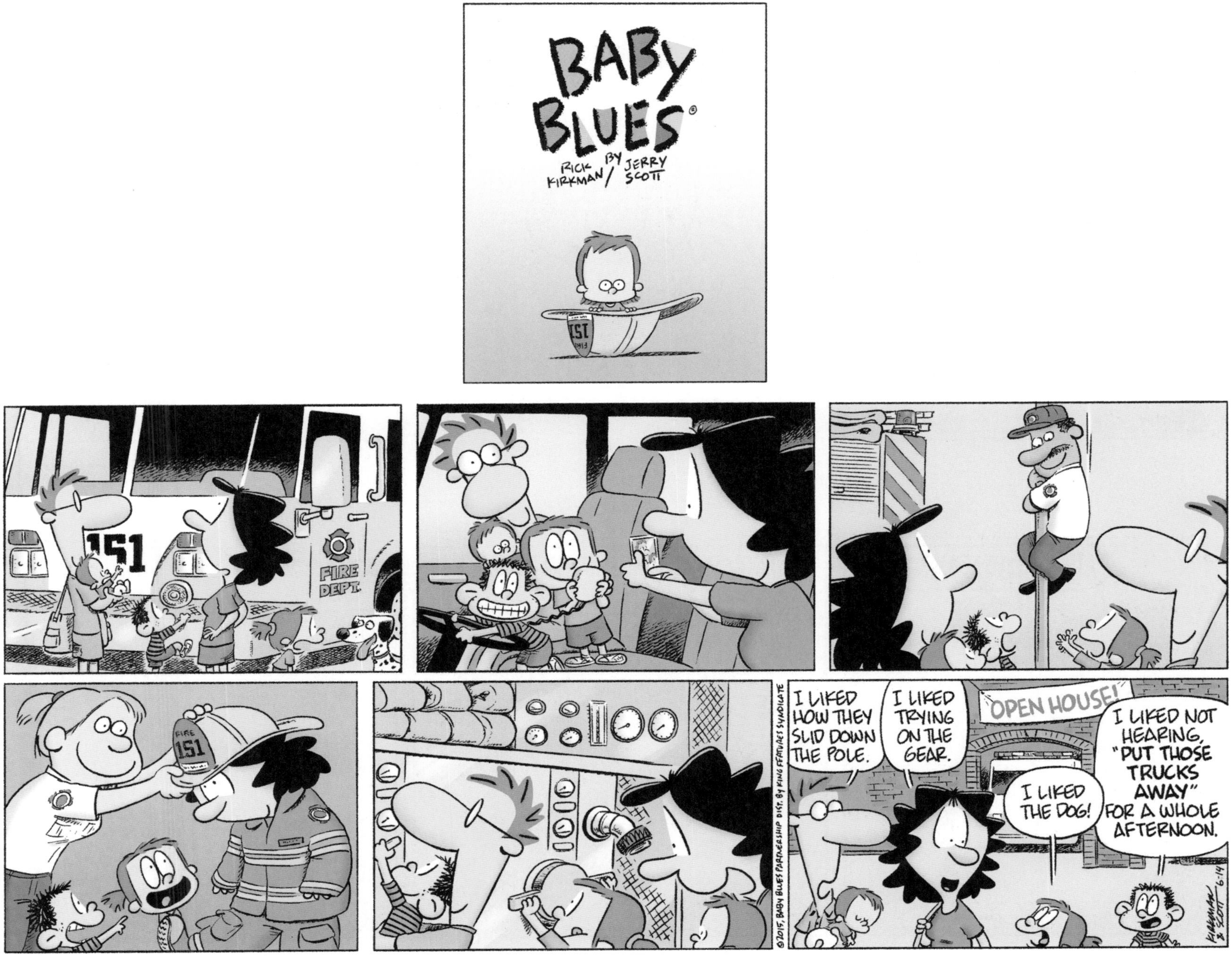
BABY BLUES®
BY RICK KIRKMAN / JERRY SCOTT
151
FIRE DEPT.
FIRE 151
I LIKED HOW THEY SLID DOWN THE POLE.
I LIKED TRYING ON THE GEAR.
OPEN HOUSE!
I LIKED NOT HEARING, "PUT THOSE TRUCKS AWAY" FOR A WHOLE AFTERNOON.
I LIKED THE DOG!
©2015, BABY BLUES PARTNERSHIP DIST. BY KING FEATURES SYNDICATE
KIRKMAN & SCOTT 6-14

Rick: I'm just going to give credit where credit is due for the art—Google image reference FTW!

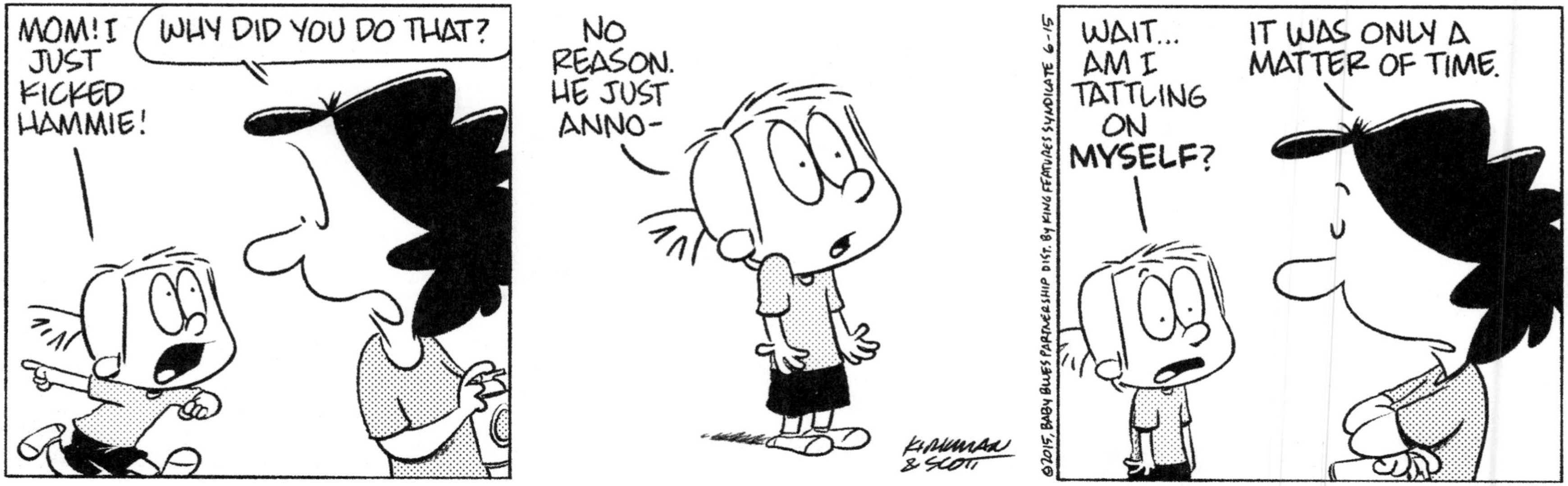
MOM! I JUST KICKED HAMMIE!
WHY DID YOU DO THAT?
NO REASON. HE JUST ANNO-
KIRKMAN & SCOTT
©2015, BABY BLUES PARTNERSHIP DIST. BY KING FEATURES SYNDICATE 6-15
WAIT... AM I TATTLING ON MYSELF?
IT WAS ONLY A MATTER OF TIME.

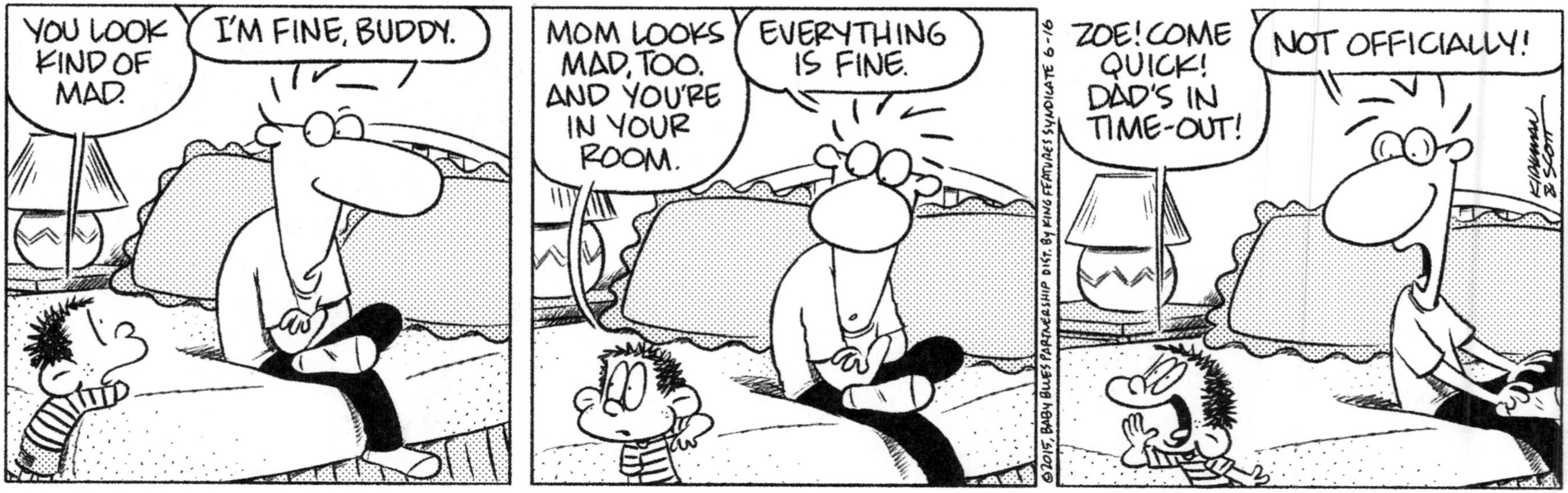
YOU LOOK KIND OF MAD.
I'M FINE, BUDDY.
MOM LOOKS MAD, TOO. AND YOU'RE IN YOUR ROOM.
EVERYTHING IS FINE.
©2015, BABY BLUES PARTNERSHIP DIST. BY KING FEATURES SYNDICATE 6-16
ZOE! COME QUICK! DAD'S IN TIME-OUT!
NOT OFFICIALLY!
KIRKMAN & SCOTT

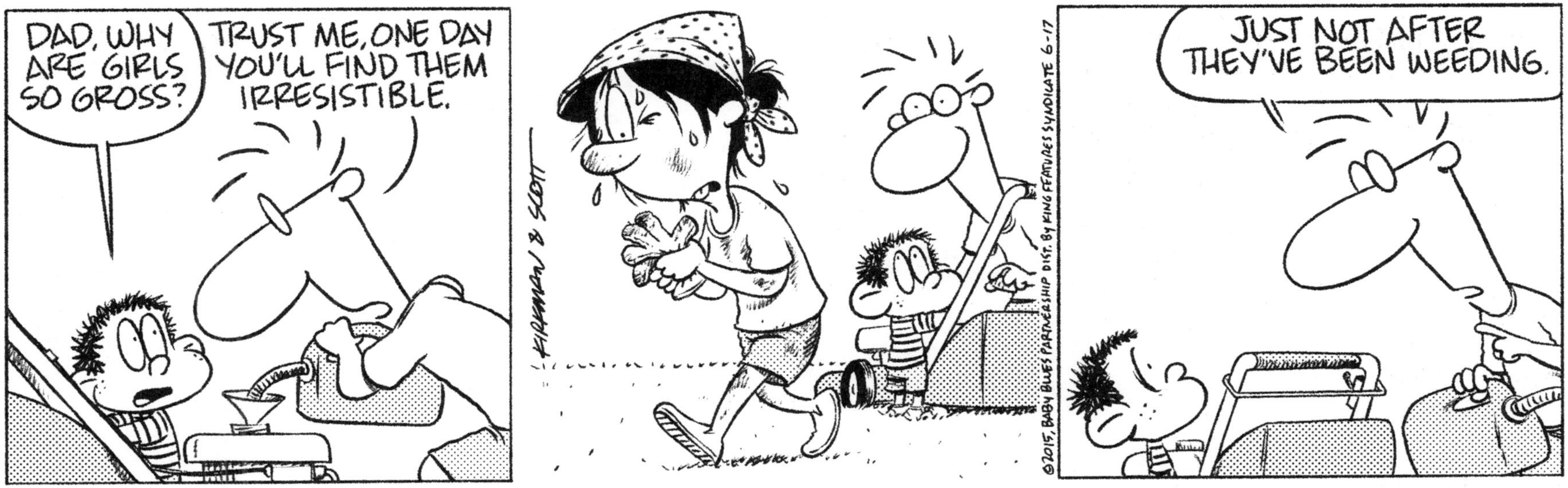
DAD, WHY ARE GIRLS SO GROSS?
TRUST ME, ONE DAY YOU'LL FIND THEM IRRESISTIBLE.
KIRKMAN & SCOTT
©2015, BABY BLUES PARTNERSHIP DIST. BY KING FEATURES SYNDICATE 6-17
JUST NOT AFTER THEY'VE BEEN WEEDING.

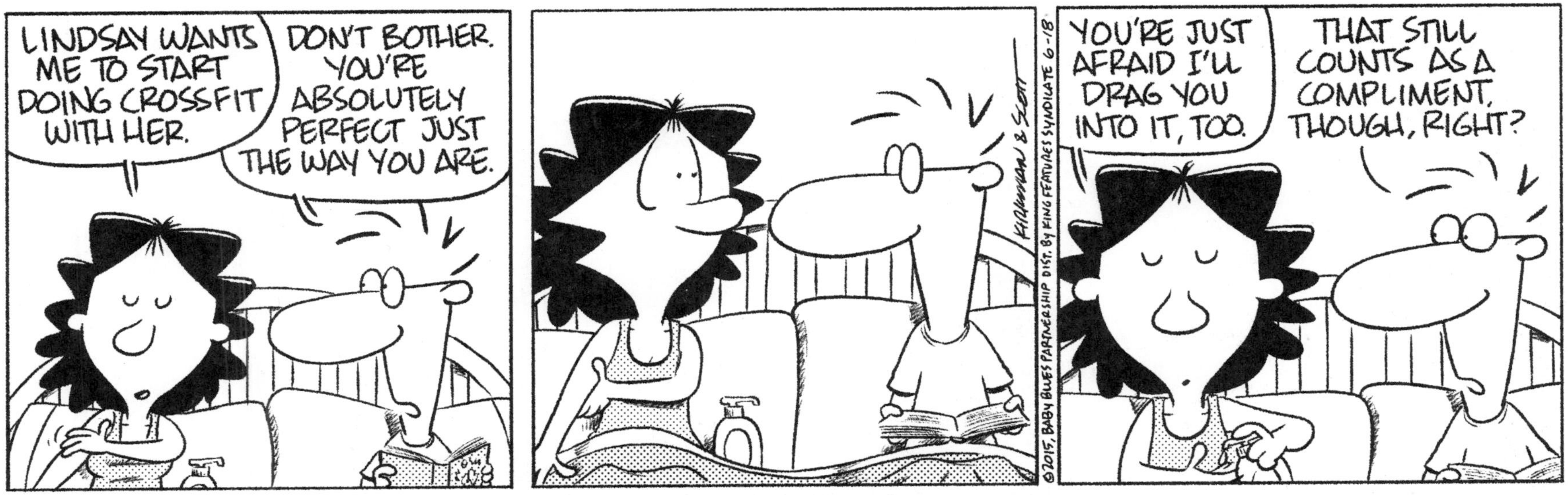
LINDSAY WANTS ME TO START DOING CROSSFIT WITH HER.
DON'T BOTHER. YOU'RE ABSOLUTELY PERFECT JUST THE WAY YOU ARE.
KIRKMAN & SCOTT
©2015, BABY BLUES PARTNERSHIP DIST. BY KING FEATURES SYNDICATE 6-18
YOU'RE JUST AFRAID I'LL DRAG YOU INTO IT, TOO.
THAT STILL COUNTS AS A COMPLIMENT, THOUGH, RIGHT?

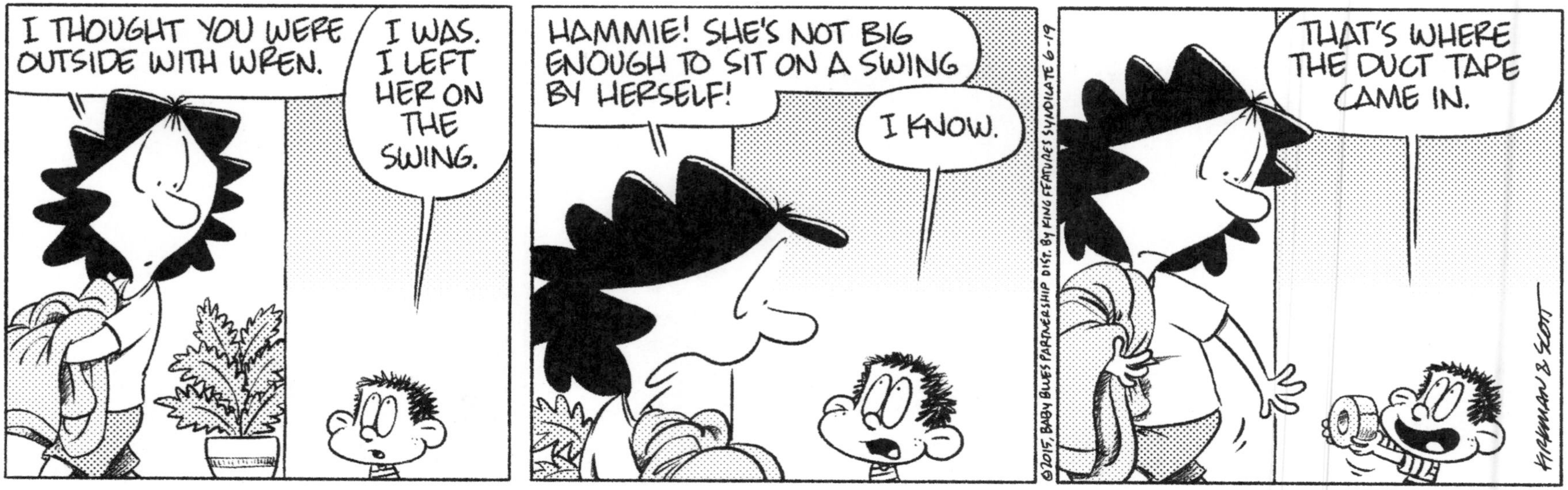
I THOUGHT YOU WERE OUTSIDE WITH WREN.
I WAS. I LEFT HER ON THE SWING.
HAMMIE! SHE'S NOT BIG ENOUGH TO SIT ON A SWING BY HERSELF!
I KNOW.
THAT'S WHERE THE DUCT TAPE CAME IN.
©2015, BABY BLUES PARTNERSHIP DIST. BY KING FEATURES SYNDICATE 6-19

Rick: From the Big Brother Handbook: A big brother must watch out for younger ones' safety. A big brother must be resourceful . . .

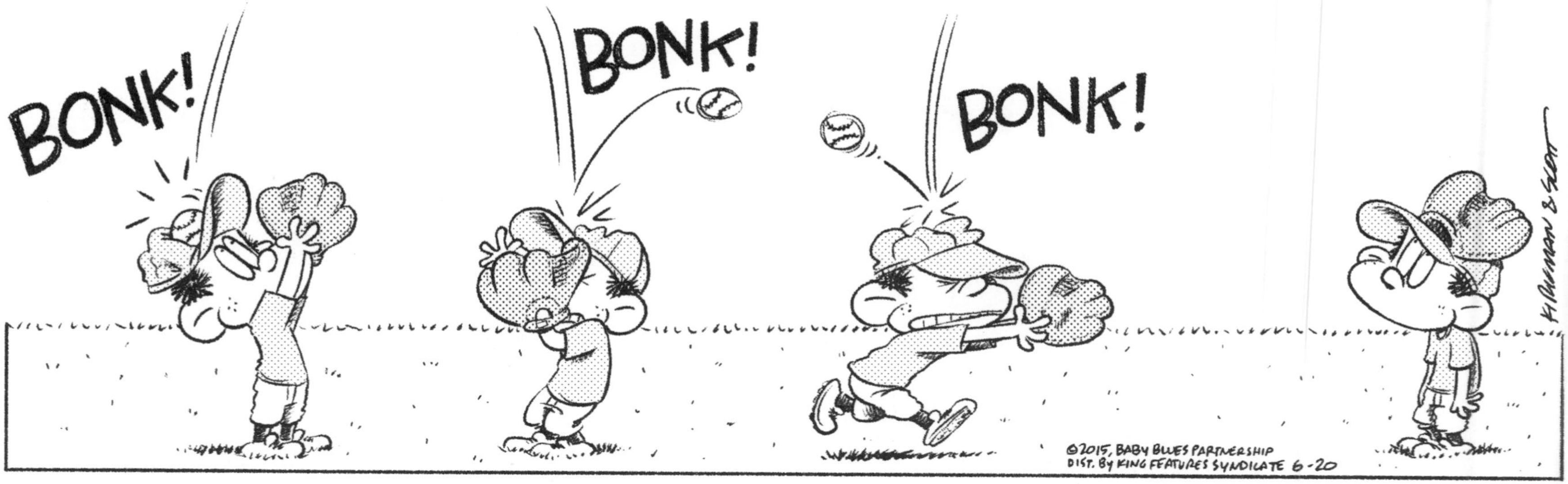
BONK!
BONK!
BONK!
©2015, BABY BLUES PARTNERSHIP DIST. BY KING FEATURES SYNDICATE 6-20

Rick: I love these action-based gags. And this was fun to tell the story in a little different way.

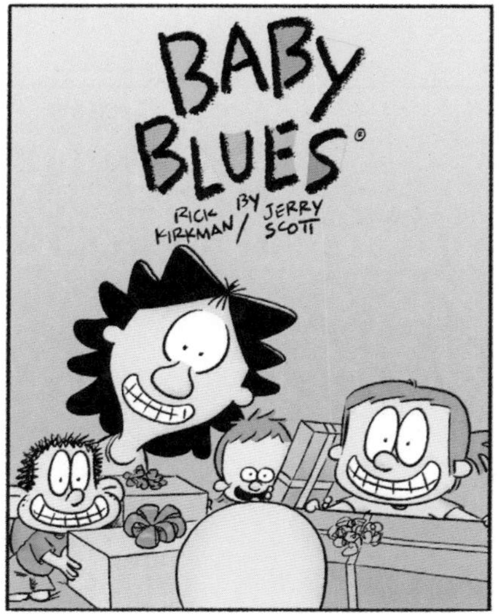
BABY BLUES®
RICK KIRKMAN / BY / JERRY SCOTT

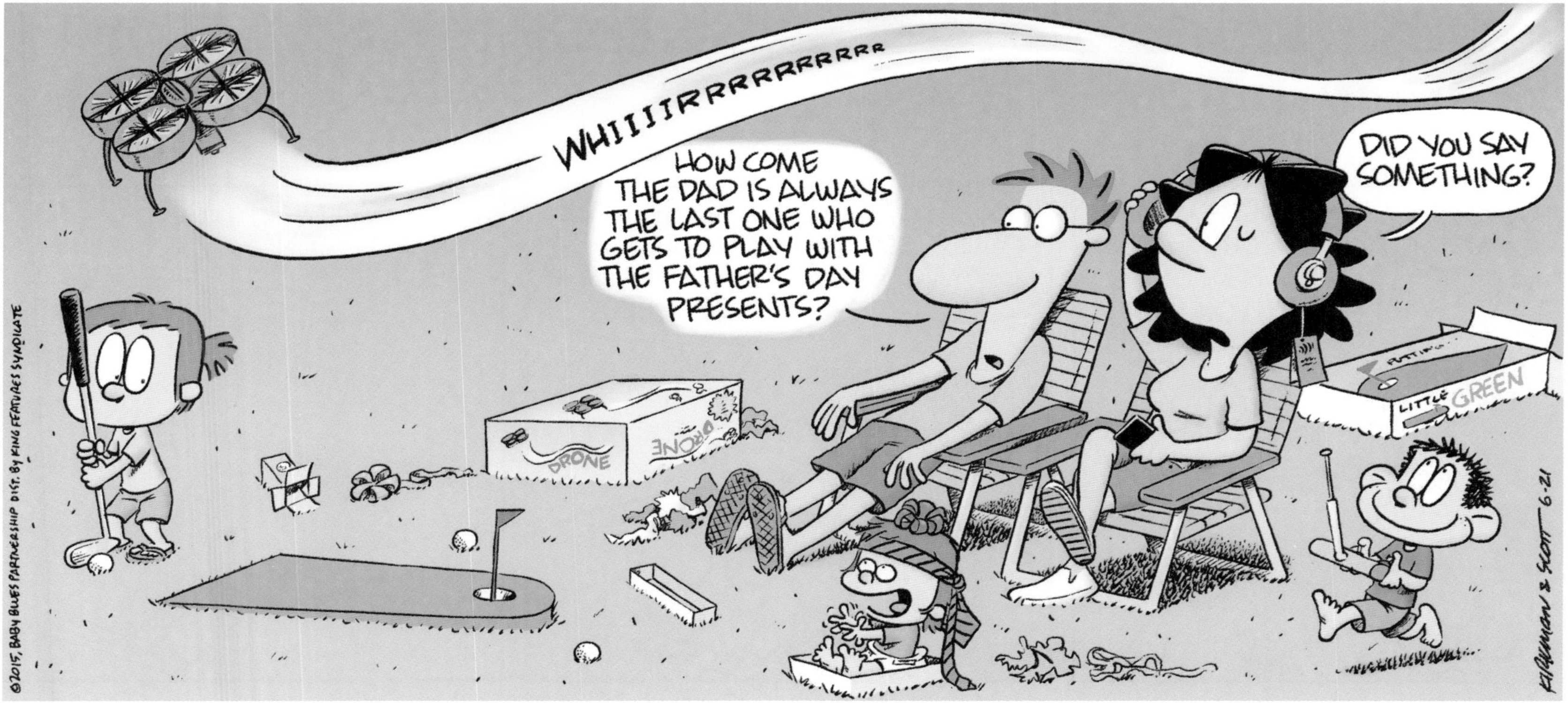
WHIIIIRRRRRRRRRRR
HOW COME THE DAD IS ALWAYS THE LAST ONE WHO GETS TO PLAY WITH THE FATHER'S DAY PRESENTS?
DID YOU SAY SOMETHING?
DRONE
DRONE
LITTLE GREEN
©2015, BABY BLUES PARTNERSHIP DIST. BY KING FEATURES SYNDICATE
KIRKMAN & SCOTT 6-21

Rick: Usually the problem is finding a way to fit everything into a strip. It was such a joy to have all that space!

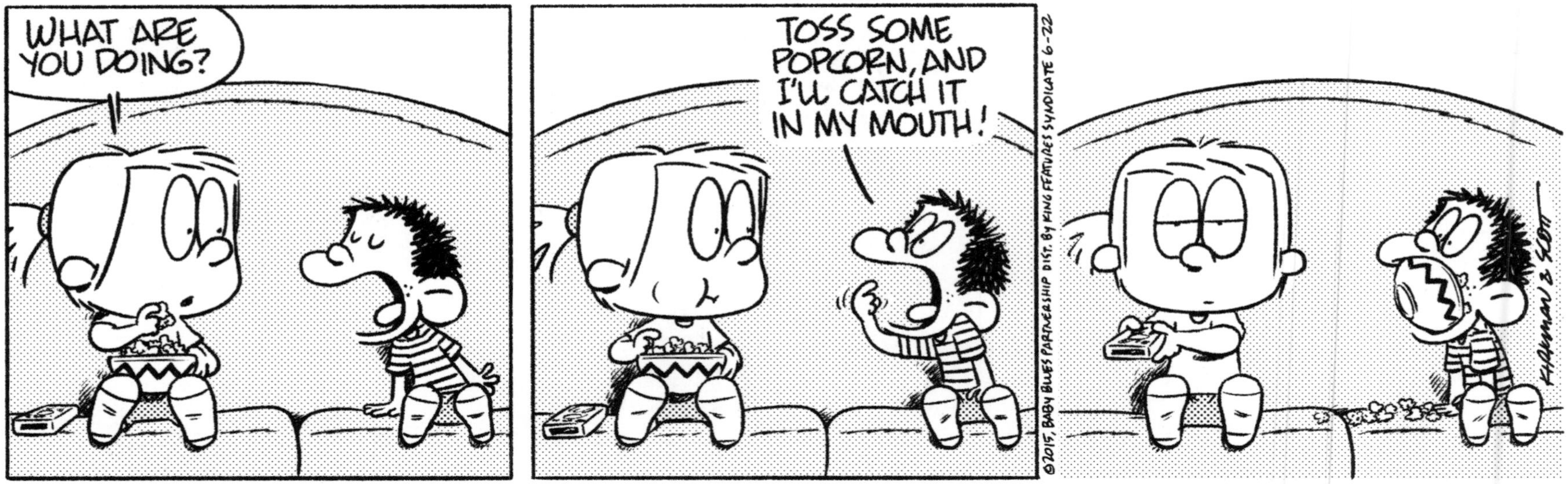
WHAT ARE YOU DOING?
TOSS SOME POPCORN, AND I'LL CATCH IT IN MY MOUTH!
©2015, BABY BLUES PARTNERSHIP DIST. BY KING FEATURES SYNDICATE 6-22
KIRKMAN & SCOTT

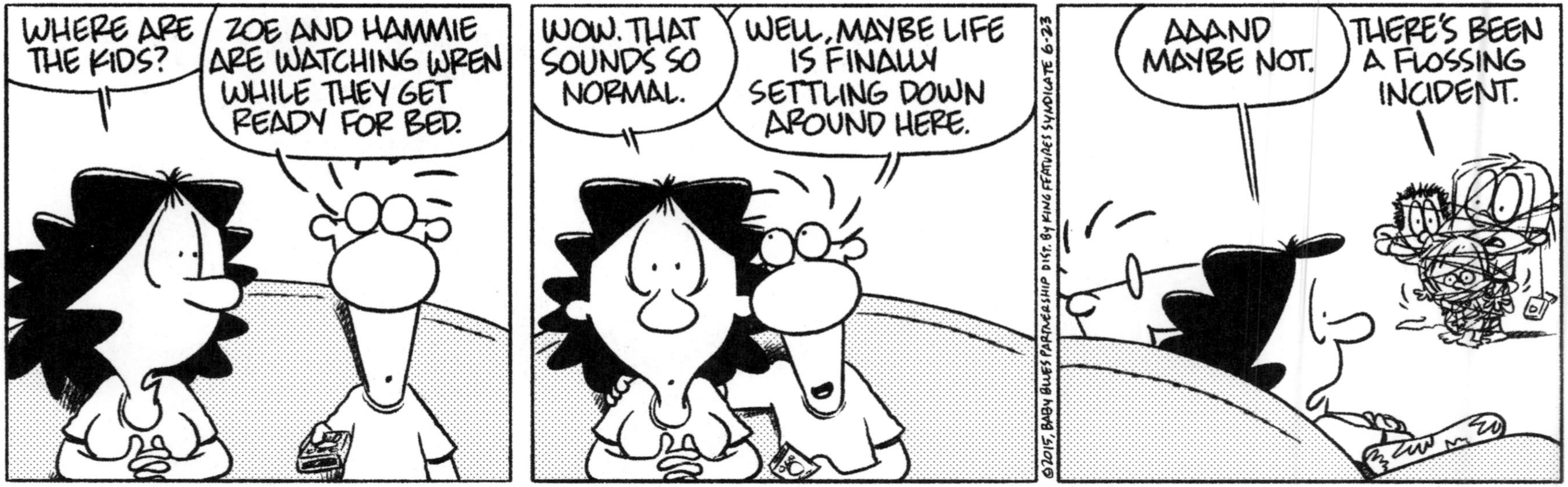
WHERE ARE THE KIDS?
ZOE AND HAMMIE ARE WATCHING WREN WHILE THEY GET READY FOR BED.
WOW. THAT SOUNDS SO NORMAL.
WELL, MAYBE LIFE IS FINALLY SETTLING DOWN AROUND HERE.
©2015, BABY BLUES PARTNERSHIP DIST. BY KING FEATURES SYNDICATE 6-23
AAAND MAYBE NOT.
THERE'S BEEN A FLOSSING INCIDENT.

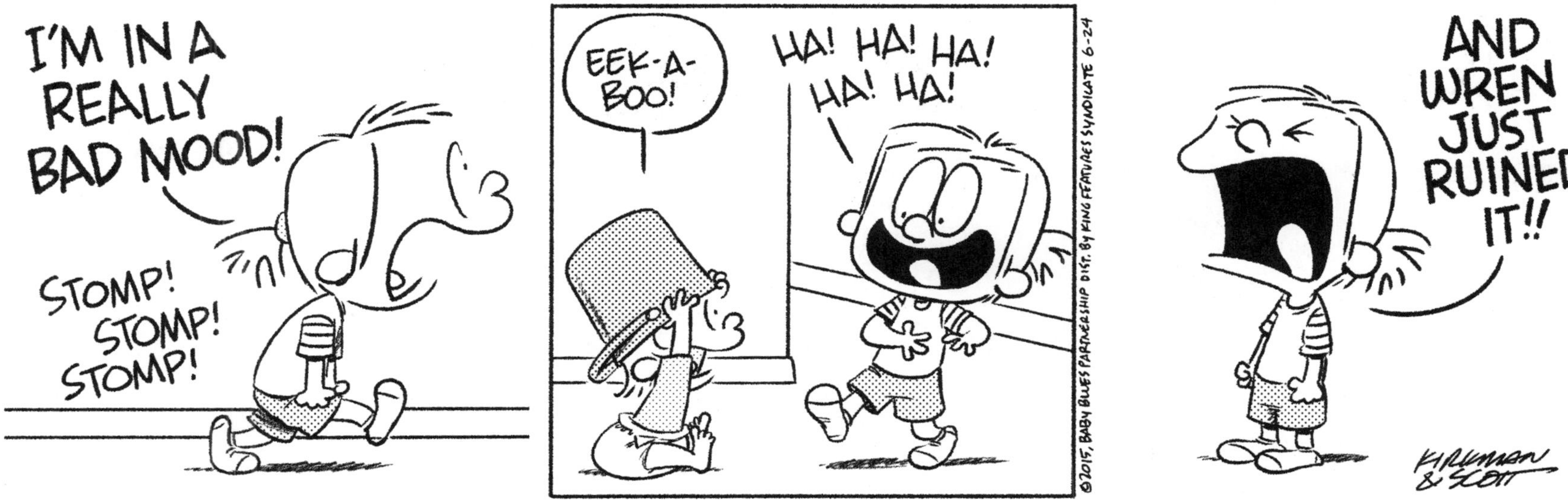
I'M IN A REALLY BAD MOOD!
STOMP! STOMP! STOMP!
EEK-A-BOO!
HA! HA! HA! HA! HA!
©2015, BABY BLUES PARTNERSHIP DIST. BY KING FEATURES SYNDICATE 6-24
AND WREN JUST RUINED IT!!
KIRKMAN & SCOTT

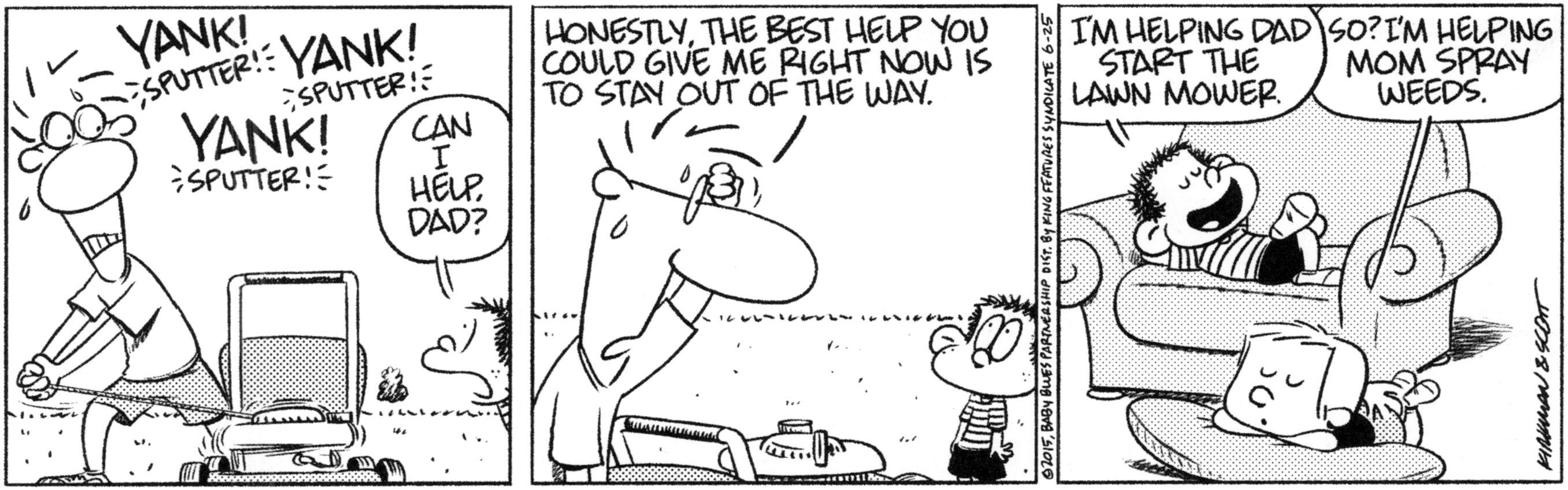
YANK! SPUTTER! YANK! SPUTTER!
YANK! SPUTTER!
CAN I HELP, DAD?
HONESTLY, THE BEST HELP YOU COULD GIVE ME RIGHT NOW IS TO STAY OUT OF THE WAY.
©2015, BABY BLUES PARTNERSHIP DIST. BY KING FEATURES SYNDICATE 6-25
I'M HELPING DAD START THE LAWN MOWER.
SO? I'M HELPING MOM SPRAY WEEDS.
KIRKMAN & SCOTT

Rick: I love their logic.

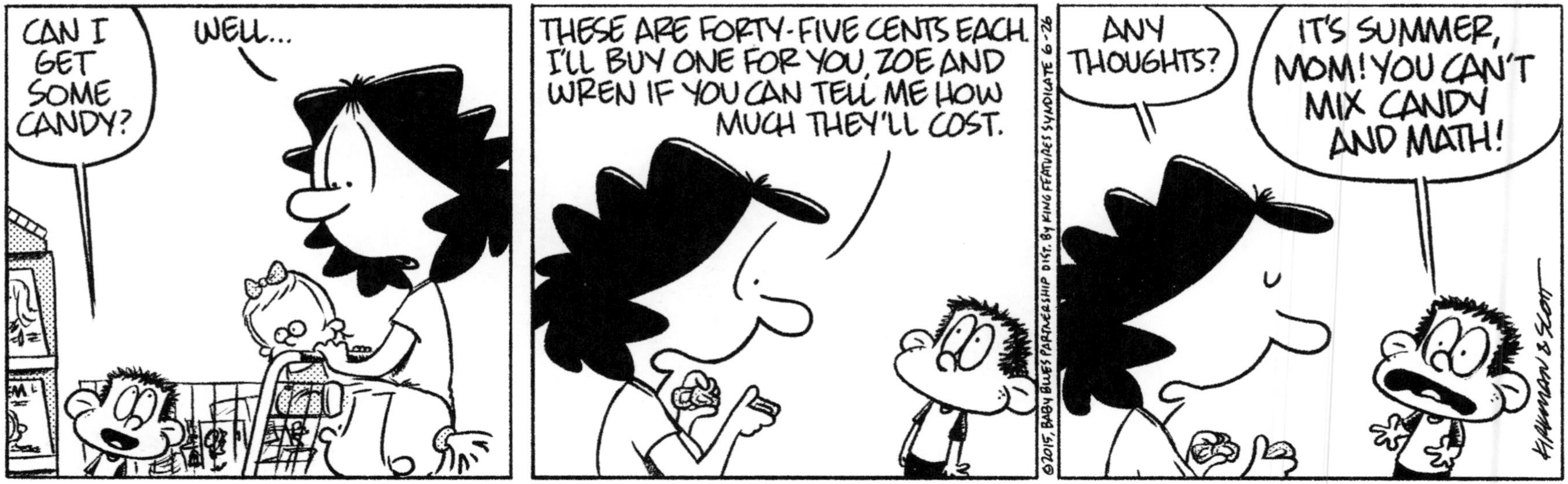
CAN I GET SOME CANDY?
WELL...
THESE ARE FORTY-FIVE CENTS EACH. I'LL BUY ONE FOR YOU, ZOE AND WREN IF YOU CAN TELL ME HOW MUCH THEY'LL COST.
©2015, BABY BLUES PARTNERSHIP DIST. BY KING FEATURES SYNDICATE 6-26
ANY THOUGHTS?
IT'S SUMMER, MOM! YOU CAN'T MIX CANDY AND MATH!
KIRKMAN & SCOTT

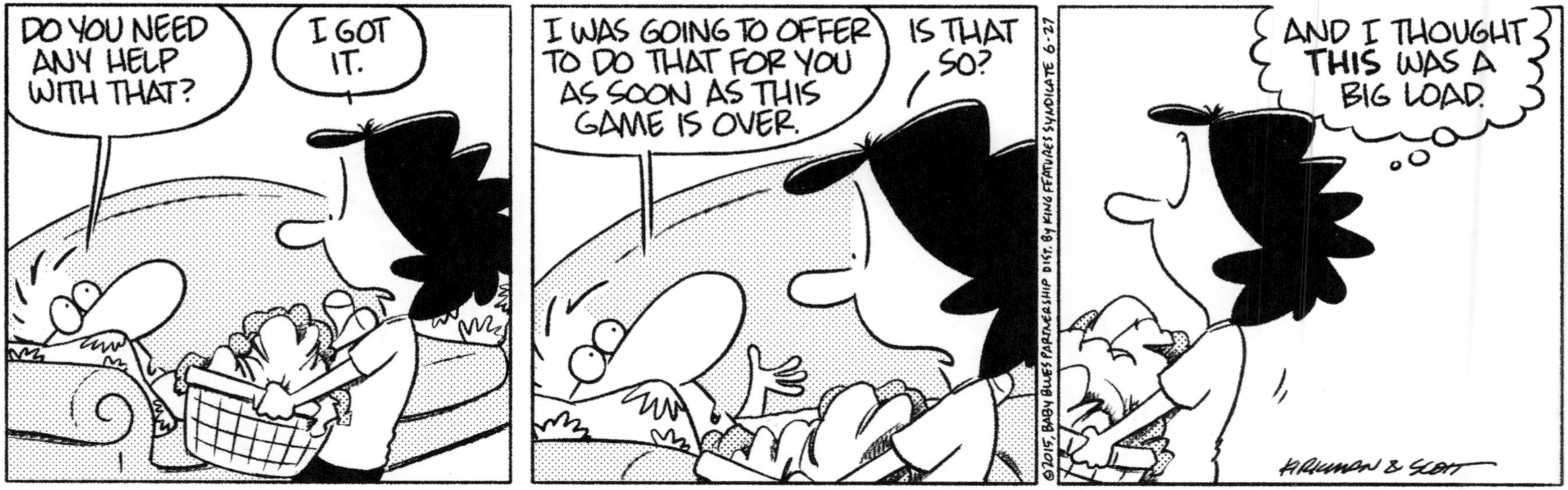
DO YOU NEED ANY HELP WITH THAT?
I GOT IT.
I WAS GOING TO OFFER TO DO THAT FOR YOU AS SOON AS THIS GAME IS OVER.
IS THAT SO?
©2015, BABY BLUES PARTNERSHIP DIST. BY KING FEATURES SYNDICATE 6-27
AND I THOUGHT THIS WAS A BIG LOAD.
KIRKMAN & SCOTT

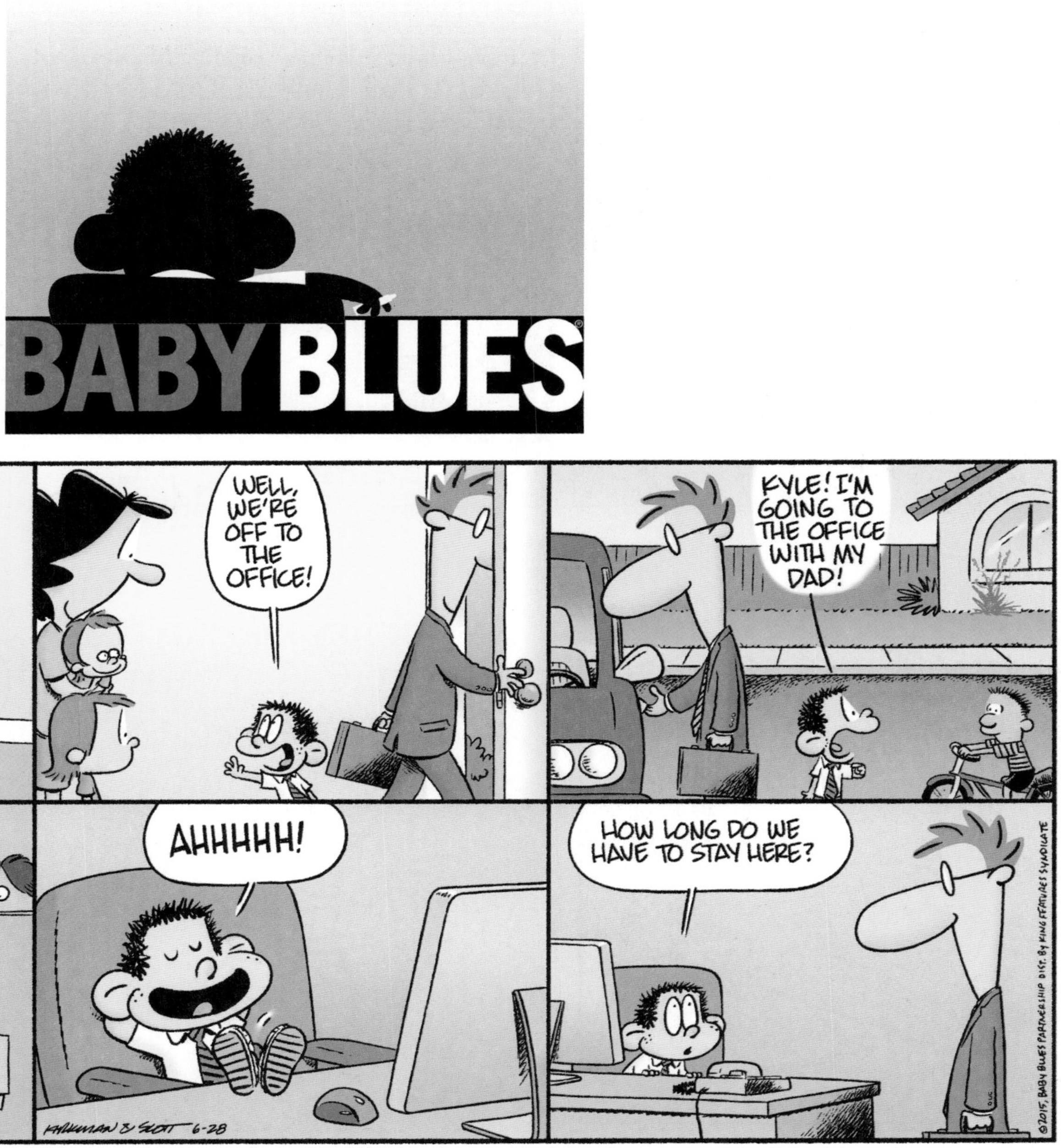
BABY BLUES
I'M GOING TO THE OFFICE WITH DAD TODAY!
WELL, WE'RE OFF TO THE OFFICE!
KYLE! I'M GOING TO THE OFFICE WITH MY DAD!
WELL, HERE WE ARE AT YOUR OFFICE!
AHHHHH!
KIRKMAN & SCOTT 6-28
HOW LONG DO WE HAVE TO STAY HERE?
©2015, BABY BLUES PARTNERSHIP DIST. BY KING FEATURES SYNDICATE

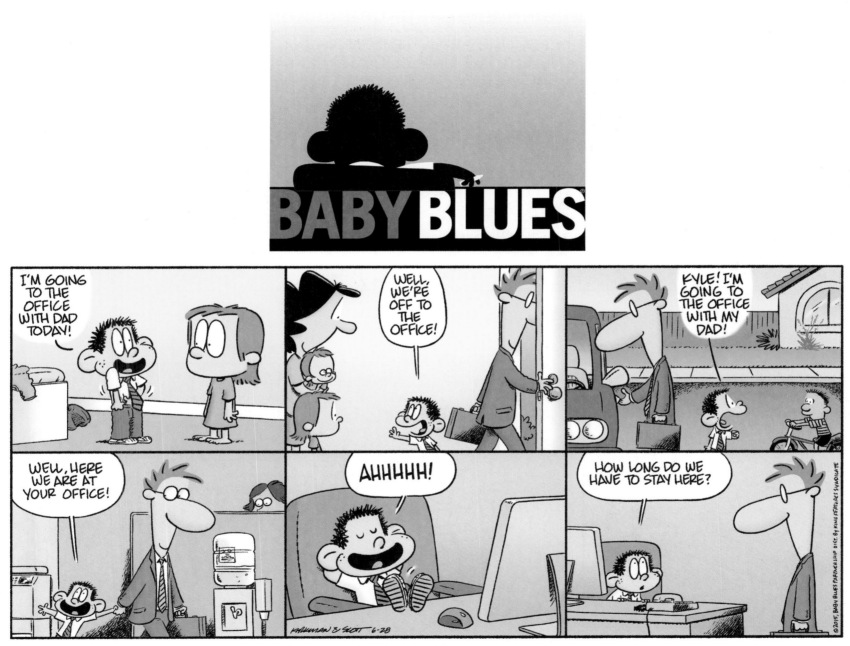

Rick: This was such a fun gag. It was begging for the *Mad Men* treatment.

Jerry: One of my favorite title panels ever.

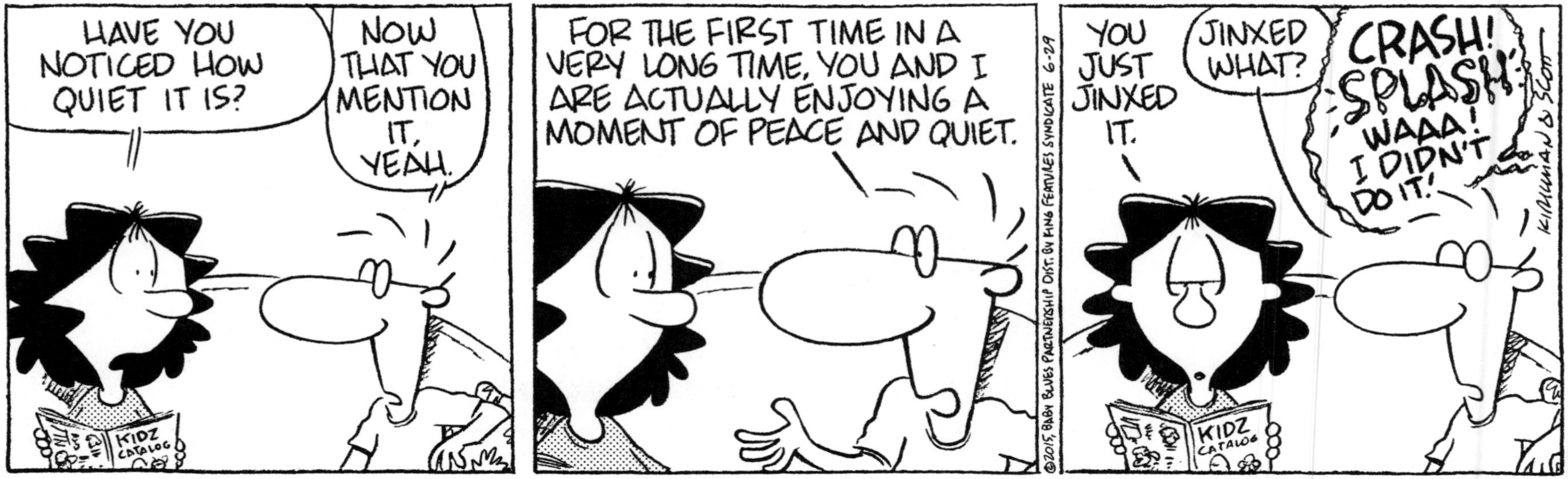
HAVE YOU NOTICED HOW QUIET IT IS?
NOW THAT YOU MENTION IT, YEAH.
KIDZ CATALOG
FOR THE FIRST TIME IN A VERY LONG TIME, YOU AND I ARE ACTUALLY ENJOYING A MOMENT OF PEACE AND QUIET.
©2015, BABY BLUES PARTNERSHIP DIST. BY KING FEATURES SYNDICATE 6-29
YOU JUST JINXED IT.
JINXED WHAT?
CRASH! SPLASH! WAAA! I DIDN'T DO IT!
KIDZ CATALOG
KIRKMAN & SCOTT

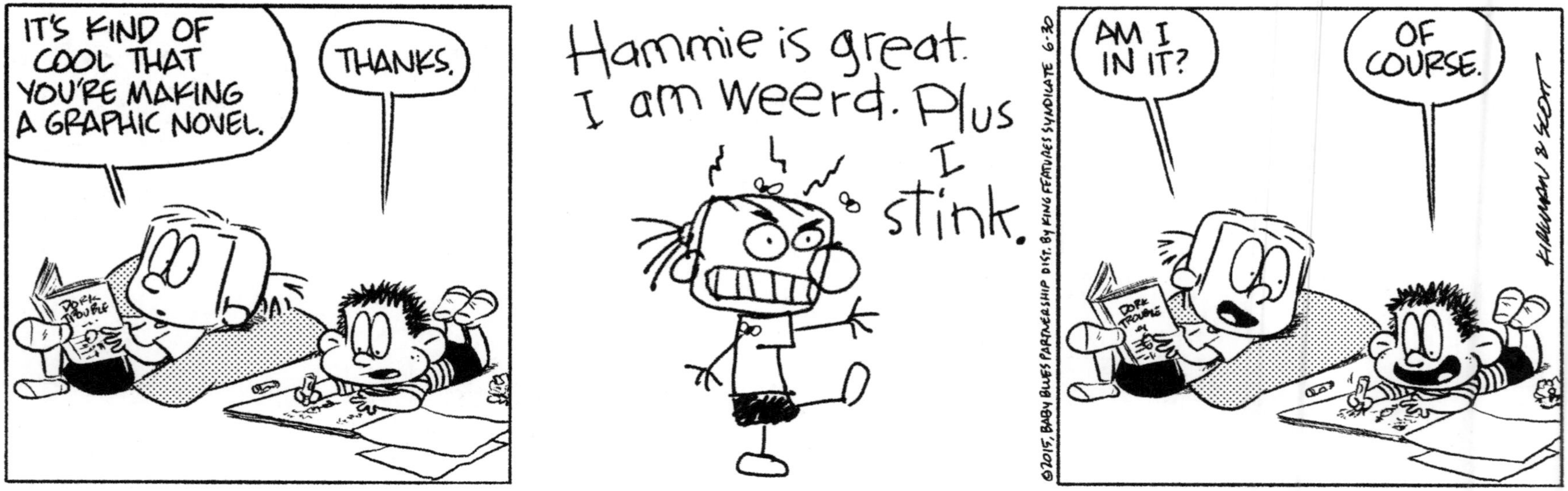
IT'S KIND OF COOL THAT YOU'RE MAKING A GRAPHIC NOVEL.
THANKS.
DORK TROUBLE
Hammie is great. I am weerd. Plus I stink.
©2015, BABY BLUES PARTNERSHIP DIST. BY KING FEATURES SYNDICATE 6-30
AM I IN IT?
OF COURSE.
DORK TROUBLE
KIRKMAN & SCOTT

Rick: Back to using my kids' art and lettering for reference.

Jerry: I started writing and illustrating long stories when I was Hammie's age. Then people told me that I should grow up and do something serious. They were wrong.

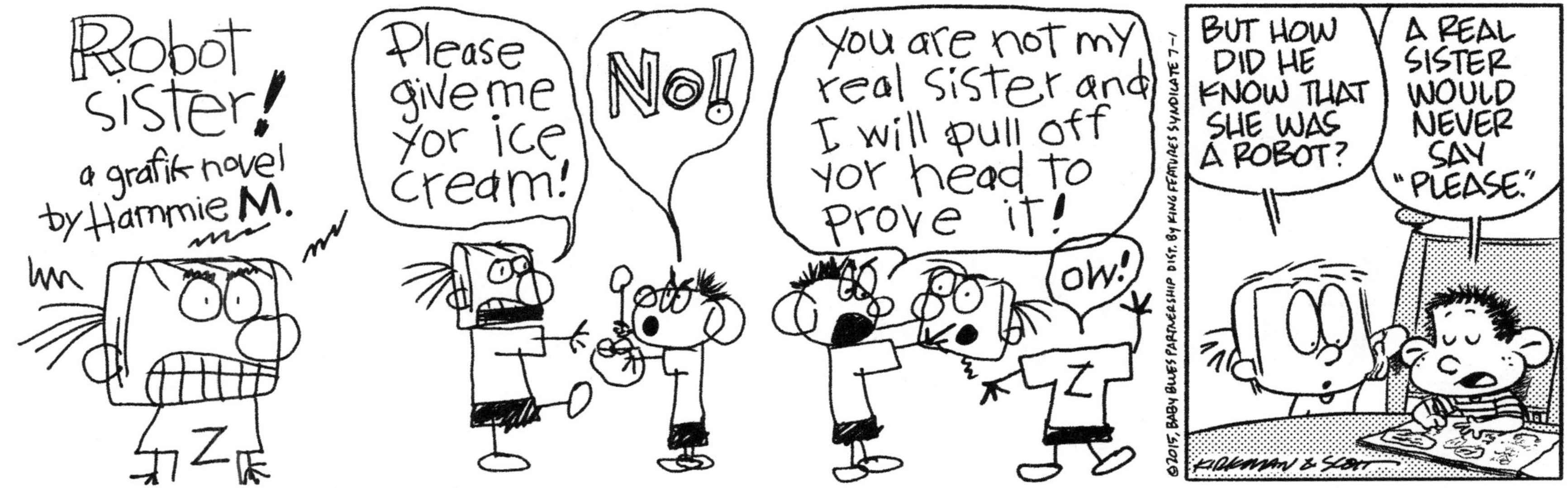
Robot sister!
a grafik novel by Hammie M.
Please give me yor ice cream!
No!
You are not my real sister and I will pull off yor head to prove it!
OW!
BUT HOW DID HE KNOW THAT SHE WAS A ROBOT?
A REAL SISTER WOULD NEVER SAY "PLEASE."
©2015, BABY BLUES PARTNERSHIP DIST. BY KING FEATURES SYNDICATE 7-1
KIRKMAN & SCOTT

Rick: I would actually like to see *Robot Sister*. It even has Zoe intrigued.

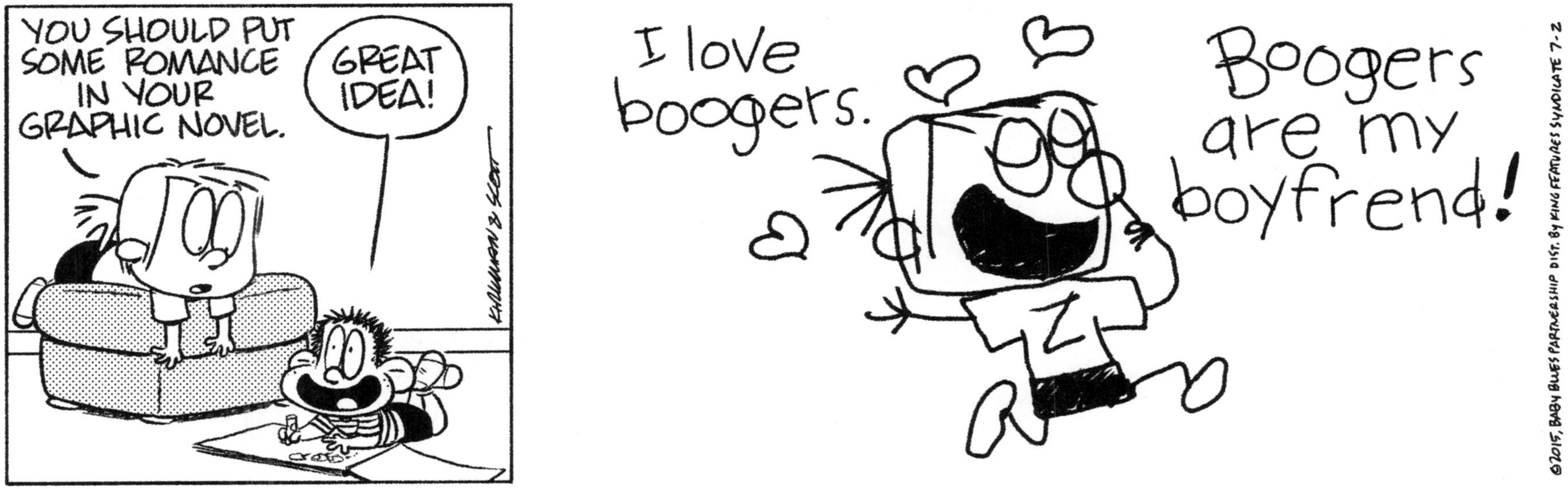
YOU SHOULD PUT SOME ROMANCE IN YOUR GRAPHIC NOVEL.
GREAT IDEA!
KIRKMAN & SCOTT
I love boogers.
Boogers are my boyfrend!
©2015, BABY BLUES PARTNERSHIP DIST. BY KING FEATURES SYNDICATE 7-2

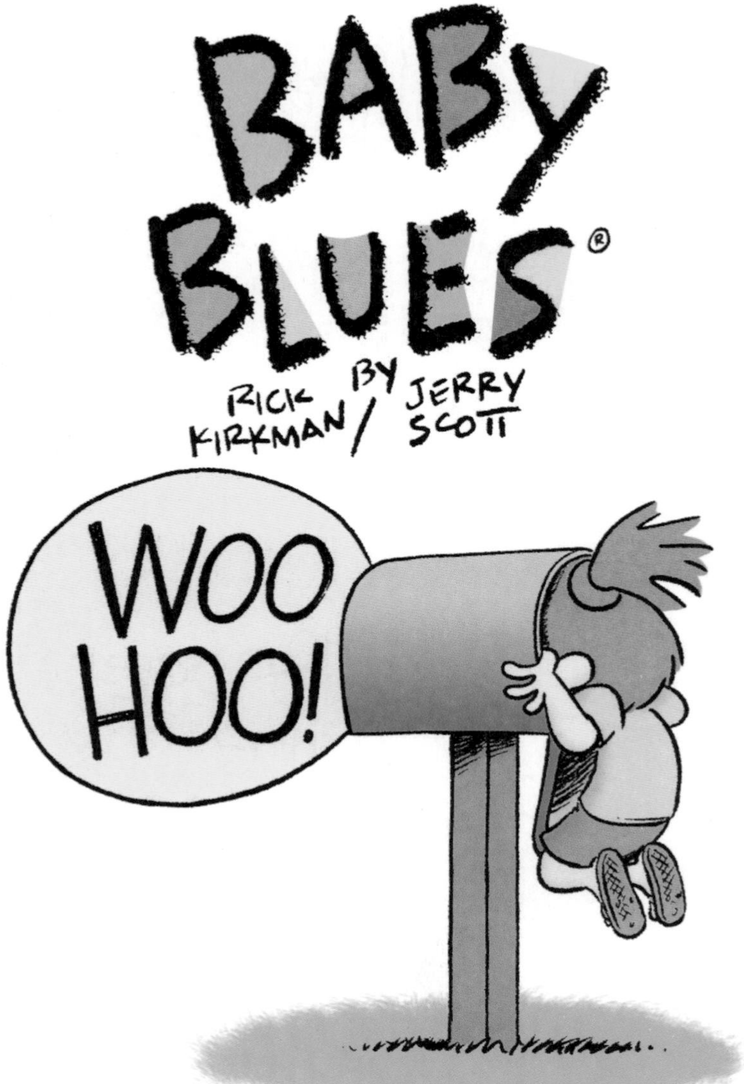
BABY BLUES®
BY RICK KIRKMAN / JERRY SCOTT
WOO HOO!

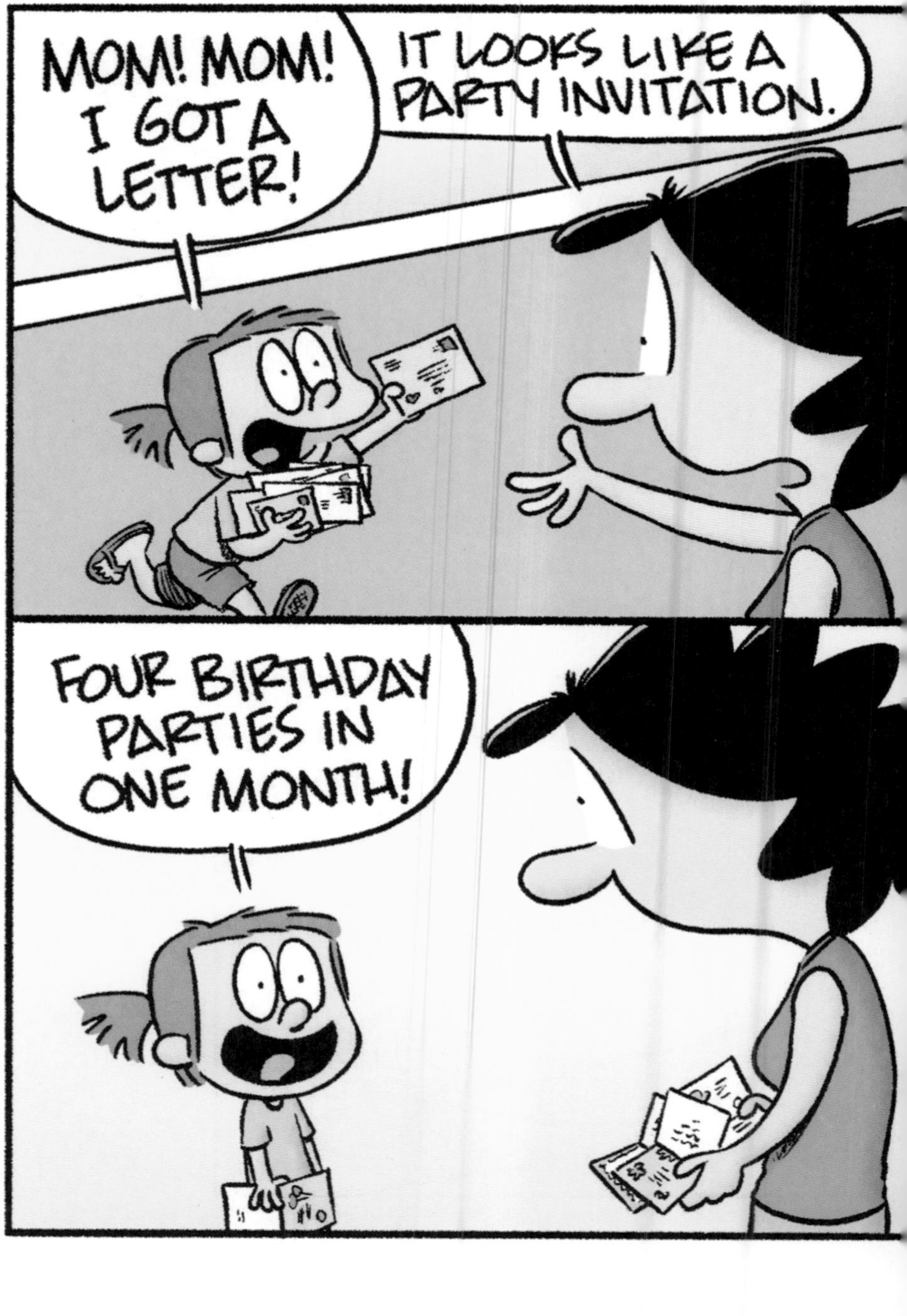
MOM! MOM! I GOT A LETTER!
IT LOOKS LIKE A PARTY INVITATION.
FOUR BIRTHDAY PARTIES IN ONE MONTH!

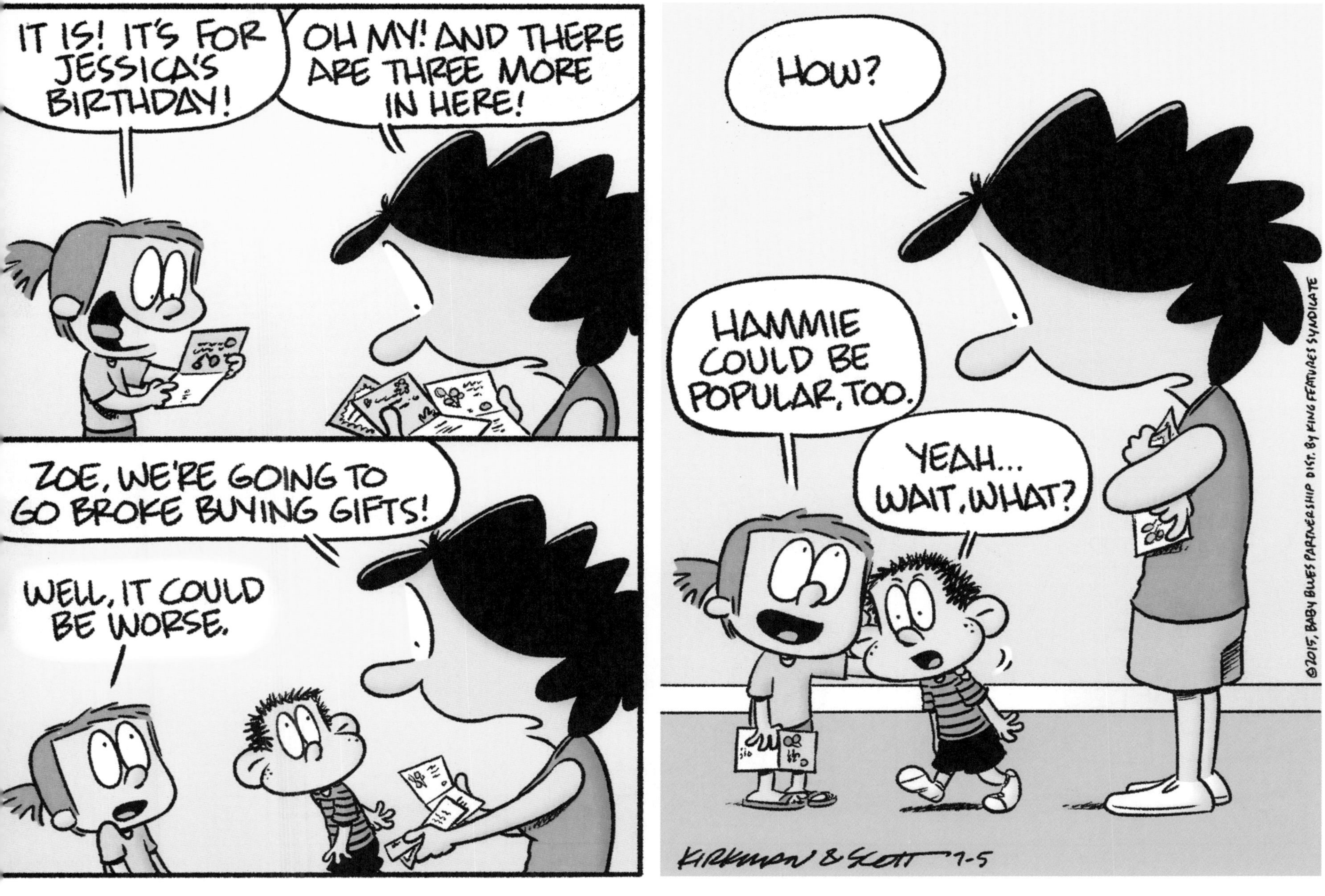
IT IS! IT'S FOR JESSICA'S BIRTHDAY!
OH MY! AND THERE ARE THREE MORE IN HERE!
ZOE, WE'RE GOING TO GO BROKE BUYING GIFTS!
WELL, IT COULD BE WORSE.
HOW?
HAMMIE COULD BE POPULAR, TOO.
YEAH... WAIT, WHAT?
©2015, BABY BLUES PARTNERSHIP DIST. BY KING FEATURES SYNDICATE
KIRKMAN & SCOTT 7-5

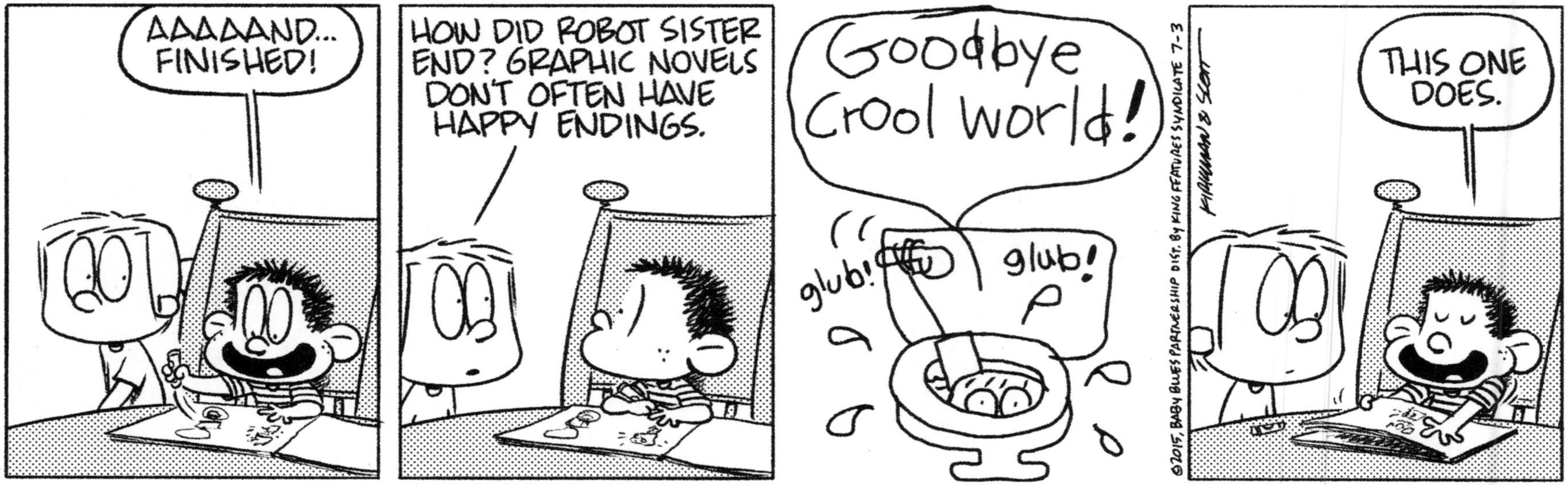
AAAAAND... FINISHED!
HOW DID ROBOT SISTER END? GRAPHIC NOVELS DON'T OFTEN HAVE HAPPY ENDINGS.
Goodbye Crool world!
glub!
glub!
©2015, BABY BLUES PARTNERSHIP DIST. BY KING FEATURES SYNDICATE 7-3
KIRKMAN & SCOTT
THIS ONE DOES.

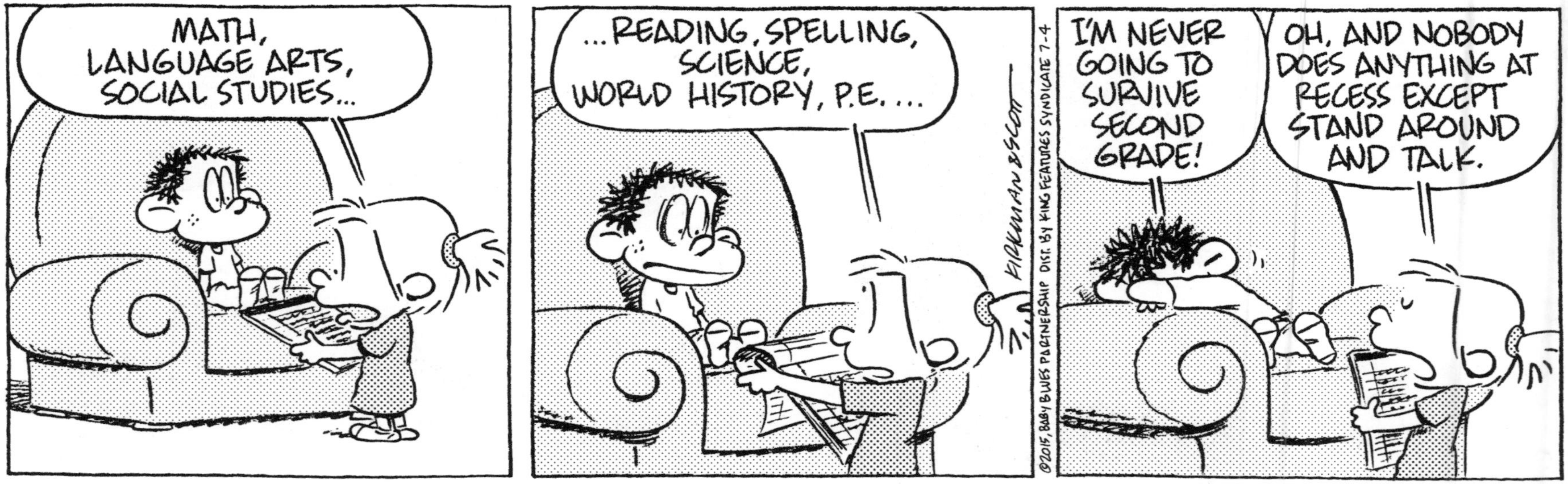
MATH, LANGUAGE ARTS, SOCIAL STUDIES...
...READING, SPELLING, SCIENCE, WORLD HISTORY, P.E. ...
KIRKMAN & SCOTT
©2015, BABY BLUES PARTNERSHIP DIST. BY KING FEATURES SYNDICATE 7-4
I'M NEVER GOING TO SURVIVE SECOND GRADE!
OH, AND NOBODY DOES ANYTHING AT RECESS EXCEPT STAND AROUND AND TALK.

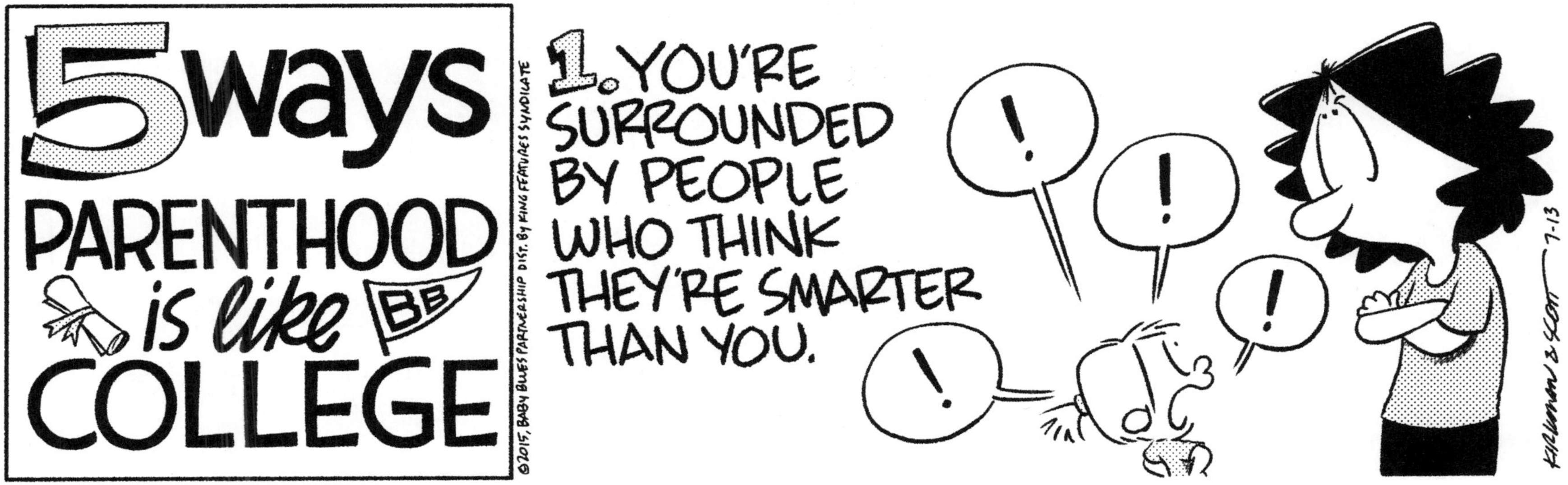
5 ways
PARENTHOOD
is like
BB
COLLEGE
©2015, BABY BLUES PARTNERSHIP DIST. BY KING FEATURES SYNDICATE
1. YOU'RE SURROUNDED BY PEOPLE WHO THINK THEY'RE SMARTER THAN YOU.
!
!
!
!
7-13
KIRKMAN & SCOTT

Rick: These kinds of series are a little deceptive. The title panels always seem to take longer than doing a regular strip, but they can be reused. And then a single image for the idea is sometimes challenging, trying to find just the right image that keeps a similar balance design-wise from strip to strip.

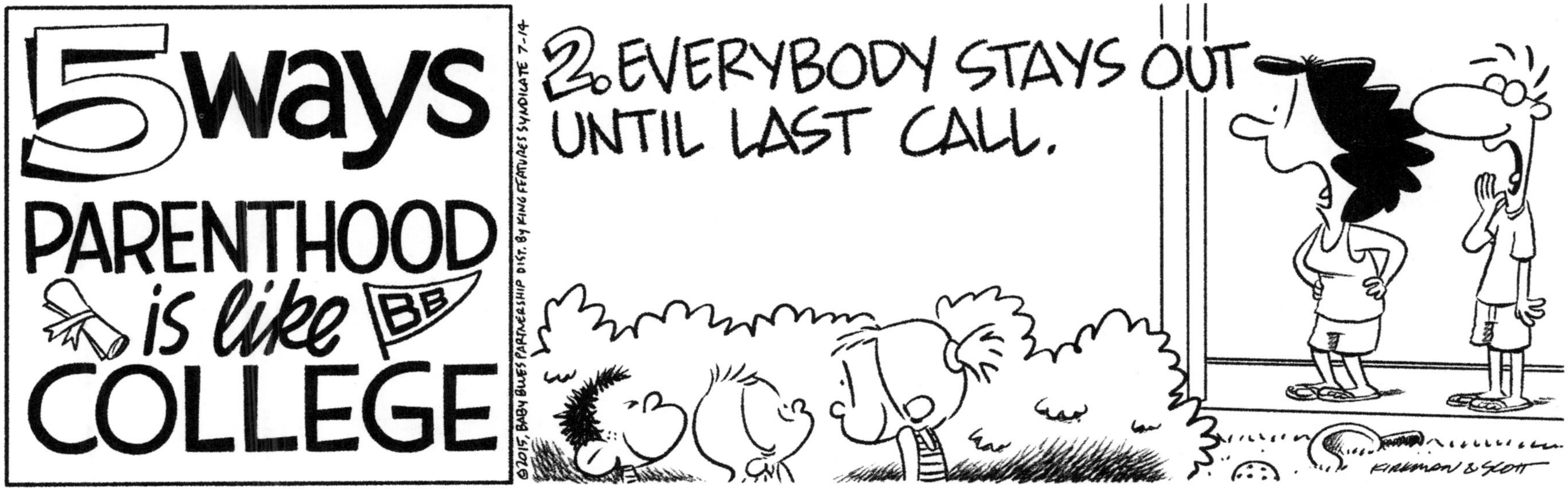
5 ways
PARENTHOOD
is like
BB
COLLEGE
©2015, BABY BLUES PARTNERSHIP DIST. BY KING FEATURES SYNDICATE 7-14
2. EVERYBODY STAYS OUT UNTIL LAST CALL.
KIRKMAN & SCOTT

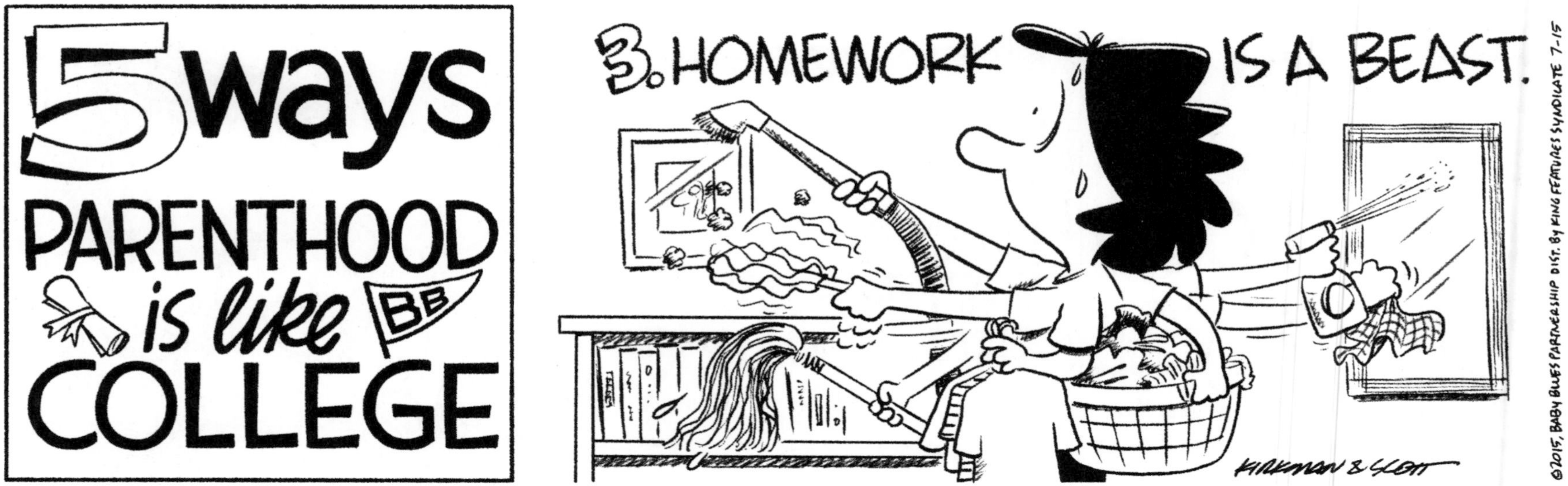
5 ways PARENTHOOD is like COLLEGE
BB
3. HOMEWORK IS A BEAST.
KIRKMAN & SCOTT
©2015, BABY BLUES PARTNERSHIP DIST. BY KING FEATURES SYNDICATE 7-15

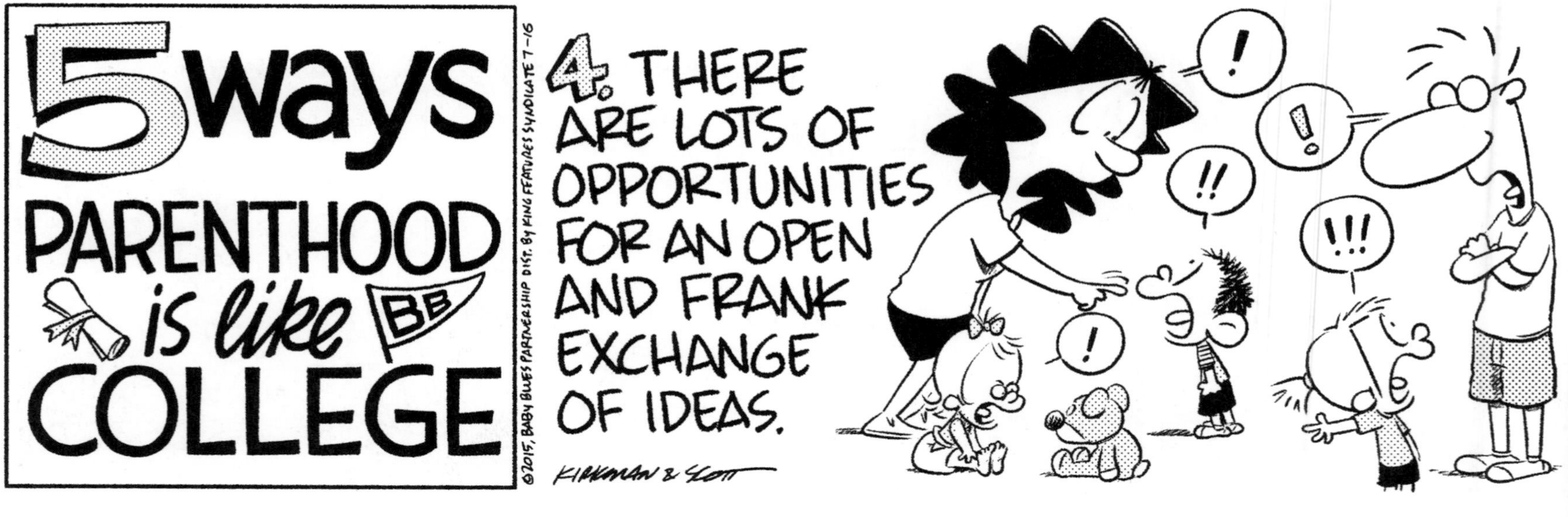
5 ways PARENTHOOD is like COLLEGE
BB
©2015, BABY BLUES PARTNERSHIP DIST. BY KING FEATURES SYNDICATE 7-16
4. THERE ARE LOTS OF OPPORTUNITIES FOR AN OPEN AND FRANK EXCHANGE OF IDEAS.
!
!
!!
!!!
!
KIRKMAN & SCOTT

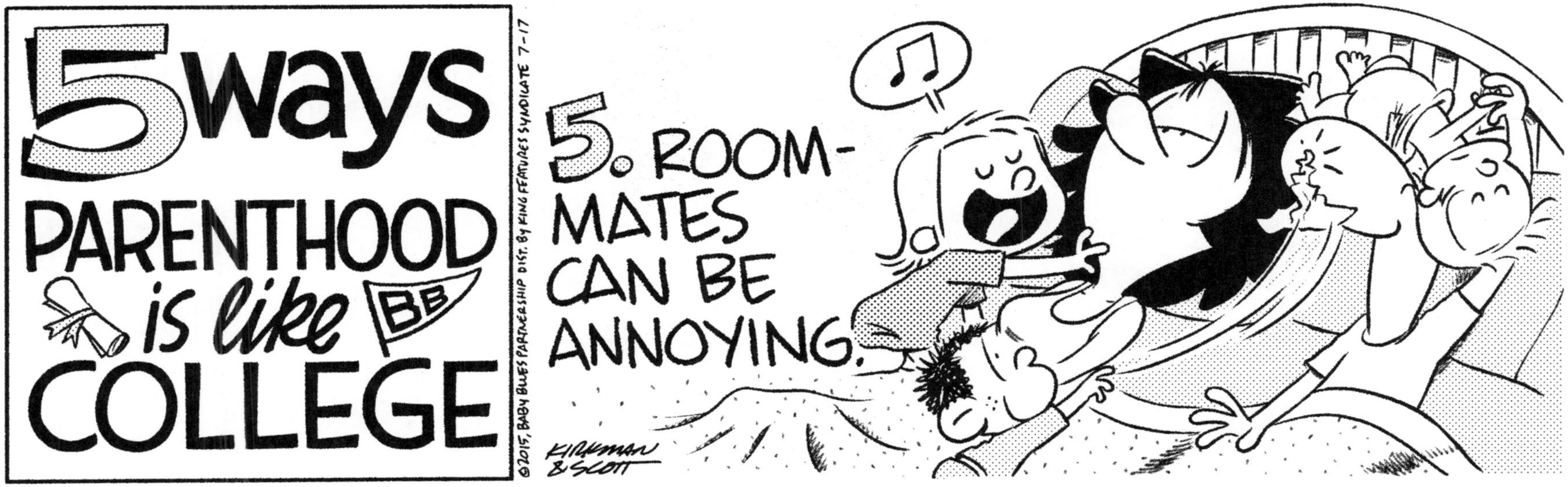
5 ways
PARENTHOOD
is like
COLLEGE
BB
©2015, BABY BLUES PARTNERSHIP DIST. BY KING FEATURES SYNDICATE 7-17
5. ROOM-
MATES
CAN BE
ANNOYING.
KIRKMAN
& SCOTT

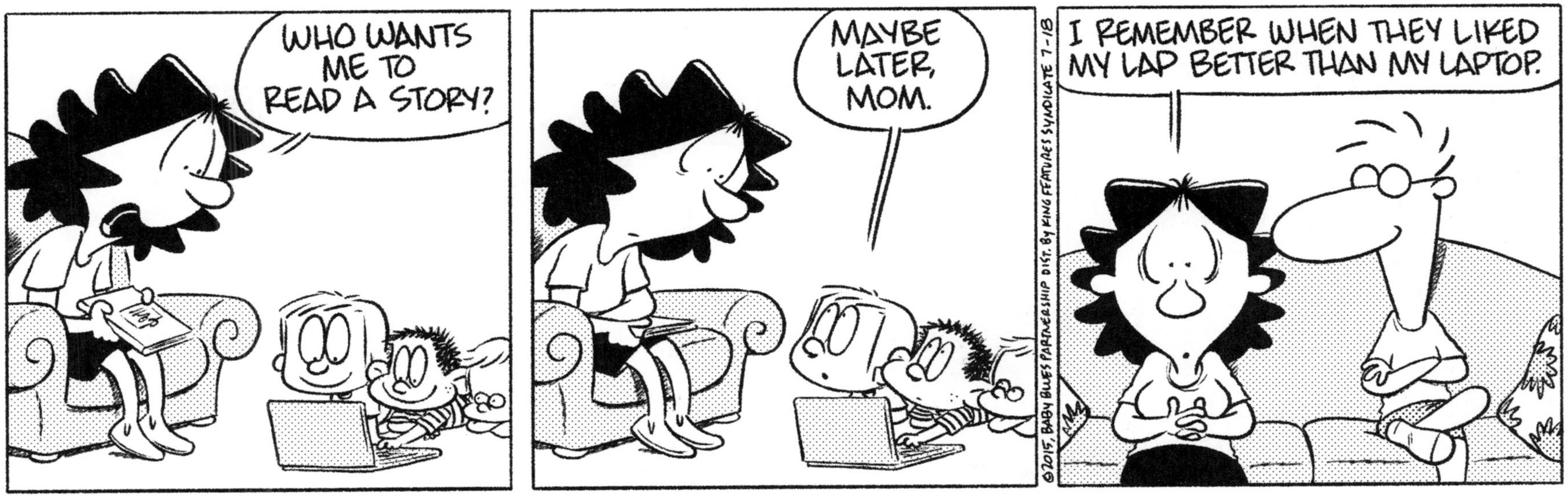
WHO WANTS
ME TO
READ A STORY?
MAYBE
LATER,
MOM.
©2015, BABY BLUES PARTNERSHIP DIST. BY KING FEATURES SYNDICATE 7-18
I REMEMBER WHEN THEY LIKED
MY LAP BETTER THAN MY LAPTOP.

Rick: This one makes me sad for Wanda.

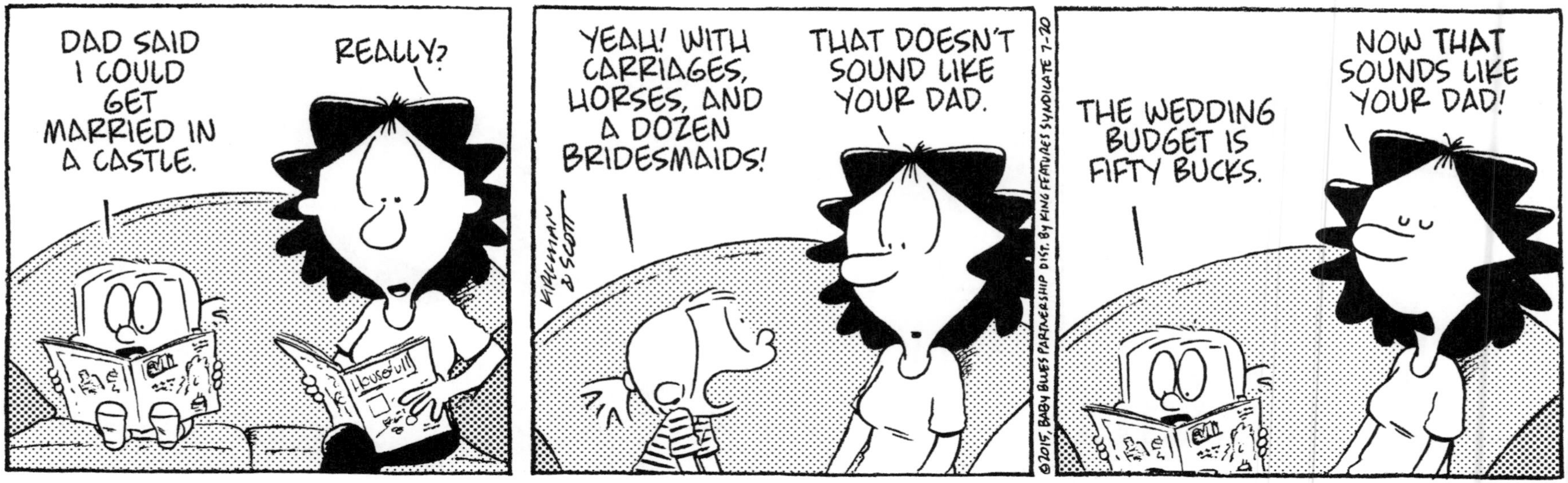
DAD SAID I COULD GET MARRIED IN A CASTLE.
REALLY?
YEAH! WITH CARRIAGES, HORSES, AND A DOZEN BRIDESMAIDS!
THAT DOESN'T SOUND LIKE YOUR DAD.
KIRKMAN & SCOTT
©2015, BABY BLUES PARTNERSHIP DIST. BY KING FEATURES SYNDICATE 7-20
THE WEDDING BUDGET IS FIFTY BUCKS.
NOW THAT SOUNDS LIKE YOUR DAD!

Jerry: Last summer Rick's father became terminally ill. Rick was overwhelmed with the responsibilities of helping his parents through that very difficult time, so we had to get creative.

Rick: All I can say is that Jerry's handling of this period of work was heroic in my eyes. He saved my deadline butt. I can't thank you enough, partner!

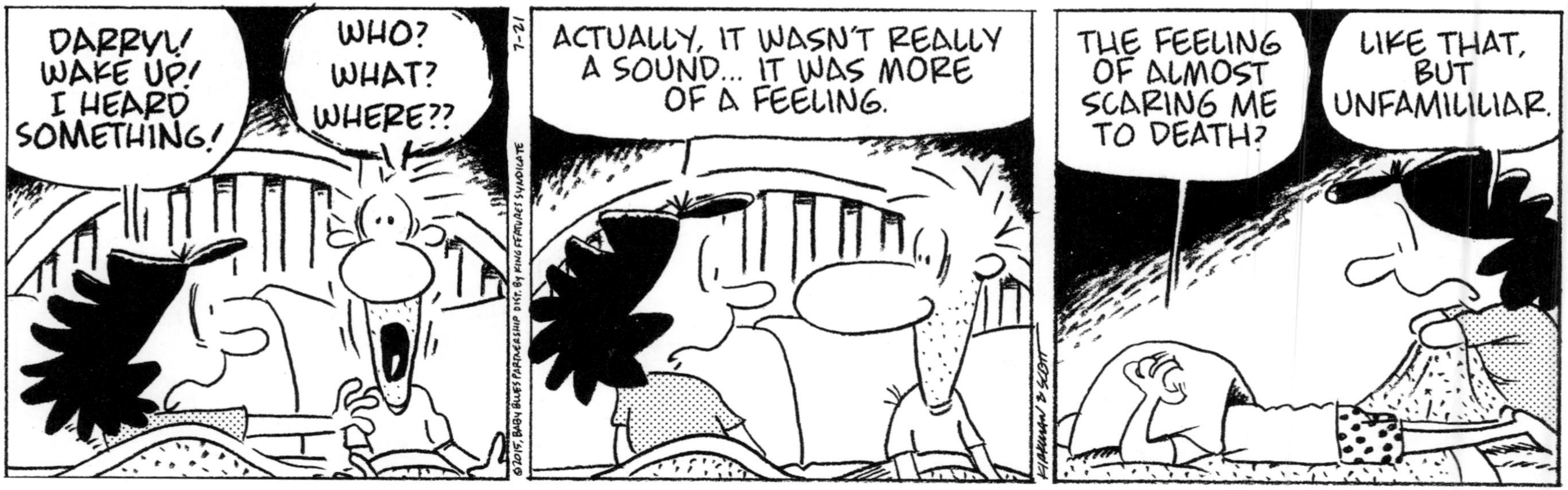
DARRYL! WAKE UP! I HEARD SOMETHING!
WHO? WHAT? WHERE??
7-21
©2015, BABY BLUES PARTNERSHIP DIST. BY KING FEATURES SYNDICATE
ACTUALLY, IT WASN'T REALLY A SOUND... IT WAS MORE OF A FEELING.
KIRKMAN & SCOTT
THE FEELING OF ALMOST SCARING ME TO DEATH?
LIKE THAT, BUT UNFAMILILIAR.

Jerry: I suppose I could have drawn the strip, but the differences in the art would have been glaringly apparent. Many of the strips on the next few pages are new ideas, but use Rick's artwork from older strips.

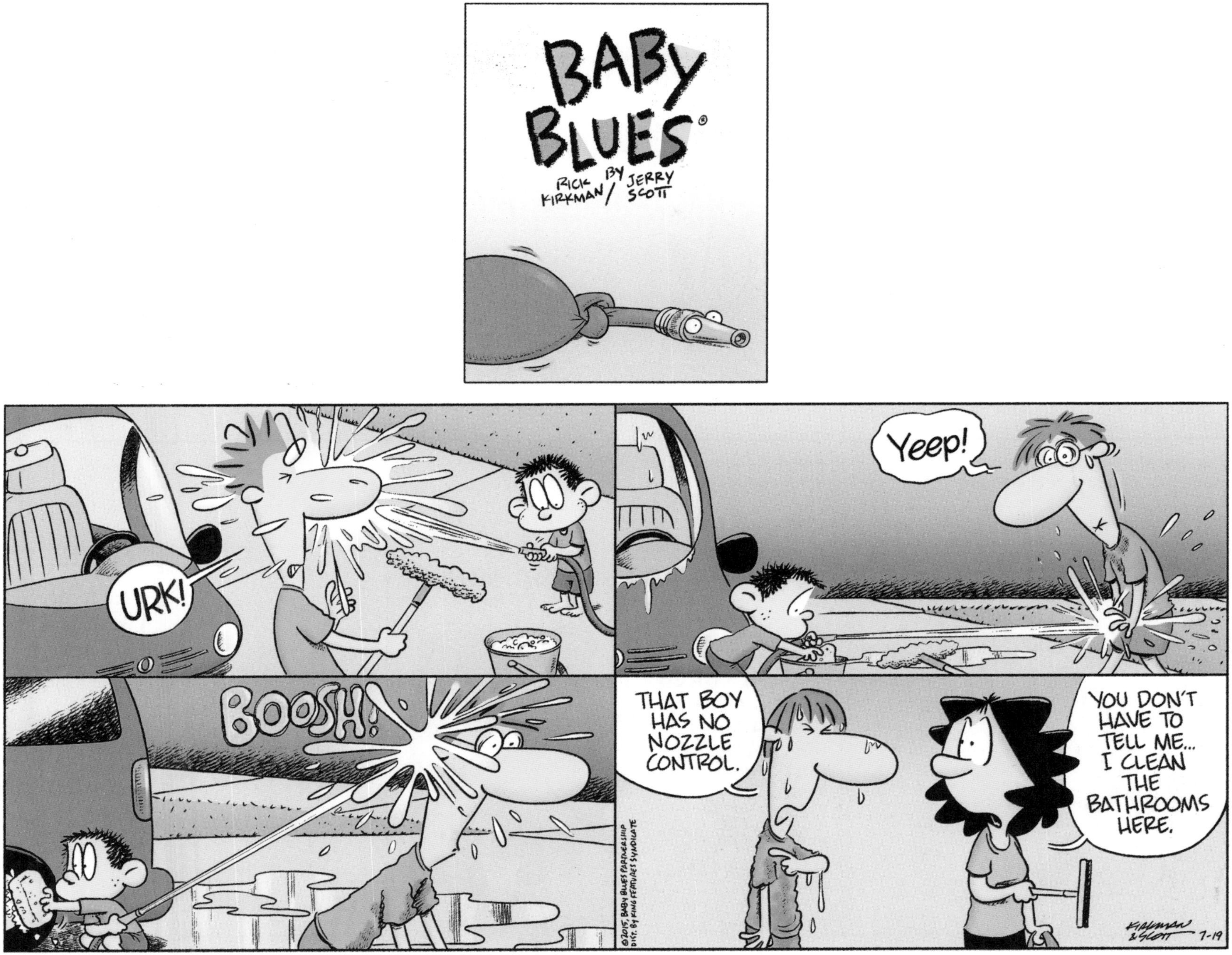
BABY BLUES®
BY RICK KIRKMAN / JERRY SCOTT
URK!
Yeep!
BOOSH!
THAT BOY HAS NO NOZZLE CONTROL.
YOU DON'T HAVE TO TELL ME... I CLEAN THE BATHROOMS HERE.
©2015, BABY BLUES PARTNERSHIP
DIST. BY KING FEATURES SYNDICATE
KIRKMAN & SCOTT 7-19

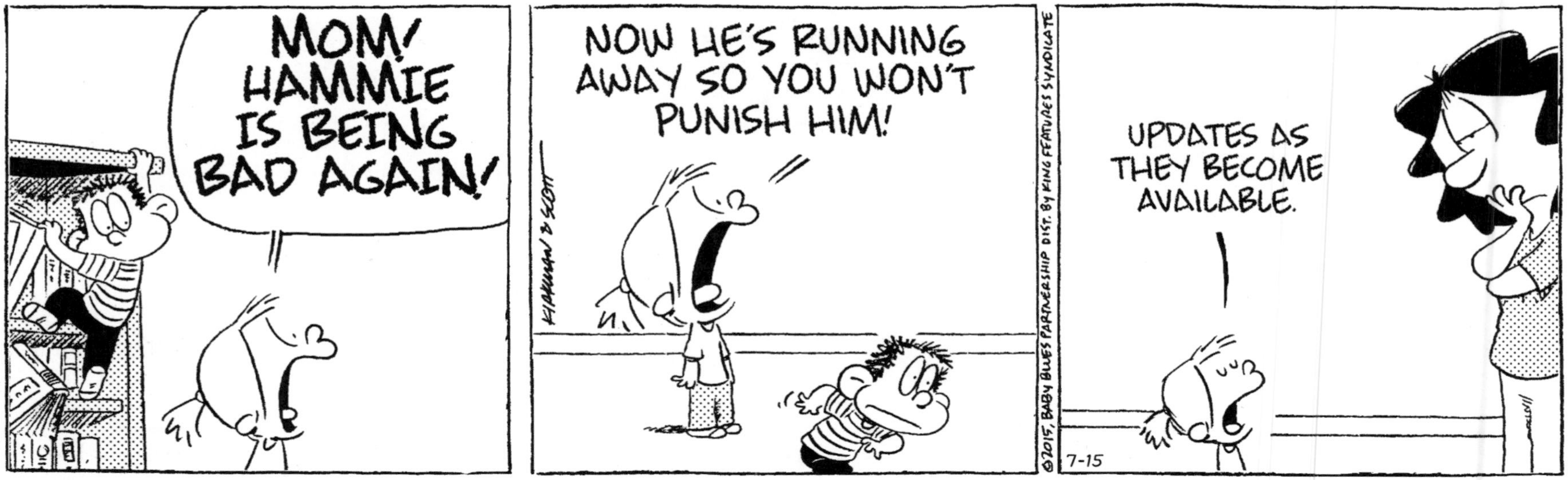
MOM! HAMMIE IS BEING BAD AGAIN!
NOW HE'S RUNNING AWAY SO YOU WON'T PUNISH HIM!
UPDATES AS THEY BECOME AVAILABLE.
KIRKMAN & SCOTT
©2015, BABY BLUES PARTNERSHIP DIST. BY KING FEATURES SYNDICATE
7-15

Jerry: I went through older strips, ignoring the dialogue and concentrating on the artwork. Once in a while the art in a particular strip would spark a new gag idea.

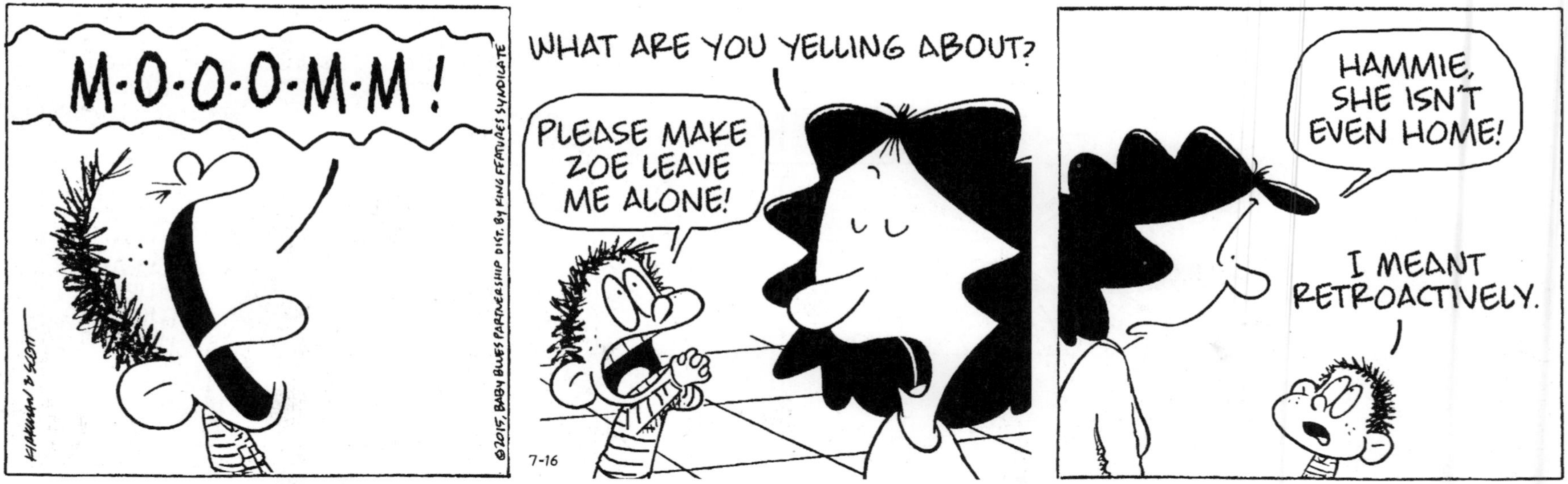
M-O-O-O-M-M!
WHAT ARE YOU YELLING ABOUT?
PLEASE MAKE ZOE LEAVE ME ALONE!
HAMMIE, SHE ISN'T EVEN HOME!
I MEANT RETROACTIVELY.
KIRKMAN & SCOTT
©2015, BABY BLUES PARTNERSHIP DIST. BY KING FEATURES SYNDICATE
7-16

Jerry: Sometimes the new idea worked with all of the art in the strip, and sometimes I had to dig around for drawings of the characters in other poses or emotion.

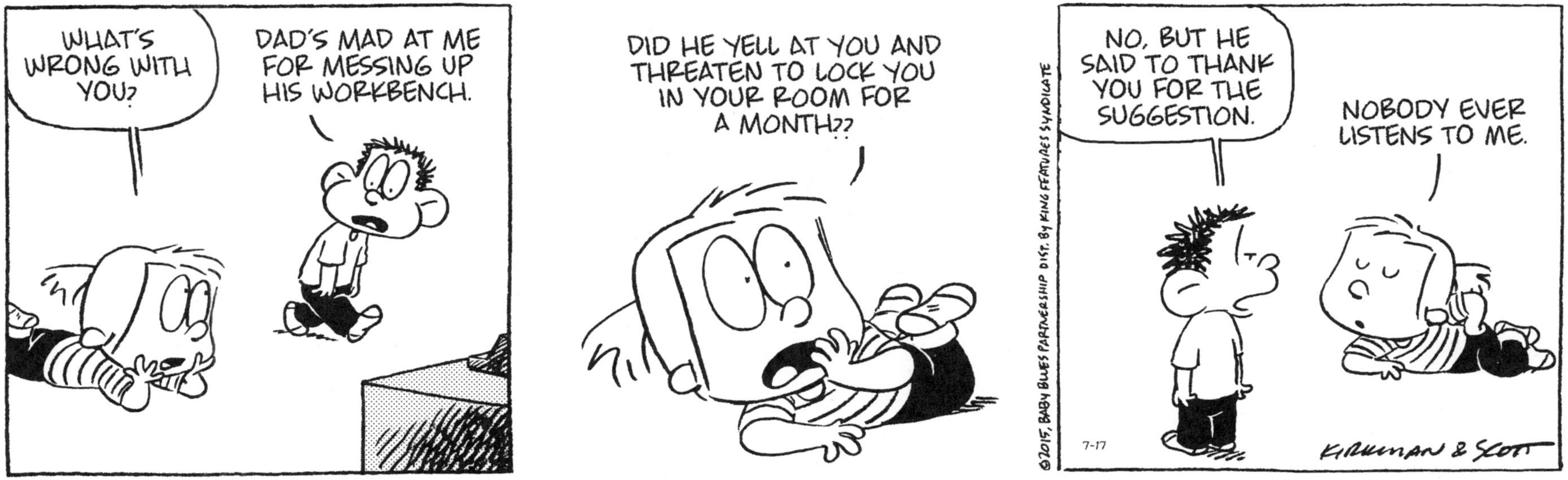
WHAT'S WRONG WITH YOU?
DAD'S MAD AT ME FOR MESSING UP HIS WORKBENCH.
DID HE YELL AT YOU AND THREATEN TO LOCK YOU IN YOUR ROOM FOR A MONTH??
©2015, BABY BLUES PARTNERSHIP DIST. BY KING FEATURES SYNDICATE
NO, BUT HE SAID TO THANK YOU FOR THE SUGGESTION.
NOBODY EVER LISTENS TO ME.
7-17
KIRKMAN & SCOTT

Jerry: I scanned Rick's lettering from previous *Baby Blues* strips and made it into two fonts: Kirkman Regular and Kirkman Bold. With a lot of scanning and a little Photoshop magic, I was able to write and assemble a few weeks' worth of strips and give Rick the time he needed.

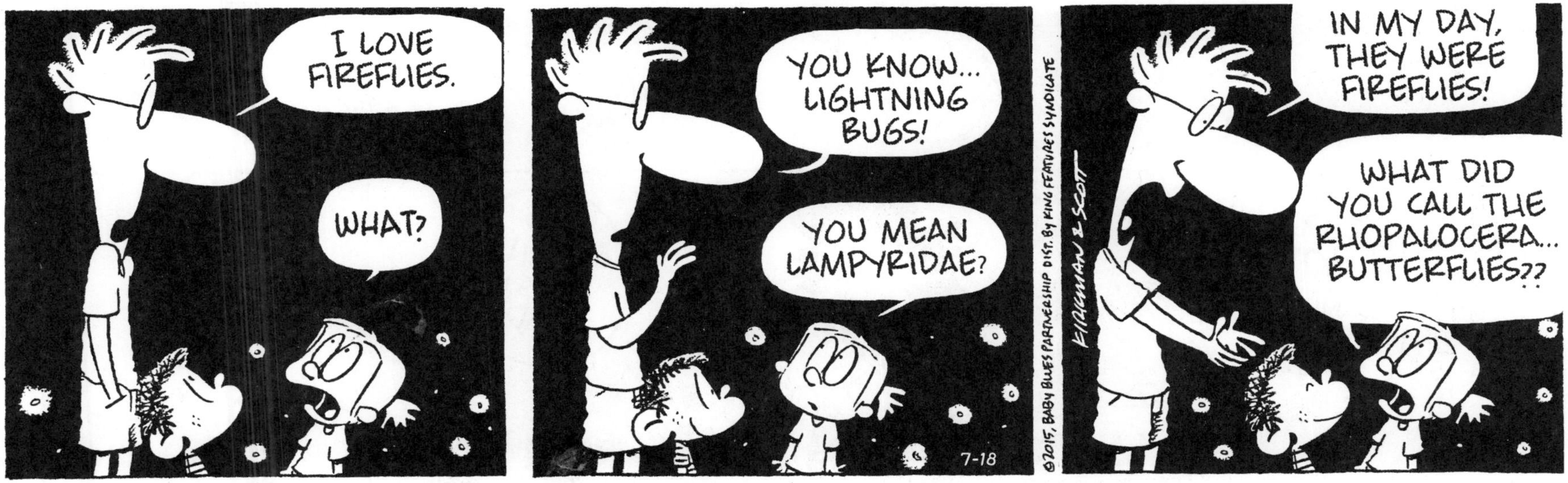
I LOVE FIREFLIES.
WHAT?
YOU KNOW... LIGHTNING BUGS!
YOU MEAN LAMPYRIDAE?
7-18
©2015, BABY BLUES PARTNERSHIP DIST. BY KING FEATURES SYNDICATE
KIRKMAN & SCOTT
IN MY DAY, THEY WERE FIREFLIES!
WHAT DID YOU CALL THE RHOPALOCERA... BUTTERFLIES??

Jerry: The experience gave me a new appreciation for how much personal expression is involved in creating a daily comic strip. Reusing existing art is not a sustainable method for us. *Baby Blues* is at its best when both of us contribute our unique talents to the creation of every strip.

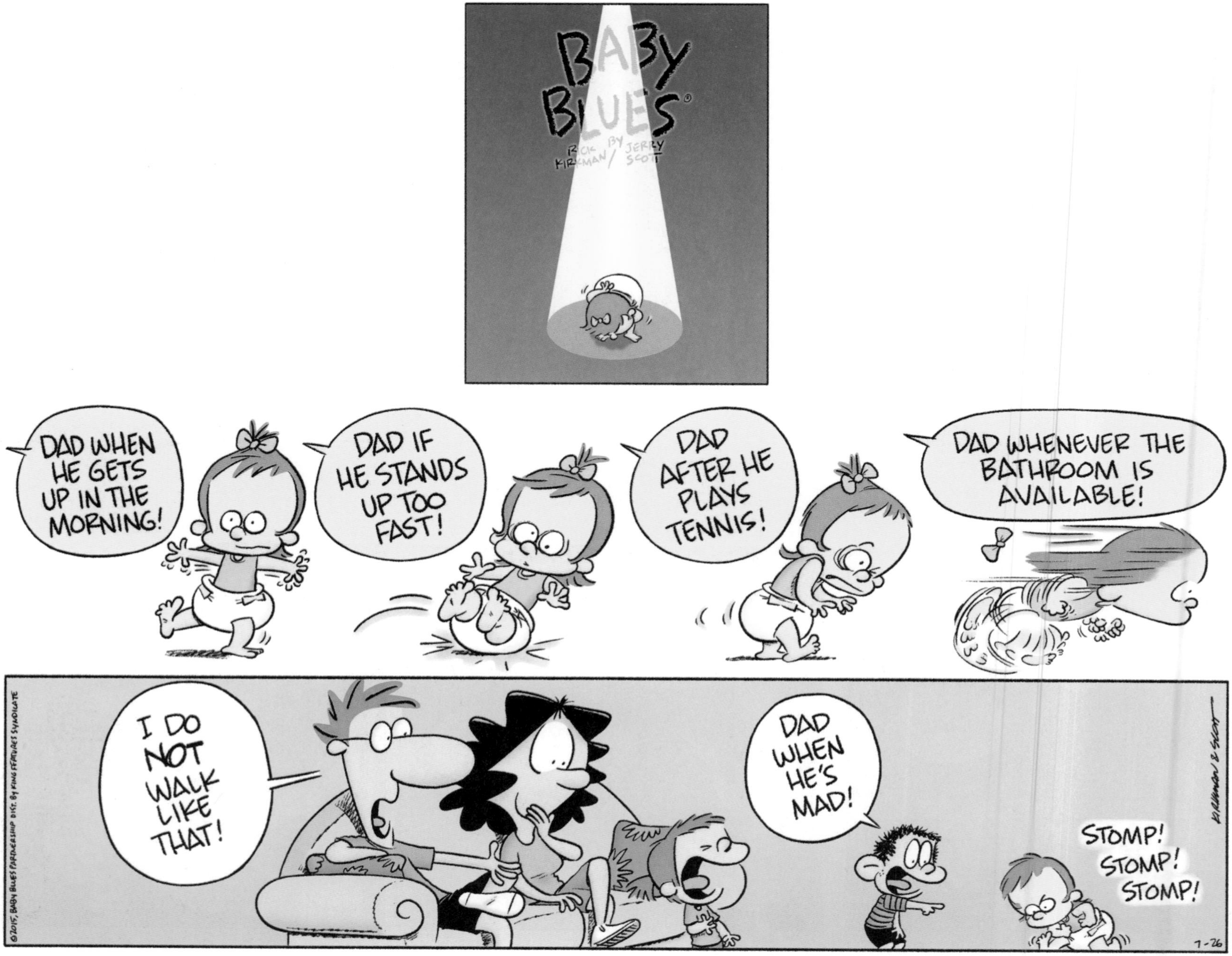
BABY BLUES®
BY RICK KIRKMAN / JERRY SCOTT
DAD WHEN HE GETS UP IN THE MORNING!
DAD IF HE STANDS UP TOO FAST!
DAD AFTER HE PLAYS TENNIS!
DAD WHENEVER THE BATHROOM IS AVAILABLE!
I DO NOT WALK LIKE THAT!
DAD WHEN HE'S MAD!
STOMP! STOMP! STOMP!
©2015, BABY BLUES PARTNERSHIP DIST. BY KING FEATURES SYNDICATE
KIRKMAN & SCOTT
7-26

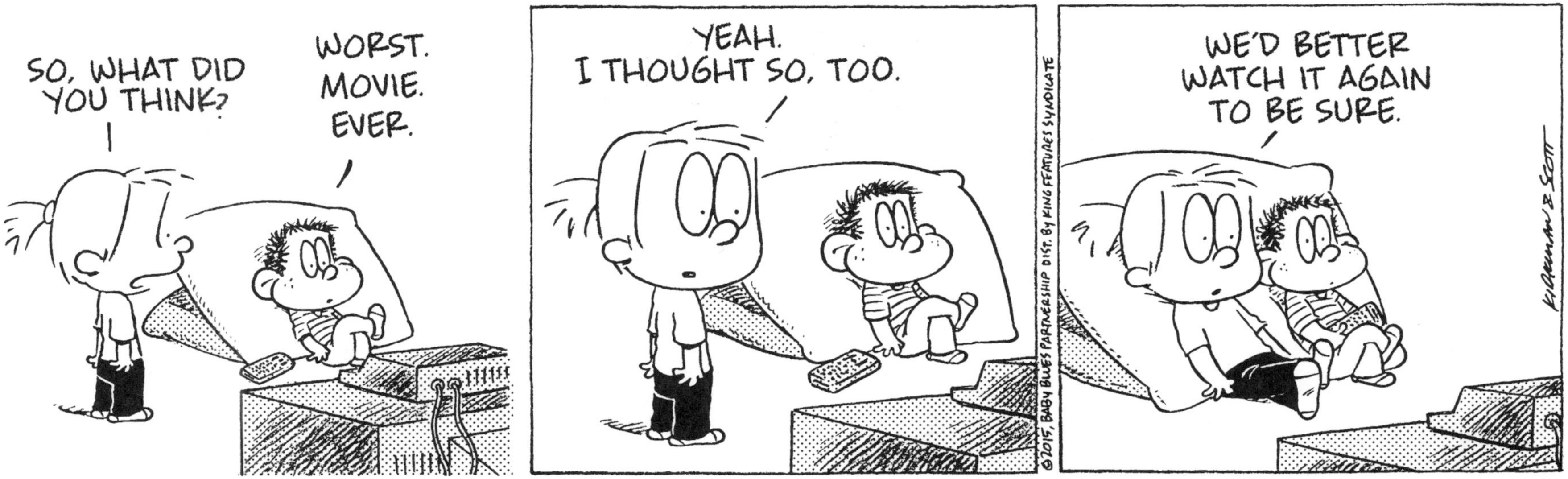
SO, WHAT DID YOU THINK?
WORST. MOVIE. EVER.
YEAH. I THOUGHT SO, TOO.
©2015, BABY BLUES PARTNERSHIP DIST. BY KING FEATURES SYNDICATE
WE'D BETTER WATCH IT AGAIN TO BE SURE.
KIRKMAN & SCOTT

Rick: Another week of the hybrid strips that Jerry put together, saving me for the second week in a row.

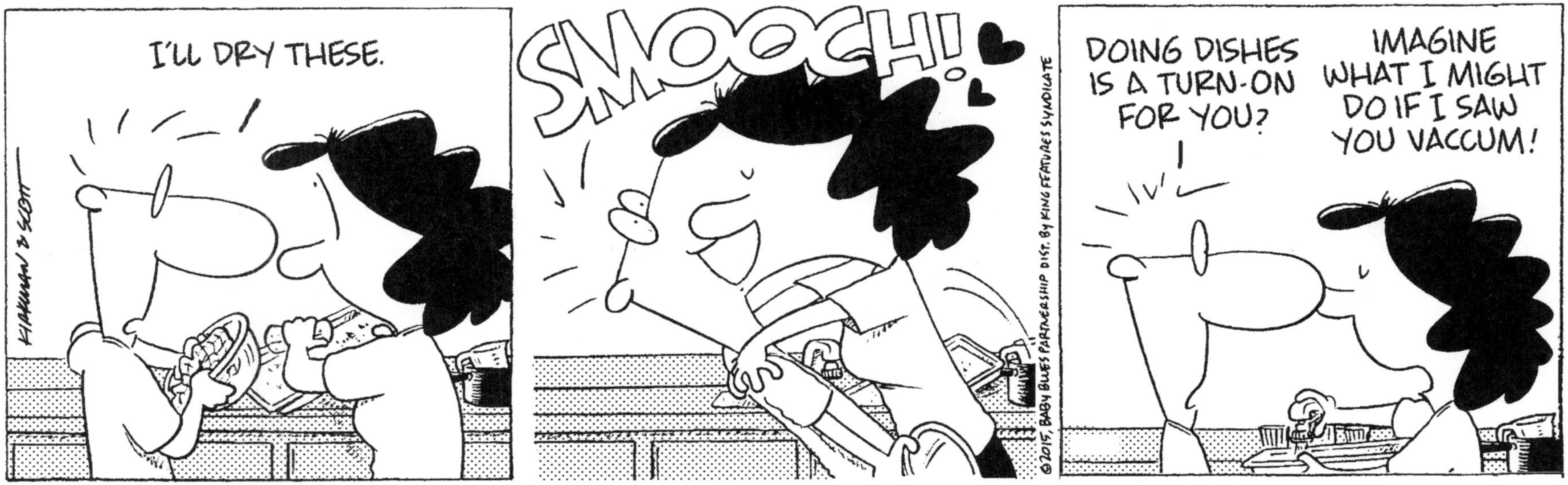
I'LL DRY THESE.
KIRKMAN & SCOTT
SMOOCH!
©2015, BABY BLUES PARTNERSHIP DIST. BY KING FEATURES SYNDICATE
DOING DISHES IS A TURN-ON FOR YOU?
IMAGINE WHAT I MIGHT DO IF I SAW YOU VACCUM!

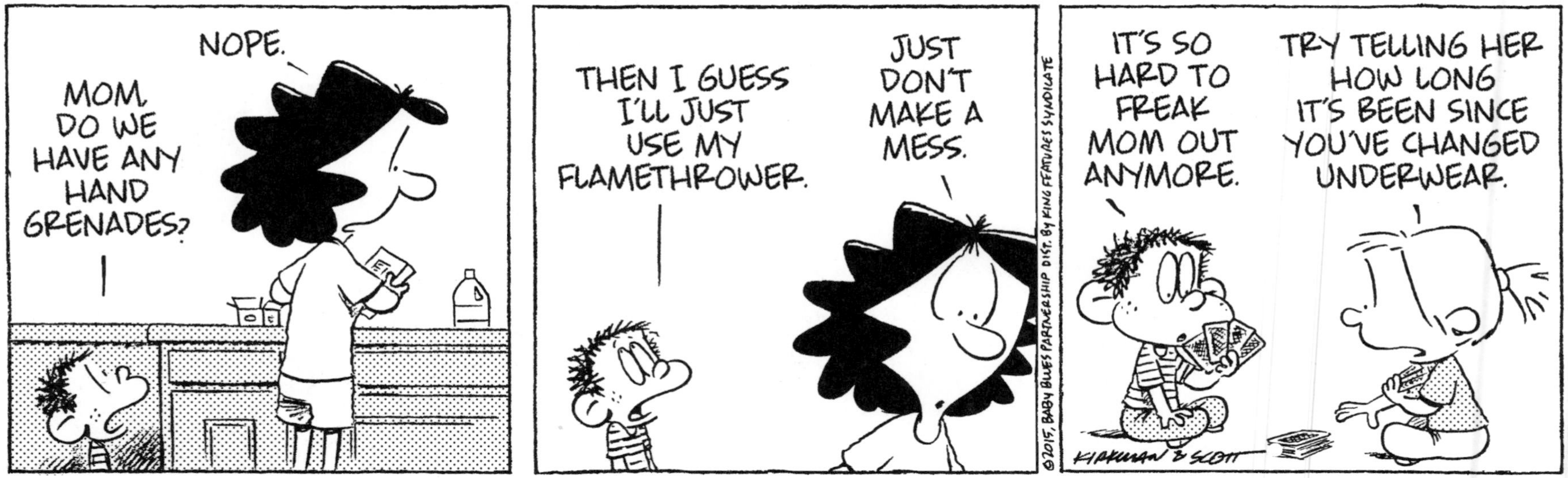
MOM, DO WE HAVE ANY HAND GRENADES?
NOPE.
THEN I GUESS I'LL JUST USE MY FLAMETHROWER.
JUST DON'T MAKE A MESS.
©2015, BABY BLUES PARTNERSHIP DIST. BY KING FEATURES SYNDICATE
IT'S SO HARD TO FREAK MOM OUT ANYMORE.
TRY TELLING HER HOW LONG IT'S BEEN SINCE YOU'VE CHANGED UNDERWEAR.
KIRKMAN & SCOTT

Rick: One of the best opening lines, ever.

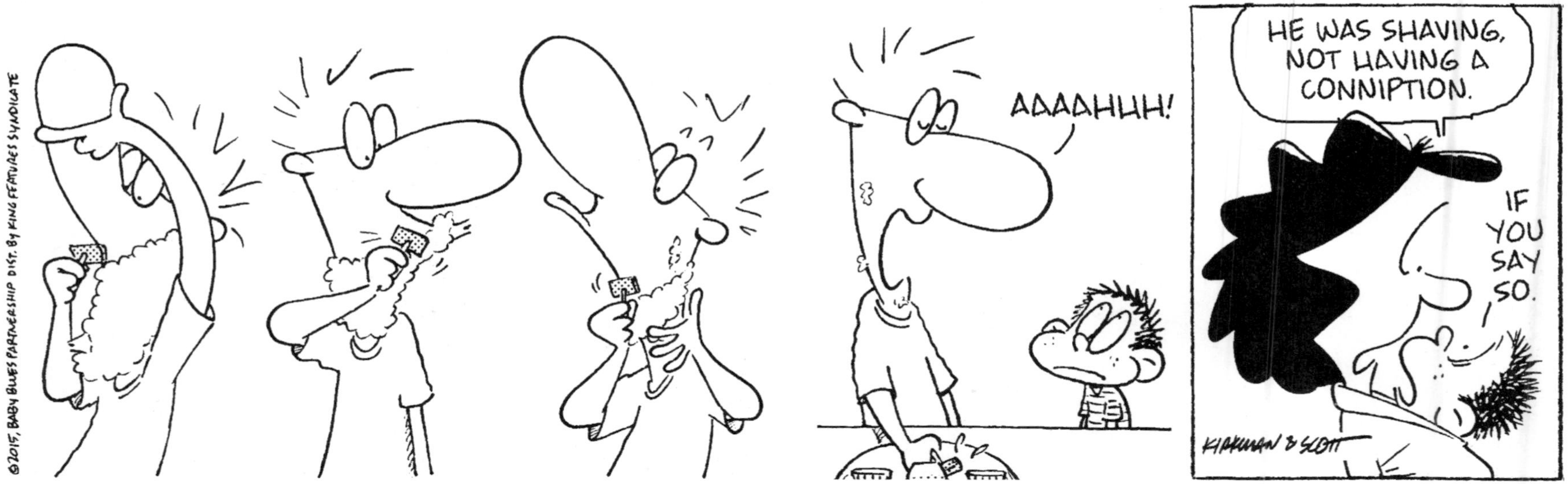
©2015, BABY BLUES PARTNERSHIP DIST. BY KING FEATURES SYNDICATE
AAAAHHH!
HE WAS SHAVING, NOT HAVING A CONNIPTION.
IF YOU SAY SO.
KIRKMAN & SCOTT

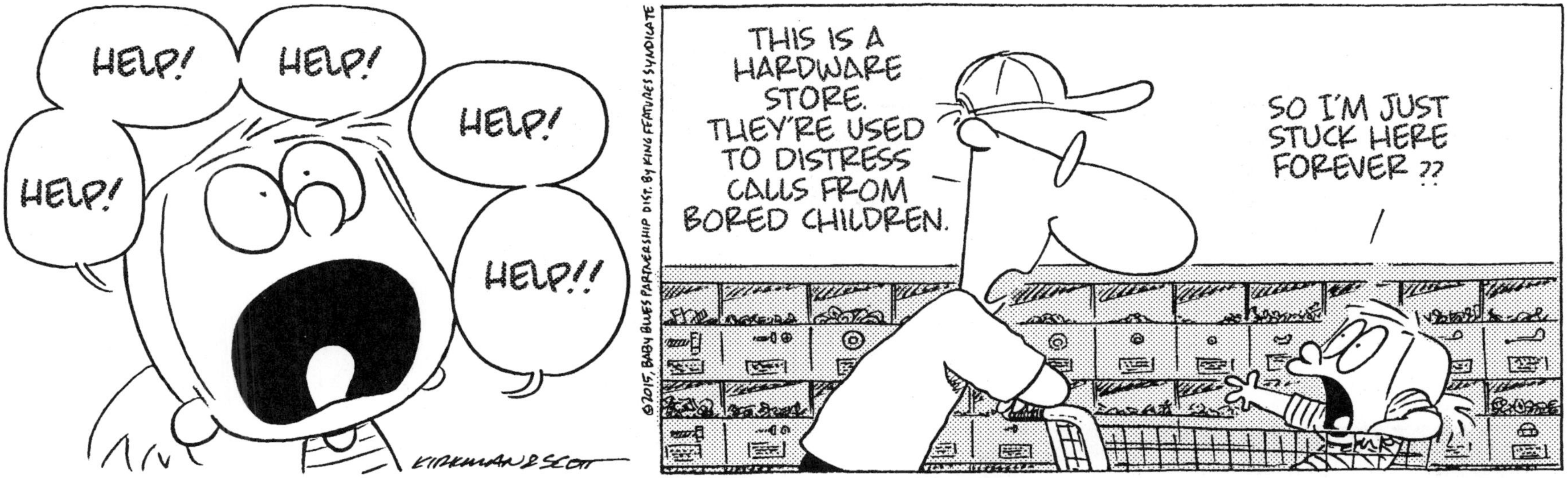
HELP!
HELP!
HELP!
HELP!
HELP!!
KIRKMAN & SCOTT
©2015, BABY BLUES PARTNERSHIP DIST. BY KING FEATURES SYNDICATE
THIS IS A HARDWARE STORE. THEY'RE USED TO DISTRESS CALLS FROM BORED CHILDREN.
SO I'M JUST STUCK HERE FOREVER ??

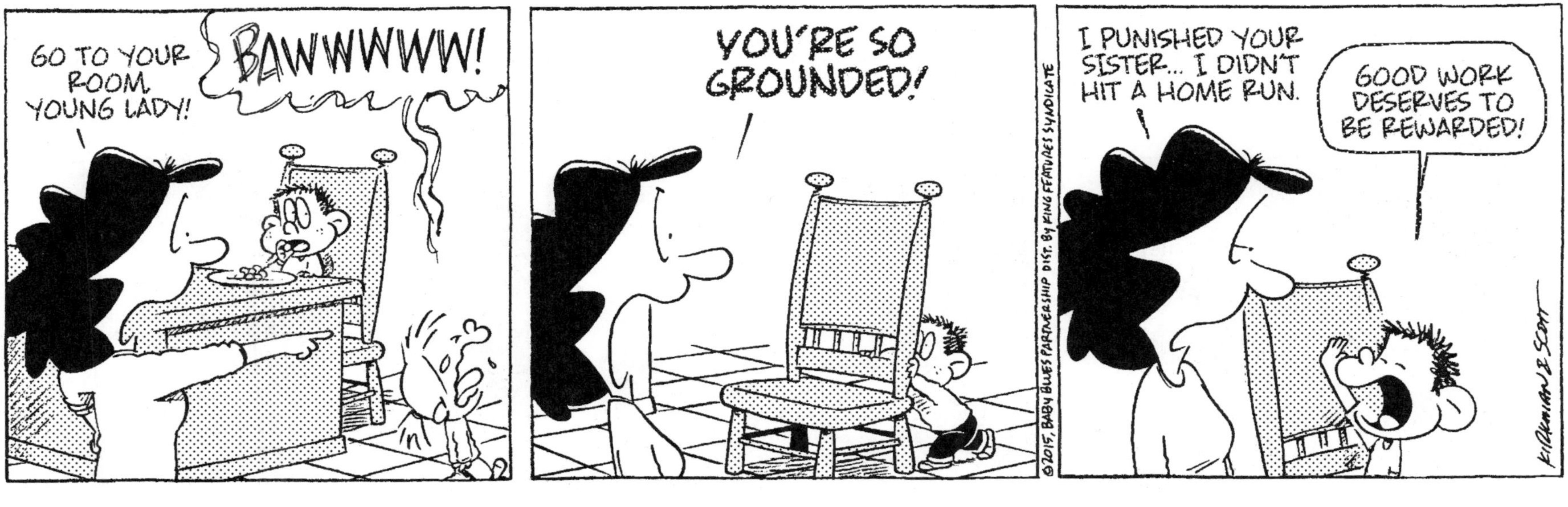
GO TO YOUR ROOM YOUNG LADY!
BAWWWWWW!
YOU'RE SO GROUNDED!
©2015, BABY BLUES PARTNERSHIP DIST. BY KING FEATURES SYNDICATE
I PUNISHED YOUR SISTER... I DIDN'T HIT A HOME RUN.
GOOD WORK DESERVES TO BE REWARDED!
KIRKMAN & SCOTT

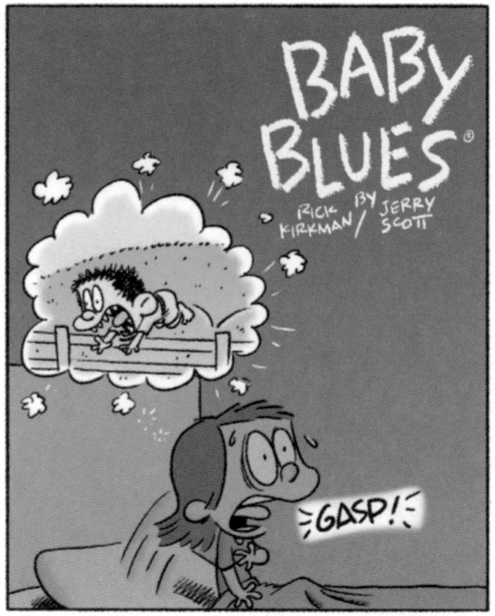
BABY BLUES®
BY RICK KIRKMAN / JERRY SCOTT
GASP!

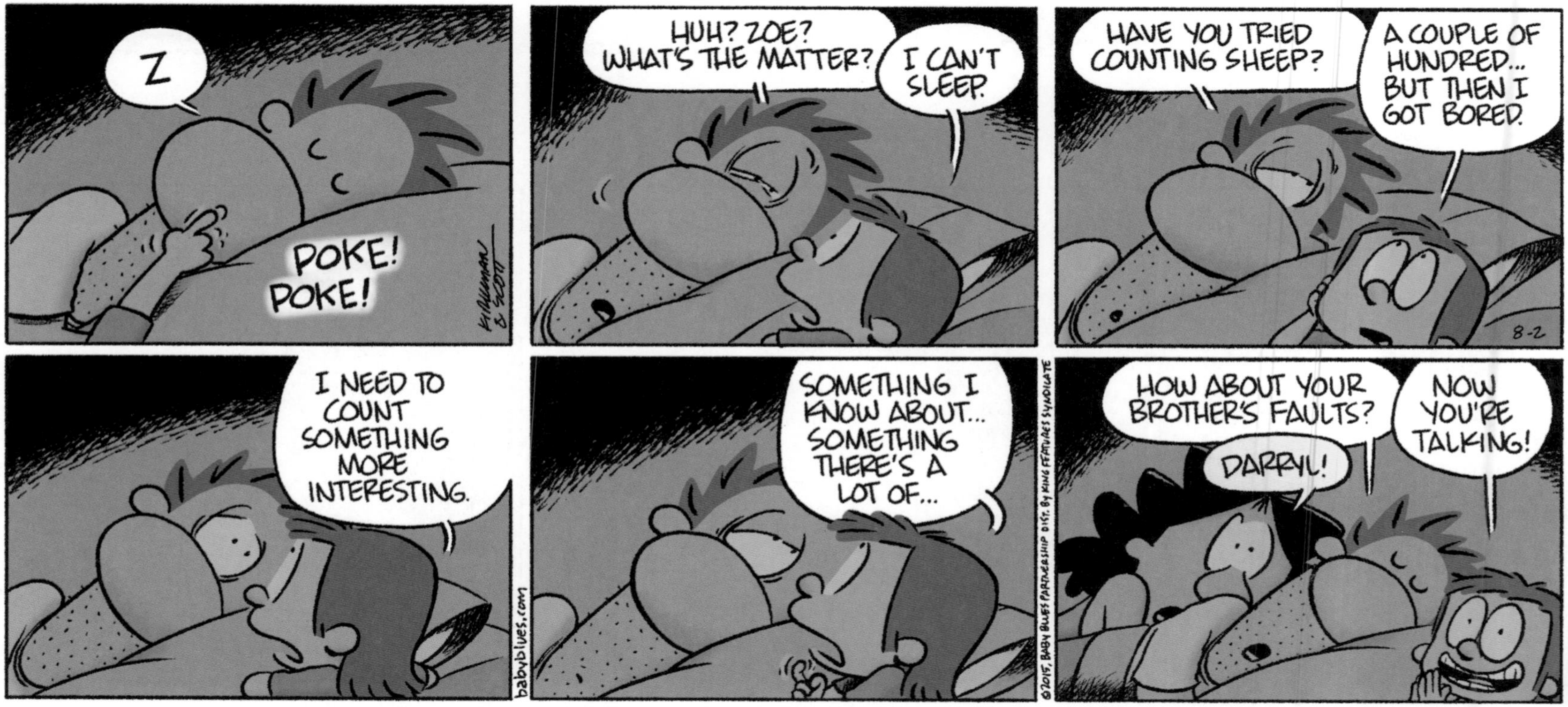
Z
POKE! POKE!
KIRKMAN & SCOTT
HUH? ZOE? WHAT'S THE MATTER?
I CAN'T SLEEP.
HAVE YOU TRIED COUNTING SHEEP?
A COUPLE OF HUNDRED... BUT THEN I GOT BORED.
8-2
I NEED TO COUNT SOMETHING MORE INTERESTING.
babyblues.com
SOMETHING I KNOW ABOUT... SOMETHING THERE'S A LOT OF...
©2015, BABY BLUES PARTNERSHIP DIST. BY KING FEATURES SYNDICATE
HOW ABOUT YOUR BROTHER'S FAULTS?
DARRYL!
NOW YOU'RE TALKING!

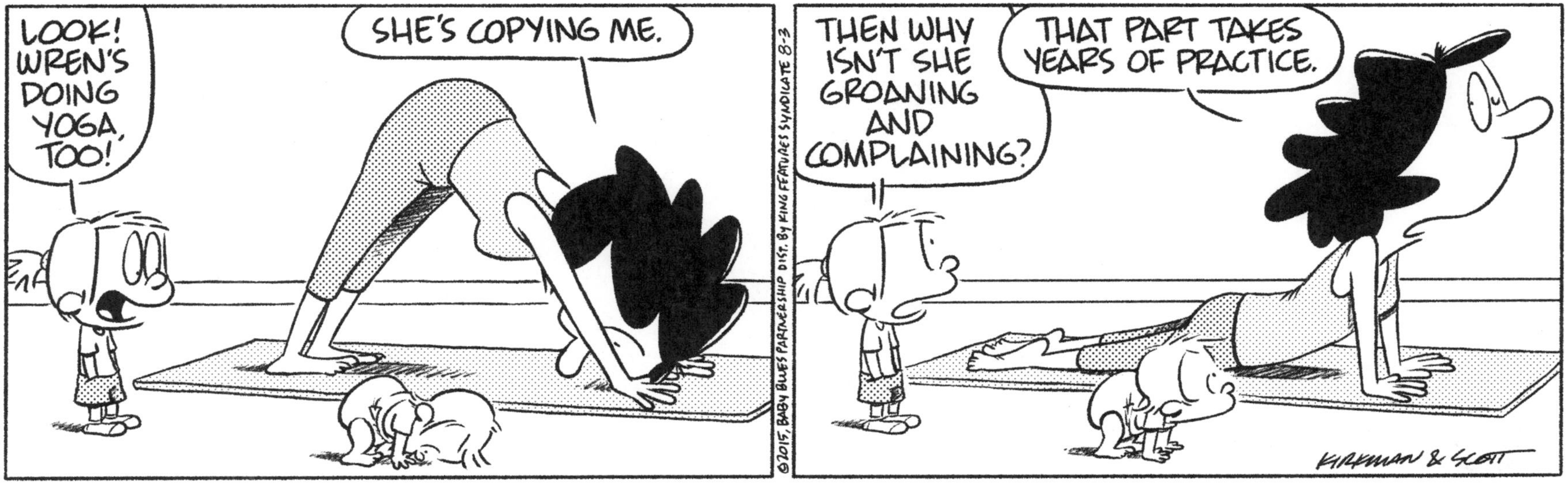
LOOK! WREN'S DOING YOGA, TOO!
SHE'S COPYING ME.
©2015, BABY BLUES PARTNERSHIP DIST. BY KING FEATURES SYNDICATE 8-3
THEN WHY ISN'T SHE GROANING AND COMPLAINING?
THAT PART TAKES YEARS OF PRACTICE.
KIRKMAN & SCOTT

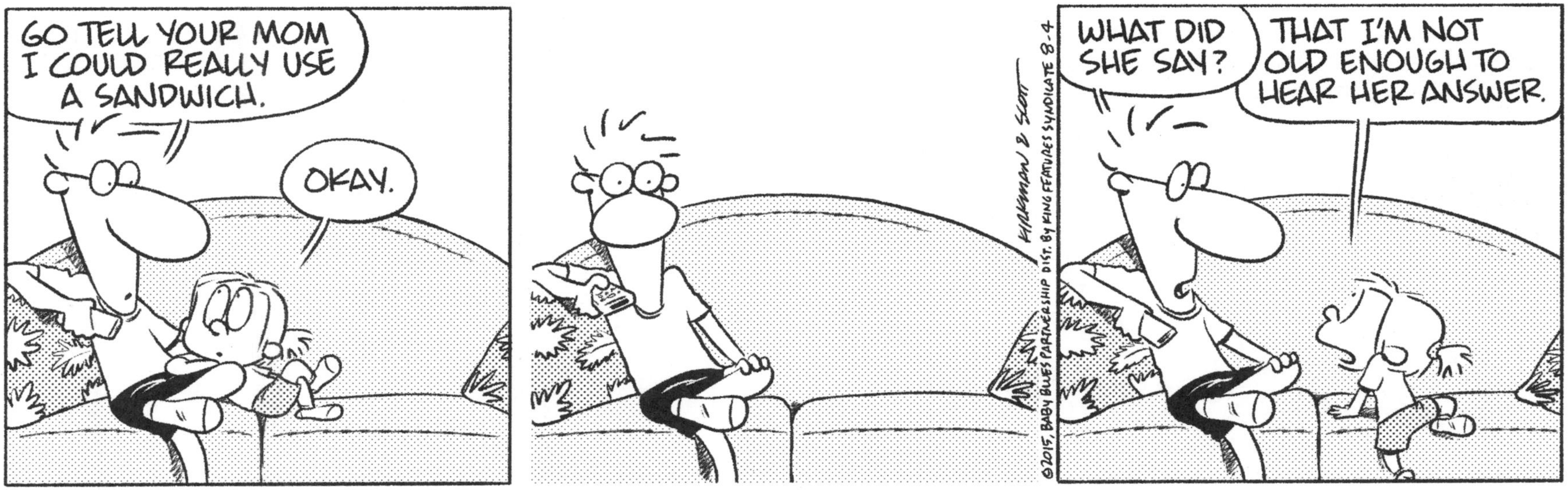
GO TELL YOUR MOM I COULD REALLY USE A SANDWICH.
OKAY.
KIRKMAN & SCOTT
©2015, BABY BLUES PARTNERSHIP DIST. BY KING FEATURES SYNDICATE 8-4
WHAT DID SHE SAY?
THAT I'M NOT OLD ENOUGH TO HEAR HER ANSWER.

Rick: He needs to be Gibbs-smacked.

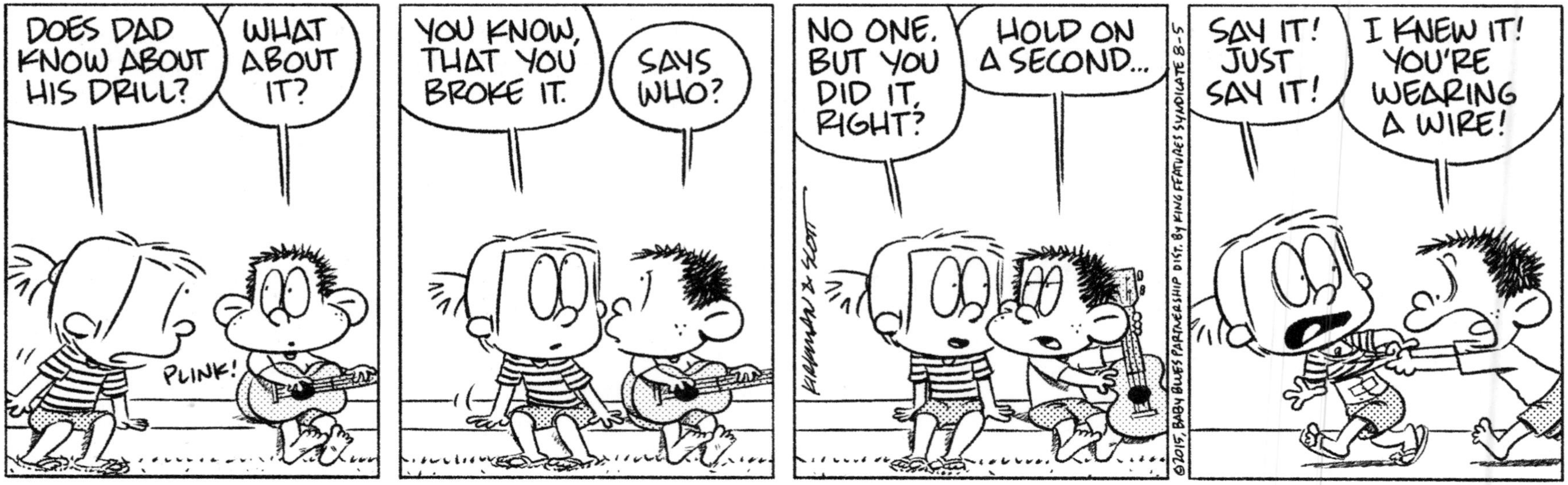
DOES DAD KNOW ABOUT HIS DRILL?
WHAT ABOUT IT?
PLINK!
YOU KNOW, THAT YOU BROKE IT.
SAYS WHO?
NO ONE. BUT YOU DID IT, RIGHT?
HOLD ON A SECOND...
SAY IT! JUST SAY IT!
I KNEW IT! YOU'RE WEARING A WIRE!
KIRKMAN & SCOTT
©2015, BABY BLUES PARTNERSHIP DIST. BY KING FEATURES SYNDICATE 8-5

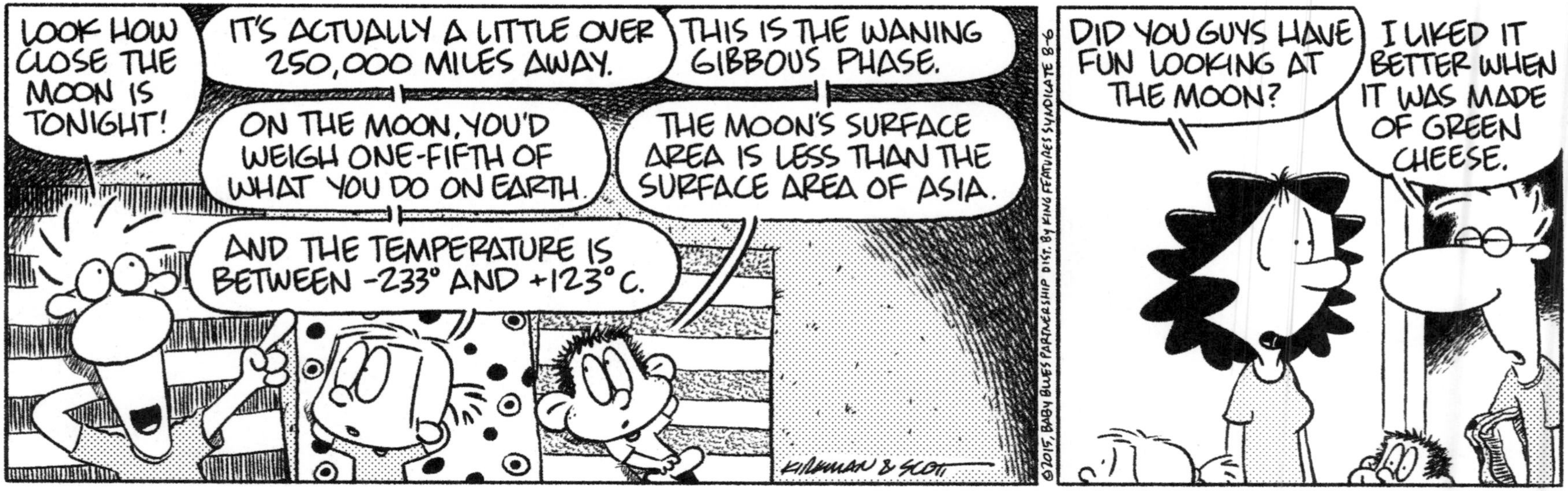
LOOK HOW CLOSE THE MOON IS TONIGHT!
IT'S ACTUALLY A LITTLE OVER 250,000 MILES AWAY.
ON THE MOON, YOU'D WEIGH ONE-FIFTH OF WHAT YOU DO ON EARTH.
AND THE TEMPERATURE IS BETWEEN -233° AND +123° C.
THIS IS THE WANING GIBBOUS PHASE.
THE MOON'S SURFACE AREA IS LESS THAN THE SURFACE AREA OF ASIA.
KIRKMAN & SCOTT
©2015, BABY BLUES PARTNERSHIP DIST. BY KING FEATURES SYNDICATE 8-6
DID YOU GUYS HAVE FUN LOOKING AT THE MOON?
I LIKED IT BETTER WHEN IT WAS MADE OF GREEN CHEESE.

Rick: Leave it to facts to ruin the moment.

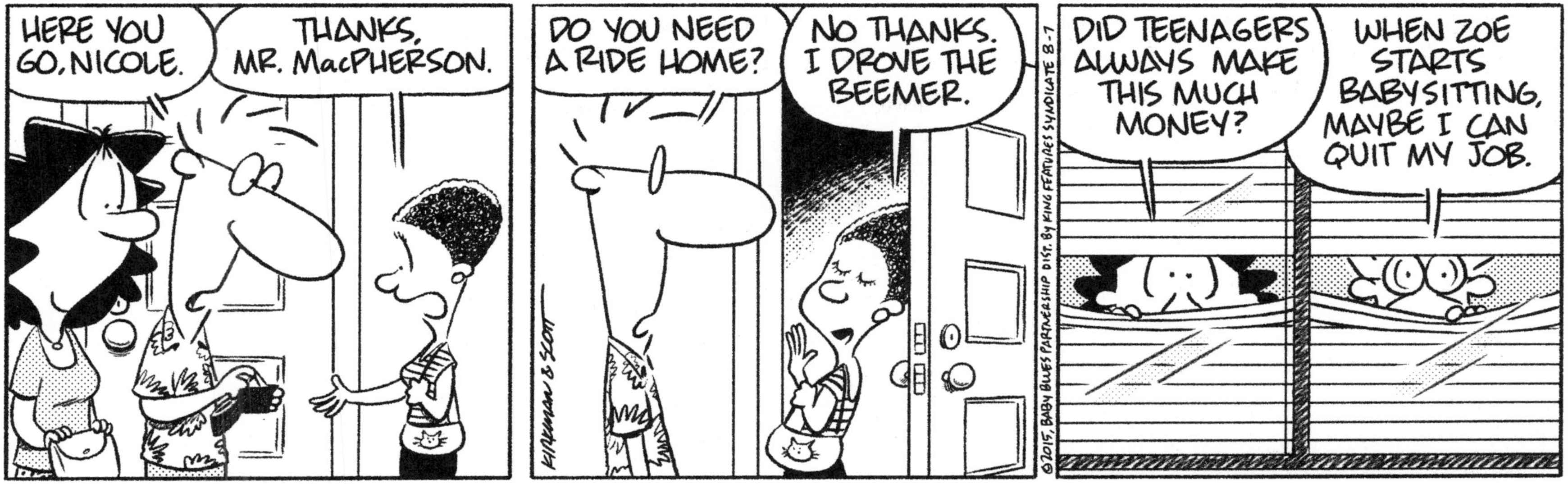
HERE YOU GO, NICOLE.
THANKS, MR. MacPHERSON.
DO YOU NEED A RIDE HOME?
NO THANKS. I DROVE THE BEEMER.
KIRKMAN & SCOTT
©2015, BABY BLUES PARTNERSHIP DIST. BY KING FEATURES SYNDICATE 8-7
DID TEENAGERS ALWAYS MAKE THIS MUCH MONEY?
WHEN ZOE STARTS BABYSITTING, MAYBE I CAN QUIT MY JOB.

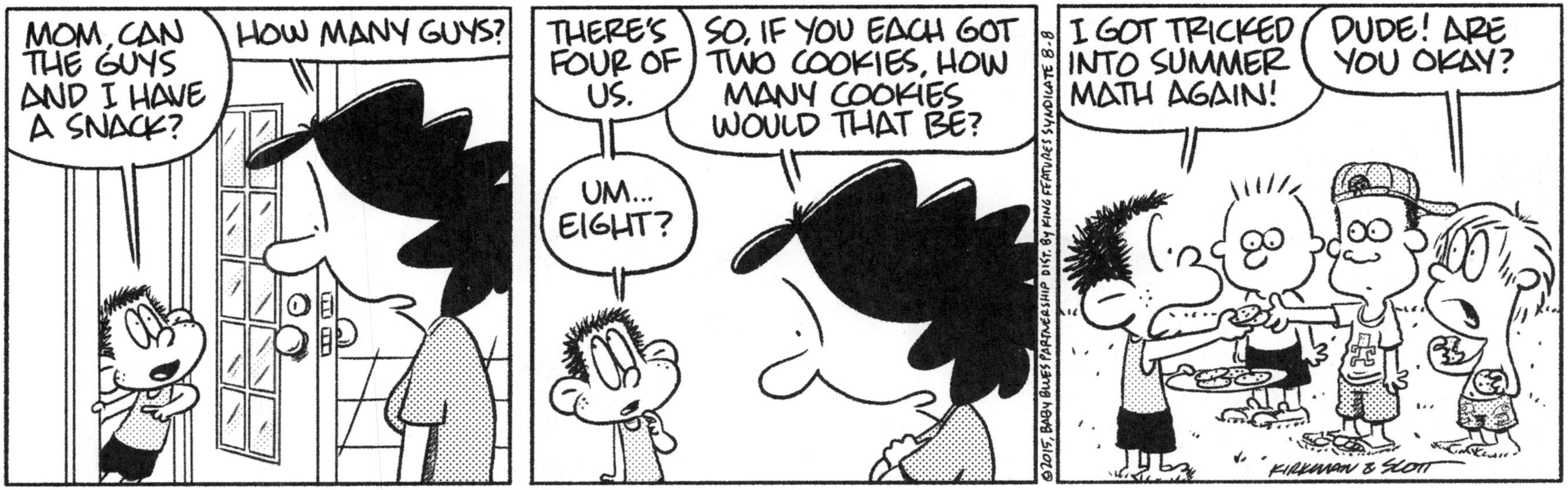
MOM, CAN THE GUYS AND I HAVE A SNACK?
HOW MANY GUYS?
THERE'S FOUR OF US.
SO, IF YOU EACH GOT TWO COOKIES, HOW MANY COOKIES WOULD THAT BE?
UM... EIGHT?
©2015, BABY BLUES PARTNERSHIP DIST. BY KING FEATURES SYNDICATE 8-8
I GOT TRICKED INTO SUMMER MATH AGAIN!
DUDE! ARE YOU OKAY?
KIRKMAN & SCOTT

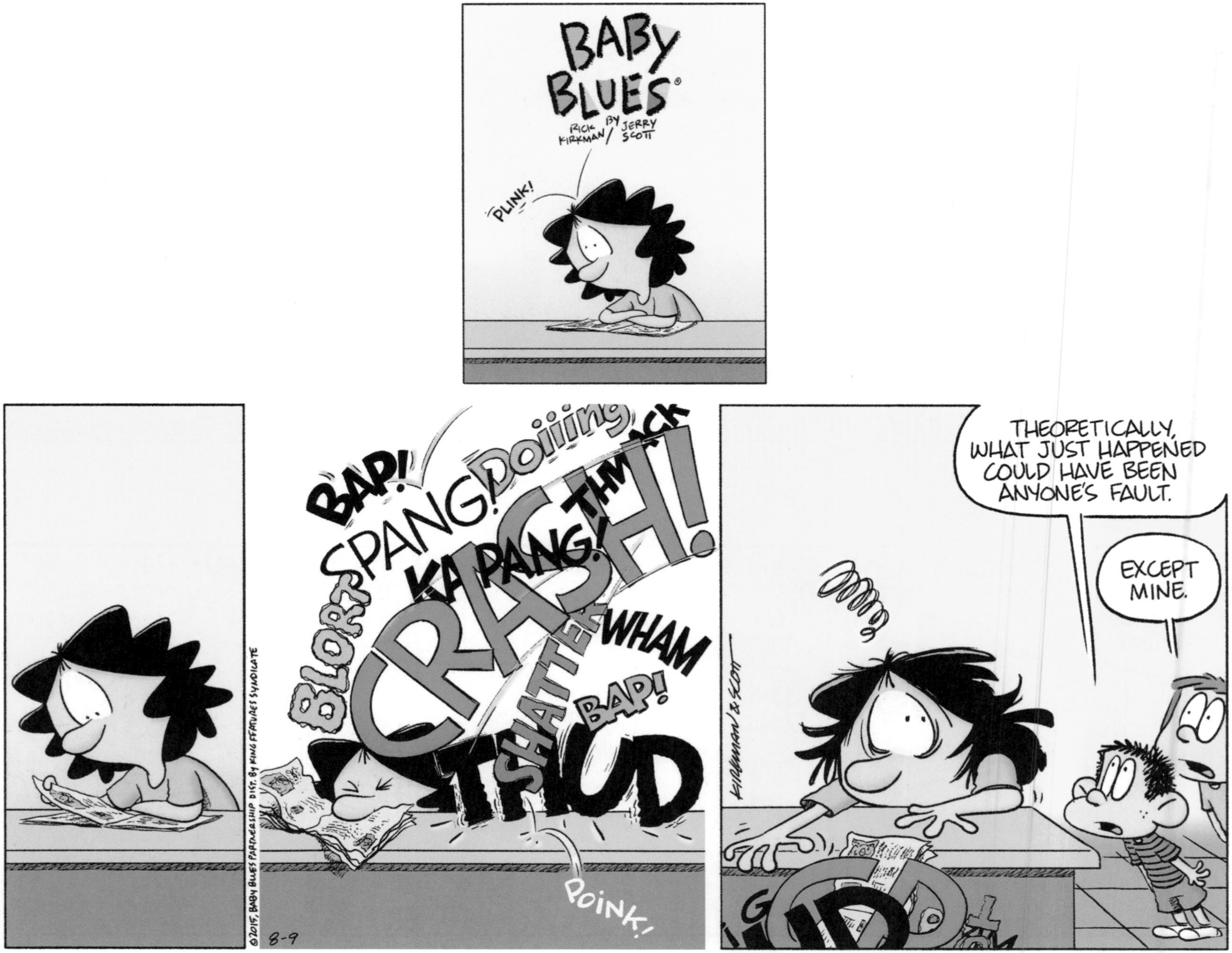

BABY BLUES®
BY RICK KIRKMAN / JERRY SCOTT
PLINK!
BAP!
BLORT
SPANG!
Doiiing
KAPANG!
THWACK
CRASH!
SHATTER
WHAM
BAP!
THUD
POINK!
©2015, BABY BLUES PARTNERSHIP DIST. BY KING FEATURES SYNDICATE
8-9
KIRKMAN & SCOTT
THEORETICALLY, WHAT JUST HAPPENED COULD HAVE BEEN ANYONE'S FAULT.
EXCEPT MINE.

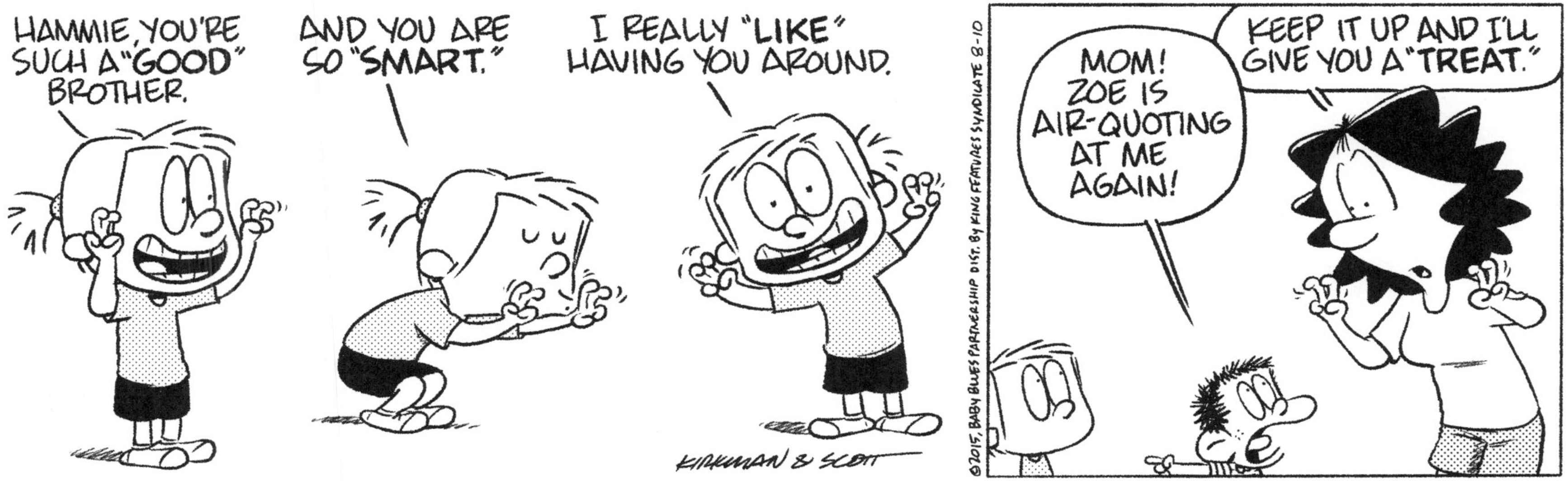
HAMMIE, YOU'RE SUCH A "GOOD" BROTHER.
AND YOU ARE SO "SMART."
I REALLY "LIKE" HAVING YOU AROUND.
KIRKMAN & SCOTT
©2015, BABY BLUES PARTNERSHIP DIST. BY KING FEATURES SYNDICATE 8-10
MOM! ZOE IS AIR-QUOTING AT ME AGAIN!
KEEP IT UP AND I'LL GIVE YOU A "TREAT."

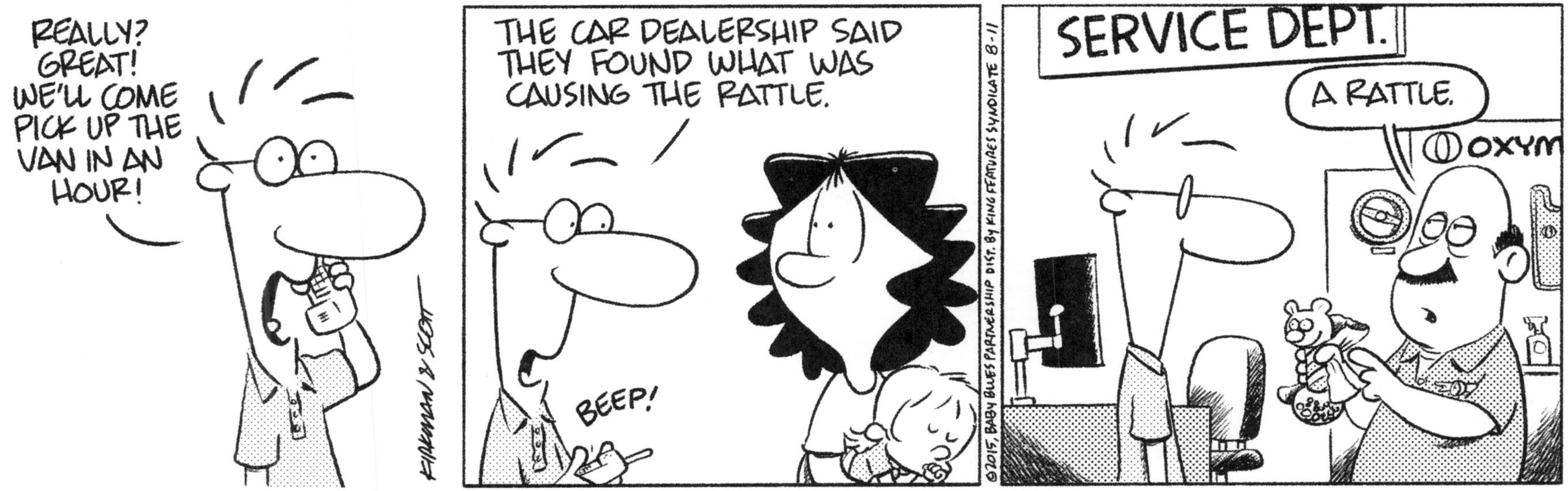
REALLY? GREAT! WE'LL COME PICK UP THE VAN IN AN HOUR!
KIRKMAN & SCOTT
THE CAR DEALERSHIP SAID THEY FOUND WHAT WAS CAUSING THE RATTLE.
BEEP!
©2015, BABY BLUES PARTNERSHIP DIST. BY KING FEATURES SYNDICATE 8-11
SERVICE DEPT.
A RATTLE.
OXYM

Rick: Probably the most embarrassing 180 bucks Darryl ever spent.

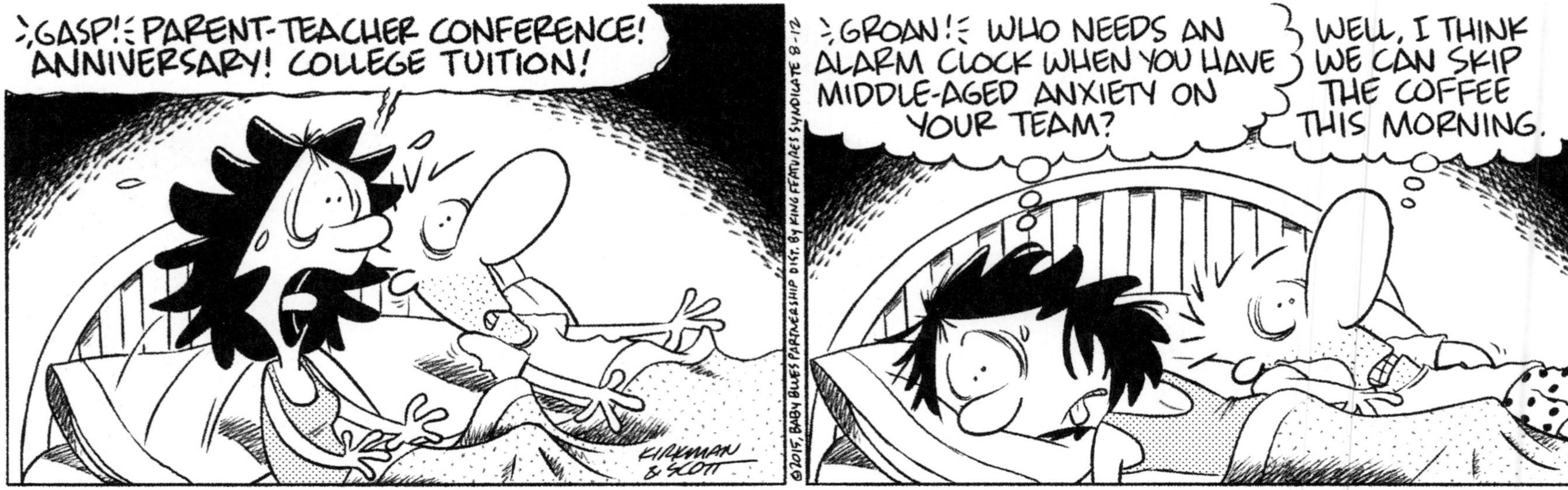
GASP! PARENT-TEACHER CONFERENCE! ANNIVERSARY! COLLEGE TUITION!
KIRKMAN & SCOTT
©2015, BABY BLUES PARTNERSHIP DIST. BY KING FEATURES SYNDICATE 8-12
GROAN! WHO NEEDS AN ALARM CLOCK WHEN YOU HAVE MIDDLE-AGED ANXIETY ON YOUR TEAM?
WELL, I THINK WE CAN SKIP THE COFFEE THIS MORNING.

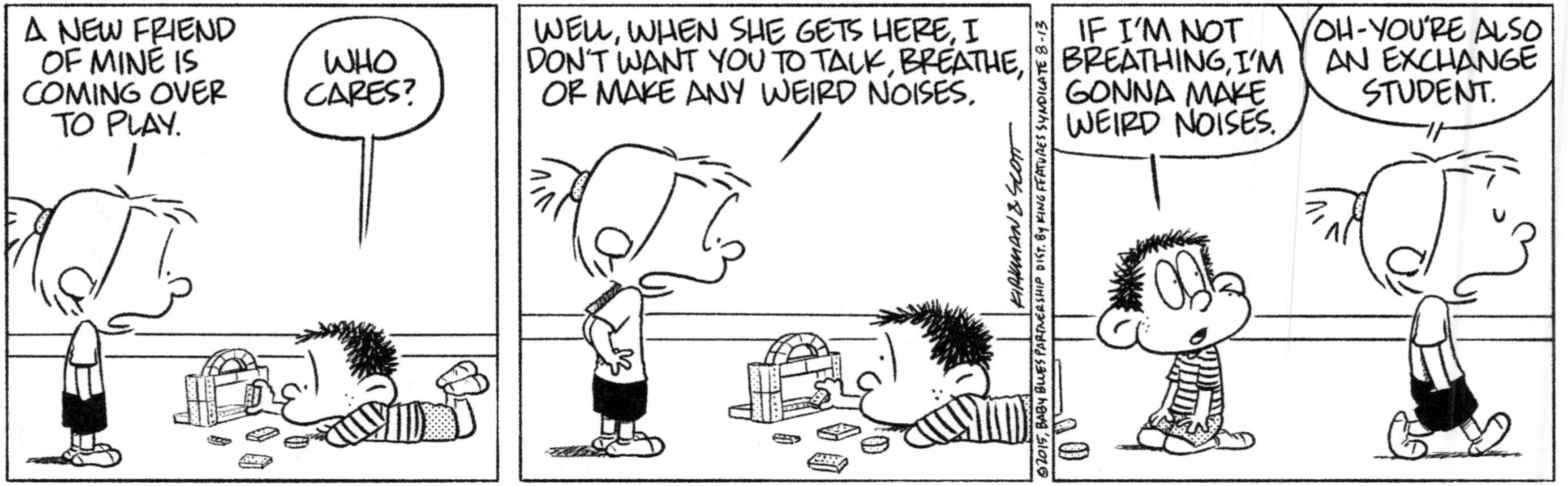
A NEW FRIEND OF MINE IS COMING OVER TO PLAY.
WHO CARES?
WELL, WHEN SHE GETS HERE, I DON'T WANT YOU TO TALK, BREATHE, OR MAKE ANY WEIRD NOISES.
KIRKMAN & SCOTT
©2015, BABY BLUES PARTNERSHIP DIST. BY KING FEATURES SYNDICATE 8-13
IF I'M NOT BREATHING, I'M GONNA MAKE WEIRD NOISES.
OH-YOU'RE ALSO AN EXCHANGE STUDENT.

Jerry: There are a lot of rules that come with being Zoe's brother.

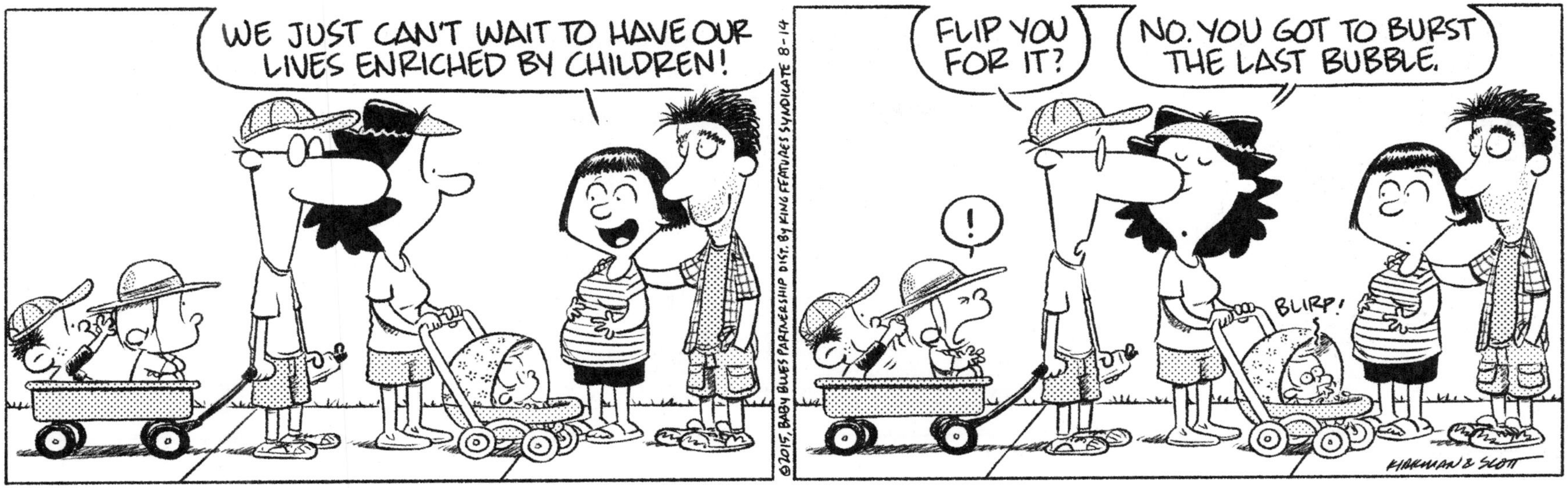
WE JUST CAN'T WAIT TO HAVE OUR LIVES ENRICHED BY CHILDREN!
©2015, BABY BLUES PARTNERSHIP DIST. BY KING FEATURES SYNDICATE 8-14
FLIP YOU FOR IT?
NO. YOU GOT TO BURST THE LAST BUBBLE.
!
BLURP!
KIRKMAN & SCOTT

Rick: This may be my favorite one-off couples. Love the gag, too. It says so much without actually saying it.

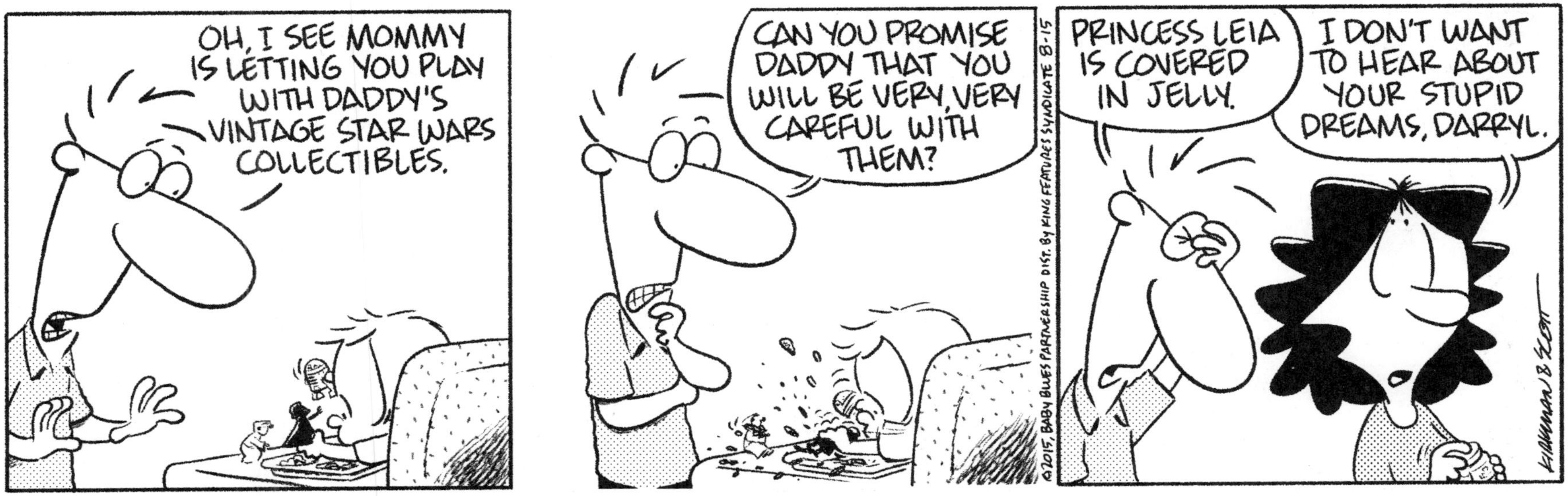
OH, I SEE MOMMY IS LETTING YOU PLAY WITH DADDY'S VINTAGE STAR WARS COLLECTIBLES.
CAN YOU PROMISE DADDY THAT YOU WILL BE VERY, VERY CAREFUL WITH THEM?
©2015, BABY BLUES PARTNERSHIP DIST. BY KING FEATURES SYNDICATE 8-15
PRINCESS LEIA IS COVERED IN JELLY.
I DON'T WANT TO HEAR ABOUT YOUR STUPID DREAMS, DARRYL.
KIRKMAN & SCOTT

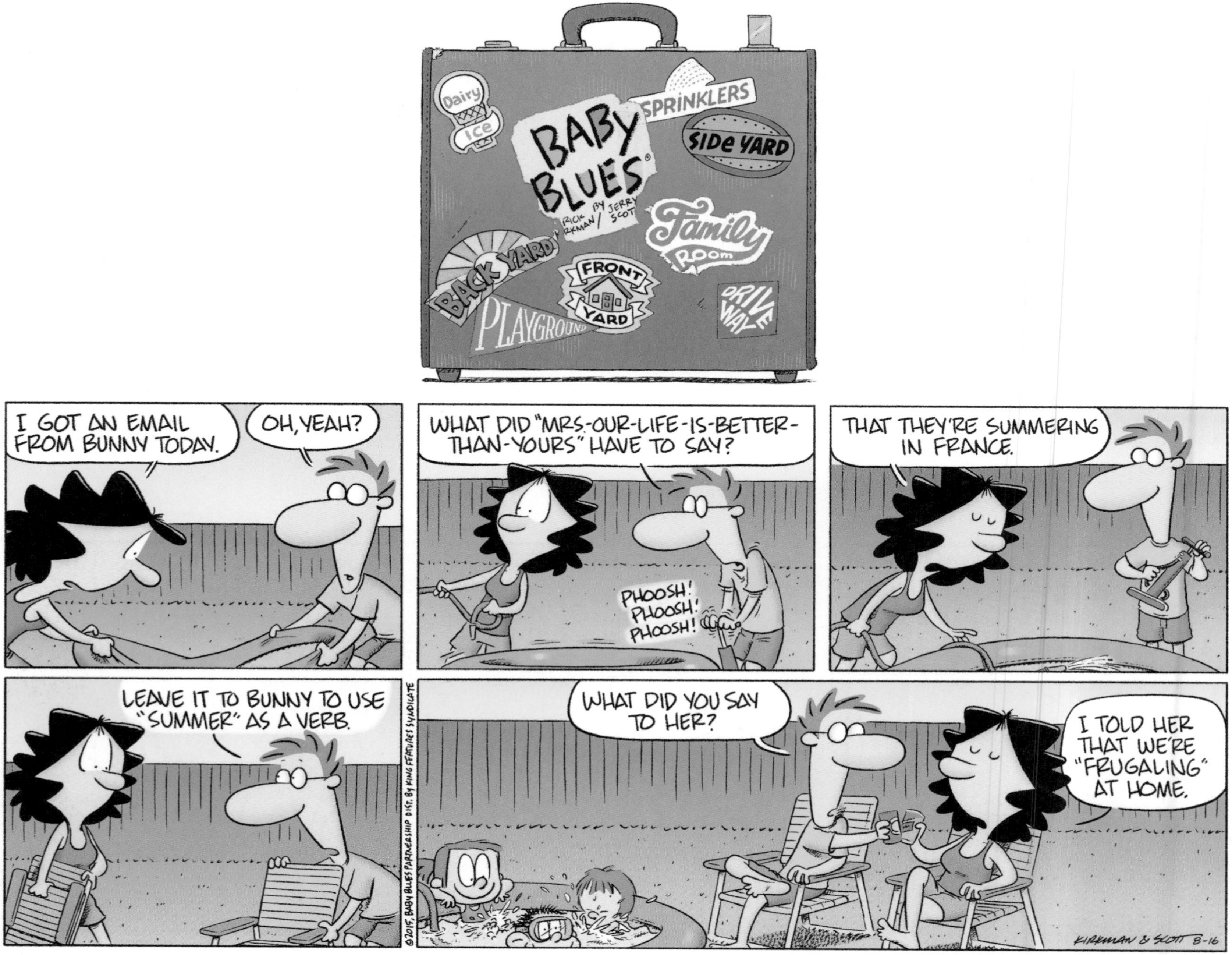
Dairy Ice
SPRINKLERS
BABY BLUES®
RICK KIRKMAN / BY JERRY SCOTT
SIDE YARD
Family Room
BACK YARD
FRONT YARD
PLAYGROUND
DRIVE WAY
I GOT AN EMAIL FROM BUNNY TODAY.
OH, YEAH?
WHAT DID "MRS.-OUR-LIFE-IS-BETTER-THAN-YOURS" HAVE TO SAY?
PHOOSH! PHOOSH! PHOOSH!
THAT THEY'RE SUMMERING IN FRANCE.
LEAVE IT TO BUNNY TO USE "SUMMER" AS A VERB.
©2015, BABY BLUES PARTNERSHIP DIST. BY KING FEATURES SYNDICATE
WHAT DID YOU SAY TO HER?
I TOLD HER THAT WE'RE "FRUGALING" AT HOME.
KIRKMAN & SCOTT 8-16

Rick: "Frugaling"—I like it.

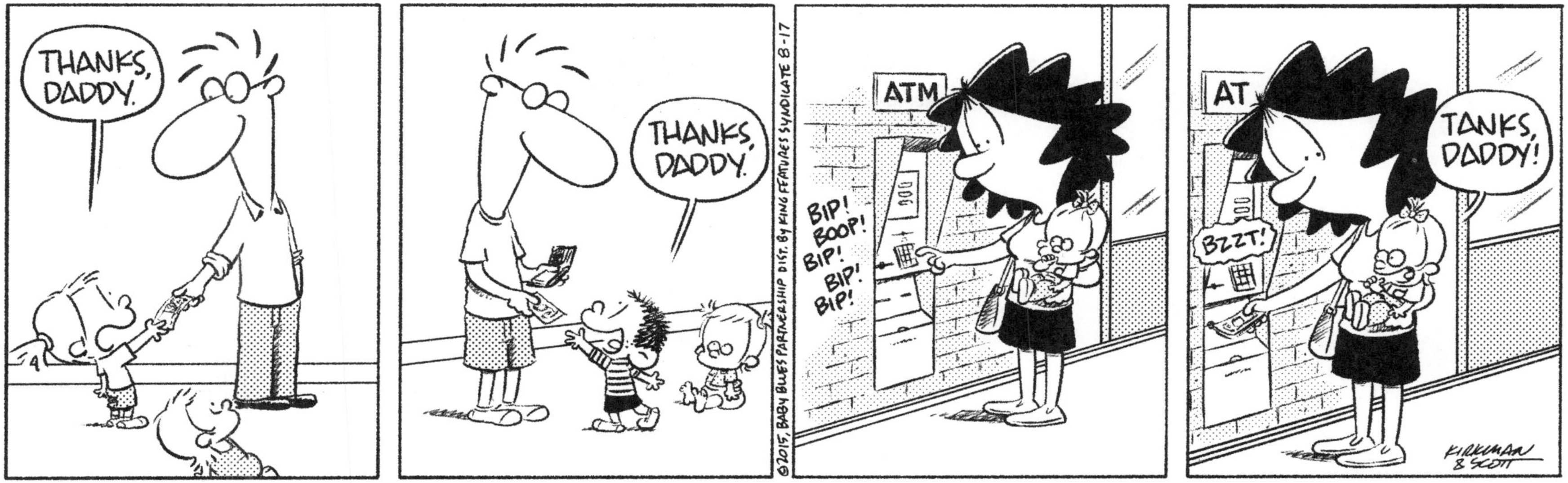
THANKS, DADDY.
THANKS, DADDY.
©2015, BABY BLUES PARTNERSHIP DIST. BY KING FEATURES SYNDICATE 8-17
ATM
BIP! BOOP! BIP! BIP! BIP!
AT
BZZT!
TANKS, DADDY!
KIRKMAN & SCOTT

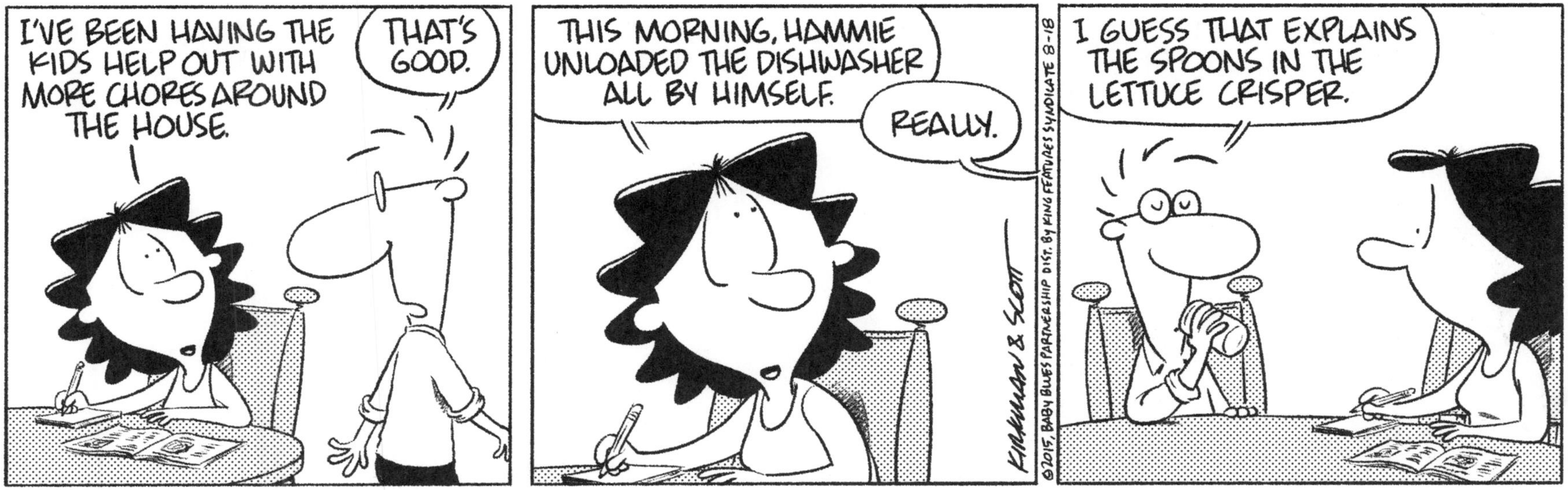
I'VE BEEN HAVING THE KIDS HELP OUT WITH MORE CHORES AROUND THE HOUSE.
THAT'S GOOD.
THIS MORNING, HAMMIE UNLOADED THE DISHWASHER ALL BY HIMSELF.
REALLY.
©2015, BABY BLUES PARTNERSHIP DIST. BY KING FEATURES SYNDICATE 8-18
KIRKMAN & SCOTT
I GUESS THAT EXPLAINS THE SPOONS IN THE LETTUCE CRISPER.

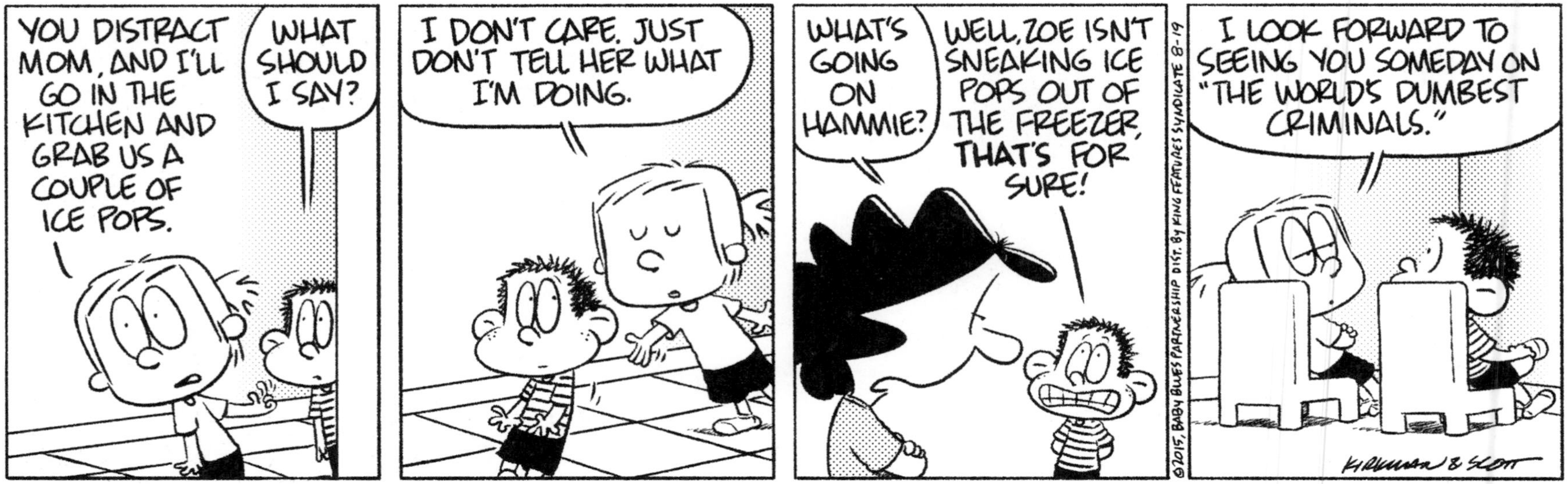
YOU DISTRACT MOM, AND I'LL GO IN THE KITCHEN AND GRAB US A COUPLE OF ICE POPS.
WHAT SHOULD I SAY?
I DON'T CARE. JUST DON'T TELL HER WHAT I'M DOING.
WHAT'S GOING ON HAMMIE?
WELL, ZOE ISN'T SNEAKING ICE POPS OUT OF THE FREEZER, THAT'S FOR SURE!
I LOOK FORWARD TO SEEING YOU SOMEDAY ON "THE WORLD'S DUMBEST CRIMINALS."
©2015, BABY BLUES PARTNERSHIP DIST. BY KING FEATURES SYNDICATE 8-19
KIRKMAN & SCOTT

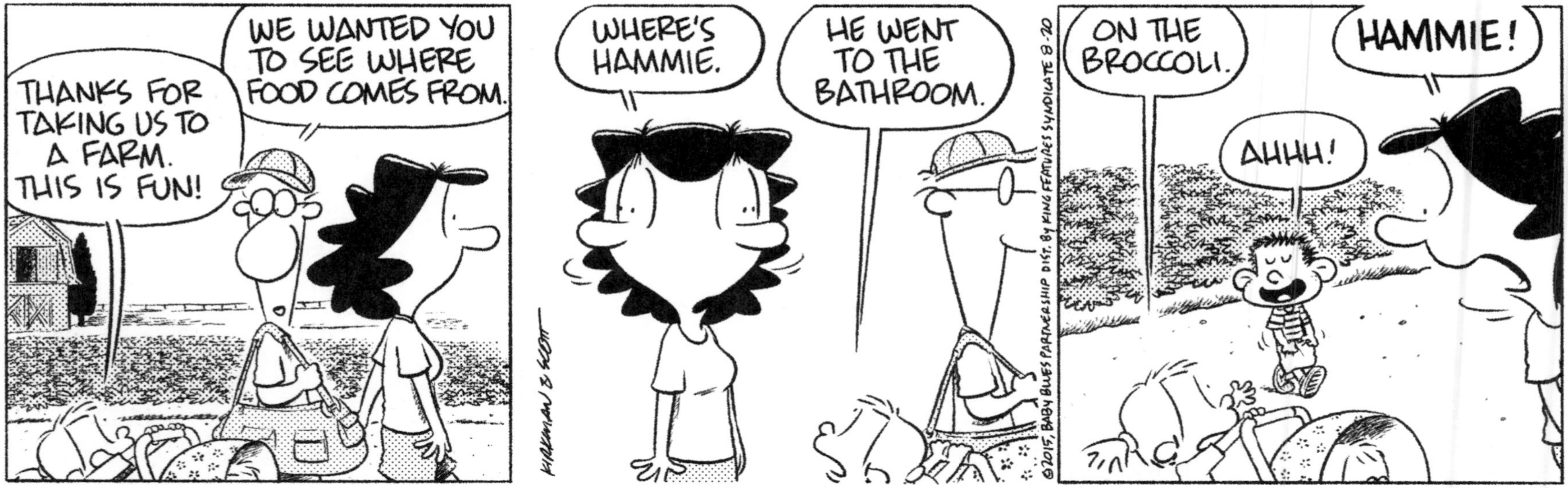
THANKS FOR TAKING US TO A FARM. THIS IS FUN!
WE WANTED YOU TO SEE WHERE FOOD COMES FROM.
KIRKMAN & SCOTT
WHERE'S HAMMIE.
HE WENT TO THE BATHROOM.
©2015, BABY BLUES PARTNERSHIP DIST. BY KING FEATURES SYNDICATE 8-20
ON THE BROCCOLI.
HAMMIE!
AHHH!

Rick: Certified organic.

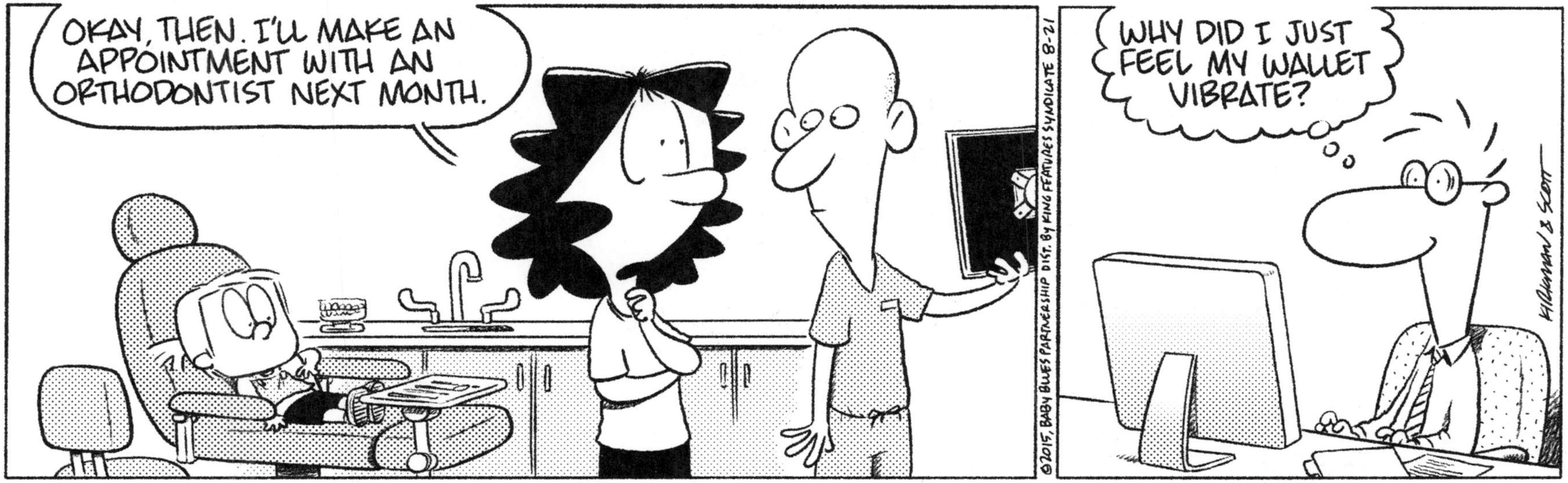
OKAY, THEN. I'LL MAKE AN APPOINTMENT WITH AN ORTHODONTIST NEXT MONTH.
©2015, BABY BLUES PARTNERSHIP DIST. BY KING FEATURES SYNDICATE 8-21
WHY DID I JUST FEEL MY WALLET VIBRATE?
KIRKMAN & SCOTT

Rick: With me, my wallet didn't vibrate—my back used to itch.

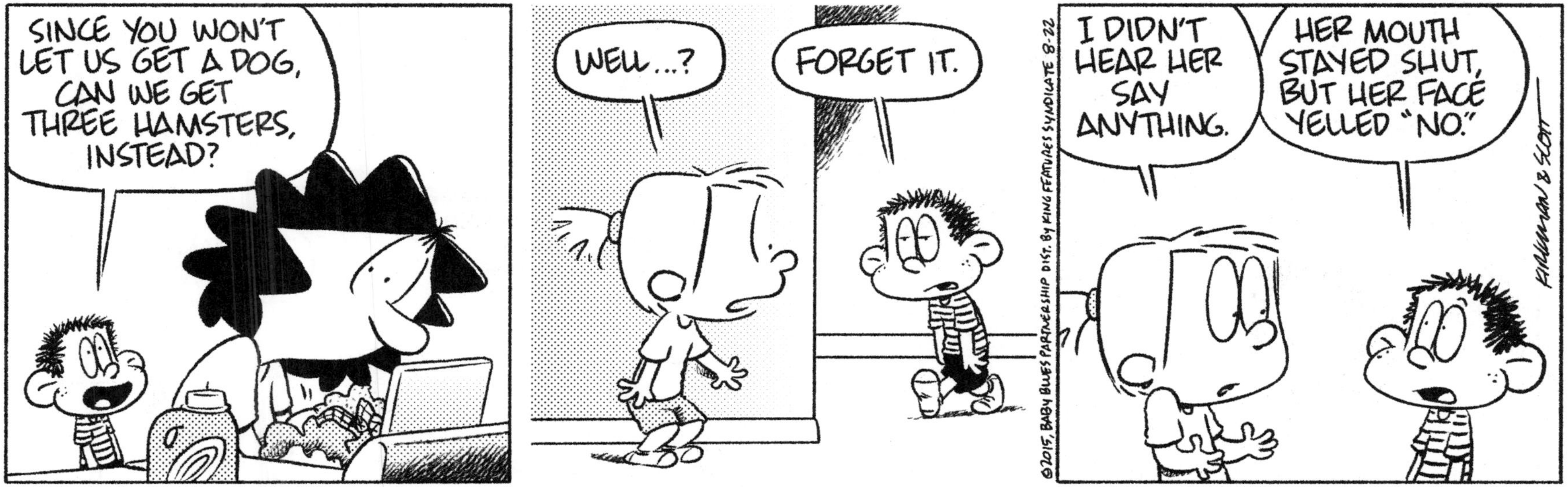
SINCE YOU WON'T LET US GET A DOG, CAN WE GET THREE HAMSTERS, INSTEAD?
WELL...?
FORGET IT.
©2015, BABY BLUES PARTNERSHIP DIST. BY KING FEATURES SYNDICATE 8-22
I DIDN'T HEAR HER SAY ANYTHING.
HER MOUTH STAYED SHUT, BUT HER FACE YELLED "NO."
KIRKMAN & SCOTT

BABY BLUES®

RICK KIRKMAN / BY JERRY SCOTT

★2.8

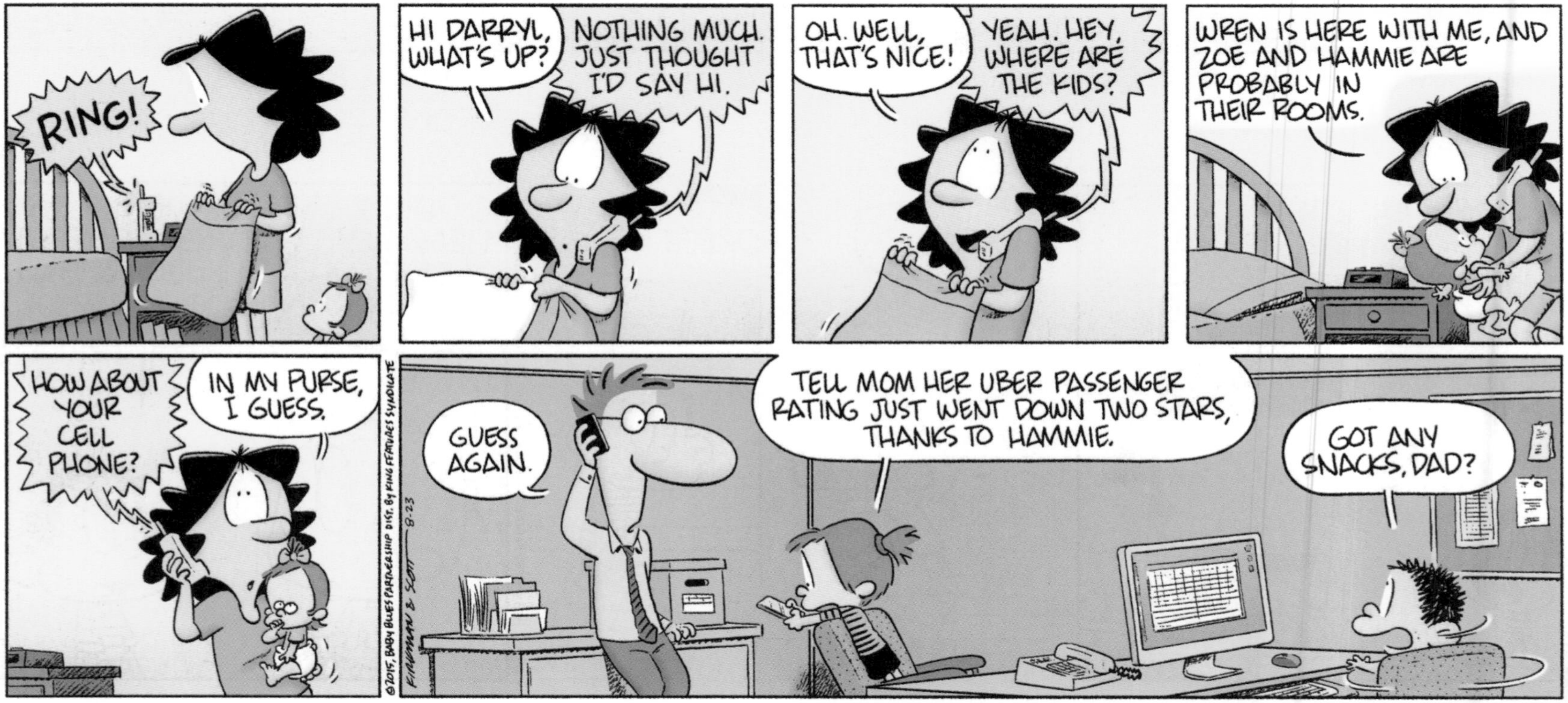
RING!
HI DARRYL, WHAT'S UP?
NOTHING MUCH. JUST THOUGHT I'D SAY HI.
OH. WELL, THAT'S NICE!
YEAH. HEY, WHERE ARE THE KIDS?
WREN IS HERE WITH ME, AND ZOE AND HAMMIE ARE PROBABLY IN THEIR ROOMS.
HOW ABOUT YOUR CELL PHONE?
IN MY PURSE, I GUESS.
GUESS AGAIN.
TELL MOM HER UBER PASSENGER RATING JUST WENT DOWN TWO STARS, THANKS TO HAMMIE.
GOT ANY SNACKS, DAD?
©2015, BABY BLUES PARTNERSHIP DIST. BY KING FEATURES SYNDICATE
KIRKMAN & SCOTT 8-23

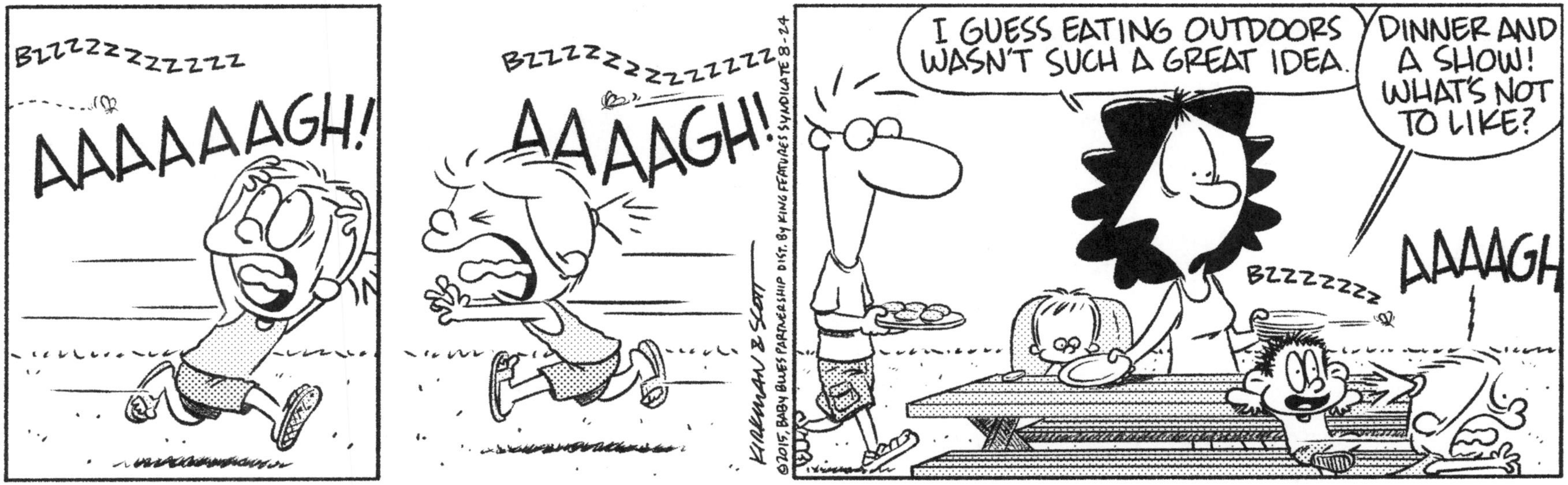
BZZZZZZZZZZZZ
AAAAAAGH!
BZZZZZZZZZZZZZZZ
AAAAGH!
KIRKMAN & SCOTT
©2015, BABY BLUES PARTNERSHIP DIST. BY KING FEATURES SYNDICATE 8-24
I GUESS EATING OUTDOORS WASN'T SUCH A GREAT IDEA.
DINNER AND A SHOW! WHAT'S NOT TO LIKE?
BZZZZZZZZ
AAAAGH

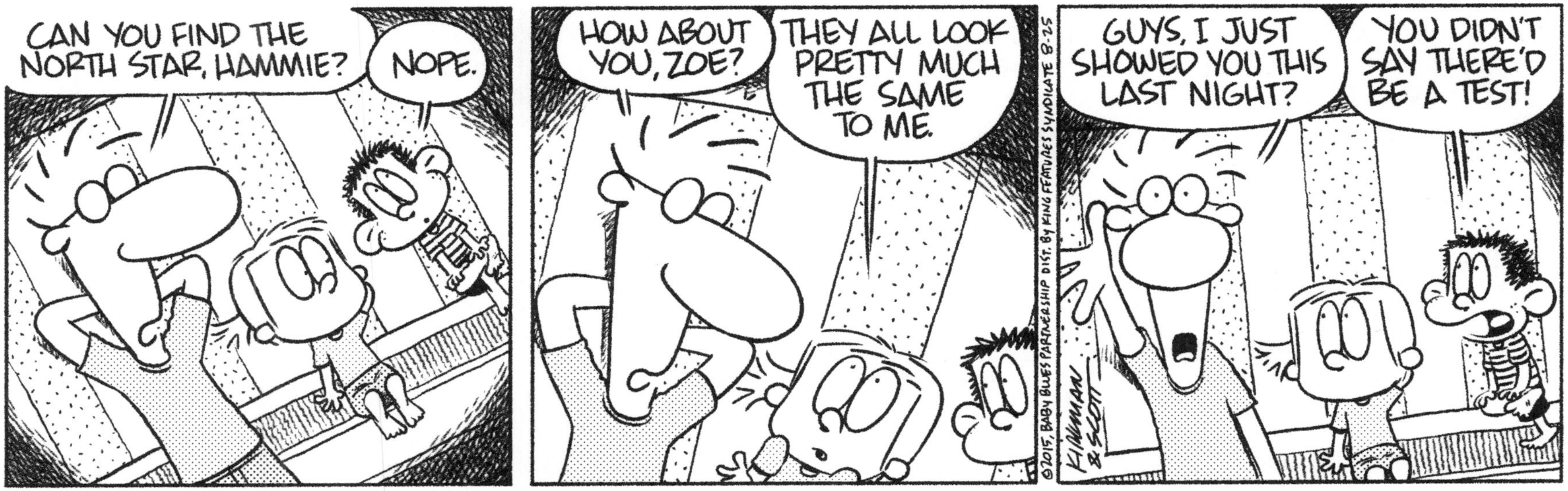
CAN YOU FIND THE NORTH STAR, HAMMIE?
NOPE.
HOW ABOUT YOU, ZOE?
THEY ALL LOOK PRETTY MUCH THE SAME TO ME.
©2015, BABY BLUES PARTNERSHIP DIST. BY KING FEATURES SYNDICATE 8-25
KIRKMAN & SCOTT
GUYS, I JUST SHOWED YOU THIS LAST NIGHT?
YOU DIDN'T SAY THERE'D BE A TEST!

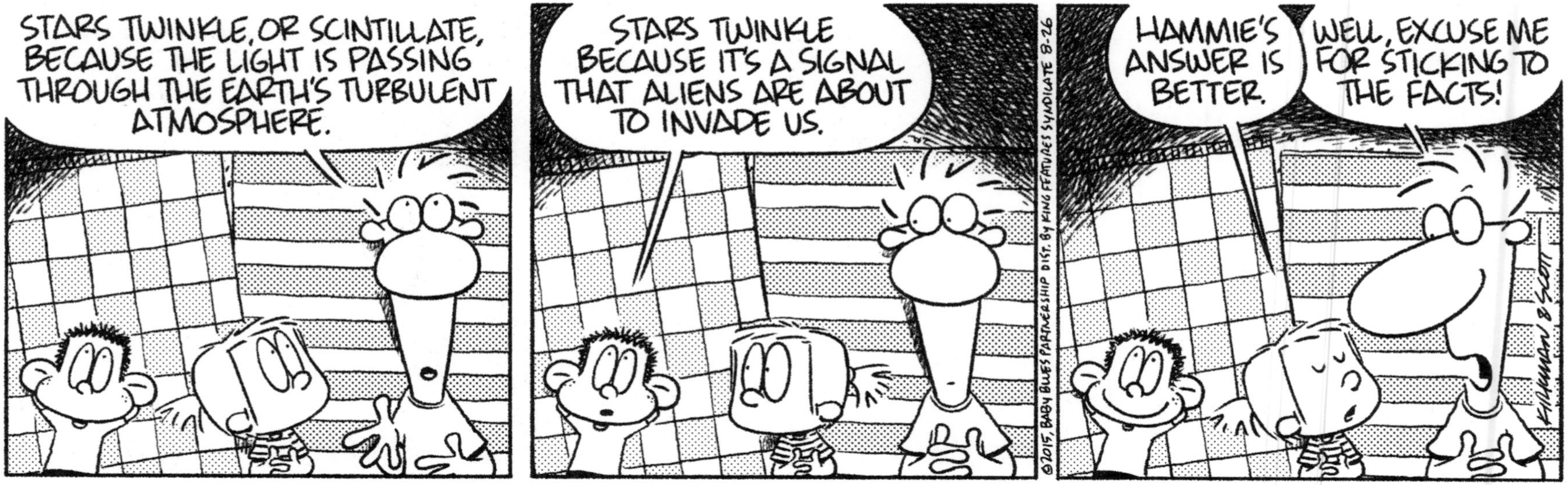
STARS TWINKLE, OR SCINTILLATE, BECAUSE THE LIGHT IS PASSING THROUGH THE EARTH'S TURBULENT ATMOSPHERE.
STARS TWINKLE BECAUSE IT'S A SIGNAL THAT ALIENS ARE ABOUT TO INVADE US.
©2015, BABY BLUES PARTNERSHIP DIST. BY KING FEATURES SYNDICATE 8-26
HAMMIE'S ANSWER IS BETTER.
WELL, EXCUSE ME FOR STICKING TO THE FACTS!
KIRKMAN & SCOTT

Rick: I'm with Zoe.

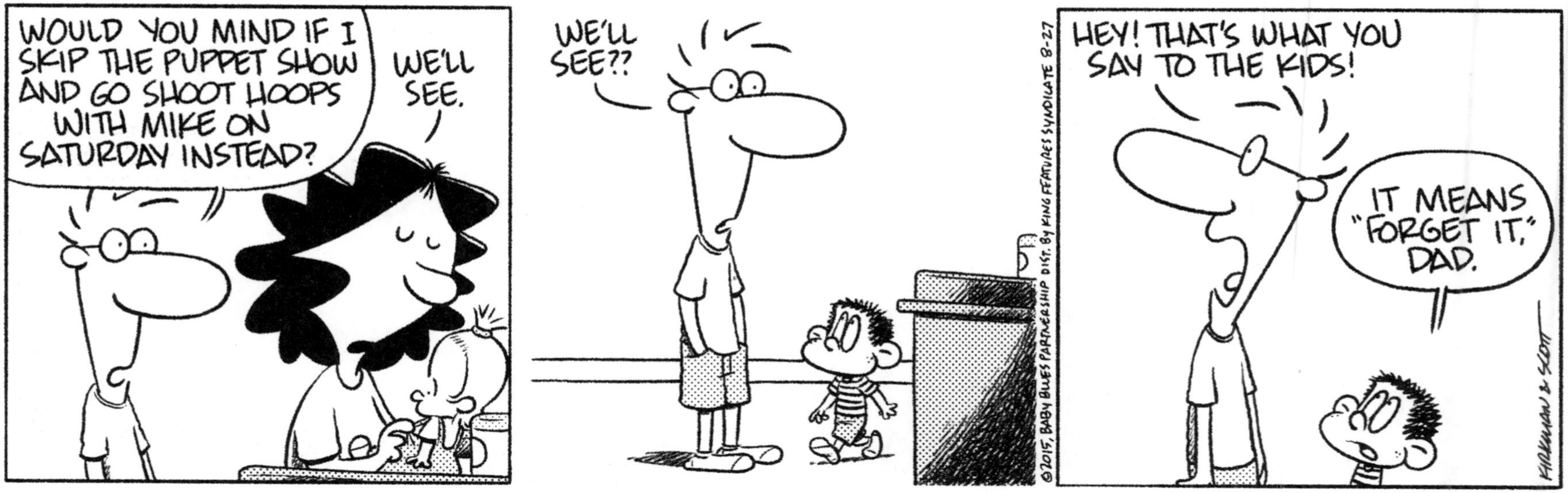
WOULD YOU MIND IF I SKIP THE PUPPET SHOW AND GO SHOOT HOOPS WITH MIKE ON SATURDAY INSTEAD?
WE'LL SEE.
WE'LL SEE??
©2015, BABY BLUES PARTNERSHIP DIST. BY KING FEATURES SYNDICATE 8-27
HEY! THAT'S WHAT YOU SAY TO THE KIDS!
IT MEANS "FORGET IT," DAD.
KIRKMAN & SCOTT

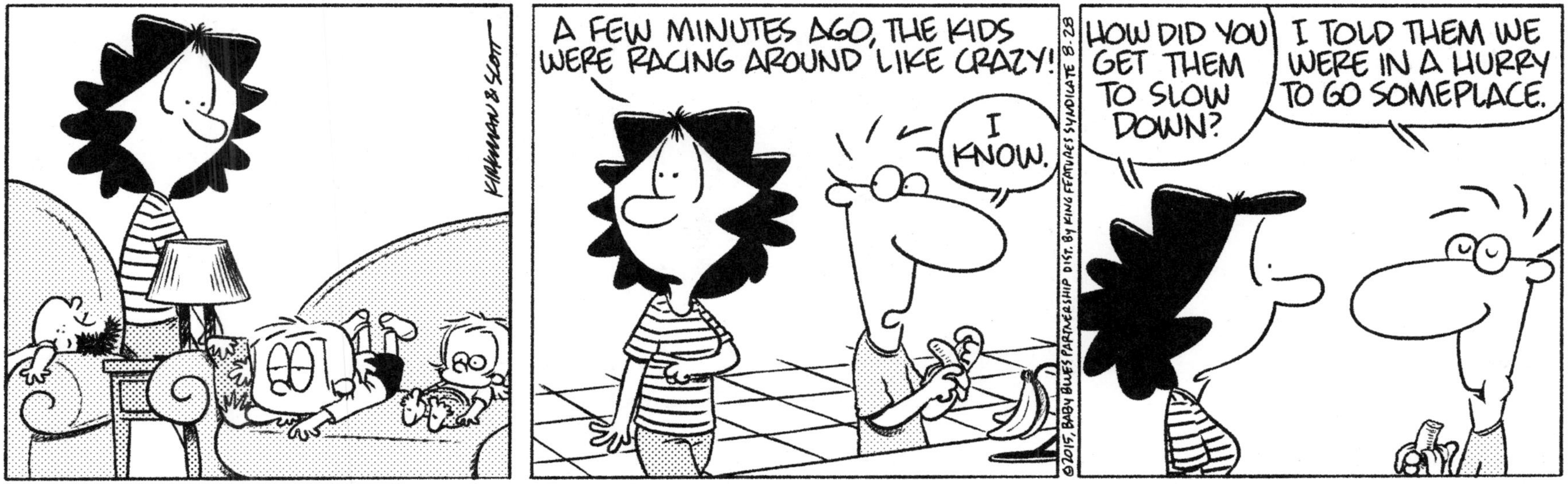
KIRKMAN & SCOTT
A FEW MINUTES AGO, THE KIDS WERE RACING AROUND LIKE CRAZY!
I KNOW.
©2015, BABY BLUES PARTNERSHIP DIST. BY KING FEATURES SYNDICATE 8-28
HOW DID YOU GET THEM TO SLOW DOWN?
I TOLD THEM WE WERE IN A HURRY TO GO SOMEPLACE.

Rick: At that moment, I was in a hurry to go someplace myself—home from a USO tour to Turkey. After twenty-five hours of flying, I finally made it.

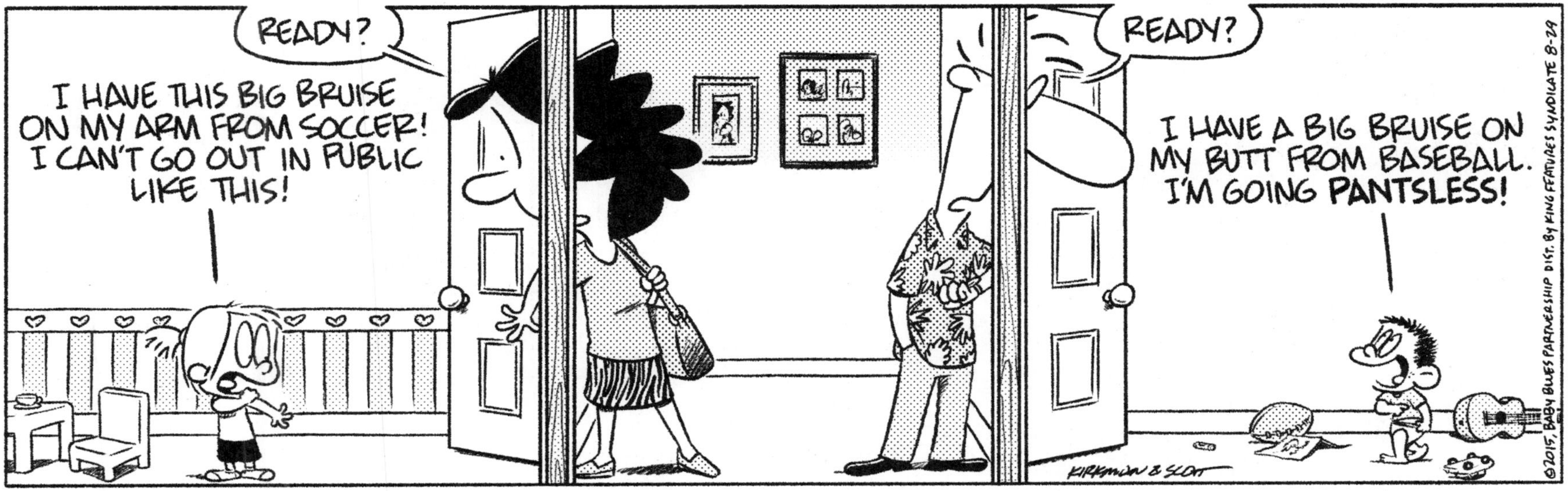
READY?
I HAVE THIS BIG BRUISE ON MY ARM FROM SOCCER! I CAN'T GO OUT IN PUBLIC LIKE THIS!
READY?
I HAVE A BIG BRUISE ON MY BUTT FROM BASEBALL. I'M GOING **PANTSLESS!**
KIRKMAN & SCOTT
©2015, BABY BLUES PARTNERSHIP DIST. BY KING FEATURES SYNDICATE 8-29

Jerry: One of my favorite layouts in a daily strip ever.

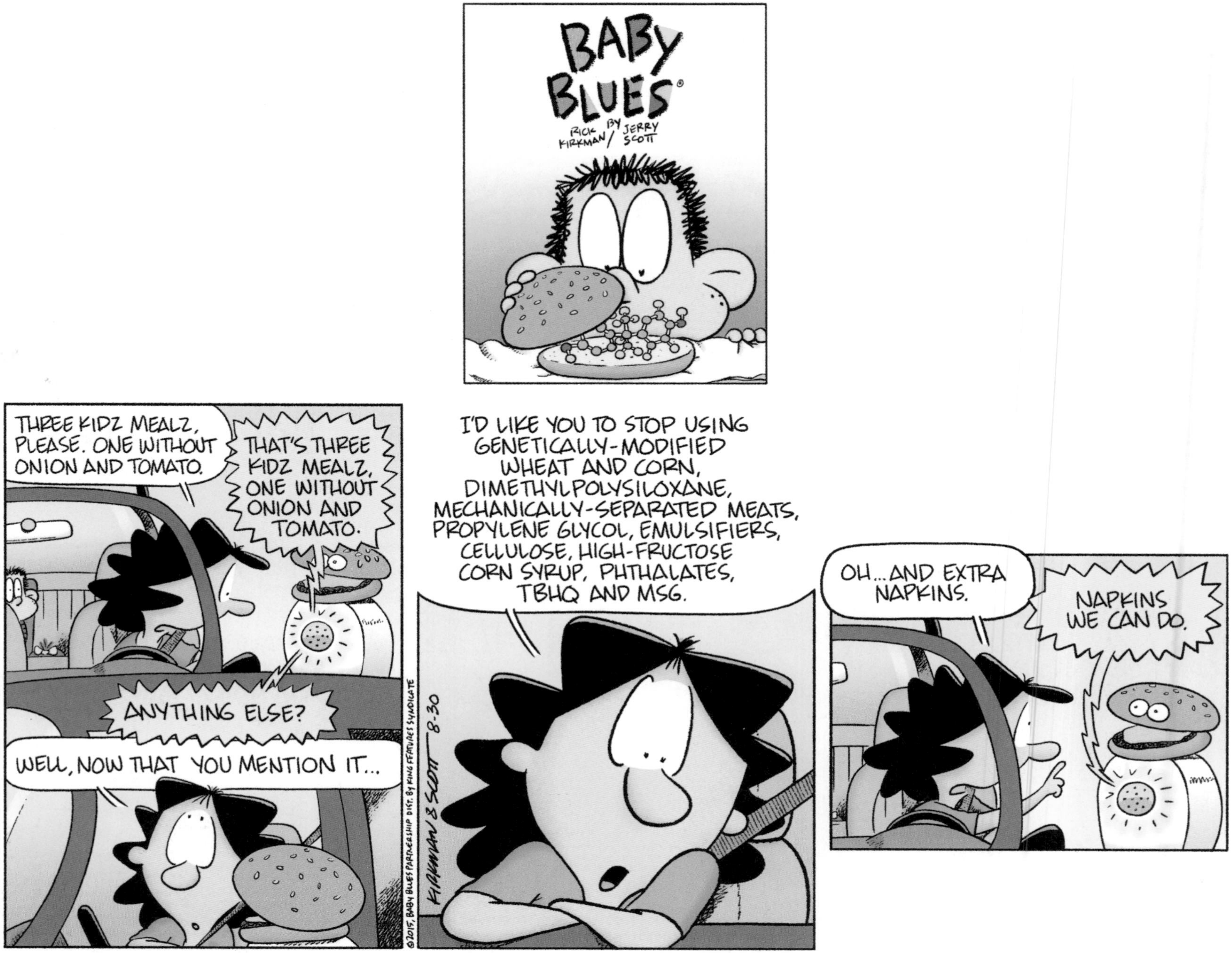
BABY BLUES®
BY RICK KIRKMAN / JERRY SCOTT
THREE KIDZ MEALZ, PLEASE. ONE WITHOUT ONION AND TOMATO.
THAT'S THREE KIDZ MEALZ, ONE WITHOUT ONION AND TOMATO.
ANYTHING ELSE?
WELL, NOW THAT YOU MENTION IT...
©2015, BABY BLUES PARTNERSHIP DIST. BY KING FEATURES SYNDICATE
KIRKMAN & SCOTT 8-30
I'D LIKE YOU TO STOP USING GENETICALLY-MODIFIED WHEAT AND CORN, DIMETHYLPOLYSILOXANE, MECHANICALLY-SEPARATED MEATS, PROPYLENE GLYCOL, EMULSIFIERS, CELLULOSE, HIGH-FRUCTOSE CORN SYRUP, PHTHALATES, TBHQ AND MSG.
OH...AND EXTRA NAPKINS.
NAPKINS WE CAN DO.

Rick: I actually looked up that molecular structure on Hammie's sandwich in the title panel . . . but now I can't remember which compound on the list it was. Maybe one of you scientists out there will know.

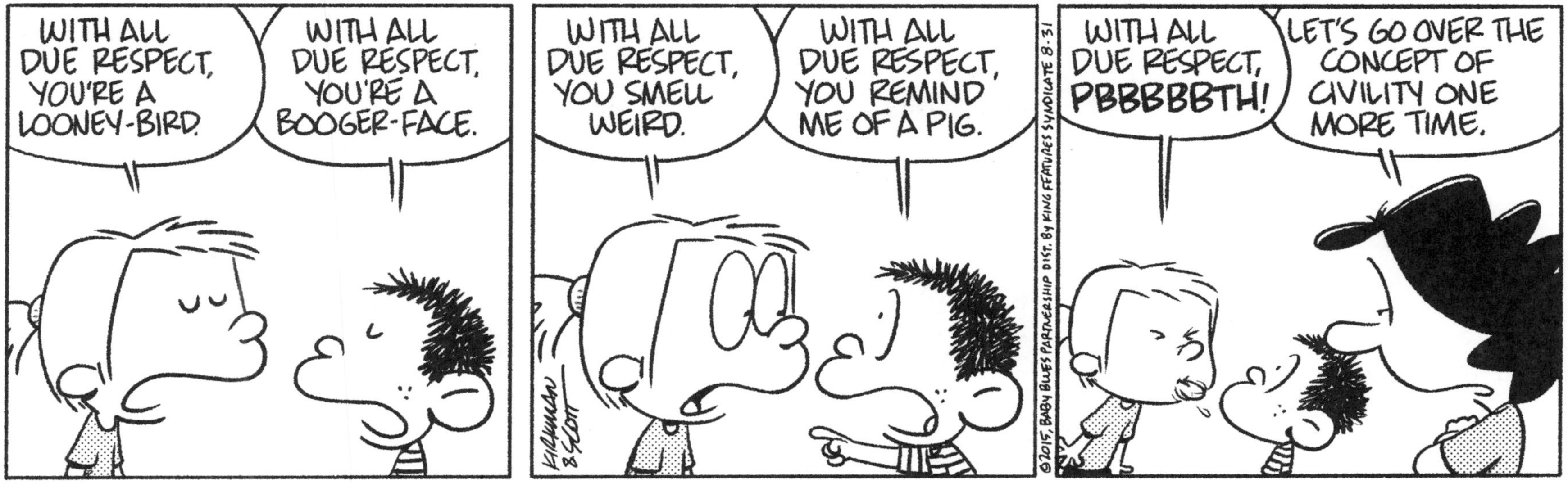
WITH ALL DUE RESPECT, YOU'RE A LOONEY-BIRD.
WITH ALL DUE RESPECT, YOU'RE A BOOGER-FACE.
WITH ALL DUE RESPECT, YOU SMELL WEIRD.
WITH ALL DUE RESPECT, YOU REMIND ME OF A PIG.
KIRKMAN & SCOTT
©2015, BABY BLUES PARTNERSHIP DIST. BY KING FEATURES SYNDICATE 8-31
WITH ALL DUE RESPECT, PBBBBBTH!
LET'S GO OVER THE CONCEPT OF CIVILITY ONE MORE TIME.

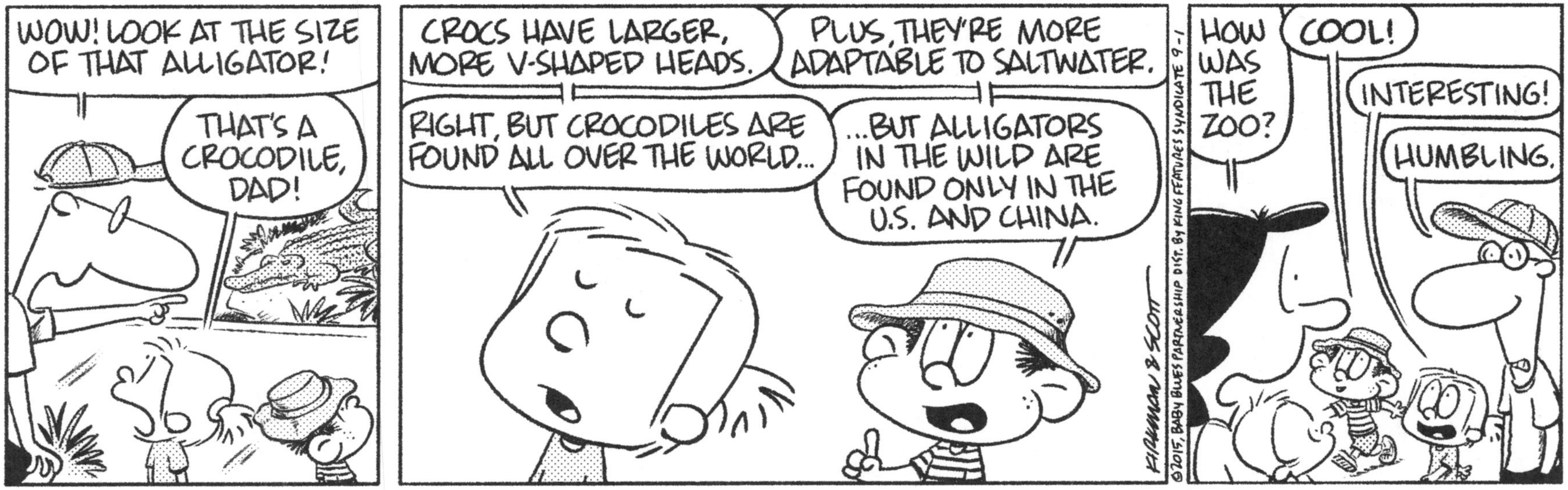
WOW! LOOK AT THE SIZE OF THAT ALLIGATOR!
THAT'S A CROCODILE, DAD!
CROCS HAVE LARGER, MORE V-SHAPED HEADS.
PLUS, THEY'RE MORE ADAPTABLE TO SALTWATER.
RIGHT, BUT CROCODILES ARE FOUND ALL OVER THE WORLD...
...BUT ALLIGATORS IN THE WILD ARE FOUND ONLY IN THE U.S. AND CHINA.
KIRKMAN & SCOTT
©2015, BABY BLUES PARTNERSHIP DIST. BY KING FEATURES SYNDICATE 9-1
HOW WAS THE ZOO?
COOL!
INTERESTING!
HUMBLING.

Rick: I learn so much from this strip.

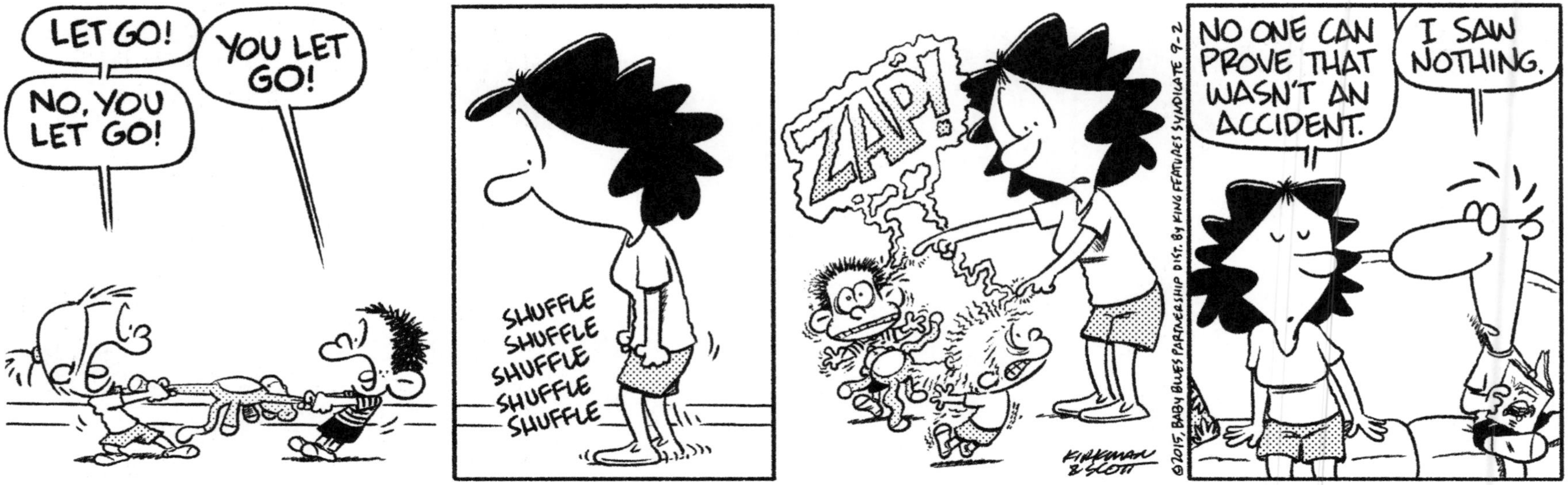
LET GO!
NO, YOU LET GO!
YOU LET GO!
SHUFFLE SHUFFLE SHUFFLE SHUFFLE SHUFFLE
ZAP!
KIRKMAN & SCOTT
©2015, BABY BLUES PARTNERSHIP DIST. BY KING FEATURES SYNDICATE 9-2
NO ONE CAN PROVE THAT WASN'T AN ACCIDENT.
I SAW NOTHING.

Rick: Poor man's Taser.

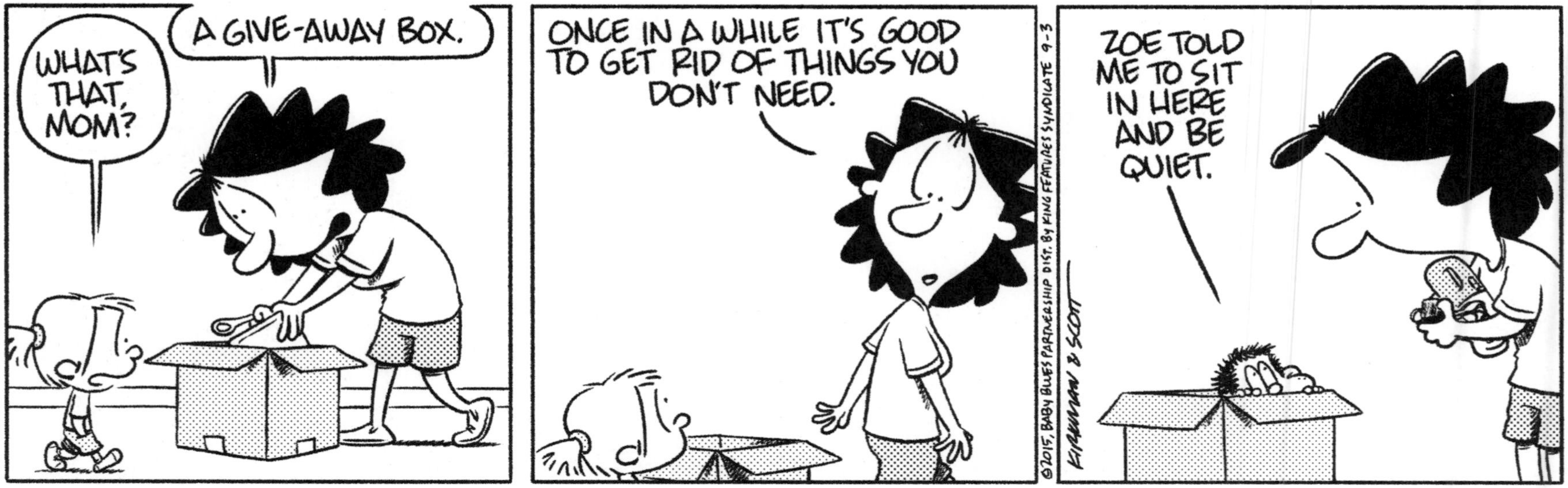
WHAT'S THAT, MOM?
A GIVE-AWAY BOX.
ONCE IN A WHILE IT'S GOOD TO GET RID OF THINGS YOU DON'T NEED.
©2015, BABY BLUES PARTNERSHIP DIST. BY KING FEATURES SYNDICATE 9-3
KIRKMAN & SCOTT
ZOE TOLD ME TO SIT IN HERE AND BE QUIET.

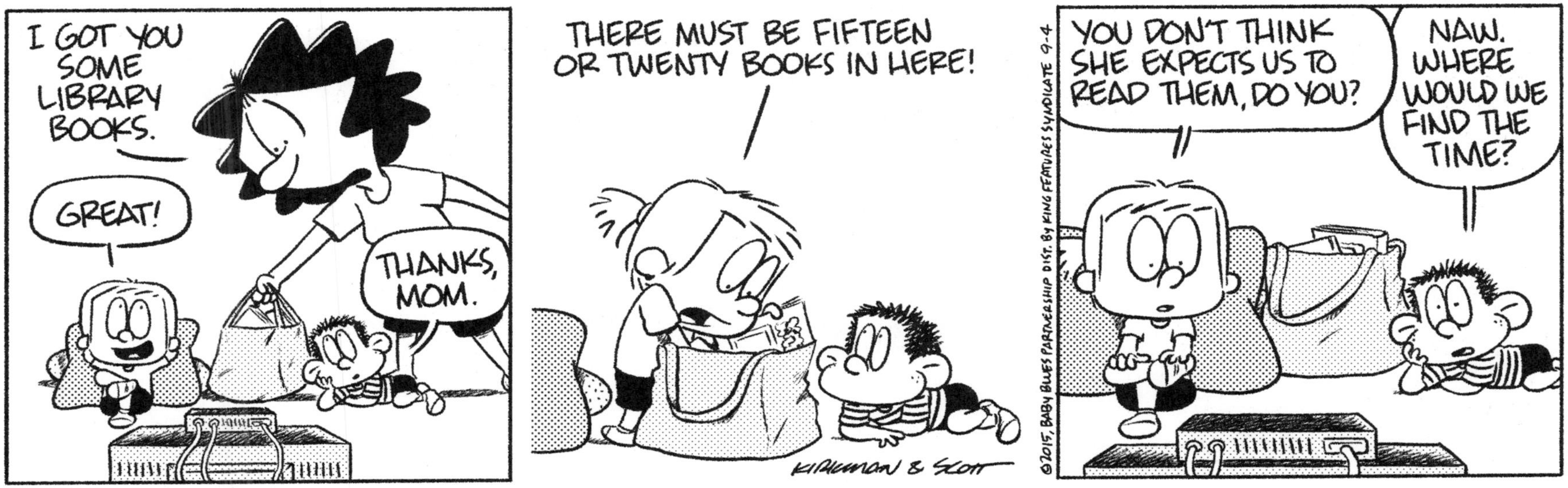
I GOT YOU SOME LIBRARY BOOKS.
GREAT!
THANKS, MOM.
THERE MUST BE FIFTEEN OR TWENTY BOOKS IN HERE!
KIRKMAN & SCOTT
©2015, BABY BLUES PARTNERSHIP DIST. BY KING FEATURES SYNDICATE 9-4
YOU DON'T THINK SHE EXPECTS US TO READ THEM, DO YOU?
NAW. WHERE WOULD WE FIND THE TIME?

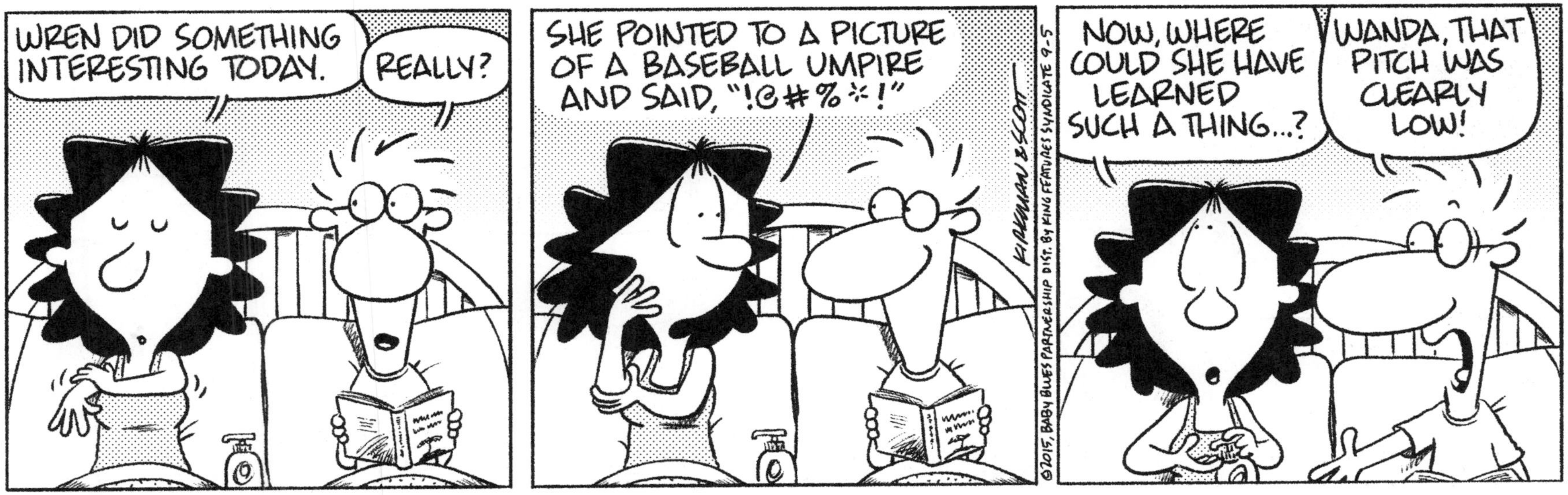
WREN DID SOMETHING INTERESTING TODAY.
REALLY?
SHE POINTED TO A PICTURE OF A BASEBALL UMPIRE AND SAID, "!@#%*!"
KIRKMAN & SCOTT
©2015, BABY BLUES PARTNERSHIP DIST. BY KING FEATURES SYNDICATE 9-5
NOW, WHERE COULD SHE HAVE LEARNED SUCH A THING...?
WANDA, THAT PITCH WAS CLEARLY LOW!

Rick: Babies don't discern, they only absorb.

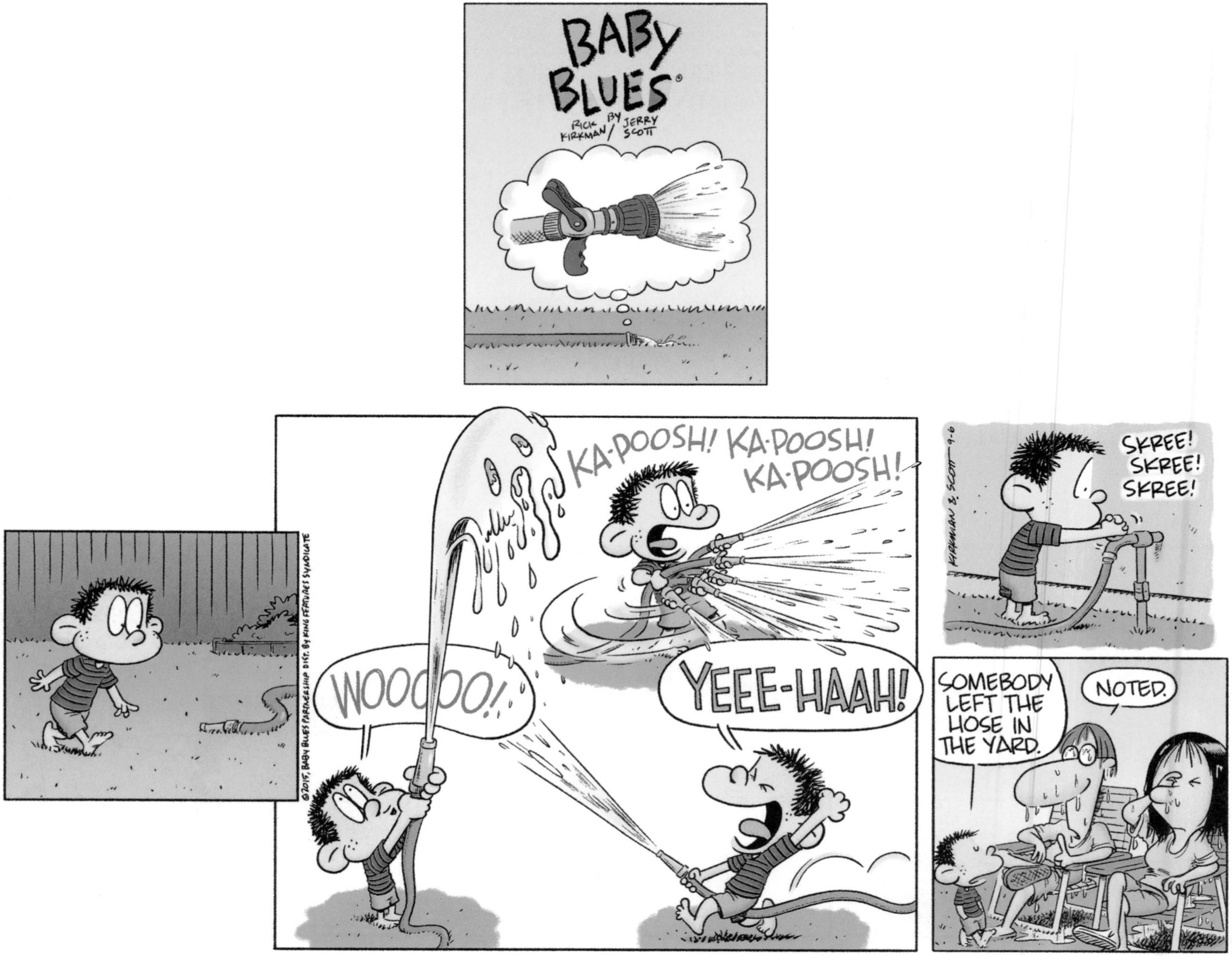
BABY BLUES®
BY RICK KIRKMAN / JERRY SCOTT
©2015, BABY BLUES PARTNERSHIP DIST. BY KING FEATURES SYNDICATE
WOOOOO!
KA-POOSH! KA-POOSH! KA-POOSH!
YEEE-HAAH!
SKREE! SKREE! SKREE!
KIRKMAN & SCOTT 9-6
SOMEBODY LEFT THE HOSE IN THE YARD.
NOTED.

Rick: Hoses can dream, too.

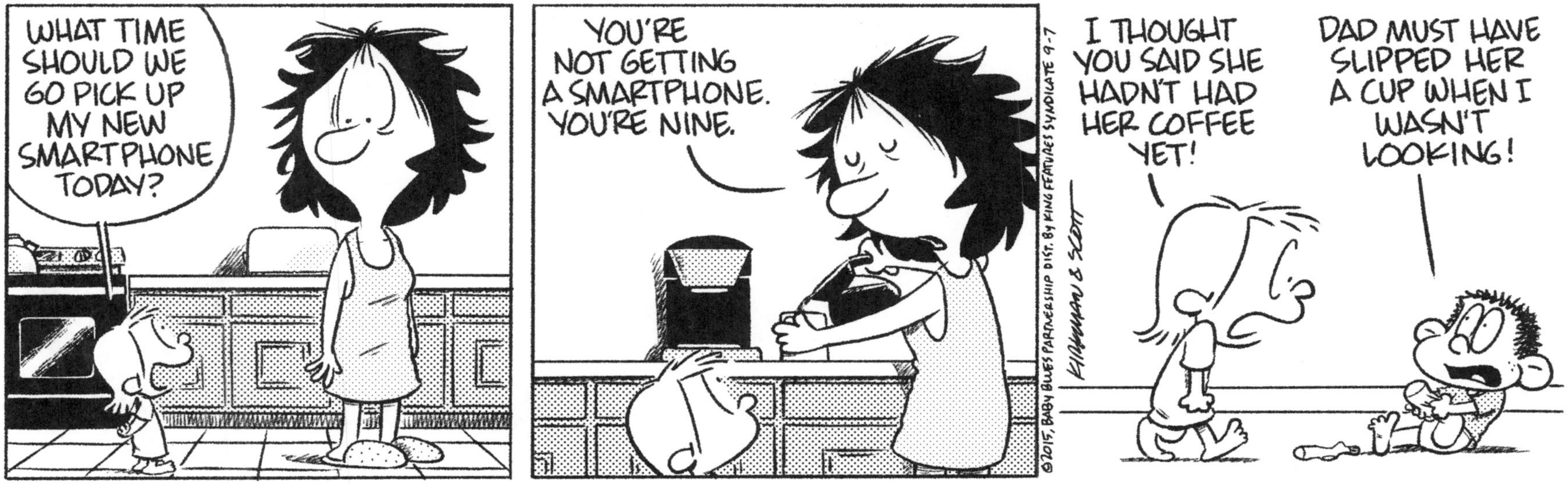
WHAT TIME SHOULD WE GO PICK UP MY NEW SMARTPHONE TODAY?
YOU'RE NOT GETTING A SMARTPHONE. YOU'RE NINE.
©2015, BABY BLUES PARTNERSHIP DIST. BY KING FEATURES SYNDICATE 9-7
KIRKMAN & SCOTT
I THOUGHT YOU SAID SHE HADN'T HAD HER COFFEE YET!
DAD MUST HAVE SLIPPED HER A CUP WHEN I WASN'T LOOKING!

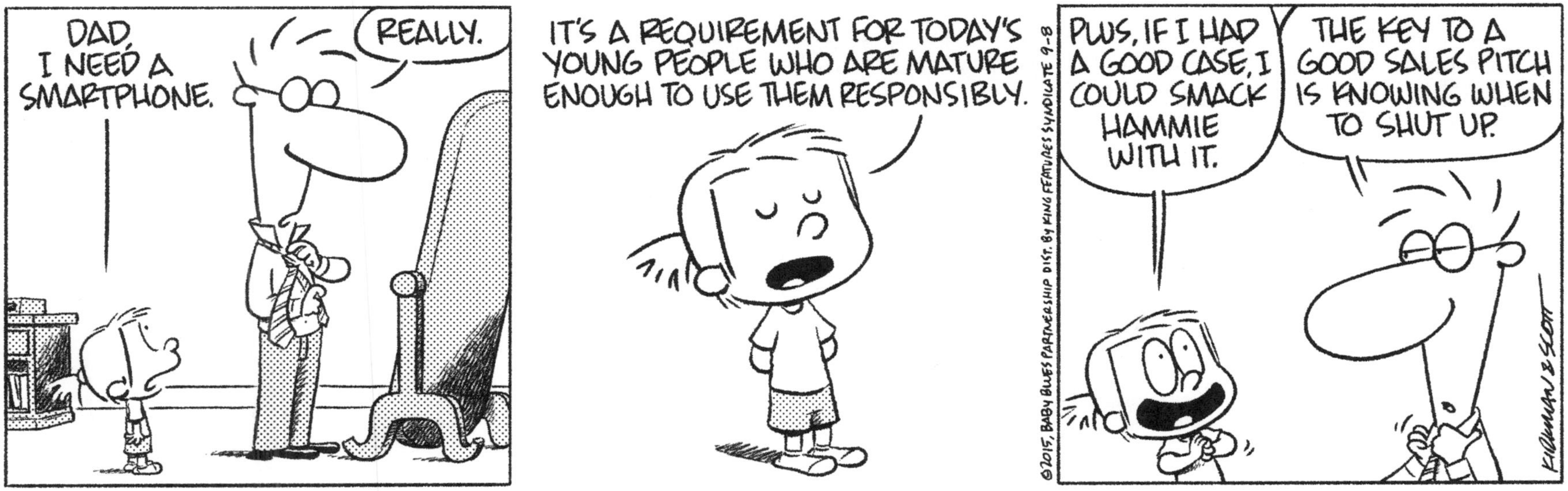
DAD, I NEED A SMARTPHONE.
REALLY.
IT'S A REQUIREMENT FOR TODAY'S YOUNG PEOPLE WHO ARE MATURE ENOUGH TO USE THEM RESPONSIBLY.
©2015, BABY BLUES PARTNERSHIP DIST. BY KING FEATURES SYNDICATE 9-8
PLUS, IF I HAD A GOOD CASE, I COULD SMACK HAMMIE WITH IT.
THE KEY TO A GOOD SALES PITCH IS KNOWING WHEN TO SHUT UP.
KIRKMAN & SCOTT

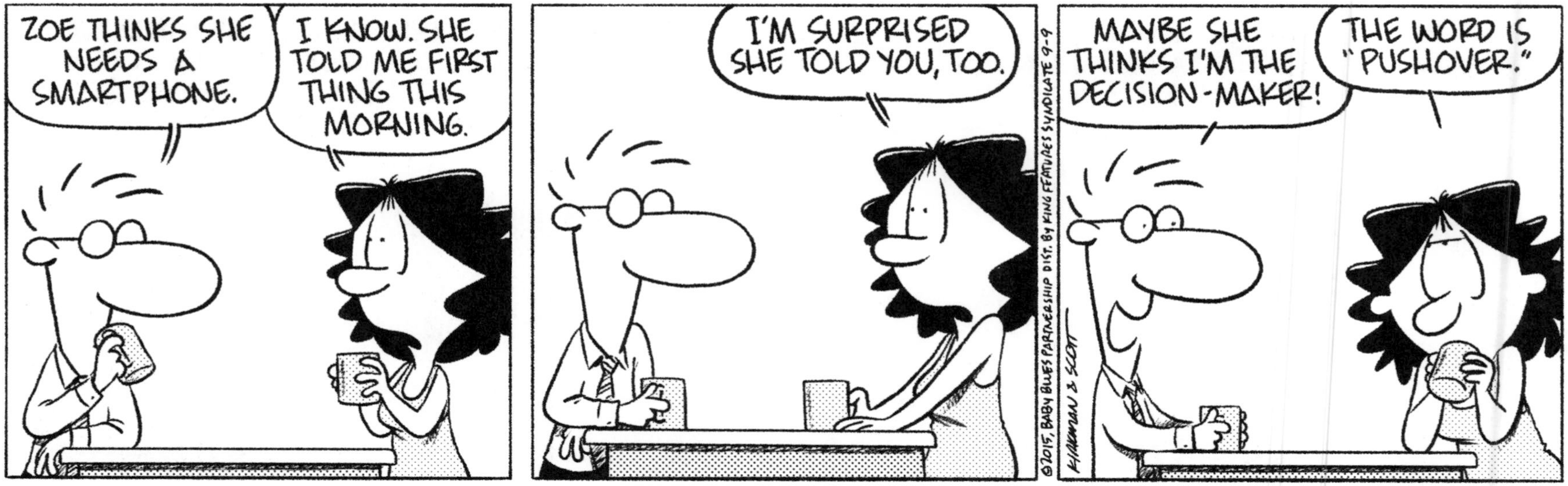
ZOE THINKS SHE NEEDS A SMARTPHONE.
I KNOW. SHE TOLD ME FIRST THING THIS MORNING.
I'M SURPRISED SHE TOLD YOU, TOO.
©2015, BABY BLUES PARTNERSHIP DIST. BY KING FEATURES SYNDICATE 9-9
KIRKMAN & SCOTT
MAYBE SHE THINKS I'M THE DECISION-MAKER!
THE WORD IS "PUSHOVER."

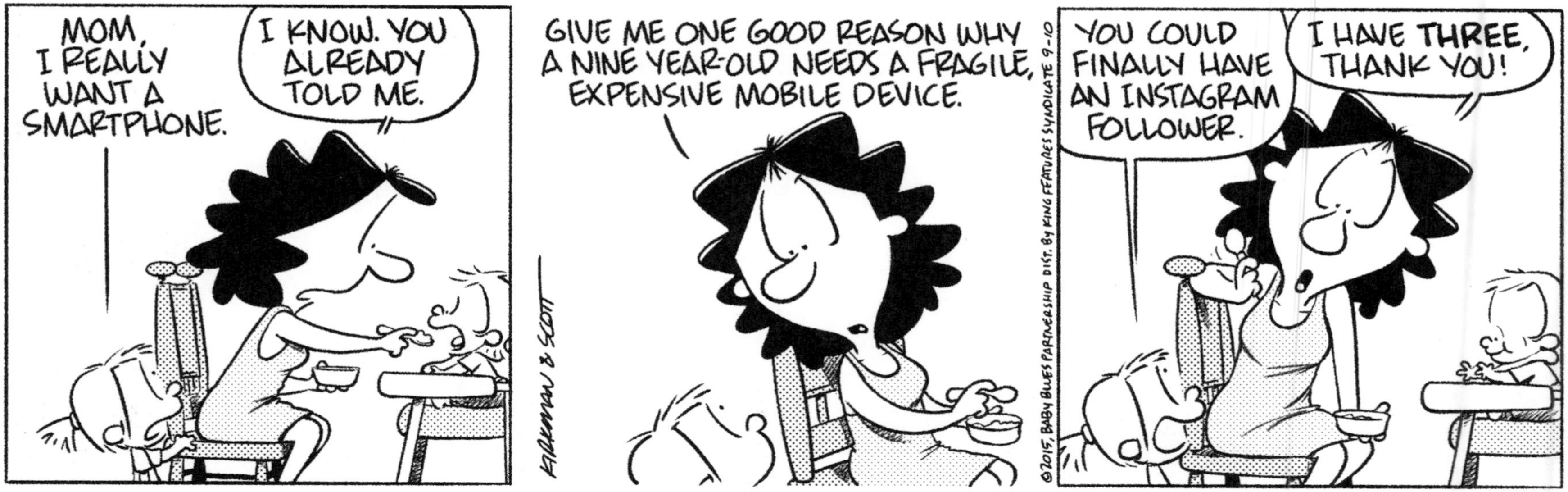
MOM, I REALLY WANT A SMARTPHONE.
I KNOW. YOU ALREADY TOLD ME.
KIRKMAN & SCOTT
GIVE ME ONE GOOD REASON WHY A NINE YEAR-OLD NEEDS A FRAGILE, EXPENSIVE MOBILE DEVICE.
©2015, BABY BLUES PARTNERSHIP DIST. BY KING FEATURES SYNDICATE 9-10
YOU COULD FINALLY HAVE AN INSTAGRAM FOLLOWER.
I HAVE **THREE**, THANK YOU!

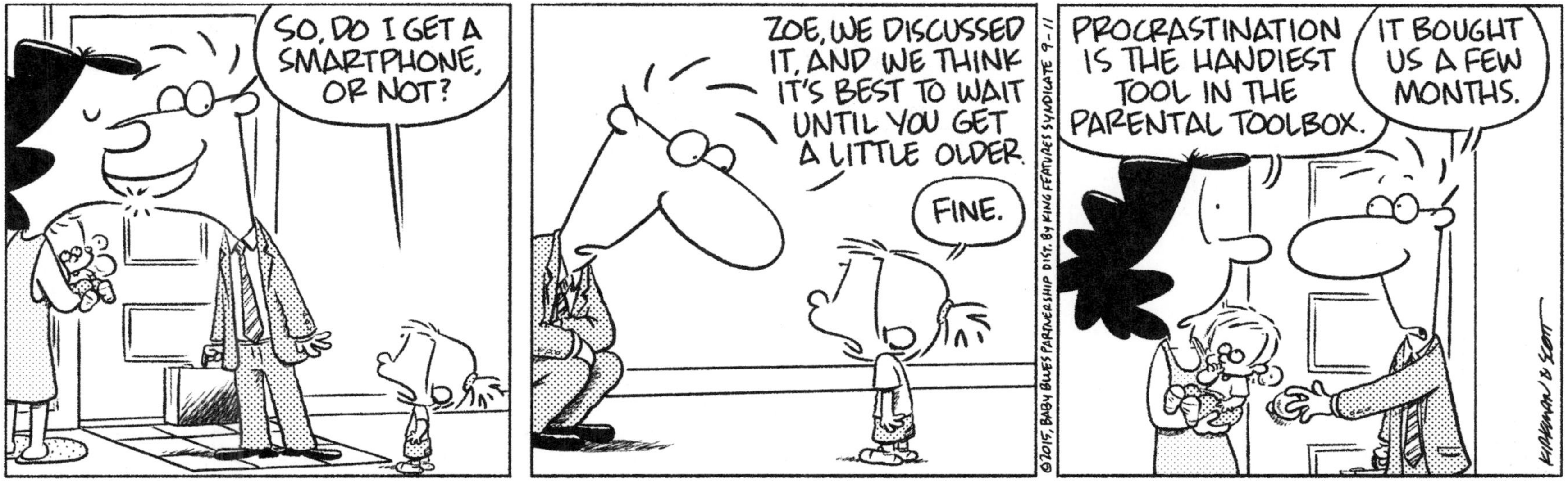
SO, DO I GET A SMARTPHONE, OR NOT?
ZOE, WE DISCUSSED IT, AND WE THINK IT'S BEST TO WAIT UNTIL YOU GET A LITTLE OLDER.
FINE.
©2015, BABY BLUES PARTNERSHIP DIST. BY KING FEATURES SYNDICATE 9-11
PROCRASTINATION IS THE HANDIEST TOOL IN THE PARENTAL TOOLBOX.
IT BOUGHT US A FEW MONTHS.
KIRKMAN & SCOTT

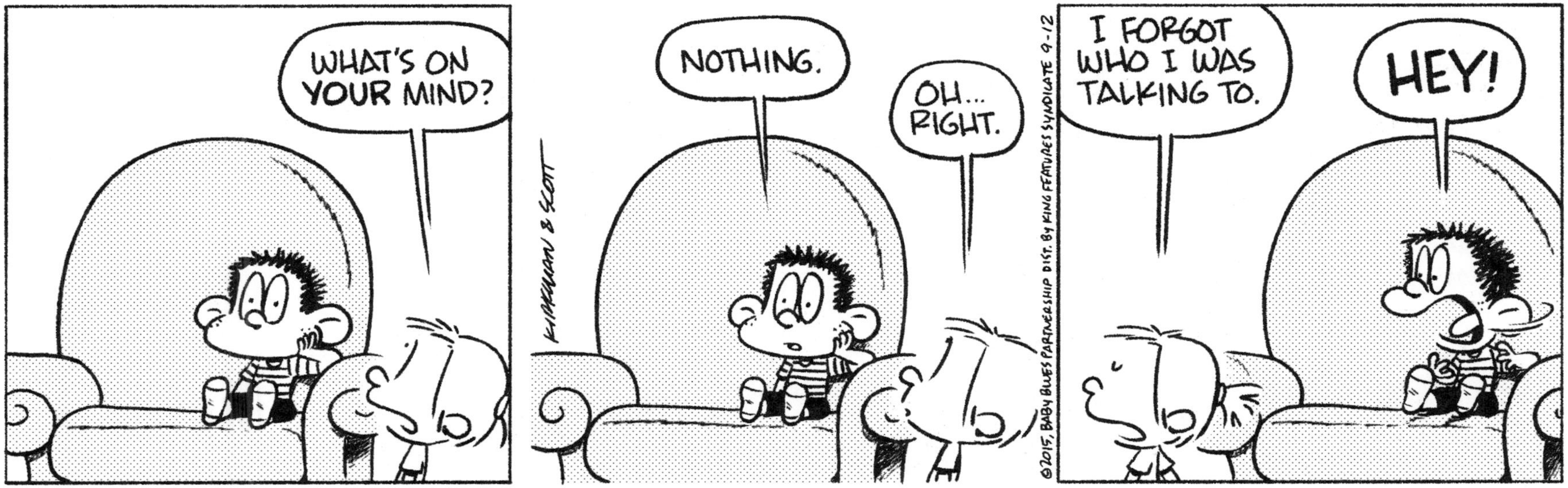
WHAT'S ON YOUR MIND?
KIRKMAN & SCOTT
NOTHING.
OH... RIGHT.
©2015, BABY BLUES PARTNERSHIP DIST. BY KING FEATURES SYNDICATE 9-12
I FORGOT WHO I WAS TALKING TO.
HEY!

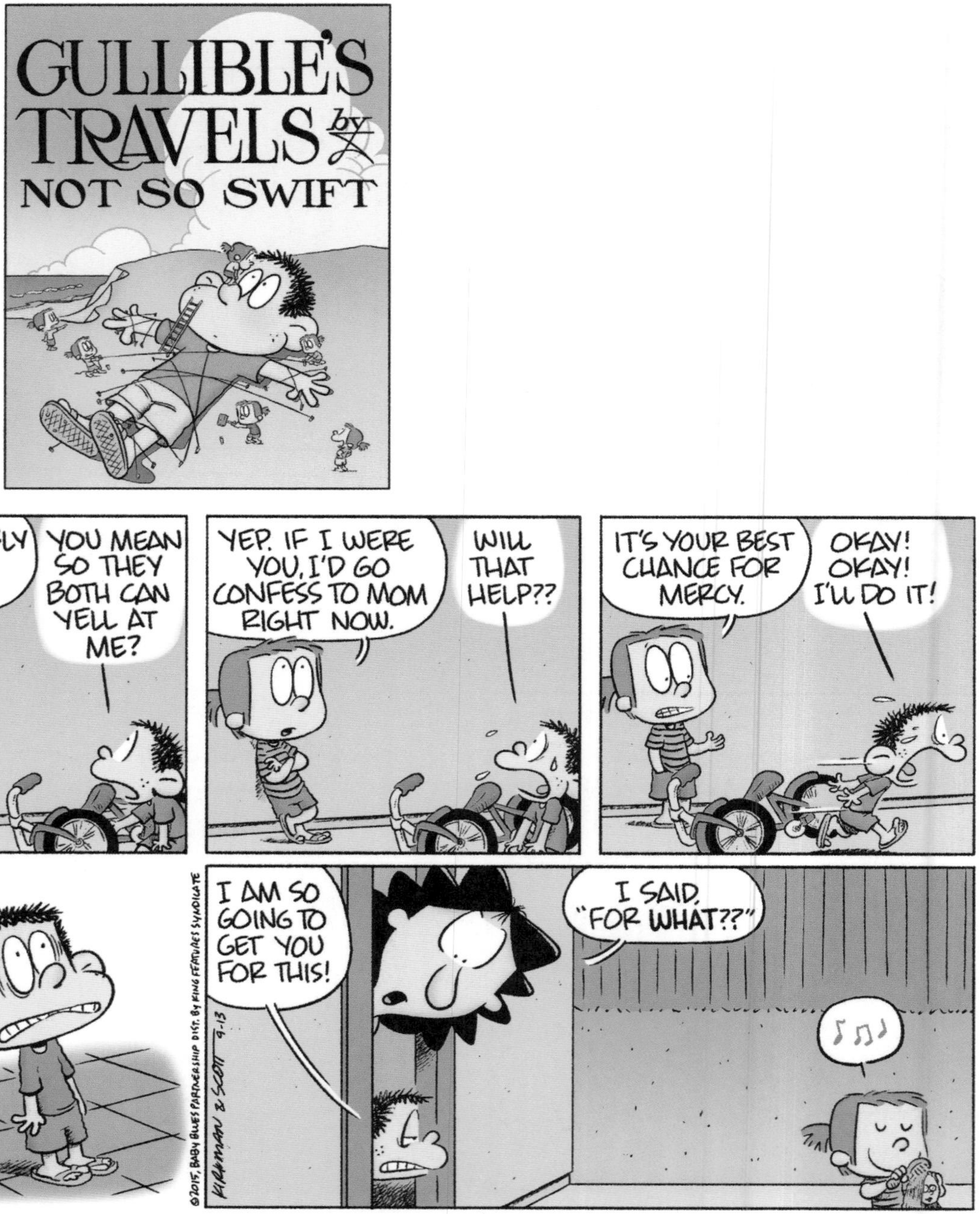
GULLIBLE'S TRAVELS by NOT SO SWIFT
BY THE WAY, I TOLD MOM WHAT YOU DID.
THEN WHY ISN'T SHE YELLING AT ME?
SHE'S PROBABLY WAITING FOR DAD.
YOU MEAN SO THEY BOTH CAN YELL AT ME?
YEP. IF I WERE YOU, I'D GO CONFESS TO MOM RIGHT NOW.
WILL THAT HELP??
IT'S YOUR BEST CHANCE FOR MERCY.
OKAY! OKAY! I'LL DO IT!
I'M REALLY, REALLY SORRY, MOM!
FOR WHAT?
UHHH...
©2015, BABY BLUES PARTNERSHIP DIST. BY KING FEATURES SYNDICATE
KIRKMAN & SCOTT 9-13
I AM SO GOING TO GET YOU FOR THIS!
I SAID, "FOR WHAT??"

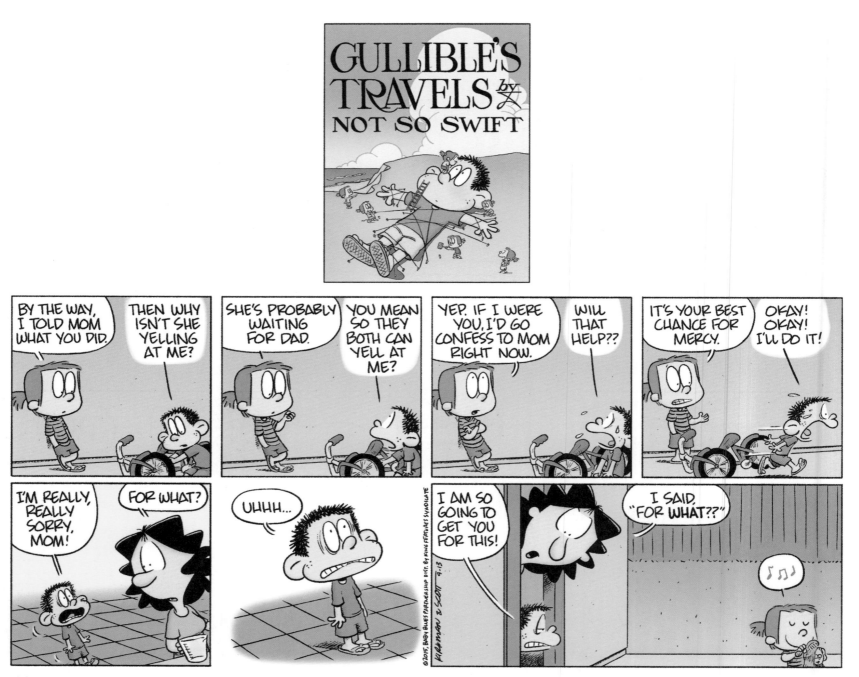

Rick: Love that gag. It called for an extra-special title panel. *Gulliver's Travels* made for a perfect malapropism. I hunted down one of the old book covers online—this being one from 1930, with illustrations by Edwin J. Prittie—and tried to replicate it. It also satisfied my love for hand-lettering.

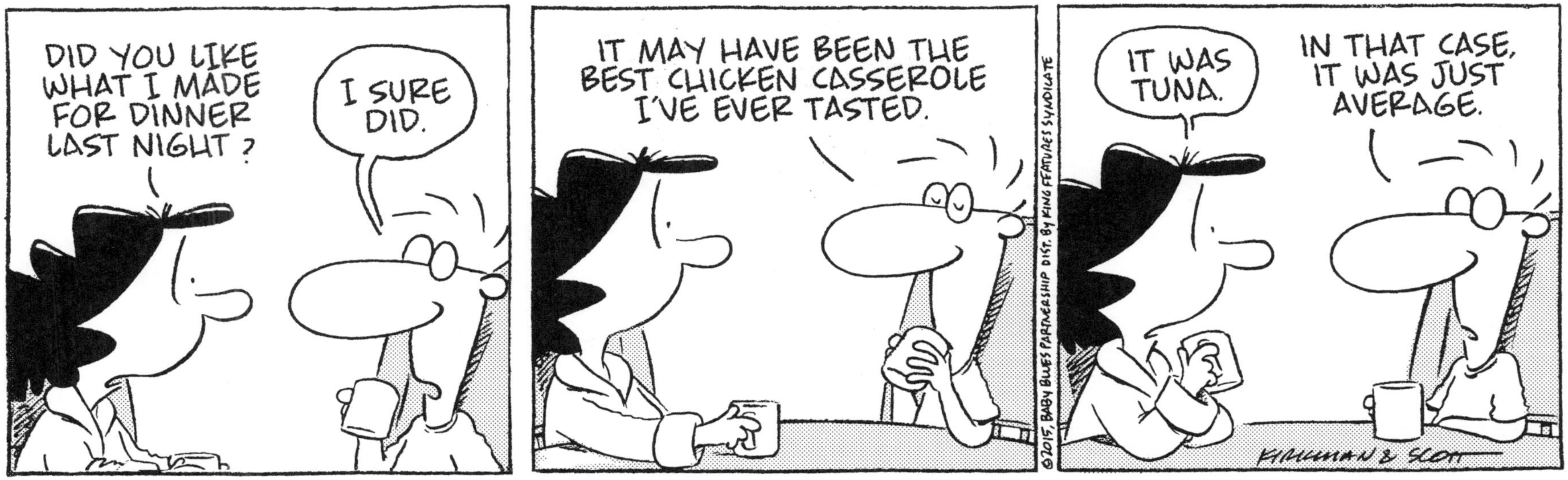
DID YOU LIKE WHAT I MADE FOR DINNER LAST NIGHT?
I SURE DID.
IT MAY HAVE BEEN THE BEST CHICKEN CASSEROLE I'VE EVER TASTED.
IT WAS TUNA.
IN THAT CASE, IT WAS JUST AVERAGE.
©2015, BABY BLUES PARTNERSHIP DIST. BY KING FEATURES SYNDICATE
KIRKMAN & SCOTT

Rick: The last of Jerry's hybrid weeks.

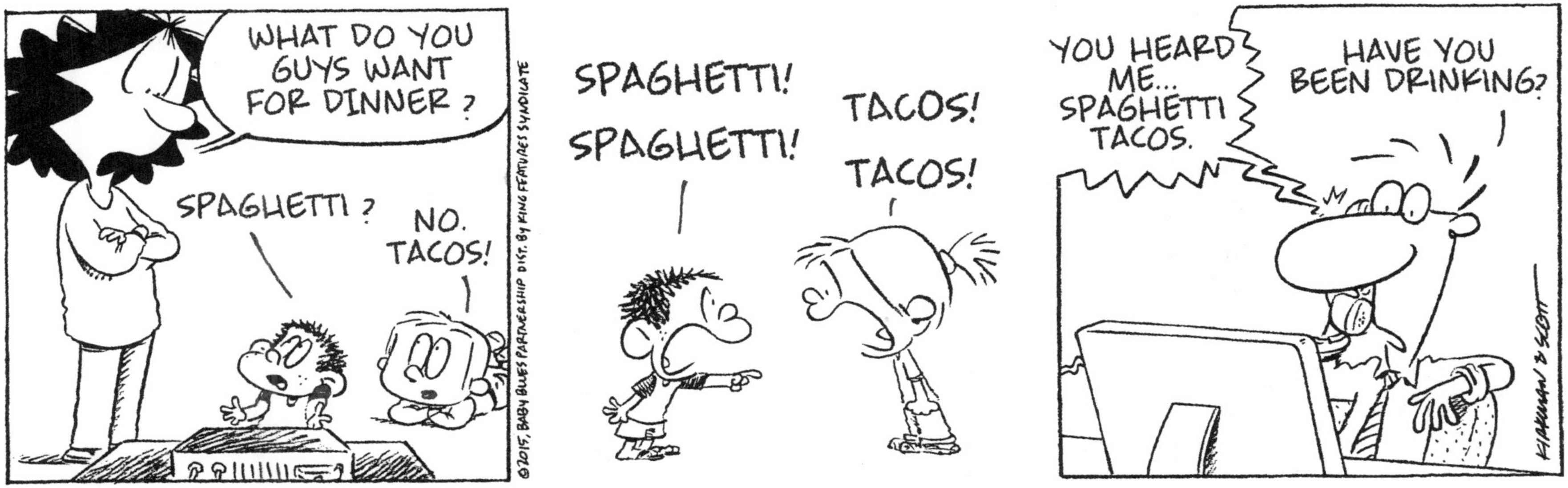
WHAT DO YOU GUYS WANT FOR DINNER?
SPAGHETTI?
NO. TACOS!
©2015, BABY BLUES PARTNERSHIP DIST. BY KING FEATURES SYNDICATE
SPAGHETTI! SPAGHETTI!
TACOS! TACOS!
YOU HEARD ME... SPAGHETTI TACOS.
HAVE YOU BEEN DRINKING?
KIRKMAN & SCOTT

Jerry: I'm going to try this the next time it's my turn to make dinner.

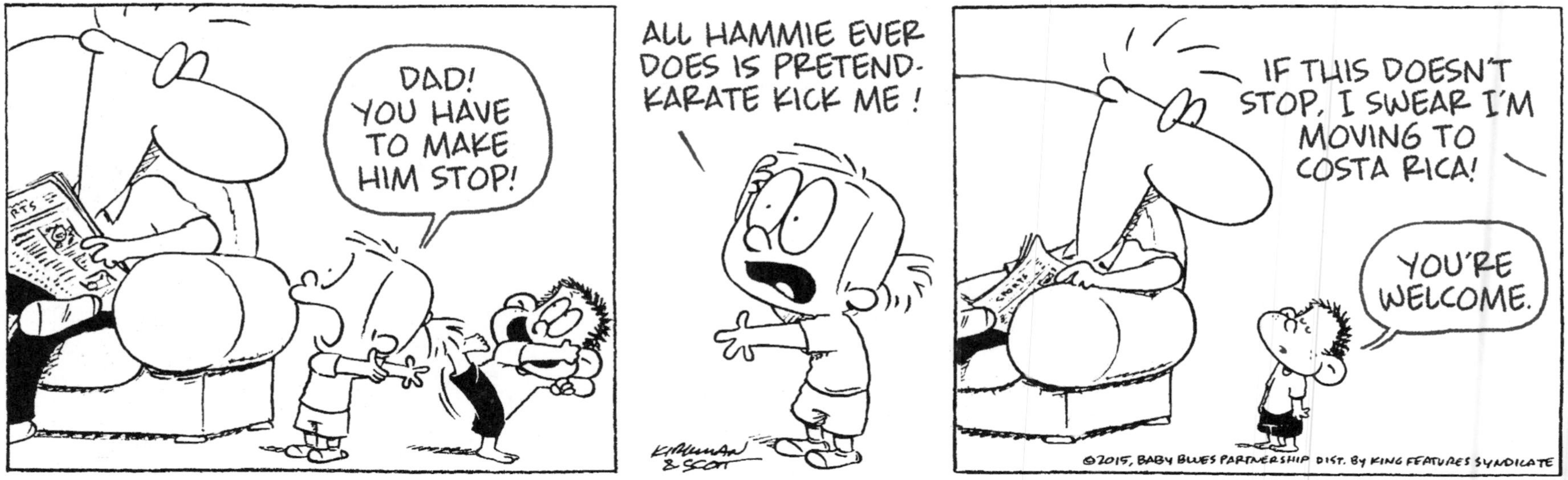
DAD! YOU HAVE TO MAKE HIM STOP!
ALL HAMMIE EVER DOES IS PRETEND-KARATE KICK ME!
KIRKMAN & SCOTT
IF THIS DOESN'T STOP, I SWEAR I'M MOVING TO COSTA RICA!
YOU'RE WELCOME.
©2015, BABY BLUES PARTNERSHIP DIST. BY KING FEATURES SYNDICATE

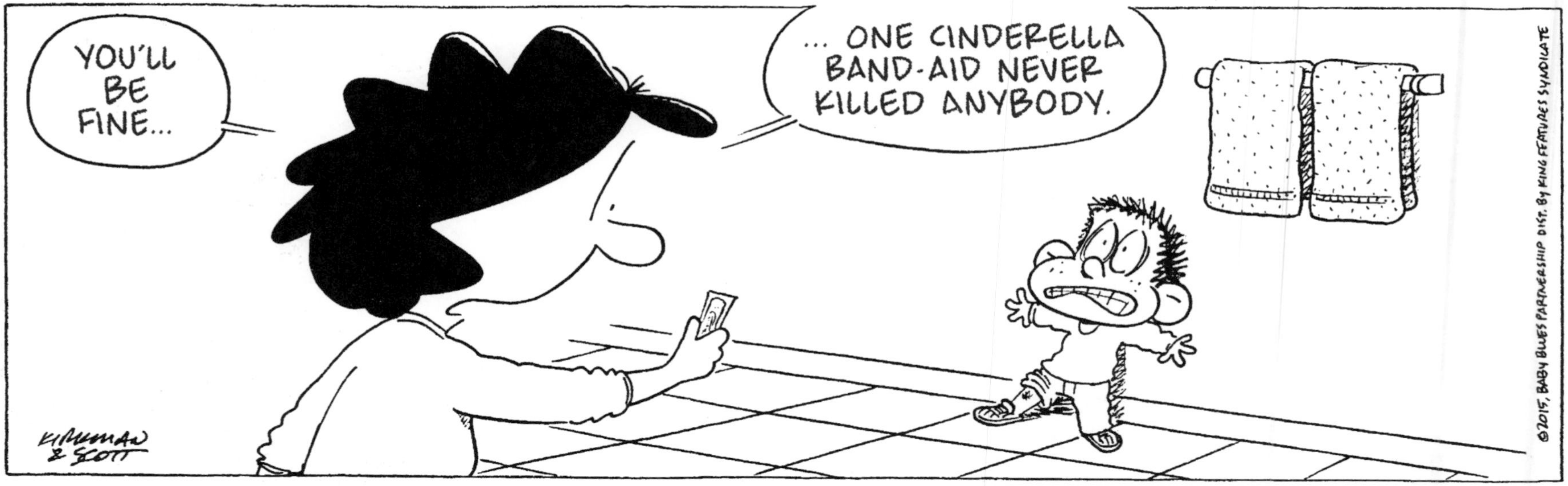
YOU'LL BE FINE...
... ONE CINDERELLA BAND-AID NEVER KILLED ANYBODY.
KIRKMAN & SCOTT
©2015, BABY BLUES PARTNERSHIP DIST. BY KING FEATURES SYNDICATE

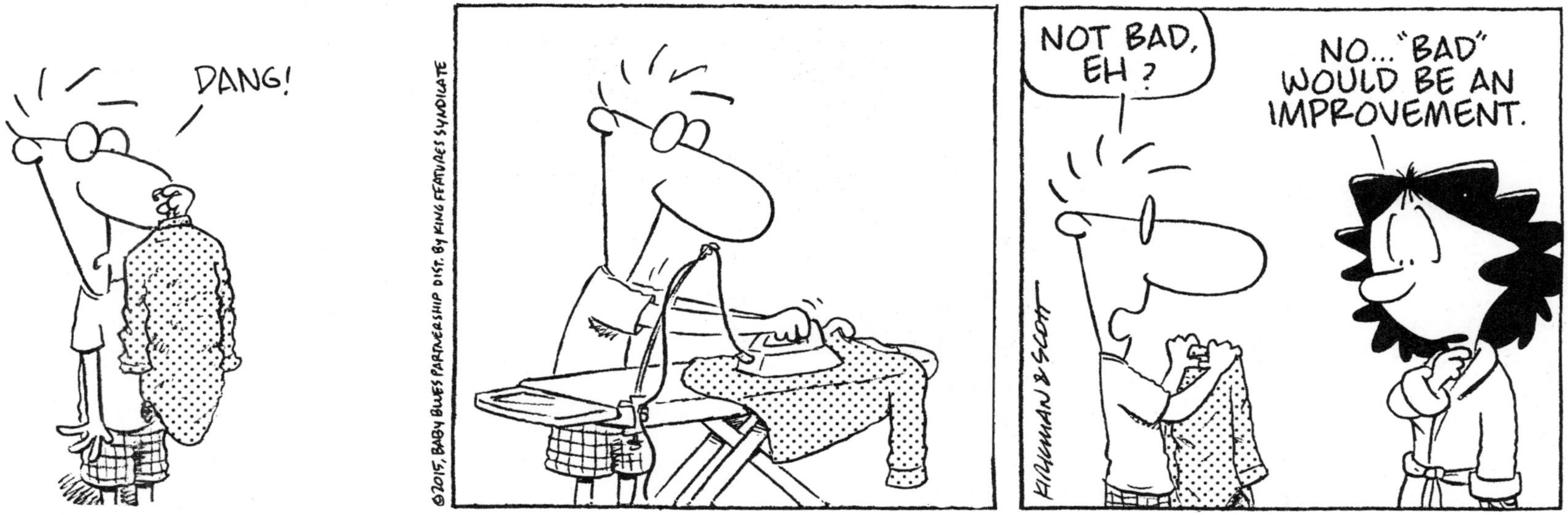
DANG!
©2015, BABY BLUES PARTNERSHIP DIST. BY KING FEATURES SYNDICATE
NOT BAD, EH ?
NO... "BAD" WOULD BE AN IMPROVEMENT.
KIRKMAN & SCOTT

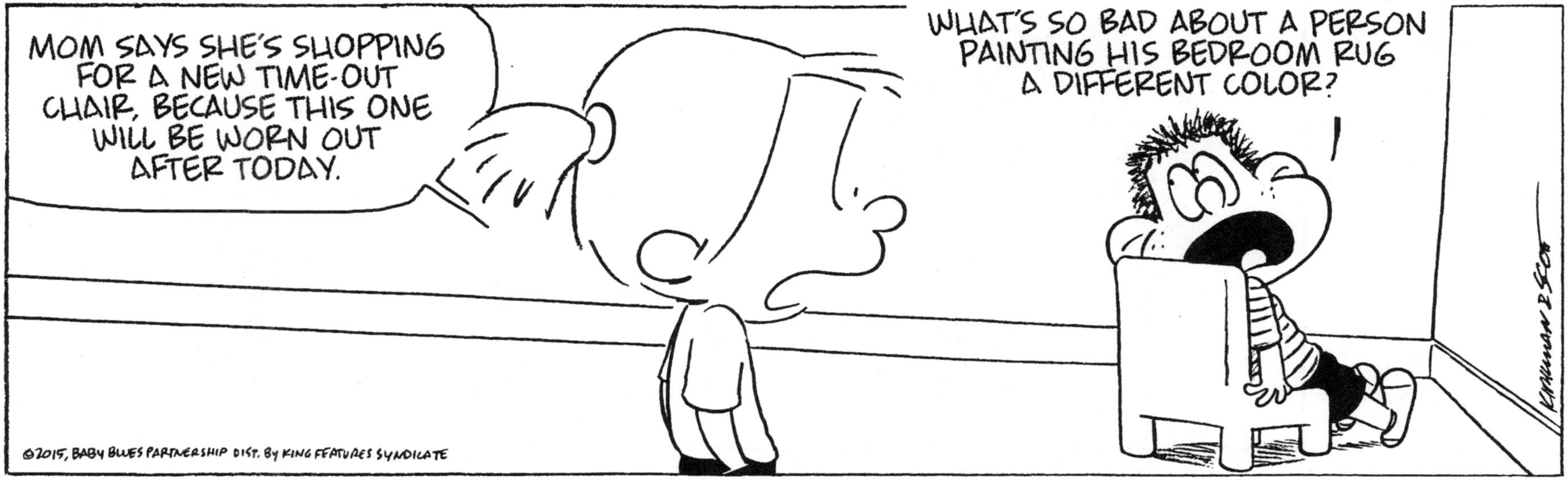
MOM SAYS SHE'S SHOPPING FOR A NEW TIME-OUT CHAIR, BECAUSE THIS ONE WILL BE WORN OUT AFTER TODAY.
WHAT'S SO BAD ABOUT A PERSON PAINTING HIS BEDROOM RUG A DIFFERENT COLOR?
KIRKMAN & SCOTT
©2015, BABY BLUES PARTNERSHIP DIST. BY KING FEATURES SYNDICATE

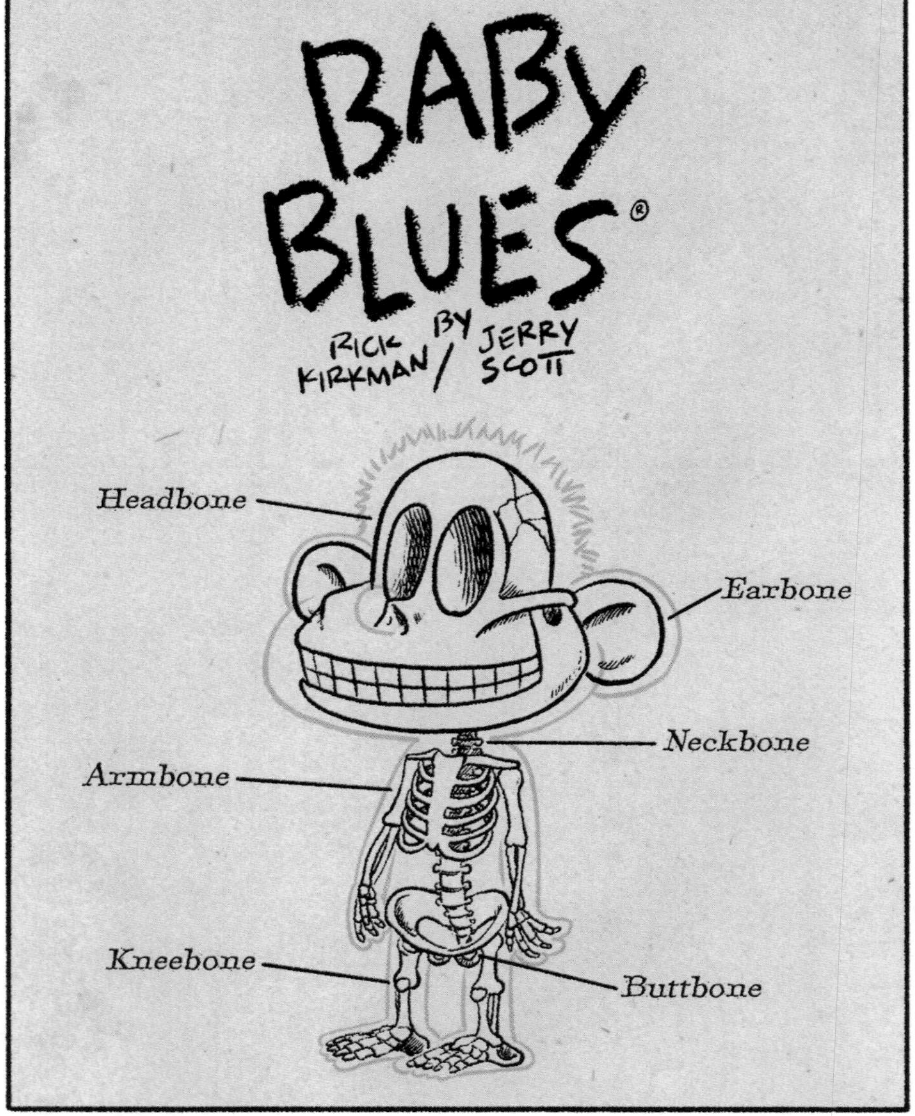
BABY BLUES®
BY RICK KIRKMAN / JERRY SCOTT
Headbone
Earbone
Neckbone
Armbone
Kneebone
Buttbone

Rick: Early on in *Baby Blues*, I drew Darryl's skeleton. It was now Hammie's turn. I strive to be anatomically correct. Take that, *Gray's Anatomy*.

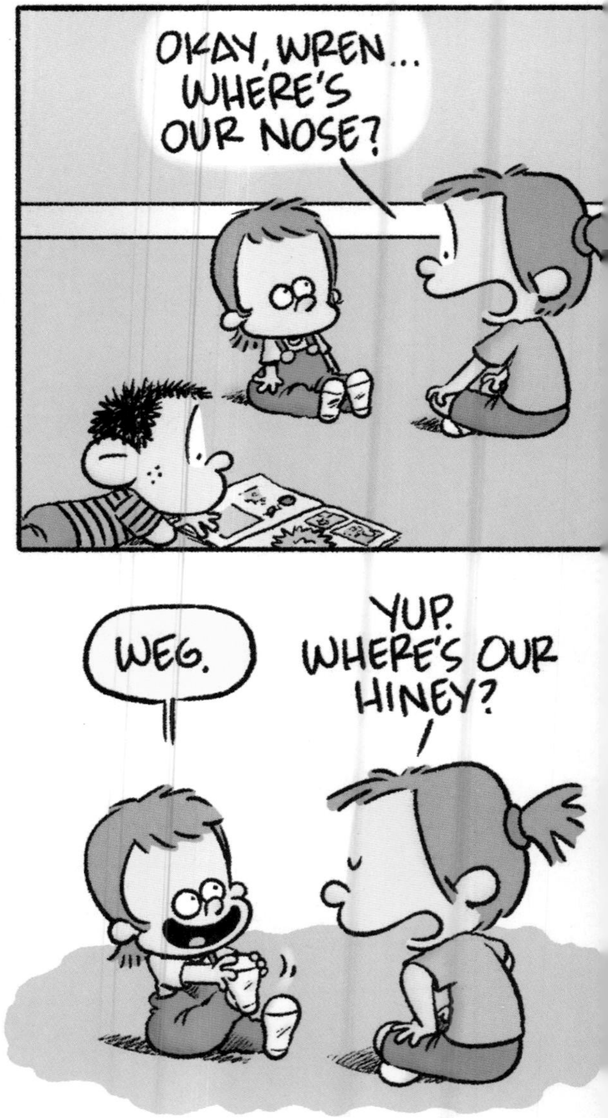
OKAY, WREN... WHERE'S OUR NOSE?
WEG.
YUP. WHERE'S OUR HINEY?

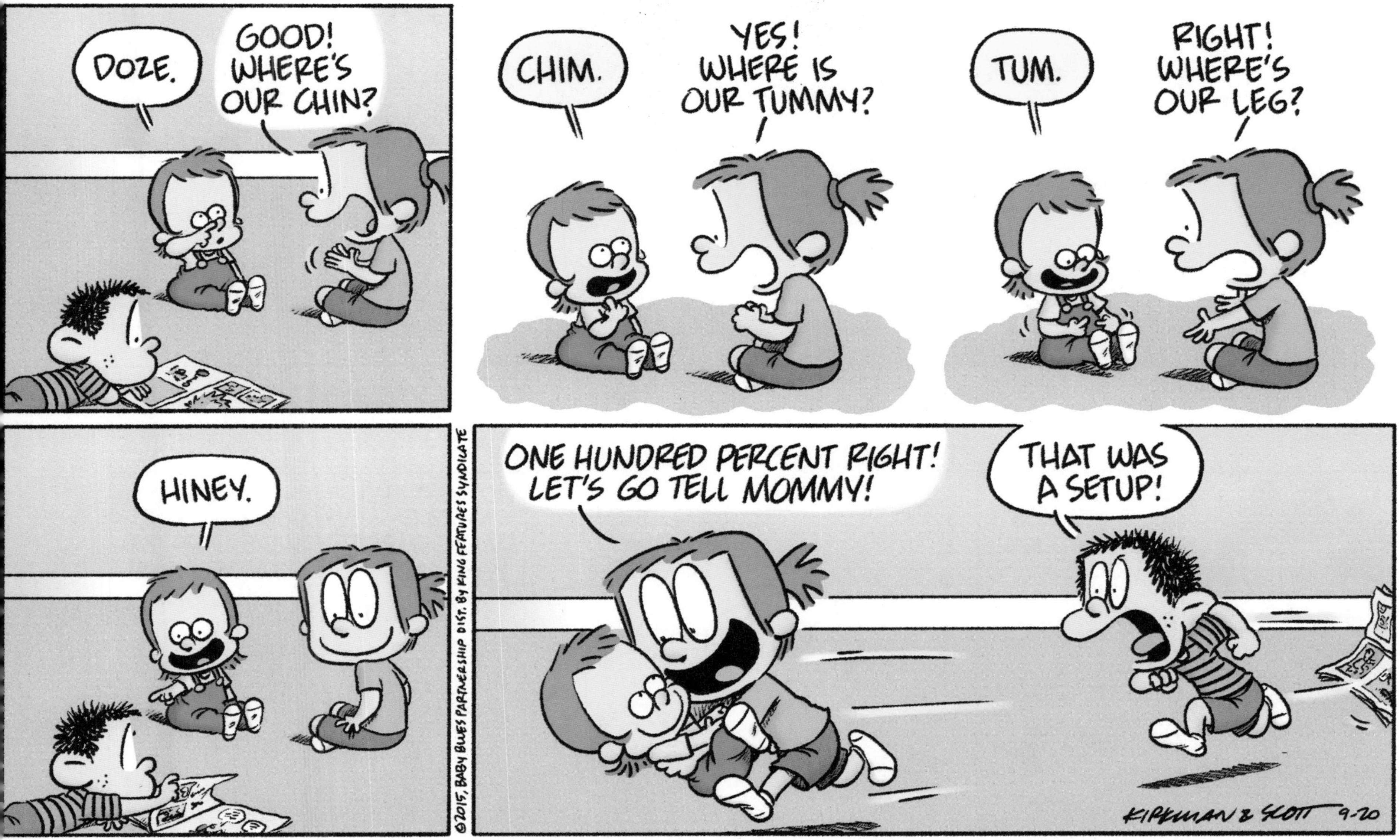
DOZE.
GOOD! WHERE'S OUR CHIN?
CHIM.
YES! WHERE IS OUR TUMMY?
TUM.
RIGHT! WHERE'S OUR LEG?
HINEY.
ONE HUNDRED PERCENT RIGHT! LET'S GO TELL MOMMY!
THAT WAS A SETUP!
©2015, BABY BLUES PARTNERSHIP DIST. BY KING FEATURES SYNDICATE
KIRKMAN & SCOTT 9-20

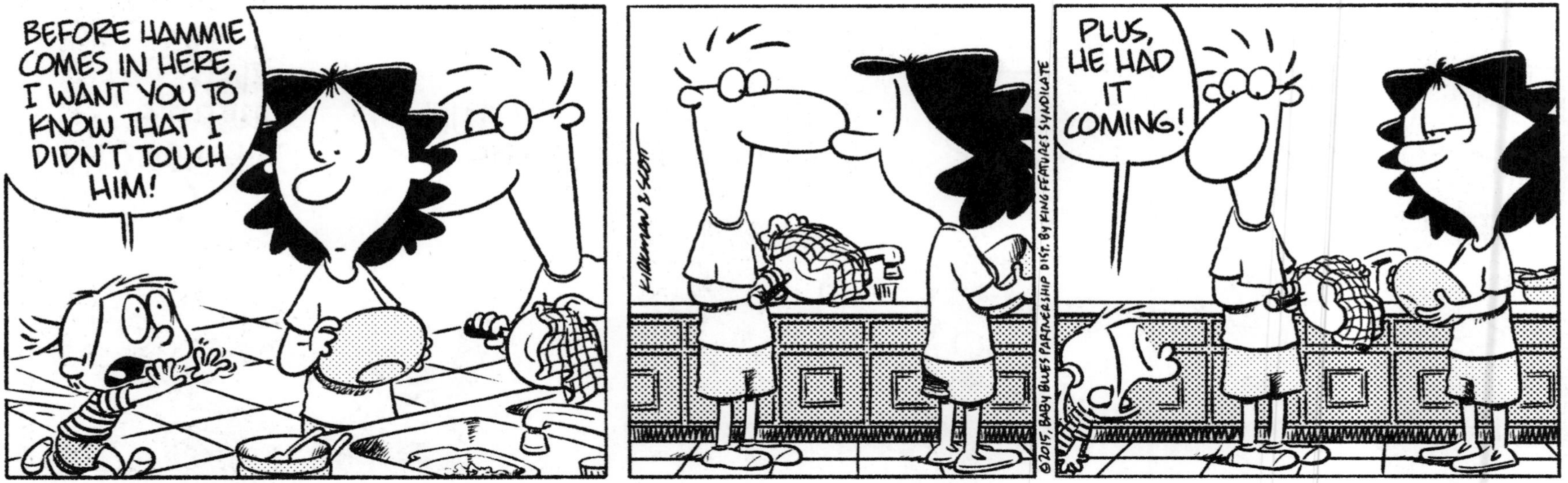
BEFORE HAMMIE COMES IN HERE, I WANT YOU TO KNOW THAT I DIDN'T TOUCH HIM!
KIRKMAN & SCOTT
©2015, BABY BLUES PARTNERSHIP DIST. BY KING FEATURES SYNDICATE
PLUS, HE HAD IT COMING!

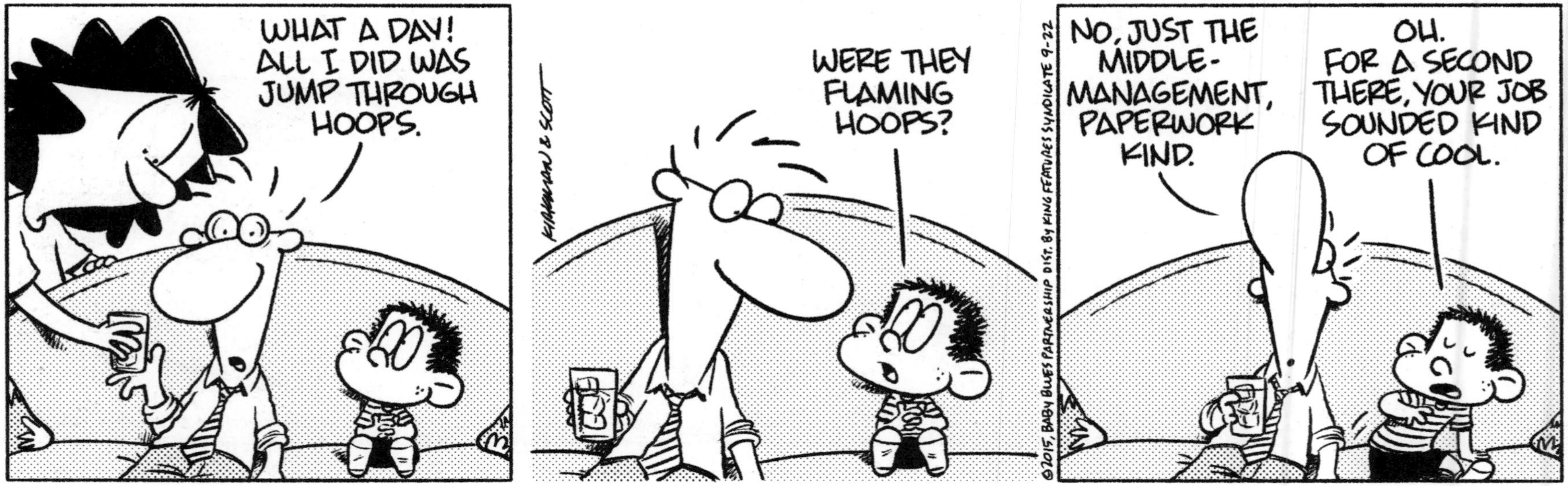
WHAT A DAY! ALL I DID WAS JUMP THROUGH HOOPS.
KIRKMAN & SCOTT
WERE THEY FLAMING HOOPS?
©2015, BABY BLUES PARTNERSHIP DIST. BY KING FEATURES SYNDICATE 9-22
NO, JUST THE MIDDLE-MANAGEMENT, PAPERWORK KIND.
OH. FOR A SECOND THERE, YOUR JOB SOUNDED KIND OF COOL.

Rick: Kids are a tough crowd.

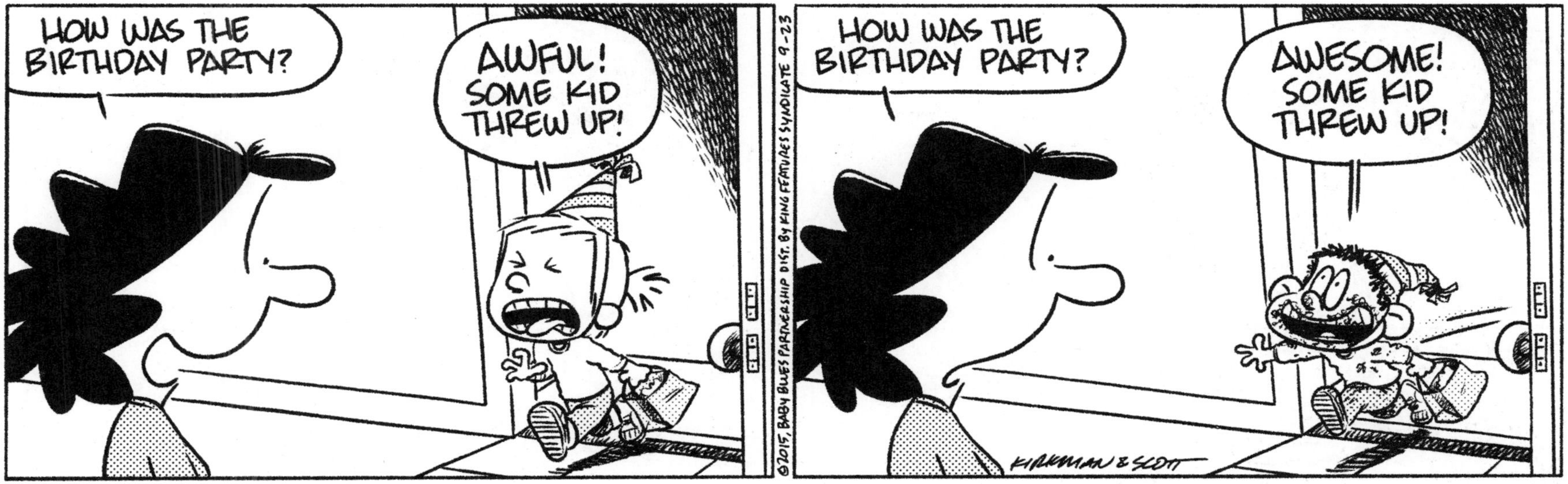
HOW WAS THE BIRTHDAY PARTY?
AWFUL! SOME KID THREW UP!
©2015, BABY BLUES PARTNERSHIP DIST. BY KING FEATURES SYNDICATE 9-23
HOW WAS THE BIRTHDAY PARTY?
AWESOME! SOME KID THREW UP!
KIRKMAN & SCOTT

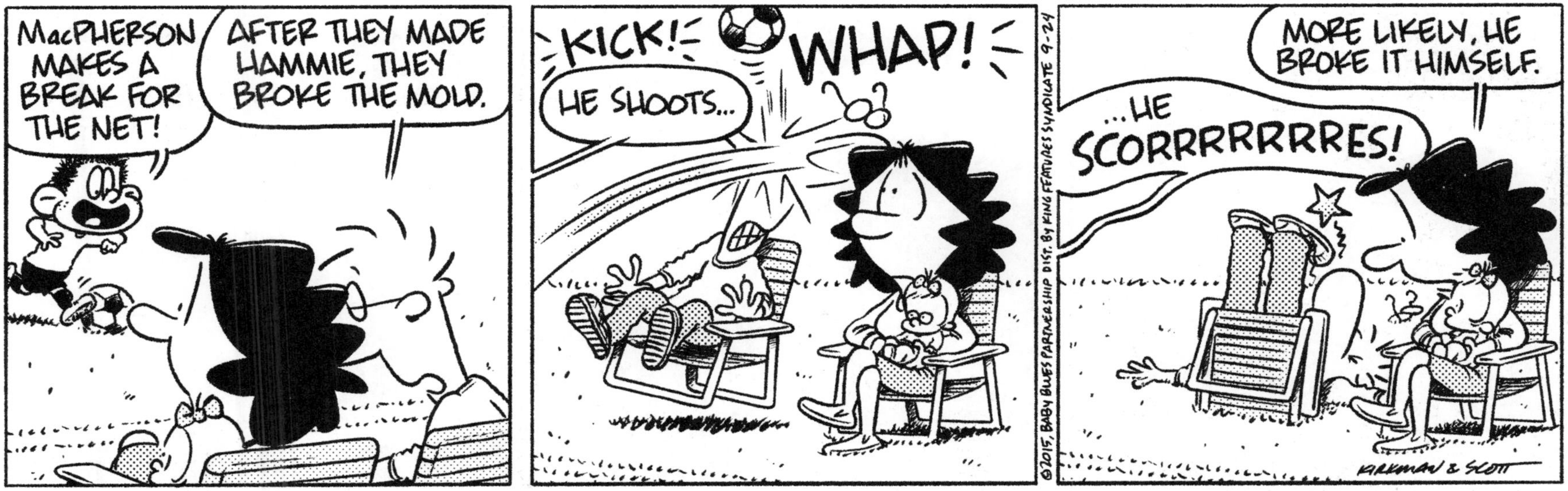
MacPHERSON MAKES A BREAK FOR THE NET!
AFTER THEY MADE HAMMIE, THEY BROKE THE MOLD.
KICK!
HE SHOOTS...
WHAP!
©2015, BABY BLUES PARTNERSHIP DIST. BY KING FEATURES SYNDICATE 9-24
...HE SCORRRRRRRES!
MORE LIKELY, HE BROKE IT HIMSELF.
KIRKMAN & SCOTT

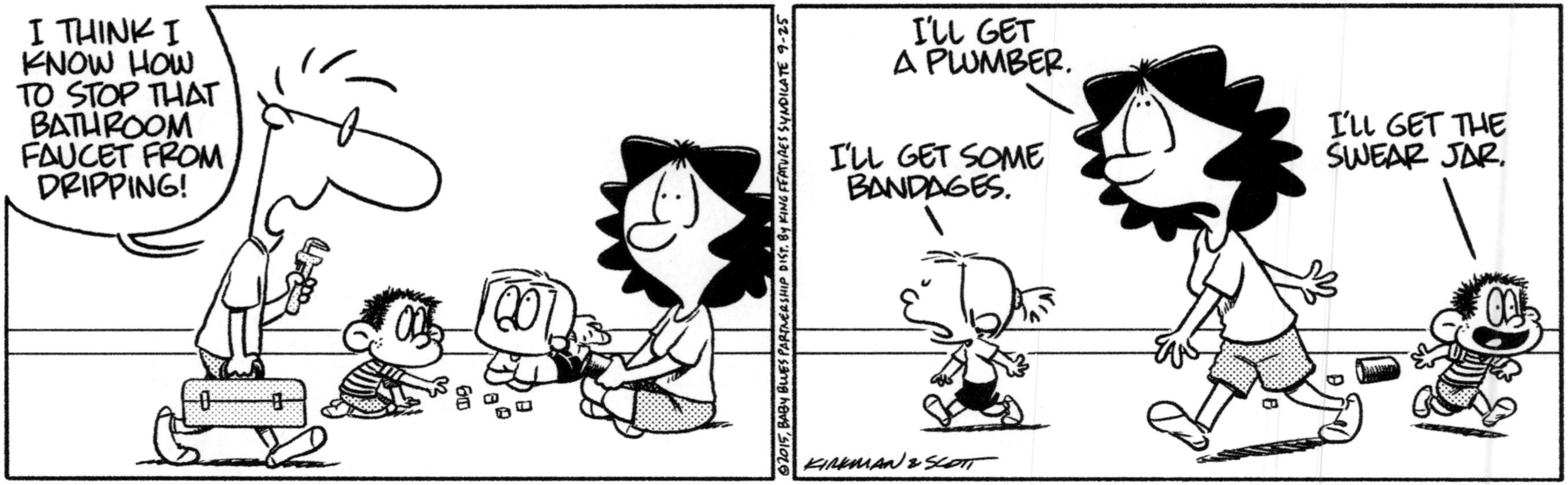
I THINK I KNOW HOW TO STOP THAT BATHROOM FAUCET FROM DRIPPING!
©2015, BABY BLUES PARTNERSHIP DIST. BY KING FEATURES SYNDICATE 9-25
I'LL GET A PLUMBER.
I'LL GET SOME BANDAGES.
I'LL GET THE SWEAR JAR.
KIRKMAN & SCOTT

Rick: Jerry must be talking to my wife.

Jerry: Rick's lack of plumbing skills is one of the most reliable joke generators I have.

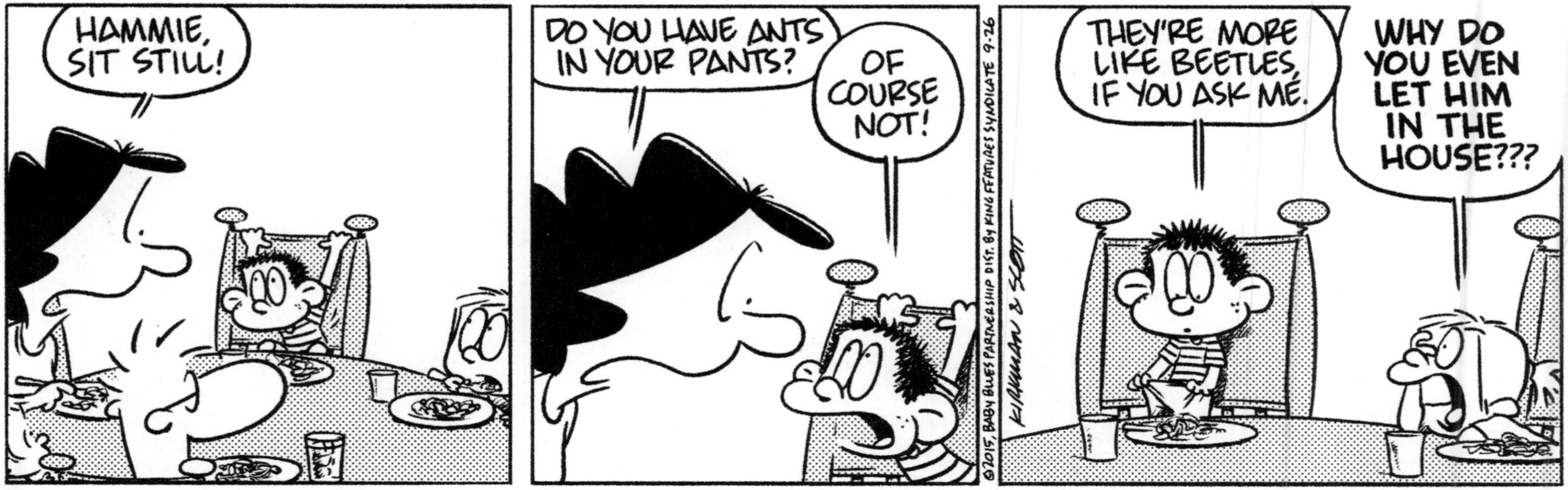
HAMMIE, SIT STILL!
DO YOU HAVE ANTS IN YOUR PANTS?
OF COURSE NOT!
©2015, BABY BLUES PARTNERSHIP DIST. BY KING FEATURES SYNDICATE 9-26
KIRKMAN & SCOTT
THEY'RE MORE LIKE BEETLES, IF YOU ASK ME.
WHY DO YOU EVEN LET HIM IN THE HOUSE???

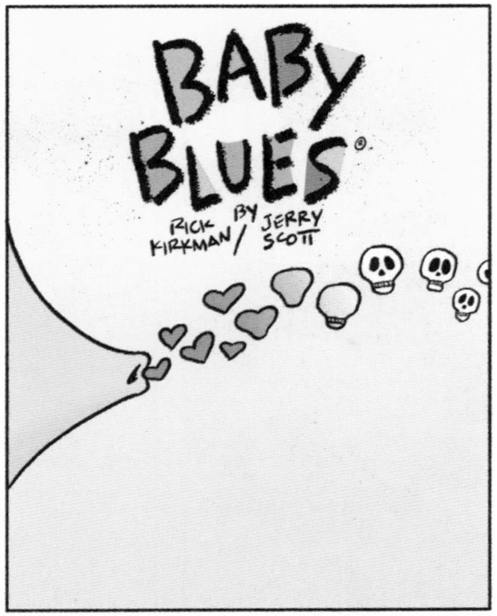
BABY BLUES®
BY RICK KIRKMAN / JERRY SCOTT

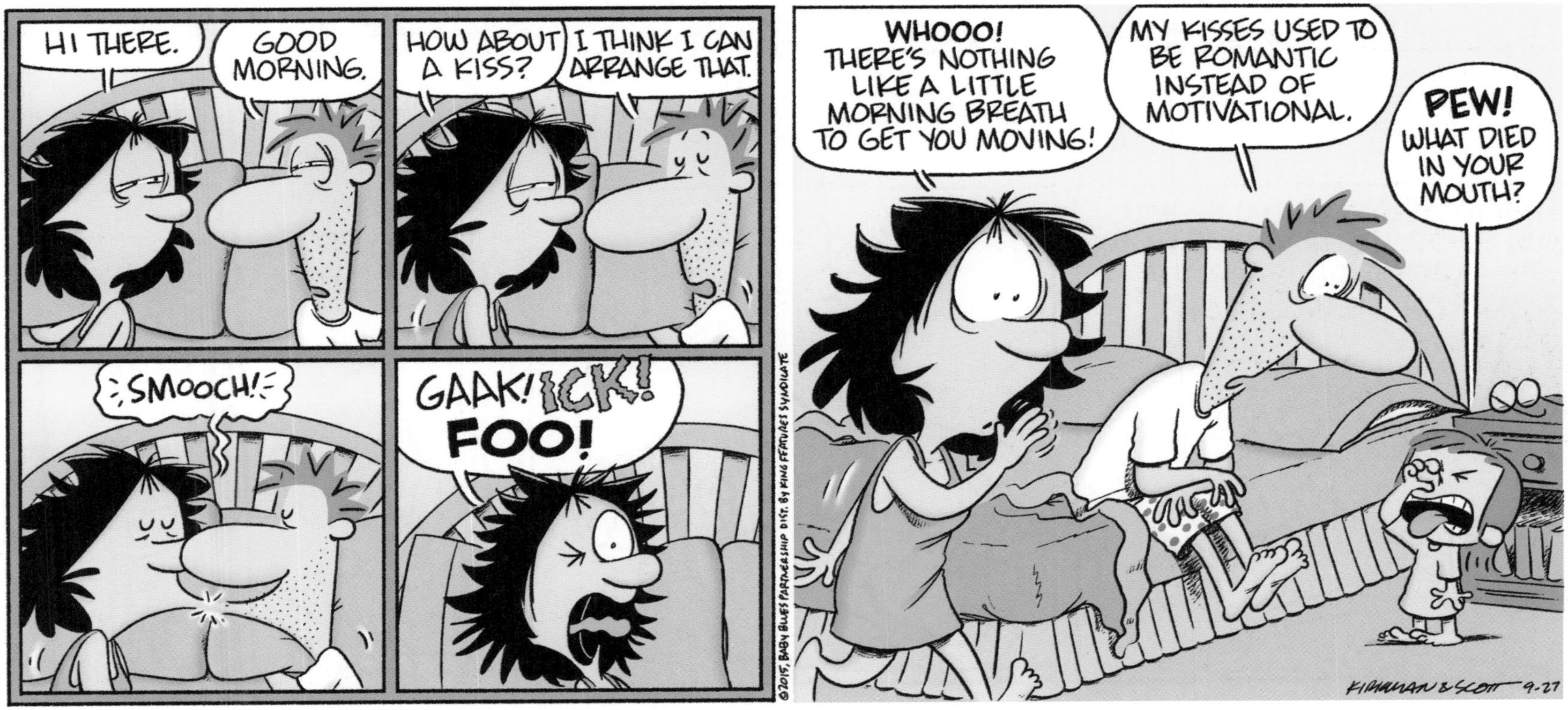
HI THERE.
GOOD MORNING.
HOW ABOUT A KISS?
I THINK I CAN ARRANGE THAT.
SMOOCH!
GAAK! ICK! FOO!
©2015, BABY BLUES PARTNERSHIP DIST. BY KING FEATURES SYNDICATE
WHOOO! THERE'S NOTHING LIKE A LITTLE MORNING BREATH TO GET YOU MOVING!
MY KISSES USED TO BE ROMANTIC INSTEAD OF MOTIVATIONAL.
PEW! WHAT DIED IN YOUR MOUTH?
KIRKMAN & SCOTT 9-27

Rick: I like the last couple drawings of Wanda here.

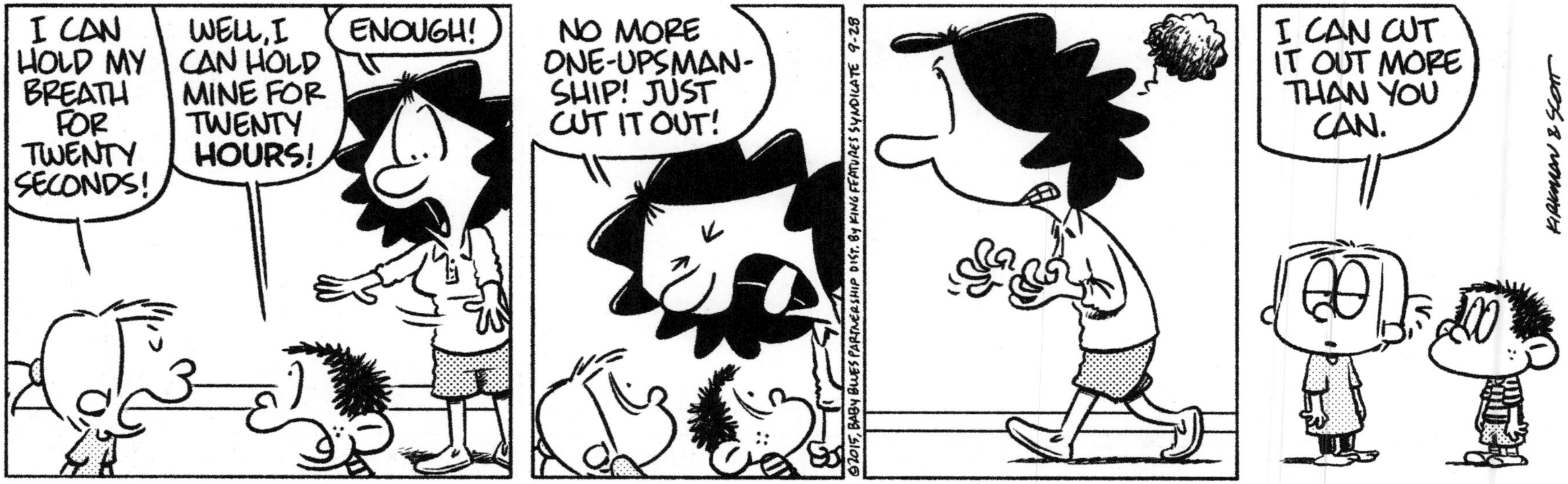
I CAN HOLD MY BREATH FOR TWENTY SECONDS!
WELL, I CAN HOLD MINE FOR TWENTY **HOURS**!
ENOUGH!
NO MORE ONE-UPSMANSHIP! JUST CUT IT OUT!
©2015, BABY BLUES PARTNERSHIP DIST. BY KING FEATURES SYNDICATE 9-28
I CAN CUT IT OUT MORE THAN YOU CAN.
KIRKMAN & SCOTT

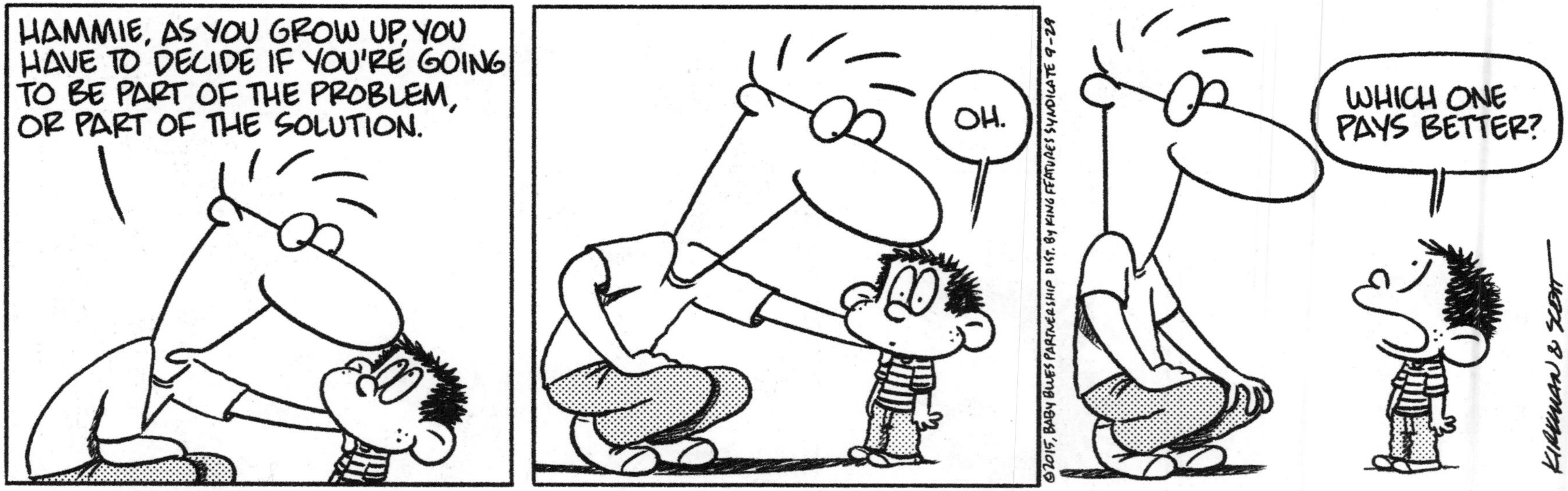
HAMMIE, AS YOU GROW UP, YOU HAVE TO DECIDE IF YOU'RE GOING TO BE PART OF THE PROBLEM, OR PART OF THE SOLUTION.
OH.
©2015, BABY BLUES PARTNERSHIP DIST. BY KING FEATURES SYNDICATE 9-29
WHICH ONE PAYS BETTER?
KIRKMAN & SCOTT

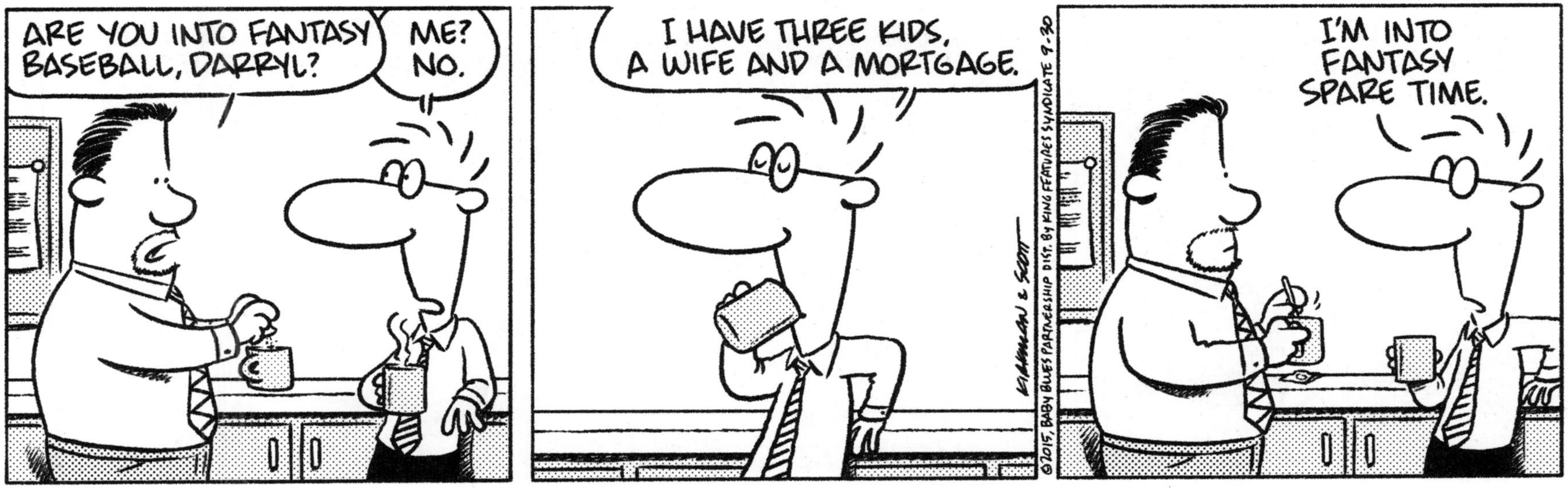
ARE YOU INTO FANTASY BASEBALL, DARRYL?
ME? NO.
I HAVE THREE KIDS, A WIFE AND A MORTGAGE.
I'M INTO FANTASY SPARE TIME.
©2015, BABY BLUES PARTNERSHIP DIST. BY KING FEATURES SYNDICATE 9-30
KIRKMAN & SCOTT

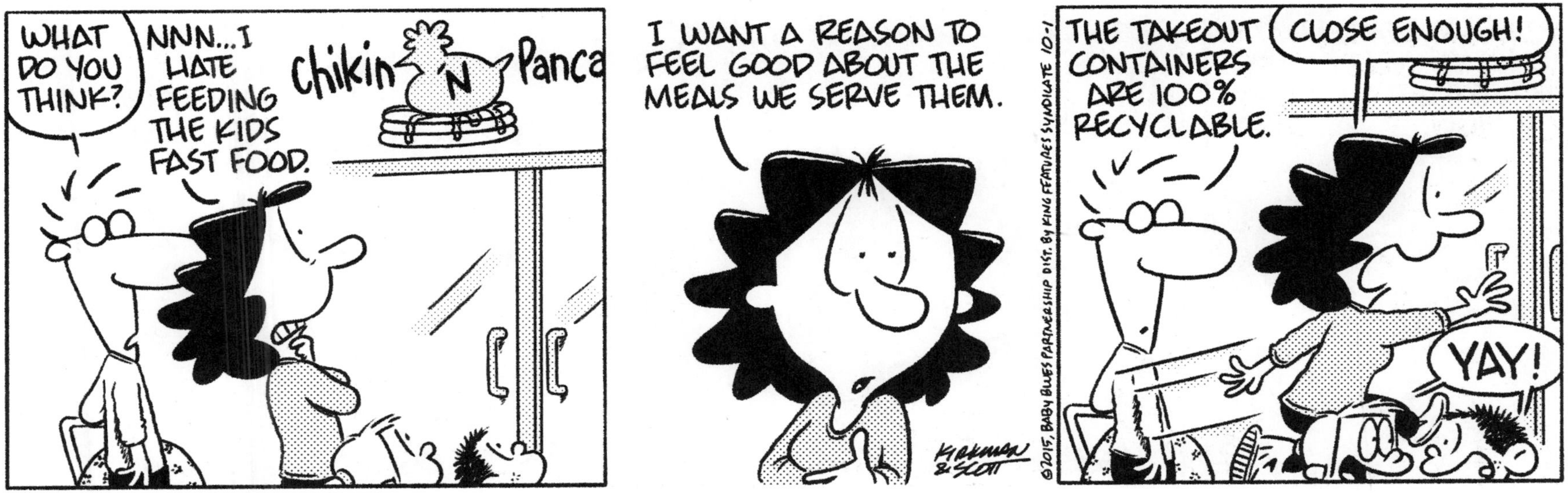
WHAT DO YOU THINK?
NNN...I HATE FEEDING THE KIDS FAST FOOD.
Chikin N Panca
I WANT A REASON TO FEEL GOOD ABOUT THE MEALS WE SERVE THEM.
KIRKMAN & SCOTT
©2015, BABY BLUES PARTNERSHIP DIST. BY KING FEATURES SYNDICATE 10-1
THE TAKEOUT CONTAINERS ARE 100% RECYCLABLE.
CLOSE ENOUGH!
YAY!

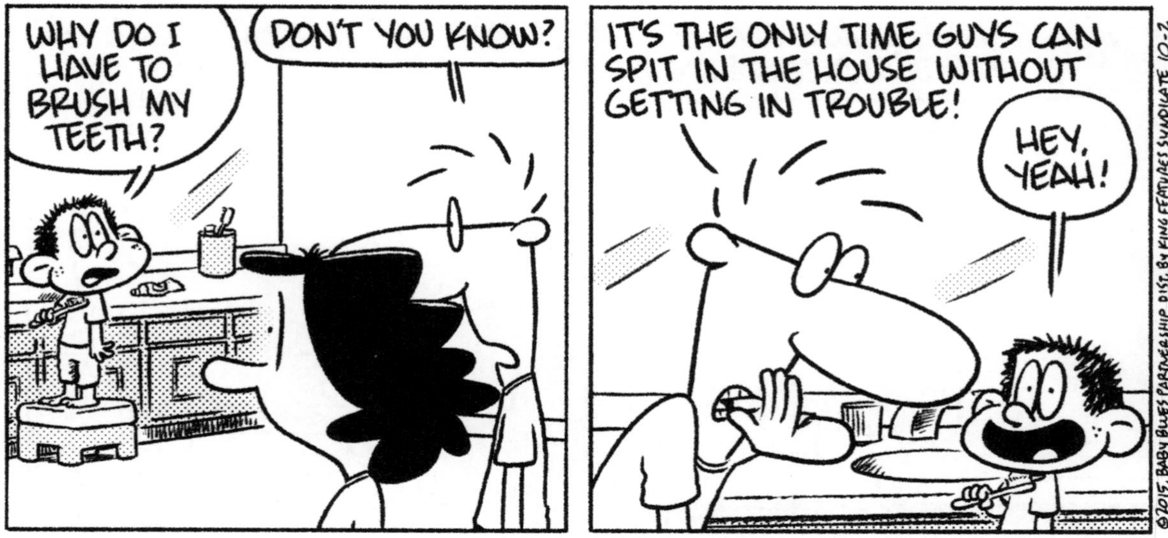
WHY DO I HAVE TO BRUSH MY TEETH?
DON'T YOU KNOW?
IT'S THE ONLY TIME GUYS CAN SPIT IN THE HOUSE WITHOUT GETTING IN TROUBLE!
HEY, YEAH!
©2015, BABY BLUES PARTNERSHIP DIST. BY KING FEATURES SYNDICATE 10-2
THAT WAS INSPIRED MALE PSYCHOLOGY!
GIRLS BRUSH THEIR TEETH FOR A DIFFERENT REASON?
KIRKMAN & SCOTT

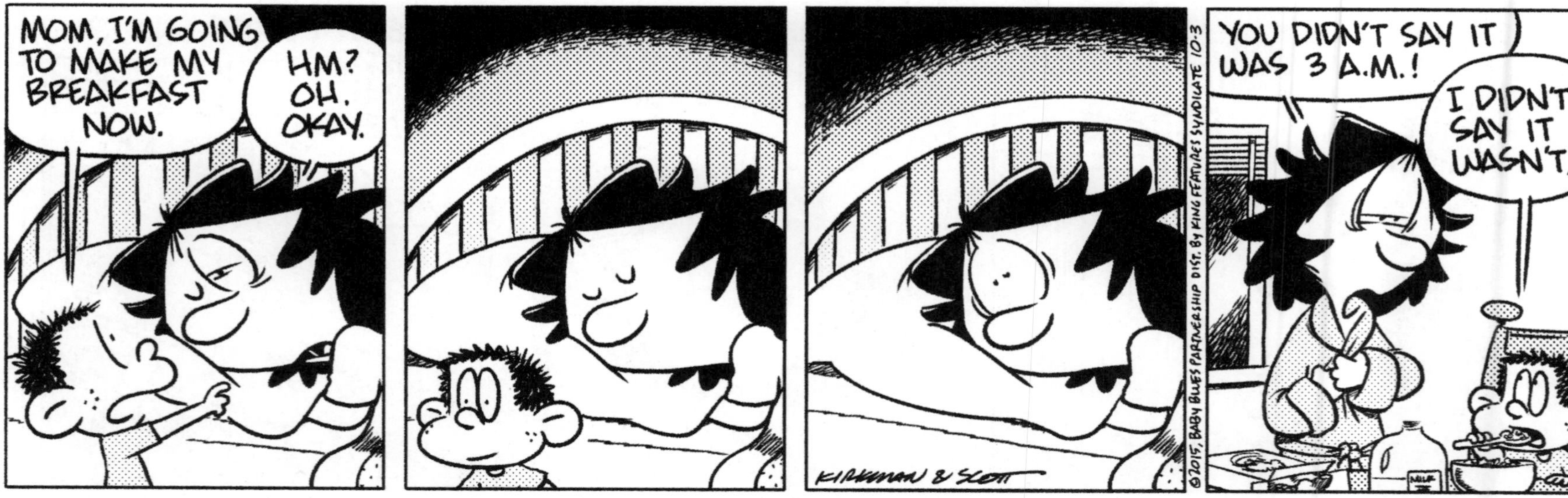
MOM, I'M GOING TO MAKE MY BREAKFAST NOW.
HM? OH. OKAY.
KIRKMAN & SCOTT
©2015, BABY BLUES PARTNERSHIP DIST. BY KING FEATURES SYNDICATE 10-3
YOU DIDN'T SAY IT WAS 3 A.M.!
I DIDN'T SAY IT WASN'T.

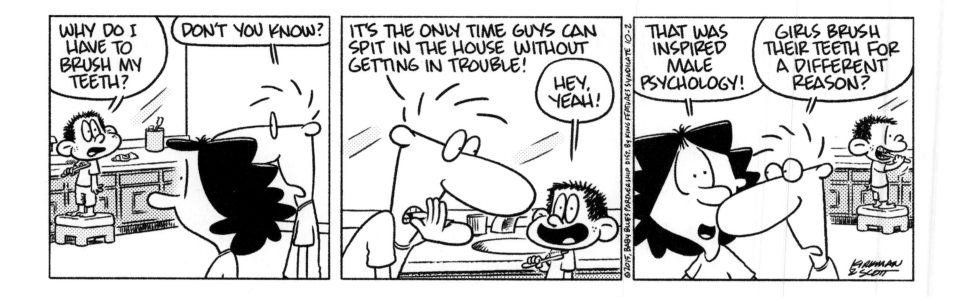

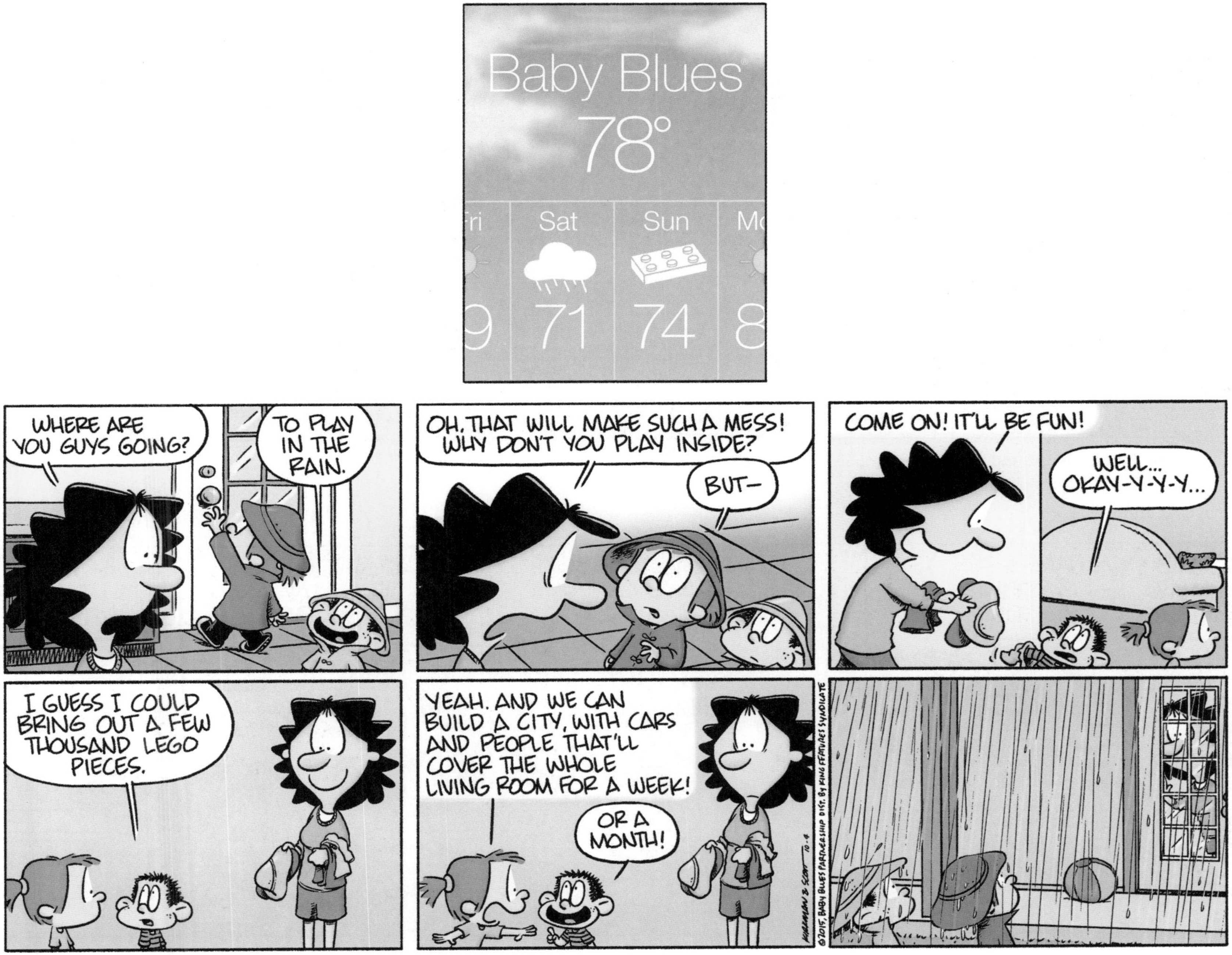

Baby Blues
78°
Fri
Sat
Sun
71
74
WHERE ARE YOU GUYS GOING?
TO PLAY IN THE RAIN.
OH, THAT WILL MAKE SUCH A MESS! WHY DON'T YOU PLAY INSIDE?
BUT–
COME ON! IT'LL BE FUN!
WELL... OKAY-Y-Y-Y...
I GUESS I COULD BRING OUT A FEW THOUSAND LEGO PIECES.
YEAH. AND WE CAN BUILD A CITY, WITH CARS AND PEOPLE THAT'LL COVER THE WHOLE LIVING ROOM FOR A WEEK!
OR A MONTH!
KIRKMAN & SCOTT 10-4
©2015, BABY BLUES PARTNERSHIP DIST. BY KING FEATURES SYNDICATE

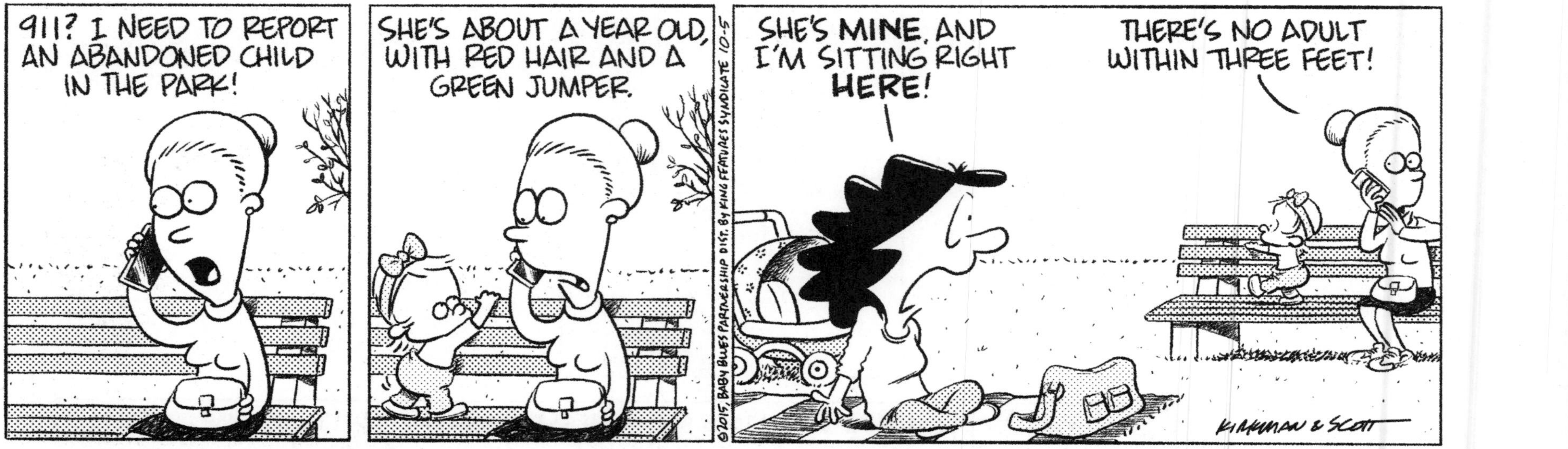
911? I NEED TO REPORT AN ABANDONED CHILD IN THE PARK!
SHE'S ABOUT A YEAR OLD, WITH RED HAIR AND A GREEN JUMPER.
©2015, BABY BLUES PARTNERSHIP DIST. BY KING FEATURES SYNDICATE 10-5
SHE'S MINE, AND I'M SITTING RIGHT HERE!
THERE'S NO ADULT WITHIN THREE FEET!
KIRKMAN & SCOTT

Rick: Where's the middle ground between being a helicopter parent and abandonment?

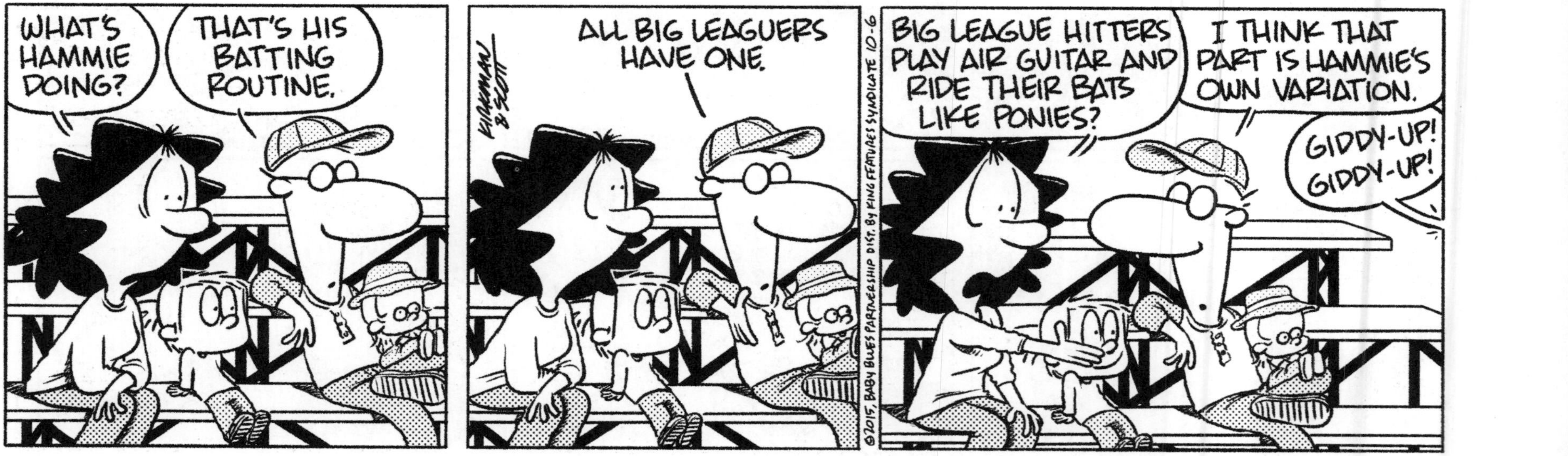
WHAT'S HAMMIE DOING?
THAT'S HIS BATTING ROUTINE.
KIRKMAN & SCOTT
ALL BIG LEAGUERS HAVE ONE.
©2015, BABY BLUES PARTNERSHIP DIST. BY KING FEATURES SYNDICATE 10-6
BIG LEAGUE HITTERS PLAY AIR GUITAR AND RIDE THEIR BATS LIKE PONIES?
I THINK THAT PART IS HAMMIE'S OWN VARIATION.
GIDDY-UP! GIDDY-UP!

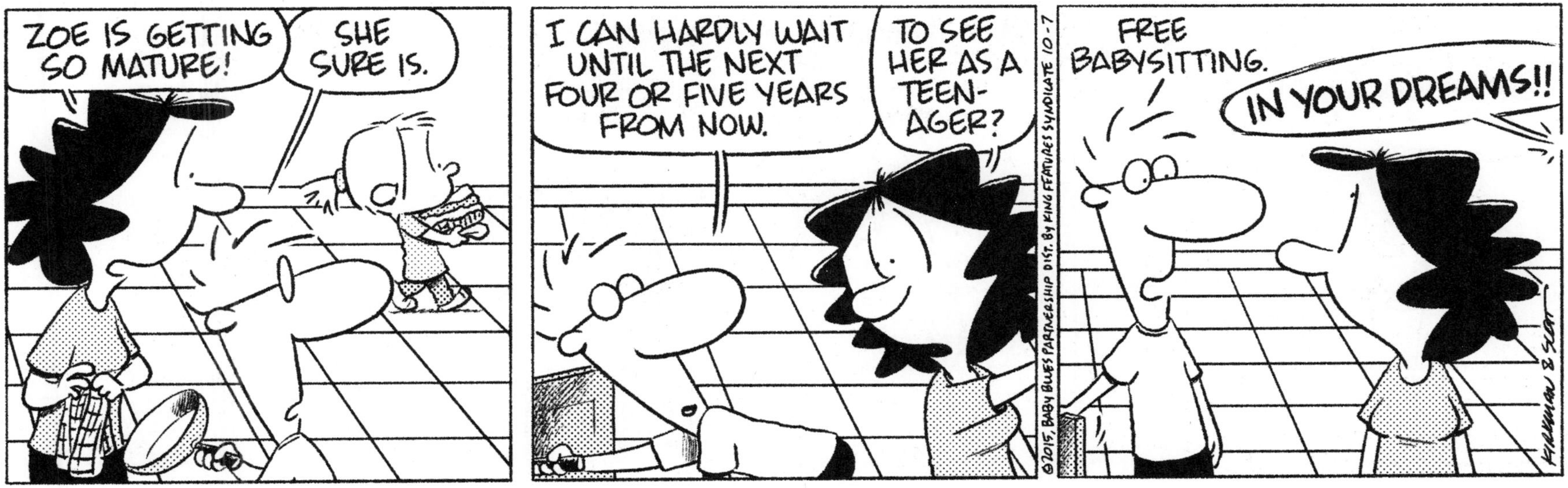
ZOE IS GETTING SO MATURE!
SHE SURE IS.
I CAN HARDLY WAIT UNTIL THE NEXT FOUR OR FIVE YEARS FROM NOW.
TO SEE HER AS A TEEN-AGER?
©2015, BABY BLUES PARTNERSHIP DIST. BY KING FEATURES SYNDICATE 10-7
FREE BABYSITTING.
IN YOUR DREAMS!!
KIRKMAN & SCOTT

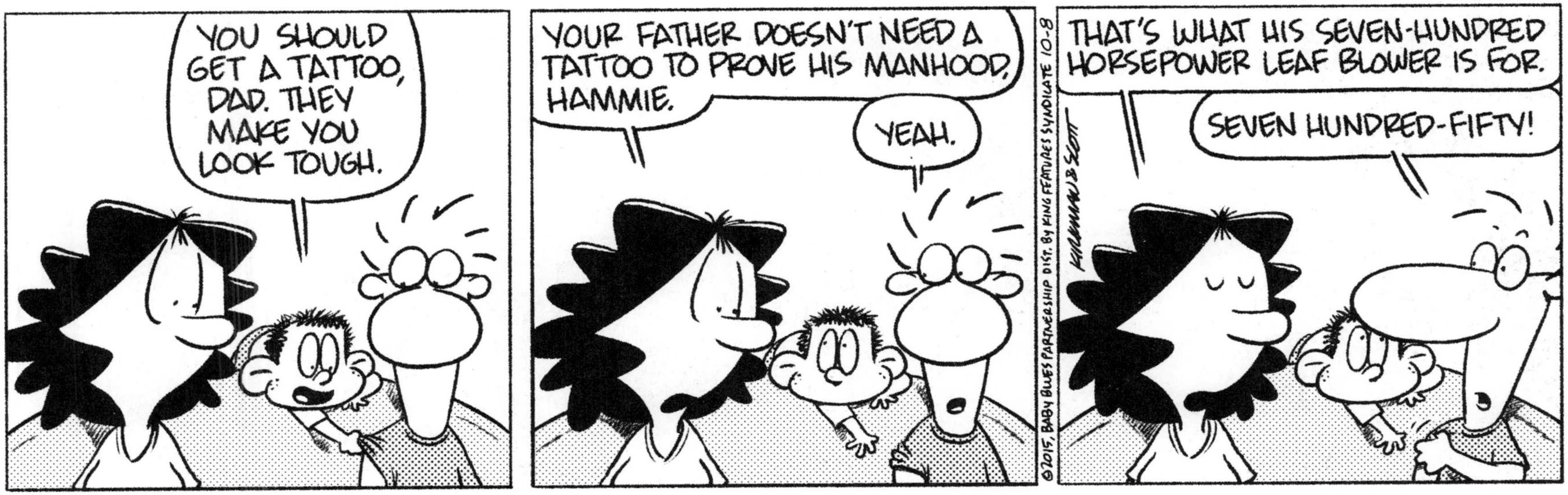
YOU SHOULD GET A TATTOO, DAD. THEY MAKE YOU LOOK TOUGH.
YOUR FATHER DOESN'T NEED A TATTOO TO PROVE HIS MANHOOD, HAMMIE.
YEAH.
©2015, BABY BLUES PARTNERSHIP DIST. BY KING FEATURES SYNDICATE 10-8
KIRKMAN & SCOTT
THAT'S WHAT HIS SEVEN-HUNDRED HORSEPOWER LEAF BLOWER IS FOR.
SEVEN HUNDRED-FIFTY!

Jerry: 750 HP leaf blower?? I want one, too!

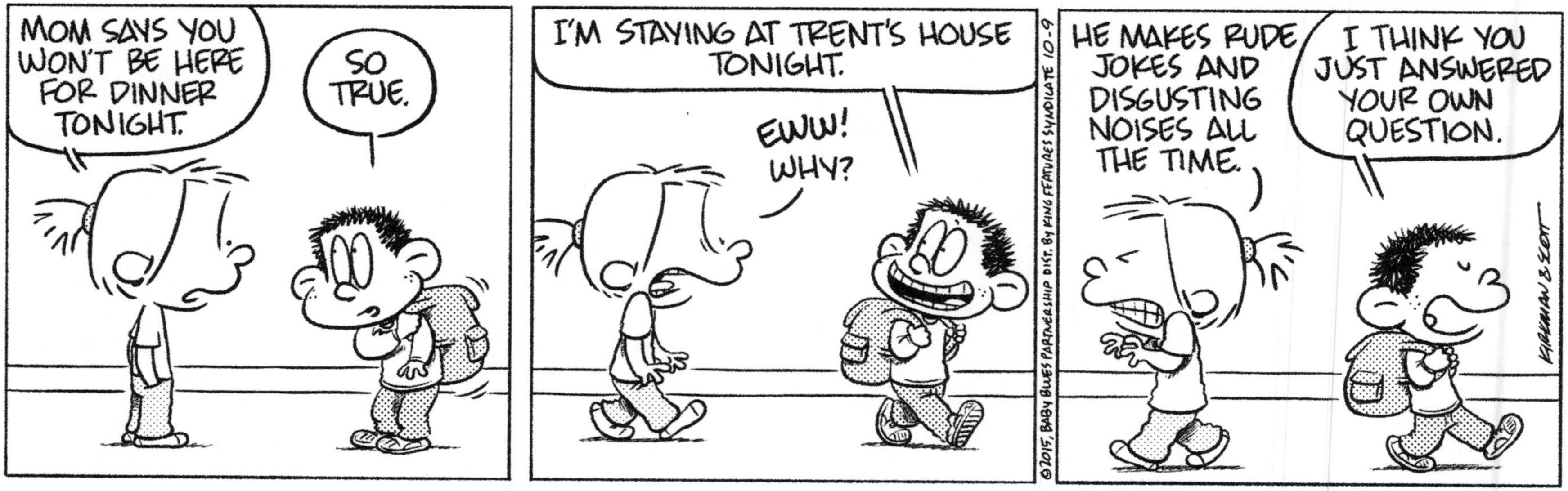
MOM SAYS YOU WON'T BE HERE FOR DINNER TONIGHT.
SO TRUE.
I'M STAYING AT TRENT'S HOUSE TONIGHT.
EWW! WHY?
HE MAKES RUDE JOKES AND DISGUSTING NOISES ALL THE TIME.
I THINK YOU JUST ANSWERED YOUR OWN QUESTION.
©2015, BABY BLUES PARTNERSHIP DIST. BY KING FEATURES SYNDICATE 10-9
KIRKMAN & SCOTT

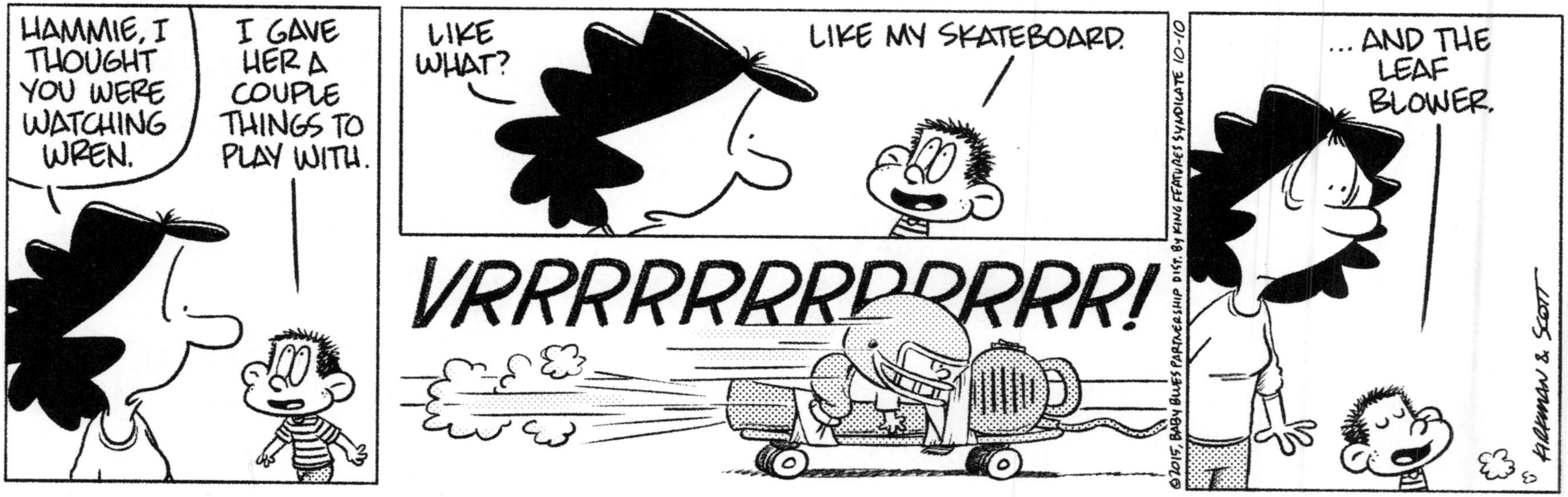
HAMMIE, I THOUGHT YOU WERE WATCHING WREN.
I GAVE HER A COUPLE THINGS TO PLAY WITH.
LIKE WHAT?
LIKE MY SKATEBOARD.
VRRRRRRRRRRRR!
...AND THE LEAF BLOWER.
©2015, BABY BLUES PARTNERSHIP DIST. BY KING FEATURES SYNDICATE 10-10
KIRKMAN & SCOTT

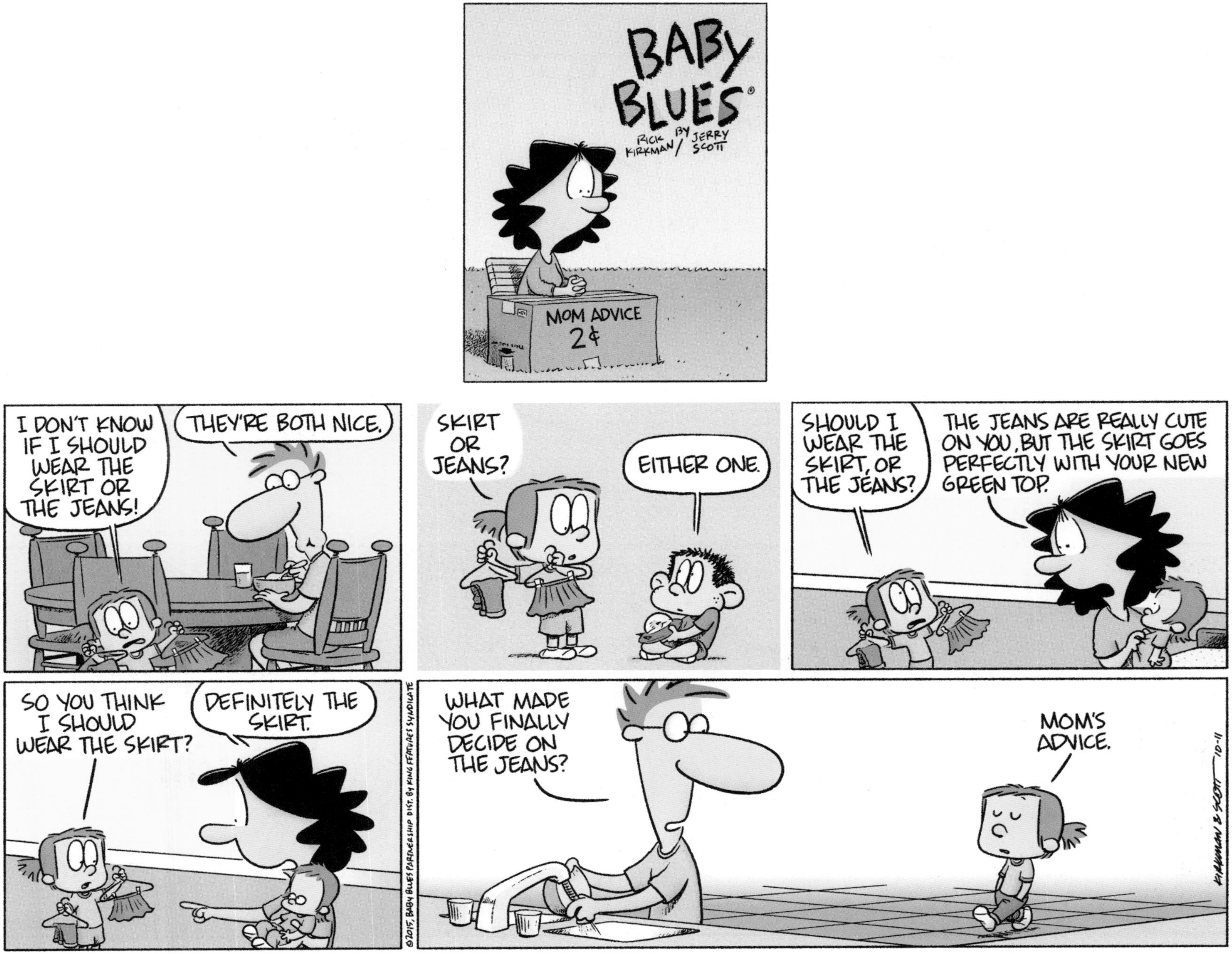
BABY BLUES®
RICK KIRKMAN / BY JERRY SCOTT
MOM ADVICE 2¢
I DON'T KNOW IF I SHOULD WEAR THE SKIRT OR THE JEANS!
THEY'RE BOTH NICE.
SKIRT OR JEANS?
EITHER ONE.
SHOULD I WEAR THE SKIRT, OR THE JEANS?
THE JEANS ARE REALLY CUTE ON YOU, BUT THE SKIRT GOES PERFECTLY WITH YOUR NEW GREEN TOP.
SO YOU THINK I SHOULD WEAR THE SKIRT?
DEFINITELY THE SKIRT.
©2015, BABY BLUES PARTNERSHIP DIST. BY KING FEATURES SYNDICATE
WHAT MADE YOU FINALLY DECIDE ON THE JEANS?
MOM'S ADVICE.
KIRKMAN & SCOTT 10-11

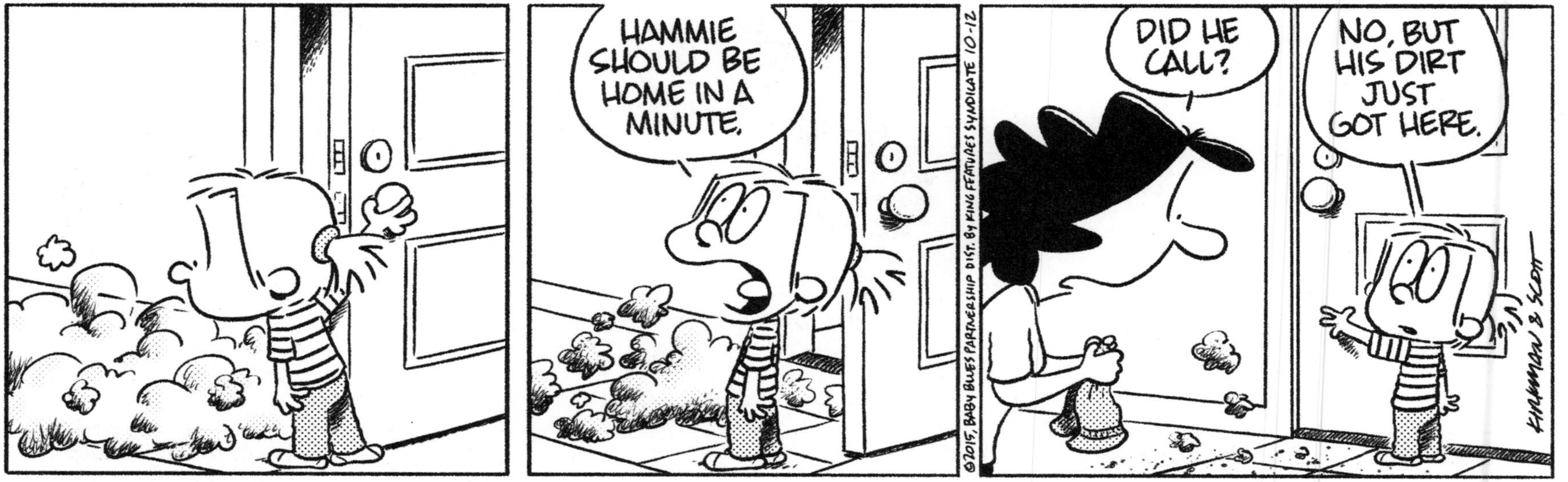
HAMMIE SHOULD BE HOME IN A MINUTE.
DID HE CALL?
NO, BUT HIS DIRT JUST GOT HERE.
©2015, BABY BLUES PARTNERSHIP DIST. BY KING FEATURES SYNDICATE 10-12
KIRKMAN & SCOTT

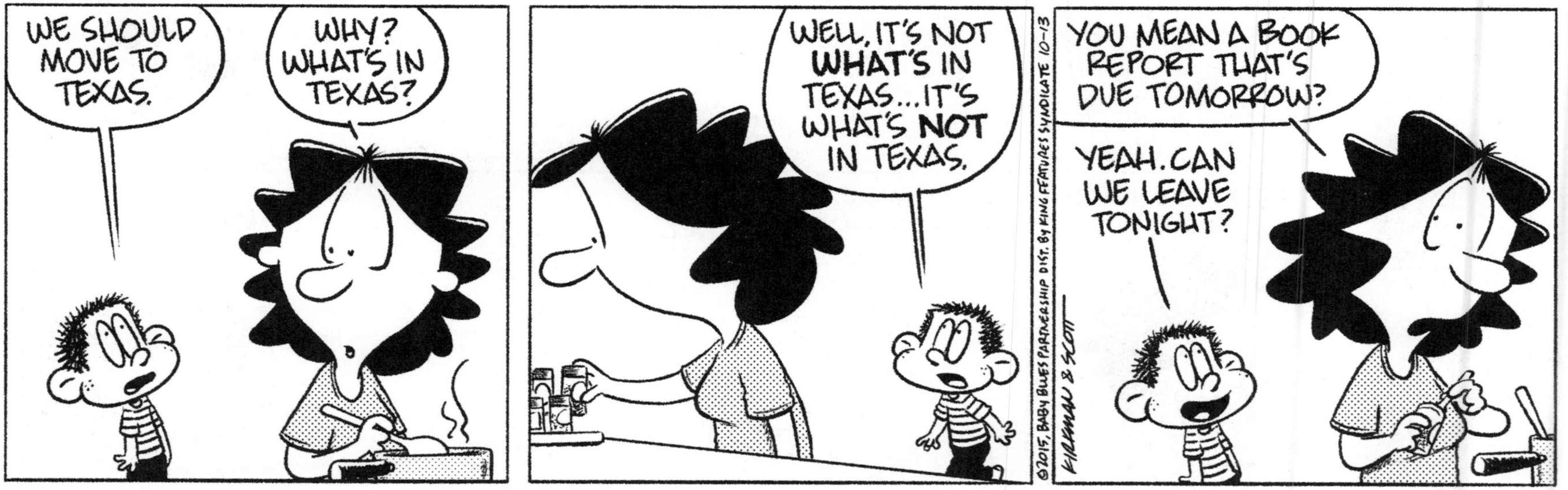
WE SHOULD MOVE TO TEXAS.
WHY? WHAT'S IN TEXAS?
WELL, IT'S NOT **WHAT'S** IN TEXAS... IT'S WHAT'S **NOT** IN TEXAS.
YOU MEAN A BOOK REPORT THAT'S DUE TOMORROW?
YEAH. CAN WE LEAVE TONIGHT?
©2015, BABY BLUES PARTNERSHIP DIST. BY KING FEATURES SYNDICATE 10-13
KIRKMAN & SCOTT

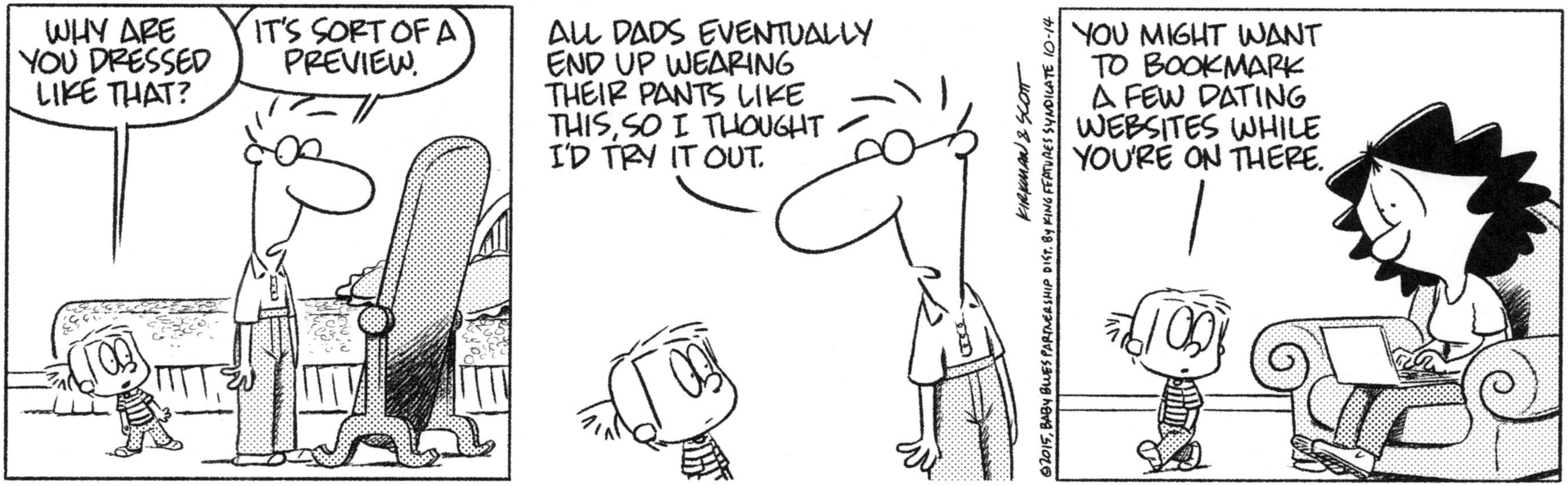
WHY ARE YOU DRESSED LIKE THAT?
IT'S SORT OF A PREVIEW.
ALL DADS EVENTUALLY END UP WEARING THEIR PANTS LIKE THIS, SO I THOUGHT I'D TRY IT OUT.
KIRKMAN & SCOTT
©2015, BABY BLUES PARTNERSHIP DIST. BY KING FEATURES SYNDICATE 10-14
YOU MIGHT WANT TO BOOKMARK A FEW DATING WEBSITES WHILE YOU'RE ON THERE.

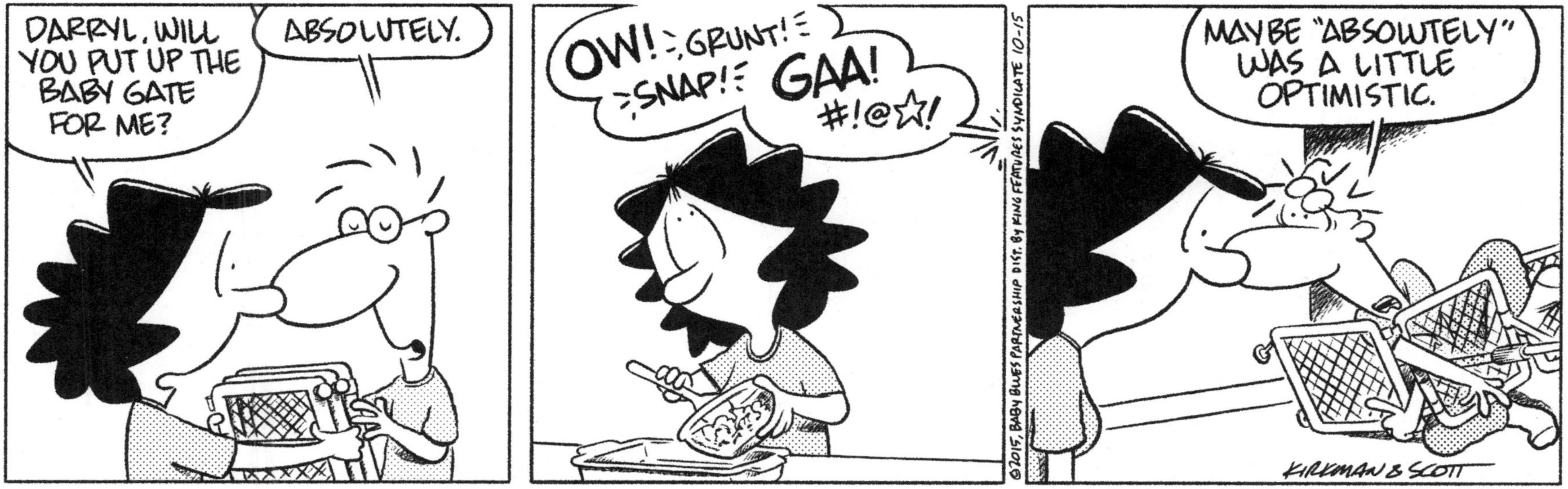
DARRYL, WILL YOU PUT UP THE BABY GATE FOR ME?
ABSOLUTELY.
OW! GRUNT! SNAP! GAA! #!@☆!
©2015, BABY BLUES PARTNERSHIP DIST. BY KING FEATURES SYNDICATE 10-15
MAYBE "ABSOWTELY" WAS A LITTLE OPTIMISTIC.
KIRKMAN & SCOTT

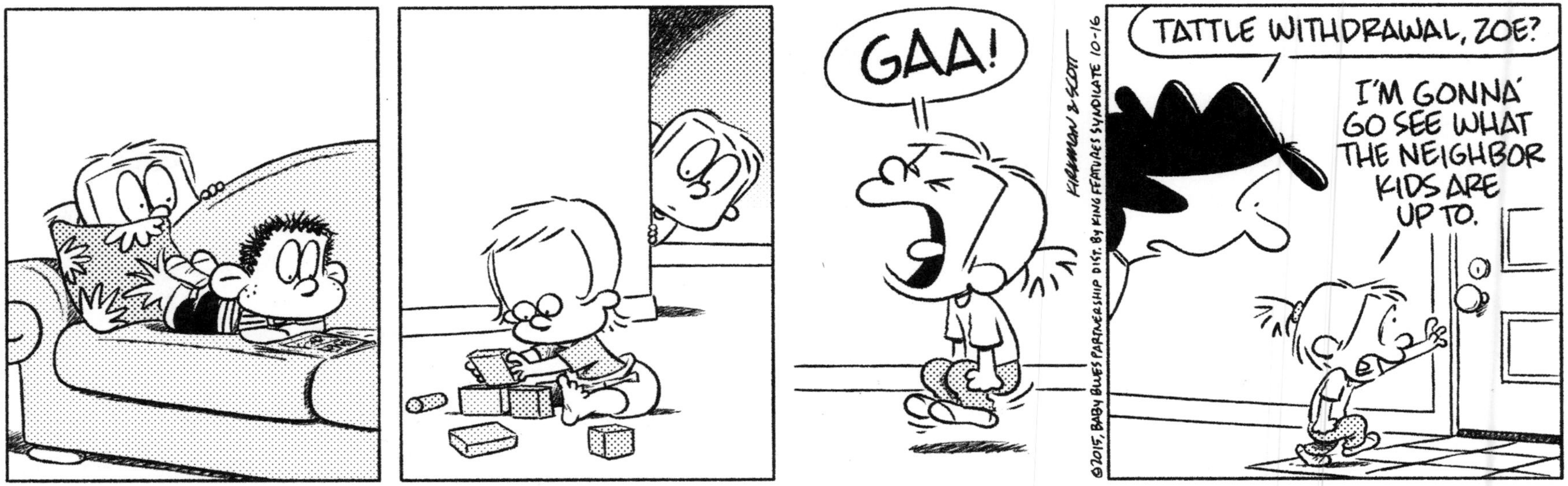
GAA!
KIRKMAN & SCOTT
©2015, BABY BLUES PARTNERSHIP DIST. BY KING FEATURES SYNDICATE 10-16
TATTLE WITHDRAWAL, ZOE?
I'M GONNA' GO SEE WHAT THE NEIGHBOR KIDS ARE UP TO.

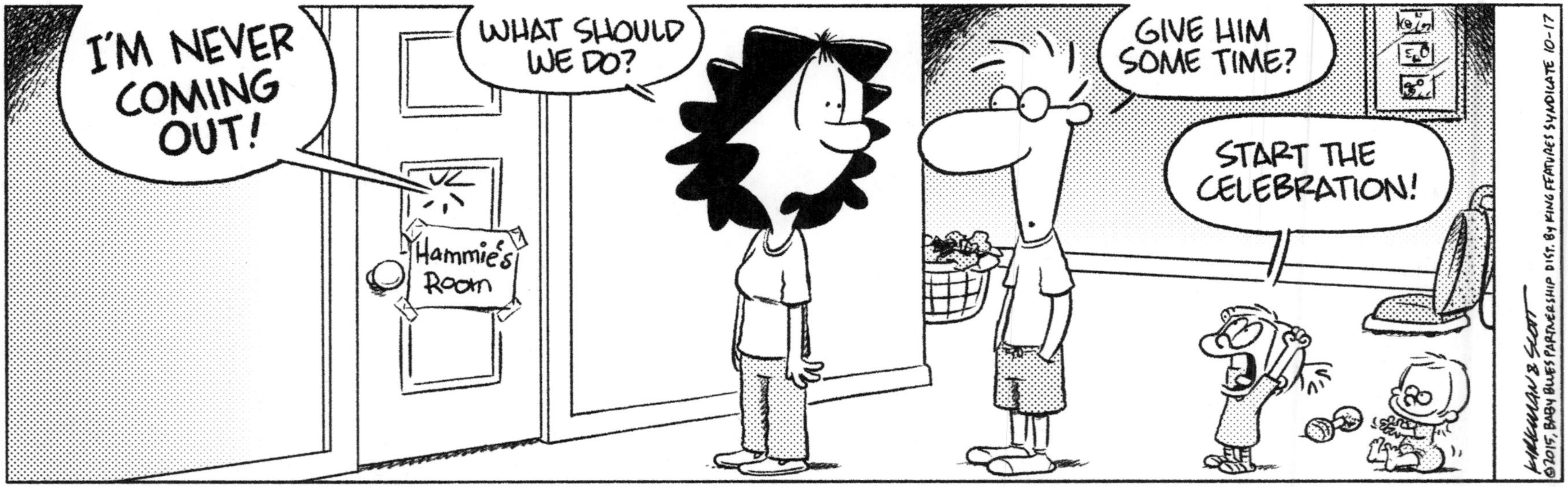
I'M NEVER COMING OUT!
Hammie's Room
WHAT SHOULD WE DO?
GIVE HIM SOME TIME?
START THE CELEBRATION!
KIRKMAN & SCOTT
©2015, BABY BLUES PARTNERSHIP DIST. BY KING FEATURES SYNDICATE 10-17

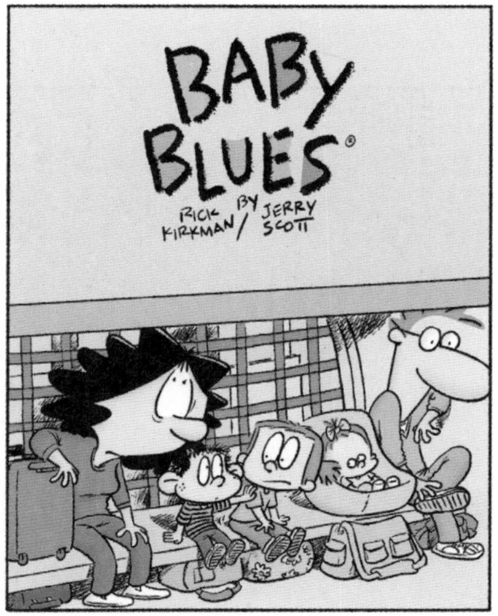
BABY BLUES®
BY RICK KIRKMAN / JERRY SCOTT

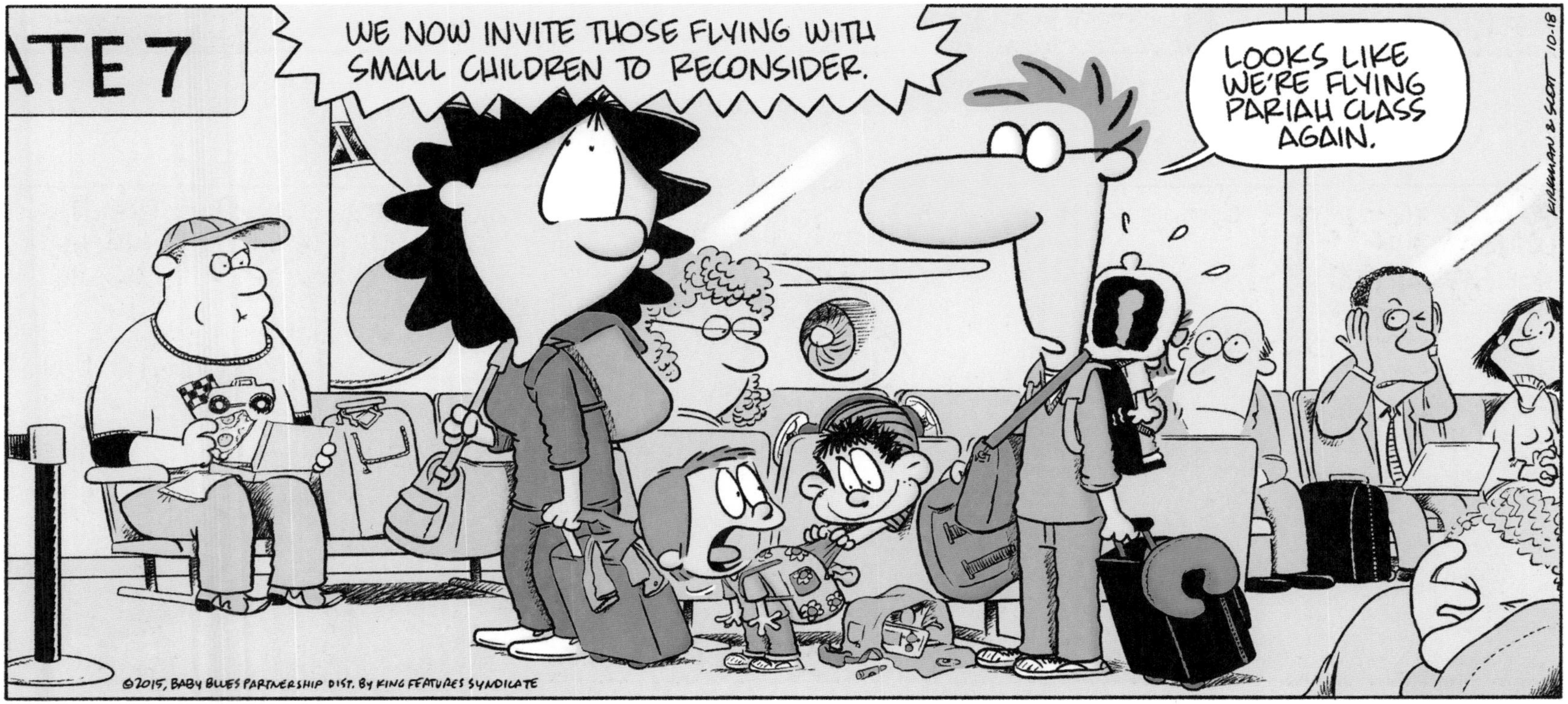
ATE 7
WE NOW INVITE THOSE FLYING WITH SMALL CHILDREN TO RECONSIDER.
LOOKS LIKE WE'RE FLYING PARIAH CLASS AGAIN.
KIRKMAN & SCOTT 10.18
©2015, BABY BLUES PARTNERSHIP DIST. BY KING FEATURES SYNDICATE

Rick: This may be my favorite Sunday strip of the year. In order to keep the focus of a busy scene on the MacPhersons, I went with a muted, limited-color range for the background, which gave the other passengers a sickly look—perfect for the situation. Since I drew this just before leaving on a ten-day USO tour overseas, I was channeling some of my dread of modern air travel. The cargo netting in the title panel is a nod to the netting on our military flights on cargo planes.

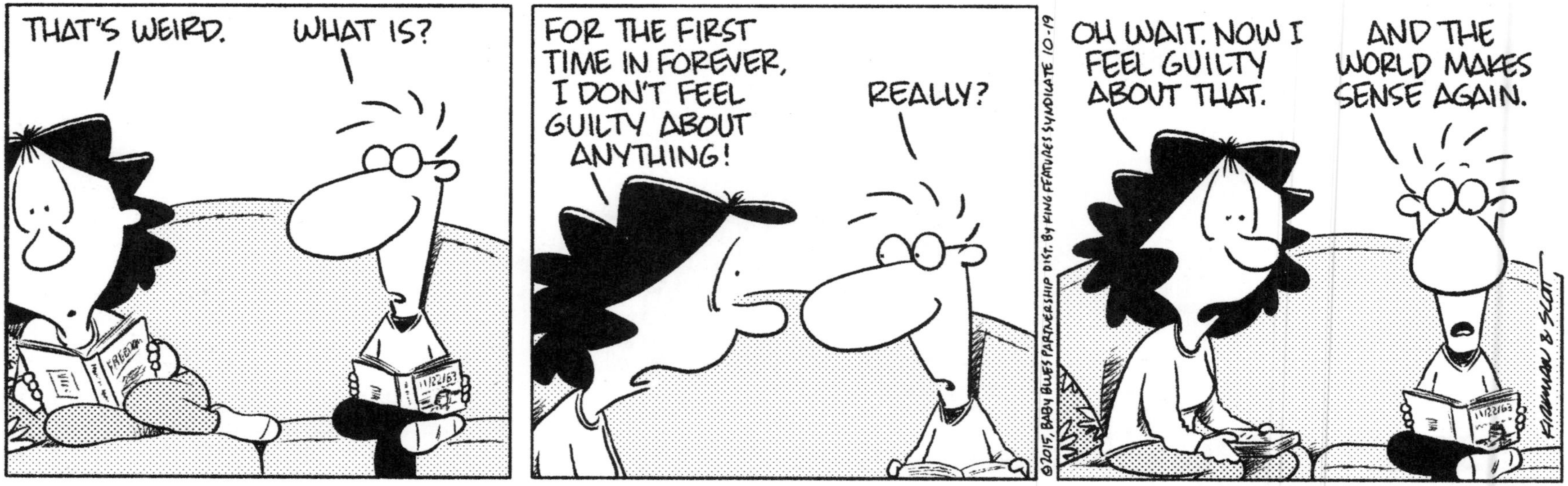
THAT'S WEIRD.
WHAT IS?
FOR THE FIRST TIME IN FOREVER, I DON'T FEEL GUILTY ABOUT ANYTHING!
REALLY?
OH WAIT. NOW I FEEL GUILTY ABOUT THAT.
AND THE WORLD MAKES SENSE AGAIN.
©2015, BABY BLUES PARTNERSHIP DIST. BY KING FEATURES SYNDICATE 10-19
KIRKMAN & SCOTT

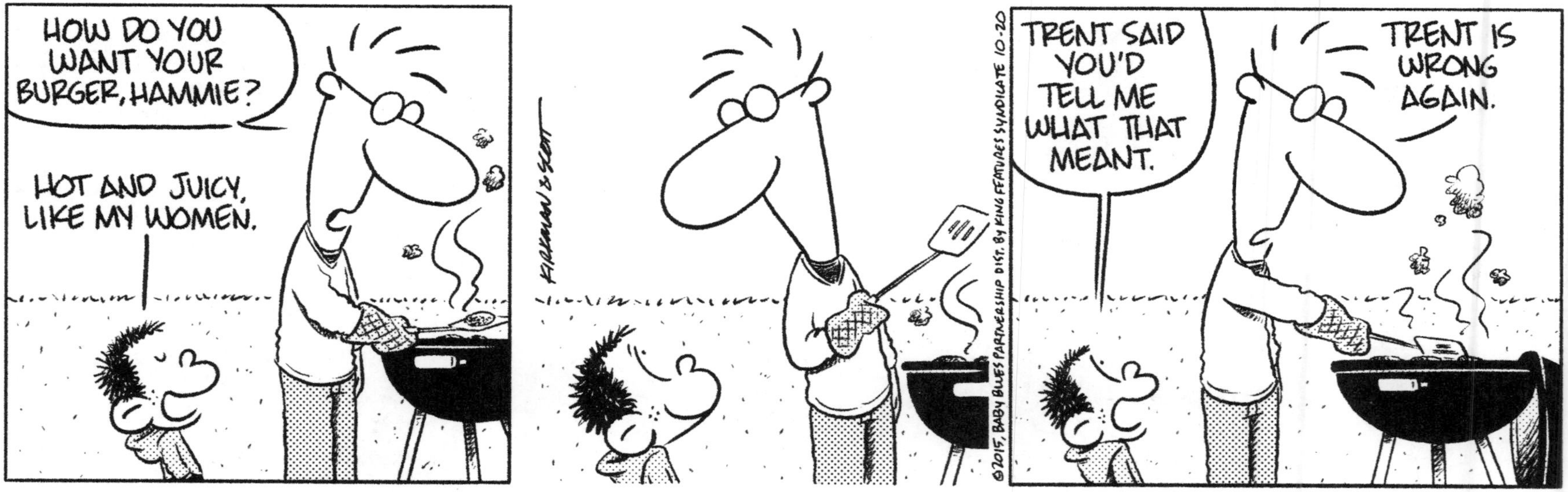
HOW DO YOU WANT YOUR BURGER, HAMMIE?
HOT AND JUICY, LIKE MY WOMEN.
KIRKMAN & SCOTT
©2015, BABY BLUES PARTNERSHIP DIST. BY KING FEATURES SYNDICATE 10-20
TRENT SAID YOU'D TELL ME WHAT THAT MEANT.
TRENT IS WRONG AGAIN.

Jerry: Quite a few folks were surprised at Hammie parroting that crude, sexist remark. But hey, if you don't hear your kid do that at least once, you're not listening.

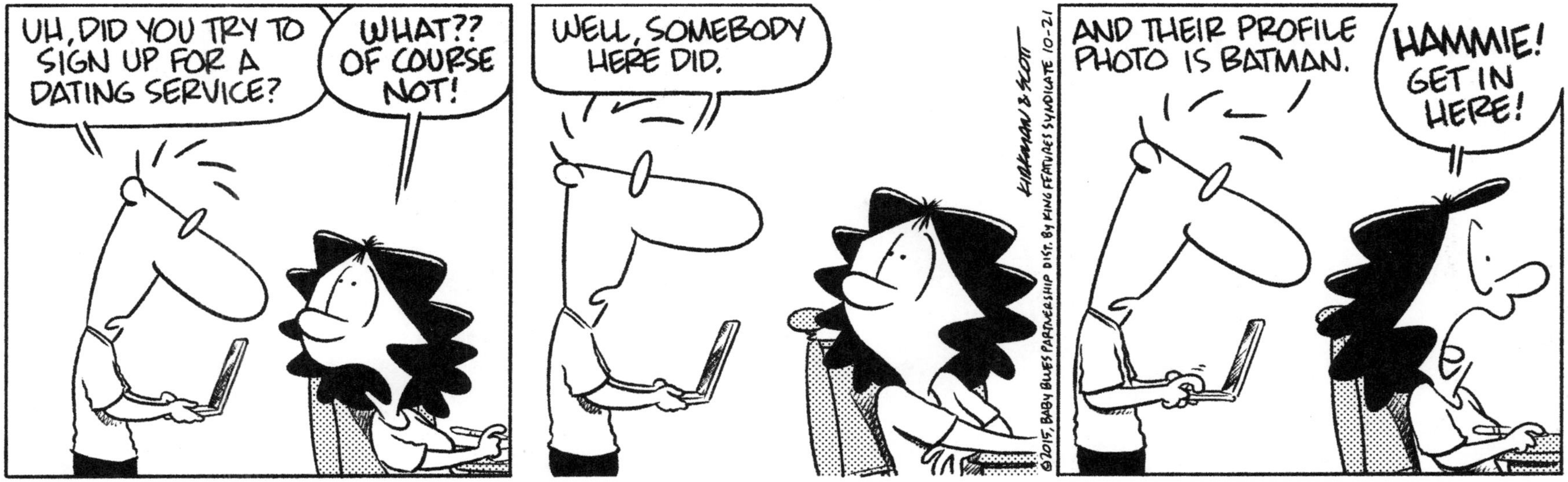
UH, DID YOU TRY TO SIGN UP FOR A DATING SERVICE?
WHAT?? OF COURSE NOT!
WELL, SOMEBODY HERE DID.
KIRKMAN & SCOTT
©2015, BABY BLUES PARTNERSHIP DIST. BY KING FEATURES SYNDICATE 10-21
AND THEIR PROFILE PHOTO IS BATMAN.
HAMMIE! GET IN HERE!

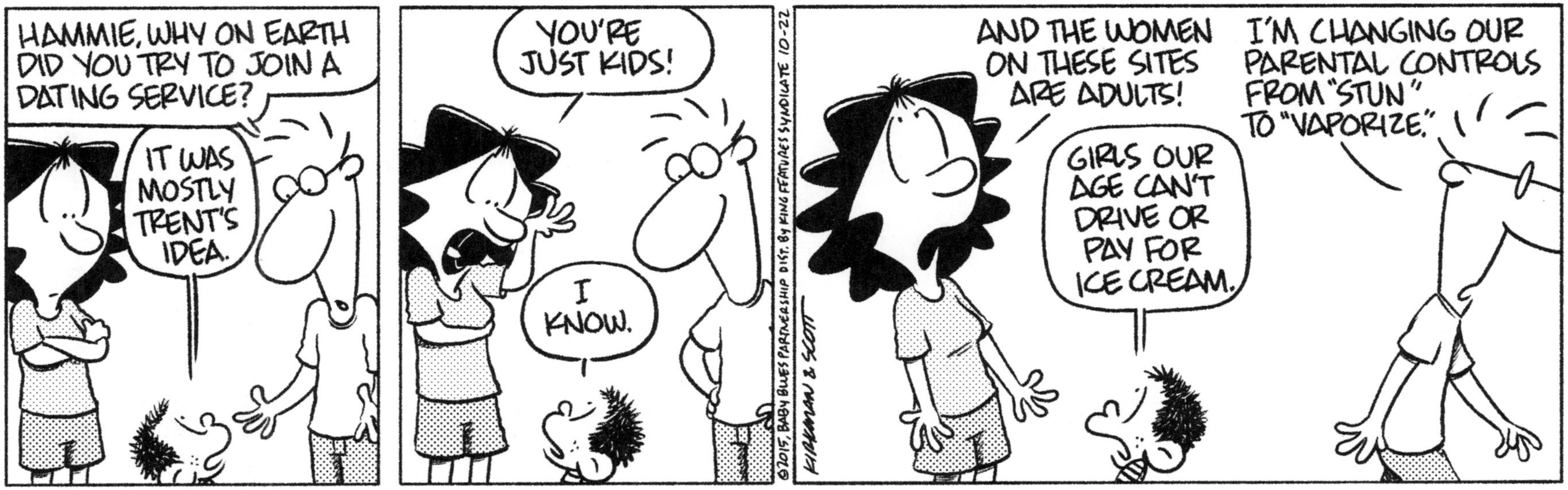
HAMMIE, WHY ON EARTH DID YOU TRY TO JOIN A DATING SERVICE?
IT WAS MOSTLY TRENT'S IDEA.
YOU'RE JUST KIDS!
I KNOW.
©2015, BABY BLUES PARTNERSHIP DIST. BY KING FEATURES SYNDICATE 10-22
KIRKMAN & SCOTT
AND THE WOMEN ON THESE SITES ARE ADULTS!
GIRLS OUR AGE CAN'T DRIVE OR PAY FOR ICE CREAM.
I'M CHANGING OUR PARENTAL CONTROLS FROM "STUN" TO "VAPORIZE."

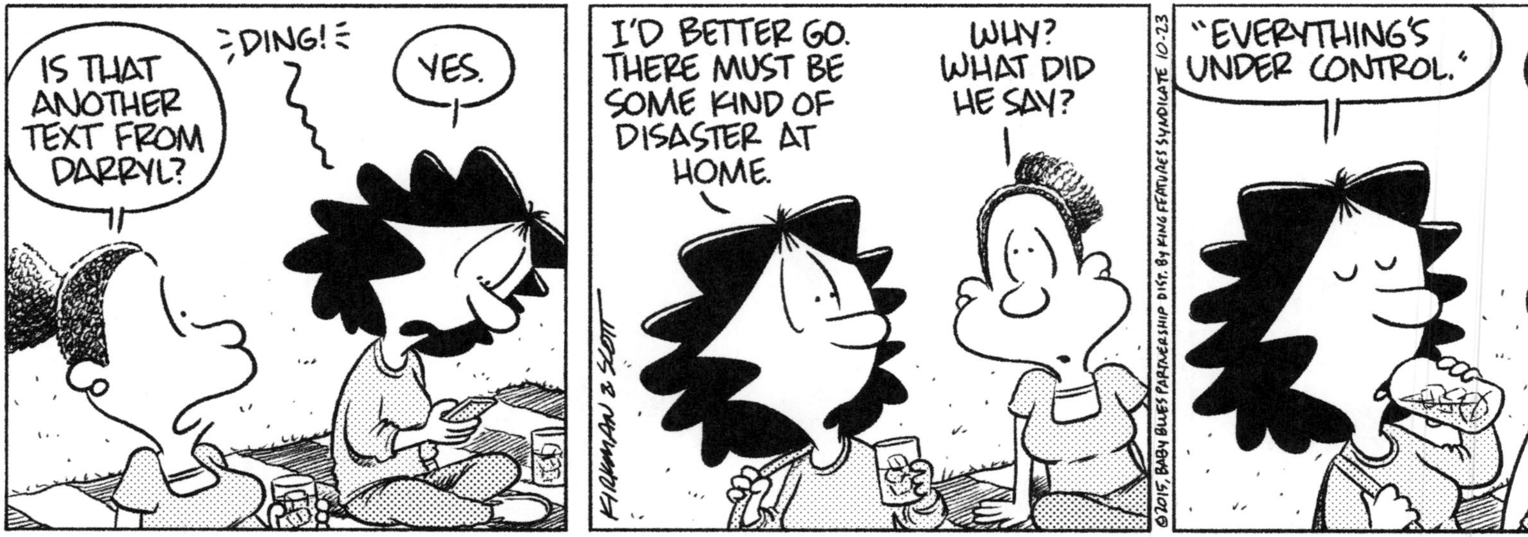
IS THAT ANOTHER TEXT FROM DARRYL?
DING!
YES.
I'D BETTER GO. THERE MUST BE SOME KIND OF DISASTER AT HOME.
WHY? WHAT DID HE SAY?
"EVERYTHING'S UNDER CONTROL."
UH-OH.
KIRKMAN & SCOTT
©2015, BABY BLUES PARTNERSHIP DIST. BY KING FEATURES SYNDICATE 10-23

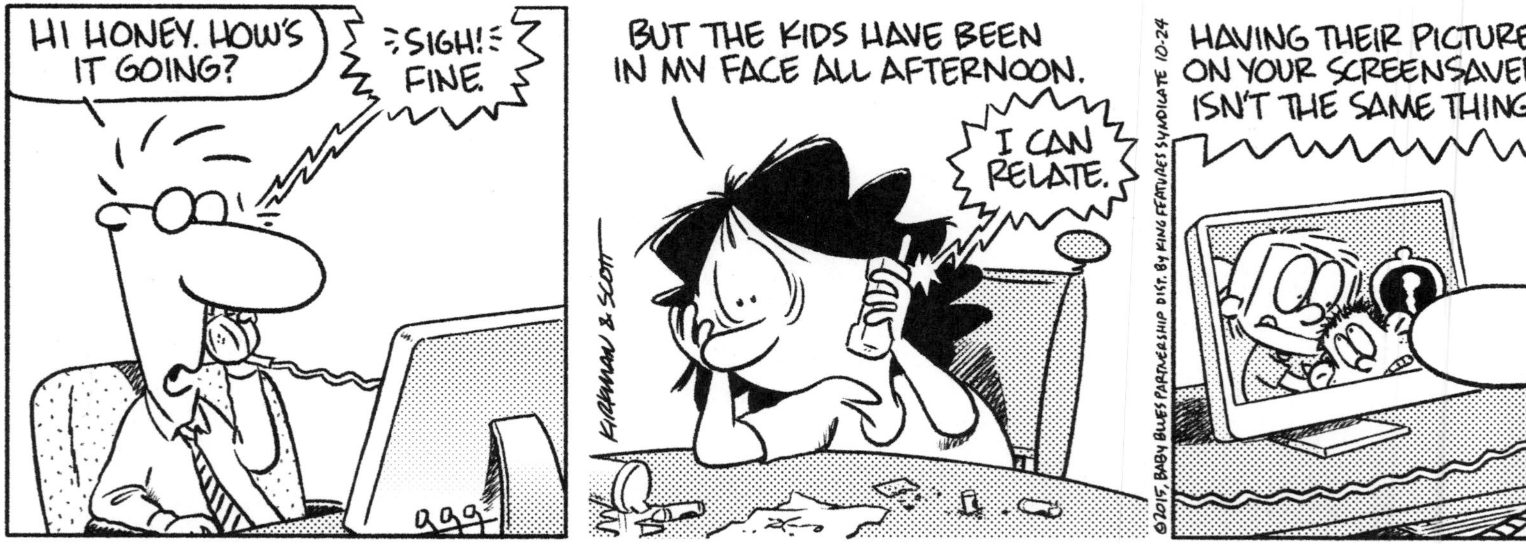
HI HONEY. HOW'S IT GOING?
SIGH! FINE.
BUT THE KIDS HAVE BEEN IN MY FACE ALL AFTERNOON.
I CAN RELATE.
HAVING THEIR PICTURES ON YOUR SCREENSAVER ISN'T THE SAME THING.
IT'S STILL TIRING.
KIRKMAN & SCOTT
©2015, BABY BLUES PARTNERSHIP DIST. BY KING FEATURES SYNDICATE 10-24

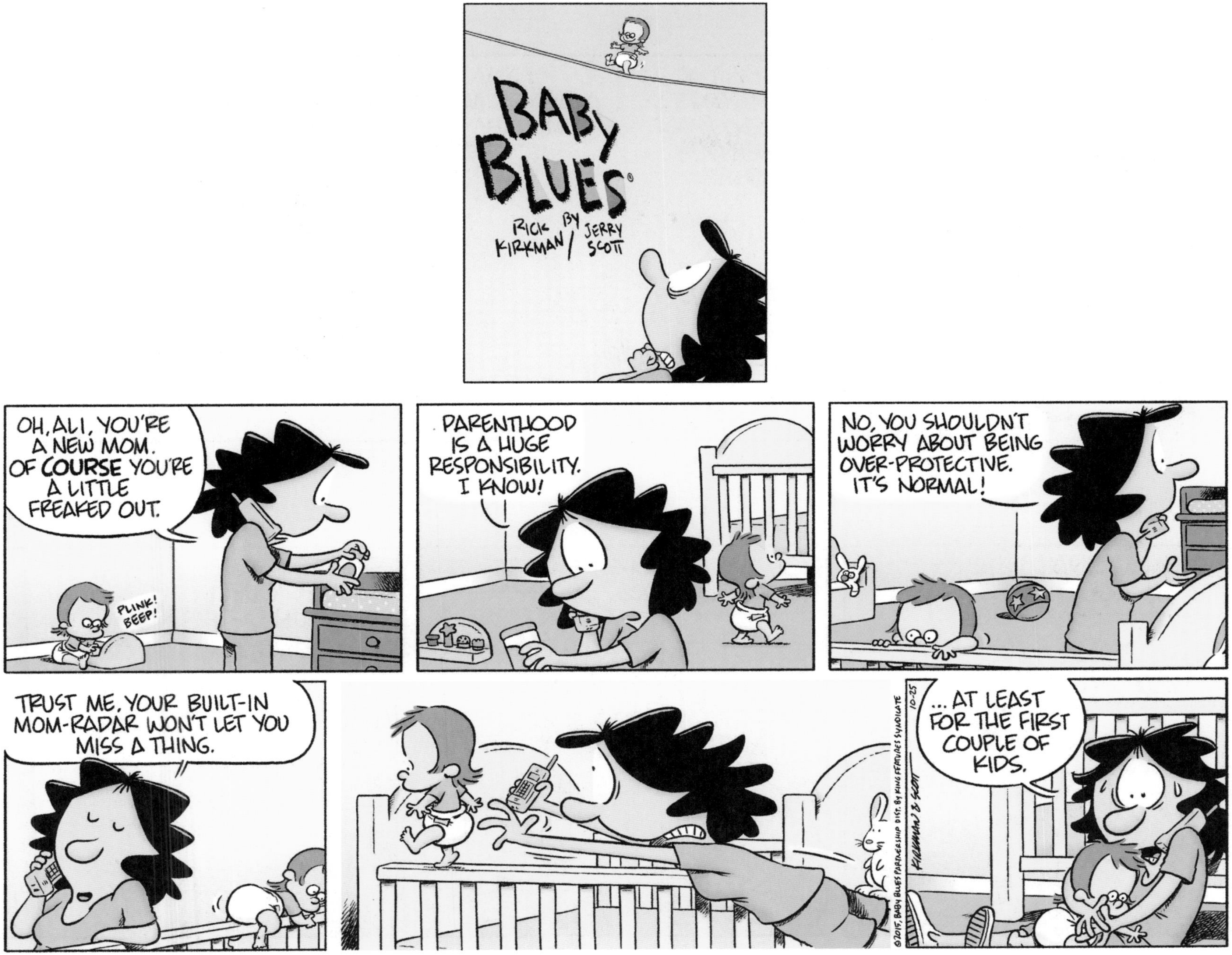
BABY BLUES®
BY RICK KIRKMAN / JERRY SCOTT
OH, ALI, YOU'RE A NEW MOM. OF **COURSE** YOU'RE A LITTLE FREAKED OUT.
PLINK! BEEP!
PARENTHOOD IS A HUGE RESPONSIBILITY. I KNOW!
NO, YOU SHOULDN'T WORRY ABOUT BEING OVER-PROTECTIVE. IT'S NORMAL!
TRUST ME, YOUR BUILT-IN MOM-RADAR WON'T LET YOU MISS A THING.
©2015, BABY BLUES PARTNERSHIP DIST. BY KING FEATURES SYNDICATE
10-25
KIRKMAN & SCOTT
...AT LEAST FOR THE FIRST COUPLE OF KIDS.

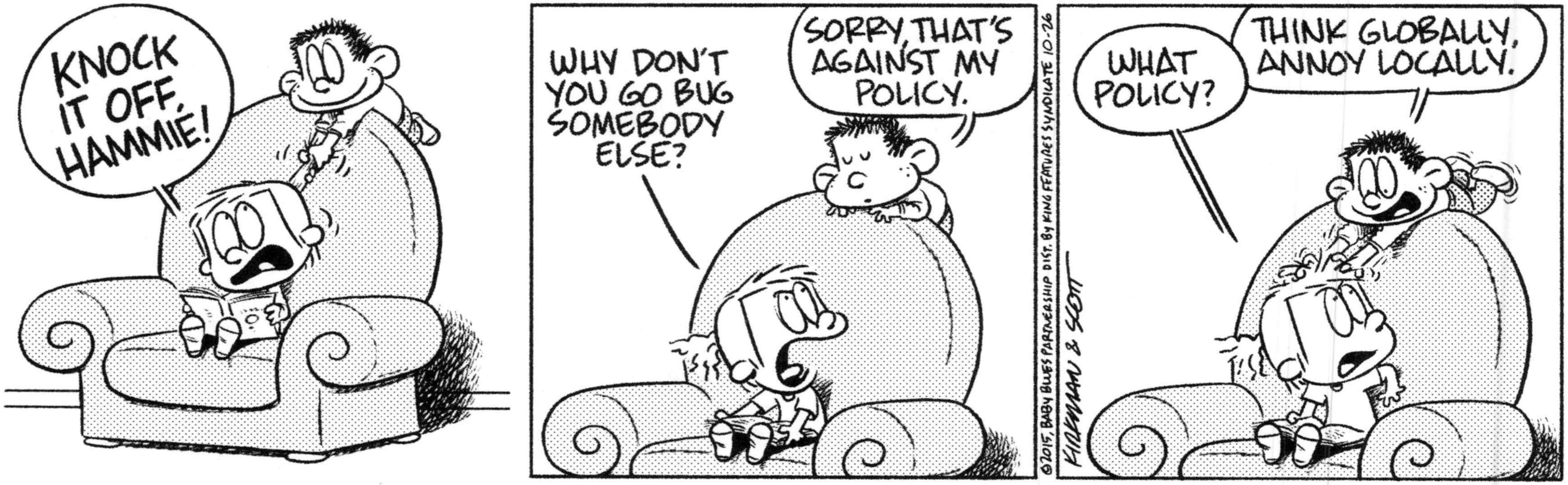
KNOCK IT OFF, HAMMIE!
WHY DON'T YOU GO BUG SOMEBODY ELSE?
SORRY, THAT'S AGAINST MY POLICY.
WHAT POLICY?
THINK GLOBALLY, ANNOY LOCALLY.
©2015, BABY BLUES PARTNERSHIP DIST. BY KING FEATURES SYNDICATE 10-26
KIRKMAN & SCOTT

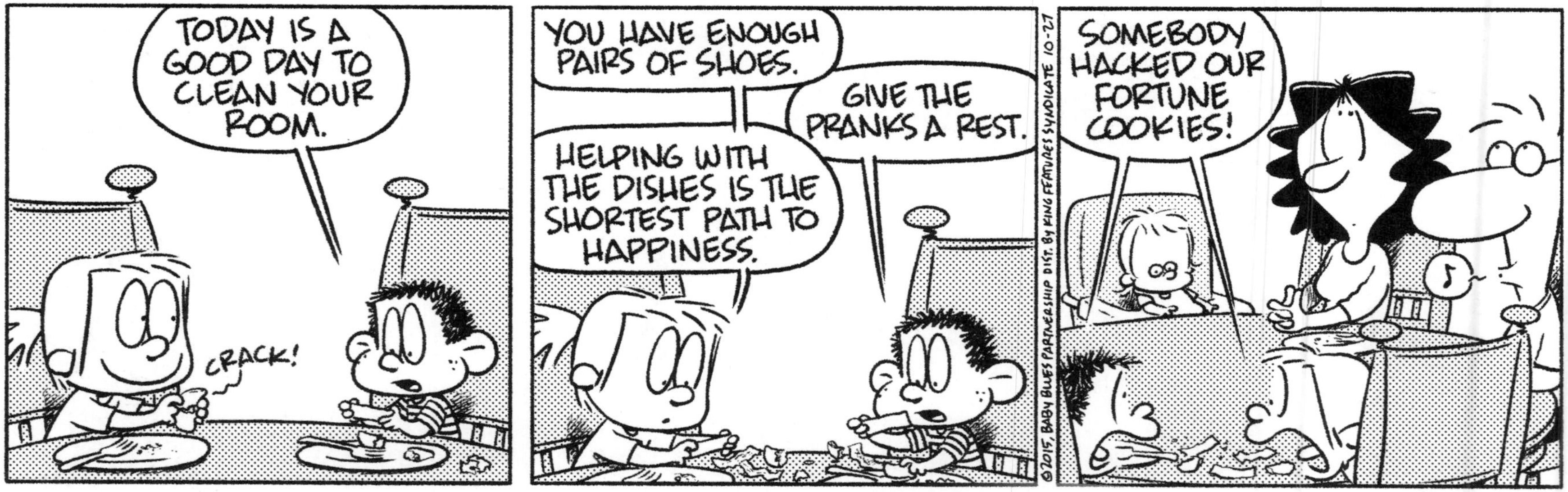
TODAY IS A GOOD DAY TO CLEAN YOUR ROOM.
CRACK!
YOU HAVE ENOUGH PAIRS OF SHOES.
HELPING WITH THE DISHES IS THE SHORTEST PATH TO HAPPINESS.
GIVE THE PRANKS A REST.
SOMEBODY HACKED OUR FORTUNE COOKIES!
©2015, BABY BLUES PARTNERSHIP DIST. BY KING FEATURES SYNDICATE 10-27

Rick: Hey, kids, those are still better than the fortunes I've been getting lately. I think the fortune-cookie industry needs to invest in some new writers. I offer Exhibits A, B and C.

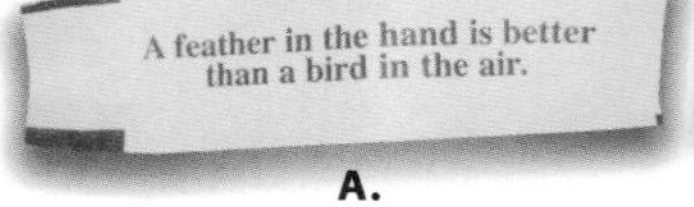
A feather in the hand is better than a bird in the air.

A.

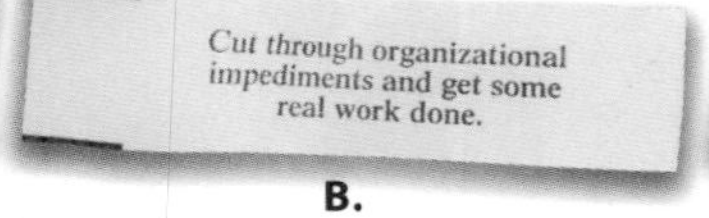
Cut through organizational impediments and get some real work done.

B.

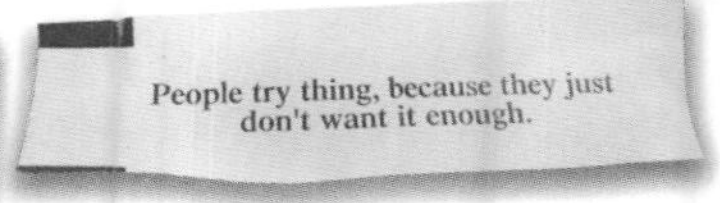
People try thing, because they just don't want it enough.

C.

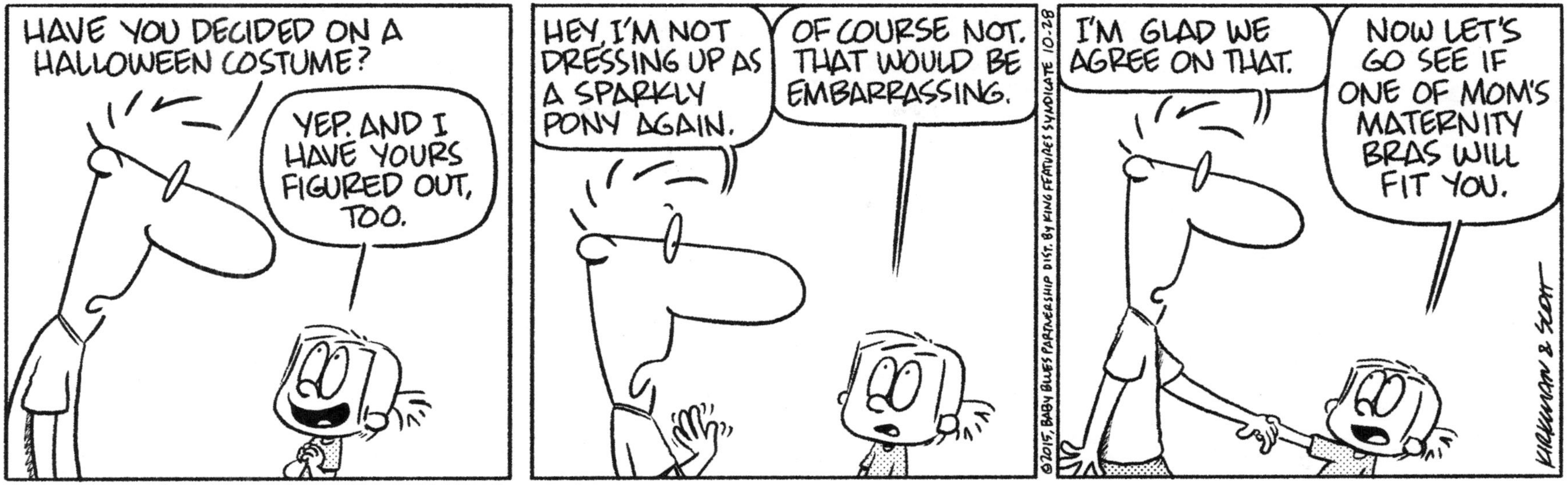
HAVE YOU DECIDED ON A HALLOWEEN COSTUME?
YEP. AND I HAVE YOURS FIGURED OUT, TOO.
HEY, I'M NOT DRESSING UP AS A SPARKLY PONY AGAIN.
OF COURSE NOT. THAT WOULD BE EMBARRASSING.
©2015, BABY BLUES PARTNERSHIP DIST. BY KING FEATURES SYNDICATE 10-28
I'M GLAD WE AGREE ON THAT.
NOW LET'S GO SEE IF ONE OF MOM'S MATERNITY BRAS WILL FIT YOU.
KIRKMAN & SCOTT

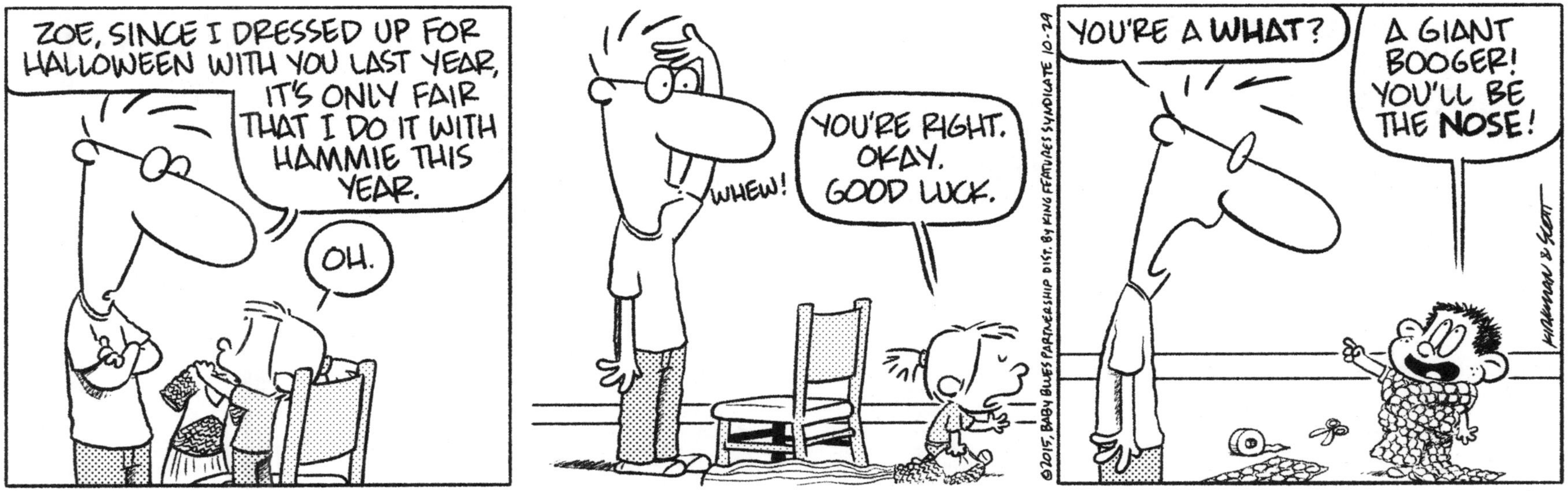
ZOE, SINCE I DRESSED UP FOR HALLOWEEN WITH YOU LAST YEAR, IT'S ONLY FAIR THAT I DO IT WITH HAMMIE THIS YEAR.
OH.
WHEW!
YOU'RE RIGHT. OKAY. GOOD LUCK.
©2015, BABY BLUES PARTNERSHIP DIST. BY KING FEATURES SYNDICATE 10-29
YOU'RE A **WHAT**?
A GIANT BOOGER! YOU'LL BE THE **NOSE**!
KIRKMAN & SCOTT

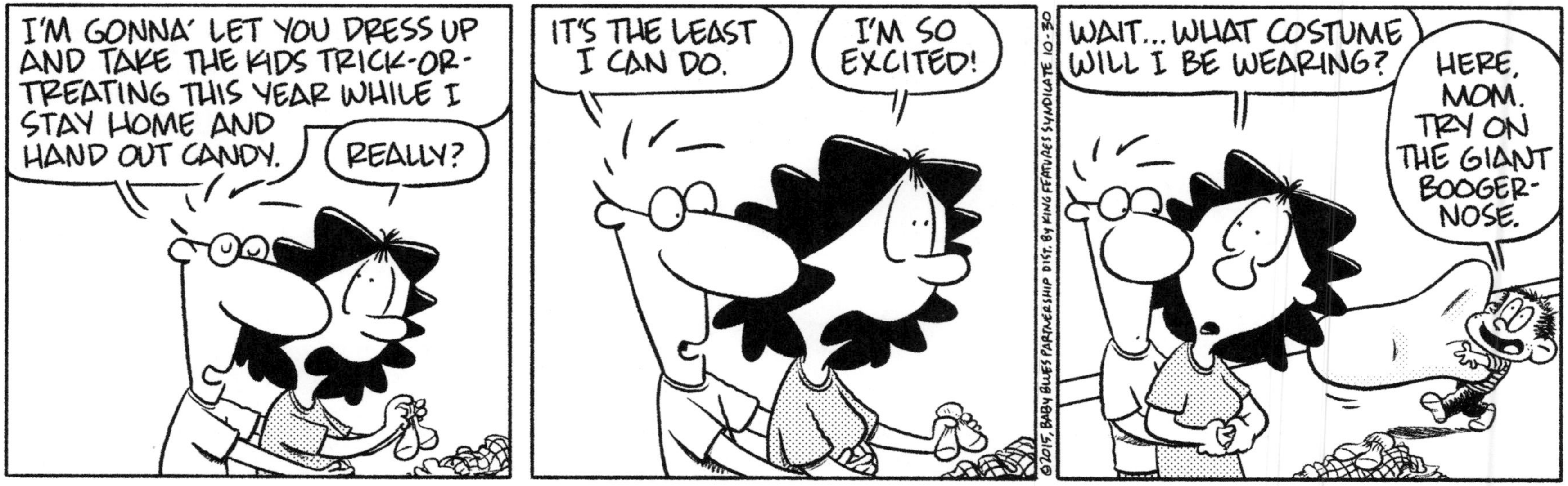
I'M GONNA' LET YOU DRESS UP AND TAKE THE KIDS TRICK-OR-TREATING THIS YEAR WHILE I STAY HOME AND HAND OUT CANDY.
REALLY?
IT'S THE LEAST I CAN DO.
I'M SO EXCITED!
©2015, BABY BLUES PARTNERSHIP DIST. BY KING FEATURES SYNDICATE 10-30
WAIT... WHAT COSTUME WILL I BE WEARING?
HERE, MOM. TRY ON THE GIANT BOOGER-NOSE.

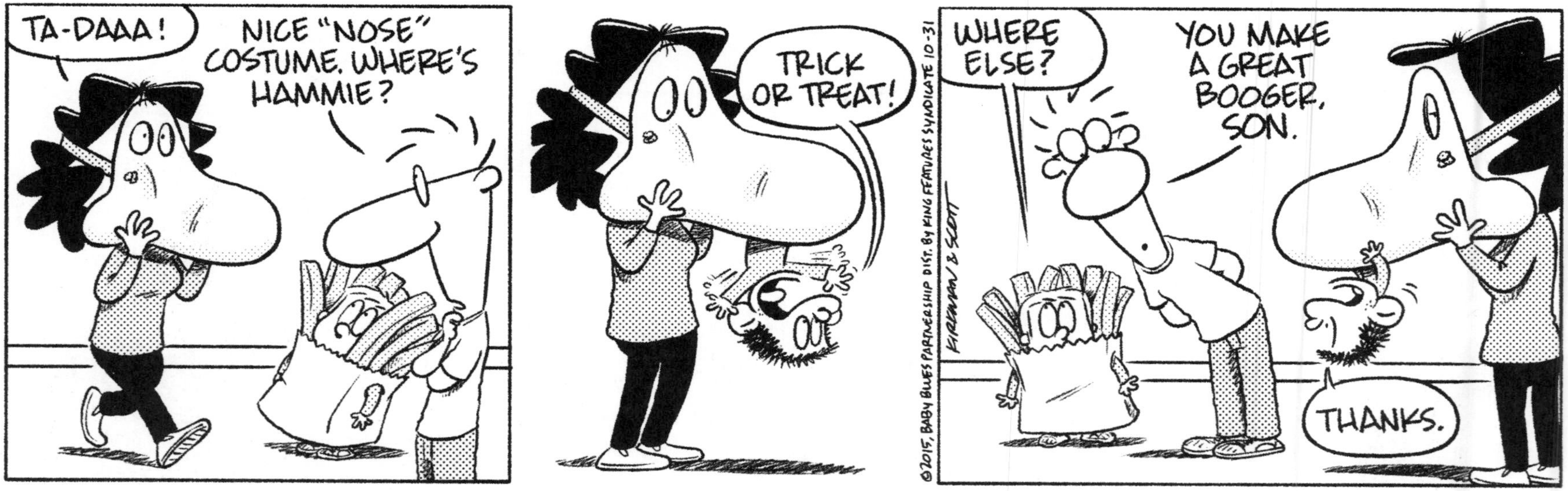
TA-DAAA!
NICE "NOSE" COSTUME. WHERE'S HAMMIE?
TRICK OR TREAT!
KIRKMAN & SCOTT
©2015, BABY BLUES PARTNERSHIP DIST. BY KING FEATURES SYNDICATE 10-31
WHERE ELSE?
YOU MAKE A GREAT BOOGER, SON.
THANKS.

Rick: In the first panel, I originally had Wanda wearing the costume lower, which was unfortunate placement. Luckily, Jerry and I noticed, and I repositioned it before the strip was sent in. Whew! Trivia: One of my daughters was actually a box of fries for Halloween.

BABY BLUES®
HAMMIE! THAT MILK IS LEAKING ALL OVER!
YEAH. THOUGHT YOU'D WANT TO KNOW.
KIRKMAN & SCOTT
©2015, BABY BLUES PARTNERSHIP DIST. BY KING FEATURES SYNDICATE 11-1

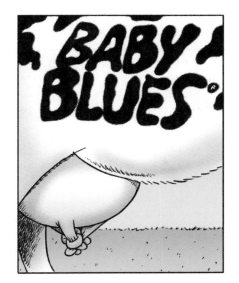

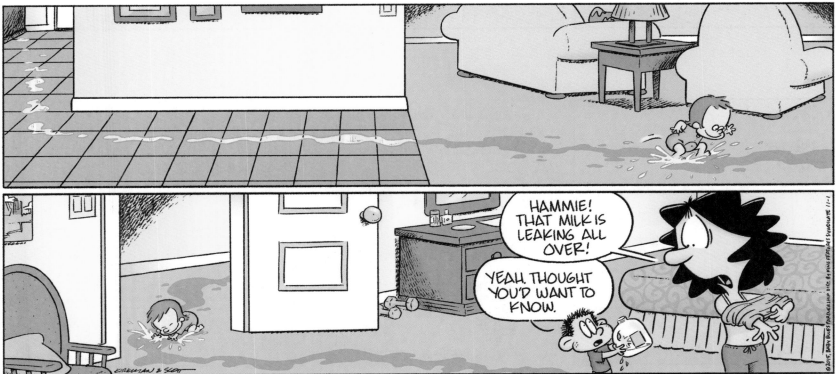

Rick: Drawing liquid on carpet is a challenge. And I used the correct number of teats on a cow this time (an old mistake that I seem to have not gotten over).

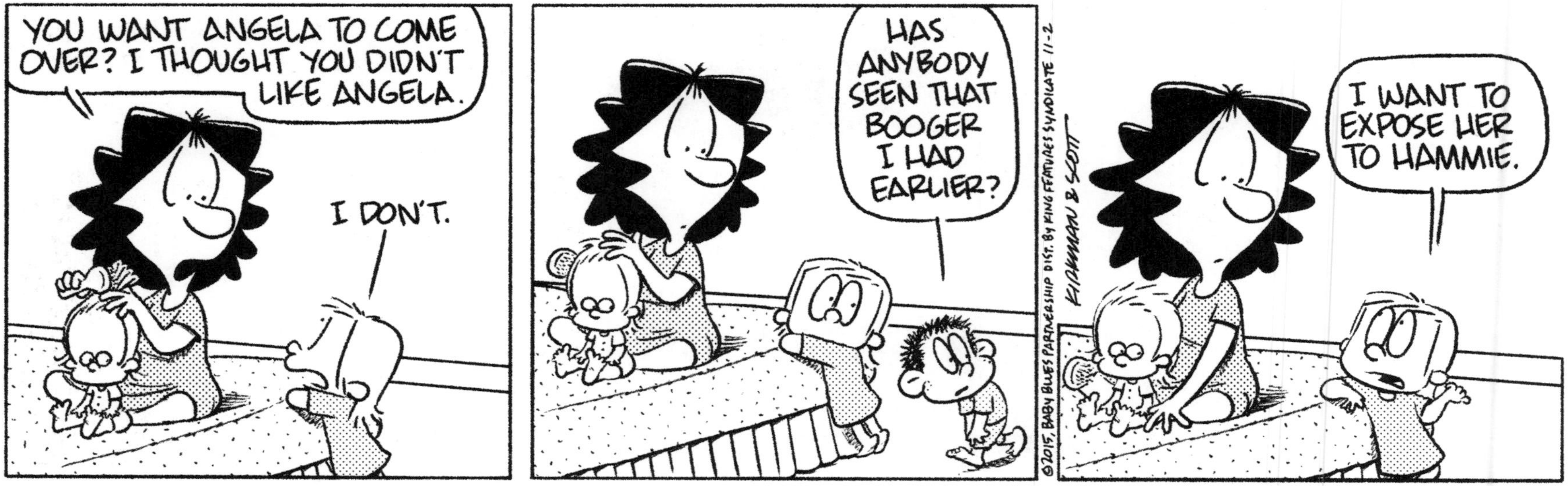
YOU WANT ANGELA TO COME OVER? I THOUGHT YOU DIDN'T LIKE ANGELA.
I DON'T.
HAS ANYBODY SEEN THAT BOOGER I HAD EARLIER?
©2015, BABY BLUES PARTNERSHIP DIST. BY KING FEATURES SYNDICATE 11-2
KIRKMAN & SCOTT
I WANT TO EXPOSE HER TO HAMMIE.

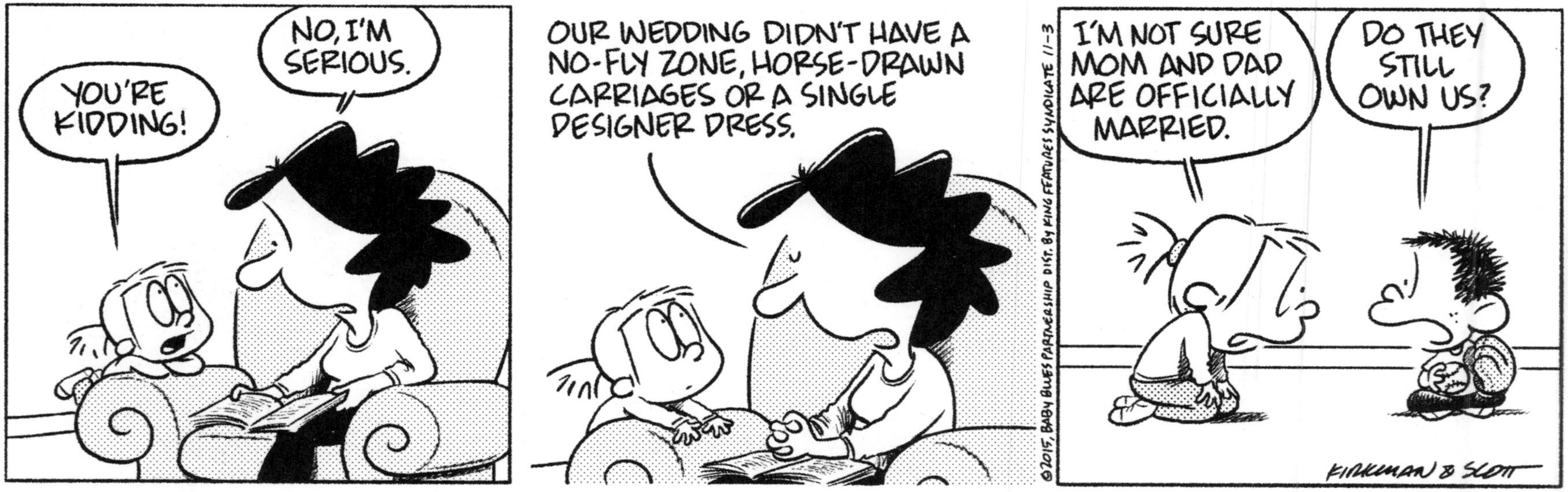
YOU'RE KIDDING!
NO, I'M SERIOUS.
OUR WEDDING DIDN'T HAVE A NO-FLY ZONE, HORSE-DRAWN CARRIAGES OR A SINGLE DESIGNER DRESS.
©2015, BABY BLUES PARTNERSHIP DIST. BY KING FEATURES SYNDICATE 11-3
I'M NOT SURE MOM AND DAD ARE OFFICIALLY MARRIED.
DO THEY STILL OWN US?
KIRKMAN & SCOTT

Rick: One of my favorite lines ever from Hammie. Nice, Jerry!

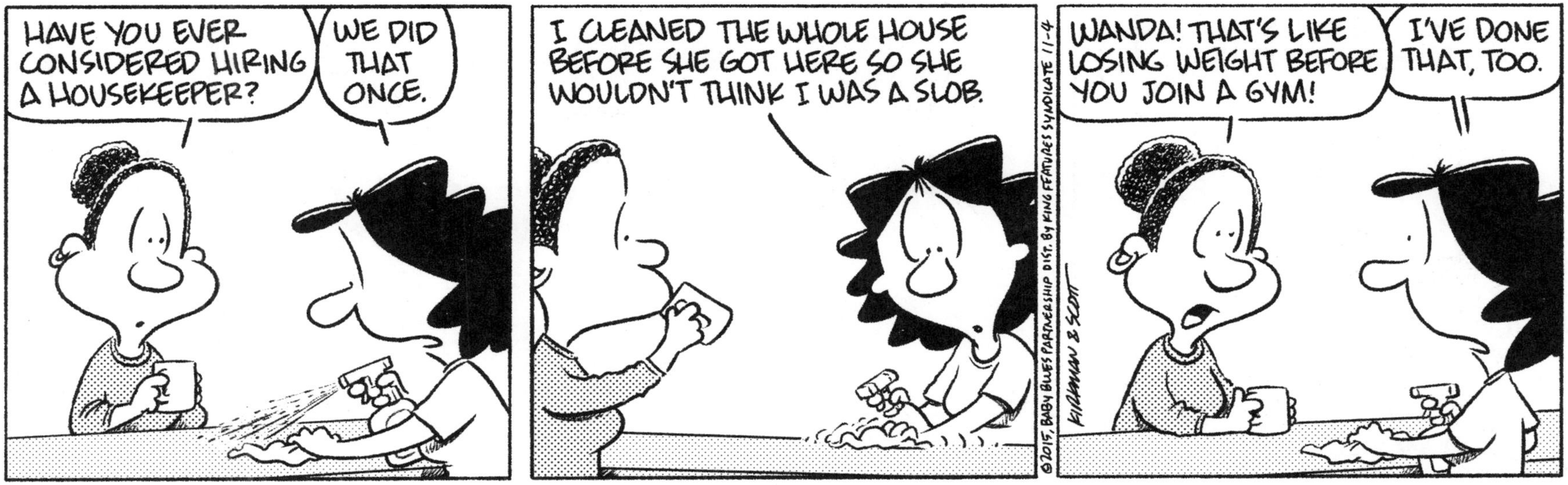
HAVE YOU EVER CONSIDERED HIRING A HOUSEKEEPER?
WE DID THAT ONCE.
I CLEANED THE WHOLE HOUSE BEFORE SHE GOT HERE SO SHE WOULDN'T THINK I WAS A SLOB.
WANDA! THAT'S LIKE LOSING WEIGHT BEFORE YOU JOIN A GYM!
I'VE DONE THAT, TOO.
©2015, BABY BLUES PARTNERSHIP DIST. BY KING FEATURES SYNDICATE 11-4
KIRKMAN & SCOTT

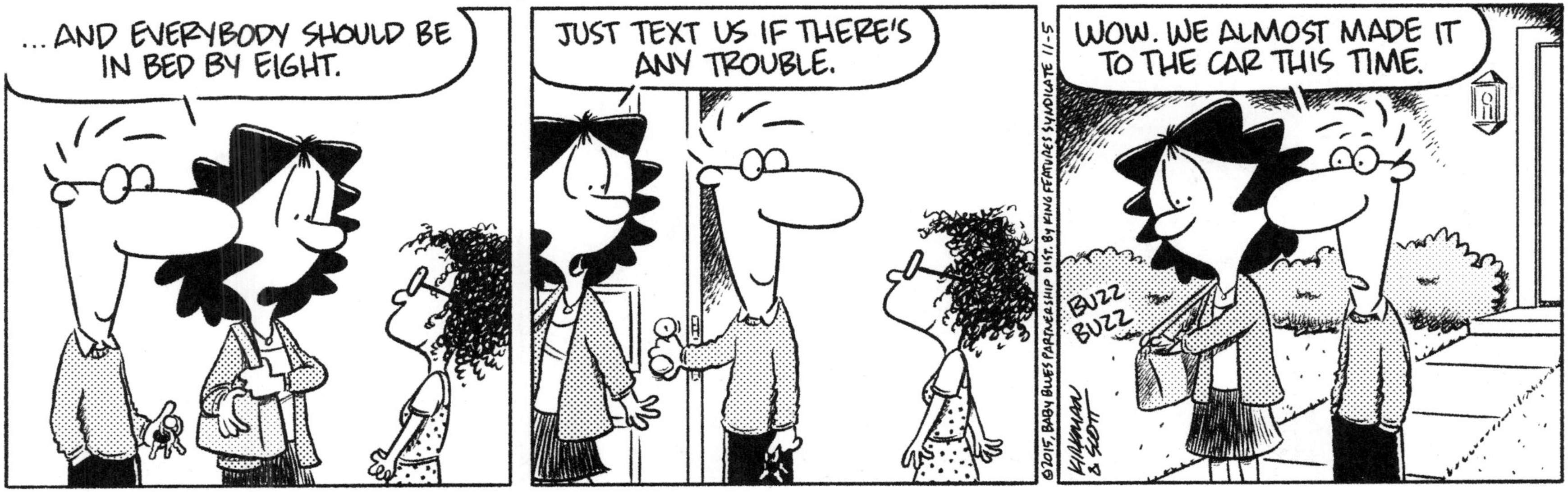
...AND EVERYBODY SHOULD BE IN BED BY EIGHT.
JUST TEXT US IF THERE'S ANY TROUBLE.
WOW. WE ALMOST MADE IT TO THE CAR THIS TIME.
BUZZ BUZZ
©2015, BABY BLUES PARTNERSHIP DIST. BY KING FEATURES SYNDICATE 11-5
KIRKMAN & SCOTT

Rick: I think I liked it better when it practically took sending out a search party to find you on date night.

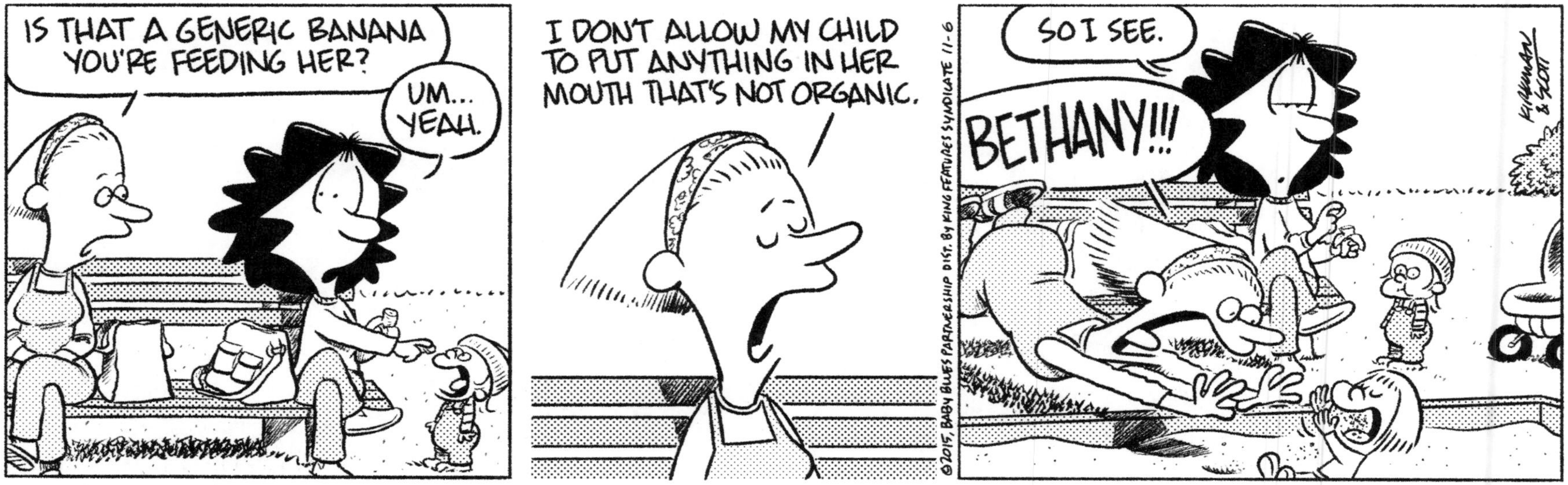
IS THAT A GENERIC BANANA YOU'RE FEEDING HER?
UM... YEAH.
I DON'T ALLOW MY CHILD TO PUT ANYTHING IN HER MOUTH THAT'S NOT ORGANIC.
©2015, BABY BLUES PARTNERSHIP DIST. BY KING FEATURES SYNDICATE 11-6
SO I SEE.
BETHANY!!!
KIRKMAN & SCOTT

Rick: Wait, that could be organic sand, depending on who's been visiting the sandbox.

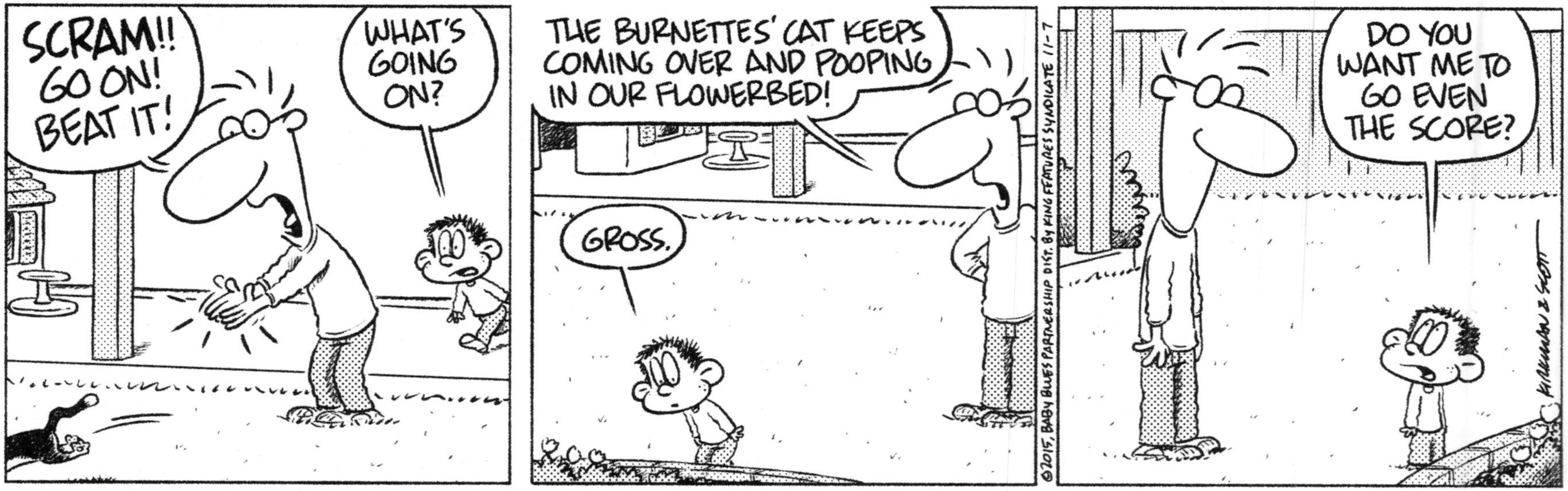
SCRAM!! GO ON! BEAT IT!
WHAT'S GOING ON?
THE BURNETTES' CAT KEEPS COMING OVER AND POOPING IN OUR FLOWERBED!
GROSS.
©2015, BABY BLUES PARTNERSHIP DIST. BY KING FEATURES SYNDICATE 11-7
DO YOU WANT ME TO GO EVEN THE SCORE?
KIRKMAN & SCOTT

Jerry: We got tons of mail on this one. There must be a lot of cat-violated flowerbeds out there.

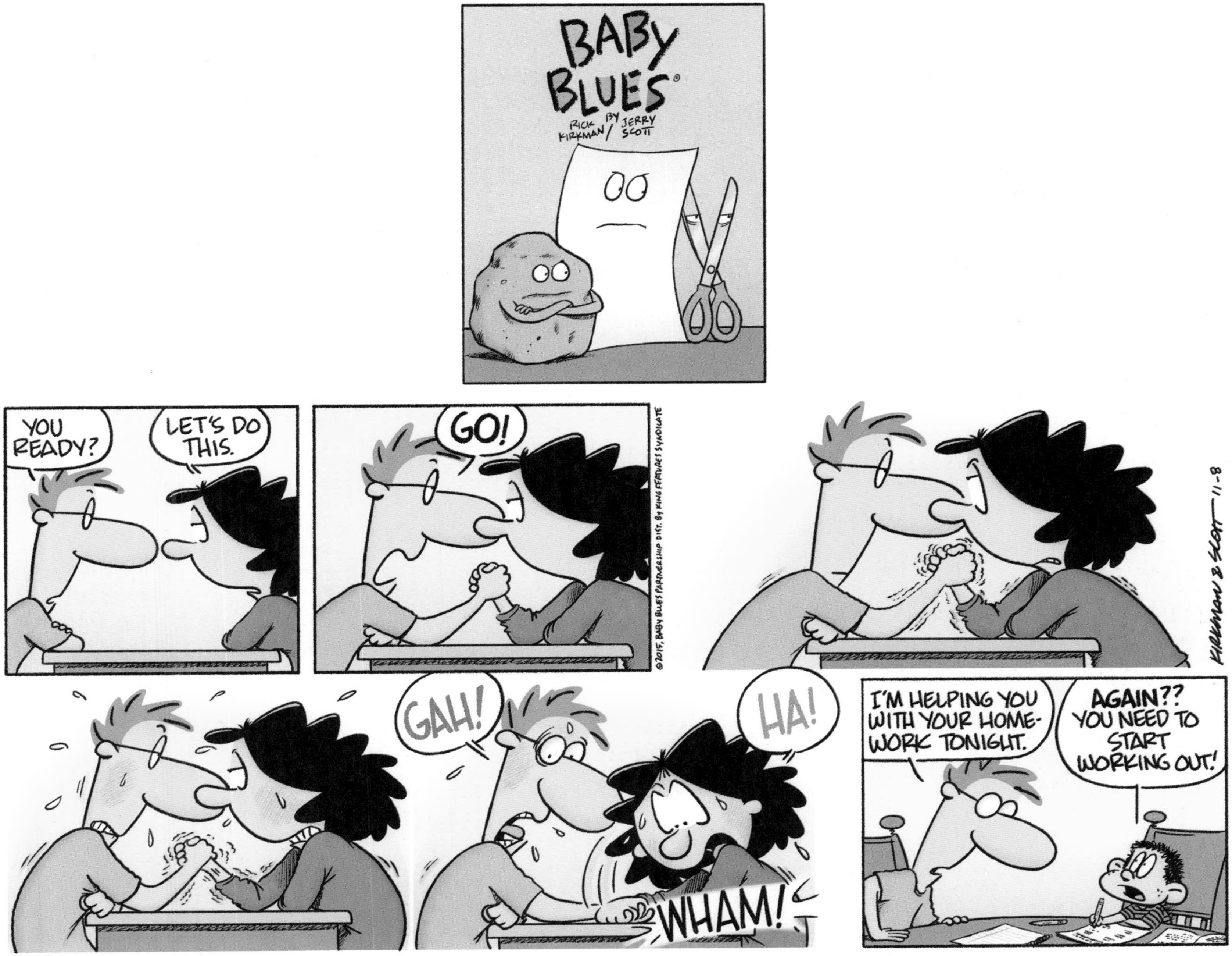
BABY BLUES®
BY RICK KIRKMAN / JERRY SCOTT
YOU READY?
LET'S DO THIS.
GO!
©2015, BABY BLUES PARTNERSHIP DIST. BY KING FEATURES SYNDICATE
KIRKMAN & SCOTT 11-8
GAH!
HA!
WHAM!
I'M HELPING YOU WITH YOUR HOME-WORK TONIGHT.
AGAIN?? YOU NEED TO START WORKING OUT!

Rick: It's not a matter of strength—it's a matter of who doesn't want it more.

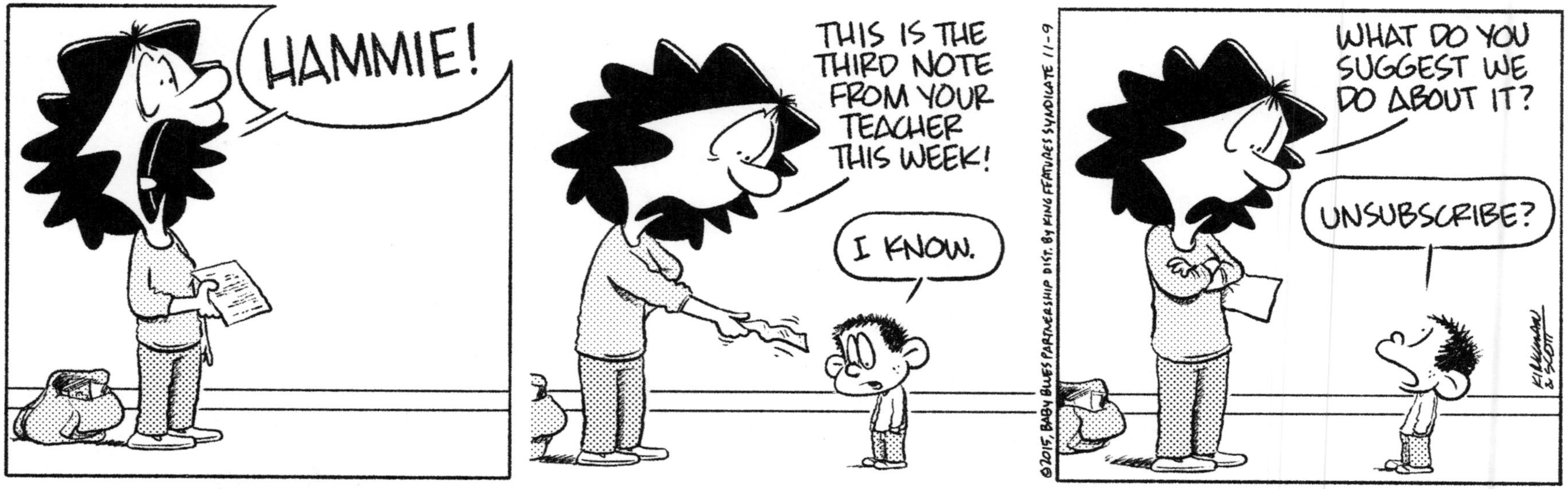
HAMMIE!
THIS IS THE THIRD NOTE FROM YOUR TEACHER THIS WEEK!
I KNOW.
©2015, BABY BLUES PARTNERSHIP DIST. BY KING FEATURES SYNDICATE 11-9
WHAT DO YOU SUGGEST WE DO ABOUT IT?
UNSUBSCRIBE?
KIRKMAN & SCOTT

Rick: I like Hammie's line of thinking.

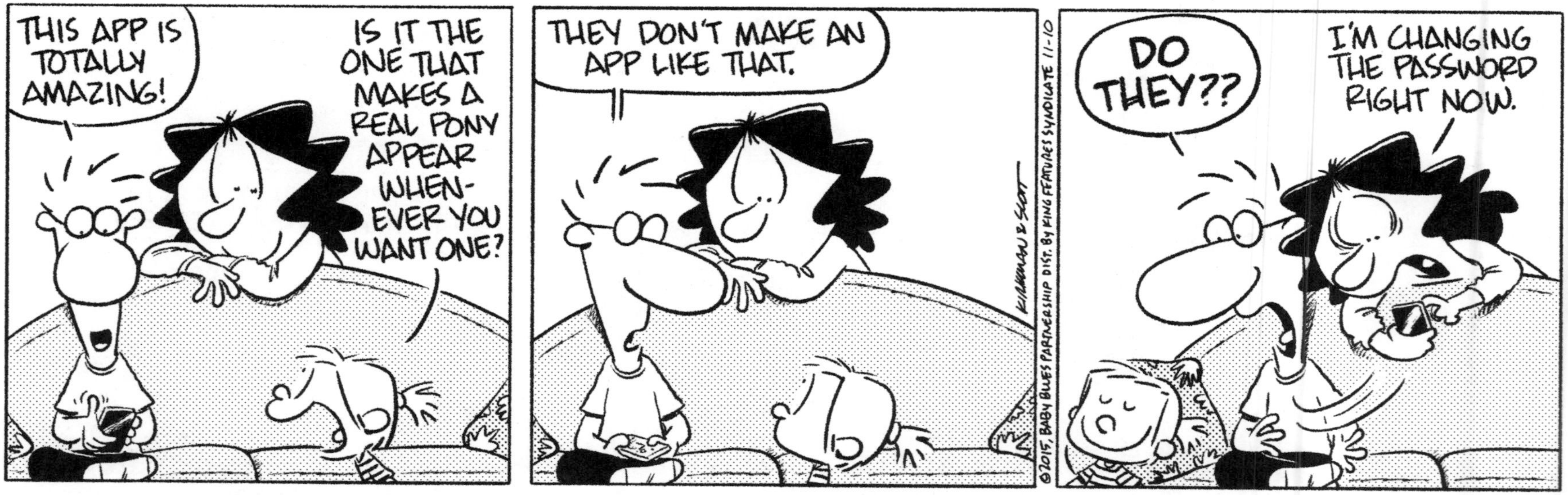
THIS APP IS TOTALLY AMAZING!
IS IT THE ONE THAT MAKES A REAL PONY APPEAR WHEN-EVER YOU WANT ONE?
THEY DON'T MAKE AN APP LIKE THAT.
KIRKMAN & SCOTT
©2015, BABY BLUES PARTNERSHIP DIST. BY KING FEATURES SYNDICATE 11-10
DO THEY??
I'M CHANGING THE PASSWORD RIGHT NOW.

Rick: There better not be an app for that.

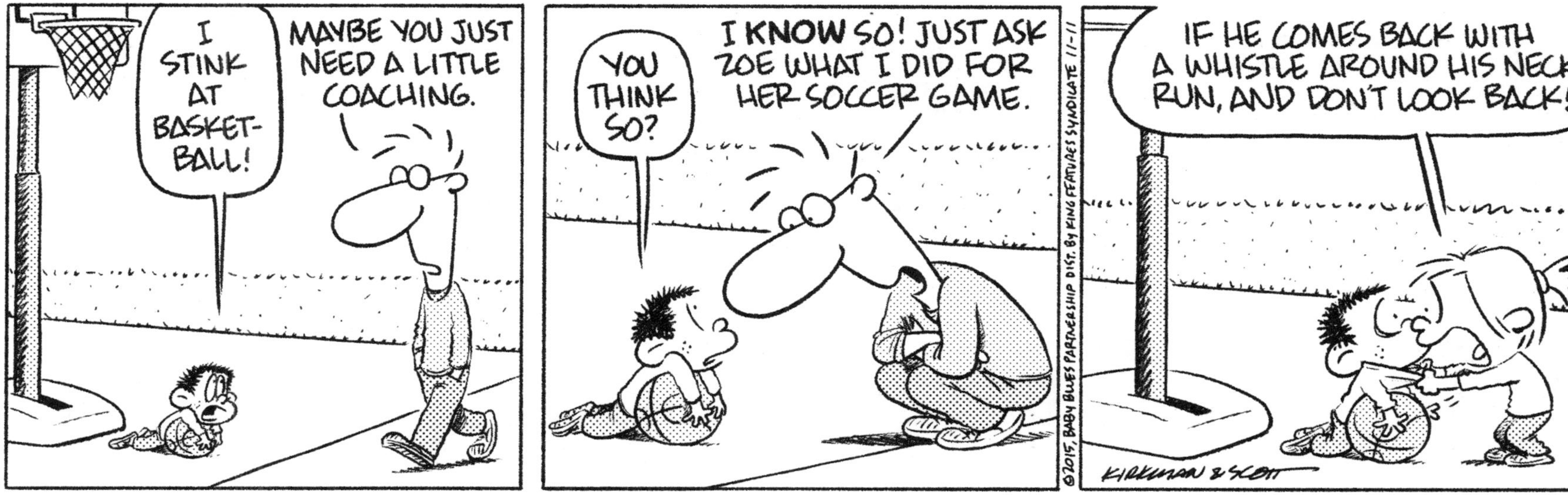
I STINK AT BASKET-BALL!
MAYBE YOU JUST NEED A LITTLE COACHING.
YOU THINK SO?
I **KNOW** SO! JUST ASK ZOE WHAT I DID FOR HER SOCCER GAME.
©2015, BABY BLUES PARTNERSHIP DIST. BY KING FEATURES SYNDICATE 11-11
IF HE COMES BACK WITH A WHISTLE AROUND HIS NECK, RUN, AND DON'T LOOK BACK!
KIRKMAN & SCOTT

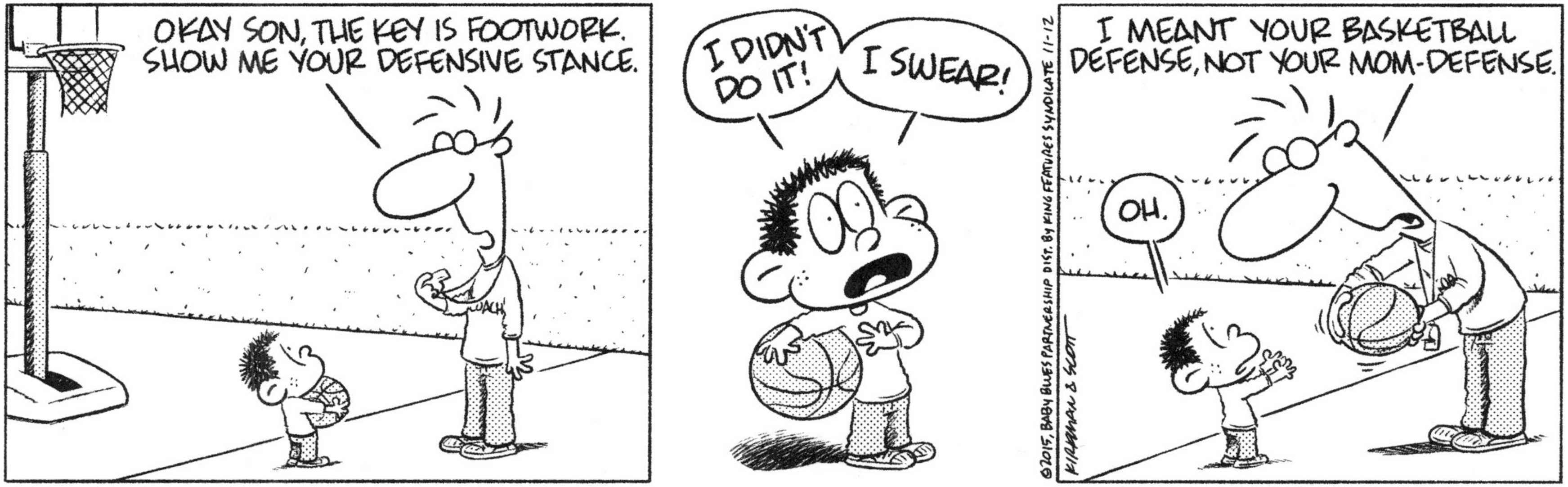
OKAY SON, THE KEY IS FOOTWORK. SHOW ME YOUR DEFENSIVE STANCE.
COACH
I DIDN'T DO IT!
I SWEAR!
©2015, BABY BLUES PARTNERSHIP DIST. BY KING FEATURES SYNDICATE 11-12
KIRKMAN & SCOTT
I MEANT YOUR BASKETBALL DEFENSE, NOT YOUR MOM-DEFENSE.
OH.

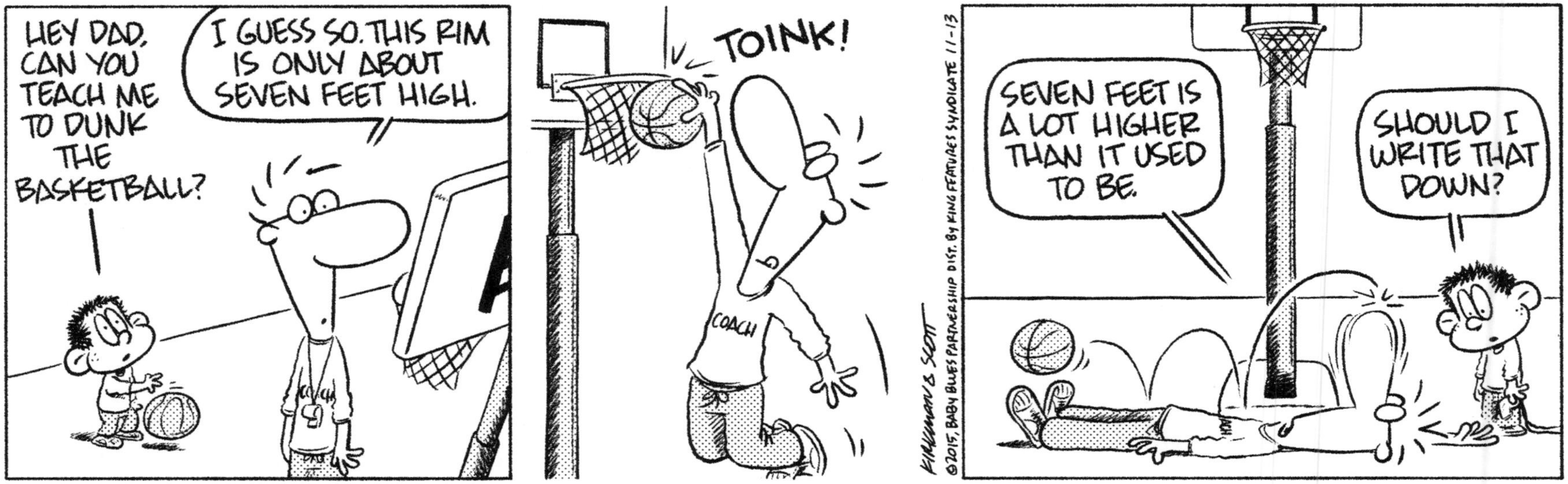
HEY DAD, CAN YOU TEACH ME TO DUNK THE BASKETBALL?
I GUESS SO. THIS RIM IS ONLY ABOUT SEVEN FEET HIGH.
TOINK!
COACH
KIRKMAN & SCOTT
©2015, BABY BLUES PARTNERSHIP DIST. BY KING FEATURES SYNDICATE 11-13
SEVEN FEET IS A LOT HIGHER THAN IT USED TO BE.
SHOULD I WRITE THAT DOWN?

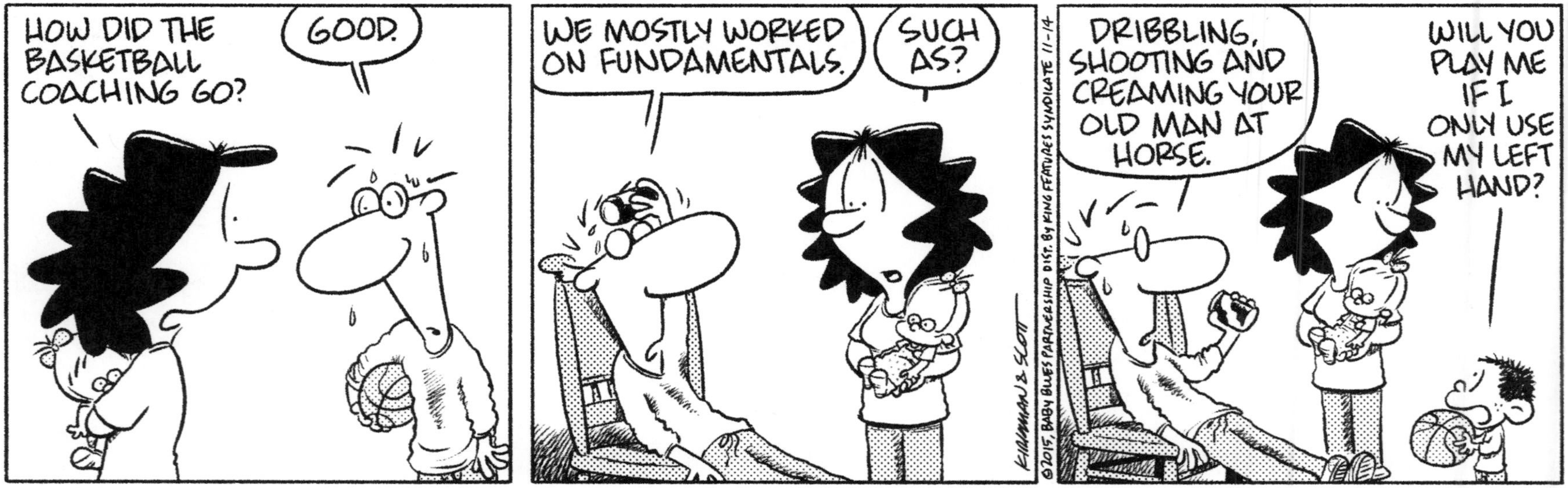
HOW DID THE BASKETBALL COACHING GO?
GOOD.
WE MOSTLY WORKED ON FUNDAMENTALS.
SUCH AS?
KIRKMAN & SCOTT
©2015, BABY BLUES PARTNERSHIP DIST. BY KING FEATURES SYNDICATE 11-14
DRIBBLING, SHOOTING AND CREAMING YOUR OLD MAN AT HORSE.
WILL YOU PLAY ME IF I ONLY USE MY LEFT HAND?

Rick: Dang! Just noticed I left "COACH" off Darryl's shirt in this strip. Maybe Darryl scraped it off after the humiliating loss. Yeah. I'm going with that.

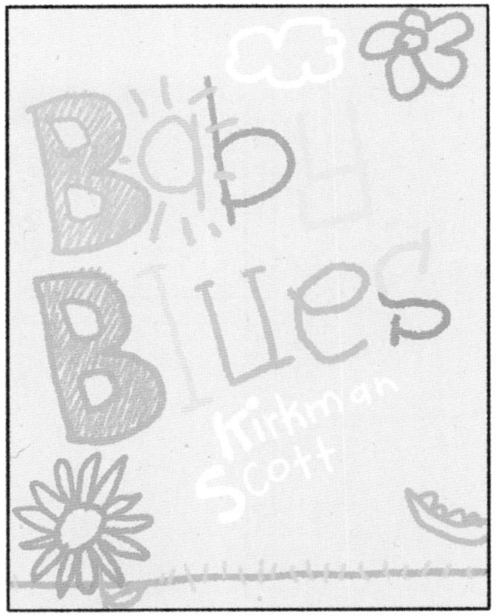
Baby
Blues
Kirkman
Scott

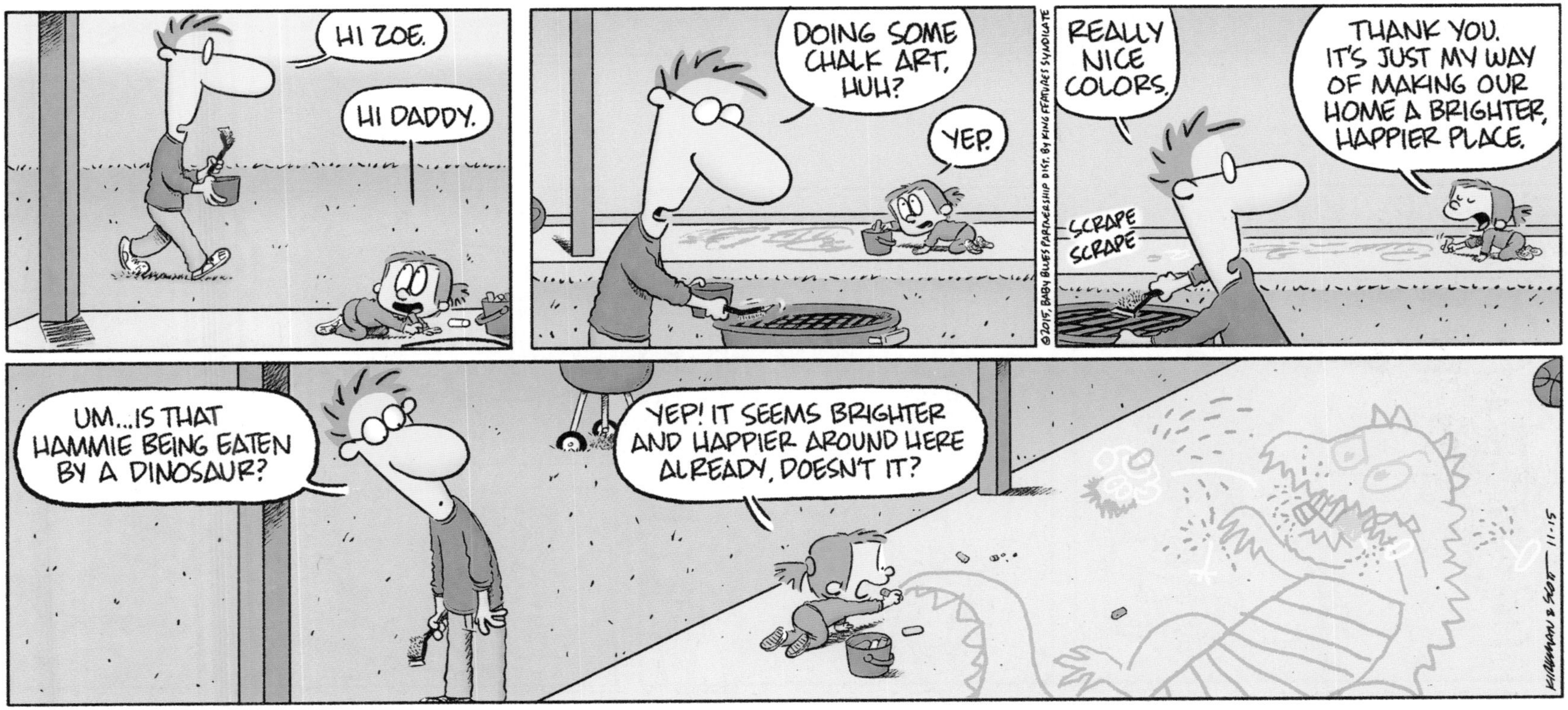
HI ZOE.
HI DADDY.
DOING SOME CHALK ART, HUH?
YEP.
©2015, BABY BLUES PARTNERSHIP DIST. BY KING FEATURES SYNDICATE
REALLY NICE COLORS.
SCRAPE SCRAPE
THANK YOU. IT'S JUST MY WAY OF MAKING OUR HOME A BRIGHTER, HAPPIER PLACE.
UM...IS THAT HAMMIE BEING EATEN BY A DINOSAUR?
YEP! IT SEEMS BRIGHTER AND HAPPIER AROUND HERE ALREADY, DOESN'T IT?
11-15
KIRKMAN & SCOTT

Rick: Hmm. Hard to pull off colored chalk on concrete in a newspaper cartoon. Oh well.

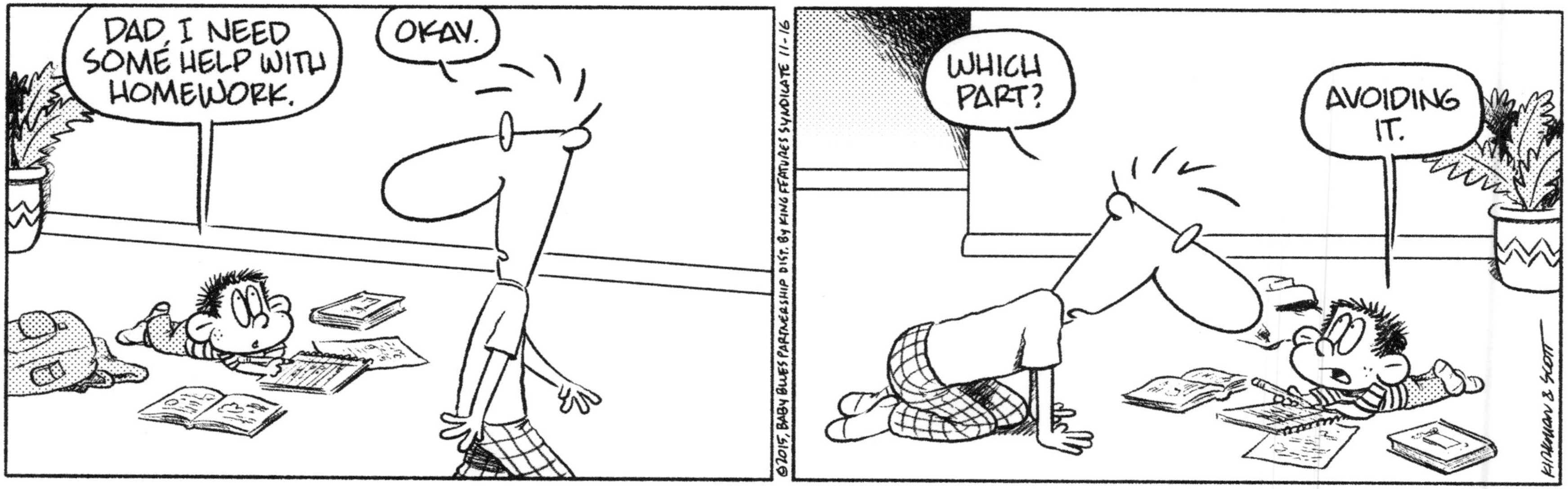
DAD, I NEED SOME HELP WITH HOMEWORK.
OKAY.
WHICH PART?
AVOIDING IT.
©2015, BABY BLUES PARTNERSHIP DIST. BY KING FEATURES SYNDICATE 11-16
KIRKMAN & SCOTT

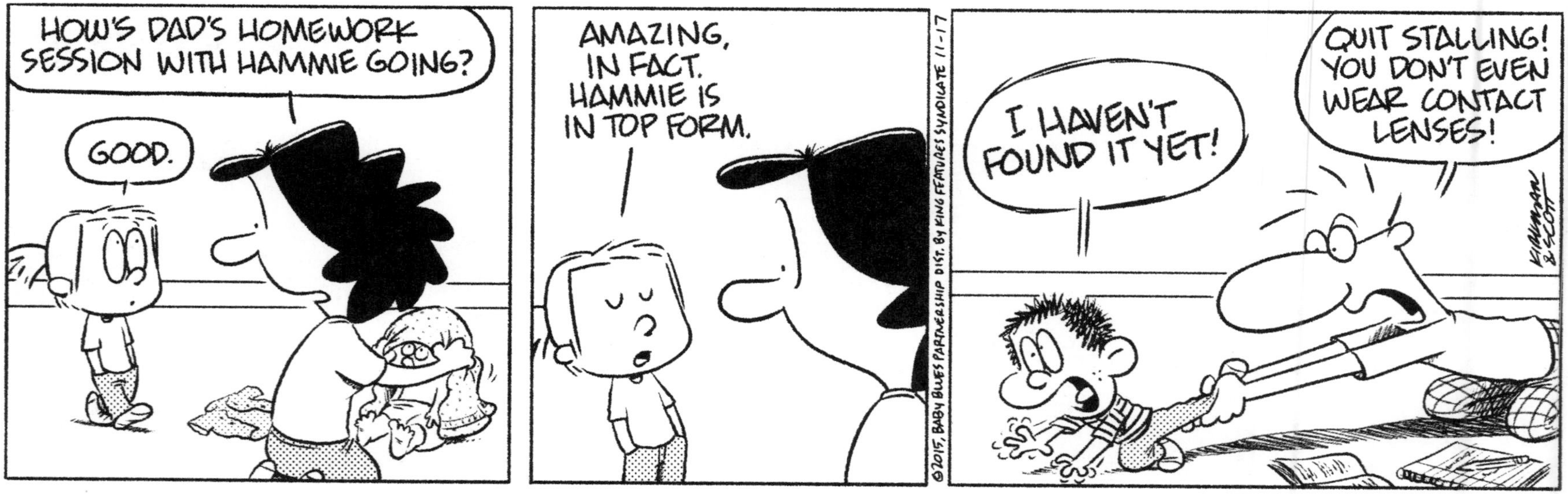
HOW'S DAD'S HOMEWORK SESSION WITH HAMMIE GOING?
GOOD.
AMAZING, IN FACT. HAMMIE IS IN TOP FORM.
I HAVEN'T FOUND IT YET!
QUIT STALLING! YOU DON'T EVEN WEAR CONTACT LENSES!
©2015, BABY BLUES PARTNERSHIP DIST. BY KING FEATURES SYNDICATE 11-17
KIRKMAN & SCOTT

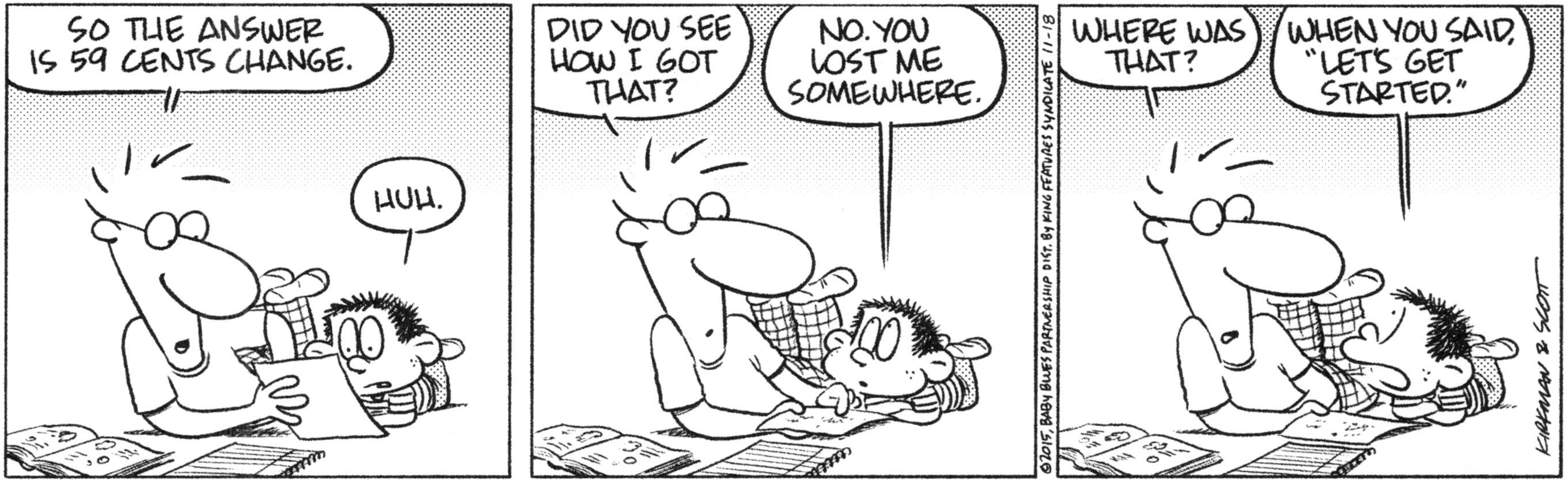
SO THE ANSWER IS 59 CENTS CHANGE.
HUH.
DID YOU SEE HOW I GOT THAT?
NO. YOU LOST ME SOMEWHERE.
©2015, BABY BLUES PARTNERSHIP DIST. BY KING FEATURES SYNDICATE 11-18
WHERE WAS THAT?
WHEN YOU SAID, "LET'S GET STARTED."
KIRKMAN & SCOTT

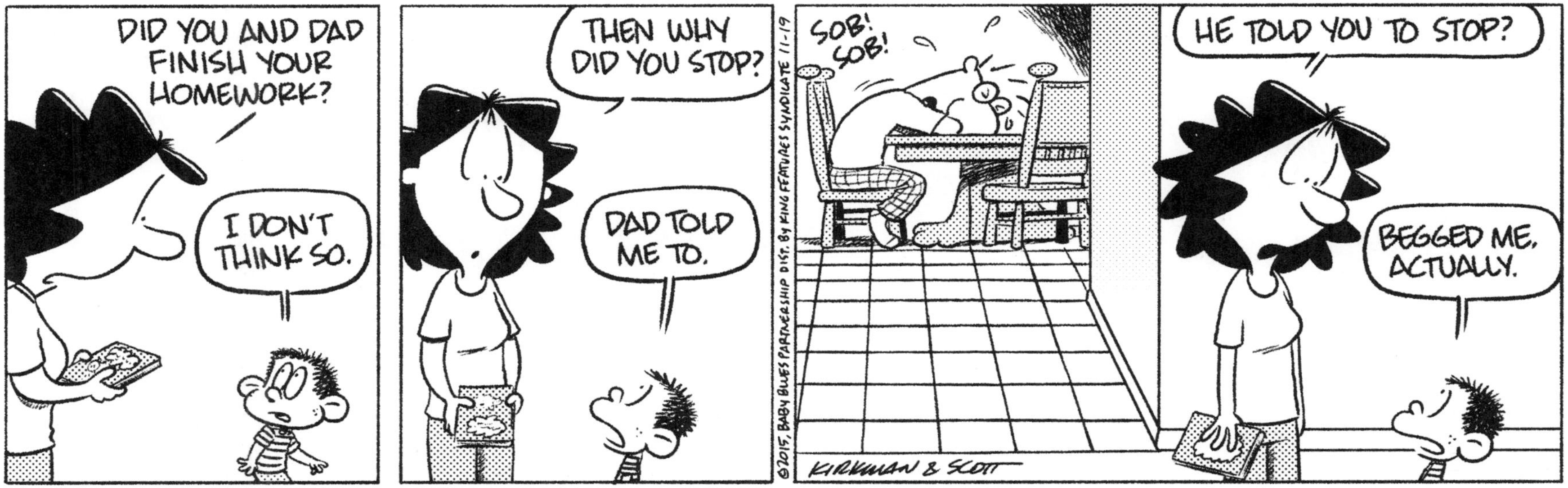
DID YOU AND DAD FINISH YOUR HOMEWORK?
I DON'T THINK SO.
THEN WHY DID YOU STOP?
DAD TOLD ME TO.
©2015, BABY BLUES PARTNERSHIP DIST. BY KING FEATURES SYNDICATE 11-19
SOB! SOB!
HE TOLD YOU TO STOP?
BEGGED ME, ACTUALLY.
KIRKMAN & SCOTT

Rick: I didn't miss homework when I graduated from school, and I didn't miss it even more when my kids graduated.

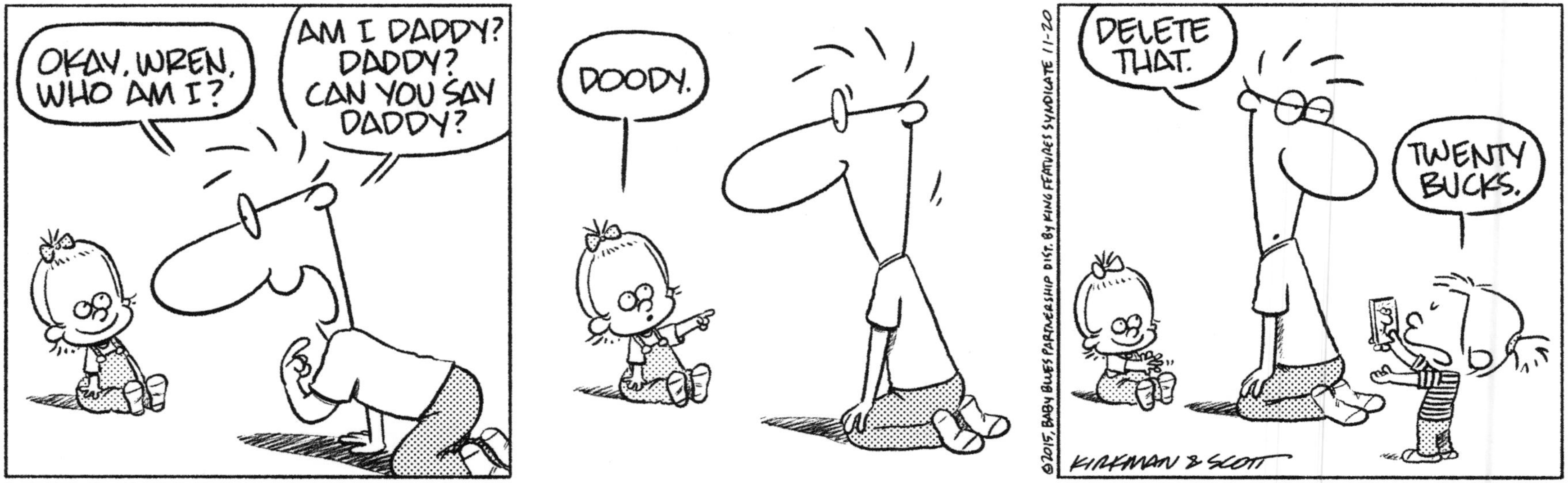
OKAY, WREN, WHO AM I?
AM I DADDY? DADDY? CAN YOU SAY DADDY?
DOODY.
DELETE THAT.
TWENTY BUCKS.
©2015, BABY BLUES PARTNERSHIP DIST. BY KING FEATURES SYNDICATE 11-20
KIRKMAN & SCOTT

Rick: Technology—enabling grade school extortionists everywhere.

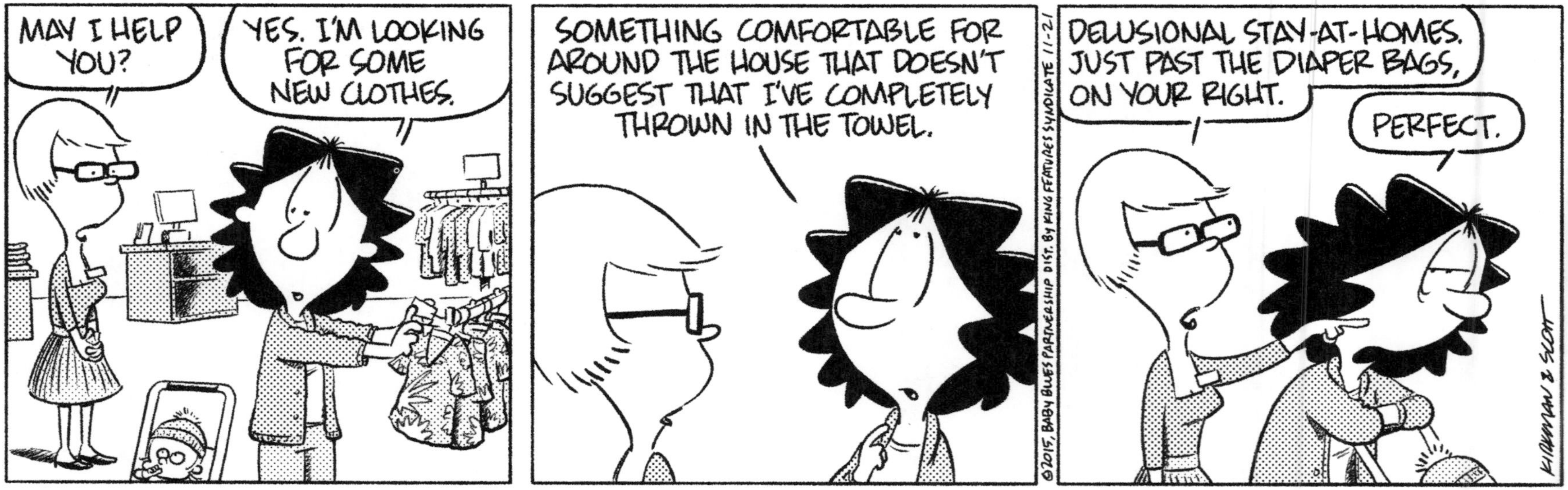
MAY I HELP YOU?
YES. I'M LOOKING FOR SOME NEW CLOTHES.
SOMETHING COMFORTABLE FOR AROUND THE HOUSE THAT DOESN'T SUGGEST THAT I'VE COMPLETELY THROWN IN THE TOWEL.
DELUSIONAL STAY-AT-HOMES. JUST PAST THE DIAPER BAGS, ON YOUR RIGHT.
PERFECT.
©2015, BABY BLUES PARTNERSHIP DIST. BY KING FEATURES SYNDICATE 11-21
KIRKMAN & SCOTT

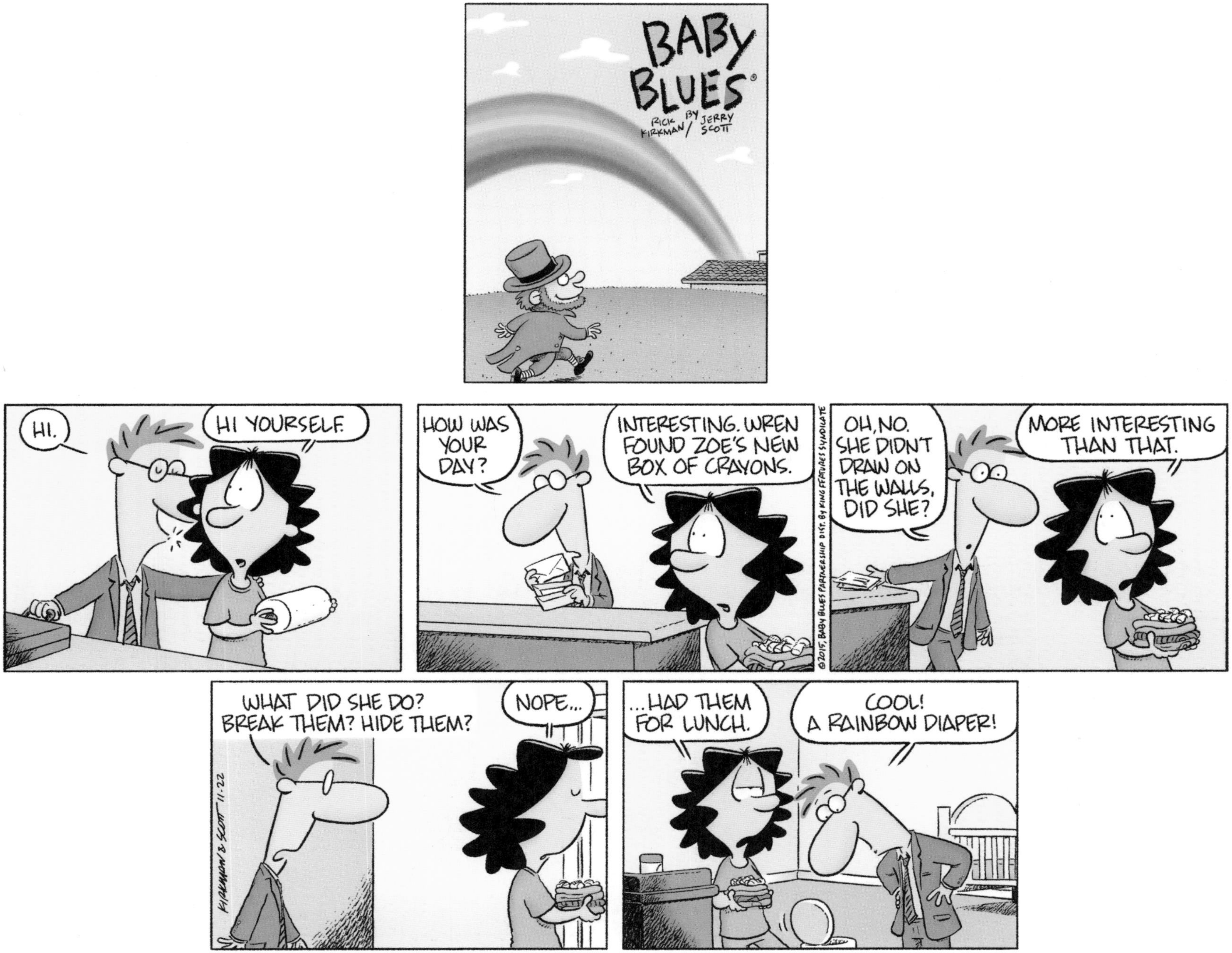
BABY BLUES®
BY RICK KIRKMAN / JERRY SCOTT
HI.
HI YOURSELF.
HOW WAS YOUR DAY?
INTERESTING. WREN FOUND ZOE'S NEW BOX OF CRAYONS.
©2015, BABY BLUES PARTNERSHIP DIST. BY KING FEATURES SYNDICATE
OH, NO. SHE DIDN'T DRAW ON THE WALLS, DID SHE?
MORE INTERESTING THAN THAT.
WHAT DID SHE DO? BREAK THEM? HIDE THEM?
NOPE...
KIRKMAN & SCOTT 11-22
...HAD THEM FOR LUNCH.
COOL! A RAINBOW DIAPER!

Rick: So thankful I could leave that to the reader's imagination.

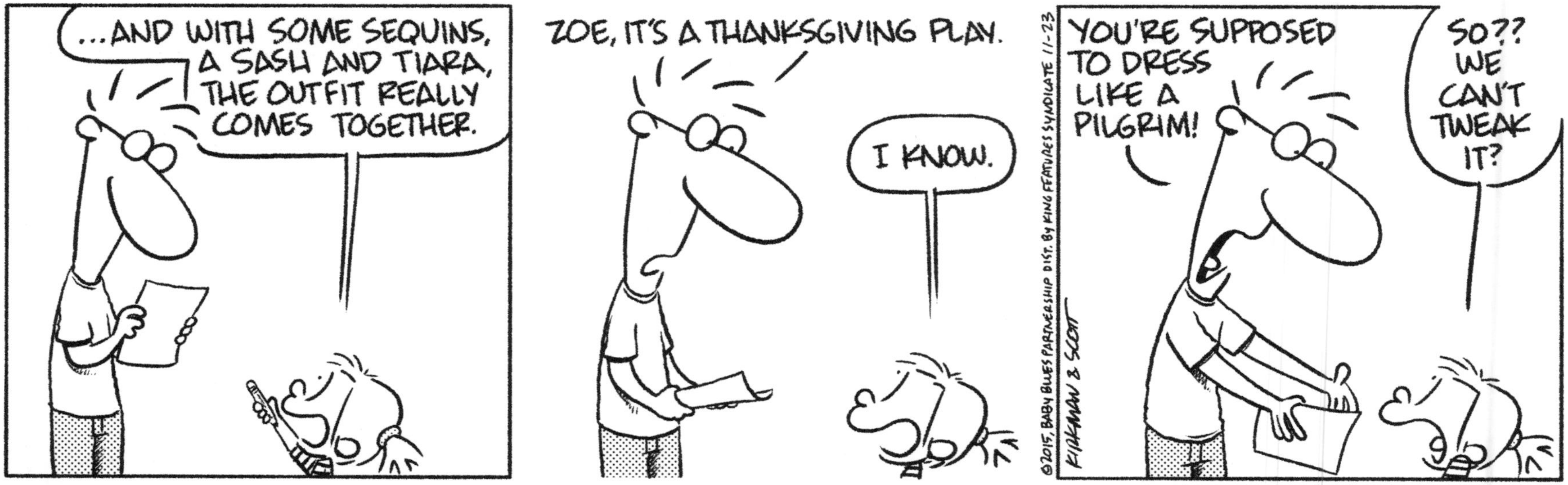
...AND WITH SOME SEQUINS, A SASH AND TIARA, THE OUTFIT REALLY COMES TOGETHER.
ZOE, IT'S A THANKSGIVING PLAY.
I KNOW.
YOU'RE SUPPOSED TO DRESS LIKE A PILGRIM!
SO?? WE CAN'T TWEAK IT?
©2015, BABY BLUES PARTNERSHIP DIST. BY KING FEATURES SYNDICATE 11-23
KIRKMAN & SCOTT

Jerry: *Pilgrims in Tiaras* . . . I'd watch that show.

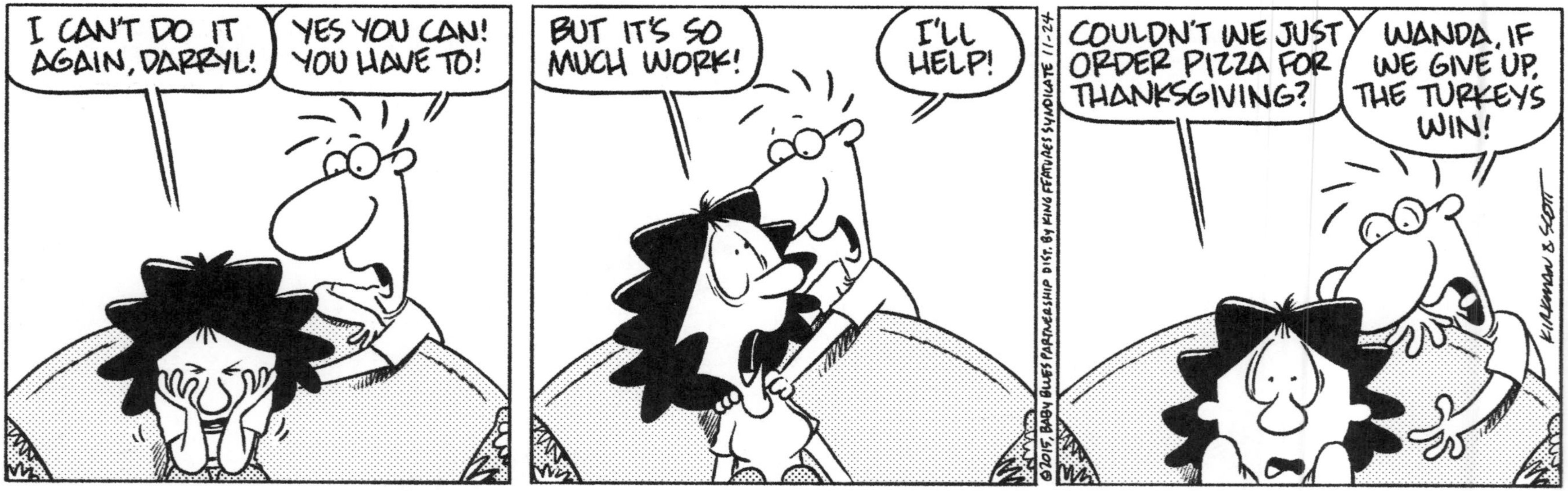
I CAN'T DO IT AGAIN, DARRYL!
YES YOU CAN! YOU HAVE TO!
BUT IT'S SO MUCH WORK!
I'LL HELP!
COULDN'T WE JUST ORDER PIZZA FOR THANKSGIVING?
WANDA, IF WE GIVE UP, THE TURKEYS WIN!
©2015, BABY BLUES PARTNERSHIP DIST. BY KING FEATURES SYNDICATE 11-24
KIRKMAN & SCOTT

Rick: How about a turkey-shaped pizza? Anybody?

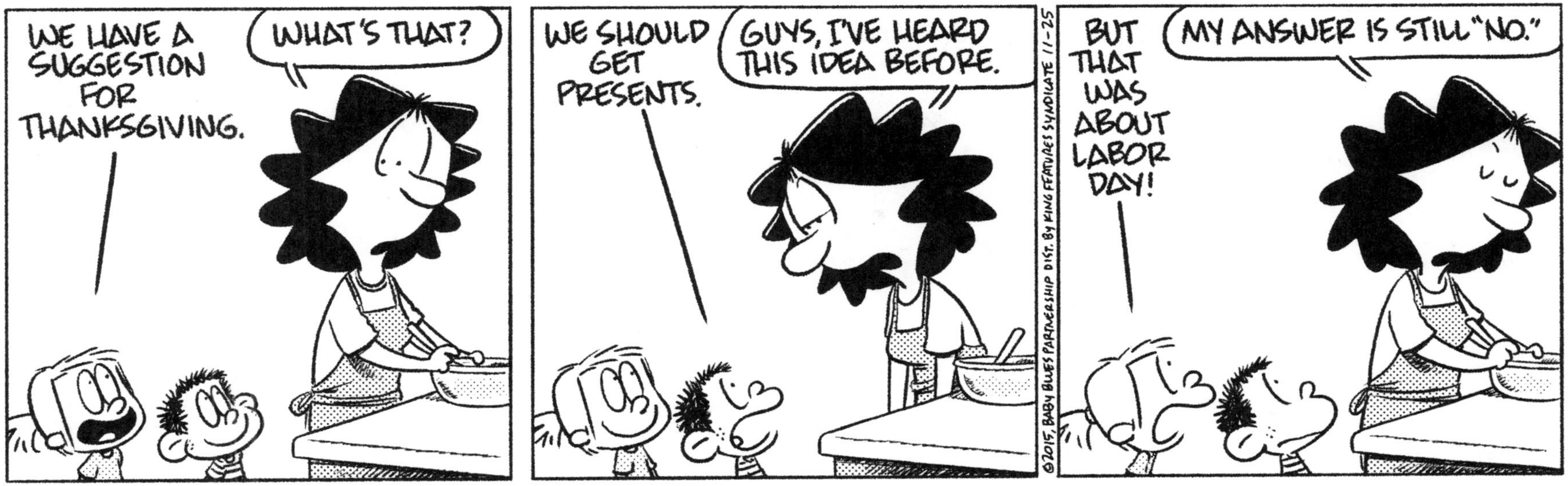
WE HAVE A SUGGESTION FOR THANKSGIVING.
WHAT'S THAT?
WE SHOULD GET PRESENTS.
GUYS, I'VE HEARD THIS IDEA BEFORE.
©2015, BABY BLUES PARTNERSHIP DIST. BY KING FEATURES SYNDICATE 11-25
BUT THAT WAS ABOUT LABOR DAY!
MY ANSWER IS STILL "NO."

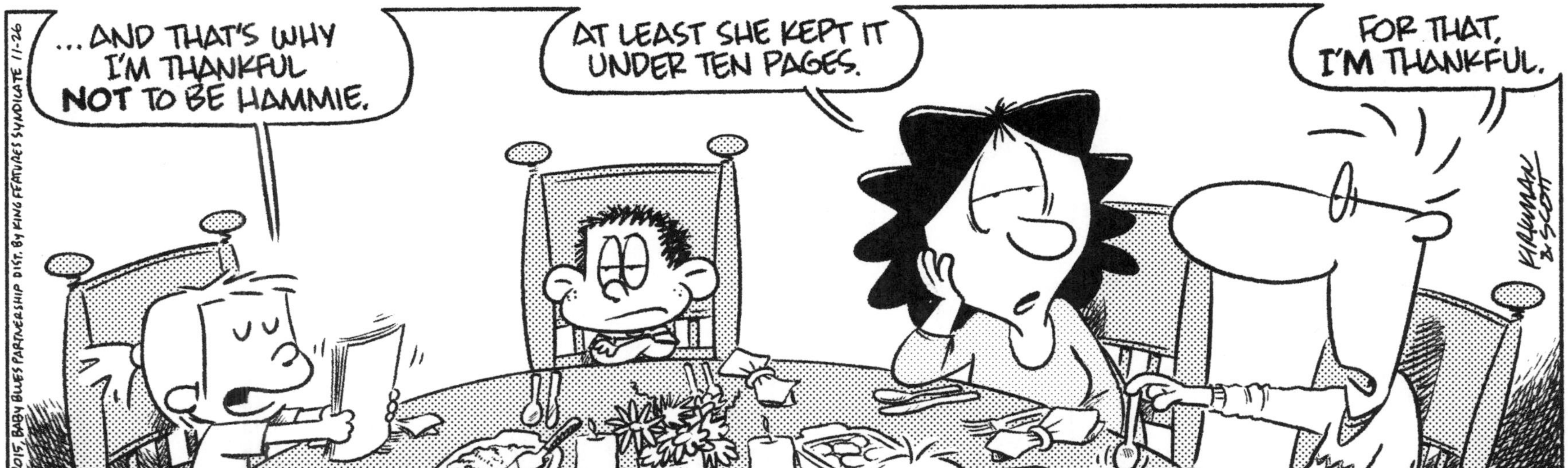
©2015, BABY BLUES PARTNERSHIP DIST. BY KING FEATURES SYNDICATE 11-26
...AND THAT'S WHY I'M THANKFUL **NOT** TO BE HAMMIE.
AT LEAST SHE KEPT IT UNDER TEN PAGES.
FOR THAT, **I'M** THANKFUL.
KIRKMAN & SCOTT

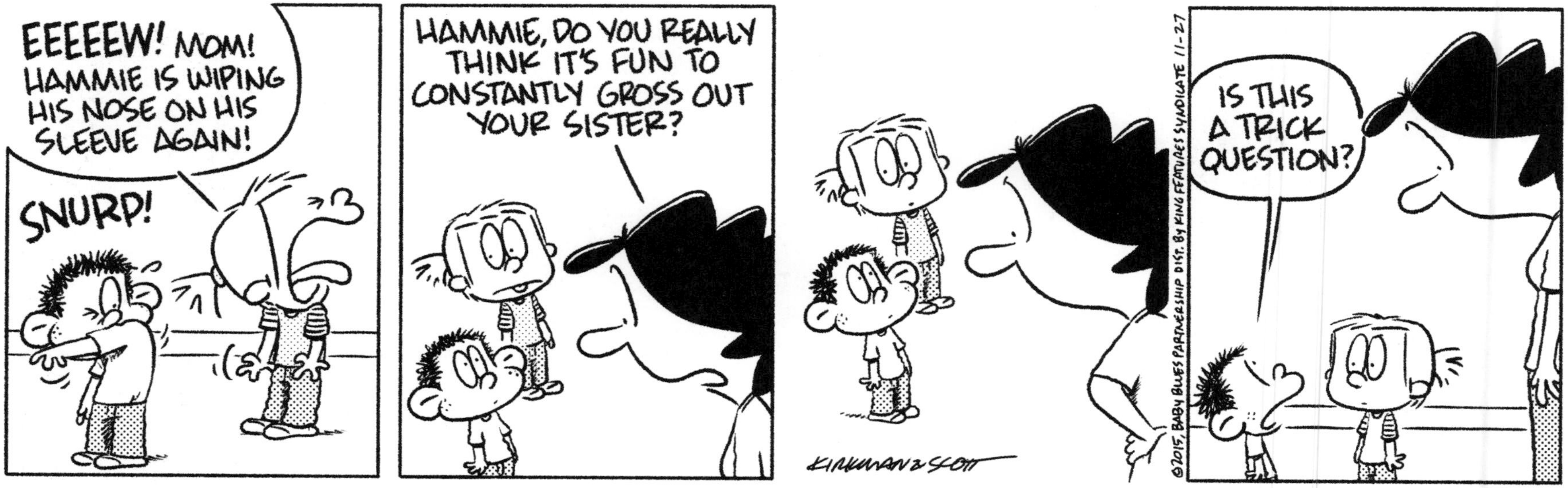
EEEEEW! MOM! HAMMIE IS WIPING HIS NOSE ON HIS SLEEVE AGAIN!
SNURP!
HAMMIE, DO YOU REALLY THINK IT'S FUN TO CONSTANTLY GROSS OUT YOUR SISTER?
KIRKMAN & SCOTT
©2015, BABY BLUES PARTNERSHIP DIST. BY KING FEATURES SYNDICATE 11-27
IS THIS A TRICK QUESTION?

Jerry: It's gotta be a trick question.

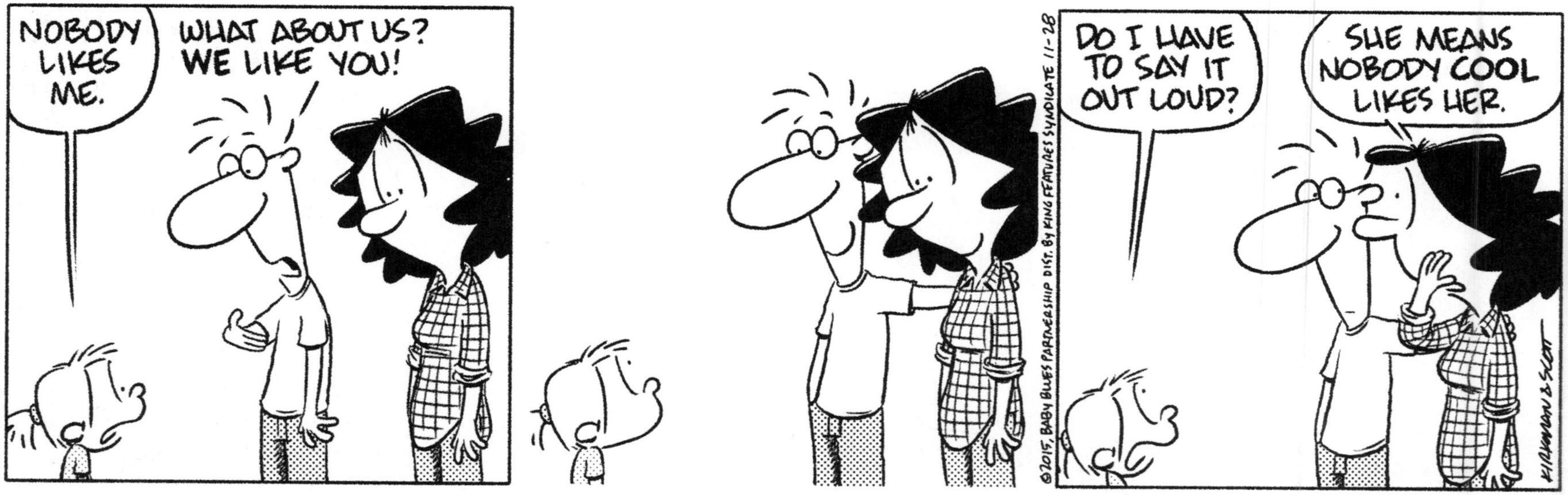
NOBODY LIKES ME.
WHAT ABOUT US? WE LIKE YOU!
©2015, BABY BLUES PARTNERSHIP DIST. BY KING FEATURES SYNDICATE 11-28
DO I HAVE TO SAY IT OUT LOUD?
SHE MEANS NOBODY COOL LIKES HER.
KIRKMAN & SCOTT

Rick: Man, she's got an early start.

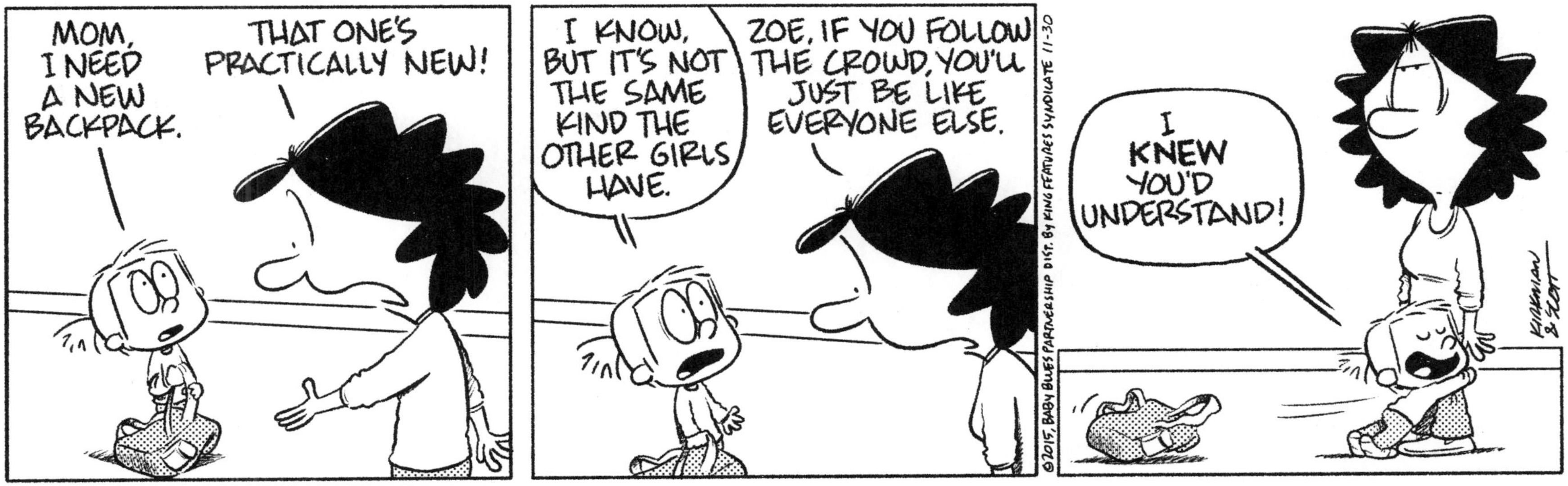
MOM, I NEED A NEW BACKPACK.
THAT ONE'S PRACTICALLY NEW!
I KNOW, BUT IT'S NOT THE SAME KIND THE OTHER GIRLS HAVE.
ZOE, IF YOU FOLLOW THE CROWD, YOU'LL JUST BE LIKE EVERYONE ELSE.
©2015, BABY BLUES PARTNERSHIP DIST. BY KING FEATURES SYNDICATE 11-30
I **KNEW** YOU'D UNDERSTAND!
KIRKMAN & SCOTT

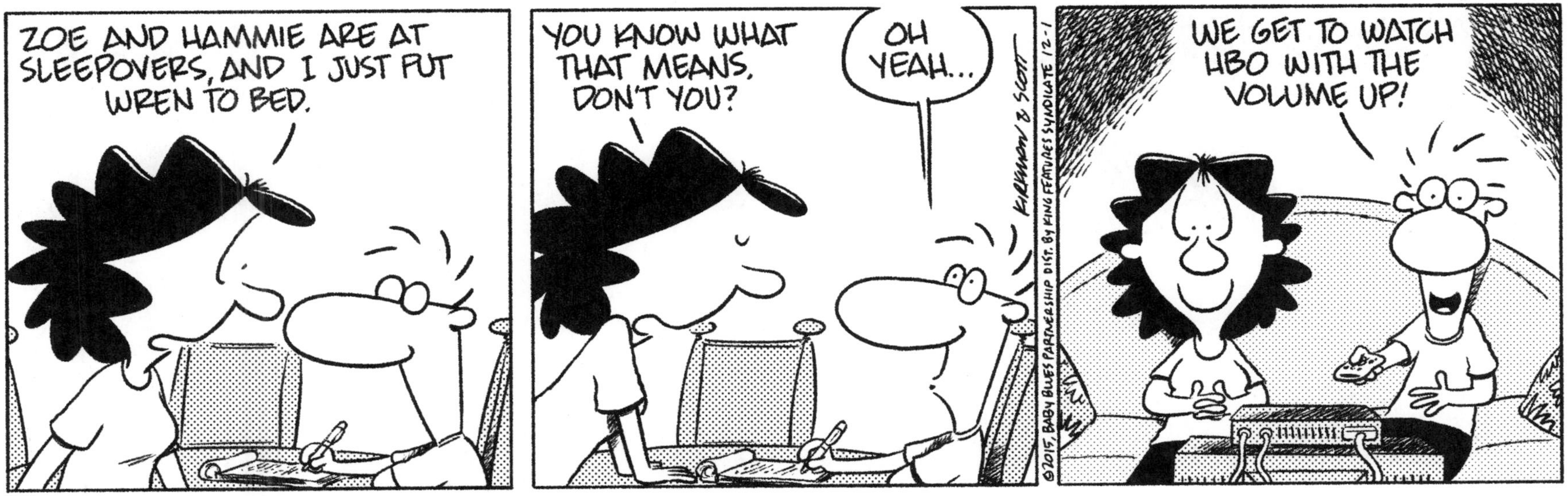
ZOE AND HAMMIE ARE AT SLEEPOVERS, AND I JUST PUT WREN TO BED.
YOU KNOW WHAT THAT MEANS, DON'T YOU?
OH YEAH...
KIRKMAN & SCOTT
©2015, BABY BLUES PARTNERSHIP DIST. BY KING FEATURES SYNDICATE 12-1
WE GET TO WATCH HBO WITH THE VOLUME UP!

Rick: It's the little pleasures . . .

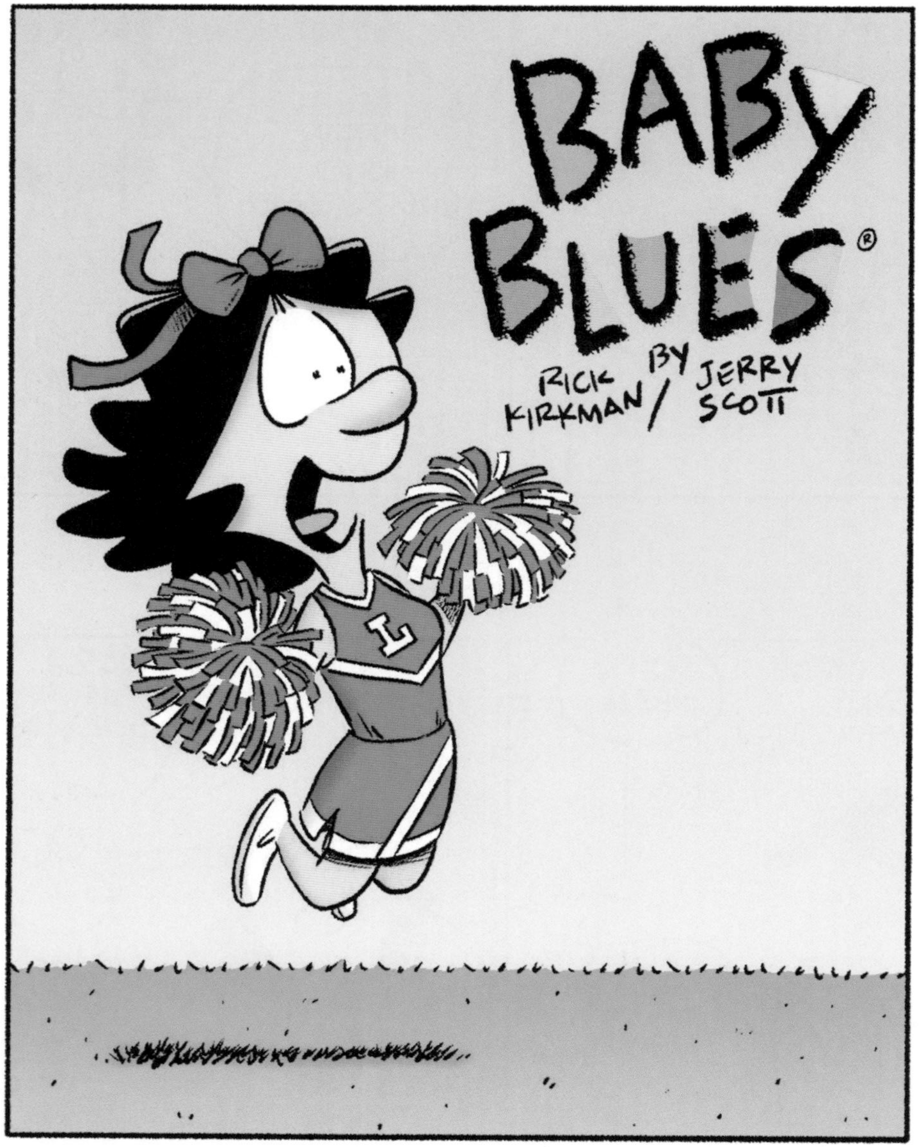
BABY BLUES®
BY
RICK KIRKMAN / JERRY SCOTT

Rick: Another example of muting the background to focus on the characters. I like the way it worked out.

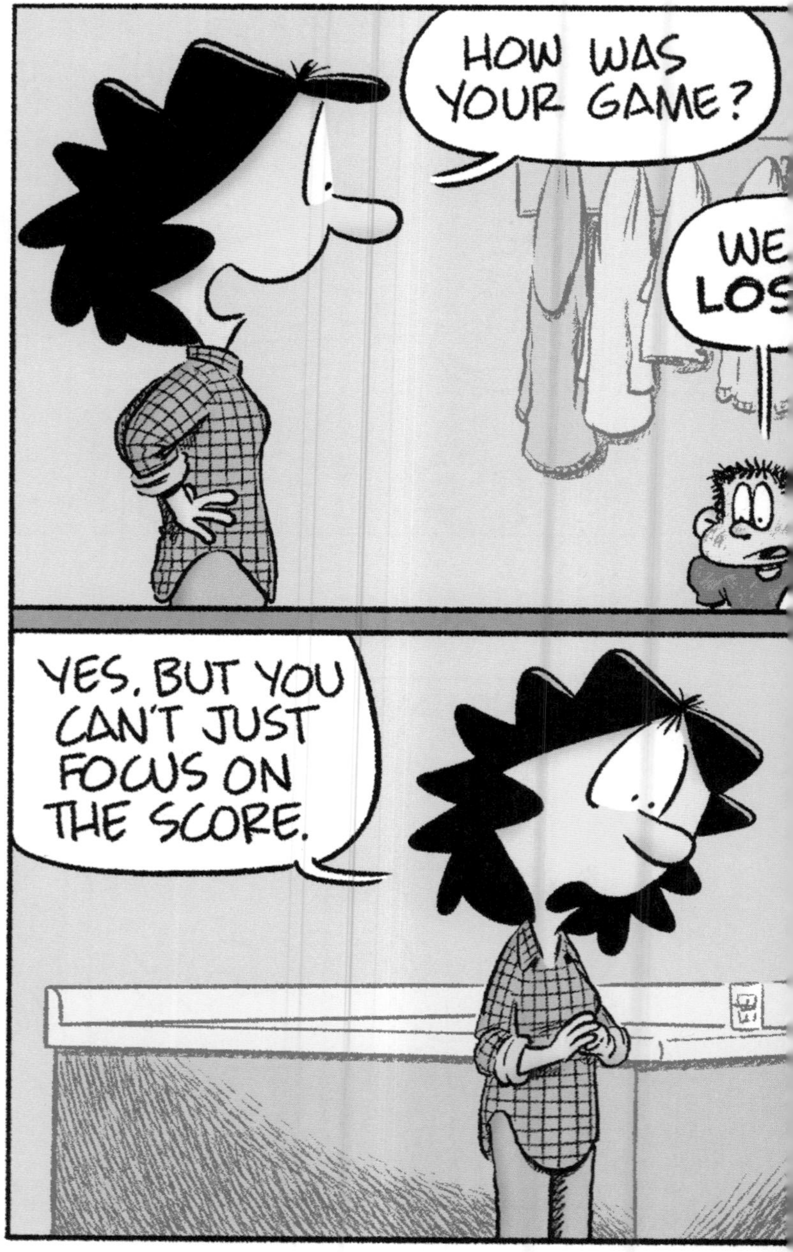
HOW WAS YOUR GAME?
WE
YES, BUT YOU CAN'T JUST FOCUS ON THE SCORE.

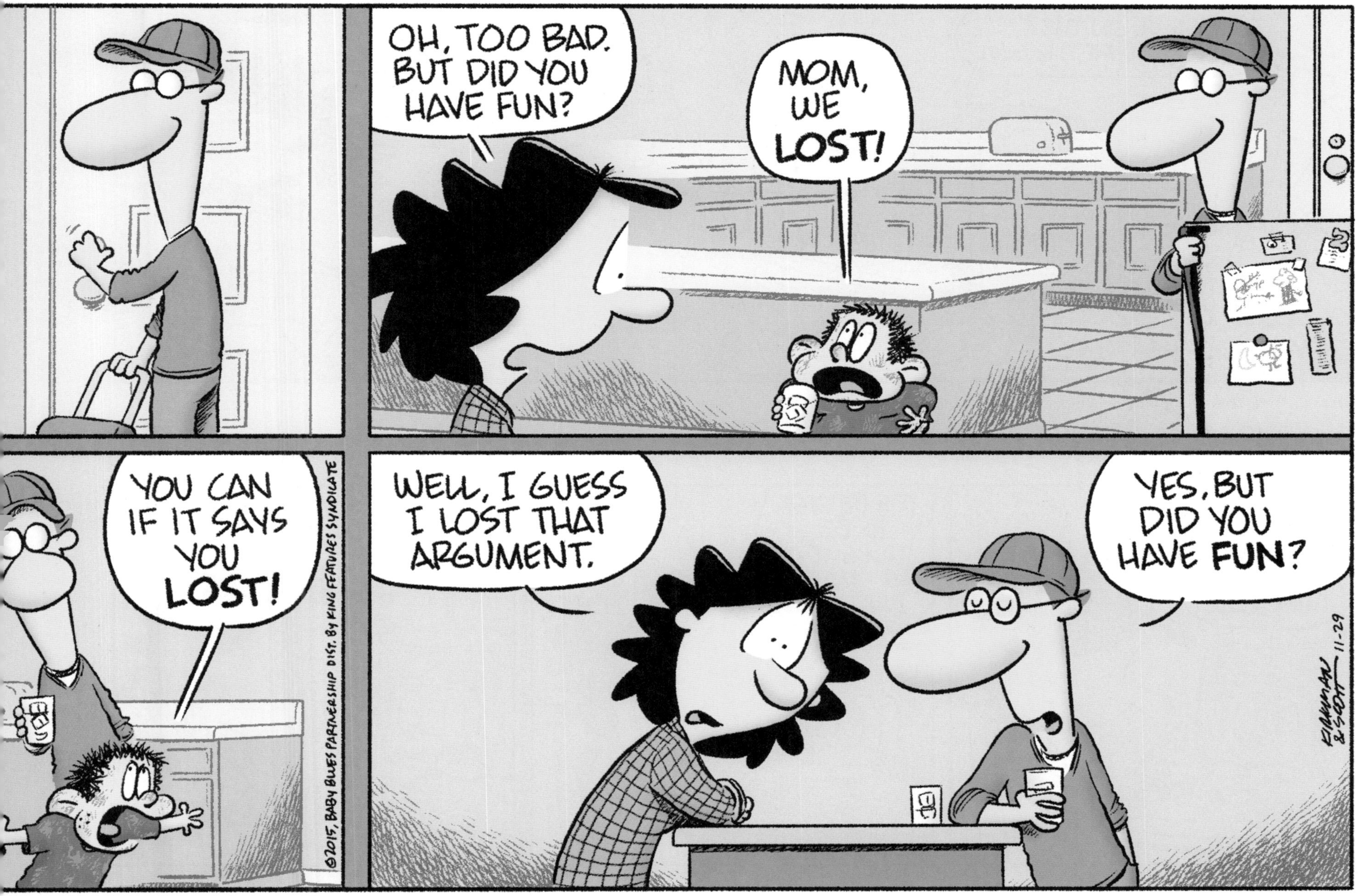
OH, TOO BAD. BUT DID YOU HAVE FUN?
MOM, WE LOST!
YOU CAN IF IT SAYS YOU LOST!
©2015, BABY BLUES PARTNERSHIP DIST. BY KING FEATURES SYNDICATE
WELL, I GUESS I LOST THAT ARGUMENT.
YES, BUT DID YOU HAVE FUN?
KIRKMAN & SCOTT 11-29

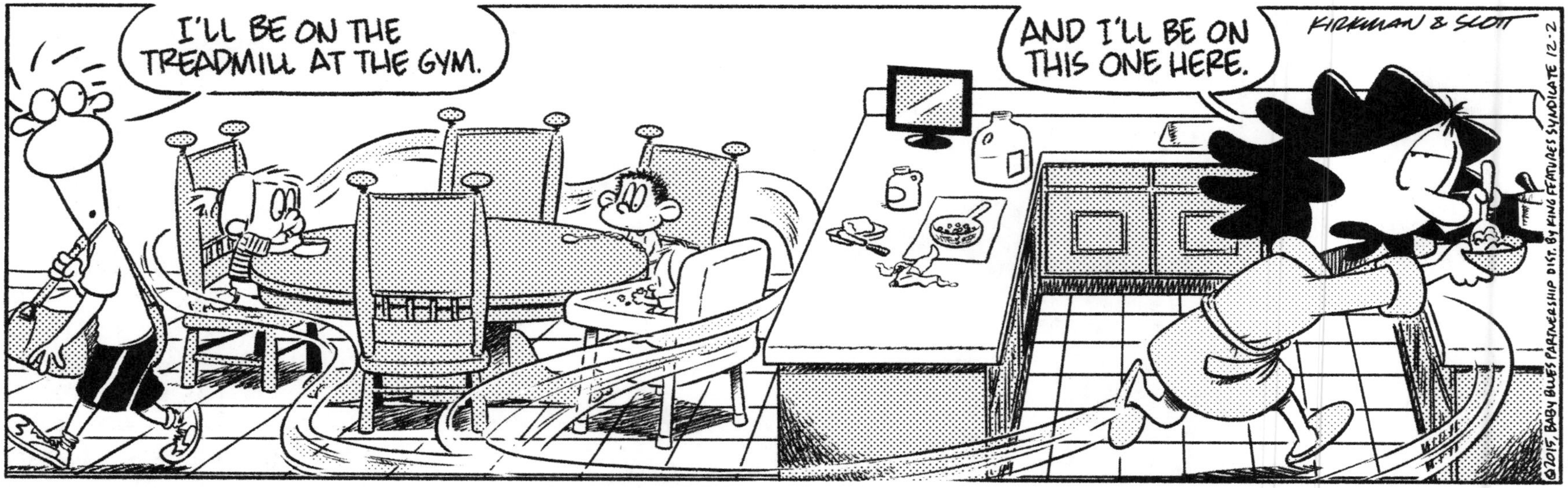
I'LL BE ON THE TREADMILL AT THE GYM.
AND I'LL BE ON THIS ONE HERE.
KIRKMAN & SCOTT
© 2015, BABY BLUES PARTNERSHIP DIST. BY KING FEATURES SYNDICATE 12-2

Rick: I admit, this one made me feel guilty.

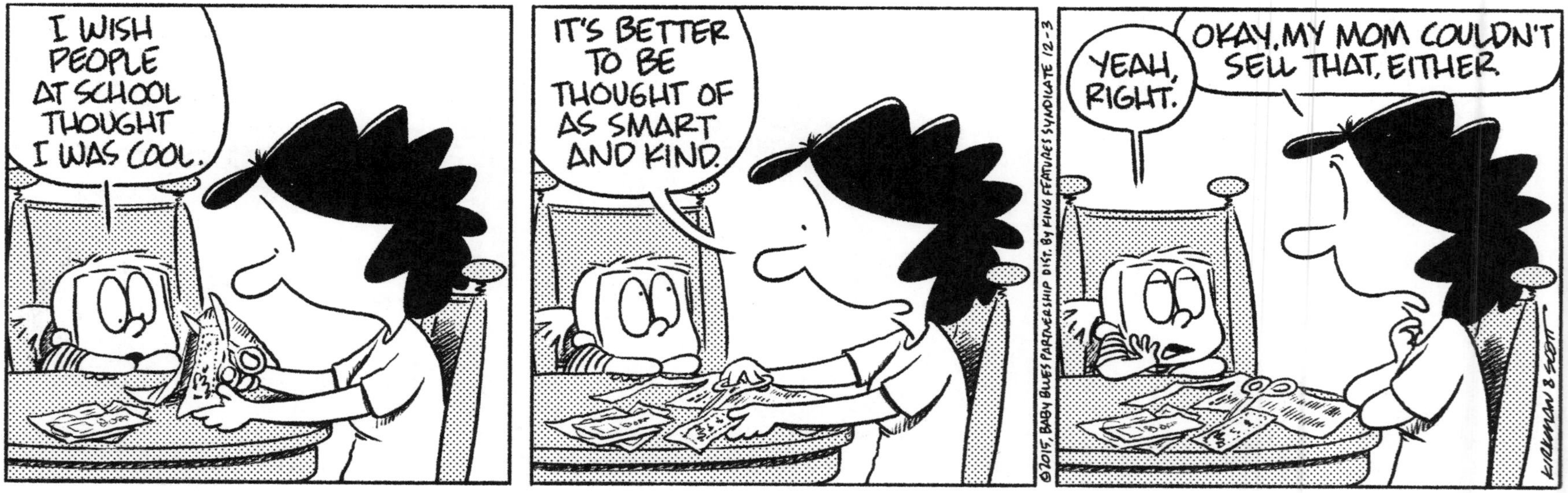
I WISH PEOPLE AT SCHOOL THOUGHT I WAS COOL.
IT'S BETTER TO BE THOUGHT OF AS SMART AND KIND.
© 2015, BABY BLUES PARTNERSHIP DIST. BY KING FEATURES SYNDICATE 12-3
YEAH, RIGHT.
OKAY, MY MOM COULDN'T SELL THAT, EITHER.
KIRKMAN & SCOTT

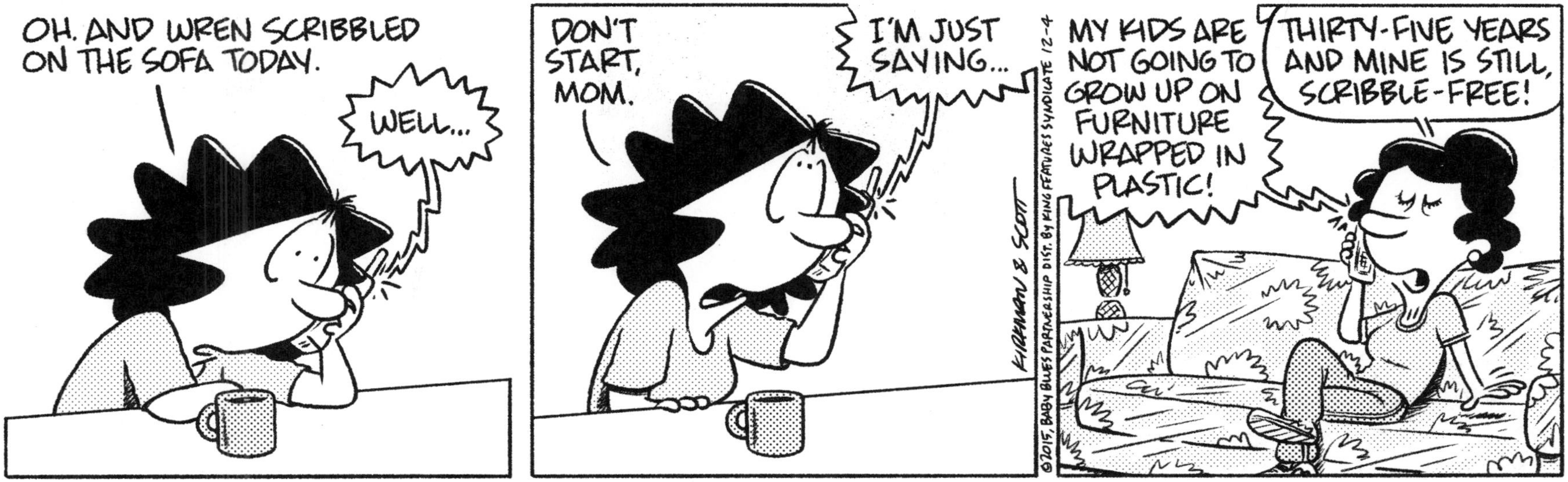
OH. AND WREN SCRIBBLED ON THE SOFA TODAY.
WELL...
DON'T START, MOM.
I'M JUST SAYING...
KIRKMAN & SCOTT
©2015, BABY BLUES PARTNERSHIP DIST. BY KING FEATURES SYNDICATE 12-4
MY KIDS ARE NOT GOING TO GROW UP ON FURNITURE WRAPPED IN PLASTIC!
THIRTY-FIVE YEARS AND MINE IS STILL, SCRIBBLE-FREE!

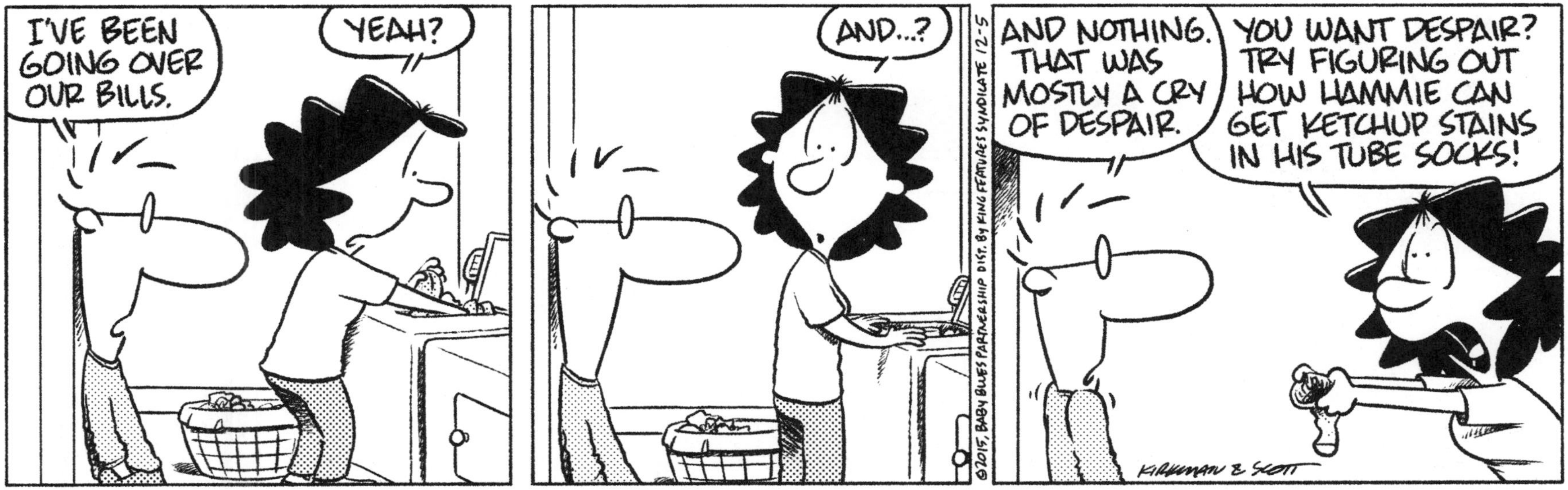
I'VE BEEN GOING OVER OUR BILLS.
YEAH?
AND...?
©2015, BABY BLUES PARTNERSHIP DIST. BY KING FEATURES SYNDICATE 12-5
AND NOTHING. THAT WAS MOSTLY A CRY OF DESPAIR.
YOU WANT DESPAIR? TRY FIGURING OUT HOW HAMMIE CAN GET KETCHUP STAINS IN HIS TUBE SOCKS!
KIRKMAN & SCOTT

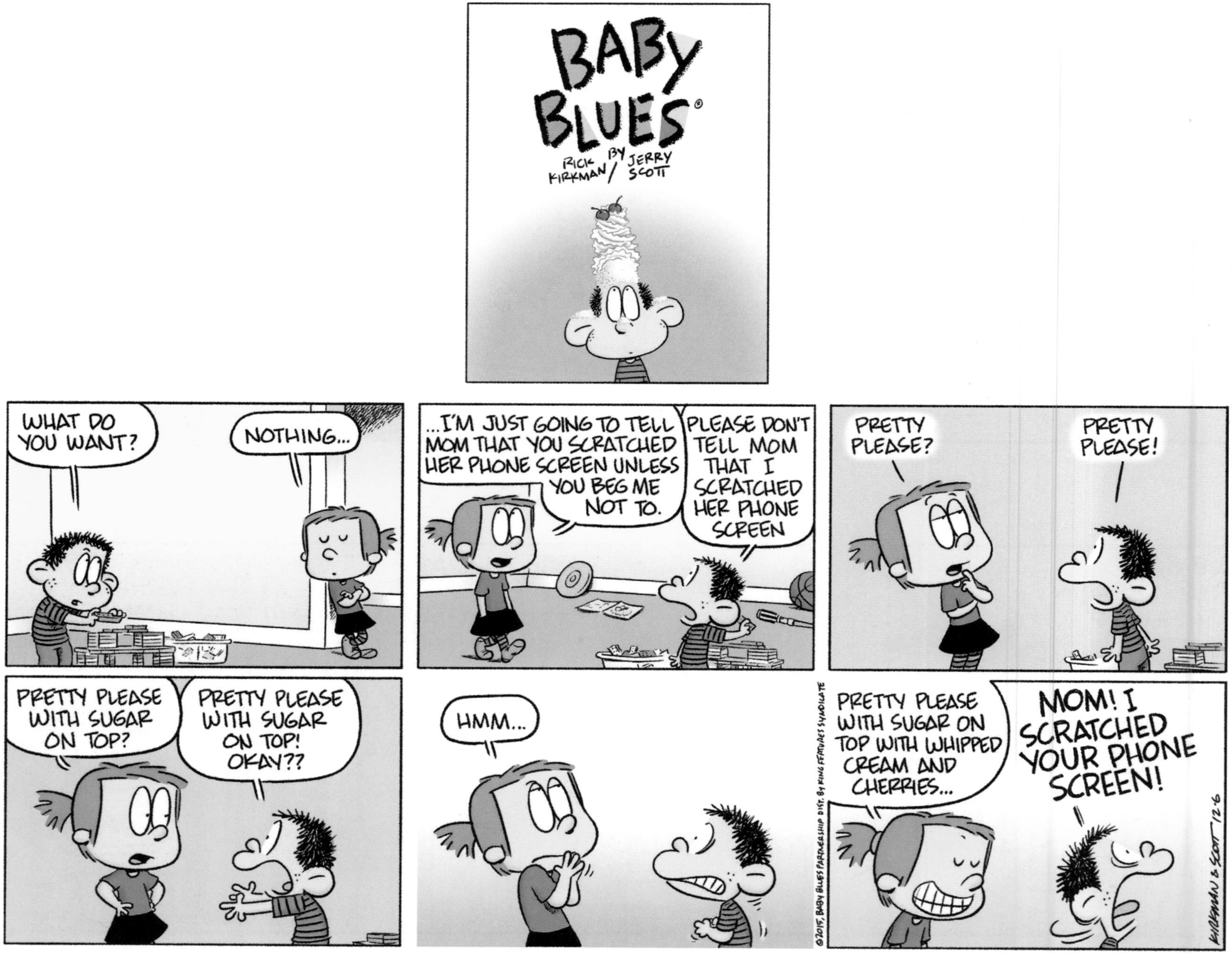
BABY BLUES®
BY RICK KIRKMAN / JERRY SCOTT
WHAT DO YOU WANT?
NOTHING...
...I'M JUST GOING TO TELL MOM THAT YOU SCRATCHED HER PHONE SCREEN UNLESS YOU BEG ME NOT TO.
PLEASE DON'T TELL MOM THAT I SCRATCHED HER PHONE SCREEN
PRETTY PLEASE?
PRETTY PLEASE!
PRETTY PLEASE WITH SUGAR ON TOP?
PRETTY PLEASE WITH SUGAR ON TOP! OKAY??
HMM...
PRETTY PLEASE WITH SUGAR ON TOP WITH WHIPPED CREAM AND CHERRIES...
MOM! I SCRATCHED YOUR PHONE SCREEN!
©2015, BABY BLUES PARTNERSHIP DIST. BY KING FEATURES SYNDICATE
KIRKMAN & SCOTT 12-6

Jerry: At some point, the payoff is more painful than the punishment.

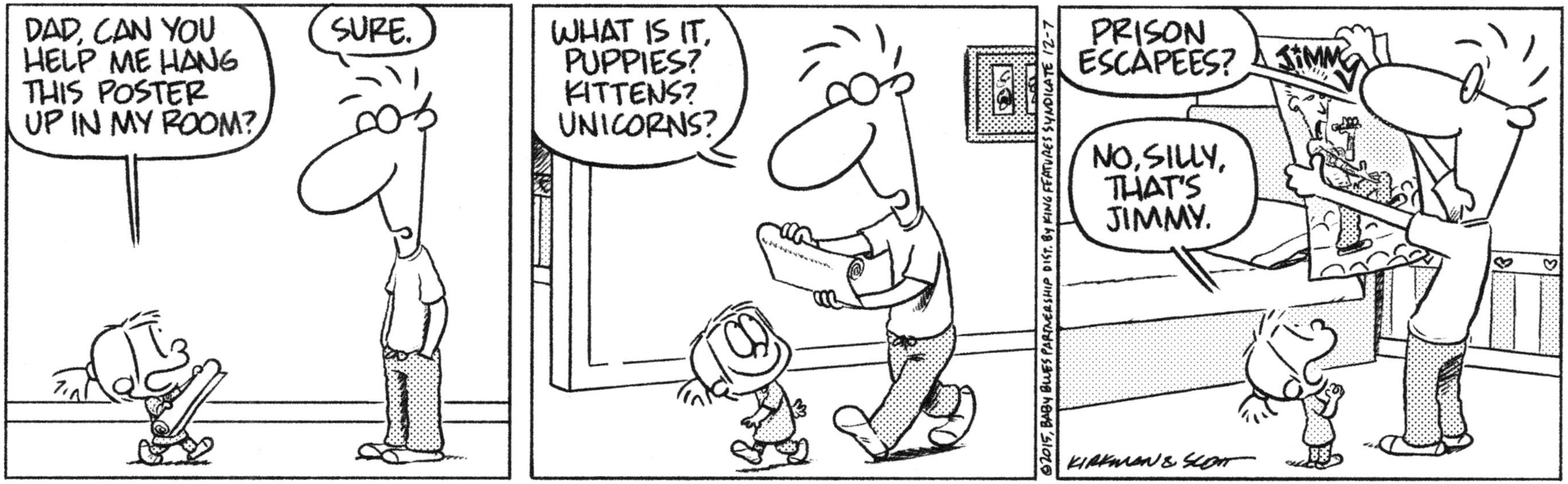
DAD, CAN YOU HELP ME HANG THIS POSTER UP IN MY ROOM?
SURE.
WHAT IS IT, PUPPIES? KITTENS? UNICORNS?
PRISON ESCAPEES?
NO, SILLY, THAT'S JIMMY.
JIMMY
©2015, BABY BLUES PARTNERSHIP DIST. BY KING FEATURES SYNDICATE 12-7
KIRKMAN & SCOTT

Jerry: In this series, Darryl is me griping about the state of popular music today.

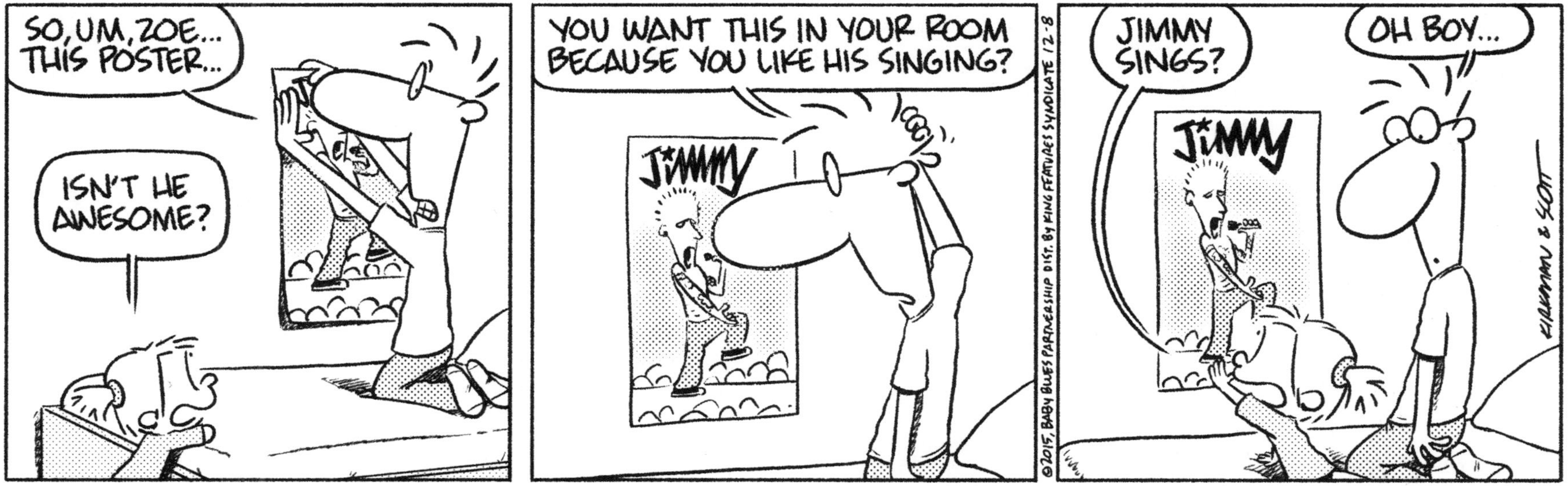
SO, UM, ZOE... THIS POSTER...
ISN'T HE AWESOME?
YOU WANT THIS IN YOUR ROOM BECAUSE YOU LIKE HIS SINGING?
JIMMY
©2015, BABY BLUES PARTNERSHIP DIST. BY KING FEATURES SYNDICATE 12-8
JIMMY SINGS?
OH BOY...
JIMMY
KIRKMAN & SCOTT

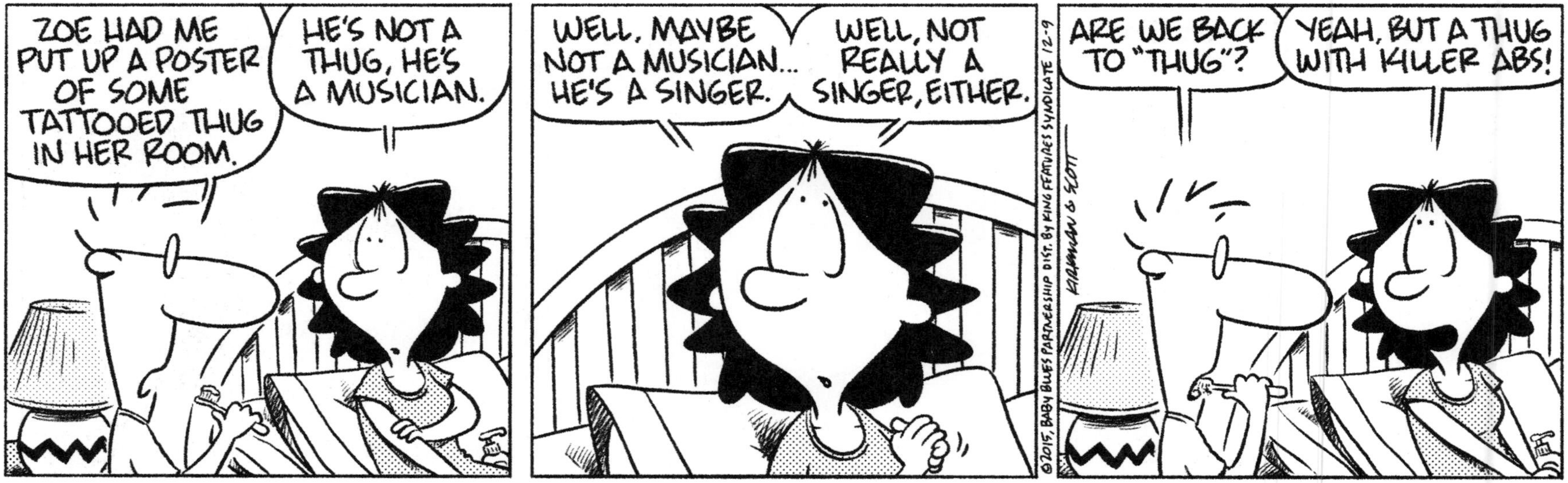
ZOE HAD ME PUT UP A POSTER OF SOME TATTOOED THUG IN HER ROOM.
HE'S NOT A THUG, HE'S A MUSICIAN.
WELL, MAYBE NOT A MUSICIAN... HE'S A SINGER.
WELL, NOT REALLY A SINGER, EITHER.
©2015, BABY BLUES PARTNERSHIP DIST. BY KING FEATURES SYNDICATE 12-9
KIRKMAN & SCOTT
ARE WE BACK TO "THUG"?
YEAH, BUT A THUG WITH KILLER ABS!

Rick: Iggy Pop was there first. Except without the tattoos. Or being a thug.

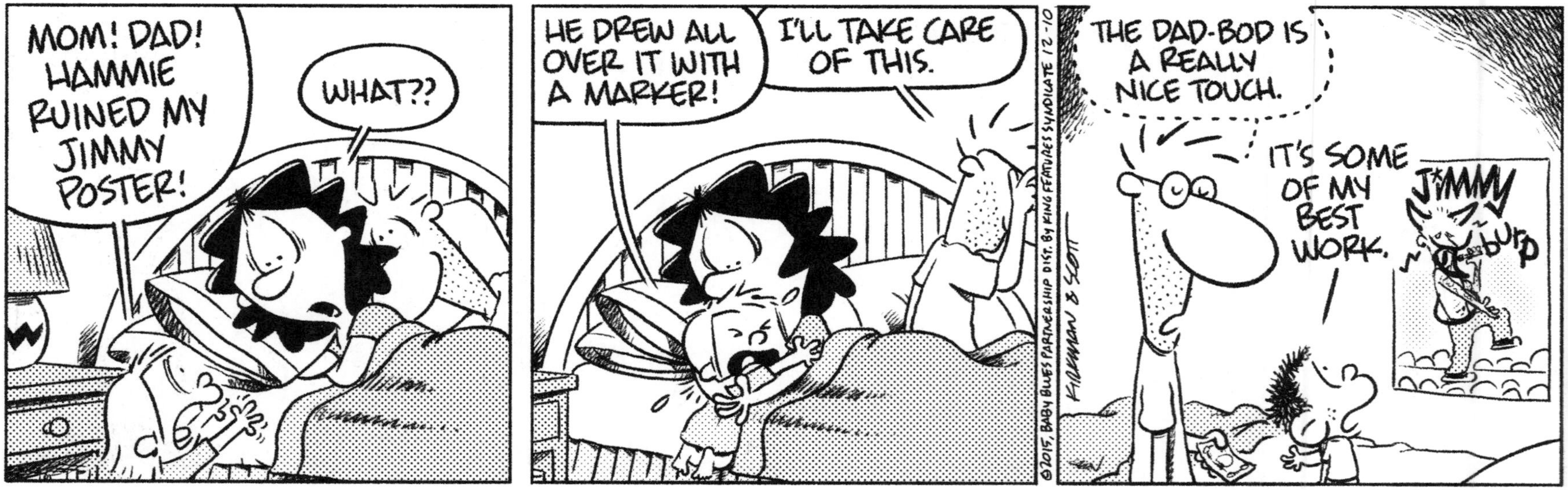
MOM! DAD! HAMMIE RUINED MY JIMMY POSTER!
WHAT??
HE DREW ALL OVER IT WITH A MARKER!
I'LL TAKE CARE OF THIS.
©2015, BABY BLUES PARTNERSHIP DIST. BY KING FEATURES SYNDICATE 12-10
KIRKMAN & SCOTT
THE DAD-BOD IS A REALLY NICE TOUCH.
IT'S SOME OF MY BEST WORK.
JIMMY

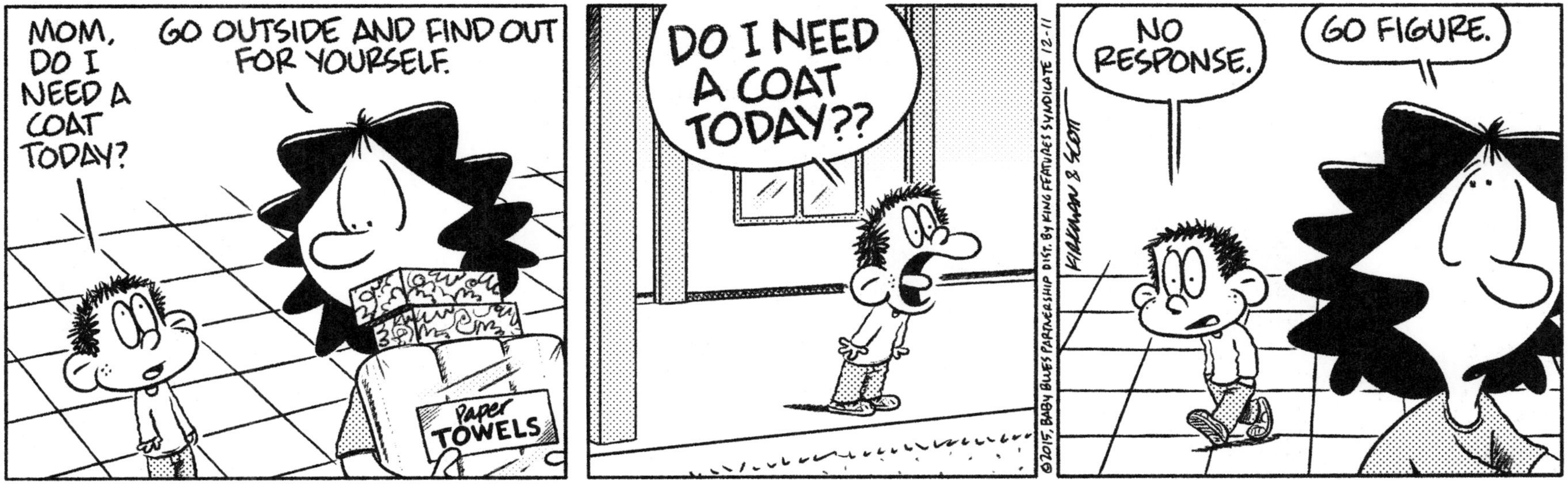
MOM, DO I NEED A COAT TODAY?
GO OUTSIDE AND FIND OUT FOR YOURSELF.
PAPER TOWELS
DO I NEED A COAT TODAY??
©2015, BABY BLUES PARTNERSHIP DIST. BY KING FEATURES SYNDICATE 12-11
KIRKMAN & SCOTT
NO RESPONSE.
GO FIGURE.

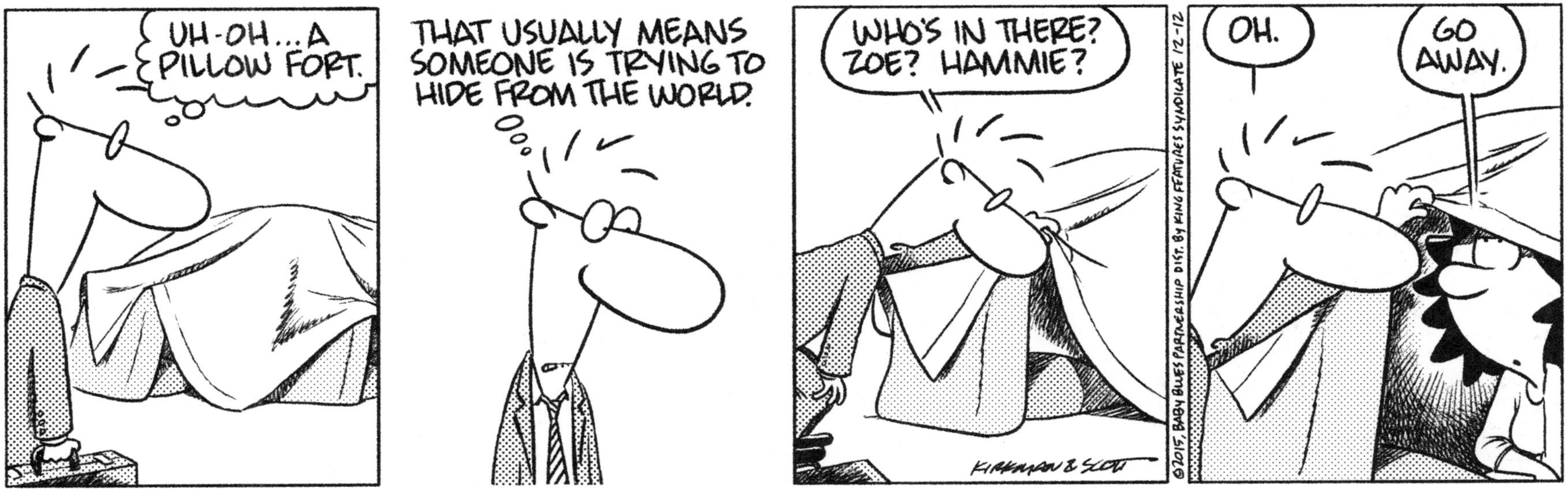
UH-OH... A PILLOW FORT.
THAT USUALLY MEANS SOMEONE IS TRYING TO HIDE FROM THE WORLD.
WHO'S IN THERE? ZOE? HAMMIE?
KIRKMAN & SCOTT
©2015, BABY BLUES PARTNERSHIP DIST. BY KING FEATURES SYNDICATE 12-12
OH.
GO AWAY.

Rick: Everyone needs access to a pillow fort sometime.

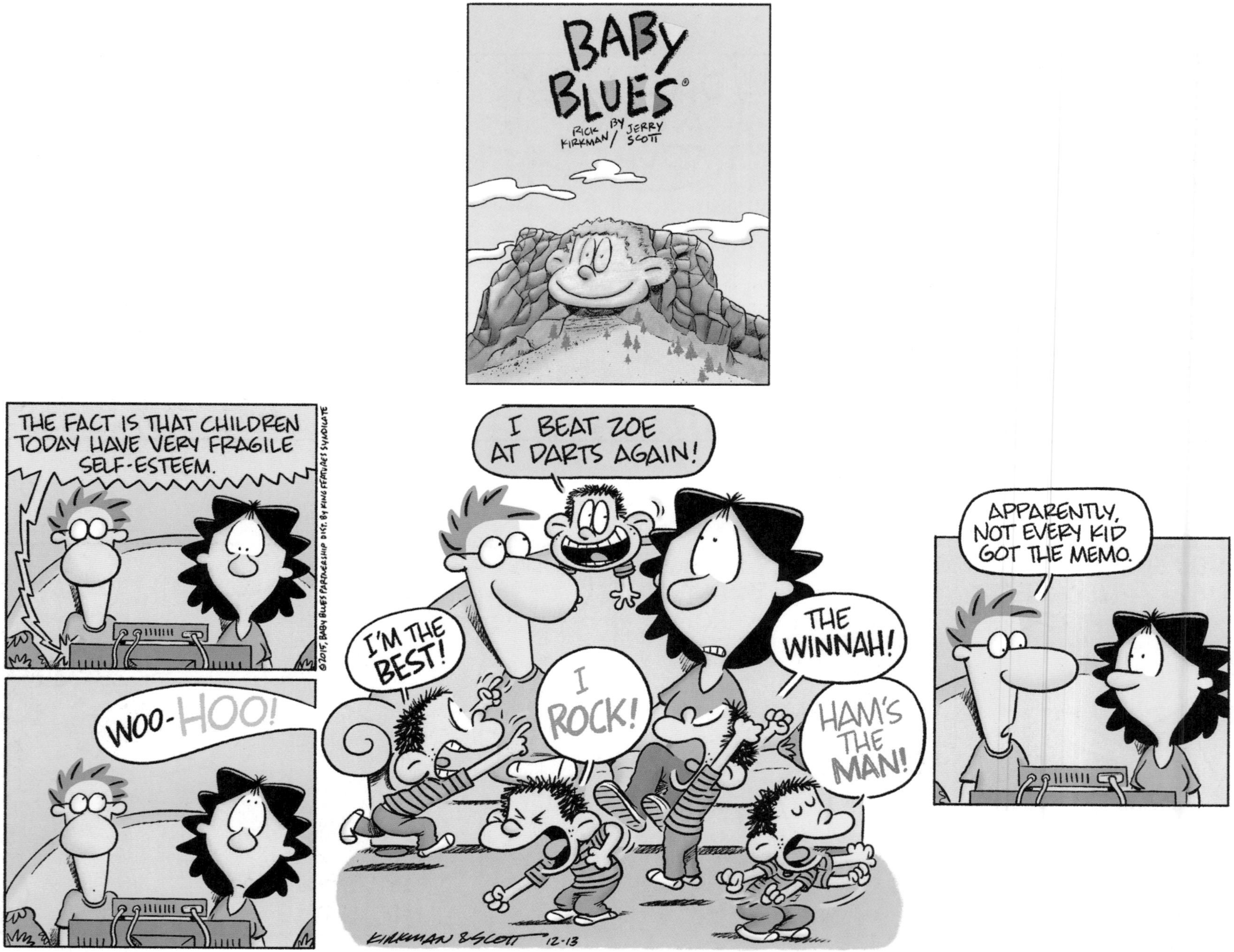
BABY BLUES®
BY RICK KIRKMAN / JERRY SCOTT
THE FACT IS THAT CHILDREN TODAY HAVE VERY FRAGILE SELF-ESTEEM.
©2015, BABY BLUES PARTNERSHIP DIST. BY KING FEATURES SYNDICATE
WOO-HOO!
I BEAT ZOE AT DARTS AGAIN!
I'M THE BEST!
I ROCK!
THE WINNAH!
HAM'S THE MAN!
KIRKMAN & SCOTT 12-13
APPARENTLY, NOT EVERY KID GOT THE MEMO.

Rick: Fun middle panel to draw with the multiple Hammies. It gives it more energy having them all in the same panel. Nice piece of stage direction from Jerry.

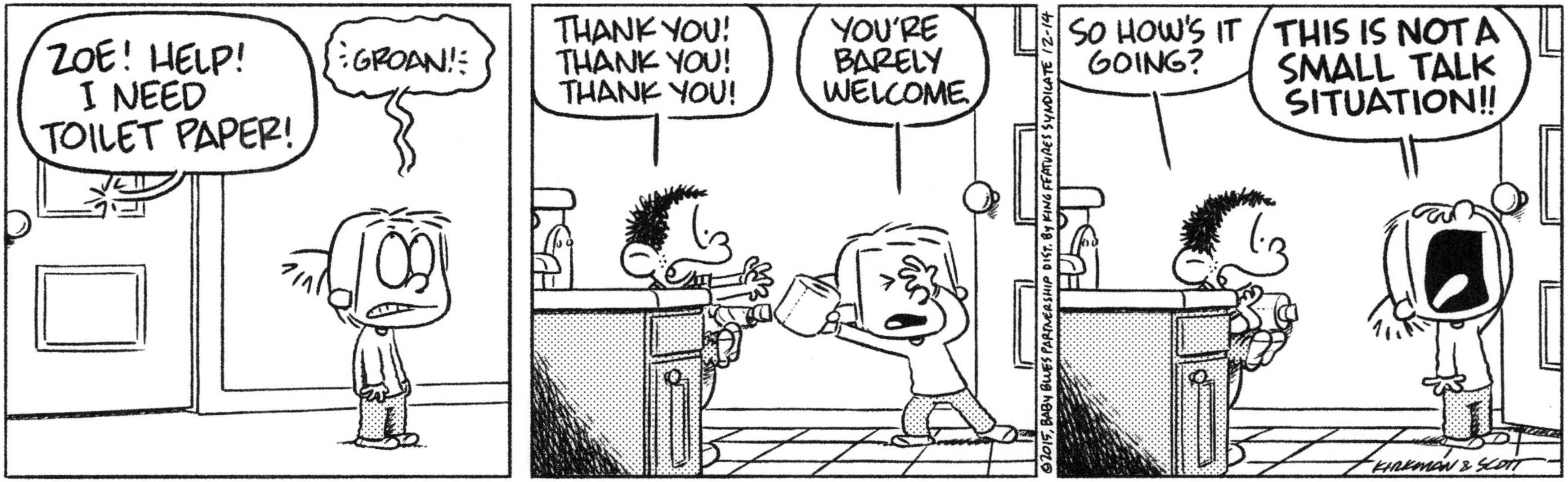
ZOE! HELP! I NEED TOILET PAPER!
GROAN!
THANK YOU! THANK YOU! THANK YOU!
YOU'RE BARELY WELCOME.
©2015, BABY BLUES PARTNERSHIP DIST. BY KING FEATURES SYNDICATE 12-14
SO HOW'S IT GOING?
THIS IS NOT A SMALL TALK SITUATION!!
KIRKMAN & SCOTT

Rick: Thank goodness for the well-positioned cabinet.

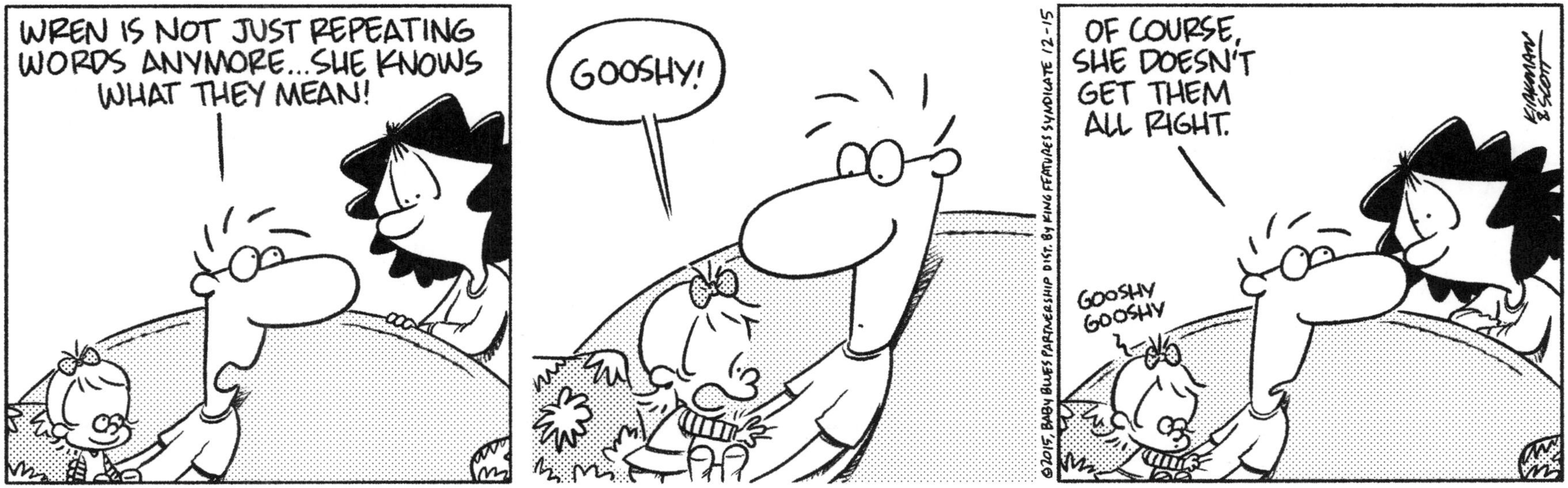
WREN IS NOT JUST REPEATING WORDS ANYMORE... SHE KNOWS WHAT THEY MEAN!
GOOSHY!
©2015, BABY BLUES PARTNERSHIP DIST. BY KING FEATURES SYNDICATE 12-15
OF COURSE, SHE DOESN'T GET THEM ALL RIGHT.
GOOSHY GOOSHY
KIRKMAN & SCOTT

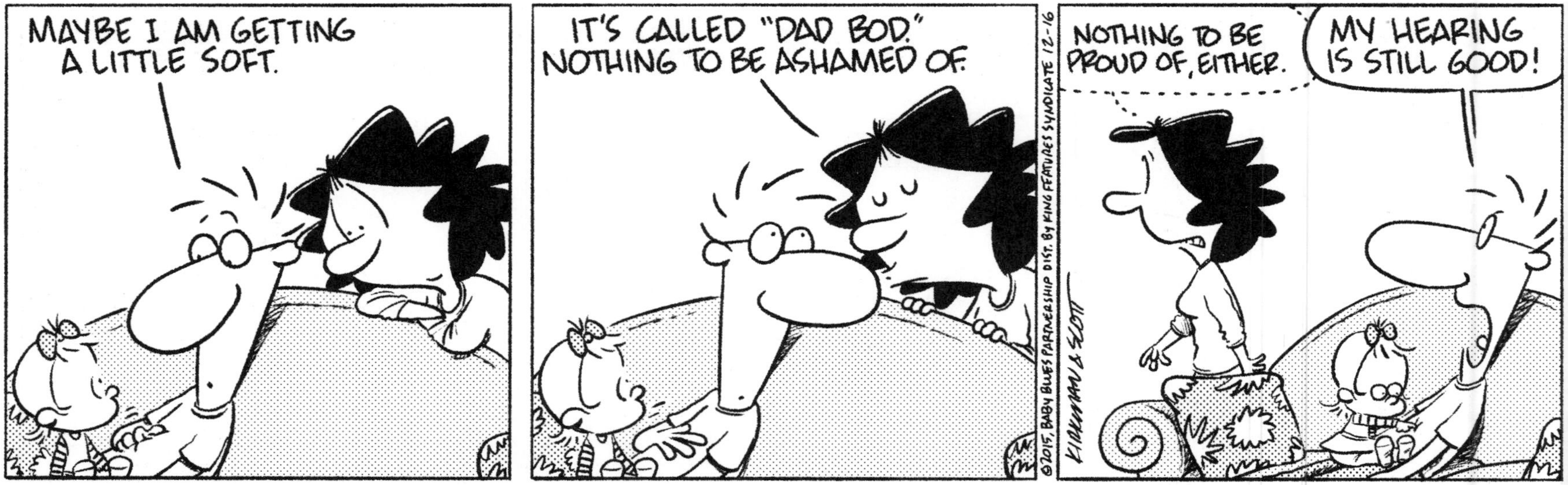
MAYBE I AM GETTING A LITTLE SOFT.
IT'S CALLED "DAD BOD." NOTHING TO BE ASHAMED OF.
©2015, BABY BLUES PARTNERSHIP DIST. BY KING FEATURES SYNDICATE 12-16
KIRKMAN & SCOTT
NOTHING TO BE PROUD OF, EITHER.
MY HEARING IS STILL GOOD!

Rick: Calling it a "Dad Bod" doesn't make me feel any better.

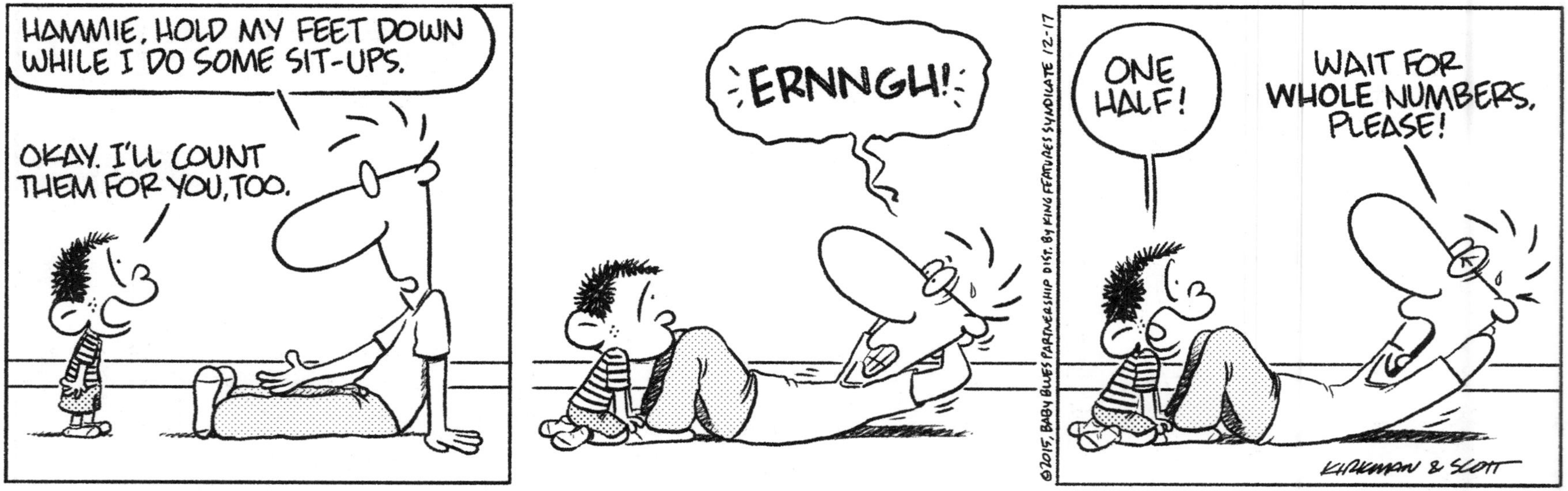
HAMMIE, HOLD MY FEET DOWN WHILE I DO SOME SIT-UPS.
OKAY. I'LL COUNT THEM FOR YOU, TOO.
ERNNGH!
©2015, BABY BLUES PARTNERSHIP DIST. BY KING FEATURES SYNDICATE 12-17
ONE HALF!
WAIT FOR WHOLE NUMBERS, PLEASE!
KIRKMAN & SCOTT

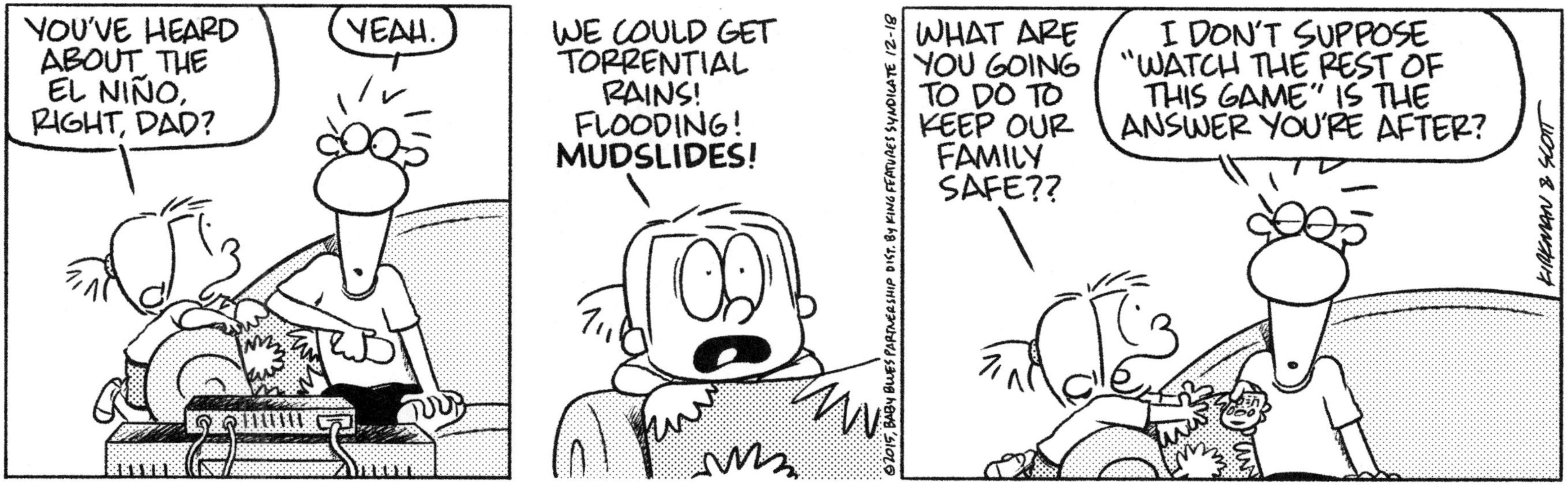
YOU'VE HEARD ABOUT THE EL NIÑO, RIGHT, DAD?
YEAH.
WE COULD GET TORRENTIAL RAINS! FLOODING! MUDSLIDES!
©2015, BABY BLUES PARTNERSHIP DIST. BY KING FEATURES SYNDICATE 12-18
WHAT ARE YOU GOING TO DO TO KEEP OUR FAMILY SAFE??
I DON'T SUPPOSE "WATCH THE REST OF THIS GAME" IS THE ANSWER YOU'RE AFTER?
KIRKMAN & SCOTT

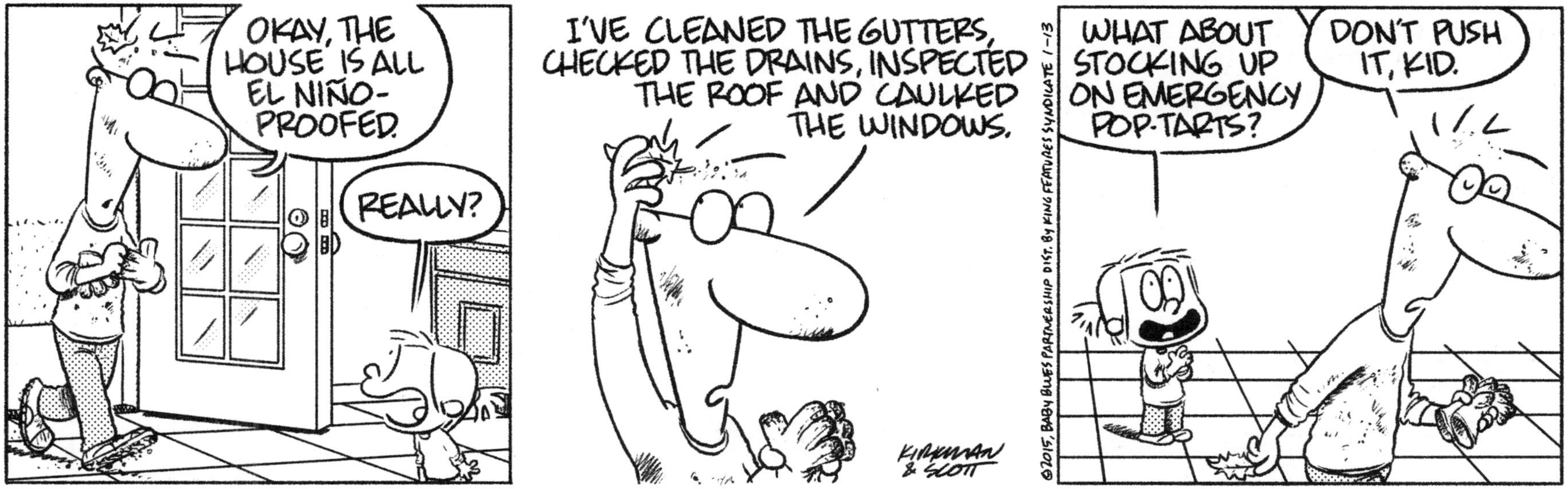
OKAY, THE HOUSE IS ALL EL NIÑO-PROOFED.
REALLY?
I'VE CLEANED THE GUTTERS, CHECKED THE DRAINS, INSPECTED THE ROOF AND CAULKED THE WINDOWS.
KIRKMAN & SCOTT
©2015, BABY BLUES PARTNERSHIP DIST. BY KING FEATURES SYNDICATE 1-13
WHAT ABOUT STOCKING UP ON EMERGENCY POP-TARTS?
DON'T PUSH IT, KID.

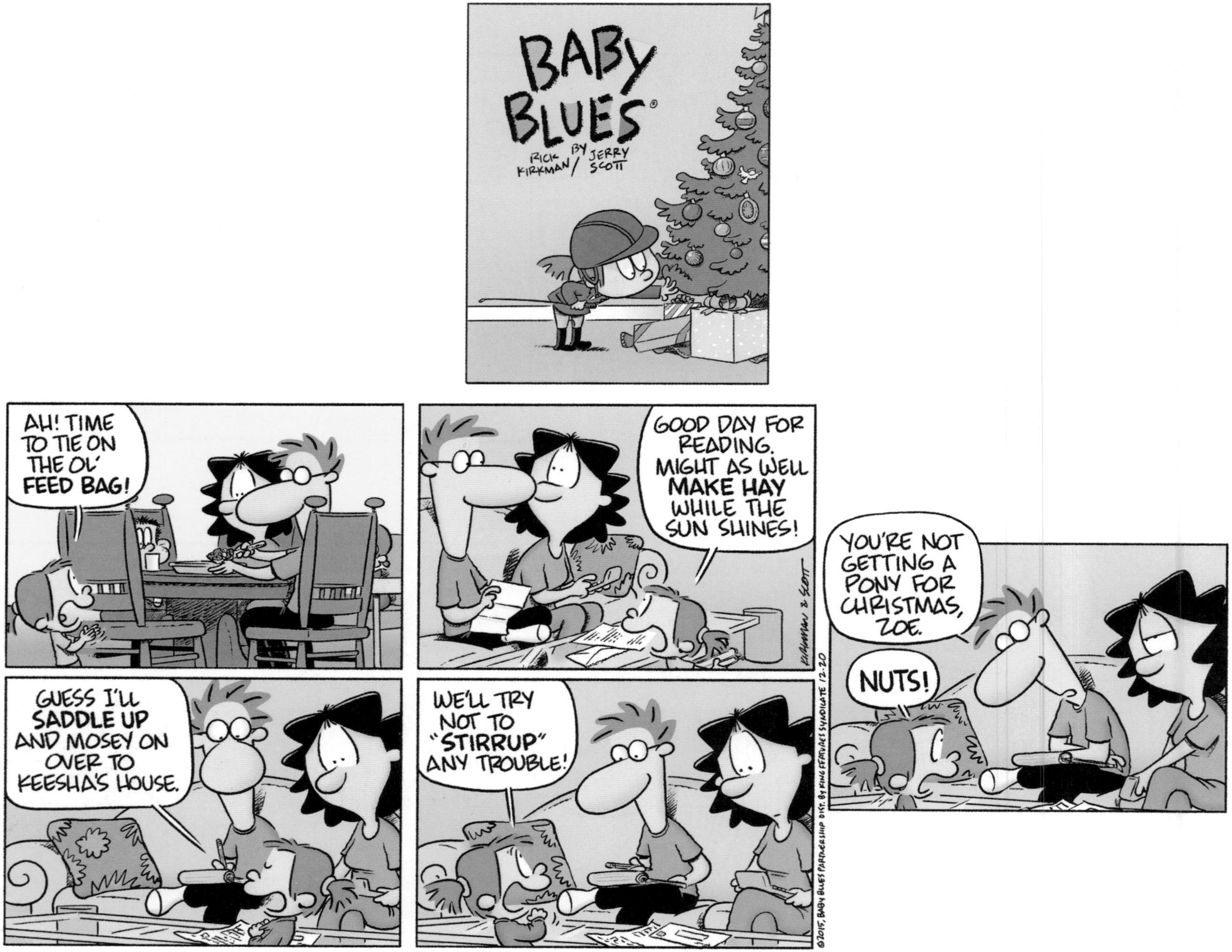
BABY BLUES®
BY RICK KIRKMAN / JERRY SCOTT
AH! TIME TO TIE ON THE OL' FEED BAG!
GOOD DAY FOR READING. MIGHT AS WELL MAKE HAY WHILE THE SUN SHINES!
KIRKMAN & SCOTT
GUESS I'LL SADDLE UP AND MOSEY ON OVER TO KEESHA'S HOUSE.
WE'LL TRY NOT TO "STIRRUP" ANY TROUBLE!
©2015, BABY BLUES PARTNERSHIP DIST. BY KING FEATURES SYNDICATE 12-20
YOU'RE NOT GETTING A PONY FOR CHRISTMAS, ZOE.
NUTS!

Rick: I hope Darryl and Wanda never give in. I hate drawing horses (only because I'm very bad at it).

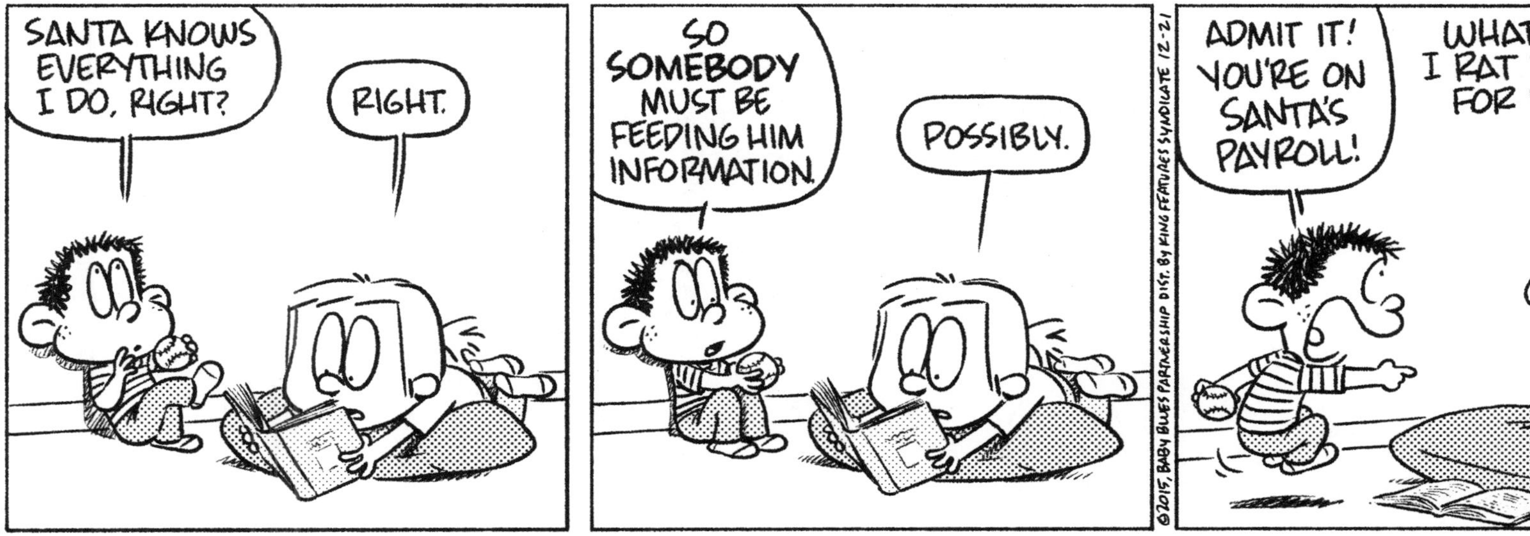

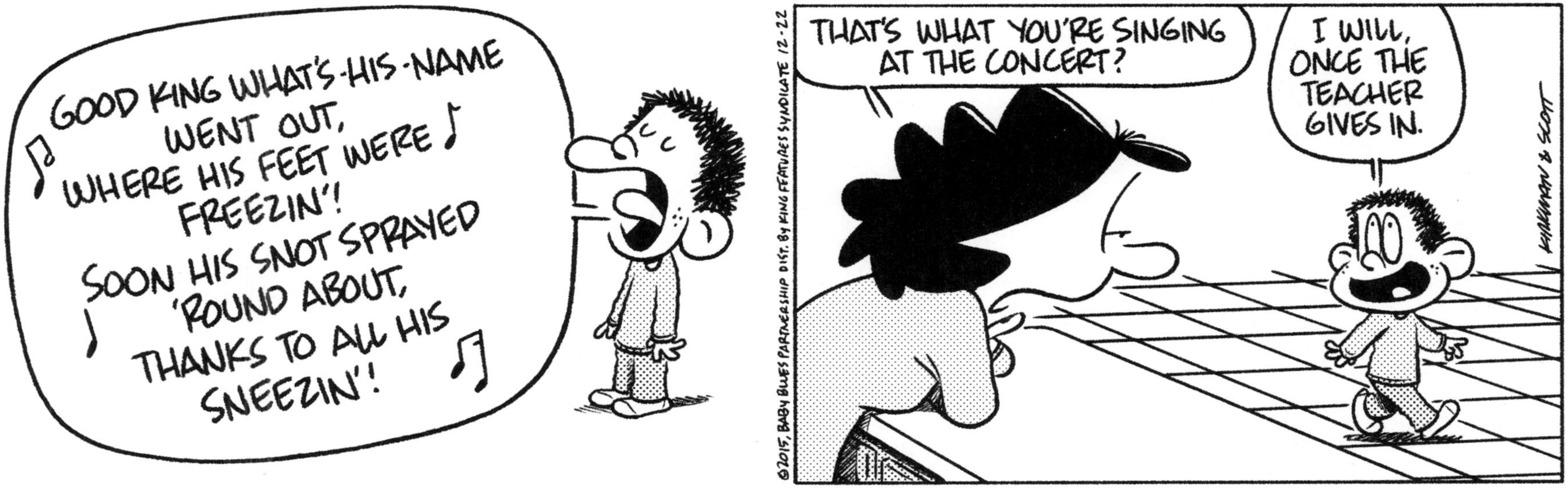

Jerry: The story of my very brief stint in the school choir.

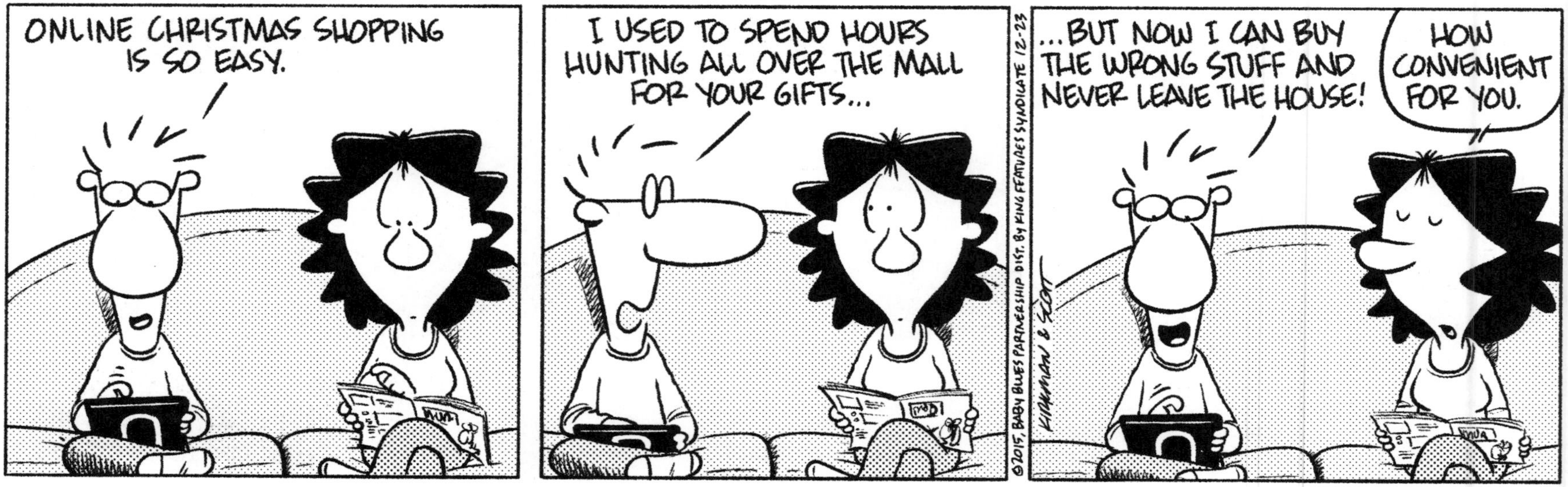
ONLINE CHRISTMAS SHOPPING IS SO EASY.
I USED TO SPEND HOURS HUNTING ALL OVER THE MALL FOR YOUR GIFTS...
...BUT NOW I CAN BUY THE WRONG STUFF AND NEVER LEAVE THE HOUSE!
HOW CONVENIENT FOR YOU.
©2015, BABY BLUES PARTNERSHIP DIST. BY KING FEATURES SYNDICATE 12-23
KIRKMAN & SCOTT

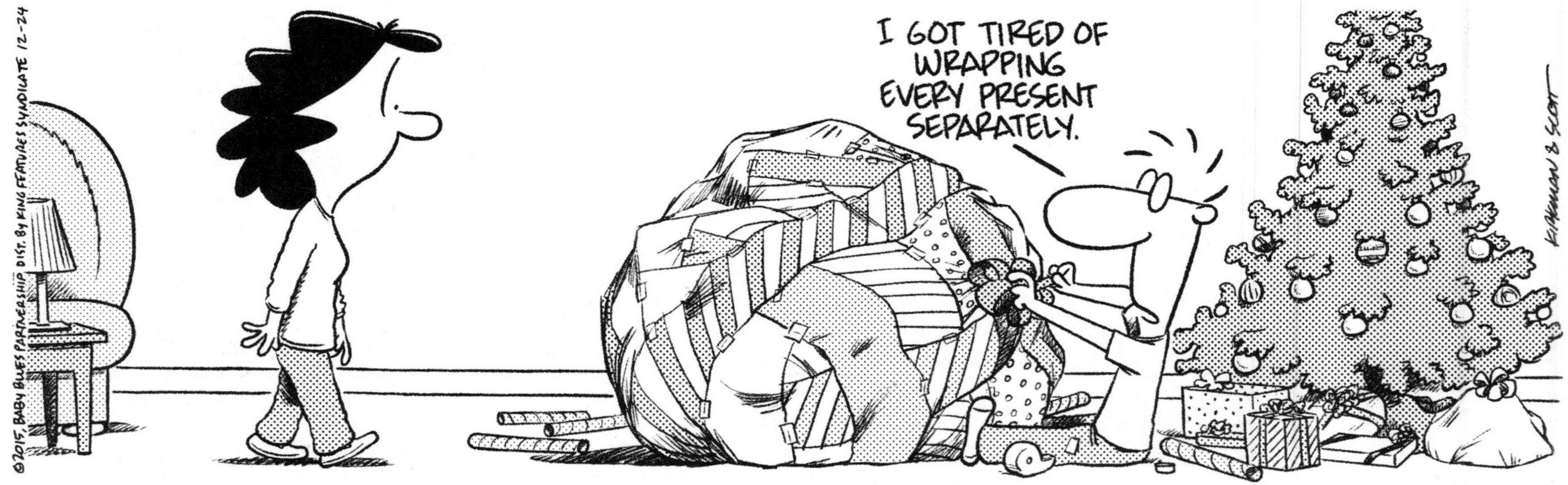
I GOT TIRED OF WRAPPING EVERY PRESENT SEPARATELY.
©2015, BABY BLUES PARTNERSHIP DIST. BY KING FEATURES SYNDICATE 12-24
KIRKMAN & SCOTT

Rick: Note to self: Remember this next year. **Jerry:** This is such a practical idea.

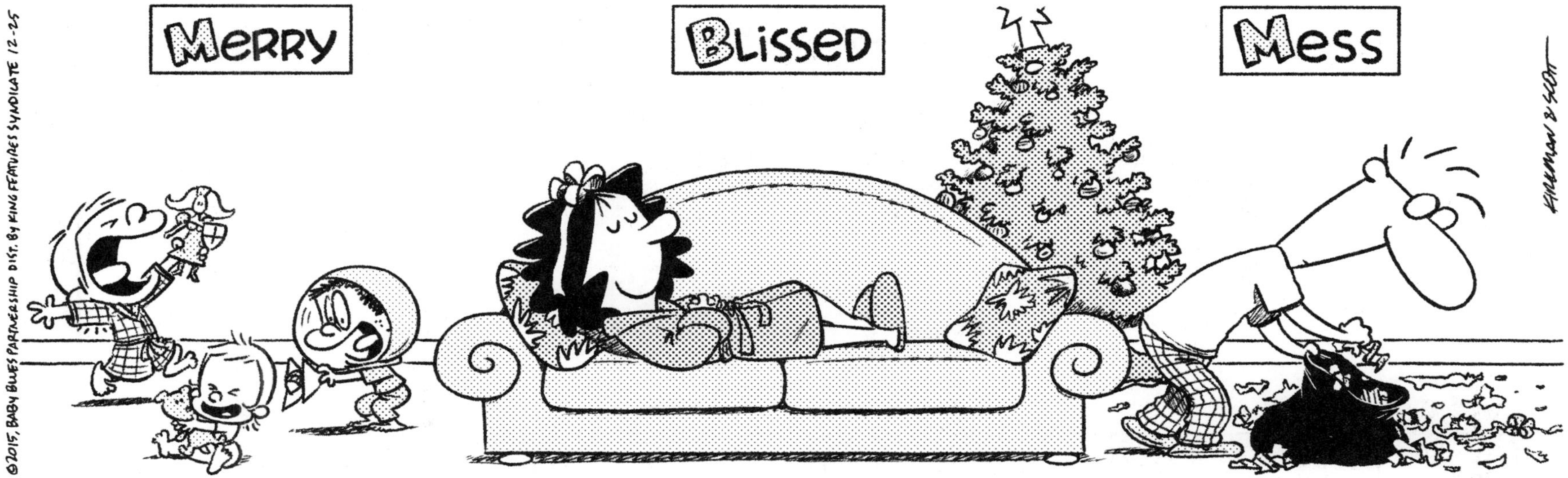
MERRY
BLISSED
MESS
KIRKMAN & SCOTT
©2015, BABY BLUES PARTNERSHIP DIST. BY KING FEATURES SYNDICATE 12-25

Jerry: I'm not wild about writing holiday strips, but I kind of like this one.

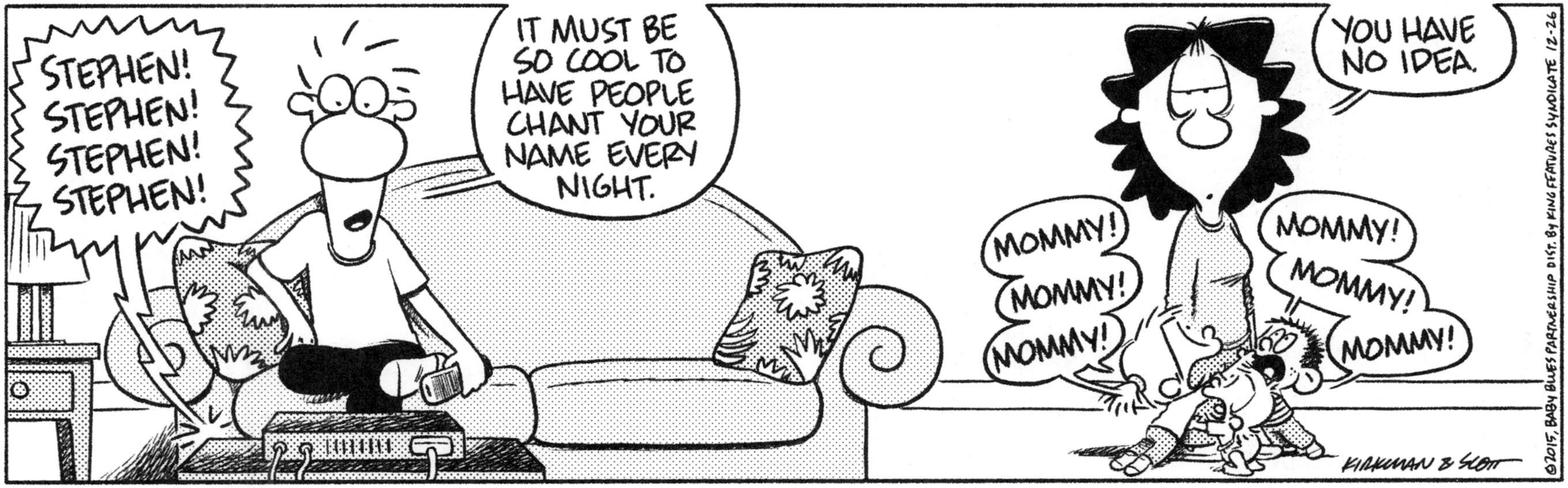
STEPHEN! STEPHEN! STEPHEN! STEPHEN!
IT MUST BE SO COOL TO HAVE PEOPLE CHANT YOUR NAME EVERY NIGHT.
YOU HAVE NO IDEA.
MOMMY! MOMMY! MOMMY!
MOMMY! MOMMY! MOMMY!
KIRKMAN & SCOTT
©2015, BABY BLUES PARTNERSHIP DIST. BY KING FEATURES SYNDICATE 12-26

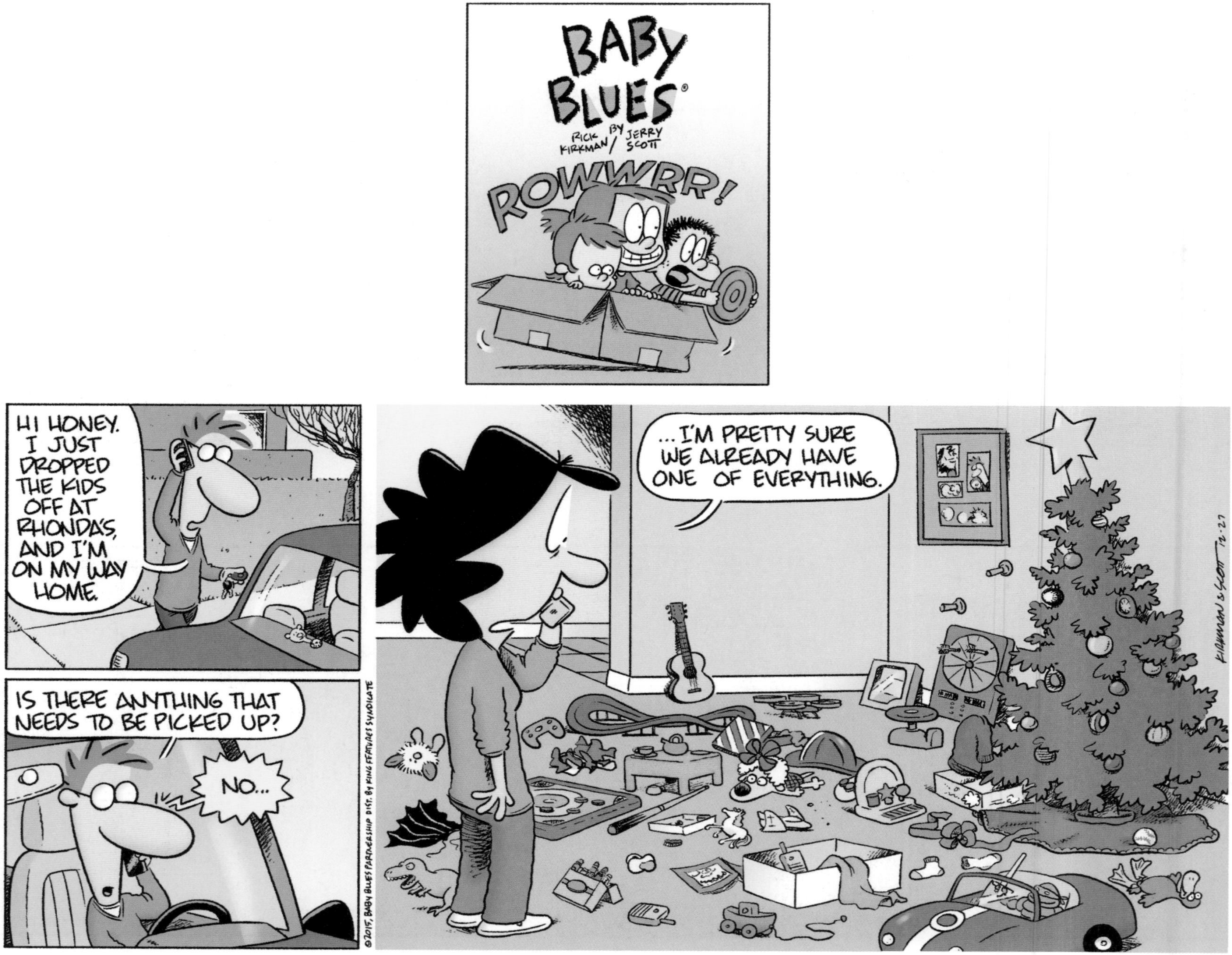
BABY BLUES®
BY RICK KIRKMAN / JERRY SCOTT
ROWWRR!
HI HONEY. I JUST DROPPED THE KIDS OFF AT RHONDA'S, AND I'M ON MY WAY HOME.
IS THERE ANYTHING THAT NEEDS TO BE PICKED UP?
NO...
...I'M PRETTY SURE WE ALREADY HAVE ONE OF EVERYTHING.
©2015, BABY BLUES PARTNERSHIP DIST. BY KING FEATURES SYNDICATE
KIRKMAN & SCOTT 12-27

Rick: And we end 2015 with more toys strewn all over the floor. Perfect.

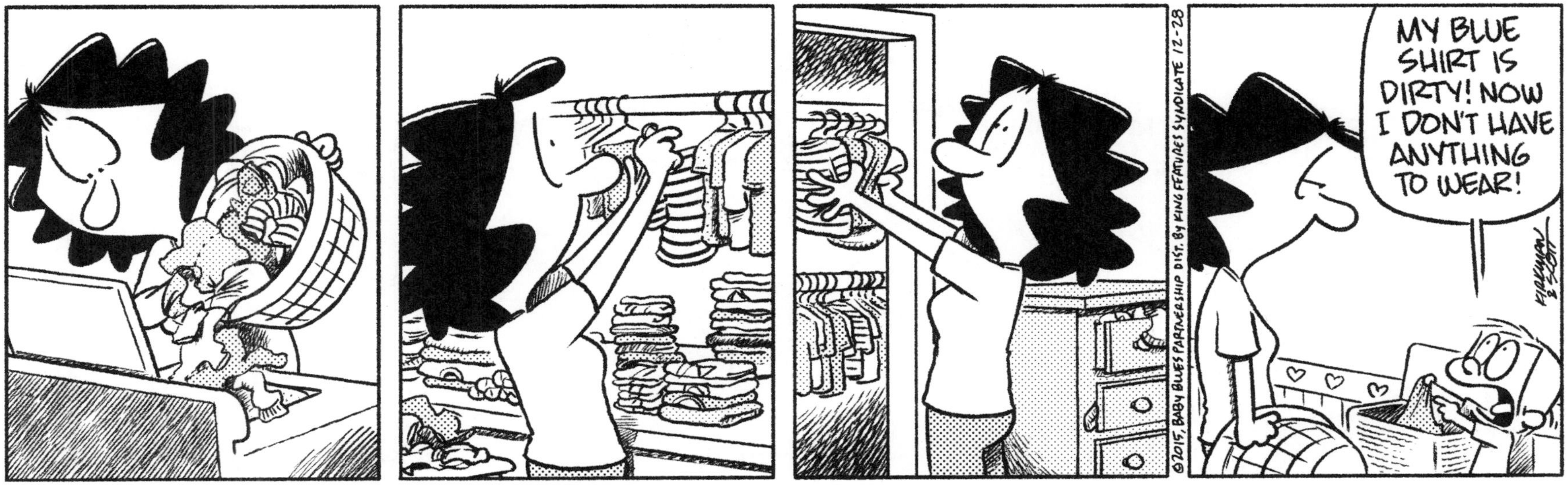
©2015, BABY BLUES PARTNERSHIP DIST. BY KING FEATURES SYNDICATE 12-28
MY BLUE SHIRT IS DIRTY! NOW I DON'T HAVE ANYTHING TO WEAR!
KIRKMAN & SCOTT

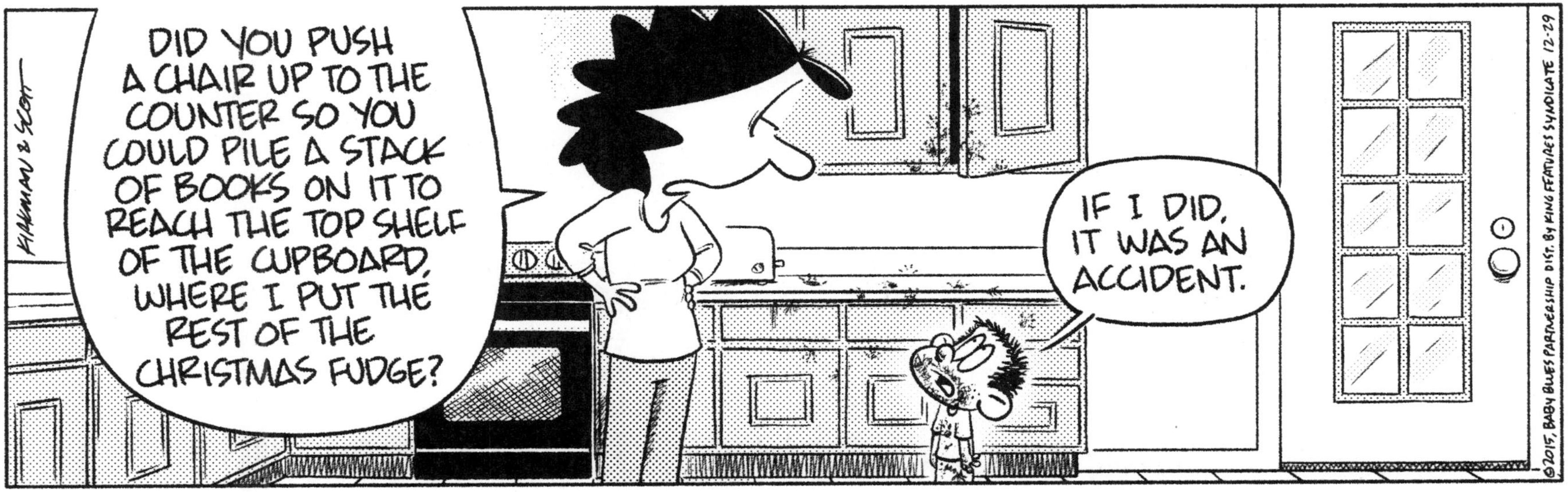
KIRKMAN & SCOTT
DID YOU PUSH A CHAIR UP TO THE COUNTER SO YOU COULD PILE A STACK OF BOOKS ON IT TO REACH THE TOP SHELF OF THE CUPBOARD, WHERE I PUT THE REST OF THE CHRISTMAS FUDGE?
IF I DID, IT WAS AN ACCIDENT.
©2015, BABY BLUES PARTNERSHIP DIST. BY KING FEATURES SYNDICATE 12-29

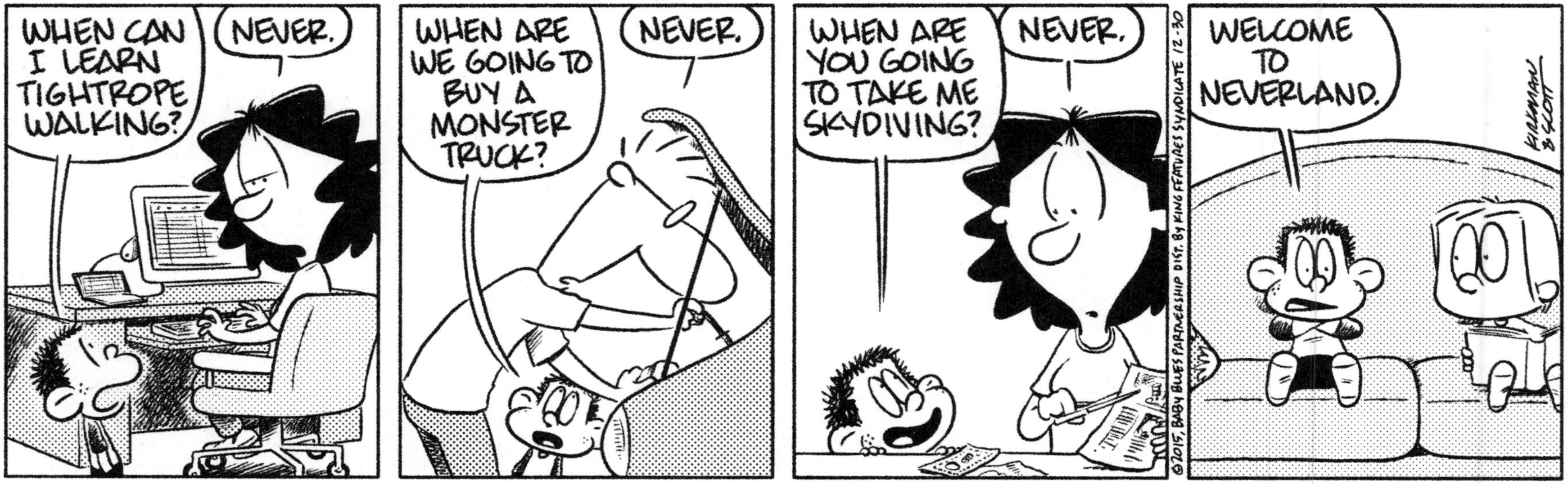
WHEN CAN I LEARN TIGHTROPE WALKING?
NEVER.
WHEN ARE WE GOING TO BUY A MONSTER TRUCK?
NEVER.
WHEN ARE YOU GOING TO TAKE ME SKYDIVING?
NEVER.
©2015, BABY BLUES PARTNERSHIP DIST. BY KING FEATURES SYNDICATE 12-30
WELCOME TO NEVERLAND.
KIRKMAN & SCOTT

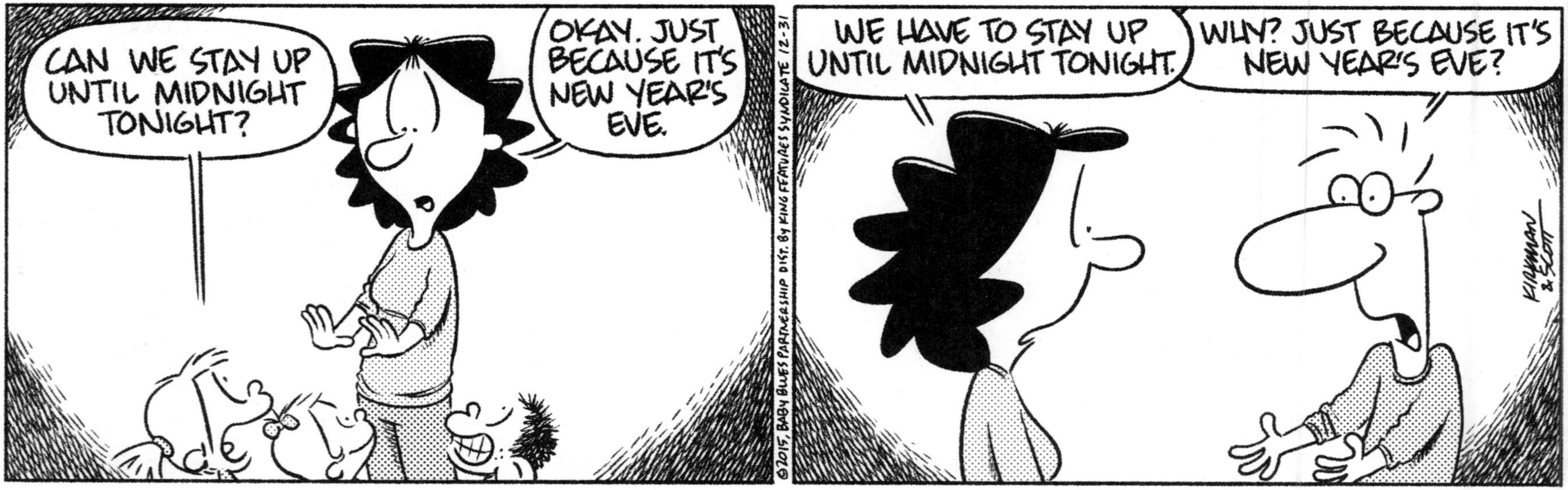
CAN WE STAY UP UNTIL MIDNIGHT TONIGHT?
OKAY. JUST BECAUSE IT'S NEW YEAR'S EVE.
©2015, BABY BLUES PARTNERSHIP DIST. BY KING FEATURES SYNDICATE 12-31
WE HAVE TO STAY UP UNTIL MIDNIGHT TONIGHT.
WHY? JUST BECAUSE IT'S NEW YEAR'S EVE?
KIRKMAN & SCOTT

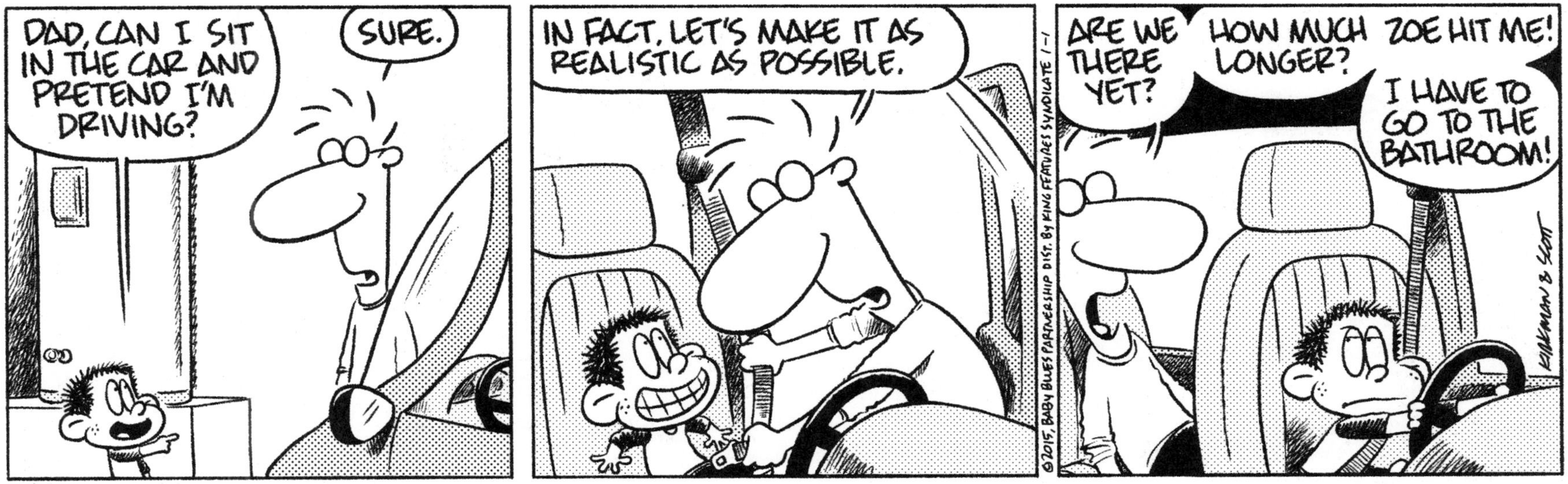
DAD, CAN I SIT IN THE CAR AND PRETEND I'M DRIVING?
SURE.
IN FACT, LET'S MAKE IT AS REALISTIC AS POSSIBLE.
©2015, BABY BLUES PARTNERSHIP DIST. BY KING FEATURES SYNDICATE 1-1
ARE WE THERE YET?
HOW MUCH LONGER?
ZOE HIT ME!
I HAVE TO GO TO THE BATHROOM!
KIRKMAN & SCOTT

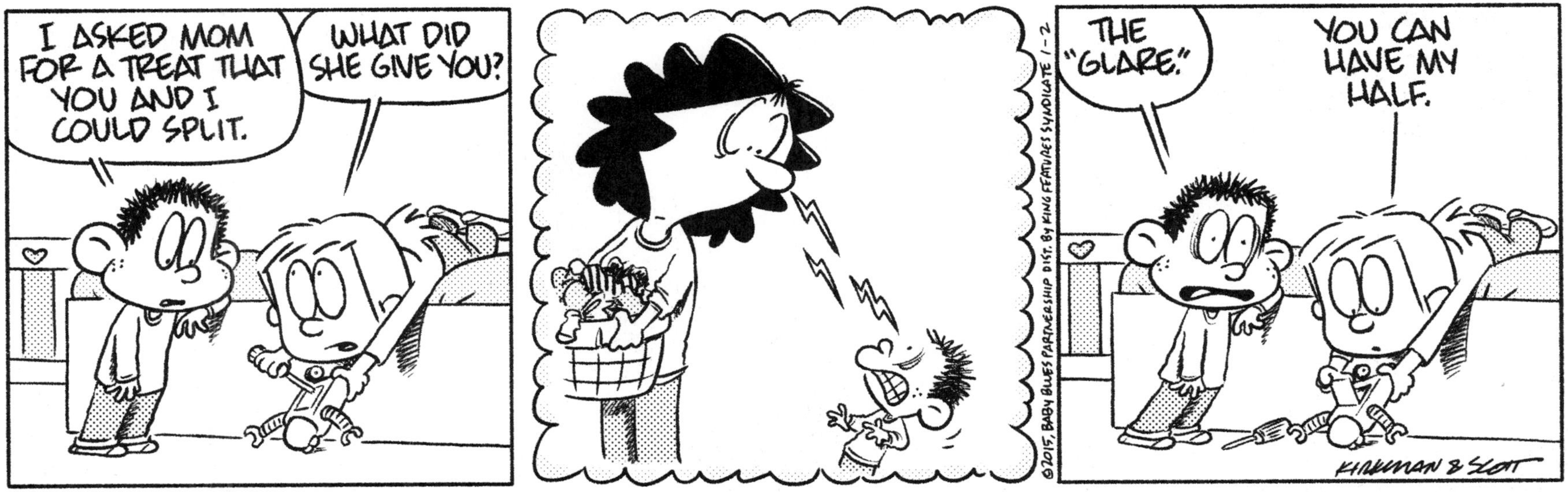
I ASKED MOM FOR A TREAT THAT YOU AND I COULD SPLIT.
WHAT DID SHE GIVE YOU?
©2015, BABY BLUES PARTNERSHIP DIST. BY KING FEATURES SYNDICATE 1-2
THE "GLARE."
YOU CAN HAVE MY HALF.
KIRKMAN & SCOTT

Andrews McMeel Publishing
a division of Andrews McMeel Universal
1130 Walnut Street, Kansas City, Missouri 64106
www.andrewsmcmeel.com

16 17 18 19 20 SDB 10 9 8 7 6 5 4 3 2 1

ISBN: 978-1-4494-7781-3

Library of Congress Control Number: 2015960044

Find *Baby Blues*® on the Web at www.babyblues.com.

ATTENTION: SCHOOLS AND BUSINESSES

Andrews McMeel books are available at quantity discounts with bulk purchase for educational,
business, or sales promotional use. For information, please e-mail the Andrews McMeel Publishing
Special Sales Department: specialsales@amuniversal.com.